The Distribution of Economic Well-Being

NATIONAL BUREAU OF ECONOMIC RESEARCH
Conference on Research in Income and Wealth

F. THOMAS
JUSTER,
editor

The Distribution of Economic Well-Being

Studies in Income and Wealth
Volume 41
by the Conference on Research
in Income and Wealth

Published for the
NATIONAL BUREAU OF
ECONOMIC RESEARCH, INC.
by
Ballinger Publishing Company
A Subsidiary of J. B. Lippincott Company
Cambridge, Mass.
1977

This book is printed on recycled paper.

Library of Congress Cataloging in Publication Data

Conference on Economic Well-Being, University of Michigan, 1974.
    the Distribution of
The distribution of economic well-being.

    (Studies in income and wealth; v. 41)
    Includes bibliographies and index.
    1. Income distribution—United States—Congresses.   2. National income—United States—Congresses.
I. Juster, Francis Thomas, 1926–   II. Title.   III. Series: Conference on Research in Income and Wealth. Studies in income and wealth; v. 41.
HC106.3.C714 vol. 41 [HC110.I5]
330′.08s   [339.2′1′0973]   76–58909
ISBN 0–87014–517–7

Relation of the National Bureau Directors to
Publications Reporting Conference Proceedings

Since the present volume is a record of conference proceedings, it has been exempted from the rules governing submission of manuscripts to, and critical review
by, the Board of Directors of the National Bureau.

(Resolution adopted July 6, 1948,
as revised November 21, 1949,
and April 20, 1968)

PREFATORY NOTE

This volume of Studies in Income and Wealth contains the papers presented at the Conference on the Distribution of Economic Well-Being, held at the University of Michigan on May 15–17, 1974. We are indebted to the University for making the Rackham Amphitheatre facilities available to us, to the Program Committee consisting of F. Thomas Juster who served as chairman and conference editor and James D. Smith, to the National Science Foundation for its support, to Ruth Ridler for preparing the volume for press, and to the late H. I. Forman for drawing the charts.

Executive Committee, 1976–77

Clopper Almon, Chairman
Laurits R. Christensen
Stanley Lebergott
Milton Moss
Joel Popkin
J. A. Sawyer
Jack E. Triplett
Dorothy Walters
Burton A. Weisbrod
Allan H. Young
Mildred E. Courtney, Secretary

Funds for the economic research conference program of the National Bureau of Economic Research are supplied by the National Science Foundation.

Contents

The Distribution
of Economic
Well-Being

F. THOMAS JUSTER

**Institute for
Social Research and
University of Michigan**

Introduction

This is the last in a recent trio of conferences, sponsored as part of the continuing activities of the Conference on Research in Income and Wealth. The focal point of these conferences was to reexamine the state of the art in National Economic Accounts Systems, the research area which originally spawned the Income and Wealth Conference in 1936.

All three conferences involved a reexamination of the basic framework of the system of Economic and Social Accounts, with an eye to updating and refining them to take account of new theoretical insights with the potential for empirical implementation and for the provision of new information. The broad focus of these meetings has been the incorporation of concepts and data which go beyond the direct recording of monetary transactions. Of course, many of the papers given at the present conference, as well as those in the previous two conferences of the trio, also consider the interpretation of conventional monetary measurements. The spirit of these conferences cannot be understood, however, without recognizing that their principal motivation was a recognition that nonmarket activities, activities which impinge differently on present and future benefits than their conventional treatment suggests, and activities which involve the public sector in one way or another are (for some purposes) not satisfactorily handled within our present economic and social accounting framework.

The first of the three meetings on economic and social accounting systems was held at Princeton in 1970 and was titled "The Measurement of Economic and Social Performance." The focus of that conference was on aggregate accounts—what activities should, could, or might be included in a broadly defined set of accounts; what the measurement

1

problems were in some of the public sectors where output is convention-ally measured by inputs; what could be done by way of accounting for and measuring environmental costs and benefits, and so on. The original idea was for a second conference to be held on the distributional consequences of this potential expansion of aggregate measures of income and material well-being. It soon became clear that a single conference would not suffice, since a range of problems concerned solely with the distributional analysis of conventional monetary aggregates required exploration. Thus, the distribution conference grew into two conferences. The first of these, "Personal Distribution of Income and Wealth," was held at Pennsylvania State University in 1972; the second was held at the University of Michigan in Ann Arbor in May of 1974.

The "Conference on the Distribution of Economic Well-Being" con-tained two special features. First, in addition to the traditional papers and comments from invited discussants, the conference organized a special session for "student papers," to which graduate students were invited to submit papers in a competition. Notification of the competition was circulated to all members of the Conference on Research in Income and Wealth, and to the chairmen of all major graduate departments in Economics. Some fifteen student papers were submitted to a panel of editors, and three were selected for inclusion in the conference proceed-ings. The three selected papers were presented at a special student papers session.

A second feature of this conference, which is common to all but the collection of papers which analyze earnings functions, is that papers are more speculative in their empirical analyses than the typical paper in other Income and Wealth conferences. The reason, of course, is the nature of the subject: we are obviously at the beginning of serious empirical work designed to implement a richer and more fully articulated set of economic and social accounts. Concerns with the overall size and distributional impact of transfers-in-kind, "consumption" of redistribu-tion, cost of automotive emission controls, environmental damage from air pollution, and so forth, evidently must be based on insights and data that are more speculative in nature than many that economists are accustomed to dealing with. Nonetheless, it is important to make a start, and this conference has clearly succeeded in doing this.

As a guide to readers of the volume, let me note that discussants have provided excellent brief summaries of the papers before embarking on their critical commentary. For this reason, I have found it neither necessary nor useful to do more than indicate the problem and the broad conclusions contained in the papers. Readers of the volume will find these summaries extremely useful in making their way through a collection of papers that, while inventive and ingenious, are often not easy reading.

The Ann Arbor Conference on the Distribution of Economic Well-Being had three principal focal points: first, a number of papers dealt with conventional distribution issues, using either unconventional concepts of output or much broader concepts of income—terms like economic welfare or economic well-being convey the appropriate flavor. Papers in this area included, "Adding In-Kind Transfers to the Personal Income and Outlay Account: Implications for the Size Distribution of Income," by Eugene Smolensky, Leanna Stiefel, Maria Schmundt, and Robert Plotnick, which emphasized a framework for the measurement of benefits received by donors (taxpayers) as opposed to donees (recipients). The basic argument is that the income distribution achieved by government transfer programs is itself a consumption good, with a value to those who provide the resources which are to be transferred. As Neenan's discussion points out, recognition that consumption benefits can accrue from income redistribution per se simply represents one illustration of the proposition that consumption benefits or disadvantages are derived from all kinds of externalities.

The paper by John Kraft and Edgar Olsen, "The Distribution of Benefits from Public Housing," focuses on the question of housing subsidies and in particular on the efficiency of in-kind versus cash transfer programs. The Smolensky et al. paper examines that same issue for a variety of in-kind programs. Kraft-Olsen find that subsidies in the form of low-rent public housing, where the subsidized product can only be accepted or rejected, have little apparent effect on the aggregate consumption of housing services, and thus appear to be a very inefficient transfer instrument. As the discussion by Henry Aaron notes, these judgments on the housing program are suspect to the degree that the housing consumption predicted in the absence of subsidies cannot be explained very well, and hence the apparent inefficiency could be attributed largely to measurement error or model misspecification.

Harold Hochman and James Rodgers in "The Simple Politics of Distributional Preference," suggest that income redistribution, like other government activities undertaken in a democratic society, can best be understood as a reflection of constituent preferences. Since the direct recipients of the redistributed transfers constitute a minority of the voting population, the paper advances a hypothesis that reconciles support for redistribution with the preferences of at least some nonrecipients. Survey data are employed to ascertain the nature of such support, and to determine whether it reflects benevolence or simply negative nonmarket interactions between donor and recipient behavior and utility functions. They conclude that a pure self-interest model is inconsistent with their data. In the discussion by Thomas Weisskopf, it is noted that the evidence does not give a persuasive edge to the benevolence motive as opposed to an alternative definition of self-interest, predicated on the desire to insure maintenance of the social status quo.

Two of the papers in the area of conventional issues unconventionally treated concern themselves with the distributional consequences of environmental costs and benefits (damage). Myrick Freeman, in "The Incidence of the Costs of Controlling Automotive Air Pollution," examines the incidence of various methods of controlling automotive emissions. He concludes that, with the exception of higher gasoline prices, all proposed methods of reducing emissions are strongly prorich in their incidence. Frank Segal notes in his discussion of the Freeman paper that this regressivity could be completely eliminated with an appropriately designed subsidy program targeted only on low-income users of automobiles.

Leonard Gianessi, Henry Peskin, and Edward Wolff, in "The Distributional Implications of National Air Pollution Damage Estimates," examine the question of environmental damage: where it impacts, and on whom. A principal contribution of their analysis is that it provides the only available quantitative measure of the distribution of air pollution damage among different localities, and demonstrates how U.S. Census Bureau data can be used to investigate distributional issues. With a mixture of data ranging from adequate to nonexistent, essential but heroic assumptions, and a good bit of ingenuity, Peskin et al. conclude that air pollution damage does not impact on the poor more heavily than the rich, and that quite possibly the reverse is true. Nancy Dorfman questions this conclusion, primarily because of the difficulties involved in defining an appropriate geographic area where air pollution damage can be assumed evenly spread, as well as because of what she views as an arbitrary and misleading method of summing damages from various types of pollutants.

Earnings functions constitute the second general area of concentration at the conference. Over the past decade and a half, a burgeoning literature, concerned with the functional determinants of earnings and income differentials, has appeared. Much of this literature starts with the assumption that observed earnings differentials reflect differential amounts of investments both in formal schooling and in on-the-job training, with schooling investments being obtained in formal schools and in the home.

In "The Anatomy of Earnings Behavior," Richard and Nancy Ruggles use a longitudinal file of individual earnings from the Social Security Administration to examine changes in the pattern of cohort earnings. They are concerned solely with market earnings in both current and constant prices, but with longitudinal aspects of those data rather than with conventional current year distributions. Among other findings, they demonstrate the existence of a great deal of year-to-year variability in the earnings of identical individuals, far more than this reader, for one, would have expected on the basis of most descriptions and analyses of the labor market. Ahmad Al-Samarrie notes that the data do not adjust for differences over time in employment covered by Social Security, and that the Ruggles analysis does not take account of differences in the size of cohorts as a possible explanation for the observed patterns of cohort earnings.

An area of continuing interest in earnings patterns is in what might be called the analysis of persistent differentials in earnings—often thought of in the context of discrimination. Finis Welch and James P. Smith in "Black/White Male Earnings and Employment: 1960–70" examine the behavior of these differentials for people at different stages of the life cycle and different levels of formal schooling. They conclude that, by any measure, blacks made significant gains relative to whites between 1960 and 1970, although a significant gap remained. The black and white earnings gap was clearly smaller for younger than for older workers, a result that the authors attribute largely to "vintage" effects of differential schooling quality. Ronald Oaxaca examines another widely discussed differential in "The Persistence of Male-Female Earnings Differentials." He finds evidence of widening differentials adverse to white women up to about 1965, with some slight indication of reversal since then. However, he reports the opposite for blacks; here the gap between female and male earnings has narrowed appreciably. In both the Welch-Smith and Oaxaca analyses of earnings differentials, the crucial factors turn out to be changes over time in both schooling attainment and schooling quality (especially for the analysis of black-white differentials) and changes in the degree to which earnings advance with age and experience (especially true for male-female differentials).

Commenting on Welch-Smith, Orley Ashenfelter suggests that the analysis of black/white earnings differentials has to explain the increase in the relative earnings of black males after the mid-1960s as well as the tendency of black females to show increases relative to white females during the period before the mid-1960s. Reduced discrimination could explain the first and increasing relative skill level the second, but we are still left with a puzzle, since both factors should apply to male as well as to female relative wage patterns through the entire period. Alvin Mickens notes the peculiar regional character of gains in black relative to white income; such gains are much more apparent in the South than elsewhere. He also points to the difficulty in the Welch-Smith analysis of dealing with the fact that 1969 was a much better year generally than 1959 and, hence, that part of the relative gains for blacks may simply be a consequence of cyclical phase. Nancy Barrett, commenting on Oaxaca, points out that a major aspect of the male-female differential concerns the increased gap between male and female wages as labor force experience grows for both—females typically tending to show less income growth. In Barrett's view, this results, at least in part, from functional discrimination—the alleged weak attachment of females to the labor force and, hence, their alleged unsuitability for managerial and other experience-dominated occupational roles.

The basic issue of how the observed earnings and income distributions are generated is examined in two papers: "Schooling, Ability, Non-pecuniary Rewards, Socioeconomic Background, and the Lifetime Distribution of Earnings" by Paul J. Taubman; and "Family Background and Lifetime Earnings," by Russell Hill and Frank Stafford.

Taubman uses an immensely rich but specialized sample (a group of males originally analyzed by Thorndike and Hagen, subsequently rein-terviewed by the NBER). His findings cannot be simply summarized, but the principal ones are that: (1) schooling and ability both make independent, and to some extent interactive, contributions to earnings; (2) occupation makes more net difference (standardizing for education and ability) than many would suppose; and (3) a number of family background and outside activity measures show up quite strongly in the determination of earnings levels and changes. The Hill and Stafford paper focuses on the role of family background in earnings functions, examining a channel of causation that has already begun to loom large in economists' thinking about the importance of inheritance in earnings functions. Hill and Stafford look specifically at the distribution of parental time inputs to children and find that more educated parents invest more time per child than do parents with lower educational attainments. (The former have fewer children but invest comparable amounts of total time.) The implications for child development, schooling attainment, and earnings, via a higher level of marketable skill, are evident.

James Morgan, in discussing the Taubman paper, notes that the difficulties of model specification suggest a number of alternative explanations for the findings. At issue is whether Taubman is testing hypotheses or ransacking data, and Morgan suggests that the latter is a more apt description. Jacob Mincer, in comments on Hill-Stafford, notes that they have barely begun the process of translating differences in inheritance (in this case, time spent by parents) into differences in earnings. In addition, Mincer notes that the very indirect procedures used by Hill and Stafford in estimating child-care time are subject to potentially serious bias.

The final subject covered at the conference proceedings concerns the distribution of wealth. Here, the paper by Lee A. Lillard, "The Distribution of Earnings and Human Wealth in a Life-Cycle Context," is concerned with implications of human capital theory for inequalities in the distribution of human wealth. The second paper, by James D. Smith, Stephen Franklin, and Guy Orcutt, "The Inter-generational Transmission of Wealth: A Simulation Experiment," is concerned with the impact of inheritance on the transmission of nonhuman or property wealth, and on the changes in wealth inequalities which result.

Lillard's paper summarizes the optimal theory of investment in human capital, estimates the implied life-cycle pattern, and computes estimated distributions of human wealth. Zvi Griliches, discussing the Lillard paper, points out a number of difficulties with the theory (largely its lack of correspondence with a number of constraints that shape the market in which these investments are made), and notes that the generating function for human wealth in Lillard's model has a sufficiently large standard error so that one cannot really tell even whether wealth is more or less evenly distributed than income.

The Smith-Franklin-Orcutt paper is a simulation experiment using the Survey of Financial Characteristics of Consumers (1962) data on wealth distribution and stochastically generated deaths from mortality rates to produce bequests and inheritances. Behavioral relationships are obtained from District of Columbia and federal data on estates. The basic conclusions are that wealth distributions are only marginally affected by even extreme inheritance tax assumptions (which is not surprising given the small number of people who pass under this tax each year) and that there is a good bit of shuffling among people within a relatively stable and highly unequal wealth distribution. John Brittain, commenting on the paper, notes some implausible findings of this simulation model (the very large gains of both very poor families and those with relatively young heads), and notes the absence of sufficient behavior relationships with a solid enough foundation to inspire confidence in the results.

The final session to be discussed is the "student paper" session, which was held during the evening of the second day of the conference. In "Labor Market Discrimination and Nonpecuniary Work Rewards," Greg Duncan of the University of Michigan examines the impact on income distribution of accounting for a collection of fringe benefits and working conditions variables. In general, Duncan finds that these rewards are more equally distributed than direct wage payments, that inequality is thereby reduced by a fuller accounting of income from work, and that at least certain persistent income differentials (male-female, in particular) are less marked if account is taken of all rewards rather than simply wages. William Johnson, from Wesleyan University, in "Uncertainty and the Distribution of Earnings," finds that income uncertainty as reflected by earnings dispersions within occupational groups, is positively associated with higher average earnings—a result consistent with the conventional view that people are risk averters. Thomas Osman, from the

University of Wisconsin at Madison, examines the wealth distribution in "The Role of Inter-generational Wealth Transfers and the Distribution of Wealth over the Life Cycle: A Preliminary Analysis." He notes that the persistent finding that wealth inequality varies little across age cohorts is inconsistent with any reasonable model of life-cycle earning and saving, and suggests that the reason may be that inter-generational transfers flow most heavily to younger age groups who already hold relatively high levels of assets. Lee Hansen's comments on all three papers are concise and perceptive.

Finally, I wish to express my appreciation to the University of Michigan for making available the excellent facilities of the Rackham amphitheater for the conference, to Peter Steiner, Dorothy Projector, Harold Shapiro, Jan Kmenta, and Harvey Brazer for chairing the various sessions, to James D. Smith of Pennsylvania State University for his work as a member of the Conference Planning Committee, to Mildred Courtney of the National Bureau of Economic Research for her invaluable assistance as Secretary of the Conference on Research in Income and Wealth, as well as for her constant prodding of both myself and authors to get things done on time, and to Antonia Kramer for keeping track of "who had not yet done what" as well as the inevitable maze of detail involved in being secretary to the Conference Chairman. H. Irving Forman drew the charts and Ruth Ridler prepared the manuscript for press.

1

EUGENE
SMOLENSKY
University of Wisconsin

LEANNA
STIEFEL
New York University

MARIA
SCHMUNDT
University of Wisconsin

ROBERT
PLOTNICK
Bates College

Adding In-Kind Transfers to the Personal Income and Outlay Account: Implications for the Size Distribution of Income

INTRODUCTION

Academic economists find, periodically, that the most pressing question they wish to answer is different from what it was just a little earlier. Each change in fashion inevitably results in a call to broaden or alter the National Income Accounts. Currently the U.S. Accounts primarily reflect

NOTE: We are grateful to the Ford Foundation (grant 700-0309) and to the National Science Foundation (grant GI36539) for financial support. Jean Behrens corrected an earlier version of the accounting system. Charles Leven made very valuable suggestions, as did Morgan Reynolds. Paul Smolensky and Margaret Helming, respectively, provided the programming and data for the simulation.

The research reported here was supported by funds granted to the Institute for Research on Poverty at the University of Wisconsin by the Office of Economic Opportunity pursuant to the provisions of the Economic Opportunity Act of 1964. The conclusions are the sole responsibility of the authors.

the question: "Will aggregate demand be sufficient to fully employ labor?" Recently, Christensen and Jorgenson, as well as Nancy and Richard Ruggles, and John Kendrick have tried to shift the emphasis to aggregate supply in response to the question: "How can the long-term growth rate be raised?" In the Christensen and Jorgenson variant, appropriately accounting for the functional distribution of income emerges as a key complementary issue. More recently the question has been: "What can be done to raise social welfare?" with a key complementary issue being appropriately accounting for the size distribution of personal income. The most recent question heightens, even more than the growth question, the ever present tension between national income as an index of wealth versus national income as an index of welfare (Nordhaus and Tobin).

This paper is in the latest fashion. It is concerned with one important issue in appropriately accounting for the size distribution of income—the treatment of in-kind transfers. Hesitantly, and with great diffidence, it puts welfare before wealth, and the size distribution before the functional distribution. Opening the accounts to welfare concepts is full of familiar complications. For example, measuring the benefits of in-kind transfers appears to require recourse to a utility function.

The paper is in two main parts. First, we offer a rationale and an illustrative set of T accounts with which to account for in-kind transfers. In the accounts, benefits are attributed both to direct recipients and to taxpayers. Second, we offer an illustrative set of numbers to show that appropriately accounting for in-kind transfers alters our view of the size distribution of income and affects aggregate measures of inequality. In-kind transfers in this paper refer only to those quantitatively large government programs which subsidize quite specific goods or services to potentially identifiable people.[1] Even this thoroughly expedient definition of in-kind transfers poses thorny theoretical issues. One fundamental question is: "Should the benefits of in-kind transfers to recipients be valued at their cost to taxpayers?" A simulation experiment suggests a surprising response. We then draw some conclusions on the desirability of expanding the number of subsidiary tables of the Personal Income and Outlay Account, in order to provide a more satisfactory picture of in-kind transfers.

I. ACCOUNTING FOR IN-KIND TRANSFERS

We shall be concerned primarily with the Personal Income and Outlay Account. Personal income is household income, where households are defined to include nonincorporated business, nonexistent businesses (to take account of imputed rental income), nonprofit institutions, and private trust and pension funds, so that charity flows can be conveniently netted out of the Commerce Department work load unless they pass through corporations or the government. Current procedures include cash transfers and the food stamp subsidy in personal income, but most of what we will call in-kind transfers appear only as purchases in Table 3.10 (Government Expenditures by Type of Function).

We shall consider here three modifications in the current procedure. The first is by now no longer controversial and we mention it merely in passing. We accept the suggestion of Nancy and Richard Ruggles and Kendrick that government capital formation and capital consumption be included in the accounts as separate items. This is important for us, because it would raise the dollar value of in-kind transfers. Indeed, for programs like public housing, in which the transfer consists largely of not charging tenants for the cost of capital consumption, nothing else makes sense.

Our second suggestion is to include in-kind transfers to direct beneficiaries in Personal Income and to value them at the minimum cash payment the recipients would accept to forgo those in-kind transfers. (Call this "recipient benefits.") The final modification we propose is to recognize that in-kind transfers benefit the givers and to assign that benefit to taxpayers. (Call this "taxpayer benefits.") These modifications are proposed both to get the totals correct and to redress a bias in the related size distribution.

The modifications of the accounts proposed in this paper (beyond the inclusion of government capital consumption allowances) apply only to the Personal Income Accounts. The Income and Product and the Government Accounts are left unchanged to permit the continued provision of data for aggregate employment demand models.

Rationale for the Suggested Modifications

Enlarging the concept of income to include in-kind transfers is a short extension of existing practice. The most basic plausible definitions of income and output—the value of money income received by factor owners and the dollar value of market output—have proven unsuitable even for narrow purposes. Accordingly, we already add selectively from nonmarketed private production. We also add money transfer payments which gives us both a better measure of aggregate demand and a measure closer to welfare. We go even further and add transfers of vouchers for goods, in particular, food stamps. Having added cash and vouchers, why not add commodities? Business in-kind transfers are probably too small to be worth the effort.[2] Government may pose the opposite problem, since, at the limit, all expenditures as well as taxes may be transfers. Still, a substantial proportion of in-kind transfers of goods and services goes to specific recipients. It certainly seems desirable to extend the concept of personal income to encompass these changes for the same reasons that cash transfers are accounted for.

Our proposed modifications, which would account for in-kind transfers at their cash equivalent values and would account for taxpayer benefits are, however, not simple extensions of current practice. If adopted, they will establish an unwelcome precedent for evaluating private goods at their cash equivalent value, ex post. Yet, if we are to have a meaningful measure of the size distribution for issues of vertical equity, or if we are to bring philanthropy, public and private, into positive economics, or even if we are to obtain sensible Engel curves for the lower end of the income distribution, we cannot logically proceed in any other way.

Conceptual Issues

Our procedure requires that we measure the cash value of in-kind transfers to recipients. A simple extension of current practice would equate recipient benefits to taxpayer costs. However, most economists expect recipient benefits to be less than taxpayer costs.[3] To the extent that this expectation is realized, following current practice would bias the distribution. Thus, we propose to measure the recipient's valuation of in-kind programs as the minimum cash transfer (ΔY) which would be necessary to get the recipient to the utility level achieved after receipt of the in-kind transfers.

The size of ΔY depends upon the functional form and parameters of the recipient's utility function as well as on the number of in-kind programs available to the recipient, the extent of the subsidies, and any possible consumption restrictions associated with the relevant public program. A utility function must be chosen to calculate ΔY, and hence an arbitrary element is introduced.

An additional major problem associated with using the ΔY valuation of recipient benefits is that it is not consistent with the valuation of other goods in the accounts. Current practice values intramarginal units at their marginal benefits, unless the good is of an all-or-nothing kind, whereas ΔY includes any consumer surplus.

Turning to taxpayer benefits, current practice regards expenditure on transfers as a burden on taxpayers rather than as a purchase which increases their welfare. Because the tax system, as conventionally measured, is mildly progressive, treating taxes in this manner biases the size distribution of disposable income toward equality. Our proposal attempts to redress this presumed bias.

Theoretical support for considering taxpayer benefits is based on the current literature on "Pareto Efficient Redistribution," which rationalizes cash and in-kind transfers by postulating that taxpayer and recipient utility functions are interdependent. Indeed, the literature assumes that the donors rationally maximize their own welfare by making transfers, cash and in kind, until the marginal cost of a transfer payment equals the marginal benefit of the payment (Hochman and Rodgers; von Furstenberg and Mueller). If we accept the assumption of rational maximizing behavior on the part of donors, the accounting framework must assume that transfers make neither the taxpayer nor the recipient worse off. It follows not only that taxpayer benefits must be measured, but also that total benefits to taxpayers must be at least equal to total cost.[4]

Once we admit the existence of benefits to taxpayers, their value must be calculated. We shall make the strong lower-bound assumption that for each in-kind program total benefits to taxpayers equal the total cost to taxpayers. That is, we assume total (as opposed to marginal) benefit taxation. This assumption implies that if recipients benefit at all, the total benefits of the program to recipients and to taxpayers exceed the total costs in the aggregate (but not necessarily at the margin).

The Modified Personal Income and Outlay Accounts

The proposed treatment of in-kind transfer programs in the Personal Income and Outlay Account is presented in this section using Medicaid and public housing as examples. The accounting procedure for *cash* transfers is presented first to establish a norm for comparison. The cash transfer entries entail only one modification, on the outlay side of the account. The in-kind transfers entries will modify both the outlay and the income sides of the accounts.[5]

Cash Transfers

Assume that the government provides 30 cash transfers in a given year, earned income is 100, the only government activity is the transfer program, and all disposable income is consumed. The Personal Income and Outlay Account would presently appear as follows:

EXHIBIT 1

Outlay		Income	
Personal consumption expenditures	100	Earned income	100
Personal tax payments	30	Government transfers to persons	30

These entries correctly value the cash transfer to the recipient, but ignore the value of the payment to the taxpayers.[6] To represent taxpayer benefits, we propose the following entries modifying what now appears on the Outlay side in the following way:

EXHIBIT 2

Outlay		Income	
Personal consumption expenditures	100	Earned income	100
Personal tax payments	30	Government transfers to persons	30
Personal consumption of redistribution	30		
Personal tax reduction due to government purchase of redistribution	−30		

On the outlay side, we treat the 30 just like any consumption purchase in the private market but the government is the intermediator, funneling the tax outlay into consumption of redistribution for the taxpayer.[7] To indicate the taxpayers' consumption benefits, we enter 30 under consumption outlays and correspondingly reduce the tax outlay. Having started from the published accounts rather than de novo, taxes must be reduced to offset the 30 added to consumption outlays.[8] The new entry also emphasizes the underlying conceptual change. Instead of a burden, the transfer is identified as a welfare-increasing purchase.

Our modification suggests that two different size distributions be calculated. The income side would be distributed by income class according to "Earned Income" and "Government Transfers to Persons" in the usual way. The outlay side would normally have the same distribution. In our accounts the outlay side is distributed according to the two categories "Personal Consumption Expenditures" and "Personal Consumption of Redistribution." To the extent that "Personal Consumption of Redistribution" is distributed differently than "Personal Tax Payments" the distribution of our Outlays will differ from the distribution of Income. The two distributions would provide an upper and lower measure of income inequality. Since we expect that taxpayer benefits are more unequally distributed than taxes, the outlay side will be more unequally distributed.

In-Kind Transfers Directly Financed

In this section we describe the procedures to be used for all directly financed in-kind transfers. To simplify the exposition, assume earned income is 100, all disposable income is consumed, and the only government activities are an expenditure of 10 for a pure public good and a transfer program that provides at no charge 30 units of medical services. Suppose ΔY is the cash equivalent value placed on this in-kind transfer by recipients.

Current accounting for the Personal Income and Outlay Account in this situation is as follows:

EXHIBIT 3

Outlay		Income	
Personal consumption expenditures	60	Earned income	100
Personal tax payments	40		

The consumption of 30 units of subsidized medical care does not appear in these accounts, but would be found in the government accounts as a government purchase.

Our proposal would recognize explicitly that this form of medical care is an in-kind type of income and consumption. The recipient cash equivalent, ΔY, would be added to personal income as "Recipient Benefits from In-Kind Transfers" and to personal outlays as "Personal (In-Kind) Consumption Expenditures." As with cash transfers, we would further consider the 30 Personal Tax Payments which financed the transfer to be a consumption purchase of redistribution services. Hence, our accounts would appear as:

EXHIBIT 4

Outlay		Income	
Personal consumption expenditures	$60 + \Delta Y$	Earned income	100
		Recipient benefits from in-kind	
Personal tax payments	10	transfers	ΔY
Consumption of redistribution	30		

The proposed accounting procedure requires slight modification for food stamps, which presently are included in personal income and outlay but at the cost to taxpayer and with no attribution of donor benefits.[9] On the income side, food stamps appear in "Government Transfers to Persons." It is therefore necessary to reduce this entry by the taxpayer cost and add in our new account, "Recipient Benefits . . . ," their cash-equivalent value.

On the outlay side, consumption must be adjusted to allow for the fact, made so explicit on the income side, that recipients may not value their increased food consumption at market prices. Furthermore, "Personal Tax Payments" should be lowered and "Consumption of Redistribution" increased by an equal amount.

In-Kind Transfers Indirectly Financed

The treatment of public housing in the accounts must differ from the preceding because the subsidy is not financed directly from tax outlays. The subsidy arises because rental income is not sufficient to amortize capital costs. The taxpayer cost is an opportunity cost rather than a direct tax outlay. The accounts as presently constructed ignore entirely the subsidized recipient benefit and the taxpayer cost, because government capital consumption is not included

Our proposed modifications require the prior assumption that the accounts have been changed to include government capital consumption and then entail further changes. We include the Income and Product and the Government Accounts to clarify the capital consumption problems.

It will facilitate the exposition of the accounting framework to use some numbers. Assume:

The gross rent (assumed equal to resource cost) which a public housing unit would obtain in the private market	74
Maintenance costs of a public housing unit	42
Rental value of public housing capital (depreciation + interest)	32
Rent charged tenants	44
Market value of subsidy to tenant	30

The following is presumed to be the current accounting practice for the rental of public housing units in the Income and Product Accounts:

EXHIBIT 5-A

Product		Income	
Personal consumption expenditures	44	Earned income	42
		Current surplus of government enterprises less subsidies	2

The Government Receipts and Expenditure Account is presumably the following:

EXHIBIT 5-B

Expenditures		Receipts	
Purchases	42	Personal tax and nontax payments	44
Current surplus, etc.	2	Nontax payments	44
		Tax payments	0

The entries appearing in the Personal Income and Outlay Account would be:

EXHIBIT 5-C

Outlay		Income	
Personal consumption expenditures	44	Earned income	42
		Current surplus of government enterprises less subsidies	2

A specific method for entering government capital consumption into the accounts has been proposed (Nancy and Richard Ruggles). This method increases total outlays and income in the Product and Government accounts, but leaves the Personal Accounts unchanged as in the following:

EXHIBIT 6-A

Product		Income	
Personal consumption expenditures	44	Earned income	42
Imputed services of durables	30	Current surplus of government enterprises less subsidies	2
		Capital consumption	30

Notice that GNP is increased by 30. On the income side of the account an addition of 30 in capital consumption is included; on the product side a new item appears, imputed services of durables, which probably ought to go into the government account.

The Government Receipts and Expenditures Account would then look as follows:

EXHIBIT 6-B

Expenditures Outlays		Receipts Income	
Purchases	42	Personal tax and nontax payments	44
Imputed services of durables	30	Imputed income from durables	30
Government surplus on income and product account	2		

Again the accounts are increased by 30 of imputed income on the income side and imputed services on the outlay side.

The following entries would appear in the Personal Income and Outlay Account:

EXHIBIT 6-C

Outlay		Income	
Personal consumption expenditures	44	Earned income	42
		Current surplus of government enterprises less subsidies	2

Our proposals would go on to assign the benefits of public housing to taxpayers on the one hand and to tenants on the other. The final table therefore is:

EXHIBIT 6-D

Outlay		Income	
Personal consumption expenditures	44	Earned income	42
Imputed services of durables to consumers	ΔY	Current surplus of government enterprises less subsidies	2
Personal consumption of redistribution	30	Capital consumption	30
		Recipient benefits from capital consumption	ΔY

The accounts for public housing differ from that of cash and voucher transfers because the subsidy is not financed directly out of taxes.[10] On the income side, an implicit cash flow from capital consumption has been added. It is this income which is transferred to tenants, and their valuation of this benefit, ΔY, must also be recorded. On the outlay side, no adjustment is made to taxes paid. The imputed services of durables are consumption expenditures assigned to tenants. The implicit transfer of 30 is entered as "Personal Consumption of Redistribution."

All other indirectly financed in-kind transfers can be treated in this way.

Summary and Conclusions on the Accounting Framework

Several principles emerge from the proposed treatment of in-kind transfers which should prove applicable when further modifications of the accounts are considered.

1. Capital consumption allowances are an important element of the redistribution process and must be carefully accounted for.
2. The double-entry nature of the accounts serves as more than a check on consistency when transfers are assumed to be Pareto efficient. The size distributions based upon the two sides provide a lower and upper bound to the degree of inequality in the distribution of income.

II. SOME ILLUSTRATIVE NUMBERS

Up to this point, the paper has stressed that in-kind transfers should be included in Personal Income, and a procedure for doing this was specified. The remainder of this paper implements the accounting system and discusses three implications for the size distribution. We wish to show first that accounting for in-kind transfers reduces income inequality compared to the distribution of cash income. Second, since recipient benefits may be less than the cost to the government, this difference is measured and its implications discussed. Finally, a technique for measuring donor benefits from in-kind transfers is implemented and the results evaluated.

At the outset, we simplify matters by setting benefits equal to costs to taxpayers. This assumption is then relaxed.

Defining and Accounting for In-Kind Transfers

A reasonable definition of an in-kind transfer would be the difference between what the taxpayer would pay for a good or service in a Lindahl equilibrium and what he does pay (Behrens and Smolensky). Every program would probably then involve some transfer. In this paper, only goods and services provided to clearly identifiable beneficiaries at other than marginal cost are called transfers. Even this approach implies a relatively broad view of what constitutes in-kind transfers. The programs that ordinarily are classed as in-kind transfers are included—food stamps, Medicaid and Medicare, public housing, and so forth. Such programs provide what we label as *consumption* in-kind benefits. Our definition also includes *investment* in-kind transfers. This category is comprised of direct expenditures on public education, subsidies, and grants to students (e.g., GI Bill and manpower programs); in short, subsidized programs which principally increase the recipient's human capital. The distinction between consumption and investment transfers is not always clear-cut; health programs could be either, for example. Since we treat both types in identical ways in our analysis, the distinction is merely an expositional convenience.

TABLE 1   Major In-Kind Transfer Programs, 1970
(Millions of dollars)

Program	Federal Expenditures	State-Local Expenditures	All Government
Consumptions transfers			
Food stamps[a]	1,577		1,577
Commodity distribution[a]	321		321
Child nutrition[b]	703	185	888
Public housing[c]	368		368
Rent supplements[b]	18		18
Medicare[d]	5,255		5,255
Medicaid[e]	2,548	2,260	4,808
Veterans hospital and medical care[b]	1,651		1,651
OEO health and nutrition[b]	123		123
Legal aid	51		51
Subtotal	12,615	2,445	15,060
Investment transfers			
Elementary, secondary and other education[f]	1,214	42,934	44,148
Higher education[f]	336	11,325	11,661
Manpower programs	1,149	98	1,247
MDTA institutional[g]	173		173
MDTA on-the-job[h]	36		36
NYC in-school[g]	41		41
NYC out-of-school[g]	21		21
Operation Mainstream	9		9
Concentrated employment[g]	82		82
JOBS[g]	82		82
Job Corps[g]	96		96
WIN[g]	50		50
Vocational rehabilitation[i]	340	98	438
Other manpower[g]	219		219
Veterans education benefits[j]	991		991
Total in-kind transfer expenditures	16,305	56,802	73,107

[a]A. Skolnik and S. Dales, "Social Welfare Expenditures," unpublished tables of the Office of Research, Social Security Administration. Total includes administrative costs and is for FY 1971.
[b]Ibid., excludes administrative costs, and is for FY 1970.
[c]Estimated value of subsidy derived from Table 3.
[d]Data from *Social Security Bulletin Annual Statistical Supplement, 1970*, Table 117, row 2; net of SMI premium cost to recipients and adjusted slightly downward since the Current Population Survey (used to derive Table 3) counts less eligibles than did the Social Security Administration. Data is for calendar year 1970. (Excludes administrative costs.)

Notes to Table 1 (concluded)

eTotal expenditure data is for calendar year 1970 and is from *Number of Recipients and Amounts of Payments Under Medicaid, 1970,* HEW, Social and Rehabilitation Services publication number (SRS) 73-03153. Allocation between federal and state-local governments is based on the average of the proportion of Medicaid expenditures found in Skolnik-Dales, for FY 1970 and 1971. (Excludes administrative costs.)

fReynolds-Smolensky, Appendix D, for FY 1970.

gData is for FY 1970 and is from U.S. Bureau of the Budget, *Special Analyses, Budget of the United States, 1972* (Washington, D.C., 1971), p. 138. (Excludes administrative costs. Expenditures adjusted to exclude estimated cash payments to participants.)

hData is for FY 1970 but on obligations basis—U.S. Department of Labor, *Manpower Report of the President, 1971* (Washington, D.C., 1971), p. 299. (Excludes administrative costs. Expenditures adjusted to exclude estimated payments to participants.)

iSkolnik and Dales, "Social Welfare Expenditures." (Excludes administrative costs. Expenditures adjusted to exclude estimated cash payments to participants.)

jAdministrator of Veterans Affairs, *1972 Annual Report,* p. 166.

In 1970 the federal government provided $16 billion in in-kind transfer benefits. State and local governments administered another $57 billion, mainly for education. The major in-kind programs (as we define them) and their costs are listed in Table 1. The dollar volume of in-kind transfers exceeded that of cash transfers, which totaled $63 billion in 1970.[11]

In what follows we restrict our attention to seven major in-kind transfer programs ($68.8 billion in 1970).[12] Implementing the proposed accounting system to record these expenditures produces the following accounts:

TABLE 2   Personal Income and Outlay, 1970 (Millions of dollars)

Outlay		Income	
Personal consumption		Earned income	
Personal consumption of cash redistribution	647,607[b]	Cash transfers	647,607[a]
Personal tax payments			
Personal savings			
		Recipient benefits from government	
Personal consumption of in-kind redistribution	68,845	in-kind transfers	68,845
	716,452		716,452

aCurrent Population Survey money income, as reported in Projector and Bretz, Table 5.

bPersonal contributions for social insurance are not deducted on the income side and, consequently, are included on the outlay side.

The Distribution of In-Kind Income

We focus here on the right-hand side of Table 2 and ask how the provision of $68.8 billion of in-kind transfers affected average household incomes and the degree of income inequality. Table 3 shows that in-kind transfers markedly increase the average incomes of all groups (col. 12). For the poorest group, the difference of $559 (col. 10) increases income by 215 percent.

There is a strong positive relationship between benefits and income. Regression indicates that a rise in cash income of 1 percent is, on the average, associated with a .22 percent gain in in-kind transfer income. An exception in this pattern for the range $6,000–$7,999 results largely from decreased Medicaid benefits after $6,000.

Consumption transfers, nevertheless, are distributed in a strongly propoor pattern (col. 5). Investment transfers, which account for 79 percent of all in-kind transfers, rise steadily with income (col. 9).

Although in-kind transfers are prorich, they are more evenly distributed than cash incomes. Hence, including them in personal income decreases the degree of "inequality." The Gini coefficient for cash income was .398; adding all in-kind benefits shifts it down to .371. Similarly, including in-kind transfers raises the share of income going to the four poorest income classes—the bottom 24 percent—from 5.2 percent to 6.5 percent. A third measure of inequality, the coefficient of variation, declines from .52 to .49 when income includes in-kind transfers.

The high level of aggregation and our use of averages obscures the fact that in any given income bracket, some households receive above-average benefits by participating in many in-kind programs, while others with nearly equal cash incomes obtain few or no benefits (Joint Economic Committee). Though the degree of equity of some individual in-kind transfer programs has been studied (Smolensky and Gomery, Feldstein), currently available data do not permit a study of this issue for the *complete system* of in-kind transfers. National data on program enrollment and benefits at the family level are needed but are nonexistent.

The data in Table 3 are meant to be illustrative of orders of magnitude only. No attempt has been made to adjust for known sources of bias (e.g., underreporting of money income in the CPS), or for inconsistencies in reporting periods (some data are for the calendar, some for the fiscal, year), and so forth. Often, distributing benefits by income class required heroic assumptions.

One slightly less obvious caveat to note about Table 3 is that it does not measure, even conceptually, the redistribution of income due to in-kind transfers. Measuring the redistribution of income due to the fisc, or any part of it, requires a quite different accounting framework. The essential element of this framework is a counterfactual which recognizes the general equilibrium interdependence between the fisc and the distribution of earned income. What is important in Table 3 is that the sum of columns 10 and 11 represents a more complete distribution of personal income.

Finally, it should be noted that human capital investments are valued at their supply price. Two comments are in order on this procedure. Though the supply price may differ from the capitalized value of the associated future earnings stream, any such difference does not affect current income. Second, the cash equivalent of the subsidy need not equal the supply price, since human capital investments are in-kind transfers.

A Simulation Approach to Benefit Weights

It has been demonstrated that in-kind benefits when valued at taxpayer cost affect measured income inequality. In this section we determine if this conclusion would be altered by valuing in-kind transfers at their cash equivalence to recipients. Our procedure is to calculate a set of scalars (benefit weights) which convert taxpayers' costs to benefits as evaluated by the recipient. A range of benefit weights for a selected list of programs is obtained via simulation.

Five programs were selected for this simulation—food stamps, public housing, rent supplements, Medicare, and Medicaid. We assume each recipient family participates in a package of in-kind transfer programs, and is enrolled in at most one housing and one medical program. A utility function, a budget constraint (Y) and maximizing behavior are assumed and the utility the family obtains is calculated. The cash income that the family would need if it were to enjoy the same level of utility but received *no* in-kind transfers, EY, is then computed. It is inferred that the bundle of in-kind benefits increased the family's welfare, measured in dollar terms, by $EY-Y$. The ratio of $EY-Y$ to the taxpayer cost of providing this set of transfers is the benefit weight.

Specifying the Utility Function

A variant of the displaced Constant Elasticity of Substitution (CES) utility function was used in this exercise.[13] Because the five in-kind programs we are concerned with involve only three commodities—food, housing, and medical insurance—the utility function has just four arguments, these three and "other." Hence, we assume

TABLE 3 Distribution of Average Household Benefits of Selected In-Kind Transfers, 1970

Income Class	Consumption Transfers					Investment Transfers				All In-Kind Transfers	Average Cash Income[g]	In-Kind Transfers as a Percent of Cash Income[g]
	Food Stamps[a]	Public Housing[b]	Medicare[c]	Medicaid[d]	Total	Elem., Sec. and Other Education[e]	Higher Education[e]	Manpower Training[f]	Total			
	(1)	(2)	(3)	(4)	(5)	(6)	(7)	(8)	(9)	(10)	(11)	(12)
$ 0–999	18	6	104	94	222	272	4	61	337	559	260	215.0
1–1,999	50	20	179	184	433	272	4	47	323	756	1,508	50.1
2–2,999	71	18	173	191	453	358	10	44	412	865	2,461	36.4
3–3,999	62	15	146	134	357	444	16	39	499	856	3,468	25.5
4–4,999	53	12	122	156	343	543	36	31	610	953	4,471	21.7
5–5,999	36	7	90	142	275	612	52	19	683	958	5,445	17.8
6–6,999	24	4	69	59	156	634	61	5	700	856	6,452	13.3
7–7,999	17	2	55	33	107	721	71	6	798	905	7,458	12.1
8–9,999	16	–	46	26	88	807	96	3	906	994	8,920	11.2
10–14,999	3	–	35	24	62	843	231	–	1,074	1,136	12,120	9.4
15–24,999	–	–	37	11	48	795	367	–	1,162	1,210	18,410	6.5
25,000+	–	–	50	–	50	744	1,171	–	1,915	1,965	35,755	5.5

[a] Assumes total food stamp subsidies equal $1,577 million as shown in Table 1. Relative distribution of benefits obtained from tabulations of the magnetic tape files of *A Panel Survey of Income Dynamics*, Institute for Social Research, Survey Research Center, Ann Arbor, Michigan, 1972.

[b] Distribution among income classes of public housing tenants obtained from U.S. Department of Housing and Urban Development, *Statistical Yearbook, 1970*, Tables 107, 112 and 148. Average subsidy based on Smolensky-Gomery, Table I-B, inflated to 1970 price level.

[c] All eligible recipients are assumed to receive the same benefit, which was computed by dividing total payments (net of premium cost) by total number of Medicare enrollees. The distribution of enrollees was derived from the *Current Population Reports*, Series P-60, #80, "Money Income in 1970 of Persons and Families," Tables 17 and 22.

[d] Table values are the sum of two separate distributions since Medicaid recipients are divided into two groups—those receiving public assistance and those not on public assistance but qualifying as "medically indigent." For the public assistance group the percentage distribution of eligible recipients among income classes was obtained from tabulations of the magnetic tape files of *A Panel Survey of Income Dynamics* (see above). Multiplying the percentage by total Medicaid payments gave the total benefits to an income class. Average household benefits for that class then equaled total class benefits divided by the total number of households in the class. For the "medically indigent" the same procedure was used, except that Medicaid eligibility was determined by comparing the household's income to the limits set by its state of residence. These limits were found in "Income and Resources Levels for Medically Needy in Title XIX Plans in Operation as of April 15, 1970," unpublished table of the Social Security Administration. Resource levels were not considered due to data limitations, but it is believed that no serious bias resulted.

[e] Drawn from Reynolds-Smolensky, Appendix D.

[f] Includes all manpower programs listed in Table 2 except "Other." For all included programs except Vocational Rehabilitation, distribution of benefits based on Tables F-5, 7, 10, 11, 12, 13, 14 of *Manpower Report*, 1971. For Vocational Rehabilitation, distribution of benefits based on Table 4 of "Characteristics of Clients Rehabilitated in Fiscal Years 1967–71," U.S. Department of Health, Education, and Welfare, Social and Rehabilitation Services, 1973.

[g] Source is Table 5 of "Measurement of Transfer Income in the CPS," by Dorothy S. Projector and Judith Bretz, in James D. Smith, ed., *The Personal Distribution of Income and Wealth* (New York: NBER, 1975).

$$(1) \qquad U = \sum_{j=1}^{4} b_j(x_j - g_j)^{\sigma - 1/\sigma} \qquad \text{if } \sigma \neq 1$$

$$(2) \qquad U = \prod_{j=1}^{4} (x_j - g_j)^{c_i} \qquad \text{if } \sigma = 1$$

where

$x_j =$ quantity of good j consumed;

$g_j =$ displacement parameter (minimum quantity consumed);

$b_j, c_j =$ parameters; and

$\sigma =$ elasticity of substitution.[14]

To proceed with the simulation, equations 1 and 2 must be given empirical content, which in turn requires identifying the c_j, g_j, b_j, and σ. To show that the c_j's are the marginal propensities to consume, assume that good 4 is "other," $g_4 = 0$, and quantity units are specified so that market prices equal unity. Maximizing equation 2 with the constraint $Y = \sum x_j$ gives

$$(3) \qquad x_j = g_j + c_j \left(Y - \sum_{i=1}^{4} g_i \right) \qquad j = 1, 2, 3$$

The parameter values of the c_j were chosen for the utility functions of five prototype families, which differ by size and/or income, from the expenditure data in the *Survey of Consumer Expenditures*, 1960-61.[15] The data themselves are observations of the money spent on $x_1, \ldots, x_4$ by family size and income, and from them we computed crude estimates of $c_1, \ldots, c_4$.

To determine the minimum consumption expenditures on each good (g_j) we solve the demand equations of (3) and obtain

$$(4) \qquad g_j = x_j - \frac{c_j}{c_4} x_4 \qquad j = 1, 2, 3$$

To identify the b_j, maximize (1), and solve the demand equations for g_j to obtain

$$(4') \qquad g_j = x_j - b_j^\sigma x_4$$

Comparing (4') to (4) shows that

$$b_j = \left(\frac{c_j}{c_4} \right)^{1/\sigma}$$

Only σ remains to be identified. The simulations were run by successively assuming $\sigma = .5, .75,$ and 1.

Maximizing Utility with the Transfer Programs

Substituting our choice of σ and our parameters into (1) and (2) produces a specific utility function for each prototype family. Assigning a particular package of in-kind benefits to a family, we maximize its utility using this estimated function, subject to the budget constraint (5) which exists when in-kind transfers are received

(5) $\quad Y = \sum_{I} (1-s_j)xp_j + \sum_{II} xp_j - \sum_{II} s_j xr_j + \sum_{III} (1-s_j)xr_j$

We are assuming units are chosen such that all prices are unity and

Y = family cash income;

s_j = subsidy rate for good j which depends on the transfer program's features and may depend on Y;

xp_j = total amount of good j consumed when family receives the assigned set of in-kind transfers;

xr_j = quantity of good j *required* to be consumed if received as an in-kind transfer. This number is constant for each recipient and is determined by the government.

I, II, III = program categories which are defined next.

As indicated in equation 5, each commodity falls into one of three categories depending upon the way in which the rules of the program affect the budget constraint.

Goods in category I are one of three types:

a. nonsubsidized ($s_j = 0$) because the family does not participate in an in-kind program providing good j;

b. "other" goods, where no subsidy is ever available, or

c. subsidized at rate s_j both on the margin and inframarginally. That is, there is no quantity restriction on the consumption of this transfer (e.g., Medicare), or some maximum limit has been set by the administrators which is larger than the amount actually desired at the subsidized price.

Category II contains commodities for which the subsidy ceases at quantity xr_j and the recipient must purchase at least xr_j, but is free to supplement this level of consumption at market prices without losing the subsidy *and does so*. In this case the family pays $(1-s_j) xr_j$ for the subsidized goods, and $xp_j - xr_j$ for the unsubsidized portion. The total cost is $xp_j - s_j xr_j$ as shown in (5). Note that $s_j xr_j$ is de facto an outright cash transfer since the subsidy does not affect the family's market behavior at the margin.[16]

Subsidized items in category III are those for which the recipient either *must* consume a prescribed fixed quantity xr_j or desires to consume this amount. Public housing, which restricts a recipient to one particular apartment, falls in this category.

Figure 1 relates the three categories to the budget constraint for a subsidized commodity. If the good is in category I, there is no relevant restraint imposed by regulation on the quantity the household can consume and the budget constraint is therefore AD. If the commodity is in category II, it is subsidized up to some quantity, xr_j, and the household must consume at least that quantity but consumes additional units purchased at the market price. Hence the household is restricted to the segment BC. In category III, the quantity the household must consume and the price it must pay are both fixed; the budget constraint collapses to point B.

Now that the budget constraint (5) has been explained, we proceed to indicate the demand functions for each category of goous obtained from maximizing utility.

(6)   *Category I* $xp_j = g_j + c_j(1-s_j)^{-\sigma}\left[\sum_{\mathrm{I}} c_i(1-s_i)^{1-\sigma} + \sum_{\mathrm{II}} c_i\right]^{-1} A$

(7)   *Category II* $xp_j = g_j + c_j\left[\sum_{\mathrm{I}} c_j(1-s_j)^{1-\sigma} + \sum_{\mathrm{II}} c_i\right]^{-1} A$

FIGURE 1   Budget Constraints for Subsidized Commodities

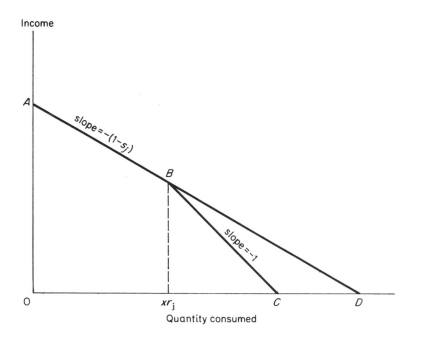

(8)   *Category III* $xp_i = xr_i$

for all σ and where

$$A = Y + \sum_{II} s_i(xr_i - g_i) - \sum_{I,III} (1 - s_i)g_i - \sum_{III} (1 - s_i)xr_i$$

The Simulations

To obtain the simulated numerical values for the xp_i from equations 6, 7, and 8, we need estimates of c_j, g_j, s_j, xr_j, Y, and σ. The first two are known from the utility function, while we chose various representative values of Y and σ. We approximated the s_j and xr_j that a prototype family would face if it participated in program j by examining the specific regulations of each of the five in-kind programs and making several assumptions.[17]

The numerical values for the xp_j are substituted into (1) and (2) to compute the family's utility U^*, given that it receives a particular set of in-kind transfers.

At this point we observe from (6) through (8) that the amount of food, shelter, and medical care (i.e., the xp_j) demanded can vary as the category in which the corresponding in-kind transfer is placed varies. In turn, this means that U^*, a function of the xp_j, is not unique. The problem is partially mitigated because one can unambiguously assign Medicare and Medicaid to category I, and public housing to III. However, food stamps may fall in either category II or category III, since the program permits a family's xp_{food} to exceed xr_{food} (II) or to be equal to it (III). The actual outcome depends upon the family's demand functions for *all four* commodities simultaneously. (Rent supplements, similarly, can be in any category.)

To deal with this simultaneity problem, all permutations of categories were considered when the transfer package at hand included food stamps and/or rent supplements. Inconsistent results were eliminated; of the remainder, the one yielding the highest utility was selected for further analysis.[18]

Having determined the recipient family's utility U^*, given its cash income and its participation in a set of in-kind transfer programs, we next compute how much money income, EY, it would need to maintain the same U^* if *no* in-kind transfers were available. We maximize (1) or (2) subject to the usual constraint that is in force when no in-kind transfers exist

(9) $$EY = \sum_{j=1}^{4} xp_j$$

This gives the quantities demanded as a function of EY

(10) $\qquad xp_j^* = g_j + c_j\left(EY - \sum_{i=1}^{4} g_i\right) \qquad j = 1, \ldots, 4$

Substituting the right-hand side into (1) or (2) produces the indirect utility function $U(EY)$. Solving

(11) $\qquad U(EY) = U^*$

gives EY^* the cash equivalent of cash income, Y, plus in-kind transfers. Hence the transfers provide a dollar benefit of $EY^* - Y$.

The taxpayer cost is

(12) $\qquad TC = \sum_{I} (s_j + p_j - 1)xp_j^* + \sum_{II,III} (s_j + p_j - 1)xr_j^*$

where market prices $= 1$ and $p_j =$ ratio of government cost price to market price. (Note that when $p_j = 1$, TC is simply the direct subsidy at market prices given to recipients.)

The benefit weight is

(13) $\qquad \dfrac{EY^* - Y}{TC}$

TABLE 4   Benefit Weights for Selected Programs

Program Package	—Two-Person Family—				Four-Person Family					
	$Y = \$2,869$		$Y = \$4,883$		$Y = \$3,414$		$Y = \$4,706$		$Y = \$6,572$	
	$\sigma = .5$	$\sigma = 1$	$\sigma = .5$	$\sigma = 1$	$\sigma = .5$	$\sigma = 1$	$\sigma = .5$	$\sigma = 1$	$\sigma = .5$	$\sigma = 1$
f	1.0	1.0	na	na	1.0	1.0	1.0	1.0	na	na
p	0.61	0.78	na	na	0.62	0.80	0.86	0.93	na	na
r	na	na	na	na	na	na	0.99	1.0	0.99	0.99
mr	0.81	0.89	0.91	0.95	na	na	na	na	na	na
md	0.64	0.76	na	na	0.67	0.78	0.74	0.85	na	na
f, p	0.72	0.85	na	na	0.90	0.95	0.94	0.97	na	na
f, r	na	na	na	na	na	na	0.98	0.99	na	na
f, mr	0.88	0.93	na	na	na	na	na	na	na	na
f, md	0.72	0.81	na	na	0.86	0.91	0.83	0.90	na	na
p, md	0.74	0.85	na	na	0.75	0.86	0.87	0.93	na	na
r, md	na	na	na	na	na	na	0.84	0.91	na	na
f, p, md	0.80	0.87	na	na	0.91	0.95	0.92	0.95	na	na
f, r, md	na	na	na	na	na	na	0.86	0.92	na	na
f, p, mr	0.85	0.92	na	na	na	na	na	na	na	na

NOTE: na = ineligible for program
f = food stamps
p = public housing
r = rent supplements
mr = Medicare
md = Medicaid

A sample of the benefit weights obtained appears in Table 4. Of the five prototype families, two were two-person households and can be thought of as elderly couples. One had a low income of $2,869 and was eligible for several transfers; the other's income of $4,883 entitled it only to Medicare. We assumed that these families would not receive rent subsidies. The three remaining families had four members and incomes of $3,414, $4,706, and $6,572.[19]

Several notable observations emerge from the table. Turning first to those instances in which households participate in only one program, one conclusion easily drawn is that the food stamp program is a de facto cash transfer. All families attach a weight of one to their benefits, because most families spend more on food than their stamp allotment even if they receive no stamps. Rent supplements can also be considered cash transfers in view of the benefit weights of .99 and 1. Public housing, in contrast, benefits the recipients less than the government's cost of providing it. For low income households, the benefit weights in the range .6 to .8 indicate that the gain from renting public housing at, say, $500 below market prices (i.e., an in-kind transfer costing $500) is between $300 and $400.[20] For the middle-income family, government housing subsidies are converted into direct consumption benefits at more efficient rates (on the order of .9). Compared to food stamps and rent supplements, the lower benefit weights for public housing presumably reflect its category III nature. Recipients must purchase the housing services of the assigned apartment, no more, no less, and this rigid requirement may create a large distortion in consumption patterns. The two medical transfers also have a wide range of benefit weights. Even though Medicaid is free, its weights are not one.

Many families that receive one of the five in-kind transfers also receive others. Because of this, the benefit weights for selected groups of in-kind transfers are also presented in Table 4. The weight for a two- or three-program bundle is not an easily computed weighted average of the several separate weights, but can only be derived independently. For example, the benefit weight of a low-income two-person family receiving both public housing and Medicaid is greater than the weight of either program taken singly. These outcomes arise because the addition of a new transfer changes the relative prices of all commodities and thereby affects the total pattern of consumption. The general tenor of these multi-transfer benefit weights is that they are on the high side. Few dip below .8 and a number are close to one.

To determine if our earlier conclusions on the impact of in-kind benefits on the size distribution could be affected by moving to a cash-equivalent basis, we modified the entries in Table 3 based on the results of Table 4. That set of benefit weights which would yield the

TABLE 5 The Distribution of In-Kind Transfers at Their Cash-Equivalent Values

Income Class	Food Stamps (1)	Public Housing (2)	Recipient (ΔY) Valuation of Consumption Benefits — Medicare (3)	Medicaid (4)	Total (5)	Taxpayer Cost of 1–4 (6)	Recipient Valuation of All In-Kind Transfers (7)	Taxpayer Cost of In-Kind Transfers (8)
$ 0–999	9	2	62	47	120	222	457	559
1–1,999	30	10	123	110	273	433	594	756
2–2,999	50	11	138	153	352	453	764	865
3–3,999	53	11	117	114	295	357	794	856
4–4,999	45	10	104	133	292	343	902	953
5–5,999	34	7	81	135	257	275	940	958
6–6,999	24	4	66	59	156	156	856	856
7–7,999	17	2	55	33	107	107	905	905
8–9,999	16	—	46	26	88	88	994	994
10–14,999	3	—	35	24	62	62	1,136	1,136
15–24,999	—	—	37	11	48	48	1,210	1,210
25,000+	—	—	50	—	50	50	1,965	1,965

maximum change in Table 3's figures was chosen for this exercise.[21] Nonetheless, Table 5 indicates relatively little change when compared with Table 3, except for the three lowest income classes. A more prorich pattern than that of Table 3 (as reproduced here in column 8) results because benefit weights generally rise with income, but the change is slight. The income elasticity of unweighted transfers is .22; after the cash-equivalent adjustment, it is .27. For the unweighted distribution based on taxpayer cost the Gini coefficient was .371; on a cash-equivalent basis it rises to .374.

Our benefit weights apply only to consumption transfers. Consequently, they have greater impact when attention is restricted to this type of transfer, as is seen when columns 5 and 6 are compared. Again, of course, benefit weight calculations modestly increase the progressivity of in-kind transfers. Unweighted consumption transfers have income elasticity of $-.46$; applying the weights increases this number to $-.33$.

Table 6 displays the proposed Income and Outlay Account when in-kind transfers are incorporated at our minimum cash equivalent values (ΔY). Compared to the earlier accounts of Table 2, ΔY is \$2,041 million (3 percent) less than the taxpayer cost. For food stamps, public housing, Medicare, and Medicaid, the only programs for which we have calculated benefit weights, the cash equivalent is 83 percent of taxpayer cost.[22]

TABLE 6   Personal Income and Outlay, 1970
(Millions of dollars)

Outlay		Income	
Personal consumption		Earned income	647,607
Personal consumption of cash redistribution	645,566	Cash transfers	
Personal tax payments			
Personal savings			
Personal consumption of in-kind redistribution	68,845	Recipient benefits from government in-kind transfers	66,804
	714,411		714,411

We have not calculated the cash-equivalent transfers for education. That the benefit weights appropriate to education may differ from 1 (at least for some income classes) is plausible enough to merit testing. Conceptually the framework developed for consumption goods is applicable, but the required assumptions are strained even more, and the data requirements are more burdensome. For example, since private education is consumed even when public education is available, public and private education must be quite different goods. Appeal to budget data, therefore, will not yield a marginal propensity to consume public education directly, if at all. This, and the many other problems are not insuperable, but the effort required to overcome them was beyond our immediate resources.

Any reasonable set of benefit weights for education would be expected to rise with income, thus accentuating the prorich character of education beyond that in Table 3. However, the weights would have to be very low at the bottom end to affect any conclusions of the study in a critical way. To turn education benefits proportional over the income range from $1,500 to $20,000, the benefit weight in the class $1,000–$1,999 would have to be as low as .14. On the other hand, introducing benefit weights for consumption goods did reduce the income of the lowest class from those transfers by almost 50 percent. If the weights at the low end of the distribution are as low for education as they may be for Medicaid, the increase in welfare of the poor due to in-kind transfers could be substantially overstated by Table 3.[23]

Though subject to considerable qualification, we conclude that our benefit weights undercut the argument that donor benefits rationalize the existence of in-kind transfers. Since in-kind transfers do not greatly alter consumption choices, they cannot be justified on donor benefit grounds.

Of course, our results are hardly definitive. Some, for example, may conclude from Tables 3 and 5 that consumption choices are importantly altered. Our failure to calculate benefit weights for education, the largest in-kind transfer and the one most likely to generate external benefits, is another limitation of the study.[24] Our estimated marginal propensities to consume were crudely derived, as were our specifications of program characteristics. Only one utility function was simulated. Other valid criticisms can also be offered. Nevertheless, we believe our results will prove robust. Our utility function is fairly flexible and was simulated with a wide range of elasticities of substitution.

Taxpayer Benefits from In-Kind Transfers:
Estimating Redistribution Services

In this section, we turn to the outlay side of our accounts and examine the effects on the size distribution of personal outlays of distributing the entry "Personal Consumption of Redistribution." Relying on our tentative simulation results, we ignore any benefits which may result from the alteration of recipient consumption patterns. We simply assume that the giving of in-kind transfers is a pure public good generating donor benefits. Hence, we can use the methodology suggested by Aaron and McGuire and Maital to quantify the taxpayer benefits from in-kind transfers. We intend these calculations to be suggestive rather than definitive.

Maital's Methodology

Assume that for persons with income y,

(14) $\quad mu(g) = t(y)\lambda(y)$

where:

$\quad mu(g) =$ marginal utility of in-kind transfer g;
$\quad t(y) =$ tax price per unit of g; and
$\quad \lambda(y) =$ marginal utility of income.

Multiplying (14) by G, the number of units of in-kind transfers, and rearranging gives

(15) $\quad Gt(y) = Gmu(g)/\lambda(y)$

Since the left-hand side is the total taxes a household with income y would be willing to pay for the benefits it receives from public goods, $Gt(y)$ is its imputed benefits, B, from giving. Making the strong assumption that all households have the same, separable utility function, $mu(g)$ is a constant across all donors since, by definition, they consume the same quantity of redistribution. Applying (15) to donors i and j and dividing i's equation by j's produces

(16) $\quad B_i/B_j = \lambda(y_j)/\lambda(y_i)$

Hence, the imputed benefits of G vary inversely with the marginal utility of income.

To apply (16) we assume, along with Aaron and McGuire and Maital, that $\lambda(y) = ay^{-\theta}$, where θ is the elasticity of marginal utility with respect to income. Hence (16) becomes

(17) $\quad B_i/B_j = (y_i/y_j)^{\theta}$

As Maital explains, estimates of θ have been obtained from many econometric studies of consumption which use CES utility functions. These studies suggest that for the United States, $\theta \doteq 1.5$.

We can compute the distribution of taxpayer benefits from equation 17, and our lower-bound assumption that the sum of the B_k equals total cost, and the additional assumption that each household has the mean cash income of its class. We then have

(18) $B_i/B_j = (y_i/y_j)^{1.5}$

and

(19) $\sum_{k=1}^{12} P_k B_k = \$68.8$ billion

where y_k = mean income of class k, P_k = number of households in class k, and \$68.8 billion = total spent on our selected set of in-kind transfers in 1970. The resulting benefits per household are shown in Table 7 (col. 1).

Column 1 indicates that taxpayer benefits are distributed in a steeply prorich pattern, a result which necessarily follows from our use of equation 18, with its income elasticity of benefits of 1.5.

To calculate the size distribution of outlays we sum "Consumption of Redistribution," the recipient value of consumption from in-kind transfers (ΔY) (col. 4), personal consumption, personal savings and adjusted personal taxes. For consumption, savings, and all personal taxes, we substitute Current Population Survey cash income (col. 3). The required adjustment to taxes was made quite explicit in Exhibit 4 where aggregate personal taxes were reduced by the value of "Consumption of Redistribution." That reduction is distributed in column 2, "Offsetting Tax Reduction," according to the incidence of all personal taxes in 1970 (Reynolds and Smolensky, Appendix C).

For each income class, the difference between personal income per household (cols. $3 + 4$) and personal outlay per household (cols. $1 + 2 + 3 + 4$) is the net sum of columns $1 + 2$.[25] In setting up our accounts, we expected that personal outlays would be more unequally distributed than personal income. That expectation was fulfilled, but the difference is small. The Gini coefficient for the size distribution of outlays (col. 5) is .382, which slightly exceeds the coefficient on personal income (.374). It appears that donor benefits add about as much to inequality as the offsetting taxes reduce it.

Some Further Comparisons

Our measures of income inequality are sensitive to the definition of income. The distribution of factor earnings plus private transfers as measured in the Current Population Survey has a Gini coefficient of .444. Adding governmental cash transfers, which yields the conventional concept of personal income, lowers the measure to .398. Our further modifications—adding in-kind transfers at their cash-equivalent value,

TABLE 7   Taxpayer Benefits and the Distribution of Personal Outlays per Household

	Consumption of Redistribution (1)	Offsetting Tax Reduction (2)	Cash Income (3)	Recipient Value of In-Kind Transfers (4)	(1) + (2) + (3) + (4) (5)
$ 0–999	4	−67	260	457	654
1–1,999	53	−67	1,508	594	2,088
2–2,999	112	−176	2,461	764	3,161
3–3,999	186	−300	3,468	794	4,148
4–4,999	273	−441	4,471	902	5,205
5–5,999	366	−540	5,445	940	6,211
6–6,999	473	−632	6,452	856	7,149
7–7,999	588	−731	7,458	905	8,220
8–9,999	770	−879	8,920	994	9,805
10–14,999	1,138	−1,143	12,120	1,136	13,251
15–24,999	2,285	−1,654	18,410	1,210	20,251
25,000+	6,179	−6,788	35,755	1,965	37,111

and taxpayer benefits with the appropriate adjustment to taxes paid—further lowers the Gini coefficient to .382.

Our accounts lead naturally to a modified concept of disposable income. To the conventional definition of consumption plus savings we add in-kind consumption at cash-equivalent value and donor benefits. The Gini coefficient for this concept of disposable income is .372 compared to a coefficient of .380 for the conventional notion.

Comparing the reduction in inequality which results from altering the definition of income suggests the following:

1. Adding governmental cash transfers to factor income plus private transfers lowers inequality by .046. In contrast, adding in-kind transfers to factor income plus private transfers lowers inequality by .011.
2. Personal Outlay as we define it has a Gini coefficient of .382, while as conventionally measured it is .398. This difference results from two opposing forces. Adding in-kind transfers to cash receipts reduces inequality by .024 but donor benefits increase inequality by .008.
3. Subtracting Personal Taxes for our concept of Personal Outlay reduces inequality by .010.

CONCLUSION

We have urged that current practice in accounting for in-kind transfers in the Personal Income and Outlay Account be altered in the following ways.

1. All government in-kind transfers accruing to clearly identifiable beneficiaries should be included. The most important omissions are the transfers which augment human capital.
2. Transfer income should be valued at the minimum cash transfer the recipients would accept to forgo the in-kind transfer.
3. The process of making the transfer should be viewed as an activity with a final output to be accounted for—a collective purchase which raises personal consumption (with an offsetting reduction in taxes).

To make more concrete what our proposals would involve, we illustrated them with a specific set of T accounts. Our proposed accounting practices could alter substantially our conceptions of the prevailing degree of income inequality. To the extent that in-kind transfers are distributed differently from cash income, the income side could show a marked change in income inequality. On the outlay side, the definition of disposable income is significantly altered, which also could shift measured income inequality.

We then provided an illustrative set of numbers to show how the size distribution of income was altered when in-kind transfers, treated our way, were distributed across income classes and added to cash income. The resulting changes were, in fact, quite small. Redistribution through in-kind transfer appears to consist of shuffling a great mass of things about, mainly in the dense middle of the distribution, with those in the lower tail gaining some.

The emphasis we put on valuing recipient benefits on a cash equivalent basis for the study of income distribution seems misplaced. Our simulations, while only suggestive, yielded rather high benefit weights. Therefore, donor benefits generated by the alteration of recipient consumption patterns cannot be important.

Our results are in no sense definitive, however, and more work could usefully be done. A low-income-household survey that determined the number of recipients receiving more than one in-kind transfer and the mix of benefits that they receive would be especially helpful. If most low-income families are in several programs, then practical concern over recipient valuations of in-kind transfers would be ended. (Of course, why we engage in such transfers when benefit weights are 1 would emerge as an important issue in public economics.) If only a small proportion of households receive transfers from more than one source, attention to consumption of subsidized commodities by low-income families would yield better income elasticities than were available for this study. Such a survey might also help to answer a variety of horizontal equity questions not otherwise tractable. The data collected would also permit rearranging households into an after-transfer distribution permitting a better understanding of the short-run effect of government on the distribution of income, when income is rather broadly defined.

An issue not yet amenable to household survey solutions is the better conceptualization, and subsequent calculation, of the set of benefit weights appropriate for education and other human-capital-augmenting public programs.

The issues surrounding the concept of donor benefits also need considerably more attention. It would be especially useful to contrast the results from assuming Pareto optimal redistribution with other models such as the median voter framework.

In summary, it seems quite acceptable to continue to account for in-kind transfers at cost (but including capital costs). The concept of in-kind transfers in Personal Income and Outlay should be broadened, however, to include education and manpower training. The notion that redistribution is an activity augmenting personal income with a concomitant reduction in taxpayer burdens requires further theoretical and empirical consideration.

NOTES

1. Since there is little reason to believe that taxes are on a marginal benefit basis, all government expenditures can be thought of as having a transfer component. In another paper, Reynolds and Smolensky have distributed all government expenditures and taxes by income size class. In that paper, however, in-kind transfers are treated in the traditional way. It would also have been consistent to enter in-kind taxes (imprisonment, compulsory school attendance, jury duty, military conscription), but no attempt was made to do so.

2. Lampman has, however, asked why receipts of insurance benefits, which he considers to be a transfer, as well as inter-household transfers are not accounted for.

3. In theory, it should be noted, the cash equivalent which recipients put on their in-kind transfers may exceed, equal, or be less than their cost to government (Schmundt, Stiefel and Smolensky).

4. Since recipient benefits are expected to be less than taxpayer costs, it may appear reasonable to value taxpayer benefits as the difference between taxpayer costs and recipient benefits. The above discussion makes it clear, however, that this method is inappropriate.

5. Schmundt, Smolensky, and Stiefel have shown that correctly measuring recipient benefits from in-kind programs (ΔY) requires simultaneously evaluating all in-kind benefits received by the recipient. For expository purposes only, the in-kind programs are treated separately.

6. We assume that there is no "stigma" or other effects associated with cash transfers which would cause the recipient to value the transfer at less than the dollar amount.

7. A more complete specification would treat the government's costs in effecting that transfer as "value added by government." That cost appears in both the current and modified accounts in "Government Purchases."

8. If we had started de novo, the two offsetting tax entries would not have appeared.

9. In recent years, the cost to the government of the food stamp program can be found primarily in line 27, other health, labor and welfare, and the column federal transfer payments and "net interest paid," of Table 3.10, "Government Expenditures by Type of Function," in the July issue of the *Survey of Current Business* and hence in the various other displays related to government.

10. Indeed, the Public Housing Authorities run a surplus on current account.

11. A. Skolnik and S. Dales, Table 1, *Social Security Bulletin*, December 1972.

12. The seven programs are food stamps, public housing, Medicare, Medicaid, elementary–secondary–other public education, higher public education, and manpower programs.

13. Of all the possible functional forms for a utility function, this is one of the few that is empirically tractable and yields demand functions consistent with economic theory (Goldberger). Recent work on consumer benefits from public housing lends empirical support to our choice (Murray).

14. In equation 1, omitting the exponent $\sigma/\sigma - 1$ simplifies calculations and does not affect the final results.

15. This procedure assumes identical utility functions for all families of a given size and income but allows them to vary across income classes and by family size.

16. An example of an in-kind transfer in this category is the school lunch program, in which a student can get a 60 cent lunch for 30 cents, but not a 40 cent lunch for 20 cents nor two 60 cent lunches, but who may bring a sandwich. Of the five programs in this simulation, food stamps can fall into this category, though they may not if the family does not exceed its food stamp allotment when buying food. Similarly, rent subsidies may or may not be in this category, depending on family consumption choices.

17. For example, federal regulations indicate that a two-person family with cash income of $2,869 in 1970 was eligible for $725 of food stamps at a cost of $583, a subsidy rate of .20. Because the family must buy all the stamps if it is to receive any, $xr = \$725$.

18. An inconsistent case exists if assigning good j to one category yields, from (6) through (8), an xp_j that contradicts the assignment. For instance, a permutation placing rent supplements in category II (where $xp > xr$) might result in $xp < xr$; this case would be excluded.

19. These income figures correspond to the income classes in the *Summary of Consumer Expenditures*, 1960–61, which are the original data, but are inflated to 1970 price levels.

20. The benefit weights on public housing are more variable than our table suggests and fall as low as .24 in one instance. Packages of transfers which contain public housing also, therefore, have quite variable, and frequently quite low, benefit weights. To a lesser extent, there is some greater variability in the weights than revealed by Table 4 for other housing programs as well.

21. Specifically, we assumed $\sigma = .5$, and (1) public-housing tenants receive no other benefits, (2) Medicare enrollees receive no other benefits, and (3) all food stamp recipients are on Medicaid and vice versa. These conditions, of course, do not reflect the true pattern of program overlap in 1970. Also a greater change in Table 3's figures could be produced by assuming, e.g., that some Medicaid recipients receive no food stamps. Our choices, however, yield the largest change of any simple set of assumptions.

   Since the simulations cover a limited income range, rough extrapolations were used to obtain a full set of benefit weights. Table 5 was constructed with the following weights:

Income Class	Public Housing	Medicare	Food Stamps and Medicaid
$0–999	0.3	0.6	0.5
1–1,999	0.5	0.7	0.6
2–2,999	0.6	0.8	0.7
3–3,999	0.7	0.85	0.85
4–4,999	0.85	0.9	0.85
5–5,999	0.95	0.95	0.95
6,000+	1.00	1.00	1.00

22. One interpretation of Table 6, obviously, is that in-kind transfers in 1970 may have wasted as much as $2 billion.

23. However, the Gini coefficient is not substantially altered when the Medicaid weights are applied to all human-investment programs.

24. See footnote 23, however.

25. This section assumed a CES utility function that is constant for all people; earlier we explicitly allowed the function to vary across income classes and by family size. Hence combining these results in Table 7 is not strictly justifiable.

REFERENCES

Aaron, H., and McGuire, M. "Public Goods and Income Distribution." *Econometrica* 28 (1970): 907–920.

Behrens, J., and Smolensky, E. "Alternative Definitions of Income Redistribution." *Public Finance/Finances Publiques* 28 (July 1974): 315–332 [No. 3–4].

Christensen, L. R., and Jorgenson, D. W. "The Measurement of U.S. Real Capital Input, 1929–1967." *Review of Income and Wealth*, Series 15, no. 4 (1969): 293–319.

———. "U.S. Real Product and Real Factor Input, 1929–1967." *Review of Income and Wealth*, Series 16, no. 1 (1970): 19–50.

Feldstein, M.; Friedman, B.; and Luft, H. "Distributional Aspects of National Health Insurance Benefits and Finance." *National Tax Journal* 25 (1972): 497–510.

Goldberger, A. S. "Functional Form and Utility: A Review of Consumer Demand Theory." 1967, processed.

Hochman, H. M., and Rodgers, J. A. "Pareto Optimal Redistribution." *American Economic Review* 59 (1969): 542–557.

Joint Economic Committee, Congress of the United States. *How Public Welfare Benefits Are Distributed in Low-Income Areas*. Studies in Public Welfare, no. 6. Washington, D.C., 1973.

Kendrick, J. W. *Economic Accounts and Their Uses*. New York: McGraw-Hill, 1972.

Lampman, R. "Social Accounting for Transfers." In James D. Smith, ed. *The Personal Distribution of Income and Wealth*. Studies in Income and Wealth 39. New York: NBER, 1975.

Maital, S. "Public Goods and Income Distribution: Some Further Results." *Econometrica* 41 (1973): 561–568.

Murray, M. P. "The Distribution of Tenant Benefits in Public Housing." University of Virginia, March 1974, processed.

Nordhaus, W. D., and Tobin, J., "Is Growth Obsolete?" In Milton Moss, ed., *The Measurement of Economic and Social Performance*. New York: NBER, 1973.

Projector, D. S., and Bretz, J. S. "Measurement of Transfer Income in the Current Population Survey." In James D. Smith, ed. *The Personal Distribution of Income and Wealth*. Studies in Income and Wealth 39. New York: NBER, 1975.

Reynolds, M., and Smolensky, E. "The Post-Fisc Distribution: 1961 and 1970 Compared." *National Tax Journal*, December 1974.

Ruggles, N., and Ruggles, R. *The Design of Economic Accounts*. New York: NBER, 1970.

Schmundt, M.; Stiefel, L.; and Smolensky, E. "When Do Recipients Value Transfers at their Costs to Taxpayers?" In I. Lurie, ed. *Integrating Income Maintenance Programs*. New York: Academic Press, 1975.

Skolnik, A., and Dales, S. "Social Welfare Expenditure, 1971–72." *Social Security Bulletin* 35 (Dec. 1972): 3–17.

———. "Social Welfare Expenditures." Unpublished tables, 1973, processed.

Smolensky, E., and Gomery, J. D. "Efficiency and Equity Effects in the Benefits from the Federal Public Housing Program in 1965." Joint Economic Committee, 92nd Congress, Second Session. Washington, D.C., 1973.

U.S. Department of Labor, Bureau of Labor Statistics. *Survey of Consumer Expenditures, 1960–61*, Supplement 3. Washington, D.C., 1966.

Von Furstenberg, G. M., and Mueller, D. C. "The Pareto Optimal Approach to Income Redistribution—A Fiscal Application." *American Economic Review* 61 (1971): 628–637.

1 ‖ COMMENTS

William B. Neenan
University of Michigan

My discussion falls into three parts: (1) a brief summary of the argumentation and conclusions of Smolensky, Schmundt, Plotnick, and Stiefel; (2) an explication of their major points; and (3) a critical evaluation of their contribution.

I

Our authors contend that the National Income Accounts should be adapted to reflect the impact of in-kind transfers on both recipients' and taxpayer-donors' income. Specifically they propose that the Personal Income and Outlay Account be altered to include in-kind transfers valued at their minimum cash value to recipients and that taxpayer benefits from redistribution be added to the outlay side of the account. Assuming "Pareto Efficient Redistribution," our authors would enter as an outlay "Consumption of Redistribution," that is, the taxpayer benefit from redistribution, with an offsetting reduction in the entry for personal taxes. The estimated minimum cash value to the recipients of a selected number of in-kind transfers is based on a simulation exercise involving utility maximization. The benefit weights derived for the in-kind transfers from this exercise are all close to unity. Our authors find that the size distribution of income is altered only slightly if in-kind transfers, evaluated in this manner, are distributed across income classes. They conclude with several qualifications of their procedures and suggestions for extending their work.

II

Our authors wish to put "welfare before wealth and the size distribution [of income] before the functional distribution" as the purpose of the national accounts. To this end they (1) propose changes in the Personal Income and Outlay Account to reflect both the benefits recipients receive from in-kind transfers and the benefits received by taxpayers from redistribution programs; and (2) provide some illustrative numbers indicating the general order of magnitude these changes make in the estimated size distribution of income.

Our authors illustrate their proposed changes in the national accounts in terms of a cash transfer program as well as medical care and public housing in-kind transfer programs. Assume that earned income is 100, that there is no saving, and that there are two government outlays, 10 for a pure public good and 30 for a program providing medical services at no charge, as shown in Exhibit 4. Under current procedures, personal consumption expenditures would be entered as

60, equal to disposable income, with personal tax outlays of 40 (10 + 30), as shown in Exhibit 4. The authors would explicitly recognize the consumption of the medical service by the recipients by adding the minimum cash value of this service to personal outlay (ΔY). Taxpayer benefits from the program would be recorded as "Consumption of Redistribution" and evaluated at the cost of the program, in this instance, 30. Offsetting this addition would be a reduction of personal taxes of 30, with a similar increase in disposable income. Thus personal taxes would be 10, the amount needed to finance the public good. On the income side, the minimum cash value of the medical service to the recipients (ΔY) is added to earned income.

The authors' proposal for the treatment of in-kind transfers from a program such as public housing, which is not directly financed by tax outlays, involves not only the procedures just discussed but also the introduction of government capital consumption into the accounts, as proposed, for example, by Nancy and Richard Ruggles, and illustrated in Exhibits 4-A, 6-B, 6-C, and 6-D.

Our authors illustrate their accounting proposals with seven programs (food stamps, public housing, Medicare, Medicaid, public elementary and secondary education, public higher education, and manpower) for which total expenditures by all levels of government in 1970 were $68.8 billion. (Total cash transfers were $63 billion in that year.) The authors believe that these seven programs are vehicles for in-kind transfers, since they provide goods and services "to clearly identifiable beneficiaries at other than marginal cost." Although these in-kind transfers, evaluated at taxpayer cost, accrue in a prorich manner, as seen in Table 3, column 10, they are indeed more evenly distributed than cash income. Hence, including them in personal income decreases the Gini coefficient from .398 to .371, as shown graphically in Figure 1.

The authors attempt to determine whether the distribution of in-kind transfers evaluated at their cash value to recipients, rather than at taxpayer cost, would become even more prorich. A range of benefit weights is calculated to convert taxpayers' costs of five programs (food stamps, public housing, rent supplements, Medicare, and Medicaid) to benefits evaluated at their cash equivalency to recipients. Each recipient family is assumed to participate in a package of in-kind transfer programs. A constant elasticity of substitution (CES) utility function, a budget constraint (Y) and maximizing behavior are assumed and the utility that the family receives is calculated. Then that cash income (EY) which will allow the family to reach this same level of utility in the absence of any in-kind transfers is computed. The difference between EY and Y is then defined as the increased welfare in dollar terms generated by the in-kind programs. The ratio of this difference (EY less Y) to the taxpayer cost of the transfer programs is the benefit weight.

Commodities in a transfer program can fall in one of three categories, depending upon the manner in which the rules governing the program affect a household's budget constraint. In category I, there is no relevant constraint imposed on the quantity of the commodity that the household can consume. In category II, a certain amount of the commodity must be consumed but additional units can be purchased at the market price. In category III, the quantity consumed and the price of the commodity are both fixed. Medicare and

Medicaid are examples of programs in category I. The food stamp program can fall in categories II or III; public housing is in category III; and rent supplements can be in any one of the categories.

Benefit weights are computed for five prototype families and several in-kind program combinations. The benefit weights shown in Table 4 range from 0.61 for public housing to 1.0 for food stamps. The weights for two- or three-program packages are generally higher than the weights for programs taken separately.

Since benefit weights generally rise with income, if in-kind transfers adjusted to their cash-equivalent basis are substituted in personal income distribution for in-kind transfers at taxpayer cost, the Gini coefficient rises but only slightly. Thus with in-kind transfers evaluated at taxpayer cost the Gini coefficient is .371; on a cash-equivalent basis it is .374. For the food stamp, public housing, Medicare, and Medicaid programs taken together, the cash equivalent is estimated to be 83 percent of taxpayer cost. Even though our authors judge that on a conceptual basis, benefits from public elementary, secondary, and higher education should be treated as in-kind transfers financed by consumption outlays for redistribution, they do not attempt to estimate weights for these programs.

Finally, the authors distribute the outlay, "Personal Consumption of Redistribution," in a manner first discussed by Aaron and McGuire. Following Maital, our authors assume that the taxpayer benefits from redistribution vary inversely with the marginal utility of income, with 1.5 the value of the elasticity of marginal utility with respect to income. On this basis, taxpayer benefits from redistribution are distributed in a steeply prorich pattern with the income elasticity of benefits necessarily being 1.5, as shown in Table 7, column 1.

Consonant with their proposal that the accounts should reflect benefits that taxpayers derive from redistribution, aggregate tax payments must be reduced by $68.8 billion, the total expenditures for those programs assumed to generate in-kind transfers in 1970. If this offsetting tax reduction is distributed according to the estimated incidence of all personal taxes in 1970, it just happens that the tax reduction in each income class very closely approximates the taxpayer benefits from redistribution allocated to the income class according to the Maital procedure (see Table 7, columns 1 and 2).

III

I am quite sympathetic with the authors' effort to introduce welfare and utility concepts into the quantitative analysis of fiscal outcomes. The theoretical public sector analysis of Samuelson, Musgrave, Buchanan, and others has long clearly pointed in this direction but only very recently have public sector quantitative studies begun to reflect this analysis. I think a significant contribution of our authors is the fact that they have grappled imaginatively with the question of income distribution and the public sector in a manner that reflects a consciously articulated behavioral base. This real accomplishment is not diminished by the fact that I feel a number of deficiencies exist in both their proposed conceptual framework and in their interpretation of some of the quantitative results. Specifically, my critique focuses on these three areas of the paper: (1) their proposed modification of the national accounting framework; (2) their adjustment of in-kind transfers to a cash-equivalency basis; and (3) their evaluation of "Personal Consumption from Redistribution," the taxpayer-donor benefits from redistribution programs.

The authors propose a new entry in the national accounts, "Personal Consumption of Redistribution," to be measured by the total cost of programs that provide goods and services "to clearly identifiable beneficiaries at other than marginal cost." Such programs are, by definition, transfer programs. I am uncomfortable with this definition of a transfer program. Take the case of public education. The beneficiaries of public education are not all clearly identifiable. Students and their families are indeed known but educational policy for decades has been built on the assumption that there are notable external benefits from elementary and secondary education. The identification and quantification of these external benefits as well as the identification of their recipients are still largely matters of conjecture. Nonetheless, to the extent that these beneficiaries do exist, they enjoy benefits at less than marginal cost and so, by our authors' definition, they are transferees. However, if such an extension of the concept of transferee is accepted, then it would seem that nearly all public services have to be defined as transfer programs. For example, the beneficiaries of national defense services, police and fire protection, the system of justice, and general government all enjoy benefits at other than marginal cost.

Further, even within the population that clearly and directly benefits from education, an additional distinction is crucial. The educational service provided to a child of an affluent family does not seem, for analytical purposes, to be an analogue either of the medical service provided to an indigent family under Medicare or of the education provided to a child of an indigent family. It can be argued that the intent of social policy is to provide medical and educational services at less than marginal cost to indigent households. However, presumably, children in affluent families are given free access to public education in the belief that by so doing some goal, say, socialization, is promoted—a goal quite distinct from redistribution. I think realism is excessively sacrificed if services such as education of the wealthy are denominated in-kind transfers along with public housing and food stamps.

A preferable procedure might be to designate first which programs can by general consensus be denominated redistributional in intent, as for example, Medicaid. Programs which seem to have some redistributional intent, such as public elementary and secondary education, can then be identified. Following this classification exercise, in-kind transfers can be estimated for either all or some fraction of the program's outlay, depending on its designation. Such a procedure is admittedly arbitrary, but I think it may be preferable to forcing programs into a redistributional mold that ill fits them.

Double-entry accounting requires a dollar-for-dollar reduction in personal taxes for each "Personal Consumption of Redistribution" entry. A reduction in taxes presumably implies an increase in households' discretionary power over income. Such an implication is plausible as long as we assume that all transfers are Pareto-efficient. However, I see no logical basis for restricting such reasoning to the transfer portion of government outlays. Must we not just as reasonably assume that all government outlays are Pareto-efficient? This assumption would then require us to create another entry, "Consumption of Public Services," which, in turn, would be offset dollar-for-dollar against personal taxes. As a consequence, all personal taxes would be eliminated from the Personal Income and Outlay Account. Public consumption would then be treated in the accounts on a par with market consumption, with the clear implication that coercion is not present in the payment of taxes. Although there is normative and undoubtedly considerable operational content to the benefit principle of taxation I think the judgment that all tax payments are discretionary expenditures is not fully justified.

These concerns with our authors' proposals for modifying the national accounts are mitigated, at least in my mind, if the proposals are not taken to require the complete elimination of current procedures. Though Occam's razor is a generally valid, even if little-used tool, I think that in this instance entities might well be multiplied. A useful measure of the distribution of welfare might well be obtained if series based on proposals similar to those of our authors were generated to supplement the current series. The complete elimination of time series data for disposable income, however, seems a high price to pay even for introducing welfare theory into the national accounts.

Our authors conclude that valuing recipient benefits on a cash-equivalent basis actually altered the size distribution of income only slightly, because they found that benefit weights are typically near unity. They infer from this result that donor benefits generated by the alteration of recipient consumption patterns must be unimportant. The authors' finding is undoubtedly valuable for policy considerations, but I am not comfortable with their dismissal of the importance to bureaucrats, if not to donors, of in-kind transfers. I suspect that the apparent long-standing preference for in-kind transfers over cash transfers must satisfy a donor wish that some attempt be made to control the spending patterns of the program recipients, or the dominance of in-kind over cash transfers may testify to the lobbying strength of such groups as the construction industry, the Farm Bureau, and the National Association of Social Workers.

Finally, there is the question of the proposed new entry, "Personal Consumption of Redistribution." Although one may feel a bit ill at ease with the preciseness of the figures displayed in Table 7, I think that their impact on the size distribution of welfare across income classes is entirely proper. Previous government benefit-incidence studies have typically ignored all external benefits whether redistributional or not and consequently have so allocated benefits that the fisc, specifically state and local fiscs, appear to redistribute welfare massively in favor of lower-income classes. Such results have generally been accepted as conventional wisdom even though it is difficult to interpret precisely what is meant by "benefits" in such a context. Certainly these benefits cannot be understood within the framework of benefit taxation. The massive benefits received by the lower-income classes in these studies, for example, cannot form the basis for assessing benefit taxes. Our authors' estimates for the personal consumption of redistribution, on the other hand, do establish a title for assessing benefit taxes.

One final observation concerning "Personal Consumption of Redistribution." What of the anomalous situation that can arise if the benefits represented by the

"Personal Consumption of Redistribution" can be increased merely by increasing the number of poor with a simultaneous increase in the dollar outlay for redistribution. As measured by "Consumption of Redistribution," it might well be that welfare in society increases pari passu with the number of poor in a society. This anomaly is dispelled, however, if it is recognized that benefit evaluation is made in a particular context with such variables as total output, income distribution, and the number of poor, all given. If these values change then the welfare measure of benefits must also be adjusted. This means, of course, that a time series of "Consumption of Redistribution" cannot be used unequivocally as an index of welfare across periods.

2

JOHN
KRAFT
Federal Energy
Administration

and

EDGAR O.
OLSEN
University of Virginia

The Distribution of Benefits from Public Housing

The federal public housing program had its origin in the United States Housing Act of 1937. At present there are more than one million public housing units occupied by more than three million people. Despite the age and size of this program, there are no published estimates of its effect on consumption patterns. Henry Aaron, Robert Bish, and Eugene Smolensky and J. Douglas Gomery have measured the benefit to a family in public housing as the difference between the market rent of its dwelling and the rent paid by the family and have made rough estimates of market rent in order to determine the distribution of direct benefits from the program. The primary purposes of this paper are to estimate the effect of the federal public housing program on the consumption patterns of its occupants and to determine the distribution of direct benefits from this

NOTE: The data underlying this study were collected in 1973 for the Department of Housing and Urban Development Housing Policy Review Task Force. We are grateful to the many people involved in their collection. The results reported here differ somewhat from those in the task force report because additional time has allowed us to make some improvements. We are also grateful to Michael Murray and participants in a seminar at the University of Michigan for critical comments and to Raymond Yacouby and Robert Berry for computational assistance.

program. These estimates are produced within the framework of a simple general equilibrium model and are based on a sample of 333 families who lived in public housing and 168 families who lived in private housing in Boston, Pittsburgh, St. Louis, San Francisco, and Washington in 1972.

I. THEORETICAL FRAMEWORK

Assume that there are two goods, housing service and nonhousing goods, and that the markets for these goods are perfectly competitive and in long-run equilibrium. Assume that the long-run supply curves in both markets are perfectly elastic.[1] These assumptions imply that the market prices of the two goods are unaffected by the public housing program.

Before proceeding, it is desirable to define the phrase housing service with some care. Housing service is a good provided in some unobservable quantity by each dwelling unit during each period of time. It is the one and only thing in a dwelling unit to which consumers attach value. More concretely, the quantity of housing service provided by a dwelling unit can be thought of as an index of all its attributes. If the private housing market is perfectly competitive, then in long-run equilibrium, each unit of housing service sold in one market sells for the same price. Hence, if we observe one apartment renting for $200 per month and another for $100 per month in the same market, then we say that the first apartment provides twice the quantity of housing service per time period that the second does.

Now let us use the assumptions made to derive formulas for calculating the effect of public housing on the consumption patterns of its occupants and the value of this program to these families. Figure 1 contains several indifference curves of one family living in public housing. In the absence of the program, this family would have some income Y and could buy as much of each good as it could pay for at prices P_h^m and P_n^m. It would select some combination (Q_h^m, Q_n^m) of the two goods. Under the public housing program, the family has been offered and has accepted a particular dwelling unit providing some quantity of housing service Q_h^g. In order to occupy this dwelling, the family must pay a certain rent $P_h^g Q_h^g$ per time period. After paying this rent, the family has enough money left to buy Q_n^g units of nonhousing goods. It is important to recognize that public housing does not change an eligible family's situation by rotating its budget line. In the two-good case, it simply adds one point to the family's budget space. Since the public housing authority could offer a family a dwelling worse than it would otherwise occupy (i.e., $Q_h^g < Q_h^m$) and charge a rent such that the family is able to increase its nonhousing consumption by more than enough to compensate for its decrease in housing consumption, the basic assumptions of the theory of consumer choice, together with the possible changes in budget spaces under the public housing program, do not imply that public housing tenants consume more housing service than they would in the absence of the program.

In the case depicted in Figure 1, the family consumes

$$100[(P_h^m Q_h^g - P_h^m Q_h^m)/P_h^m Q_h^m] \text{ percent}$$

FIGURE 1 The Effect of Public Housing on a Family's Consumption Pattern and Well-Being

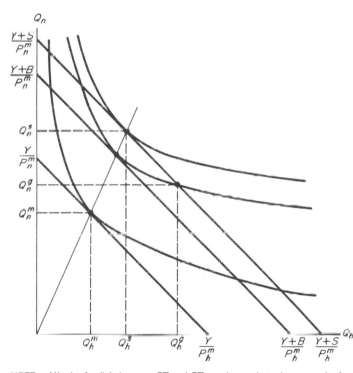

NOTE: Y is the family's income, P_h^m and P_n^m are the market prices per unit of housing service and nonhousing goods, Q_h^m and Q_n^m are the quantities of housing service and nonhousing goods consumed by the family in the absence of the public housing program, Q_h^g and Q_n^g are the quantities of housing service and nonhousing goods consumed by the family under the program, B is the value of the program to the family, S is the difference between the market value of the goods consumed by the family under the program and the family's income, O_h^s and O_n^s are the quantities of housing service and nonhousing goods that the family would consume were it given an unrestricted cash grant equal to S instead of its eligibility for public housing.

more housing service than it would have consumed in the absence of the public housing program. In addition the family spends

$$P_h^m Q_h^m - P_h^g Q_h^g$$

less on housing. As a result, it consumes a greater quantity of nonhousing goods. To be precise, it consumes

$$100[(P_n^m Q_n^g - P_n^m Q_n^m)/P_n^m Q_n^m] \text{ percent}$$

more nonhousing goods. Since there are only two goods, everything that the consumer does not spend on housing service is spent on nonhousing goods. Hence,

$$P_n^m Q_n^g = Y - P_h^g Q_h^g$$

and

$$P_n^m Q_n^m = Y - P_h^m Q_h^m$$

The proportional change in the total quantities of housing service and nonhousing goods for a set of families living in different cities can be calculated by formulas 1 and 2 where the subscript i indicates the ith family and the subscript j indicates the jth city. We write each formula in two ways to point out that our quantity indexes are arrived at by dividing expenditure figures by price indexes.

$$(1) \qquad \frac{\sum\limits_{j=1}^{k} \sum\limits_{i=1}^{r_j} (Q_{hij}^g - Q_{hij}^m)}{\sum\limits_{j=1}^{k} \sum\limits_{i=1}^{r_j} Q_{hij}^m} = \frac{\sum\limits_{j=1}^{k} \sum\limits_{i=1}^{r_j} [(P_{hj}^m Q_{hij}^g / P_{hj}^m) - (P_{hj}^m Q_{hij}^m / P_{hj}^m)]}{\sum\limits_{j=1}^{k} \sum\limits_{i=1}^{r_j} (P_{hj}^m Q_{hij}^m / P_{hj}^m)}$$

$$(2) \qquad \frac{\sum\limits_{j=1}^{k} \sum\limits_{i=1}^{r_j} (Q_{nij}^g - Q_{nij}^m)}{\sum\limits_{j=1}^{k} \sum\limits_{i=1}^{r_j} Q_{nij}^m} = \frac{\sum\limits_{j=1}^{k} \sum\limits_{i=1}^{r_j} [(P_{nj}^m Q_{nij}^g / P_{nj}^m) - (P_{nj}^m Q_{nij}^m / P_{nj}^m)]}{\sum\limits_{j=1}^{k} \sum\limits_{j=1}^{r_j} (P_{nj}^m Q_{nij}^m / P_{nj}^m)}$$

Notice that these formulas incorporate an implication of our assumptions that all markets are perfectly competitive and in long-run equilibrium, namely, that within each city all consumers pay the same price per unit of housing service and the same price per unit of nonhousing goods. However, it is not presumed that either price is the same in all cities.

There is some unrestricted cash grant B which, if given to this family in place of its eligibility for public housing, would make the family as well off as it is under the public housing program. This is what we mean by the benefit (or value) of the program to the family. Obviously, the value of the program to this family depends on its indifference map. In order to estimate the benefits of the program to families living in public housing, we assume that all such families have a utility function of the form

(3) $U = Q_h^a Q_n^{1-a}$

For a family having this utility function, Joseph De Salvo[2] has shown that

(4) $B = (P_h^m Q_h^g / a)^a [(Y - P_h^g Q_h^g)/(1-a)]^{1-a} - Y$

The mean benefit to a set of families occupying public housing is obtained by computing the benefit to each family and calculating the mean of these numbers. Mean benefit cannot be obtained by substituting the mean values of a, Y, $P_h^m Q_h^g$, and $P_h^g Q_h^g$ into (4).

Under the assumptions made in this section, the effect of the program on aggregate consumption of housing service and nonhousing goods by the public housing tenants in our sample and the benefit to each family can be calculated from a knowledge of each family's income, its expenditure on housing under the public housing program and in its absence, the market rent of its public housing unit, the parameter of its indifference map, and the differences in the market prices of housing service and nonhousing goods in different cities. We know the income of, and the rent paid by, a sample of public housing tenants. The U.S. Department of Labor produces cross-sectional indexes of housing and nonhousing prices. We must predict how much each family would spend on housing in the absence of the program, the parameter of its indifference map, and the market rent of its public housing unit.

II. PREDICTION OF THE PARAMETER OF A FAMILY'S INDIFFERENCE MAP AND ITS HOUSING EXPENDITURE IN THE ABSENCE OF THE PUBLIC HOUSING PROGRAM

The "parameter" a is simply the proportion of income spent on housing by a consumer with the preferences (3) facing the budget constraint

$P_h Q_h + P_n Q_n = Y$

We assume that a depends in part on certain family characteristics but is not identical for all families which are the same with respect to these characteristics. Specifically, we assume

(5) $a = b_0 + b_1 R + b_2 S + b_3 N + b_4 A + u$

where $R = 1$ if the head of household is nonwhite and 0 if white, $S = 1$ if the head of the household is female and 0 if male, N = number of persons in the household, A = age of the head of the household, and u = a random variable with mean zero and variance independent of these family characteristics.[3] Therefore, the best linear unbiased predictor of a for a family selected at random is

$$\hat{b}_0 + \hat{b}_1 R + \hat{b}_2 S + \hat{b}_3 N + \hat{b}_4 A$$

where the $\hat{b}$'s are the least-squares estimators of the b's in (5), based on a sample of families who buy both goods in the private market.

We had data on the housing expenditure, income, number of persons, and the age, race, and sex of the head of 168 households living in Boston, St. Louis, San Francisco, and Washington just prior to their admission to public housing. These data were used to estimate a relationship of the form (5) for each city separately and for all cities combined. The

TABLE 1   Estimated Relationships between Rent–Income Ratio and Family Characteristics

	Boston	St. Louis	San Francisco	Washington	Combined
Constant	.3726	.2830	.3959	.4788	.4364
	(2.89)	(2.16)	(2.39)	(4.57)	(5.89)
Race of head of household	−.0688	–	−.0598	–	−.0668
	(−.97)	–	(−.72)	–	(−1.61)
Sex of head of household	.0886	.1758	.0172	.1311	.0979
	(1.47)	(2.30)	(.26)	(2.49)	(3.19)
Numbers of persons in household	−.0193	−.0080	.0109	−.0307	−.0164
	(−2.18)	(−.69)	(.54)	(−2.95)	(−2.95)
Age of head of household	.0013	−.0016	−.0010	−.0023	−.0009
	(0.76)	(−.74)	(−.49)	(−1.39)	(−1.06)
Mean rent-income ratio	.35	.34	.35	.39	.36
Number of observations	40	48	40	40	168
R^2 (adjusted)	.26	.14	−.08	.22	.10
Standard error	.15	.17	.19	.14	.17

NOTE: All families in the samples for St. Louis and Washington were nonwhite.

estimated coefficients, t-scores, and other statistics are reported in Table 1. We also had data on the characteristics of 333 families living in public housing in these four cities and Pittsburgh. The characteristics of the public housing tenants living in Boston, St. Louis, San Francisco, and Washington were substituted into the equations for these cities to predict the proportions of their incomes that they would devote to housing in the absence of the public housing program. Since we had no data on families living in private housing in Pittsburgh, we used the relationship based on data from all four cities to make predictions for public housing tenants in this city.

Each family's predicted rent-income ratio was multiplied by its income to predict how much the family would have spent on housing in the absence of the program.

III. PREDICTION OF THE MARKET RENT OF A PUBLIC HOUSING UNIT

Robert Gillingham has estimated relationships between market rent and housing characteristics in each of the five cities, using data for 1960.[4] The housing characteristics included were age of structure; number of rooms; number of bathrooms; condition of unit; inclusion in rent of furnishings, refrigerator, air conditioning, and stove; the presence of hot running water, central heat, covered parking, and elevator; number of persons in unit; and race of the head of the household. We tried to obtain data on these characteristics for the 333 public housing units in our sample. There were some gaps in the data. Most importantly, year built was not reported for the 120 leased existing units in the sample. We assumed that the age of each of these units was equal to the median age of private housing in the same city. In all, somewhat less than 5 percent of the desired information was missing and was filled in with well-educated guesses. The information on the characteristics of the public housing units in the sample was substituted into Gillingham's equations to predict the market rents of these units in 1960. Bureau of Labor Statistics (BLS) time-series housing price indexes were used to adjust these predictions to 1972.

IV. EMPIRICAL RESULTS

We know the income of, and the rent paid by, a sample of 333 families living in public housing. There are cross-sectional indexes of housing and nonhousing prices. The parameter of each family's indifference map, its housing expenditure in the absence of the program, and the market rent of its public housing unit have been predicted. The sample means of $P_h^g Q_h^g$, $P_h^m Q_h^m$, $P_h^m Q_h^g$, and Y are \$74, \$132, \$148, and \$450 per month. The sample mean of a is .32.

Using equations 1 and 2, we estimate that public housing tenants in this sample consumed 11 percent more housing service and 18 percent more nonhousing goods than they would have consumed in the absence of this program.[5] Of course, different families experienced different percentage changes in their consumption of the two goods. Indeed, we estimate that 33 percent of these families occupied worse housing and 9 percent spent less on other goods.

The usual arguments for housing subsidies imply that the attainment of an efficient allocation of resources, preferred by everyone, to the allocation in the absence of subsidies requires that recipients consume more housing service and less nonhousing goods than they would consume were they allowed to choose any combination of goods with the same market value as the combination consumed under the housing subsidy program. Therefore, it is important to compare Q_h^g and Q_h^s in Figure 1. Table 2 presents the distribution of the variable

$$100(Q_h^g - Q_h^s)/Q_h^s = 100(P_h^m Q_h^g - P_h^m Q_h^s)/P_h^m Q_h^s$$

for the families in this sample. We estimate that public housing is more stimulative of housing consumption than cash grants for a bare majority (54 percent) of these families. Therefore, the effect of public housing on consumption patterns appears to be inconsistent with the rationale of this program for a substantial minority of its direct beneficiaries.

Formula 4 was used to estimate the value of the public housing program to each family in the sample. The mean of these numbers is \$54 per month.[6] Had each of these families been allowed to consume any combination of goods with the same market value as the combination that it consumed under the program, the mean benefit would have been \$74 per month.[7] The difference is a manifestation of the tremendous distortions in consumption patterns under the program from the viewpoint of public housing tenants. These distortions are evident in Table 2.

If there had been no cost of administering the public housing program and no inefficiency in producing housing service under the program, then \$74 would have been the mean cost incurred by taxpayers on behalf of the families in this sample. All existing estimates (Smolensky 1968, pp. 94–101; Olsen 1968, pp. 69–78; Muth 1973, pp. 7–20; Kraft and Olsen 1973, pp. 11–38) suggest that it costs more than a dollar to produce a dollar's worth of housing service under the conventional and turnkey variants of public housing. Therefore, even if the cost of administering a

TABLE 2 Distribution of Deviations of Housing Consumption under the Public Housing Program from Housing Consumption with Unrestricted Cash Grants

Percentage Deviations	Percentage of Families in Sample
Less than	6.6
−49 to −40−49	6.0
−39 to −30	6.6
−29 to −20	8.4
−19 to −10	6.9
−9 to 0	11.4
0 to 9	12.0
10 to 19	8.7
20 to 29	6.9
30 to 39	7.8
40 to 49	6.3
More than 49	12.3

program of unrestricted cash grants was as great as the cost of administering the public housing program, the mean cost incurred by taxpayers on behalf of the families in this sample was probably greater than $74 per month. By giving these families unrestricted cash grants, it would have been possible to induce each family to consume a combination of goods that it considered to be as satisfactory as the combination consumed under the public housing program, while reducing the cost to taxpayers by at least 27 percent.

The preceding results are not based on a random sample from the population of families in public housing. Furthermore, the characteristics of the families in this sample differ significantly from the characteristics of all public housing families. Some of these differences are reported in Table 3.

In order to get better estimates of mean tenant benefit and proportional changes in consumption of housing service and nonhousing goods for the entire program, we regressed each of these variables on family characteristics, using data in the sample, and substituted the mean characteristics of all public housing families into these estimated

TABLE 3 Comparison of Characteristics of all Public Housing Families with Public Housing Families in Sample

Characteristics	Sample	Universe
Mean monthly income	$450	$289
Mean number of persons	4.8	3.3
Mean age of head of household	39	49
Percentage of households headed by nonwhite	86	60
Percentage of households headed by female	60	72

SOURCE: The mean age of head of household for the entire population of households in public housing was estimated from the age distributions in Tables 108 and 113 of the *1971 HUD Statistical Abstract*. The other means and percentages for the universe of households in public housing were estimated by Susan Kete of the U.S. Department of Housing and Urban Development.

relationships.[8] In effect, we argue that, although the characteristics of the families in the sample differ significantly from the characteristics of all families in public housing, the relationships between the variables of interest and family characteristics in the sample are good estimates of the relationships for the population.[9] The estimated coefficients, t scores, and other statistics are reported in Table 4. Substituting the mean characteristics of all families in public housing into the first two equations yields estimates of 33 and 14 percent for the changes in aggregate consumption of housing service and nonhousing goods. This compares with estimates of 11 and 18 percent based on the sample alone. These estimates lead us to believe that the increase in aggregate consumption of housing service is greater for all families in public housing than for the families in our sample and that the program distorts consumption towards housing for substantially more than 54 percent of all public-housing tenants. Substituting the mean characteristics of all families in public housing into the third equation leads us to conclude that mean tenant benefit for the entire program is $81 per month.

An estimated relationship between net tenant benefit and family characteristics is also useful for analyzing the distribution of benefits among families in public housing. For this purpose, we estimated the following relationship:

$$(6) \quad B = 130.19 - .149Y - .000079Y^2 + 16.74N - .910N^2$$
$$\quad\quad (4.05) \quad (-3.55) \quad (-2.75) \quad\quad (3.38) \quad (-2.22)$$

$$\quad\quad -.305A - .0010A^2 - 15.11S - 22.53R$$
$$\quad\quad (-.21) \quad (-.06) \quad (-2.21) \quad (-2.46)$$

$$R^2 \text{ (adj.)} = .52;$$
$$S = 56$$

The numbers in parentheses are t scores.

Since we were able to reject at the 5 percent level of significance the hypothesis that the coefficients of the squared terms are all zero, we conclude that there are nonlinearities in the relationship between mean tenant benefit and family characteristics. Equation 6 indicates that mean benefit varies inversely with income and directly with family size for families of less than nine persons. We can be moderately confident that households headed by females receive smaller benefits than households headed by males and that nonwhite households receive smaller benefits than white households. The hypothesis that net tenant benefit varies with the age of the head of the household can be rejected at the 5 percent level of significance. Table 5 shows that if we do not hold constant other characteristics, mean benefit increases with income at the lowest income levels and decreases with income at higher levels.

TABLE 4 Regressions of Weighted Proportional Changes in Consumption and Tenant Benefit on Family Characteristics

	Weighted Proportional Change in Housing Consumption	Weighted Proportional Change in Nonhousing Consumption	Net Tenant Benefit
Constant	.991	.0539	179.39
	(9.87)	(1.55)	(11.08)
Monthly income	−.00232	.00058	−.252
	(−25.72)	(18.48)	(−17.33)
Race of head of household	.0372	−.0963	−20.17
	(.65)	(−4.85)	(−2.19)
Age of head of household	.00145	−.0022	−.541
	(.90)	(−3.88)	(−2.09)
Number of persons in household	.0755	−.0189	7.62
	(8.53)	(−6.15)	(5.34)
Sex of head of household	−.465	.206	−16.86
	(−10.93)	(13.92)	(−2.46)
Mean of regressand	.11	.18	54
Number of observations	333	333	333
R^2 (adjusted)	.67	.57	50
Standard error	.35	.12	.57

NOTE: *t*-statistics are in parentheses.

TABLE 5 The Distribution of Benefits from Public Housing by Income Class in 1972

Income Class (1)	Mean Income of Households in Sample (2)	Mean Benefits to Households in Sample (3)	Standard Deviation of Benefits to Households in Sample (4)	Number of Households in Public Housing (5)	Number of Households in U.S. (6)	Percentage of Households Served by Program (7)	Mean Benefits to All Households in U.S. (8)	Standard Deviation of Benefits to All Households in U.S. (9)
$ 0–999	$ 960	$ 478	$336	26,000	1,758,000	1.5	$ 7	$ 71
1,000–1,999	1,655	885	412	283,000	3,812,000	7.4	66	257
2,000–2,999	2,569	1,095	380	249,000	4,320,000	5.8	64	272
3,000–3,999	3,491	1,170	432	184,000	3,958,000	4.7	55	265
4,000–4,999	4,347	1,070	614	124,000	3,844,000	3.2	34	218
5,000–5,999	5,318	781	634	73,000	3,759,000	2.0	16	141
6,000–6,999	6,408	421	609	46,000	3,624,000	1.2	5	81
7,000–7,999	7,467	141	563	28,000	3,846,000	0.7	1	48
Totals				1,055,000	68,537,000			
Means	5,397	649						

NOTE: Columns (5), (6), and (7) are taken from Table 30 of Chapter 4 of *Housing in the Seventies*. All dollar amounts in this table are annual.

Not only does mean benefit vary inversely with income among families living in public housing, after taking account of the effects of other characteristics, but also such families are on the average poorer than those not served by the program. In 1972, the median annual income of all families in the United States was more than $10,000, whereas it was less than $3,000 for families in public housing.

Behind these measures of central tendency lie some disturbing variances which reflect unfavorably upon the equity of the public housing program. The estimate of the standard deviation of the error term in regression 6 suggests that we should expect roughly one-third of a set of families that are the same with respect to the five characteristics included in the regression to receive benefits deviating from the mean by at least $56 per month. This enormous variance in benefits to similarly situated families in public housing can also be seen in column 4 of Table 5. In part, these differences in benefits are due to the great variance in the desirability of different public housing units. Among families that are the same with respect to the five characteristics, some occupy new units in excellent condition while others live in deteriorating older units.

As important as the large variance in benefits to similarly situated families who get into public housing is the fact that most families at the lowest income levels receive no benefits. Indeed, most of the neediest families are not served, while many less needy families are served. Table 5 indicates that about 50 percent of the families in public housing have annual incomes in excess of $3,000, while 95 percent of all families in the United States with annual incomes less than $3,000 are not served by the program.

Combining data in columns 3 through 7, we are able to estimate the mean and standard deviation of benefits to all households in each income class. This mean benefit first rises and then falls with income. While these standard deviations are smaller than the standard deviations of benefits among families who get into public housing, the coefficients of variation are much larger.

NOTES

1. This assumption is consistent with the finding of Richard Muth (1960, pp. 42–46), but Frank de Leeuw and Nkanta Ekanem find price elasticities of long-run supply between 0.3 and 0.7.
2. The Cobb-Douglas indifference map is appealing because it yields an explicit formula for calculating benefits. Other widely used indifference maps do not yield such a formula. In these cases, it is necessary to solve a different nonlinear programming problem for each family in order to estimate its benefit. The Cobb-Douglas indifference map is roughly consistent with empirical evidence on the demand for housing service which suggests that the price elasticity of demand is approximately equal to minus one and the permanent-income elasticity is about equal to one. Unfortunately, our data

include current income but do not contain a good proxy for permanent income, and estimates of the current-income elasticity are substantially less than one. In order to test our specification (3), we estimated the parameters of a displaced Cobb-Douglas indifference map,

$$U = (Q_h - b_h)^a (Q_n - b_n)^{1-a}$$

of which equation 3 is a special case. We rejected at the 5 percent level of significance the hypothesis that both displacement parameters are zero. Michael Murray has estimated the parameters of a generalized Constant Elasticity of Substitution (CES) indifference map using current income. The Cobb-Douglas indifference map is also a special case of the generalized CES. Murray rejected at the 5 percent level of significance the Cobb-Douglas specification. Clearly, we have sacrificed accuracy for simplicity in estimating benefits.

3. We tested for nonlinearities by estimating a relationship including age of head of household and number of persons squared. For all four cities we could not reject at the 5 percent level of significance the hypothesis that the coefficients of these two variables are both equal to zero.

4. It should be noted that the coefficients of determination range in value from 0.55 to 0.75. The regressand in these regressions is the natural logarithm of gross rent, and data on individual dwelling units are used.

5. In response to Henry Aaron's closing remark, it should be noted that the accuracy of these estimates depends on the accuracy with which the *mean* housing expenditure in the absence of the program and the *mean* market rent have been estimated. This depends upon, but is not the same thing as, the accuracy with which the housing expenditures of individual families and the market rents of individual dwellings can be predicted. With 333 observations, the means can be estimated with much greater accuracy than the values for individuals.

6. It is common to use aggregate data to estimate the mean benefit of a government program to a set of families. Substituting the sample means of a, $P_h^m Q_h^g$, $P_h^g Q_h^g$, and Y into formula 4 yields $72 per month. Obviously, the results of this procedure can be very misleading.

7. The most frequently used measure of the benefit of a government program to a family is the excess of the market value of the goods consumed under the program over the market value of the goods that would have been consumed in its absence. Seventy-four dollars is the mean of these differences for our sample. Since this measure assumes that an individual is indifferent between all combinations of goods with the same market value, it is clearly cruder than the measure used in this paper which only assumes that an individual is indifferent between all dwelling units with the same market value.

8. The proportional changes in aggregate consumption of housing service and nonhousing goods are equal to the means of the weighted proportional changes for individual families, where the weights are the ratio of each family's consumption of the good to mean consumption. That is

$$\sum_{i=1}^{n} (Q_i^g - Q_i^m) \Big/ \sum_{i=1}^{n} Q_i^m = (1/n) \sum_{i=1}^{n} \left[Q_i^m \Big/ \left(\sum_{i=1}^{n} Q_i^m / n \right) \right] [(Q_i^g - Q_i^m)/Q_i^m]$$

These weighted proportional changes in consumption are the dependent variables in the regressions reported in Table 4. Substituting the mean characteristics of the households in our sample into these estimated relationships yields the estimates of the proportional changes in aggregate consumption already reported.

9. Two possibly important objections to this assumption are that the rent schedules and the age and, hence, quality distributions of public housing units are likely to be different between local housing authorities in the sample and other local housing authorities.

REFERENCES

Aaron, Henry J. *Shelter and Subsidies.* Studies in Social Economics. Washington, D.C.: The Brookings Institution, 1972.

Bish, Robert L. "Public Housing: The Magnitude and Distribution of Direct Benefits and Effects on Housing Consumption," *Journal of Regional Science* 9 (Dec. 1969): 425–438.

de Leeuw, Frank, and Ekanem, Nkanta F. "The Supply of Rental Housing." *American Economic Review* 61 (Dec. 1971): 807–817.

De Salvo, Joseph S. "A Methodology for Evaluating Housing Programs." *Journal of Regional Science* 11 (Aug. 1971): 173–185.

Gillingham, Robert F. "Place-to-Place Rent Comparisons Using Hedonic Quality Adjustment Techniques." Ph.D. diss., University of Pennsylvania, 1973.

Kraft, John, and Olsen, Edgar O. "An Evaluation of Public Housing." Oct. 1973, processed.

Murray, Michael. "The Distribution of Tenant Benefits in Public Housing." *Econometrica* 43 (July 1975): 771–788.

Muth, Richard F. "The Demand for Non-Farm Housing." In Arnold C. Harberger, ed., *The Demand for Durable Goods.* Chicago: University of Chicago Press, 1960.

————. *Public Housing: An Economic Evaluation.* Evaluation Studies. Washington, D.C.: American Enterprise Institute for Public Policy Research, 1973.

Olsen, Edgar O. "A Welfare Economic Evaluation of Public Housing." Ph.D. diss., Rice University, 1968.

Smolensky, Eugene. "Public Housing or Income Supplements—The Economics of Housing for the Poor." *Journal of the American Institute of Planners* 34 (Mar. 1968): 94–101.

Smolensky, Eugene, and Gomery, J. Douglas. "Efficiency and Equity Effects in the Benefits from the Federal Public Housing Program in 1965." In *Benefit-Cost Analyses of Federal Programs,* a compendium of papers submitted to the Subcommittee on Priorities and Economy in Government of the Joint Economic Committee of the Congress of the United States. Washington, D.C., 1973.

U.S. Department of Housing and Urban Development. *1971 HUD Statistical Yearbook.* Washington, D.C., 1972

————. *Housing in the Seventies.* Washington, D.C., 1974

U.S. Department of Labor, Bureau of Labor Statistics. *Three Budgets for an Urban Family of Four Persons: 1969–70.* Supplement to Bulletin No. 1570-5.

————. *The Consumer Price Index: U.S. City Average and Selected Areas.* Monthly.

2 | COMMENTS

Henry Aaron
The Brookings Institution and University of Maryland

Economists have long argued that subsidies should be provided in cash rather than in kind if the objective is to maximize the increase in the recipient's

---

NOTE: The views expressed are those of the author, and not necessarily those of the officers, trustees, or other staff members of the Brookings Institution or the University of Maryland.

well-being. As a number of authors have recently pointed out, this conclusion does not follow if those who are paying for the subsidy care about the items which the recipient consumes as well as (or instead of) his general well-being. Others have argued that society may be a better custodian of the rights of children than are parents, and that restriction of subsidies to items consumed jointly by the household (e.g., housing) or that bulk larger in the utility functions of children than in those of adults (e.g., food) may be warranted. Still others have held that the decision about which goods should be allocated through the market, which through other means, and which through some combination is itself a political judgment, in the making of which no automatic presumption in favor of market allocation is warranted. Indeed, Schmundt, Stieffel, and Smolensky have shown that if consideration is accorded to opinions about the consumption mix of beneficiaries held by persons other than the recipient, then transfers that do not distort consumption (i.e., unrestricted income transfers) are, in general, suboptimal.

However these issues are resolved, it is important to know how much particular subsidies do distort consumption choices of recipients. In such calculations, it is necessary, in principle, to take account of all other subsidies in measuring distortions, although in practice this counsel of perfection is usually ignored.

The paper by John Kraft and Edgar Olsen is an important step in the effort to estimate the inefficiencies of in-kind subsidies viewed solely in terms of the tastes of recipients. This paper grew out of evaluations performed within the Department of Housing and Urban Development to determine whether federal housing subsidies should be extended, revised, or abolished. Kraft and Olsen proceed by noting that public housing enlarges the choice set of recipients by one point. Access to public housing enables recipients to buy a certain quantity of housing at a subsidized price. In principle, this quantity of housing may be greater or less than the recipient would consume, and the rent charged may be greater or less than recipients would pay, in the absence of public housing. All that is required for the tenant to accept public housing is that he enjoy increased utility from the quantity of public housing and the quantity of other goods that can be purchased after the subsidized rent has been paid.

To clarify what Kraft and Olsen have done, consider the following simple identities

C = total cost of supplying public housing

$-N$ = inefficiencies of supplying public housing (may be positive or negative)

M = market value of public housing

$-S$ = subsidy to tenants

R = rent paid by tenants

Clearly the net financial cost of public housing to various governments is $N + S$, but the welfare cost of public housing is less to the extent that S improves tenant utility. Some unrestricted cash transfer, T, would put the potential public housing tenant on the same indifference surface as does public housing. If $S - T = Z$ measures the consumption inefficiency of public housing, $N + Z$ measures its welfare cost. Kraft and Olsen measure Z. They ignore N, which was treated in other HUD studies.

Kraft and Olsen computed M by modifying and applying hedonic price indexes (estimated by Robert Gillingham) to the physical characteristics of 333 public housing units. Given R from public housing records, S then is a residual. To calculate Z, T must be estimated, which requires that Kraft and Olsen obtain the household's utility function.

They do so by assuming a Cobb-Douglas utility function of two goods, housing and other goods. The exponent of housing in this function is also its budget share. Kraft and Olsen estimate the proportion of income public-housing tenants would spend on housing if they rented on the unsubsidized market from a regression of this share on race, sex, and age of household head, and household size of a sample of low-income households from whom data were collected just before their admission to public housing in Boston, St. Louis, San Francisco, and Washington. These functions are used to calculate how much residents of public housing with various characteristics would spend on housing if they did not live in public housing. Given this share, the Cobb-Douglas utility function is specified (since the budget share of housing equals its exponent). It is then easy to calculate the unrestricted transfer T that would be just as attractive as access to public housing. Kraft and Olsen estimate that $S = \$74$, $T = \$54$, and that therefore the consumption inefficiency of public housing, Z, was about 27 percent among sampled households.

Kraft and Olsen next regress the estimated change in housing and other consumption and estimated net benefit of sampled households on various household characteristics. Based on mean values of these characteristics for all public-housing tenants, they conclude that the distortion of consumption is considerably greater for all households than for sampled households.

Kraft and Olsen also estimate that net tenant benefit T first rises then falls with tenant income, presumably because the distortive effects of public housing are greater and, hence, the additions to utility are smaller as incomes tend toward zero. As incomes rise beyond a certain point, so do rents, thus reducing net benefits.

Finally, they observe that these inefficiencies do not occur so much because public housing *on the average* increases housing consumption more than consumption if the government gives S in cash, but rather because some households are forced to consume too much and some to consume too little. In fact, public housing induces a bare majority, 51 percent, of sample households to consume more housing than they would if given S in cash.

The conclusion is clear though unstated. For the sampled households, public housing distorts consumption but increases it no more on the average than would an unrestricted transfer. Whatever might be said on behalf of a program that increased housing consumption of most families, little can be said for one that capriciously distorts it. Some other form of housing assistance must be better, and housing allowances spring to mind. While I agree with the conclusion, I have serious qualms about the analysis.

My comments fall into two categories. The first concerns the possibility of bias in the point estimates Kraft and Olsen present. The second concerns the standard error that surrounds those estimates.

1. The fraction of income households would freely spend on housing is crucial to the analysis. This fraction is based on regressions using data for households just prior to their admission to public housing. The proportion of the variance in the housing income ratio explained by these regressions is remarkably low [one R^2 (adjusted) is negative, the others range from .14 to .26]. This means that most of the variance in the housing-income ratio is due to other factors. The method that Kraft and Olsen have used converts these unexplained variances into estimates of distortion by public housing.

An example will illustrate the problem. Assume that we estimate the rent-income ratio for a sample of households as a function of several variables, exactly as Kraft and Olsen did, and that the regression explains, say, 20 percent of the variance in the rent-income ratio. Assume now that this sample moves into public housing and that each family consumes exactly the same amount of housing as it would have consumed if it had been given S in cash. By definition there is no distortion in housing consumption; $S = T$ and $Z = 0$. Yet if we estimate the distortion from the *predicted* rent-income ratio, in a manner analogous to that used by Kraft and Olsen, we will conclude that 80 percent of the variation in rent-income ratios is the result of distortion caused by public housing. This problem vanishes only if the equation predicting the rent-income ratio has an R^2 of 1.0, and it is directly proportional to the amount by which R^2 is less than 1.0. One must hold suspect calculations which are based on regressions that leave at least three-quarters of the variation in the rent-income ratio unexplained, and which, in effect, charge as distortions of public housing the difference between the actual rent-income ratio and such an estimated value.

There are two other reasons why, I think, Kraft and Olsen overestimate distortion. First, one would expect that families with above-average tastes for housing would show positive residuals in the equation that estimates rent-income ratios, and would be more likely than families with lower tastes to accept public housing only if it were better than average (and, of course, relatively cheap). The reverse argument suggests that households with below-average tastes for housing would differentially end up in lower-quality public housing units. By ignoring both such assortative effects, Kraft and Olsen tend to overestimate distortion.

But even if distortion is overestimated, any distortion is too much if public housing does not cause more housing to be consumed than would an unrestricted cash transfer. I think there is reason to suspect that Kraft and Olsen underestimate the impact of public housing on housing consumption.

The rent-income ratio of households just before admission to public housing is likely to be abnormally high. It is more likely that the current measured income of such households is below rather than above normal income. Kraft and Olsen acknowledge that using measured income may cause problems. In fact, they understate the increase in housing consumption to the extent that the ratio of housing consumption to current income exceeds the ratio of housing consumption to normal income.

Second, Kraft and Olsen use a convenient construct, developed, I think, by Muth, that defines a unit of housing service as whatever $1 buys. It is a very useful approach and I have used it, as has Olsen, in previous work. The rationale for using this construct is that under conditions of equilibrium, the marginal utility of $1 spent by the tenant on each feature of the house must be equal and must equal the cost of providing it. Those of us who feel that the housing industry is fairly competitive have no trouble accepting this assumption for aggregative analysis. However, I think that it is unacceptable at the micro level.

Unless all households are in equilibrium all the time, the marginal value to particular households of the various features of a housing unit may not equal the market value of these features. Even if we are willing to apply hedonic indexes estimated for market housing to public housing, there is no reason to think that public-housing tenants value the particular bundle of features public housing units contain in the same way as the market would. In other words, there is no way of knowing whether a public-housing tenant, who if given S would have spent exactly M on housing, would have chosen public housing—with its peculiar set of features often unavailable in the free market—or market housing if both had a market value of M and rented for M. Once again, however, there is some reason to think that households that cared less than average for the features that public housing had in greatest supply would be less likely to end up in public housing. Conversely, one would expect that households that liked the features of public housing more than average would be more likely to end up in public housing.

2. The estimates presented in the Kraft-Olsen paper are consistently insignificant. Not only are the relationships between rent-income ratios very loose (8 coefficients out of 14 are smaller than their standard errors), but, more importantly, the estimates of the impact of public housing on consumption of housing and of other goods and the estimates of the net tenant benefit are so unreliable that one cannot reject any of the following hypotheses for particular households at even unimpressive levels of significance:

1. that housing consumption doubles;
2. that housing consumption declines 50 percent;
3. that housing consumption goes up more than nonhousing consumption;
4. that housing consumption goes up less than nonhousing consumption; or
5. that net benefits of public housing are negative.

Having worried about the same questions Kraft and Olsen address in their paper, and having gotten nowhere, I admire the ingenuity and the care that they have demonstrated. I also have preconceptions about the desirability of sub-sidies, tied to housing demand rather than to supply, which I know they share. I look forward to evidence in support of our views that is free of the questionable elements of the current paper. In the meantime, we should all be grateful for the step forward that their effort represents.

3

HAROLD M.
HOCHMAN
City University
of New York

and

JAMES D.
RODGERS
Pennsylvania State
University

The Simple Politics of Distributional Preference

Income redistribution, in its many facets, poses extraordinarily difficult and complex problems for both normative and positive economics. For normative economics, it has, until recently,[1] meant irreconcilable conflict. With regard to how much redistribution should occur, scholars, notwithstanding long debate, remain agnostic, as they have been since Lord Robbins shattered the scientific illusion of classical utilitarianism.[2]

For positive economics, the realm of this paper, efforts to interpret redistribution have exposed the limited extent of our progress in over-

NOTE: When this paper was written, Hochman was visiting lecturer in the Graduate School of Public Policy, University of California at Berkeley. Denis Aitken, William Bicker, Mickey Levy, Edward Neuschler, and Ted Radosevich deserve credit for assistance with the data. Research support from the National Science Foundation is gratefully acknowledged: Hochman's grant was GS-33244X; Rodgers' was GS-33224X. Data for this study, originally collected by the Field Research Corporation, were provided by the State Data Program of the Institute of Governmental Studies, with the assistance of the Survey Research Center, University of California at Berkeley. These organizations are not responsible for the analysis and interpretation of data appearing here.

coming the conundrums of empirical measurement and modeling. The measurement problem itself poses two broad problems. One relates to the adequacy and availability of data and the other to the conceptual difficulties encountered in determining the incidence of public expenditures. While there exist studies of the redistributive impact of individual programs,[3] general-equilibrium problems have befuddled efforts to develop convincing estimates of the overall amount of redistribution.[4]

The development and empirical testing of positive theoretical models intended to explain the extent to which individuals and communities choose to engage in income redistribution has also produced but limited progress. Existing positive research can be divided into two parts, one dealing with transfers carried out in the private sector (through charity, donations of time, and intergeneration gifts)[5] and the other, on which this paper focuses, with income redistribution through government programs.

In a society with a democratic government,[6] there are at least two different, though complementary, ways in which the analysis of public redistribution may be approached. The first inquires into how much redistribution will occur and what its pattern may be expected to be.[7] The second starts with the overall pattern of redistribution produced by an existing government, or by the existence of a particular redistributive program, and attempts to construct a theory to account for it. In one sense these two approaches are similar. Both call for a theory that contains not only a model of individual behavior subject to constraints, but also a model of the political process through which preferences for goods and services with "public" characteristics are transmitted. The difference is that the first approach asks a question that is open-ended, while the second starts with a particular pattern of redistribution.

This paper adopts the second approach. Its concern is with explaining, in terms of individual preferences, public redistribution to low-income persons—to be specific, those distributional adjustments, taken as a group, that are commonly referred to as "welfare" programs.

A number of recent papers have argued that income redistribution, through tax-financed, poverty-alleviating income transfers, may represent a collective response to the existence of nonmarket interactions between the poor and the nonpoor, the nonpoor being concerned, for a variety of reasons, with the well-being, or the consumption-leisure choices, of the poor.[8] One ground on which this explanation of income transfers has been criticized is that transfer recipients, as well as taxpayers, have the franchise, so that observed transfers may well be attributable to the political power of the former rather than to the preferences of the nonpoor.[9] Thus, provided that transfer recipients exercise their right to vote, the conventional assumption of universal independent preferences, combined with direct or representative decision making by majority rule, may in itself be sufficient to account for transfers to the poor.

While we have no intention of denying that transfer recipients, through voting, will support programs that provide them with benefits, either monetary or in kind, the thrust of our argument will be that the support of recipients, given the voting rules in force, cannot itself account for the existence of such programs. This does not mean that self-interest considerations play no part in generating support for redistribution to the poor. But it does mean that something must be present, in addition to simple recipient self-interest, to account fully for the redistribution that is observed.

The remainder of this paper presents the analytical basis for these remarks and some evidence of individual preferences which seems to support them. In Part I, we discuss the basis of nonrecipient support for redistribution. Part II contains a model of redistribution in direct democracy. In Part III, this model is extended to a setting of indirect or representative democracy, and we explore how much nonrecipient support the enactment of redistribution requires. In Part IV, an effort is made to derive real-world measures of distributional preference from the responses of a panel of California citizens to queries about welfare spending and other redistributive expenditures. In Part V, the implications of these responses are examined in terms of the political models developed in Parts II and III. Part VI, set at a more general level, offers a few concluding remarks about the line of reasoning pursued in this paper.

I. THE BASIS FOR NONRECIPIENT SUPPORT FOR REDISTRIBUTION

A major theme of this paper is that the political base on which support for redistribution rests extends well beyond its direct recipients. We imply by this that many nonrecipients do not behave like simplistic "economic men," concerned with their own disposable incomes and the goods and services these incomes can buy for own-use, and nothing else.

Some nonrecipients, of course, may support redistribution to the poor for reasons that seem almost as straightforward as those of recipients. A nonrecipient may support welfare programs because (a) he expects, with high probability, to himself be a direct recipient at some future time; (b) he may derive income from some activity that is favorably affected by such redistributive programs (e.g., farmers presumably have higher incomes because of food stamps, and social workers receive higher salaries because of Aid to Families with Dependent Children); or (c) he may view transfer programs as substitutes for transfers he would otherwise feel obliged to make privately, entirely on his own (e.g., persons with parents drawing Old Age Assistance).

But the basis of nonrecipient support for redistributive programs may extend beyond simple self-interest. Transfers to the poor may be viewed, as mentioned earlier, as a collective response to nonmarket interactions between the status or activities of the poor and nonpoor members of the community. Such nonmarket interactions may take several forms. Nonrecipients may be concerned, for a variety of reasons, with the well-being of the poor, or at least interested in seeing that all individuals have access to minimum amounts of certain commodities and services, such as food, housing, and medical care. Thus, the individual's utility function may include, as an argument, the welfare (or some proxy for welfare like income) of other persons, as in

(1) $$U^A = U^A(Y^A, Y^C)$$

As specified in (1), A's utility function includes not only his own income, Y^A, but C's income, Y^C. With this specification, A will desire to make a transfer to C whenever the rate at which he is willing to trade increments in own-consumption for increments in C's consumption (his marginal rate of substitution between own-consumption and C's) exceeds the rate at which such trades can be made. In the N-person case, where such demands are satisfied (for familiar reasons) through the political process, A may well feel that welfare spending, as financed by taxation, satisfies this condition. Alternatively, if A cares about C's consumption pattern, e.g., with the food or housing that C consumes, the specification of A's utility function will be

(2) $$U^A = U^A(X_1^A, \ldots, X_n^A, X_1^C)$$

where $X_1^A, \ldots, X_n^A$ are the rates of consumption of each of the n goods consumed by A and X_1^C is the amount of X_1 which C consumes. In this case, A will favor transfer activities aimed at increasing C's consumption of the particular commodities with which he, A, is concerned. He will tend to favor, say, price subsidies for consumption of these goods to programs providing C with cash payments.[10]

Nonmarket utility interactions may also arise, however, because A sees the existence of poverty as a source of negative externalities. Although A may not "care" about C for C's own sake, he may be affected adversely by particular aspects of C's behavior. In such cases, transfers for him are a kind of input used to "produce" a reduction in such social maladies as crime and public health inadequacies.

In the discussion that follows, actions directed to the reduction of such negative externalities, as well as to the maximization of own-consumption (as opposed to utility) or to the minimization of private costs (payments for goods and services, directly or through taxes) are considered to be based on self-interest. Thus, if all individuals act only on self-interest, to be more precise, "narrow" self-interest, nonrecipient support for redistributive transfers must derive from nonmarket utility interactions that are negative or from the motives described as (a) and (b) in our first set of examples.

On the other hand, we define behavior which results from *positive* nonmarket interactions among utility functions as *benevolence*. Nonrecipient support for redistributive transfers that derives from utility inter-dependencies, as described in the two-person example of equation 1, and from the motive described as (c) are included in this category.

Our discussion of the implications of nonrecipient support for redistribution concerns itself only with the existence, not the pattern, of benevolence. At issue is whether individuals, through the mechanisms of public choice, support transfer programs that enable others to augment their consumption, not whether the beneficiaries are relatives or friends or anonymous persons, identified only by, say, inferior income status.

Note also that benevolence, in our definition, is fully consistent with the maximization of own-utility. Individuals support transfers that are based on benevolence because they reflect preferred income allocations. Such transfers are, then, a matter of "rational" calculus, consistent with the private utility functions of the actors. It is for this reason that such choices can be accommodated within the corpus of economic theory.

Nothing that we say implies that benevolence is based on altruism. Altruism, which Webster's dictionary defines as "unselfish concern for the welfare of others," relates to motivation, not preference, and implies something more; namely, selflessness. Strictly speaking, therefore, in an analysis grounded in the postulate that choice is "rational," in the sense of being consistent with an objective function that is internal to the individual, altruism is an empty box.

II. REDISTRIBUTION IN DIRECT DEMOCRACY

This section begins our attempt to determine the circumstances under which a political democracy may be expected to produce redistribution to the poor. It deals, as a first step, with the simple but revealing case of direct democracy, in which the political community votes directly in referenda on public programs rather than for representatives who vote on such programs in legislatures. Part III then turns to the more complex and realistic case of representative democracy.

One important determinant of the amount of redistribution is the voting rule through which the community reaches its decisions. If unanimity is required, preference independence and income certainty, taken together, suffice to rule out all redistribution. Only if the unanimity requirement is relaxed can redistribution occur in a model that abstracts from both interdependent preferences and uncertainty. More plausible, however, is the assumption that simple majority rule prevails, implying that a motion will be adopted if favored by $(N+1)/2$ of the voters. What we wish to determine is whether, with this voting rule, redistribution favoring the poor is likely to be enacted.

Assume that (a) each person has one vote and (b) the distribution of income among persons is unequal. One might predict, then, following Anthony Downs (1957), that the 51 percent of the voters with the lower incomes would enact a tax on the 49 percent with the higher incomes and transfer the proceeds to themselves, each member of the "coalition" receiving an equal share of the redistributive pie.

A three-person model provides the simplest example that can illustrate this kind of redistributive outcome of direct democracy. Suppose three voters, A, B, and C, have initial incomes of Y^0_A, Y^0_B, and Y^0_C, where $Y^0_A > Y^0_B > Y^0_C$. By assuming away incentive effects so that each party maintains his market income at Y^0, regardless of which redistributive policies are adopted, the situation can be characterized as a constant-sum game. If income redistribution among the three members of the community is the only issue with which public choice deals, and if revenue is obtained from the members of the group through the taxation of income at a single tax rate, t, the characteristic function of this game can be identified in terms of the payoffs to the various coalitions that may form.

(3)   *i.* $V(A) = V(B) = V(C) = 0$

       ii. $V(A, B) = tY_c$; $V(A, C) = tY_b$; $V(B, C) = tY_a$

No payoff is available to one-member coalitions such as $V(A)$. Two-member coalitions receive an amount tY_i, where the income that is taxed is that of the excluded party. Since $Y^0_A > Y^0_B > Y^0_C$, the payoffs in the three possible two-member coalitions are ranked as $V(B, C) > V(A, C) > V(A, B)$. The highest payoff is earned by the coalition (B, C) which excludes A, the highest-income voter, and this result is the basis for the Downsian conclusion that the 51 percent coalition will consist of the voters with the lowest incomes in an N-voter model.

The second part of this Downsian solution, which specifies that B and C will share equally in the gains, is not necessarily compelling. To obtain this result, one seems forced to make some very special assumptions about expectations. *B* and *C*, for example, may anticipate that unequal sharing would significantly enlarge the chance of their coalition proving unstable. The prospect that the (*B*, *C*) coalition will disintegrate and permit the formation of another coalition from which one of them is excluded must be assumed so unfavorable that neither will risk demanding a disproportionate share of the coalition gains. There is no compelling reason, however, why either *B* or *C* must be so risk averse.[11]

We may now inquire how likely it is that the redistribution that democratic societies effect on behalf of the poor will reflect the kind of coalition that emerges in our example, viz., a (*B*, *C*) coalition with equal sharing. Clearly, one of the main problems with this is that the maximum income at which a voter can remain eligible for transfers in the real world is far below the median. A substantial number of those at the top of the bottom 51 percent receive zero cash transfers and, absent all interdependencies positive or negative, would vote for transfers only if they view the existence of such programs as a means of generating private income (i.e., as suppliers) or as a kind of insurance against the hazard of becoming impoverished.[12] That these motives apply for all those in the bottom 51 percent of voters with incomes too high to be eligible for redistributive transfers is open to considerable doubt. Those nonrecipients who see private gain in transfer programs, after accounting for their shares of the tax costs, are unlikely to be more than a very small minority of the voting population. Nor is the receipt of welfare payments now treated as a right to which persons are "entitled." The barriers erected to exclude the "undeserving" poor from recipient status and to prevent cheating serve also to reduce the insurance value of the programs to those who are not poor. There is, moreover, no reason for the nonpoor to content themselves with programs that provide only insurance benefits, as they would surely be better off with actual transfers. For various reasons then, existing welfare programs, in which means tests exclude a large number of voters with incomes below the median from benefits, are not easily accounted for by the simple Downsian coalition hypothesis.

Within the context of a direct democracy model, what alternative hypothesis can we invoke to account for transfers to the poor? One alternative is to assume that voters with above-median incomes have utility functions that reflect interdependence. This being the case, they may support and willingly consent to finance transfers to that one-fifth to one-quarter of the population that they classify as poor.

As far as the theory of redistribution in direct democracy is concerned, what does such nonrecipient support imply? In terms of our three-person model, the fact that high-income *A* may derive benefits from transfers can be examined on the assumption that such benefits are greater if the recipient is low-income *C*, rather than *B*. This would be true, presumably, if the source of A's benefits is positive utility interdependence, as in equations 1 and 2. It would also be true if A perceives a link between low income and crime.

On these assumptions, it is clear that a coalition of A and C is much more likely, relative to one of B and C, than it was in the previous analysis. B's support need no longer be obtained to enact a transfer program, and A has an incentive to break up a (B, C) coalition if it should form, not just to reduce his tax bill, but to assure that the transfers will be used in what he thinks to be a more appropriate way (going just to C instead of to B as well as C).

These conclusions may now be applied to an N-voter model. If some individuals with above-average incomes benefit from income transfers to the poor, a phenomenon that simple self-interest models, with no recognition of externalities, are hard put to explain, ceases to be a mystery. Given a transfer program which restricts net payments to, say, the low 20 percent of the income distribution, it is very difficult to assure the support of a majority in a model which ignores utility interdependence. But recognition of nonrecipient support surmounts this difficulty.

III. REDISTRIBUTION IN REPRESENTATIVE DEMOCRACY

Political models in which public decisions are made by popular vote describe but a limited number of real-world situations. The lion's share of collective decisions are made in representative bodies. Thus, it is to an analysis of the redistributive policies that may be expected to emerge from such representative assemblies or legislatures that we now turn.

Consider a hypothetical community of 25 persons, divided geographically into five equal parts, among which there is no short-run mobility.[13] These parts can be considered districts, provinces, counties, or states. In each district one person is elected by simple majority vote to serve as member of the community's legislature. It is assumed that this person clearly perceives the preferences of the majority responsible for his election and honors these preferences when voting in the legislature. Decisions in the legislature are also made by simple majority rule and, for purposes of the present argument, on an issue-by-issue basis with no vote trading. Finally, the legislature concerns itself only with policies explicitly designed to redistribute income—its jurisdiction is a kind of special district with a distributional mandate.

Assume initially that voters, as in the Downs model, have independent preferences and that no person fails to exercise the franchise.[14] Thus, each voter unfailingly votes for the candidate who supports programs that yield him the largest positive fiscal residual (the transfers he receives less the taxes he pays). A description of the decision-making process implicit in these assumptions is provided in Figure 1. Each column represents one

FIGURE 1

D_1	D_2	D_3	D_4	D_5
X	X	X	O	O
X	X	X	O	O
X	X	X	X	X
O	O	O	O	O
O	O	O	O	O

of the five districts, D_1 to D_5, and the five cells in each column represent the five voters in this district. A representative is elected by majority vote from each district, and the assembly therefore contains five representatives. In Figure 1, an X is displayed in a cell if the voter approves and votes for a proposal; an O is displayed if the voter opposes it. As is apparent from Figure 1, with simple majority rule, both in voting for representatives and in voting on legislation, a motion *may* be enacted if favored by a *minimum* of nine voters. This is because three representatives must vote for enactment, and each, to be elected, must be favored by at least three constituents.[15]

To illustrate the implications of such a model, we may examine several situations. These differ in their assumptions about (a) the number of people eligible for transfers and (b) their dispersion among the districts. Throughout, the redistributive program is assumed to be explicit, with upper-income groups being taxed at a uniform rate t and the receipts being distributed uniformly to those with incomes below some specified level. We are not concerned with what this level is or how it is decided, but take it as given. In the illustrations that follow, each person in each district is either eligible for transfers and thus designated "poor" and identified by an X, *or* pays taxes to finance transfers, in which case he is called "rich" and is identified by an O.

A distribution of poor voters among districts like that represented in Figure 1 illustrates the situation in which the number of "poor" people (assuming simple self-interest—no utility interdependence—on the part of the rich) required to enact redistribution is at its minimum of nine. If one of the poor were to shift from D_1 to, say, D_4, the redistributive proposal would fail. Hence, it is clear that the spatial distribution of supporters is crucial. Another way of demonstrating this is to consider the situation represented by Figure 2. Here, even though the "poor" number sixteen, they are unable to vote themselves income transfers from the wealthy.

FIGURE 2

D_1	D_2	D_3	D_4	D_5
X	X	X	X	X
X	X	X	X	X
O	O	O	X	X
O	O	O	X	X
O	O	O	X	X

The general implication of these illustrations is that redistribution is bound to be enacted, no matter what the distribution of the poor among districts, if their number exceeds sixteen—with a population of twenty-five and majority rule in force—and that redistribution will never occur if the poor are less than nine. However, if the poor number between nine and sixteen, inclusive, their distribution among districts determines whether redistribution will occur. In the general case of K districts, each with N persons, at least 25 percent of the population must be poor if redistribution on their behalf is to occur, and it is enacted in this case only if the poor are evenly distributed over $(K + 1)/2$ districts and absent entirely from the remaining $(K - 1)/2$.[16]

Now consider the implications of utility interdependence on the part of the nonrecipient rich. Assume, for the sake of argument, that there is no negative externality basis for redistribution, so this interdependence is entirely a matter of benevolence. If there are more than sixteen poor, the effect of introducing such interdependence into the twenty-five person model is nil, inasmuch as redistribution would be enacted in any case. However, with sixteen poor or less, interdependence can bring about redistribution which would not occur without it. This effect can be illustrated for two extreme cases:

    a.   If there are sixteen poor, distributed as in Figure 2, only one of the nonrecipients in D_1, D_2, or D_3 must be benevolent, to a degree sufficient to be made better off by redistribution, to reverse the outcome.

b. With, say, but one poor person in each district, a much higher proportion of nonrecipients must be benevolent, as Figure 3 illustrates.

FIGURE 3

D₁   D₂   D₃   D₄   D₅

X	X	X	X	X
O	O	O	O	O
O	O	O	O	O
O	O	O	O	O
( )	O	O	O	O

Here, six is the minimum number of benevolent nonrecipients (the minimum of nine supporters minus the three poor blokes in any three of the other five districts). The maximum number of rich who can be benevolent without assuring legislative enactment of redistribution is eleven, the maximum of sixteen less the five poor, distributed one to a district.[17]

For the relevant cases (situations in which the number of poor is less than seventeen), the implications of nonrecipient benevolence can conveniently be summarized in a table of "minimum requirements," such as Table 1. While the transfer recipients must number at least nine (must exceed 32 percent of the population) with no benevolence, its introduction can reduce the minimum number of recipients to one. The implicit arithmetic is simple. In political effect, the rich, if benevolent, are perfect substitutes for poor recipients. Depending on the overall spatial distribution of supporters, a benevolent minority among the nonpoor can assure the passage of legislation that transfers income to the poor, and this minority need be nowhere near so large as it must be with the same decision rule in direct democracy.[18]

Several issues of practical policy and constitutional politics can be discussed in terms of this model. The first is the impact of reapportionment as a means of long-run recourse open to a defeated opposition on the redistributive outcome. At one level of analysis, the answer to this question must remain indeterminate. To know the effects of reapportion-

TABLE 1 Number of Benevolent Rich Required for Enactment of Redistributive Legislation

Number of Poor (Actual Transfer Recipients)	Poor as a Percentage of Community	Number of Benevolent Rich to Ensure Enactment		Percentage of Rich Who Are Benevolent		Percentage of Benevolent Rich in the Community Population	
		Minimum	Maximum	Minimum	Maximum	Minimum	Maximum
17 (or over)	68	0	0	0	0	0	0
16	64	0	1	0	11	0	4
15	60	0	2	0	20	0	8
14	56	0	3	0	27	0	12
13	52	0	4	0	33	0	16
12	48	0	5	0	38	0	20
11	44	0	6	0	43	0	24
10	40	0	7	0	47	0	28
9	36	0	8	0	50	0	32
8	32	1	9	6	53	4	36
7	28	2	10	11	56	8	40
6	24	3	11	16	58	12	44
5	20	4	12	20	60	16	48
4	16	5	13	24	62	20	52
3	12	6	14	27	64	24	56
2	8	7	15	30	65	28	60
1	4	8	16	33	67	32	64

ment, one must specify the initial situation, the specific inter-district reallocation of voters that it contemplates, and the constitutional constraints under which it operates. But a specific example can illustrate some of the possibilities.

Suppose that the legislature has passed a redistributive proposal and that Figure 4 illustrates the distribution of its supporters, consisting of both the poor and the benevolent rich (denoted by B). In this setting, reapportionment that shifts any individual from district D_4 to D_5 (or vice versa) can have no effect, for both of these districts are opposed to redistribution in any case. But the outcome may be quite different if reapportionment affects one of the districts in which a majority supports redistribution. If, for example, reapportionment shifts a benevolent person from D_3 to D_4, it changes to one in which three out of five representatives (those from D_3, D_4, and D_5) oppose redistribution, resulting in its termination.

FIGURE 4

D_1	D_2	D_3	D_4	D_5
X	X	X	B	B
X	X	X	O	O
B	B	B	O	O
B	O	O	O	O
O	O	O	O	O

At another level of analysis, the possibility of reapportionment, at least in a long-run sense, may make redistribution more difficult to effect. This is true, for example, if significantly less than 50 percent of the community supports redistribution, while a decision to reapportion requires but a simple majority among the electorate. To see this, one need only observe that if, say, only nine persons out of twenty-five secure the enactment of a redistributive program, a substantial majority opposes it. If reapportionment can be carried out in any manner whatsoever, no matter how arbitrary, it is an easy matter for this majority to bring about the redistricting needed to terminate the program. In the real world, of course, reapportionment is constrained by rules governing the geographical basis of representation, rules which require, for example, spatial continuity within jurisdictions. This constraint limits the efficacy of reapportionment as a means of recourse to a defeated majority. Still, on the average, the prospect of reapportionment does increase the minimum level of overall support under which redistribution is likely to be enacted.[19]

Metaphorical swords, however, usually have two edges. Just as the possibility of reapportionment can limit the ability of a minority as small as 9/25 to secure enactment of a redistributive program, so it can also prevent a minority of 9/25 from blocking the passage of such a program. Reapportionment can, for example, easily convert the situation in Figure 2, in which redistribution is favored by 16/25 of the population but fails, into a situation in which redistribution will occur.

It should be noted, finally, that reapportionment can make the outcome of collective decision making in representative democracy more like the outcome under direct democracy only if apportionment decisions are themselves decided by a simple majority rule. In contrast, if, say, three-fourths of the population must approve reapportionment, its potential impact is nullified.

A related issue, similarly elucidated by our model, concerns the effect of the spatial distribution of potential recipients, the poor, on the likelihood that a transfer program will be enacted. Put a bit more pragmatically, it is relevant to ask whether the poor are likely to enjoy more political success (obtain larger per capita transfers) if they are dispersed across districts or concentrated. Our model suggests that this question is relatively easy to resolve. In the absence of nonrecipient support, neither concentration nor an even distribution among districts benefits potential recipients. Where there are ten such persons, the implications of an even distribution of two per district and the concentration of all ten in but two districts are the same—redistributive proposals will fail. To make the most of their numbers, potential recipients must be "semidispersed."[20]

Clearly, the model of representative democracy that this section has presented is innocent of many of the realities of collective decision making. A number of complications are, therefore, apparent. Two of these, hitherto ignored, are discussed here, together with some modifications that they might require.

The first complication is that collective decisions are often outcomes of a logrolling process in which representatives trade votes on different issues. To gain support on issues on which they hold strong views, representatives may either vote for legislation to which they (and, on our assumptions, their constituents) are mildly opposed or vote against legislation which they mildly favor. Such behavior immediately takes us beyond the confines of our simple single-issue model and poses the question of when an extension of the model to accommodate logrolling is essential to the analysis of redistribution through the public sector. What we can point out here is that to the extent that all constituents have intense feelings (either positive or negative) about redistribution relative to other issues, logrolling is not likely to be an important factor.

A second complication, also with some real-world importance, is that rates of voter participation, obviously much less than 100 percent, tend to vary directly with income. The analytic equivalent of such variation in voter participation, in terms of our model, is a disproportionate reduction in population, which eliminates more potential voters with low incomes than with high incomes. Other things equal, inverse voter participation reduces the ability of the poor to gain income transfers through use of the political process. By raising the minimum proportion of nonpoor who must favor a redistributive proposal to obtain its legislative enactment, it increases the importance of nonrecipient support in accounting for observed transfers to the poor.

IV. EVIDENCE OF DISTRIBUTIONAL PREFERENCE

Other things being equal, direct recipients of income transfers, together with those who think themselves likely to become recipients, can be expected to look favorably upon redistributive programs. To assure this, one needs only the comfortable assumption that the marginal utility of net increments in disposable income (the difference between transfers and perceived taxes) is sufficient to offset any implied costs in terms of lost privacy associated with the transfer process itself.[21]

But preferences of nonrecipients, which are transmitted through a political process that sets out to define new programs or to propose changes in the level or content of existing programs, are less transparent. In representing nonrecipient demands, one may, to start, presume that the capacity and taste for redistributing income vary with conventional socioeconomic and demographic indexes. Thus, even if all nonrecipients have identical tastes for redistribution, their willingness to transfer income—the "effectiveness" (marginal relevance) of their demands—will vary with these indexes (in other words, income and other claims, implied by family size, age, and so on, on nonrecipient resources).

Unfortunately, data that indicate the incidence of utility interdependence, benevolent or other—much less the critical levels the enactment of redistributive motions require—are not only difficult to delineate, but are difficult to obtain. Indeed, even if such data were identifiable, the fact that political institutions do not generate data in the required form precludes definitive investigation. Since what one has to work with is fragmentary and imperfect, little choice remains but to arm oneself with such tenuous assumptions about patterns of preference interdependence as seem to fit the evidence and institutions and to proceed.

To examine redistribution in direct democracy, one can turn to, as Wilson and Banfield (1964) have done, voting patterns in public expenditure referenda with redistributive overtones, involving school tax decisions or the capital financing of such facilities as a general hospital with a low-income clientele.[22] Or, in examining referendum voting on such measures as Proposition I (the California tax initiative rejected in November 1973, which proposed the constitutional restriction of public expenditures), one may introduce into the relationship variables used to explain the voting outcomes in precincts or census tracts that putatively reflect utility interdependence, as Levy (1974) has done. Where inference about the prevalence and strength, much less the political significance, of interdependencies is at issue, however, these procedures have a number of drawbacks. Citizen perceptions of the implicit distributional implications of the proposals under study are bound to be imperfect, not just because voters differ in fiscal sophistication, but because such effects are inherently unclear. This may not only affect how people vote but whether they vote. Moreover, the data examined, which represent averages for voting precincts or census tracts, can only provide evidence of central tendency, indicating median voting behavior (in terms of income, education, or other indicators of preference) within such political units. Our political models, on the other hand, indicate that it is the distributional preferences of critical minorities that determine whether proposed redistributive measures are successful. While it is possible to infer something about the size and composition of such minorities from cross-section voting data, provided detailed information on voter characteristics within political units exists, this is at best a tricky business.

Thus, to study actual and (for political acceptance) necessary levels of nonrecipient support for redistribution, it seems worthwhile to seek data in which the individual voter is the unit of observation. Periodic polls of a sample of California voters by the Field Research Corporation appear to be a workable mine of such data. Several of the Field polls conducted during 1970 (in May, August, and November) posed a variety of questions, designed to ascertain attitudes toward government expenditures in general and toward welfare spending in particular, to just over half of their samples of more than 1,100 voters. The focus on welfare spending, the most obvious means of redistribution to the poor, was attributable to the fact that Governor Reagan had made welfare reform a major issue in his reelection campaign. A defect of these data is that they measure intention, without enforcement of performance, rather than revealed preference. In one sense, however, this is a virtue, for it eliminates the distortions of actual distributional preferences that occur in candidate voting, where there is issue packaging, and in logrolling, which figures significantly in legislative decision making.[23]

Distributional preferences, as implied by responses to the welfare spending questions of the 1970 California polls, are summarized in Table 2. Income is the primary classification variable, in recognition of its importance in determining whether utility interdependencies are marginally relevant, and whether respondents are likely to be welfare recipients.[24] The sample responses have been recalculated (producing but minor changes of a percentage point or two) to reflect California population weights, which are, aside from vagaries of voter participation, measures of voting strength. Though the May, August, and November samples from which the data were compiled included different respondents, the responses are assumed to be comparable.

Within each income group (summarized in rows 1 through 3 of Table 2), the responses may be interpreted as the data of a simple cumulative function, though one for which the variable which interests us, attitude toward spending, is qualitative and discontinuous. The family of such functions (one for each income-bracket column in Table 2) describes variation, with income, in respondent satisfaction with particular welfare spending levels, relative to the existing level and to a regime in which there would be no welfare program at all. Rows 1 through 3 of the table each indicate a different respondent attitude. Row 1 measures the percentage of respondents who believe that some level of welfare spending (a level which is greater than zero but by an unspecified amount) must be considered a "moral imperative." Such persons responded with "agree strongly" or "agree somewhat" to the statement: "In spite of some waste in the welfare program, it would be morally wrong to do away with it." Row 2 indicates the proportion who consider the present level of welfare spending either "adequate" (that is, not too frugal) or "insufficient" (that is, desiring that it be increased). Taken together, we interpret these respondents as viewing the present level as "not unduly generous." This is obviously a weaker and more inclusive indication of support than that registered in row 3 by respondents who think that the present level of welfare spending is insufficient and desire more.

On inspection, a number of implications seem clear. First, only a small percentage of persons in any income bracket oppose any and all welfare spending. Only 11 percent do not feel that it is a "moral imperative" to maintain *some* positive level of welfare spending.

Second, in each of the three rows there is in general a systematic break in the relationship between the response percentages and income at roughly $7,000, and this income is interpreted as the breakpoint between the actual and potential welfare recipient population and the nonrecip-

TABLE 2 Derivation of Distributional Preferences from Reactions to Statements on Welfare Spending (Sample percentage responses weighted to reflect California population)

	Less than 3 (10%)	3–5 (10%)	5–7 (11%)	7–10 (21%)	10–15 (27%)	15–20 (14%)	More than 20 (6%)	All (100%)
1. Moral imperative	92	96	96	88	87	93	82	89
1a. Not moral imperative	8	4	4	12	13	17	18	11
2. Present level not unduly generous (adequate or insufficient)	82	64	79	63	60	65	61	66
2a. Present level adequate	44	26	39	44	36	39	47	39
3. Desire more spending	38	38	40	19	25	25	14	27
4. Helps prevent crime	75	68	58	49	48	47	26	65
5. (1) – (4)	18	28	37	39	39	46	56	24
6. Provide housing to those who can't afford it	71	63	49	50	39	42	32	46
7. (1) – (6)	21	33	47	38	48	51	50	43
8. (5) – (6)*	(53)	(35)	(12)	(11)	nil	4	24	(22)
9. Able-bodied men should not collect welfare	72	86	76	78	82	74	79	79
10. (1) – (9)	20	9	19	10	5	19	3	10

NOTE: All questions except those in rows 6 and 11 are from the August 1970 poll. Lines 6 and 11 are from the November 1970 poll. Defects in comparability, in addition to those attributable to sample composition, arise because the November (but not the August) poll permitted "undecided" responses (which we treat as "disagreement"). The following explanation relates to the various rows.

1. Welfare is a moral imperative. Reactions of "agree strongly" and "agree somewhat" to the statement: "In spite of some waste in the welfare program, it would be morally wrong to do away with it." Response that welfare is a moral imperative is taken to imply the marginal relevance of some utility interdependence.
   1a. The complement of 1.

2. Response that "more" spending is desired or current level of spending is "adequate" to the question: "Where should welfare, relief, and poverty programs fit in government spending?" implies that respondent does not believe the current level of the program to be unduly generous.
   2a. Response that current level of spending is "adequate."

3. Response that "more money" should be spent.

4. Reaction of "agree strongly" or "agree somewhat" to statement that "if I weren't for welfare, there would be a lot more stealing, burglaries, and other crime." Interpreted as the upper limit on support for welfare spending that is based on narrow self-interest rather than benevolence.

5. The difference between percentage responses under 1 and 4. Interpreted as lower limit of support for welfare that is benevolence-based.

6. Reactions of "agree strongly" and "agree somewhat" to "it's only fair for government to provide good housing for people who can't afford it."

7. The difference between the percentage responses under 6 and 1.

8. The difference between the percentage responses under 5 and 6. Asterisk indicates that the percentages contain negative percentages.

9. Reactions of "agree strongly" and "agree somewhat" to "no able-bodied man who is healthy enough to work should be allowed to collect welfare."

10. The difference between the percentage responses under 1 and 9.

ient population.[25] The decline in what appear, on the whole, to be favorable attitudes toward welfare spending may be interpreted as reflecting a rise, with income, in its net "price," more than sufficient to offset any increases in "tastes" for redistribution. Several factors contribute to this: (a) direct variation of the tax cost of income transfers with marginal tax rates and (b) inverse variation with income of the monetary benefit of transfers, because the probability of ever being poor declines and welfare programs consequently become a much worse form of insurance.

Third, only in the $3,000 to $5,000 group (where the figure is 25 percent) do less than 36 to 47 percent believe that the existing level of welfare spending is "adequate," a characterization that implies an absence of any demand for increases in such programs. The difference between the 25 percent response rate in this group ($3,000 to $5,000) and the 44 percent response in the lowest group (less than $3,000) seems to be primarily a matter of differences in age composition and in experience with the inadequacies of existing levels of welfare payments.[26]

In examining Table 2, one might inquire why prowelfare sentiment is less than unanimous in those income groups in which direct recipients are likely to be concentrated. Higher levels of redistributive transfers are, after all, in their apparent private interest. Doubtless, a part of the answer is that the Field polls inquired about attitudes toward welfare spending and not, more inclusively, about redistributive transfers or, in even more general terms, about income transfers, including those like social security, which are at least partially (even if more in perception than fact) annuities financed by prior social insurance payments. Some of those in the lowest income groups are, moreover, transients who had incomes that were below long-run expectations in the year concerned. Others, such as the "working poor," may well have taken the survey questions literally, interpreting them as referring to a particular package of welfare programs, monitored through complex rules and regulations that they consider unpalatable. These rules may have made them ineligible or made their participation so uncomfortable that they registered negative responses even though they could be quite favorably disposed toward such familiar systems of "no strings" income transfers as the Family Assistance Plan or a demogrant system of the type proposed by Senator McGovern in 1972. Without probing deeper through further questions (an alternative not available to us) there is no way of telling which of these motivating factors were operative, or to what degree.

The responses themselves offer little in the way of precise basis for inferring the motives of nonrecipient support. In this regard, agreement that "it would be morally wrong to do away with" welfare spending is of some help, inasmuch as it does indicate benevolence, as we have defined it, but it does so, strictly speaking, only for marginal departures from program levels of zero. As Part I has indicated, however, benevolence, deriving from a sense of fairness or caring about the well-being of others, is but one basis of nonrecipient support.[27]

The role of negative externalities, grounded in a distaste for behavior patterns associated with absolute or relative deprivation, must also be considered. It should be stressed that these need not be founded on a dislike of the poor. They may derive, for example, from presumed implications of poverty for the stability of the social and political fabric, or the quality of community life.

A crude, though suggestive, attempt to distinguish positive or benevolent interactions from negative utility interactions as the basis for nonrecipient support of welfare spending is made in rows 4 and 5 of Table 2. For hints into the real-world operation of the models of democracy that Parts II and III have presented, these rows contain some of our most interesting data. Reactions to the statement: "If it weren't for welfare, there would be a lot more stealing, burglaries, and other crime," are recorded in row 4. Among nonrecipients, agreement with this statement (responses of "agree strongly" and "agree somewhat") is here interpreted as an indication of support for redistribution (a belief that welfare spending is desirable) on grounds of negative utility interactions and not on grounds of benevolence. The strong inverse relationship between income and agreement that "welfare prevents crime" is worth noting. It suggests that those most experienced with crime (which in prevalence varies inversely with neighborhood quality and, thus, income) seem most convinced that the statement is correct.

As far as negative interactions deriving from crime itself are concerned, these figures are, of course, at most an upper limit—more likely an overstatement—to which nonrecipient support does not derive from benevolence. Here, however, for the sake of argument, we treat the responses in row 4 as a proxy for all negative sources of nonrecipient support.

Differences between the responses to "welfare is a moral imperative" (row 1) and "welfare prevents crime" (row 4) are reported in row 5. These derived figures are then our measures (in a sense, minimum measures) of the frequencies with which benevolence itself is a factor in distributional preferences, in the sense that nonrecipients prefer *some positive* level of welfare spending.[28] That "net" benevolence, thus measured, varies directly with income is what one would expect if "concern for the well-being of others" is a normal good.

The frequencies in row 5 rise from 18 percent among respondents with incomes under $3,000 to 56 percent among those with $20,000 or more. Among all those who are presumed to be nonrecipients (those over

$7,000) its range is 39 to 56 percent, and its average incidence is 47 percent.[29] However, since some respondents who agree that "welfare prevents crime" did not consider it a moral imperative, the deductions row 4 provides are too large. The 47 percent figure should, therefore, be adjusted upward by 3 percent, producing a corrected estimate of 50 percent. In the context of our political models, in which low frequencies of nonrecipient benevolence can be crucial, this minimum estimate of the incidence of benevolence in nonrecipient preferences must be considered quite significant.

The substantive focus changes in row 6 to the form in which non-recipients prefer their redistributive transfers to the poor to be made. At issue here (and in the remaining rows of Table 2) is whether the levels of self-perceived well-being of recipients—or alternatively, their consumption patterns or work-leisure choices—are the basis of donor concern.

In models of democracy without benevolence, all transfers will be in cash. Transfers in cash provide a wider range of consumption options and will be preferred by recipients who enact redistribution on their own behalf. On the other hand, in models with benevolence (or negative utility interactions), nonrecipient preferences are also relevant, both in determining whether redistribution will occur and in establishing its form and amount. If nonrecipient support does not derive from concern with the self-perceived well-being of transfer recipients, but extends to the sources or uses of their incomes, cash transfers may no longer be preferred. Specifically, if the utility interdependence of the marginal donor in the coalition required to enact a redistributive motion is of the particular-commodity type, the preferred transfers will be in kind and not cash. Row 6, taking up this issue, indicates nonrecipient reactions of "agree strongly" or "agree somewhat" to the statement posed in the November 1970 poll that "it's only fair for government to provide good housing for people who can't afford it." Because a different sample was used in November, comparisons with the August responses for inference about patterns of benevolence and the preferred form of income transfers must be taken with a large grain of salt. Still, provided one has a bit of a speculative bent, such comparisons are enlightening.

The responses in row 6 can be interpreted loosely as evidence of donor concern with the consumption patterns rather than the general well-being of recipients. In the housing case, this might have any of a number of sources: concern with how well recipients are housed, an objection to the aesthetics of ill housing or, to stretch a point, an aversion to the implications of housing inadequacies for social behavior. For the moment, there is no need to discriminate among these explanations; it can simply be assumed that the response frequencies in row 6 are an upper limit on the incidence of particular-commodity interdependence, as opposed to general and nonspecific utility interdependence with which we are concerned here.[30]

Our specific interest in this connection is with the interpretation that might be given of the responses of individuals with incomes above the breakpoint, which is, in this case, $5,000 rather than $7,000. Among such respondents, 38 to 51 percent of those agreeing that welfare is a moral imperative did *not* express the opinion that government is obligated to provide good housing for those who cannot afford it (see row 7). The theory suggests two possible reasons for this. Either these respondents were concerned with the overall welfare and not the consumption patterns of the poor, *or* they were not concerned with the poor at all, but supported welfare spending because of a belief that it prevents crime or ameliorates other undesirable side effects of poverty. To "net out" the effects of such negative interactions, we then deducted the "provide housing" responses from the calculated "net" benevolence levels (in row 8) rather than deducting them only from the "moral imperative" frequencies (as in row 7). Of course, "helps prevent crime" and "good housing" are not mutually exclusive as this procedure taken by itself implies. Many observers would argue that the housing component of welfare spending plays a major role in its effect on crime. Row 8's "net" estimates of benevolence, attributable to general and nonspecific, rather than particular-commodity utility interdependence, are minima in two ways: first, because the "prevents crime" frequencies place an upper limit on nonrecipient support that is not attributable to benevolence; and second, because of overlap among responses to the "prevents crime" and "provide housing" queries.

Taken at face value, the *negative* net frequencies in row 8 of Table 2 suggest that nonrecipient support for redistribution is (strictly) a matter of particular-commodity interdependence for respondents with incomes between $5,000 and $10,000. From $10,000 to $15,000, the net figure is effectively zero and warrants a similar interpretation. Over $15,000, however, it rises from 4 percent to a maximum of more than 24 percent among respondents with incomes over $20,000.[31] This is a large enough frequency to suggest with some force that donor concern with the self-perceived well-being of welfare recipients is a normal good which holds little interest at or near the breakpoint between recipients and nonrecipients but which is in significant demand among voters in the top decile of the income distribution. This inference, based on the indications of distributional preference summarized in Table 2, lends strength to the argument (developed elsewhere)[32] that support of redistribution by the rich, in the coalitions required to enact welfare programs, varies directly with income and is disproportionately derived from those donors with the highest incomes.

Another key issue in the investigation of distributional preference is whether nonrecipient donors are concerned with levels of self-perceived welfare among the recipient population or with the potential levels of their money incomes.[33] Donor aversion to work disincentives is evident in public discussion of redistributive proposals (in connection, for example, with the family assistance legislation and, in particular, with income-maintenance experimentation) and is corroborated by the almost uniformly positive poll responses to the statement that "no able-bodied man who is healthy enough to work should be allowed to collect welfare" (summarized in rows 9 and 10 of Table 2).[34]

Within the present frame of reference, the differences between non-recipient responses on the "moral imperative" and "able-bodied man" issues may be taken as evidence of a minimum level of interdependence in which the recipient's welfare, pure and simple, rather than his earned income is what counts. The average of these differences, which vary but little across income classes, approximates 10 percent. This contrasts with the 50 percent estimate of the incidence of "net" benevolence implied by the differences between the responses to the "moral imperative" and "welfare prevents crime" statements. It may, therefore, in a very rough sense, be interpreted as a lower limit on the extent to which nonrecipient supporters of welfare spending are likely to support a simple program of cash transfers containing no work requirement provisions.

V. IMPLICATIONS OF NONRECIPIENT SUPPORT UNDER DIRECT AND INDIRECT DEMOCRACY

This section examines with the derived evidence from the California polls the degree to which nonrecipient support for welfare spending (or opposition to it) is essential to its enactment. We do this by treating the queries posed to the California sample in the May and August 1970 polls as though they were referenda or legislative motions. The relevant responses, classified by respondent income, are reported in row number 3 of Table 2 and in Table 3. Table 4 displays the levels of nonrecipient support required for enactment of each of these motions, under a variety of decision rules, given the levels of support that recipient groups have evinced.[35] These decision rules range from a minimum of one-fourth to a maximum of three-fourths. One-half is obviously the operative require-ment for the overall population for a referendum decided under direct democracy with majority rule. One-fourth and three-fourths define the limiting cases for the model of indirect democracy developed in Part II. Population distribution and apportionment are, however, seldom favorable enough to permit these minimum coalitions to pass or block any motion. Thus, from a practical standpoint, limits of one-third and two-thirds seem more sensible, and even these may well be too wide.

In May 1970 poll interviewees were asked (in separate open-ended questions) which, if any, of a list of eight government programs categories involving large expenditures of money they would like to see "increased or kept at the same level of spending" or "reduced in spending." Table 3 summarizes the frequencies with which the respondents mentioned welfare spending.[36] Since some 7 percent of the interviewees mentioned welfare spending in neither case, some inconsistency is reflected in the responses. The inconsistency decreased with income, producing an upward bias in the support level required to enact a legislative motion proposing an increase in welfare spending and a downward bias in the level of nonrecipient support required to defeat it.[37]

The legislative motions implicit in the May 1970 questions for which distributional preferences are indicated (in Table 3) are set out in rows 1a, 1b, 2a, and 2b of Table 4. The right-hand side of this table reports

TABLE 3 Responses to Distributional Preference Questions on May 1970 Poll
(Sample percentage responses weighted to reflect California population)

| | —————— Income ($1,000) and Income Distribution —————— (in parentheses) | | | | | | | |
	Less than 3 (10%)	3–5 (10%)	5–7 (11%)	7–10 (21%)	10–15 (27%)	15–20 (14%)	More than 20 (6%)	All (100%)
1. Increase or maintain the same	64	75	67	59	56	52	43	59
2. Decrease	18	15	22	37	40	37	57	34
3. Inconsistent: no mention of welfare in (1) or (2)	18	9	11	4	4	10	–	7

NOTE: The explanation relates to the various rows.

1. Frequency with which "welfare spending" was mentioned by respondents when interviewer stated: "Here is a list of some government programs which require large expenditures of money. Which would you like to see increased or kept at the same level of spending?" The query was open-ended, and the responses were neither mutually exclusive nor constrained, either by a budget limitation or by a requirement that priorities be specified.

2. Responses to: "Here is a list of government programs which require large expenditures of money. Which would you like to see reduced in spending?" The same comments apply as in row 1.

3. No mention of welfare in either of the above responses, reflecting implicit inconsistency. Note that this inconsistency is, on the average, lower for the income groups of $7,000 and above.

TABLE 4   **Referenda Implicit in Attitudes toward Welfare Spending**
(Sample percentage responses weighted to reflect California population)

Implicit Referenda on Welfare Spending	—Income[a]— Less than $7,000 (32%)	More than $7,000 (68%)	Required Support among Those with Incomes of $7,000 or More to Achieve Indicated Population Support Level 1/4	1/3	1/2	2/3	3/4
Questions on May 1970 Poll							
1a. Increase or maintain the same	68	55	8	19	43	66	78
1b. "Don't" decrease	81	60	3	14	38	61	73
2a. Decrease	19	40	27	39	62	86	97
2b. "Don't" increase or maintain the same	32	45	22	34	57	81	92
Questions on August 1970 Poll							
3a. Spend more	39	22	19	31	55	80	92
3b. "Don't" spend more	61	78	8	20	45	69	81

NOTE: The population is apportioned between the 32 percent with incomes "less than $7,000" and the 68 percent with incomes "$7,000 and above." This breakpoint, we assume, distinguishes between respondents who, given current economic status, are or have a significant likelihood of becoming welfare recipients. The choice of $7,000 rather than $5,000 as the breakpoint between the current and potential "poor" (recipients) and the "rich" (individuals who are unlikely to become recipients) is based on an apparent discontinuity in the responses, thus in distributional preferences, at this income level.

Figures in the right-hand half of Table 4 indicate percentage levels of support among the population with incomes of "$7,000 or more" required to achieve the indicated overall level of support (across all income groups) for the implicit referenda on welfare spending listed at the far left.

Support levels indicated in 1a and 2b are derived from reactions (and the negative complement of reactions) to: "Here is a list of government programs which require large expenditures of money. Which would you like to see reduced in spending? Which would you like to see increased or kept at the same level of spending?" and its negative complement. These questions were asked in the May 1970 poll.

Required support levels in 3a and 3b are derived from the response of "more money" to "Where should welfare, relief, and poverty programs fit in our government spending?" and its negative complement. This question was asked in the August 1970 poll.

[a]The figures in parentheses are population weights.

levels of nonrecipient support required for this enactment. For both the "increase or maintain" and the "decrease" questions, required support levels for the negative complement ("don't decrease" and "don't increase or maintain") have also been calculated to delimit the significance of the response inconsistencies discussed above. Inspection of

Table 4 indicates that the inconsistencies were not very important, since their effect, which was to produce differentials of approximately 5 percent across the board in nonrecipient support requirements, was not very important.

The necessary levels of nonrecipient support in a referendum on whether "more money" (as distinct from enough to "increase or maintain" the present level) ought to be spent on welfare programs are reported in rows 3a and 3b of Table 4. These figures are derived from the August 1970 responses summarized in row 3 of Table 2 and discussed in Part IV. Although, as mentioned earlier, the composition of the May and August samples differed, so that the responses are not strictly comparable, these outcomes are consistent with what one would expect, given an inverse relationship between the extent to which utility interdependence is relevant at the margin and the price of acting upon it. Still, the low level of support for higher welfare spending ("more money") among respondents with incomes of "less than $7,000" is puzzling. One possible explanation is that the August queries were not phrased in the open-ended language of the May questions but in terms of spending priorities, thus imposing an implicit but rough budget constraint into the calculus of the respondents.

In understanding Table 4, it is useful first to think of the implicit referenda as if they had been proposed in a regime of direct democracy, with enactment requiring overall support of 50 percent. In this case, enactment of an increase in welfare spending requires support (given, as the first column indicates, 39 percent support among the "poor") from 55 percent of the nonrecipient rich, while the assent of but 40 percent (a rough average of the 38 and 43 percent in rows 1a and 1b) is required to pass a motion to "increase or maintain." To effect a "decrease" in welfare spending, on the other hand, 60 percent of the "rich" (a rough average of 62 and 57 percent) must consider the present level of welfare spending too high.

These figures may now be contrasted with the actual frequencies. In fact, only 22 percent of the "rich" would like to see welfare spending increased, while 40 to 45 percent would like it decreased. However, virtually 60 percent, the same proportion enactment requires, favor its being "increased or maintained." There seems then a clear implication (to the extent the California samples are representative) that the existing level of welfare spending is stable,[38] at least under simple majority rule. The fact that nonrecipient support levels of three-fifths to four-fifths are required to pass on all two-thirds positive motions, and roughly a one-third minority among nonrecipients is in all cases sufficient to block any two-thirds motion for change in the present level of welfare spending, supports this conclusion.[39]

Under indirect democracy, the required levels of overall support may range, in theory, from 25 to 75 percent. In consequence, the variety of possible levels of required nonrecipient support multiplies. With a given decision rule, and the information Table 4 contains, one may work through the prospects of each motion, under whatever assumptions about voter participation (among recipients and nonrecipients) and the "optimality" of the spatial distribution of supporters (apportionment) he may wish to make. Since the character of this exercise is clear, specific discussion does not seem necessary at this juncture.

It is now possible to return to our crude estimate of the lower limits on "net" nonrecipient benevolence and "nonrecipient support for a cash transfer" program without work requirements and inquire, speculatively, into their implications for the likely success of proposals to institute transfer programs. Recall that the first limit, 50 percent, was derived from the "moral imperative" and "welfare prevents crime" responses and the second, 10 percent, from the deduction of the "able-bodied man" (implying a concern with the effects of income transfers on work incentives) from the "moral imperative" responses. The former can then be interpreted as a lower bound on the extent of nonrecipient support for some sort of cash redistribution program, whereas the latter indicates the minimum level of nonrecipient willingness to support such a program without imposing work requirements.

That some program of cash transfers can be enacted, whatever the decision rule, seems apparent if 50 percent is the operative limit of nonrecipient benevolence. Even the 10 percent figure, which permits some defection of recipients, is likely to be consistent with enactment if, as the case may be in representative democracy, only one-third of all voters must agree. However, the data, as available, provide no grounds on which to base estimates of the magnitude of such programs.

As indicated in the earlier discussion, the limits in themselves simply indicate prevalence and do not measure the significance or marginal relevance of benevolence at the current level of welfare spending, the base to which the implicit motions considered in Table 4 refer. To ascertain this, we require a heroic assumption about the rate at which income transfers beginning from a base of zero succeed in internalizing benevolence. To this end, assume for the sake of argument that the basis for nonrecipient support for income transfers to the poor is simple positive utility interdependence, that all welfare spending at the start is in cash, and that the initial level of cash transfers from which departures are being considered internalizes half the benevolence that would be present at a zero level of transfers. The implied operative limits of nonrecipient support for marginal changes in the initial level of cash transfers (as distinct from maintenance of the program at its current level) are then 25 and 5 percent.

The levels of required nonrecipient support spelled out in Table 4 indicate, in this case, that in direct democracy (in a referendum decided by simple majority rule) there is no "positive" motion to "increase or maintain" the level of transfer programs that could pass. But, depending upon the spatial distribution of their supporters, the same motions, set forth under representative democracy, might well stand some chance of success. If, for example, the distribution of supporters is ideal, so that overall support of but 25 percent is required, motions to "increase or maintain" and "spend more" would both do well. This also seems true for the former if one-third support is required.[40] On motions to decrease welfare spending, the benevolence limits imply that three-fourths support is simply unattainable and that other, less restrictive support levels, such as two-thirds, are unlikely to be attainable.

Admittedly, such argumentation is tenuous, as it must be, given the character of the evidence at our disposal. It does, nonetheless, suggest directions in which research must proceed if our practical understanding of the workings of democratic political process is to be meshed with theoretical models of public choice that attempt to interpret it. What is needed, first, as in discussing more conventional topics, are better structural models, with tangible counterparts in empirical evidence. To characterize democratic processes in terms of such models, one requires a consistent body of microdata, capturing the preferences of the individual actors upon which politics builds. To obtain such data, a suitable panel must be subjected to a carefully structured series of questions, capable of measuring gradations in preference and linking choice, grounded in such preference, to the price and reward systems implicit in public policies. The applicability of such data would be much less limited than that grounded in hypothetical binary choices. For the researcher interested in distributional preferences, the best of all worlds would provide matched data, relating preferences, as discerned through such surveys as the California polls that we have used, and voting through which such preferences are revealed.[41] It is obvious that this is a great deal to ask. And as if it were not already enough, or too much, the ambitious scholar may even hope for data that relate the choices of legislators and legislatures, adjusted somehow for their constituents.[42]

VI. CONCLUSION

The classical preoccupation with income distribution enjoyed a renascence in the 1960s. In motivation, this was largely pragmatic, a matter of discomfort with the apparent coexistence of social deprivation and general prosperity, rather than analytic interest in the empirical dimensions of an elusive social optimum. Disenchanted with the structure and the outcome of prevailing property rights, which define claims to human and nonhuman capital, some writers went so far as to suggest that distributive justice requires a radical restructuring of social institutions, holding that there is no way in which the social and economic system, in its present form, can accommodate the adjustments they think "necessary." Others, more cautious, and, frankly, more committed to liberal values, argued that more redistribution would occur if only the democratic political process and the social programs it produces could be made to more accurately reflect the "true" preferences of the voters from whose consent they derive.

For the practicing social scientist, which way of posing these issues is more accurate is less interesting than the question of which is more open to inquiry. To us, the apparent stability of a distributional outcome that conforms with voter preferences seems sufficient to make the investigation of redistribution as a matter of public choice, within a predefined system of rights and rules, the prior research topic. It seems more efficacious to make use of familiar concepts and methods, even when they can be adapted only with difficulty to current concerns, than to disregard them and seek, like Lancelot, a new paradigm.

Recently within the public choice frame of reference, some considerable effort has been devoted to the normative question of how much income redistribution is appropriate, and whether its form should be cash or kind. Treatment of the positive counterpart of this issue, the effort to determine the kinds of preferences reflected by income transfers carried out through private charity and public programs, has been much less satisfactory. As means of explaining redistribution, the basic deficiency of traditional neoclassical analysis resides in its formulation of the objectives, thus the preferences, which motivate voters and politicians. The requirement that rational behavior be consistent with simple self-interest, in particular, makes it far more difficult than need be to explain redistributive activities. The appropriate extension of the neoclassical paradigm, which permits more realistic interpretation of redistribution, introduces choices which reflect benevolence into the objective function.

In the present paper, we have developed this theme by building utility interdependence into models of redistribution in direct and indirect democracy. Perhaps our most significant conceptual finding is that widespread, much less universal, benevolence need not be postulated in order for its impact on the distributional outcome to be substantial. We have also attempted, using data from poll responses, to determine some of the dimensions of nonrecipient support for redistributive transfers through welfare spending. We believe the results are quite striking and offer support for assertions about the existence of benevolence and the significance of its impact on redistributive outcomes.

NOTES

1. See Aaron and von Furstenberg (1971), Becker (1969), Buchanan (1968), Goldfarb (1970), Hochman (1971), Hochman and Rodgers (1969, 1970, 1971, 1973, and 1974), Johnston (1972), Mishan (1972), Musgrave (1970), Olsen (1969, 1971a, 1971b), Pauly (1970), Peterson (1972), Rodgers (1973), von Furstenberg and Mueller (1971).
2. Robbins (1932), pp. 136–143.
3. For example, an estimate of the redistributive effects of the U.S. farm program is given in Schultze (1972).
4. See McGuire and Aaron (1970) and Gillespie (1965).
5. See Becker (1969), Dickinson (1962), Hochman and Rodgers (1973), and Schwartz (1971).
6. By a democratic system of government, we mean a set of institutional arrangements governing the procedures through which a community arrives at collective decisions in which individuals compete for the votes of a broadly based electorate. On the appropriateness of defining political democracy in this way, see Schumpeter (1942), Chapters 21 and 22.
7. Since an infinite number of transfer patterns are consistent with any total amount of redistribution, any discussion of this subject must also specify who pays and who receives. But the level of redistributive activity has some importance independent of its pattern, since it gives an indication of the proportion of resources that the community is devoting to transfer activities. For a discussion suggesting that a society, with certain institutions and rules, may be caught in a prisoner's dilemma and excessively engage in these activities, see Tullock (1971a).
8. See the references cited in note 1.
9. See Buchanan (1972).
10. For more detailed consideration of these nonmarket interactions in the two-person and N-person cases, see Hochman and Rodgers (1969), Rodgers (1973), and Rodgers (1974).
11. The essential difficulties in the view that (B, C) with equal sharing is the most likely outcome of the redistribution "game" can be seen by examining this solution more closely and comparing it with some alternatives. If the (B, C) coalition forms and votes to tax A, collecting tY_A, B and C, with equal sharing, each receive $tY_A/2$. The redistribution pattern in each period is then $(-tY_A, tY_A/2, tY_A/2)$. Whether this represents a stable solution depends on the deals that B and C, respectively, can strike with A, the expectations of each party about the behavior of the others, and the aversion of each party to the uncertainties associated with instability.

    To consider one possibility, A could bribe either B or C to forsake the coalition and to join with him. If either B or C were offered anything more than $tY_A/2$, either would be willing to defect the (B, C) coalition. At first sight, the bargaining range might appear to be between tY_A and $tY_A/2$, for C must receive at least $tY_A/2$ in a coalition with A, while A would be agreeable to a coalition with C that costs him anything less than tY_A. But this potential gain to A and C from forming a coalition as an alternative to (B, C) actually understates the potential gain, since the (A, C) coalition can also tax B, obtaining an additional tY_B. If, then, an (A, C) coalition forms, it would clearly be possible, even with no redistribution from B, for both A and C to be better off. But with redistribution from B, both A and C stand to gain even more. If C is content with $3/4$ tY_A and $1/2$ tY_B, A will suffer a net income loss of only $3/4$ $tY_A - 1/2$ $tY_B = t(3/4 \ Y_A - 1/2 \ Y_B)$. Moreover, if $tY_B \geqq 1/2 \ tY_A$, A need pay nothing at all to C in order for C to be better off in a coalition with A than in (B, C). But before the reader gets the impression that an (A, C) coalition is more stable, he should note the possibility that B might be able to induce A to foresake C by agreeing to give A a sizable amount of his income. The possibilities are endless. Indeed, the situation is not unlike price warfare among a group of oligopolistic firms; and the outcome is indeterminate for much the same reasons.

12.   The notion that income redistribution through the fiscal structure may, in part, serve the function of income insurance has a substantial intellectual history and is much discussed in the literature. See, for example, Buchanan and Tullock (1962), Chapter 13, and the summary discussion in Rodgers (1974).

13.   This assumption rules out the location effects on which the Tiebout thesis focuses (1954). Implications of redistribution for location are described and discussed in recent papers by Buchanan (in Hochman and Peterson 1974) and Pauly (1972).

14.   Later in the analysis, we drop this assumption and consider the significance of voter participation rates and variation in such rates across income classes.

15.   In general, with K districts, each containing the same odd number of people, n, the minimum number who must favor legislation for its adoption, is given by $[(K+1)/2][(n+1)/2]$. Thus, the smallest fraction of voters who must support a proposal to insure its adoption by the legislature is given by

$$\frac{\left(\dfrac{K+1}{2}\right)\left(\dfrac{n+1}{2}\right)}{Kn} = 1/4(1+1/K+1/n+1/Kn)$$

As n and $K \to \infty$, the last three terms in the right-hand parentheses drop out and the value of this expression approaches 25 percent. See Buchanan and Tullock (1962), pp. 220–221. We have borrowed our diagrammatic representation from them.

16.   With a bicameral legislature, in which constituent sets in the two houses overlap, the minimum percentage is likely to be higher. However, consistencies in voting, as between representatives of the same district in the two houses, and offsets across districts imply that it is unlikely to come at all close to doubling.

17.   Note that the payment per recipient will differ in cases (a) and (b) if the tax cost of redistribution is the same for each nonrecipient. Suppose that the tax rate on the rich is a flat 10 percent, that rich persons all have incomes of $20,000 and that each poor person has an income of $4,000. Then in case (a) the nine nonrecipients each pay $2,000 and the payment to each poor person is $18,000/16 or $1,125. The single rich person who is benevolent gives up $2,000 to see the incomes of each of the sixteen poor persons raised by $1,125. Each of the other nonrecipients is made worse off since they have independent preferences. In case (b), if the benevolent rich distributed are such that only six are required to enact redistribution, the total tax collected is $20 \times \$2,000 = \$40,000$, and each poor person receives $\$40,000/5 = \$8,000$.

18.   Table 1 also illustrates how small differences in benevolence may produce substantial differences in the degree to which societies (contrast, for example, Sweden, Great Britain, and the U.S.) pursue egalitarian social policies.

19.   Related to this, for distributional adjustments at subnational levels of government, is the observation that voters, if dissatisfied with distributional connotations, can move

away. This is the phenomenon of "voting with one's feet" on which the so-called Tiebout thesis rests. One implication of utility interdependence, justifying redistributive income transfers, is that the structure of local communities is more stable than a public choice model with independent preferences might suggest. As potential transfer recipients enter a community, responding to the generosity of its welfare levels, the price of liberalism rises, leading marginal supporters of redistributive activity to emigrate and making any given level of redistributive activity more costly for those who remain. This process feeds upon itself. In these circumstances, whether redistribution will be maintained at its initial level depends on the conflicting population flows, with recipients moving in and erstwhile nonrecipient supporters moving out.

20. For the case of racial integration, this suggests that partial dispersal of the ghetto, limited to jurisdictions in which the formation of sympathetic coalitions is feasible, may be a much more effective means of increasing the political power of the minorities than the reinforcement of concentration (ghetto-gilding) or equi-proportional representation (total integration).

21. With respect to welfare spending, there are only a few obvious cases in which this assumption, with nontrivial likelihood, might be expected to fail. One is where the welfare authorities apply a "man in the house rule" or pry into private morals in screening applicants for "Aid to Dependent Children." Another is where inquiries into financial status offend potential recipients of, say, "Old Age Assistance." Even in these circumstances, however, it seems unlikely that the implied costs in terms of privacy will predominate for any more than a minority of the individuals concerned.

22. Note, however, that the examples Wilson and Banfield (1964) have cited need not be redistributive in the larger sense. Favorable votes, as for the hospital, need not imply benevolence or "public-regardingness" at all, but a desire to drain off the low-income population, permitting more effective segregation of community health facilities by income or race.

23. In general, it seems preferable to ask the reader to grant our awareness of the problems inherent in the sampling techniques of the Field Surveys, through which the data were derived, and just as important, the objective imperfections of the questions. Exhaustive presentation of qualifications, already too familiar to anyone who has worked with such data, would add little but boredom.

24. Unfortunately, to the best of our knowledge, the poll did not ask whether the respondent was or had been a welfare recipient.

25. Consider, for example, the difference between the 38 to 40 percent support for an increase in welfare spending among those with incomes of less than $7,000 and the 14 to 25 percent levels of support among those with incomes of $7,000 or more.

26. In the under $3,000 bracket, 72 percent of the respondents were sixty years of age or older, while only 49 percent of these in the $3,000 to $5,000 bracket were over sixty. A larger proportion of elderly respondents may feel that welfare is inadequate because fewer are likely to be recipients of both welfare and social security, and retirees, even if receiving social security, may not identify with welfare recipients. However, Radosevich (1974), in a careful study of nonsupport among the probable net recipients, found that age itself did not seem to account for such deviant responses. What seemed important, rather, was the interaction between age and level of education, inasmuch as nonsupport was more likely among those with high school or less than three years of college (as opposed to even less or more education).

27. One might also, as we mentioned in Part I, attribute a portion of nonrecipient support for welfare to government employees or others with a private interest in the magnitude of public programs. Aside from utility interdependence or insurance, however, there seems no reason for government employees, except for those who are direct suppliers of welfare spending, to be more favorably disposed to it than the average voter.

Indeed, if welfare competes with other uses of public funds, the incentives that face government employees who are not directly involved in supplying welfare services are quite the opposite.

28. This ignores support which derives from expectations of income insurance benefits and the support, based on self-interest, of government welfare workers. Both these sources of demand are likely to be small, the former because few people with 1970 incomes over $7,000 are likely to view welfare programs as providing more than the remotest possibility of potential direct benefits, and the latter for the reason already given, because the proportion of social workers in the total population is small.

29. In examining row 5, note that the rise in net benevolence with income runs counter to the decrease in the percentage of respondents who considered welfare spending a moral imperative.

30. Implicitly, we are assuming here that the housing responses are an adequate proxy for all types of particular-commodity interdependence, as we did with the crime responses and negative utility interactions. As a source of income augmentation, recipients, other things being equal, may be expected to view such in-kind transfers as inferior to cash, though they will certainly prefer them to nothing at all. If sophisticated, however, they may realize that the dollar value of transfers obtainable in kind, if interdependence is of the particular-commodity type, may well exceed that of transfers obtainable in cash.

31. Presumably, this maximum would be even larger with a more detailed income breakdown above $20,000.

32. See Hochman and Rodgers (1969), Section IV.

33. See Rodgers (1973), Peterson (1973), and Zeckhauser (1971).

34. That these responses were not unanimous may be attributed to recognition of the income deficiencies of some "working poor" and to the failure of this statement to discriminate between voluntary and involuntary unemployment.

35. Part V maintains the assumption that those with incomes of less than $7,000 are recipients and those with incomes of $7,000 or more are nonrecipients. This may well be an oversimplification. The issues the California polls posed were in terms of attitudes toward spending or public spending generally rather than in terms of income redistribution. The reasons why "recipient" groups are not unanimous in their support of motions proposing that welfare spending be increased or maintained have been discussed earlier.

36. Since these questions as posed were open-ended, the mention of welfare spending may be taken to imply that the respondent did not think it insignificant. That welfare reform was, as noted earlier, an issue in the ongoing gubernatorial primary campaign must certainly have strengthened such feelings.

37. One may speculate on the reasons for such inconsistencies, though they are of doubtful importance here. Such explanations include, for example, imperfect tax-consciousness (varying inversely with income) and general indifference. Surprising though it may seem for some respondents wishing to limit the number of their responses to open-ended questions, welfare spending may have been less salient than, say, education, the environment, and law enforcement.

38. Whether the present level of spending is stable because respondents are more comfortable with a program level to which they have been accustomed and thus favor the status quo, or viewing the political process as rational, as we have, because this level accurately reflects median voter demand, is beyond the informational capabilities of the data at hand.

39. As William Niskanen has pointed out, the two recent presidential candidates who took strong, though opposing, positions on the adequacy of present levels and systems of

welfare spending, Senators Goldwater and McGovern, were both soundly defeated. While this bit of circumstantial evidence supports our inference that the present level of welfare spending is stable, at least in terms of distributional preference, the reasons why one should not overstress it are obvious.

40. In general, Table 4 indicates that motions to "increase" or "increase and maintain" welfare spending have a somewhat better chance of success, given the parameters, than motions to decrease it.

41. It would be useful to find out if individuals, some months after voting, would repeat their choices if given the opportunity to do so. The 1973 and 1974 Gallup and Harris polls assessing the popularity of President Nixon were, to be sure, evidence of modified preference attributable to changes in perceived "prices" and "rewards."

42. Davis and Jackson (1974) provide an example of this, but make no use of underlying data on individual preferences.

REFERENCES

Aaron, Henry, and von Furstenberg, G. M. "The Inefficiency of Transfers in Kind, The Case of Housing Assistance." *Western Economic Journal* 9 (June 1971): 184–191.

Becker, G. S. "A Theory of Social Interactions." Department of Economics, University of Chicago, Sept. 1969.

Bicker, W. E. "Public Attitudes and Opinions of the Current Welfare System and Components of the Proposed Family Assistance Plan." Findings of a study undertaken for the Department of Health, Education, and Welfare. Institute of Governmental Studies, University of California at Berkeley, July 1970.

Buchanan, J. M. *Public Finance in Democratic Process*. Chapel Hill: University of North Carolina Press, 1967.

———. "What Kind of Redistribution Do We Want?" *Economica* 35 (May 1968): 185–190.

———. "Who Should Distribute What in a Federal System?" In H. M. Hochman and G. E. Peterson, eds., *Redistribution Through Public Choice*. New York: Columbia University Press, 1974, pp. 22–42.

———. "The Political Economy of the Welfare State." Research Paper # 808231-1-8. Center for Study of Public Choice, Virginia Polytechnic Institute and State University, June 1972.

Buchanan, J. M., and Tullock, Gordon. *The Calculus of Consent*. Ann Arbor: University of Michigan Press, 1962.

Downs, Anthony. *An Economic Theory of Democracy*. New York: Random House, 1957.

Dickinson, Frank G., ed. *Philanthropy and Public Policy*. New York: Columbia University Press, 1962.

Fry, B. R., and Winters, R. F. "The Politics of Redistribution." *American Political Science Review* 64 (June 1970): 508–522.

Gillespie, W. Irwin. "Effect of Public Expenditures in the Distribution of Income." In R. A. Musgrave, ed., *Essays in Fiscal Federalism*. Washington, D.C.: The Brookings Institution, 1965.

Goldfarb, R. S. "Pareto Optimal Redistribution: Comment." *American Economic Review* 60 (Dec. 1970): 994–996.

Hochman, H. M. "Individual Preferences and Distributional Adjustments." *American Economic Review* 62 (May 1972): 353–360.

Hochman, H. M., and Rodgers, J. D. "Pareto Optimal Redistribution." *American Economic Review* 59 (Sept. 1969): 542–557.

———. "Pareto Optimal Redistribution: Reply." *American Economic Review* 60 (Dec. 1970): 997–1002.

———. "Is Efficiency a Criterion for Judging Redistribution?" *Proceedings of the International Institute of Public Finance*. Leningrad Congress, 1971, pp. 1236–1248.

———. "Brennan and Walsh Reconsidered (Mutt and Jeff Ride Again)." *Public Finance Quarterly* 1 (Fall 1973): 359–371.

Johnston, John. "Utility Interdependence and the Determinants of Redistributional Public Expenditures." Ph.D. diss., Duke University, 1972.

Levy, Mickey. "A Study of Voting on the California Proposition I Referendum." Graduate School of Public Policy, University of California at Berkeley, 1974.

McGuire, M. C., and Aaron, Henry. "Public Goods and Income Distribution." *Econometrica* 38 (Nov. 1970): 907–920.

Mishan, E. J. "The Futility of Pareto-Efficient Distribution." *American Economic Review* 62 (Dec. 1972): 971–976.

Musgrave, R. A. "Pareto Optimal Redistribution: Comment." *American Economic Review* 60 (Dec. 1970): 991–993.

Olsen, E. O. "A Normative Theory of Transfers." *Public Choice* 6 (Spring 1969): 39–58.

———. "Some Theorems in the Theory of Efficient Transfers." *Journal of Political Economy* 79 (Jan./Feb. 1971): 166–176.

———. "Subsidized Housing in a Competitive Market: Reply." *American Economic Review* 61 (Mar. 1971): 220–224.

Olson, Mancur. *The Logic of Collective Action*. Cambridge: Harvard University Press, 1965.

Pauly, M. V. "Income Redistribution as a Local Public Good." *Journal of Public Economics* 2 (Feb. 1973): 35–58.

———. "Efficiency in the Provision of Consumption Subsidies." *Kyklos* 23 (Mar. 1970): 33–57.

Peterson, G. E. "Welfare, Workfare, and Pareto Optimality." *Public Finance Quarterly* 1 (July 1973): 323–338.

Radosevich, Ted. "An Estimation of Non-Support Among Probable Net Recipients of Income Transfers, State Data Program of the Institute of Governmental Studies." Institute of Governmental Studies, University of California at Berkeley, 1974.

Robbins, Lionel. *An Essay on the Nature and Significance of Economic Science*. London: Macmillan, 1932.

Rodgers, J. D. "Distributional Externalities and the Optimal Form of Income Transfers." *Public Finance Quarterly* 1 (July 1973): 266–299.

Rodgers, J. D. "Explaining Income Redistribution." In H. M. Hochman and G. E. Peterson, eds., *Redistribution Through Public Choice*. New York: Columbia University Press, 1974, pp. 165–205.

Schumpeter, J. A. *Capitalism, Socialism, and Democracy*. New York: Harper and Bros., 1942.

Schultze, C. L. *The Distribution of Farm Subsidies: Who Gets the Benefits?* Washington, D.C.: The Brookings Institution, 1971.

Schwartz, R. A. "Personal Philanthropic Contributions." *Journal of Political Economy* 78 (Dec. 1970): 1264–1291.

Tiebout, C. M. "A Pure Theory of Local Expenditures." *Journal of Political Economy* 64 (Oct. 1956): 416–424.

Tullock, G. "The Cost of Transfers." *Kyklos* 24 (1971a): 629–643.

———. "The Charity of the Uncharitable." *Western Economic Journal* 9 (Dec. 1971b): 379–392.

Wilson, J. Q., and Banfield, E. C. "Public Regardingness as a Value Premise in Voting Behavior." *American Political Science Review* 58 (Dec. 1964): 876–887.

Zeckhauser, R. "Optimal Mechanisms for Income Transfers." *American Economic Review* 61 (June 1971): 324–334.

3 ‖ COMMENTS

Thomas E. Weisskopf
University of Michigan

I. SUMMARY

Hochman and Rodgers (H & R), in their paper on "The Simple Politics of Distributional Preference," are concerned with "explaining, in terms of individual preferences, public redistribution to low-income persons" and, in particular, with explaining "those distributional adjustments taken as a group that are commonly referred to as 'welfare' programs" (p. 72). Observing that (in the United States, at least) the actual recipients of welfare transfers are not sufficiently numerous to cause a system of direct or representative democracy to institute such programs against the will of all nonrecipients, H & R focus their attention on the sources of *nonrecipient support* for redistribution which must be present to account for the existence of welfare programs.

The paper explores three related but separable topics. Part I considers potential sources of nonrecipient support for redistribution. Parts II and III construct and analyze simple models of redistribution under direct and representative democracy in order to determine how much nonrecipient support is necessary for the enactment of redistribution programs. Part IV attempts to use the results of certain public opinion polls to assess the actual sources and magnitude of nonrecipient support for redistribution in the United States, and Part V examines whether or not this support is sufficient to account for the enactment of U.S. welfare programs when considered in the framework of the models of democracy previously constructed.

1. Sources of Nonrecipient Support for Redistribution (Part I.) H & R distinguish three major categories of such support: simple self-interest, concern for others, and negative externalities. *Simple self-interest* can arise from: (a) the expectation of becoming a recipient at a future time; (b) participation in activities whose income potential is affected favorably by the demand

shifts accompanying redistribution; or (c) the prospect of having public transfers substitute for otherwise unavoidable private transfers to dependents. *Concern for others* can be characterized by an individual utility function including as an argument not only the individual's own income but also the income of another person, or some variable that contributes positively to the welfare of another person. *Negative externalities* can generate nonrecipient support for redistribution when it is expected that redistribution will help to reduce the impact of certain social maladies (e.g., crime, disease) on nonrecipients.

Among these sources of nonrecipient support for redistribution, H & R introduce a significant distinction between those involving "narrow self-interest" and those involving "benevolence." "Narrow self-interest" is said to underlie support due to sources (a) and (b) of simple self-interest, as well as support due to negative externalities. The term "benevolence" is used to characterize support due to source (c) of simple self-interest and support due to concern for others. H & R emphasize that both of these basic motives—"narrow self-interest" and "benevolence"—are perfectly consistent with a rational calculus based on the maximization of own-utility by individuals; their analysis can therefore be grounded in the corpus of orthodox economic theory.

2. Models of Redistribution under Democracy (Parts II and III.)

H & R seek "to determine the circumstances under which a political democracy may be expected to produce redistribution to the poor" (p. 75) first by considering the simple case of direct democracy and then by turning to the more complex case of representative democracy. Under direct democracy with simple majority rule, it would take a 51 percent coalition of voting citizens to enact a redistributive program. In the absence of nonrecipient support, such a coalition would have to be formed by the 51 percent of voters with the lowest incomes. As H & R observe, such a model cannot explain existing welfare programs in the United States because large numbers of voters with incomes below the median are excluded from welfare benefits. Either the voting behavior of many nonrecipients is governed by considerations other than simple self-interest, or the direct democracy model is inapplicable to welfare-program decision making in the United States, or both.

H & R go on to note that direct democracy is in fact rarely exercised in real-world situations; most collective decisions are made in representative bodies. They then construct a model of the decision-making process in which voters in separated districts elect district representatives by majority vote. These representatives, in turn, vote directly by majority rule on explicit redistributive programs, taxing all persons above a given income level and redistributing the proceeds uniformly to all persons below that level.

In such a model of representative democracy, the circumstances under which a redistribution program will be enacted depend not only on the number of citizens who favor it but also on their distribution among districts. In general, H & R show that there is a minimum proportion of voter support α which is necessary to pass a bill under *optimal* spatial distribution, and a minimum proportion β which will get the bill passed under *any* spatial distribution. As the number of voters and districts increase, the values of α and β approach 25 percent and 75 percent, respectively.

H.& R draw several conclusions from this model. First, in a representative democracy a smaller proportion of voter support can (under certain circumstances) enact redistributive programs than in a direct democracy; one might be able to explain existing welfare programs in the United States on the basis of minority support from recipients plus a limited number of nonrecipients. Second, reapportionment of districts brought about by a defeated majority can make the outcome of collective decision making in a representative democracy more like the outcome of direct democracy *if* reapportionment decisions themselves require less than β in total voter support. Finally, the optimal spatial distribution of a political minority—from the point of view of their political power in a representative democracy—is neither concentrated nor evenly distributed, but "semidispersed."

H & R mention two significant limitations of their model when confronted with real-world processes of decision making in democracies. One is the model's failure to take into account the process of logrolling, in which votes are traded on different issues. H & R suggest that this is not important insofar as feelings about redistribution are much more intense than feelings about other issues. The second problem cited is the model's failure to account for differential rates of voter participation, which tend to be directly related to income. But H & R suggest that it would be easy to adjust the model for this phenomenon, treating variations in voter participation as analytically equivalent to corresponding reductions in voter population in each income class.

3. Empirical Evidence on Distributional Preferences (Parts IV and V.) In this section H & R seek to derive and apply empirical evidence on voter attitudes toward redistribution, using the results of several opinion polls on welfare spending conducted with a sample of California voters in 1970. Their primary purpose is to obtain measures of the nature and extent of nonrecipient support for welfare programs (viewed as an imperfect proxy for generalized redistribution to the poor). The results of the poll were classified by income class; because of strong discontinuities in responses, an income level of $7,000 was identified as the breakpoint between nonrecipients and actual or potential recipients of welfare transfers.

The poll results show that large majorities of all income classes consider some amount of welfare spending as a "moral imperative," but the level of welfare spending considered adequate is on the whole inversely related to the respondent's income level. H & R focus particular attention on the relationship between the percentage of voters viewing some welfare spending as a "moral imperative" and the percentage of voters who believe that welfare spending helps prevent crime. Among nonrecipients, the latter percentage is interpreted as an upper limit on a measure of the frequency with which distributional preferences reflect self-interest arising from negative externalities. The difference between the two percentages (subject to a minor correction) is interpreted as a lower limit on a measure of the frequency with which distributional preferences reflect "benevolence" rather than "narrow self-interest." This minimum indicator of "benevolence" varies directly with income and averages around 50 percent for the nonrecipient population.

H & R consider their finding of such a high level of "benevolence" a highly significant one in the context of their models of democratic decision making. They also take satisfaction from the fact that the positive correlation between income and "benevolence" is consistent with a utility-maximization model in which benevolent transfers are a normal good.

H & R then go on to examine the question of whether nonrecipient concern about welfare recipients is based upon the recipients' general level of self-perceived utility or applies to their particular sources and uses of income. The percentage of voter support for public provision of housing to those who cannot afford it is interpreted as an upper limit on nonrecipient preference for particular-commodity rather than general-utility concern. This percentage is subtracted from the previously derived percentage measuring "benevolence" to get a new measure representing a lower limit on nonrecipient concern for the general welfare of the poor. This lower limit rises with the income class of nonrecipients from negative figures to a maximum of about 25 percent in the highest income class. H & R infer that "donor concern with the self-perceived well-being of welfare recipients is a normal good" (p. 93) and that support of redistribution by nonrecipients "is disproportionately derived from those donors with the highest incomes" (p. 93).

Finally, H & R address themselves to the issues of whether nonrecipient donors are concerned with the self-perceived welfare or the money income of recipients. The percentage of voters agreeing that able-bodied men should not collect welfare is subtracted from the percentage believing in some welfare spending as a "moral imperative" to get a measure of the "lower limit on the extent to which nonrecipient supporters of welfare spending are likely to support a simple program of cash transfers containing no work requirement provisions" (p. 94). This measure averages about 10 percent and does not vary with income class.

In Part V (pp. 94–99), H & R go on to estimate tentatively the degree to which nonrecipient support is actually needed in order to pass motions concerning welfare spending. Using referenda considered implicit in further sample polling in California in 1970, H & R calculate the support required from nonrecipients to reach total support levels ranging from 25 percent to 75 percent (the limits on required voter support to enact motions in a representative democracy). The results indicate that to reach a total support level of 50 percent, motions to increase welfare spending require 55 percent support from nonrecipients, while motions to decrease welfare spending require 60 percent support from nonrecipients. Both of these support levels exceed by a considerable margin the corresponding actual frequencies suggested by nonrecipient responses to the polling; H & R draw the implication that current levels of welfare spending are stable under a system not too far from simple majority rule.

Finally, H & R attempt to bring to bear their estimates of nonrecipient "benevolence" (lower limit: 50 percent) and nonrecipient preference for cash transfers (lower limit: 10 percent) on the prospects for enacting transfer programs. These estimates suggest that some program could be enacted, but they say nothing about the magnitude of the program or the marginal preferences of nonrecipients at current levels of spending. At this point, H & R must introduce some strong assumptions about the structure of nonrecipient preferences in order to conclude (ever so tentatively) that a motion to increase the level of transfer programs might have a chance to pass in a favorably distributed representative democracy.

In their concluding remarks, H & R underline the weakness of their empirical evidence and urge further work both on constructing theoretical models and on collecting a suitable body of microdata to estimate and to apply the models.

II. CRITIQUE

H & R have written an article that is in many ways ingenious, and I trust that it will be considered an interesting contribution to its particular field of research. As one who is not very familiar with work in this field, I shall find it difficult to separate criticism of assumptions and practices common to most researchers in the field from criticism of H & R's work in particular. Indeed, I suspect that much of my criticism will really be applicable to the field as a whole. If so, I hope it will be understood that I am not singling out H & R for reprobation, but rather that I am raising a few basic issues that seem to me to call for more careful thought by all researchers in this area.

I shall divide my comments into three sections: a discussion of the authors' models of democratic decision making, an analysis of the authors' use of the concept of "benevolence," and some concluding observations.

1. Models of Democracy The models of direct and representative democracy constructed by H & R in Parts II and III are very neatly and cogently developed. The analysis of representative democracy, in particular, leads to some interesting implications that, if not exactly counter-intuitive, are nonetheless far from obvious at the start. I have no criticism to make at the level of logical consistency and mathematical accuracy.

However, I do feel that H & R's analysis reflects an extraordinary degree of naiveté about the way the political process works in a real-world "democracy" such as that of the United States. H & R are aware that they are imposing certain simplifying assumptions on their model of representative democracy; the most important of these are spelled out (Pt. III). After concluding their analysis they cite two major "complications"—logrolling and variable rates of voter participation—which might affect the conclusions that they draw. But one is left with the impression that no other major factor would interfere with the validity of their results.

Completely ignored by H & R is any hint of a relationship between economic and political power, other than one mediated by actual voter participation. In this era of Watergate, it should hardly need to be stressed that a realistic analysis of the American political process must deal with the various mechanisms whereby the rich can translate their economic power into disproportionate influence on political decisions. Whether through the financing of political campaigns, the organization of lobbying efforts, influence over the mass media, and so on, the economically powerful can have a decisive influence on what questions are submitted for political decision making, on the form in which they are posed, and on the outcome of any votes.

Indeed, how can models of representative democracy of the kind used by H & R begin to explain the numerous cases of "antiwelfare" programs that characterize contemporary American society? Through tax loopholes, subsidies, special treatment, and so forth, many high-income Americans are able to bring about redistribution in their own favor at the expense of the great majority of citizens in the low-income and/or middle-income classes. To explain such phenomena one must deal seriously with the vastly unequal distribution of effective political power that characterizes the American system of democracy.

H & R might suggest that "differential voter effectiveness" could be incorporated into their model in the same way that variable voter participation rates could. But this would beg the question—for the model itself does nothing to illuminate the immensely important links between economic and political power.

A second important criticism of H & R's model of the political process is that it is rooted in the dominant liberal conception of a system of independent voters, with independently determined and consistently articulated preferences. Yet the presumption of "voter sovereignty" in democratic politics seems to this critic to be no more tenable than the presumption of "consumer sovereignty" in capitalist economies. Although each individual votes in isolation, he/she is continuously bombarded with opinion-molding influences ranging from overt propaganda to subtle persuasion. The result is that rational and predictable utility maximization (however broadly construed) may have great difficulty emerging in even the most (formally) democratic of political systems.

2. Self-interest and Benevolence H & R make much of the distinction between "narrow self-interest" and "benevolence" as independent motives for nonrecipient support of redistributive programs. Both of these words are highly charged with moral connotations. "Narrow self-interest" suggests a kind of scheming egoism which is morally repugnant. "Benevolence" suggests admirable and virtuous behavior: "an inclination to do good; kindliness," according to Webster's dictionary. H & R insist that their notion of "benevolence" is not associated with altruism and its suggestion of selflessness (p. 75), but their most important category of benevolence—concern with the welfare of others, for their own sake—certainly suggests altruistic behavior.

Words *do* matter. Much of H & R's concern focuses on the extent of "benevolence" on the part of nonrecipients of welfare spending, i.e., the middle and upper classes. Indeed, one of the most significant conclusions reported by H & R is a remarkably high (at least 50 percent) incidence of "benevolence" among nonrecipient classes in the United States. An implication of this finding—perhaps not conscious on the part of the authors, but certainly part of the message conveyed by their article—is that the American system is blessed with a happy correlation of wealth and virtue. This is a political message and a conservative one.

Here I want to do more than draw attention to the danger of using value-laden terms and the difficulty of pursuing politically neutral social-science research. I want to suggest that the political issues bound up with the authors' research may well have affected their interpretation of the data. For it seems to me that the inferences they draw from the voter-attitude polls are biased in overemphasizing the "benevolence" of the middle- and upper-income classes and consequently exaggerating the potential for equity in the American social order.

H & R derive their critical quantitative measure of "benevolence" from differences in the polled responses to two statements, the first implying that welfare is a moral imperative and the second implying that welfare prevents crime. The measure of "benevolence" thus obtained is inflated by at least two sources of bias. First, agreement with the statement "in spite of some waste in the welfare program, it would be morally wrong to do away with it" (note to Table 2) may reflect a variety of attitudes other than a genuine interest in redistribution. Respondents might feel that, once instituted, a welfare program should not suddenly be abolished because of the commitments and expectations generated by it. Respondents might feel that as a statement of general principle they should espouse what appears to be a laudably "Christian" attitude, without necessarily being prepared to pay for the cost of the programs implied.

More serious, however, is the bias introduced by treating agreement with the statement: "If it weren't for welfare, there would be a lot more stealing, burglaries, and other crime" (note to Table 2) as the upper limit on support for redistribution for reasons other than benevolence. Crime is only one of many possible sources of negative externalities that might induce the middle and upper classes to support redistributive transfers in their own self-interest. Not only should specific social maladies such as disease and drug traffic be added to the list, but more generally, I would think that a concern for maintaining the overall stability of the social system (from which they benefit) would motivate the middle and upper classes to alleviate conditions of poverty that might lead to social and political turmoil. Indeed, the history of American welfare spending suggests that it is precisely when threats to the social order arise that redistributive programs get enacted and implemented (see, for example, Frances Piven and Richard Cloward, *Regulating the Poor*, 1972). To suggest that this is the result of "benevolence" rather than enlightened self-interest seems to me to distort words or to misread history.

Ignoring the above reasons for suspecting that their estimate of the incidence of benevolence is much too high, H & R actually regard their estimate as a *minimum* measure. This is apparently because a positive response to the welfare-prevents-crime statement, contrary to the assumption on which their numerical calculation is based, need not necessarily exclude the motive of "benevolence." Self-interested concern about negative externalities may coexist with some degree of "benevolence" in the same individual. To the extent that this is true, and ceteris paribus, the incidence of "benevolence" would be underestimated by the H & R procedure.

Currently available data do not permit one to determine the precise quantitative significance of this last source of misestimation; I should very much doubt that it offsets the effects of the sources of upward bias in H & R's estimate of the incidence of "benevolence." But even if it does so, it does nothing to offset the downward bias in H & R's estimate of the incidence of self-interested concern about negative externalities. Such concern is clearly far more important than suggested by H & R. And it follows that inquiry into political support for redistribution in a society such as ours should focus much more attention on the perceived self-interest of the middle- and upper-income classes.

My emphasis on "self-interest" rather than "benevolence" as a motivating force should not be attributed to a generalized cynicism about human nature. On the contrary, I believe that human beings have an immense potential for benevolence. The problem is that this potential may be frustrated by the particular institutional framework within which individuals act. In a capitalist society, one is expected to act in, and one is rewarded for acting in, one's narrow self-interest. To act in a benevolent manner is to act counter to the logic of the system, very possibly to one's own detriment. It is therefore only realistic to expect that under capitalism self-interest will play a much more important role than benevolence. And it follows that a greater degree of benevolence can only be expected under a very different socioeconomic system, with a very different pattern of values and incentives.

3. Conclusion   In their own conclusion (Part VI), H & R introduce a radical/liberal dichotomy of the kind that has almost become de rigueur in contemporary writing in the social sciences. Radicals "suggest that distributive justice requires a radical restructuring of social institutions" (p. 100); liberals "argue that more redistribution would occur if only the democratic political process . . . could be made to more accurately reflect the 'true' preferences of the voters" (p. 100). As a longtime member of the Union for Radical Political Economics, I accept H & R's characterization of the radical position on distributive justice and I espouse it. Yet at the same time, I see no reason to disagree with the liberal argument cited by H & R. If the American democratic political process could be made more truly democratic, I have no reason to doubt that more redistribution would occur than at present. This follows directly from my observation that the American political process is one which now grants vastly disproportionate political power to the rich vis-à-vis the poor.

I believe that there are two principal questions—one normative, one positive—that really divide radicals and liberals in their approach to the issue of distribution: (1) What constitutes "distributive justice"? and (2) What would it take to make the American political process truly democratic? The radical response to each question would involve a much greater departure from the current American status quo than would the liberal response.

H & R's posing of the radical/liberal dichotomy is thus misleading. Their subsequent comments also seem to me very questionable. H & R imply that their characterization of the liberal approach to the issues is much more "open to inquiry" than the radical approach (p. 100). Why is not a potentially radical restructuring of social institutions open to inquiry? Why is the investigation of distributional preferences "within a predefined system of rights and rules" the prior research issue? I need hardly emphasize the conservative conception of the role of the intellectual which is reflected in such remarks.

4

NANCY D. RUGGLES
National Bureau of Economic Research

and

RICHARD RUGGLES
National Bureau of Economic Research
and Yale University

The Anatomy of Earnings Behavior

INTRODUCTION

Earnings from wages and salaries constitute two-thirds of the total personal income received by households and more than half of the total of all payments generated by the gross national product. As the economy grows and develops, wage and salary earnings also change. Increases in the population bring more wage and salary earners into the labor force. Retirements and deaths reduce the labor force. Productivity increases lead to increased earnings, and changes in labor force participation also have major effects. In the shorter run, changes in the level of economic activity and differences in the rate of inflation affect the behavior of total earnings and of the earnings of different social and economic groups. A better grasp of these relationships is needed, to understand both why total wage and salary earnings as they appear in the national accounts change

NOTE: This research was supported by National Science Foundation Grant Project GS-33956.

as they do and how different socioeconomic groups gain or lose, both in absolute terms and relative to one another.

The degree of disaggregation currently available in the national income accounts is not sufficient to provide a basis for this type of analysis. Although wage and salary earnings are given quarterly by industry, no information is provided on the age, sex, and race of the wage and salary recipients; on the size distribution of wage and salary earnings; on exits from and entrants into the labor force; or on the distribution of changes in earnings among different socioeconomic groups. Information of this type is needed in order to elucidate the processes of evolutionary economic change and the effects upon such evolutionary change of short-run changes in the level of economic activity and inflation. However, abandonment of the national income accounting approach is no solution. Independent studies of age profiles, lifetime earnings patterns, sex and race differentials in earnings, labor force participation, size distribution of earnings, and changes in income of different socioeconomic groups would lead to a maze of conflicting observations that would be impossible to integrate into a cohesive whole. Ideally, one would like to be able to disaggregate total wage and salary earnings into components that would permit evaluation of the importance of different factors relative to one another and to the behavior of total earnings.

THE NATURE OF THE LEED FILE

A partial solution to this problem can be found in the LEED file of the Social Security Administration (SSA). The SSA has created a one percent sample of the social security files in such a way that it yields a Longitudinal Employee-Employer Data (LEED) file. In each year, the reports by employers for all social security numbers ending in a given series of digits are selected and matched over time to provide a complete set of employee-employer records for each individual in the sample. Such a procedure not only brings together all of the information pertinent to a given individual, but it also automatically brings in the new entrants into the labor force in the proportion in which they occur, and the absence of employee-employer records automatically reflects exits. The basic information provided on each individual includes age, sex, and race, and for each quarter of every year, the amount of wages paid to the individual by each employer. There is, however, a cutoff point established in the social security law beyond which wages are no longer reported. Since the Federal Insurance Contribution Act (FICA) tax is applied against total earnings as they are paid, the effect of this provision is to stop the reporting of income at the point in the year when the limit for any one employer is reached. If an individual is receiving earnings from several employers, each would be reported separately, and the limit would apply to each individually. Although the Social Security Administration does compute an estimate of total earnings for the year in those instances where the limit is reached before the end of the year, it is obvious that the early part of the year will be more fully reported than the later part, and the estimates for these early quarters will more fully reflect the national totals. For the purposes of this study, therefore, the analysis will be confined to the first-quarter data, which are relatively unaffected by the taxable limit, and which, in addition, reduce the influence of seasonality.

It should be pointed out that the LEED file does not contain various sorts of social and demographic information which would be very useful in the analysis of earnings behavior. Thus, for example, no information is provided on education, occupation, or marital status of individuals; the data, furthermore, refer solely to total earnings paid, and no information is provided on the number of hours worked. Thus, earnings may be low either because the wage rate is low or because the employee worked for only a fraction of the period or on a part-time basis.

Despite these deficiencies, however, the LEED file is still a rich source of data. It is an extremely large sample, equal in magnitude to the 1 percent Census Public Use Samples. In contrast to the Public Use Samples, however, it follows each individual over a substantial period of time (1957–69), so that year-to-year changes for specific individuals or groups can be observed. Although other panel history sample surveys are being developed, most of them cover very much smaller samples and cannot be successfully disaggregated to show the anatomy of the total wage bill in the national economy.

The social security system covers about 90 percent of total wage and salary employment. Certain government employees are excluded, and there are a small number of other groups who, like the railroad employees, have their own pension system, or who are not covered by any system. As is indicated in Table 1, the percentage of wage and salary earners covered by social security rose from 87 percent to 90 percent over the period covered by the LEED file. The same table compares the total wage and salary figures reported in the national accounts by the Bureau of Economic Analysis (BEA) with the wage and salary figures derived from the LEED file. The LEED coverage gradually increased from 80 percent of the national accounts wage and salary earnings total in 1957 to 85 percent in 1969. This total is somewhat lower than the social security employment coverage, partly because of the processing procedures used in the creation of the LEED file. The Social Security Administration points out that it creates the LEED sample in September of the year

TABLE 1   Coverage of Social Security LEED File

| | Percent of Total Employment | | | Wage and Salary Earnings | | |
| | Total Reported to SSA | Not reported to SSA | | BEA Total | LEED File | LEED as Percent |
		Government	Other	(billion $)		of BEA
1957	87	8	5	237	189	80
1958	88	7	5	235	190	81
1959	88	7	5	253	204	81
1960	89	6	5	269	219	81
1961	89	6	5	271	223	82
1962	89	7	4	290	241	83
1963	89	7	4	305	252	83
1964	89	6	5	324	270	83
1965	89	6	5	347	285	82
1966	89	6	5	380	315	83
1967	90	7	3	412	347	84
1968	90	7	3	448	379	85
1969				492	417	85

SOURCE: Percentages of total employment:
"The 1% Sample Longitudinal Employee-Employer Data File," Social Security Administration, Office of Research and Statistics, Division of Statistics, Statistical Operations Branch, November 1971, page 3.
BEA wage and salary earnings:
1957–64   "The National Income and Product Accounts of the United States 1929–1965—Statistical Tables," Supplement to *The Survey of Current Business*, August 1966, Table 2.1, pages 34 and 35.
1965–67   *Survey of Current Business*, July 1969, Table 2.1, page 26.
1968–69   *Survey of Current Business*, July 1971, Table 2.1, page 26.
LEED wage and salary earnings:
Tabulated from LEED 1% file—summary figures multiplied by 100.

following the year to which the data refer, and that any items that are posted after this date are excluded. It is difficult to estimate the exact amount of undercoverage which results from this procedure, and it may differ considerably from year to year, but it is likely to be from 2 to 4 percent. Another source of difference may lie in the fact that the government employees who are not included in the LEED file have higher than average earnings.

From the point of view of year-to-year change, the earnings reflected in the LEED file track the national accounts wage and salary earnings very well. The gradual rise in the percentage of earnings covered from 80 to 85 percent in all probability reflects the combined effect of the increased number of people covered by the social security system and changes in the timing of updating procedures. In terms of sampling reliability, the LEED 1 percent sample is of course quite large, starting with 515,000 cases in 1957 and rising to 700,000 cases in 1969.

SPECIFIC QUESTIONS TO BE INVESTIGATED

The LEED file provides a basis for investigating a wide variety of questions. In view of the lack of information on such things as hours worked, education, and family status, it is not possible to develop a full-fledged model of wages and labor force participation with the LEED material alone. Nevertheless, the LEED file is capable of providing new insights relating to certain specific aspects of earnings and labor force participation. This paper will confine itself to four sets of questions relating to specific variables. These are:

1. age-earnings profiles and birth cohort lifetime patterns of earnings;
2. sex and race differentials in both age-earnings profiles and birth cohort patterns of earnings;
3. work history at different points in the life cycle for different sexes and races; and
4. the distribution of earnings by size for different age-race-sex groups, its change over time, and the effect of changes in the level of economic activity and in prices on the distribution of earnings and labor force participation.

AGE

Age-earnings profiles have been the focus of considerable interest by economists. It has long been recognized that earnings rise with age up to a point, and then level off and decline. This phenomenon underlies many of the human-capital models which attempt to explain the observed differentials in terms of human investment by both the wage earner and the employer. The most comprehensive and reliable age profiles available up to now have come from the Census records, although even small samples do reveal the general patterns in broad outline. What has been lacking is an understanding of how the age-earnings profiles shift from year to year as the age composition of the population changes and as the level of economic activity and prices change, and as long-run economic growth takes place. Since the LEED file is available yearly for the period 1957 to 1969, it can be used to ask how age-earnings profiles do shift over time, and whether these shifts are sensitive to differing sizes of entering cohorts and different economic conditions.

A second question with respect to age is how earnings change from the point of view of birth cohorts, rather than from the perspective of age-earnings profiles. In recent years, the topic of lifetime earnings of specific birth cohorts has aroused increasing interest because of the realization that individuals are, in fact, treated quite differently at different points in the life cycle, receiving different levels of income and having different financial responsibilities. The LEED file is particularly well suited to analyze the pattern of earnings for a twelve-year segment of the lives of individual cohorts, and to discover whether there is a significant difference in these lifetime patterns. There is a real need to link the analysis of shifts in age-earnings profiles over time with the relative behavior of different birth cohorts over time. These two questions are in fact different aspects of the more central question of the relation of age to earnings.

SEX AND RACE

Questions relating to sex and race differentials have also been central to the analysis of earnings and labor force participation. There have been many studies of such differentials, some of which have attempted to assess the extent of discrimination, defined in terms of differences in earnings of individuals with similar qualifications in the same occupation but with different race and sex characteristics. This sort of analysis is outside the scope of the present study. The sex-race differentials which are observed in the LEED file may result from a large variety of factors, including differences in occupation, education, labor force participation, and discrimination, and it is not possible to isolate the different factors. It is important, however, to recognize that, whatever their roots, there are major sex and race differentials, which result in different amounts of earnings for different individuals. With the LEED data, it is possible to ask how age-earnings profiles differ for the different sex and race groups, and how these profiles have shifted over the period from 1957 to 1969. The answer to these questions can throw considerable light on whether or not the gross differentials between sex and race groups are, in fact, being systematically reduced by increased educational opportunities and a reduction in discrimination. In this connection, it is also possible to trace out the lifetime earnings patterns of different birth cohorts for individual race and sex groups, to ascertain whether there are characteristic differences in the shapes of these functions, and whether generalizations can be made about such patterns in terms of the nature of the groups involved.

WORK HISTORY

There are a number of questions relating to work history that can be answered by the data in the LEED file. For example, it is useful to ask how the different sex and race groups enter and exit from employment over their life cycle. Men traditionally enter the labor force in their teens or early twenties, and leave it only through death or retirement. Women, on the other hand, may leave the labor force during the childbearing years, and then may or may not reenter it. Detailed evidence on the age pattern of entrance and exit based on a large sample has not been readily available. The LEED data can cast considerable light upon the nature of this pattern for both white and nonwhite females.

There are also other questions relating to work history to which the LEED data can provide answers. For each individual, it can be ascertained whether he is working at all in a given quarter, and whether his employer is the same or different from the one reported in some other specific period. Thus, a work history can be developed which reflects exits from and entrants to employment from one year to the next, and shows as separate groups those individuals who retain the same employer and those who change employers. The question of exits and entrants is highly related to employment turnover or instability, and to the pattern of younger people coming into the labor force and older people leaving it. Differences in age, race, and sex patterns throw light on questions of labor force participation by different groups at different stages in their life cycles. For instance, is it true that it is the tendency for labor force entrants to come in at a low wage and for those who exit to leave at a high wage that makes possible increases in wages to all workers without a corresponding increase in the total wage bill? Although hours worked are not available in the LEED file, it is possible to see whether an individual's total earnings increased or decreased from one period to the next. Such increases and decreases will, of course, reflect changes in both wage rates and hours worked. Moving from part-time to full-time work may result in very large increases in earnings, and from full time to part time will result in large decreases. Changes in overtime work may also have a major impact on the change in earnings. Changes in wage rates should, in general, result in increases in earnings rather than decreases, but on the average, such increases would not be expected to be large. Examination of the increases and decreases in earnings for individuals with unchanged employers can, therefore, cast some light on the question of how important changes in labor force participation are for individuals who remain employed. Such questions are central to analyzing why the wage bill changes as it does under different economic conditions.

DISTRIBUTION OF EARNINGS BY SIZE

The distribution of average annual earnings by size is, of course, directly related to the question of earnings differentials according to age-sex-race groups. Specifically, it may be asked whether the observed higher male wages come about through a greater variance in the size distribution of their income. In other words, does the male distribution include low- as well as high-income earners, or is the whole range of male earnings higher? Does the size distribution of earnings become more unequal with advancing age, and is this true for all sex and race groups?

Finally, does the size distribution of income differ significantly over time, and at different levels of economic activity? This final set of questions relates to the effects of changes in the level of economic activity and the price level upon earnings and labor force participation. The questions which will be asked relate to who benefits and who loses in periods of slow growth and small wage increases, compared with periods of higher growth and larger wage increases. In all periods, some individuals gain and others lose. The question which is being asked here relates to differences in the number of people who gain and lose, and the differential effects on different age, sex, and race groups. Only by such analysis, expressed in real terms, can the loss or gain resulting from tightening down or speeding up economic activity be assessed.

AGE AND EARNINGS

Age-earnings profiles for the period 1957–69 can be derived from the LEED file by single years of age. These are shown in Figure 1. The successive age-earnings profiles for the different years shift upward, the lowest representing the year 1957, and the highest the year 1969. From this chart it becomes apparent that the shift from year to year is highly dependent upon economic conditions. The year 1958, for example, shows no significant upward shift over the year 1957; in fact the two age-earnings profiles overlap. Similarly, in the mild recession of 1961 the age-earnings profile also failed to shift upward significantly. In contrast,

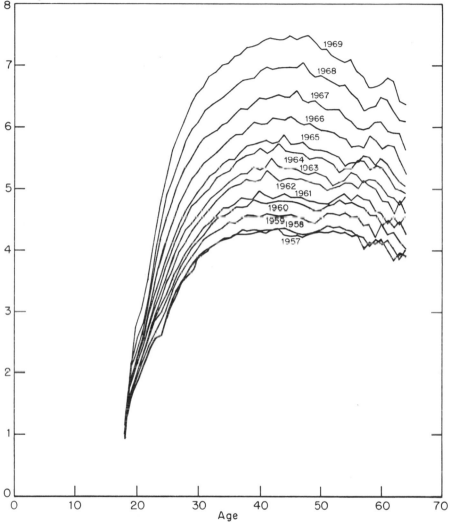

**FIGURE 1 Age-Earnings Profiles, 1957–69
(Current dollars)**

Earnings (thousand dollars)

in each year from 1966 through 1969 there was a strong upward shift in the profile reflecting a sharp rise in earnings for all age levels.

From Figure 1, it would appear that the profile is considerably less flat in the ages from 35 to 60 in more recent years than it was in 1957. In other words, those in the middle age groups would appear to have gained relatively more than those either younger or older. The age-earnings profiles shown in Figure 1 are, however, not completely smooth and regular. Inasmuch as they are based on a very large sample, the irregularities deserve consideration. Thus, for example, the profile for 1969 shows a sharp dip in earnings for those of age 58, born in 1911, relative to those immediately older or younger. This dip can in fact be traced back for this birth cohort in the profiles for previous years, suggesting that for some reason this cohort was retarded relative to those around it. This was the birth cohort which entered the labor force in approximately 1930, and it is not unreasonable to assume that the labor market conditions at the time of their entry had a significant depressing effect on their earnings, relative to those who preceded them and were already established in the labor market. In contrast, the cohort who were born a decade later and came into the labor market in 1940 are high relative to the cohorts surrounding them and seem to have enjoyed this advantage continuously. Especially sharp peaks for this birth cohort can be seen in the profiles for the period 1961 to 1965.

The average earnings shown in Figure 1 are in terms of current year prices, and to the extent that consumer prices were rising the chart overstates the upward shift of age-earnings profiles in real terms. In Figure 1A average earnings of each year are deflated by the consumer price index, using 1957 as a base. The successive annual profiles in Figure 1A are much closer together than those in Figure 1, indicating that a substantial part of the observed earnings increases from 1957 to 1969 did not reflect increases in real earnings. It is interesting to note that in real terms the age-earnings profile for the year 1958 is lower than that for 1957, indicating that even the employed workers in the 1958 recession suffered a real decline in income.

The earnings patterns for all birth cohorts born in the period from 1904 to 1941 are shown in Figure 2. Each line in this diagram shows the average earnings over the period 1957–69 for a single-year birth cohort. The points plotted in this figure are of course the same as those in Figure 1. In Figure 1, however, the points for all ages in a given year are connected, yielding a cross-section picture. In Figure 2, points for a given birth cohort for all years are connected, thus tracing out the experience of given groups through time. The relation between Figure 1 and Figure 2 can be easily seen if one considers that the age profile shown for the year 1969 can be obtained by connecting the end points of the birth cohort earning patterns.

In Figure 2, the lack of change in earnings from 1957 to 1958 appears as a sideways movement in earnings patterns; this same sideways movement is exhibited again for the period 1960 to 1961. The ripples in the earnings pattern lines indicate slackening in the rate of increase of earnings due to slowing down of economic activity. The earnings patterns for the cohorts born in 1911 and 1921 are labeled explicitly on Figure 2; as can be seen, these are the cohorts which respectively lagged behind and led adjacent cohorts, and appeared as dips and peaks in Figure 1.

If the age cohort earnings patterns are deflated by the consumer price index, the individual age cohort earnings patterns rise much more slowly, and the difference in the rate of increase with age becomes more apparent. This is shown in Figure 2A. From 1957 to 1958, the earnings of all cohorts 35 years old and over declined. Less drastic slowdowns in the increase in earnings can be seen for a number of other years.

FIGURE 1A   Age-Earnings Profiles, 1957–69 (1957 dollars)

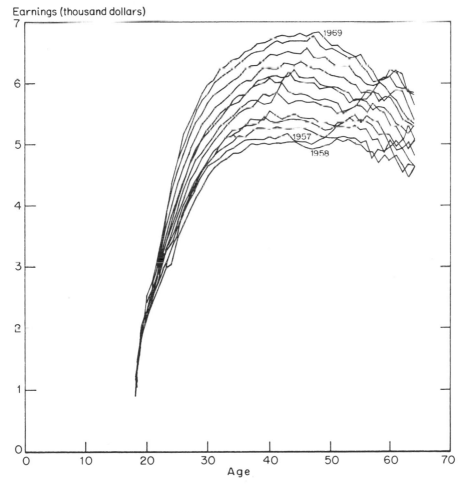

FIGURE 2 Age-Cohort Earnings, 1957–69 (Current dollars)

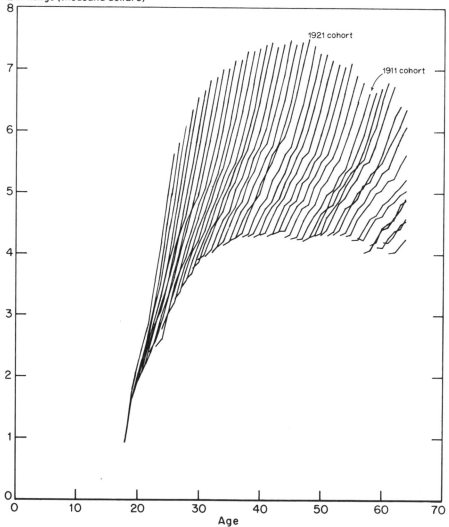

**FIGURE 2A Age-Cohort Earnings, 1957–69
(1957 dollars)**

Earnings (thousand dollars)

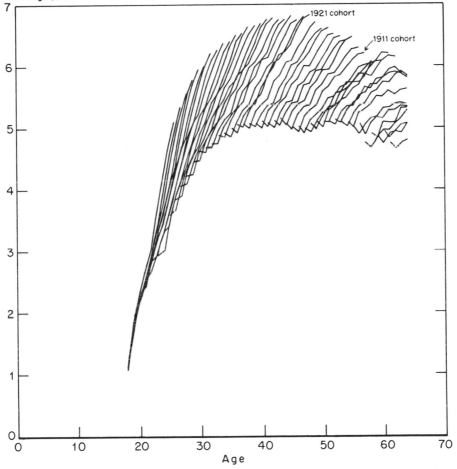

The interrelation of the earnings patterns of different birth cohorts can be seen more easily when they are plotted by calendar year, rather than age. Figure 3 shows the earnings patterns for people who were born in 1940, 1928, 1916, and 1904. At the beginning of the period, these people were aged 17, 29, 41, and 53. By the end of the period, they were 29, 41, 53, and 65. In 1957, the average earnings of the 1904 and 1916 cohorts

FIGURE 3 Earnings Patterns of Four Birth Cohorts, 1957–69 (Current dollars)

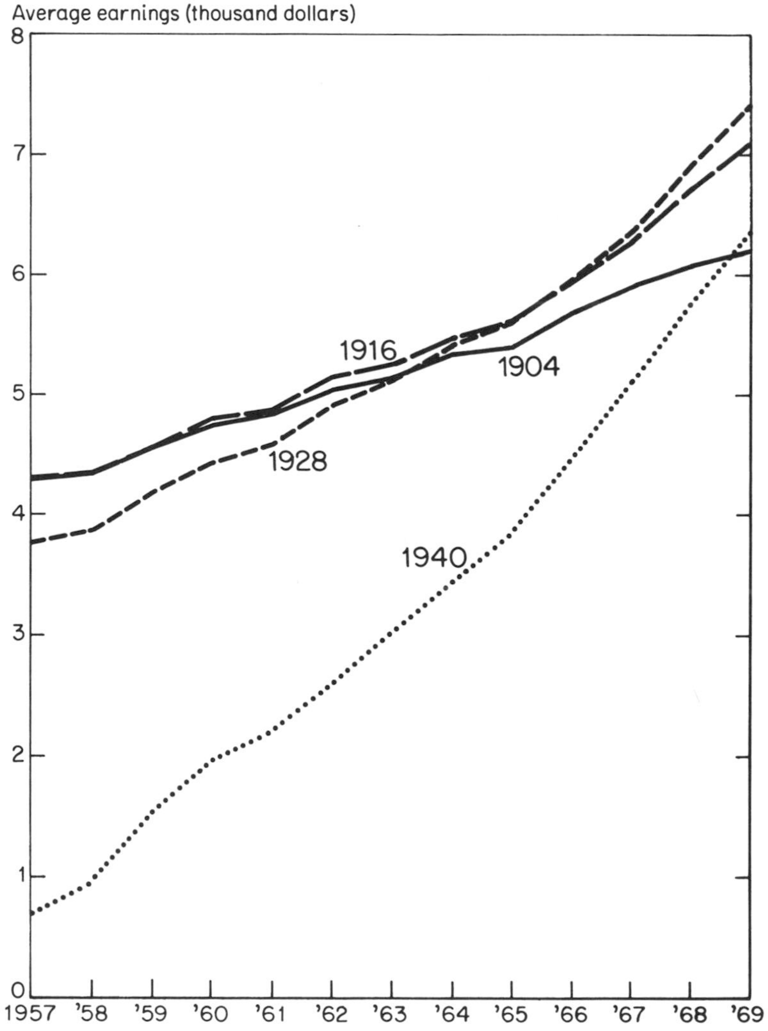

Average earnings (thousand dollars)

were almost identical, and they exhibited the same pattern of growth for the next two years. After that, however, the 1904 cohort rose somewhat more slowly, and in 1963, when its members were 59 years old, its earnings were equaled by those of the faster-rising 35 year olds of the 1928 cohort. This 1928 cohort was also increasing faster than the 1916 cohort, and caught up with the latter by 1965, going on to be the top in average earnings from then on. The 1940 cohort, which of course started out the lowest of all in 1957 when they were 17 years old, increased rapidly throughout the period, catching up with the 1904 cohort in 1968 when they were 28 and those in the older group were 64. The striking point of Figure 3 is that younger cohorts successively overtake older cohorts, and in turn are themselves overtaken by still younger cohorts. The variance which existed among cohorts when they were at ages ranging from 17 to 53 became considerably reduced when they all advanced to the age range 29–65.

In relating the age-earnings profiles to the earning patterns of specific birth cohorts, the leveling off and decline in average earnings shown by the cross-sectional age-earnings profile is in marked contrast with the continual rise in earnings exhibited by every birth cohort up to the point of retirement at age 65. The shape of the age-earnings profile results from the differential rates of earnings increase at different points in the life cycle. The effect of economic conditions appears in a substantially reduced rate of earnings increase for all birth cohorts in periods of recession and unemployment, but substantial increases in output and employment do not appear to have as much influence.

If the earning patterns of specific birth cohorts are measured in real terms (as shown in Figure 3A), the rate of increase for all of the cohorts is substantially reduced, and for the oldest cohort (those born in 1904) an actual decline in real earnings takes place in the last several years, i.e., after age 65. No significant real decline takes place prior to that age, however, except in periods of recession.

SEX AND RACE DIFFERENTIALS

The discussion of age-earnings profiles and birth cohort earnings patterns to this point has treated the population as a whole, without respect to either sex or race. It is well known, however, that significant sex and race differences do exist. The differences in age-earnings profiles are striking. Figure 4 shows the age-earnings profiles by race and sex for the year 1969; this figure is a decomposition of the total age-earnings profile shown in Figure 1. For white males, the peak average earnings in 1969

Earnings Patterns of Four Birth Cohorts, 1957–69 (1957 dollars)

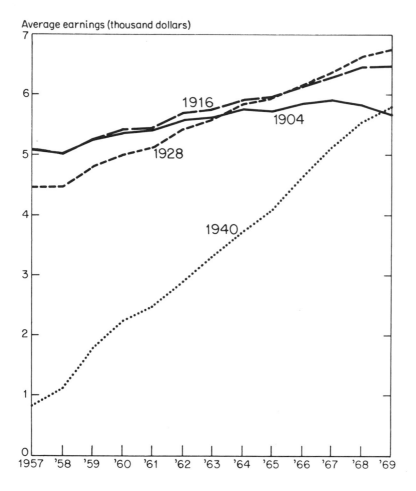

Average earnings (thousand dollars)

were received by those in the late forties, and substantial differentials existed over the ages from 30 to 65. For nonwhite males, the highest income was received in 1969 by those in their late thirties. Although the level of nonwhite male earnings is lower than that for white males, the general shape of the age profile is quite similar. For all ages and both races, male earnings are substantially greater than female.

Besides being substantially below that for both groups of males, the age-earnings profile for white females is very different in shape. After an

FIGURE 4 Age-Earnings Profiles by Race and Sex, 1969

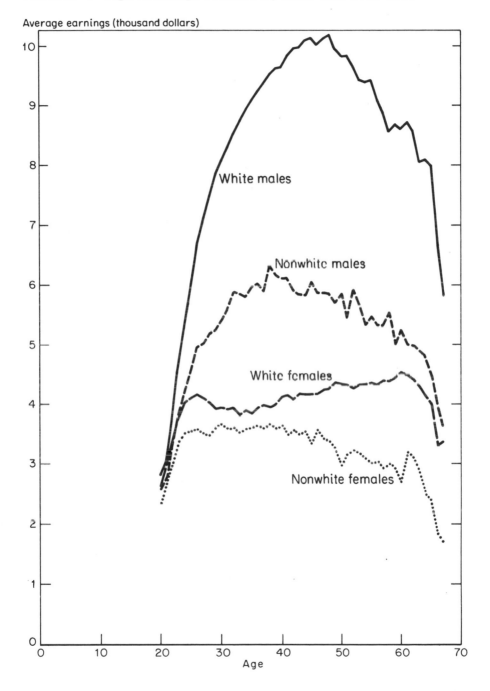

Average earnings (thousand dollars)

White males

Nonwhite males

White females

Nonwhite females

Age

initial rise up to the mid-twenties, the age-earnings profile drops until the mid-thirties, after which time there is a gradual rise to age 60. This pattern is undoubtedly influenced by the withdrawal of women during the childbearing ages. There appears to be a mix effect in which the net exit of women with higher incomes is greater than the net exit of women with lower incomes. Table 2 illustrates this pattern for white women aged 24.

TABLE 2　Number of White Women Aged 24 in Social Security Covered Employment by Income Class

Income Group	Number 1963	Exits 1963	Entrants 1964	Percent Net Change
$　1–999	585	292	261	−5.3
1,000–1,999	535	194	156	−7.1
2,000–2,999	814	206	139	−8.2
3,000–3,999	932	204	105	−10.6
4,000–4,999	730	129	55	−10.1
5,000–5,999	275	48	21	−9.8
6,000–6,999	82	10	6	−4.9
7,000–7,999	20	6	1	−25.0
8,000 and over	4	0	0	0
Total	3,979	1,089	744	−8.7

SOURCE:　Based on detailed tabulations of Appendix Table A-3.

It should be pointed out that this decline in the age-earnings profile of white females does not mean that there is a corresponding decline in the lifetime patterns of birth cohorts passing through these age groups. During the year 1963 more than 27 percent of the women 24 years old exited from employment, while only 18 percent of the women employed in the first quarter of 1964 had not been employed in the first quarter of 1963. Thus, of women who were 24 years old in 1963, the number employed declined by approximately 9 percent from 1963 to 1964. As Table 2 shows, this decline was sharper for women in higher earnings groups than for those in lower earnings groups. It seems reasonable that this effect may be due to the higher family-income status of women who are themselves receiving higher earnings. The decision to leave employment because of childbearing is probably related to the level of income enjoyed by the family. Women in low-income families who themselves are receiving low incomes cannot afford to stop working.

For nonwhite females, the ages of highest income are between 30 and 40, a range over which there is no appreciable difference. After that, as in the case of nonwhite males, the earnings for older age groups are lower. It should be pointed out that the age-earnings profiles reflect the influence of historical changes on lifetime patterns. It is doubtless true that the occupations and industries in which the different sex and race groups are employed have different lifetime patterns. It is also true, however, that in recent years these occupations and industries have been changing, especially for the younger age groups, which suggests that the age profiles can be expected to change in shape in the future.

A comparison of the percentage change in average earnings by sex and race over the period 1957–69 for specific age groups is shown in Table 3.

TABLE 3 Percent Change in Average Earnings by Age,
Sex, and Race, 1957–69

Age	White Male	White Female	Nonwhite Male	Nonwhite Female
20–24	54	52	77	106
25–29	75	66	90	124
30–34	74	59	92	110
35–39	76	59	92	109
40–44	80	67	90	107
45–49	84	64	92	108
50–54	76	64	99	98
55–59	71	72	79	105
60–64	69	86	83	130
Average	73	67	86	107

SOURCE: Based on Appendix Table A-1.

This table provides a measure of the extent to which gross differentials among the various groups have changed. The most striking feature of this table is the relative improvement in the position of nonwhite females. They averaged an increase of 107 percent over the period 1957–69, and in almost every age group exceeded the increases shown for other groups. In contrast, the position of white females improved the least. Overall, their earnings rose by only 67 percent. From age 55 onward, however, white females did better than white males, and after 60 even better than nonwhite males. Nonwhite males did better than white males at all ages, increasing by over 90 percent between the ages of 25 and 54. In general, then, the gross differentials by race narrowed in the period 1957–69 for all age groups, with black women making the largest relative gains. White females, however, dropped behind; the gross differential between them and white males increased for all ages up to 55.

The earnings patterns for specific birth cohorts can also be broken down by race and sex. This is done in Figures 5 and 5A. The four sections of these figures represent a disaggregation by race and sex of the earnings patterns for birth cohorts shown in Figures 3 and 3A. It is apparent that the sex and race differentials in earnings patterns are established in the early years; as the 1940 birth cohort shows, well before age 29. White female earnings are on a par with those of white males up to age 22, after which time the earnings of white males increase much faster than those of white females; the latter are surpassed by nonwhite males by the age of 26. The rate of increase of white and nonwhite females over the period as a whole was remarkably similar. The patterns for all race and sex groups in the older cohorts reveal the expected slowing in the rates of increase, but again it is striking that no birth cohort for any race or sex suffers a decline in earnings over any part of its life cycle, and the relative positions of the different sex and race groups are essentially maintained throughout.

In this connection, it may be noted from Figure 5A that the average real earnings of older nonwhite males do drop significantly in periods of mild recession. Thus, in the three older birth cohorts there is a substantial decline in both 1958 and 1961 for this group. For white males, there was a decline in real earnings for the oldest cohort in 1958, but for females the earnings patterns are relatively undisturbed by the recessions.

WORK HISTORY

Individuals' employment history varies considerably over their lifetimes. The LEED file cannot capture the complete pattern in all of its detail; it does not include the self-employed, many of the employees of state and local governments, most federal employees, railroad employees, and those employed in some other small uncovered occupations. Nevertheless, as was indicated in Table 1, the coverage is quite high, so that an analysis of the work history of specific birth cohorts does provide information on the lifetime pattern of employment.

Determination of the size of the birth cohort raises certain problems. Actual birth data are not suitable, because of the mortality, immigration, and emigration which take place prior to the age of legitimate employment. Census data are more appropriate, but for younger age groups they suffer from substantial underreporting. In the 1970 Census, for example, it is estimated that total underreporting was of the order of 2.5 percent, i.e., 5 million persons, and it is generally conceded that the most serious underreporting occurs in the highly mobile groups—the young, the male, the nonwhite. For instance, the number of 20-year-old nonwhite males reported in the 1960 Census was 23 percent below the number of 30-year-old nonwhite males reported in the 1970 Census. Understatement on a somewhat smaller scale also exists in the 1960 Census for young whites (12 percent for males, 9 percent for females), but for older age groups the discrepancy between the 1960 and 1970 censuses is in line with expected mortality. Although it would be possible to adjust the birth cohort size to reflect mortality, it is perhaps more useful to treat it as a form of withdrawal from employment, somewhat analogous to permanent retirement.

The expected lifetime employment pattern for males is one in which the percentage employed increases during the initial years due to individuals entering the labor force for the first time, levels off in the adult years, declines somewhat due to mortality in the middle and later years, and declines sharply at the point of retirement. For females, childbearing can be expected to have a significant impact on the lifetime employment pattern. Figure 6 presents the observed lifetime employment patterns for four different birth cohorts. These cohorts have been selected so that, taken all together, they cover the ages from 17 through 65. The pattern within a cohort reflects the actual experience of that cohort in the years from 1957 to 1969.

For males, the expected pattern does emerge. The break between the 1940 and 1928 cohorts may be due in large part to Census understatement of the size of the younger population cohort. If the cohort is, in fact, larger than shown in the Census, the percentage of this cohort employed in covered occupations would be correspondingly lower, and would be more in line with the 1928 cohort. It is, of course, quite legitimate for employment percentages for these two cohorts to be different at the point of the break, since one represents the situation for 29-year-olds in 1969, whereas the other represents 29-year-olds in 1957. In the experience of the 1928 birth cohort, it can be seen that the employment of nonwhite males dropped in the recession of 1958, but rose substantially above that of white males in the subsequent prosperity of the late 1960s. The striking feature of the 1916 and 1904 birth cohorts is the substantial decline in the percentage employed, similar for both nonwhite and white males. The decline starts in the early forties, and increases thereafter, until at the conventional retirement age of 65 only about a quarter of the cohort is still employed in covered occupations.

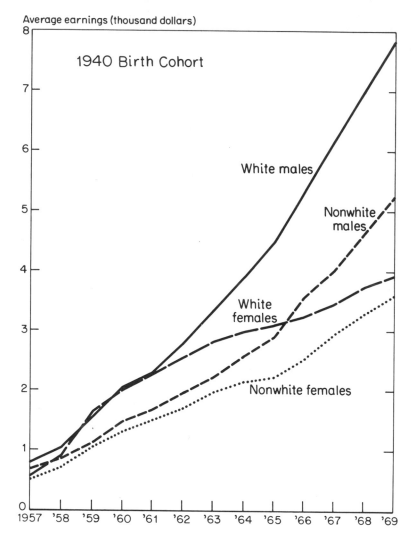

FIGURE 5 **Earnings Patterns by Race and Sex for Selected Birth Cohorts, 1957–69: Section 1 (Current dollars)**

Average earnings (thousand dollars)

1940 Birth Cohort

White males

Nonwhite males

White females

Nonwhite females

1957 '58 '59 '60 '61 '62 '63 '64 '65 '66 '67 '68 '69

For white females, the percentage employed declines from age 21 through age 28, reflecting withdrawals for raising families. Starting in the early thirties, the percentage employed increases continually to the mid-fifties. Only after that does the decline set in, and it is more gradual than that of males. During the childbearing ages, the percentage employed dropped from 46 percent to 27 percent. Since, in fact, the data

Earnings Patterns by Race and Sex for Selected Birth Cohorts, 1957–69: Section 1 (1957 dollars)

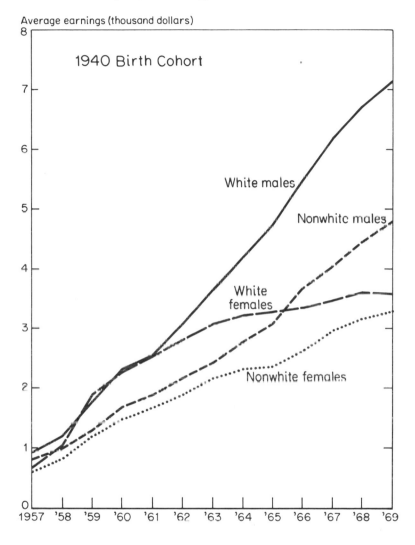

Average earnings (thousand dollars)

1940 Birth Cohort

White males

Nonwhite males

White females

Nonwhite females

shown here pertain only to covered employment, the actual percentage employed probably exceeded this by at least another 6 or 7 percentage points. Thus, approximately three-fifths of the number of women initially employed are employed throughout this period. Although the higher percentage of women employed at the end of the 1940 birth cohort in comparison with the beginning of the 1928 birth cohort may be explained

FIGURE 5 (continued): Section 2

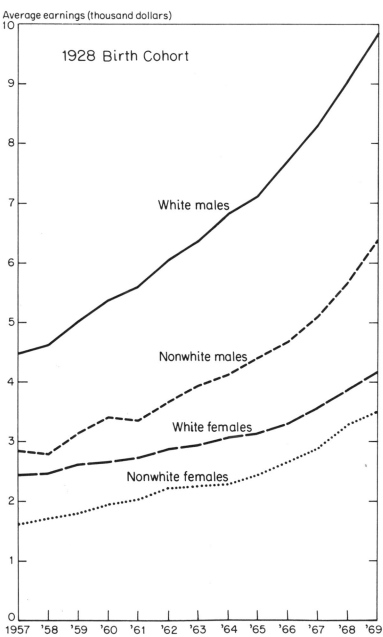

Average earnings (thousand dollars)

1928 Birth Cohort

White males

Nonwhite males

White females

Nonwhite females

FIGURE 5A (continued): Section 2

Average earnings (thousand dollars)
9
8
7
6
5
4
3
2
1
0
1928 Birth Cohort
White males
Nonwhite males
White females
Nonwhite females
1957
'58
'59
'60
'61
'62
'63
'64
'65
'66
'67
'68
'69

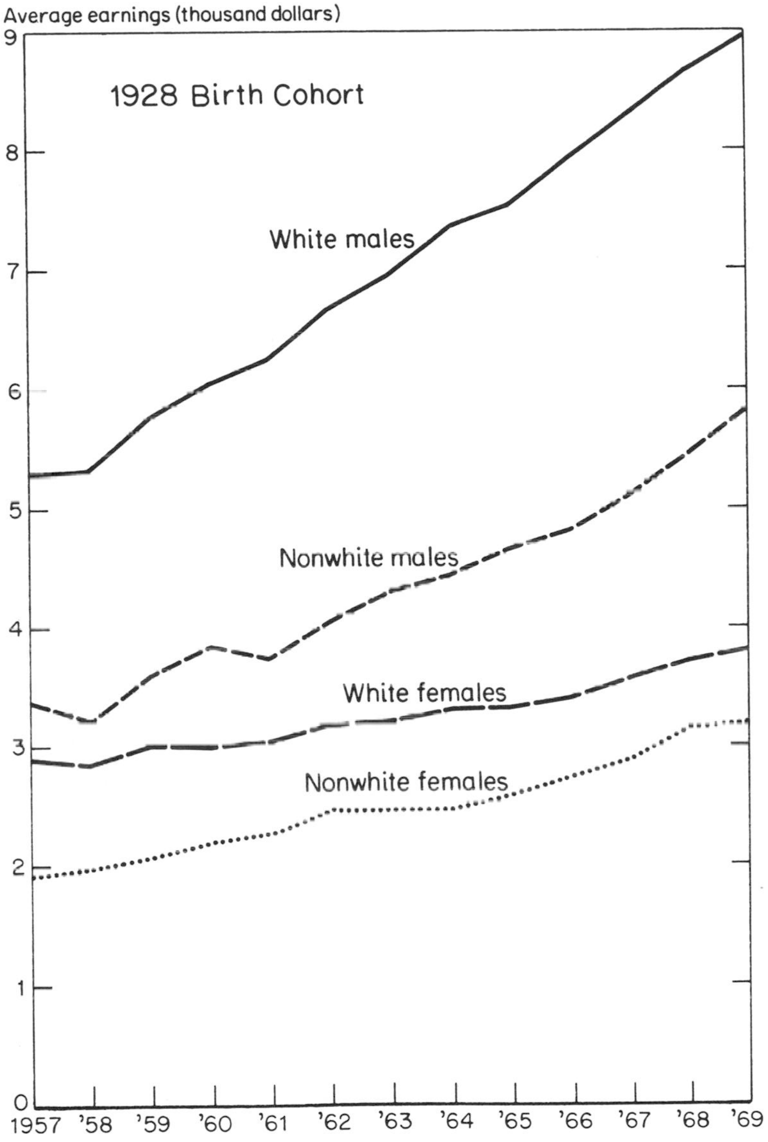

in part by Census underenumeration, underenumeration is substantially less for women, and this same relation between cohorts can be observed between the other pairs of cohorts as well. This suggests that there is a successive increase in the percentage employed by each successive younger cohort.

FIGURE 5 (continued): **Section 3**

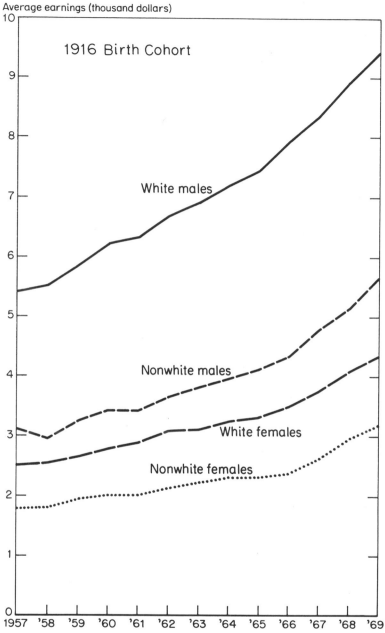

Average earnings (thousand dollars)

1916 Birth Cohort

White males

Nonwhite males

White females

Nonwhite females

Average earnings (thousand dollars)

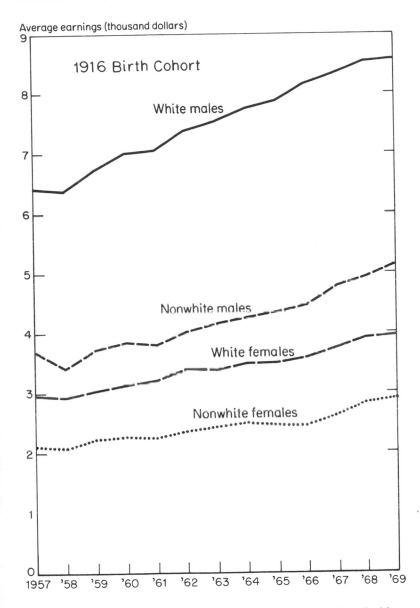

Nonwhite women do not follow the pattern either of white women or of males. Their employment in the earlier years is substantially lower, but it increases steadily even during the childbearing ages. At age 25, it equals that of white women, and it continues to rise thereafter. As in the case of

FIGURE 5 (concluded): Section 4

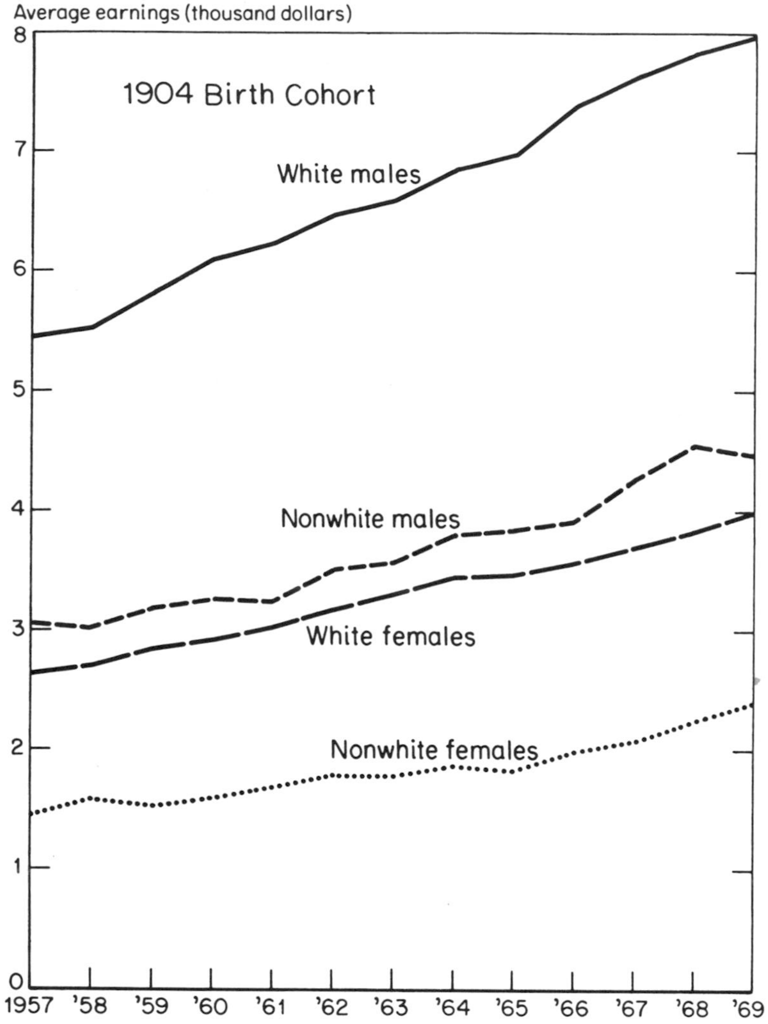

Average earnings (thousand dollars)
8
7
6
5
4
3
2
1
0
1904 Birth Cohort
White males
Nonwhite males
White females
Nonwhite females
1957
'58
'59
'60
'61
'62
'63
'64
'65
'66
'67
'68
'69

white women, this increase extends into the mid-fifties. In the oldest cohort, the employment of nonwhite women is almost identical with that of white women.

The percent-employed data, however, do not adequately reveal the year-to-year work-history changes. It is interesting to ask how people move in and out of employment in the various age groups, and to determine the relative importance of workers with single employers over time. Table 4 presents this information by race and sex for three age

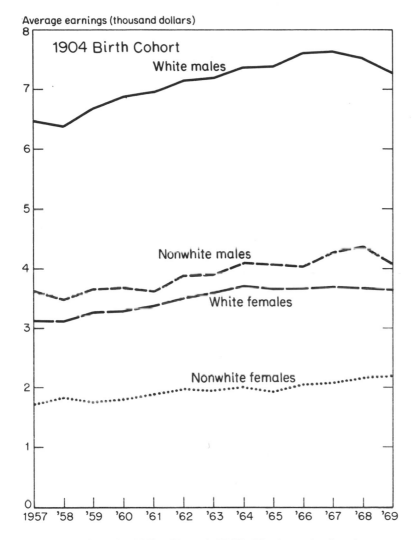

Average earnings (thousand dollars)

1904 Birth Cohort

White males

Nonwhite males

White females

Nonwhite females

groupings in 1957–58 and 1968–69. An exit, for the purposes of this table, is a person who was employed in the first quarter of the initial year, but for whom there is no record of employment in the first quarter of the following year. An entrant is a person for whom there is no record of employment in the first quarter of the initial year, but who is employed in the first quarter of the following year. Persons having unchanged single employers in both years can also be identified, since the establishment identification number is given in the social security records. It should be

FIGURE 6   Percent of Cohort Employed by Race and Sex for Selected Birth Cohorts, 1957–69

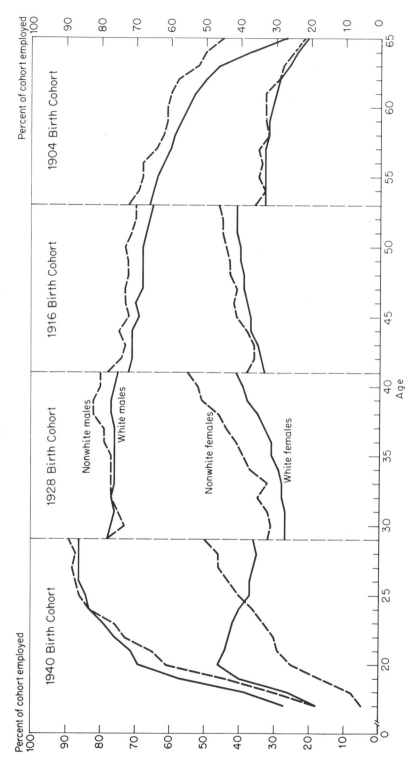

borne in mind that the observations relate to a period of one quarter, and the absence of an employer report signifies that an individual was not employed in social-security–covered employment at any time during the quarter. On the other hand, the presence of an employer report does not necessarily mean that the person was fully employed during the whole quarter. Even a single week of employment within the quarter would be sufficient to generate an employer record. In view of this extended period over which the employment measurement is made, the number of exits and entrants is quite high. As many as 30 percent of females under age 24 exit in a single year; the smallest percentage of exits shown for any group in Table 4, about 7 percent, relates to males in what is presumably their period of highest employment, ages 25–59. Predictably, entrants are highest in the early age groups, and lowest in the ages after 60. About 35 to 40 percent of the younger age groups, and 60 to 70 percent of the middle and older age groups, have single, unchanged employers in successive years. The older age group does not appear to have significantly lower continuity of employment than the middle group.

With respect to sex differences, females do have a higher level of entrants and exits than do males. A more detailed age grouping would, of course, reflect the initial high entry, subsequent exit during the childbearing period, and gradual reentry from age 30 onward. In the period over age 60, the work-history pattern of females is amazingly similar to that of males.

In terms of race, nonwhites also have higher entry and exit rates, and a somewhat lower percentage with single employers, but these racial differences also fade out in the most advanced age group.

The work-history data thus suggest substantial churning of individuals in and out of employment, and the LEED data undoubtedly understate the actual amount of this churning, since lapses of employment which are less than one quarter are not captured. These changes in employment have implications for the change in total earnings. The employer is relieved of paying anything to those who leave his employment. On the other hand, he becomes now responsible for paying those who enter employment. In a static system, one would expect that the salaries of those who were retiring would be larger than those of new entrants, so that, on balance, employers would make a saving, which would be distributed among the employed workers as seniority increases. In this manner, everyone could receive an increase in pay without any increase in total earnings. In an expanding system, however, the larger size of new cohorts will mean that employment will be expanding, so that the payment to those entering may be larger than the saving on those retiring. In periods of increasing unemployment, on the other hand, one would expect that exits due to layoffs and reduced hirings would result in some

TABLE 4 **Work History of Employed Workers 1957–58 and 1968–69 (Percent)**

	Total Initial Year	Exits	Entrants	Unchanged Single Employers	Changed and Multiple Employers
1957–58:					
Under 25					
White male	100	17	26	44	40
White female	100	30	38	41	29
Nonwhite male	100	22	29	40	38
Nonwhite female	100	37	52	38	24
25–59					
White male	100	9	7	66	25
White female	100	17	18	64	19
Nonwhite male	100	11	11	55	43
Nonwhite female	100	21	20	59	20
60 and over					
White male	100	21	8	66	13
White female	100	21	12	67	12
Nonwhite male	100	20	7	63	17
Nonwhite female	100	20	12	61	17
1968–69:					
Under 25					
White male	100	12	32	36	51
White female	100	25	45	37	38
Nonwhite male	100	16	39	32	52
Nonwhite female	100	28	41	36	36
25–59					
White male	100	7	6	73	20
White female	100	14	16	64	22
Nonwhite male	100	10	10	52	38
Nonwhite female	100	15	18	56	29
60 and over					
White male	100	18	7	66	16
White female	100	19	8	69	12
Nonwhite male	100	11	7	58	30
Nonwhite female	100	21	11	59	20

SOURCE: Based on detailed tabulations of Appendix Tables A-1 and A-2.

net saving to the employer. The extent and magnitude of these changes in earnings are reflected in Table 5. In three years, 1957, 1960, and 1962, the reduction through exits did in fact exceed the increase through new entrants; this effect was primarily the result of recession and increasing unemployment. In two additional years, 1958 and 1963, there was an exact balance. In the remaining years, entrants' earnings exceeded exits' earnings, for some years by a substantial amount.

Payments to persons employed by unchanged single employers also contribute to the change in total earnings. It is illuminating to divide these people into two groups: those whose earnings decreased from one year to the next, and those whose earnings increased. Decreases in earnings come about mainly by reduction in overtime or shifting to part time. As Table 5 shows, decreases in earnings are not insignificant. From 1957 to 1958, the magnitude of decreases in earnings was almost equal to that of increases in earnings, and even in the most expansionary year, decreases were over one-third the size of increases. What this suggests is that the earnings of a substantial body of individuals are actually reduced even in periods of expansion. The net change in the earnings of people with changed or multiple employers also shows the same sort of pattern.

The process by which the total earnings in one year change to a new level of total earnings in the following year thus includes a variety of factors. The change from 1957 to 1958, for example, appears to be quite minor, from $189 billion to $190 billion, but the component elements involved in this change are quite large. Certainly the patterns of work history and the change in the structure of employment are considerably more important in determining total earnings than the average movement of the wage rate.

THE SIZE DISTRIBUTION OF EARNINGS

As a first approach to analyzing the behavior of the size distribution of earnings, it is useful to determine the effect upon that distribution over time of those individuals who leave employment (exits), and those who enter (entrants), as well as the changes in earnings of those who are continuously employed. Given the age profile of earnings, one might expect that those who exit from employment would have quite a different distribution of income from those who enter. Specifically, it would seem reasonable that those who leave employment would, on the average, have substantially higher incomes, and the variance of the size distribution of their earnings would be larger. Those who enter employment might be

TABLE 5 Year-to-Year Change in Total Earnings by Type of Change, 1957–69 (Billions of dollars)

Initial Year	1957	1958	1959	1960	1961	1962	1963	1964	1965	1966	1967	1968
Initial total earnings	189	190	203	218	222	241	252	270	285	315	347	379
Earnings of exits	−16	−14	−13	−16	−15	−16	−16	−16	−16	−19	−22	−24
Earnings of entrants	+14	+14	+15	+13	+16	+15	+16	+18	+21	+23	+24	+27
Decreases by unchanged employers	−10	−7	−7	−10	−7	−9	−8	−11	−11	−10	−12	−12
Increases by unchanged employers	+11	+16	+15	+14	+18	+16	+19	+18	+26	+27	+31	+34
Net change by changed and multiple employers	+1	+4	+5	+3	+7	+5	+7	+6	+10	+11	+11	+13
Final total earnings	190	203	218	222	241	252	270	285	315	347	379	417
Final Year	1958	1959	1960	1961	1962	1963	1964	1965	1966	1967	1968	1969

SOURCE: Based on Appendix Tables A-1 and A-2.

expected to be similar to each other, with lower earnings and smaller variance. An examination of what actually takes place, however, is presented in Table 6. The surprising finding is that, for all groups, exits and entrants have very much lower levels of income than do those who remain employed. This strongly suggests that the exits and entrants are not primarily those entering the labor force for the first time and those retiring from it permanently, but rather lower-paid individuals who come in and go out of employment on a transient basis. It is true that for white males the level of earnings for exits is generally higher than for entrants, but for white females the difference is very much smaller, and it is practically nonexistent for nonwhite males and females.

TABLE 6 Quartile Distributions of Earnings, 1957–58 and 1968–69, for Exits, Entrants, and Persons Employed Both Years, by Race and Sex

	1957–58			1968–69		
	Bottom Quartile	Median	Top Quartile	Bottom Quartile	Median	Top Quartile
White males						
Entrants	$ 700	$1,700	$3,600	$ 800	$1,900	$4,500
Exits	800	2,100	4,000	900	2,700	5,900
Employed both years	2,900	4,500	6,000	4,200	6,900	9,500
White females						
Entrants	500	1,300	2,400	700	1,800	3,400
Exits	600	1,400	2,500	700	1,900	3,700
Employed both years	1,600	2,600	3,500	2,300	3,800	5,200
Nonwhite males						
Entrants	500	1,200	2,300	700	1,700	3,500
Exits	500	1,300	2,300	600	1,700	3,600
Employed both years	1,700	2,700	4,000	2,400	4,300	6,400
Nonwhite females						
Entrants	500	1,000	1,700	700	1,700	3,200
Exits	500	1,000	1,700	600	1,400	2,800
Employed both years	1,000	1,700	2,500	1,600	3,000	4,300

SOURCE: Based on detailed tabulations of Appendix Table A-2.

Abstracting from the effect of exits and entrants, Figure 7 shows the change in the size distribution over time for employees with unchanged employers. In general, there has been some increase in inequality in the size distribution over time. Using the interquartile range as a percentage of the mean as a measure, dispersion increased from 1957 to 1968 from .69 to .77 for white males, from .73 to 76 for white females, from .85 to .93 for nonwhite males, and from .88 to .90 for nonwhite females. Such changes in inequality are not large, but they all are in the same direction. The differences among race and sex groups in inequality are also not large, with white males and females being the most equal, and nonwhite males and females the most unequal.

The age composition of the various race-sex groups obviously affects this measure of the dispersion of the size distribution of earnings. As Table 7 shows, if the quartile distributions are examined within specific

TABLE 7   Dispersion of Earnings by Age, Sex, and Race, 1968
(Persons employed in both 1968 and 1969)

	First Quartile	Median	Third Quartile	Quartile Difference as Percent of Mean
White males				
Age 60	$5,200	$7,400	$10,000	65
Age 45	6,200	8,500	11,500	62
Age 30	5,300	7,300	9,300	55
All ages	4,200	6,900	9,500	77
White females				
Age 60	2,900	4,100	5,700	68
Age 45	2,300	3,400	4,700	71
Age 30	2,500	4,000	5,500	75
All ages	2,300	3,800	5,200	76
Nonwhite males				
Age 60	3,300	4,700	6,600	70
Age 45	3,700	5,400	7,600	72
Age 30	3,500	4,800	6,700	67
All ages	2,400	4,300	6,400	93
Nonwhite females				
Age 60	1,100	2,300	3,600	109
Age 45	1,800	3,000	4,400	87
Age 30	2,100	3,400	4,800	79
All ages	1,600	3,000	4,300	90

SOURCE: Based on detailed tabulations of Appendix Table A-2.

FIGURE 7 Distribution of Earnings by Quartiles, 1957–69

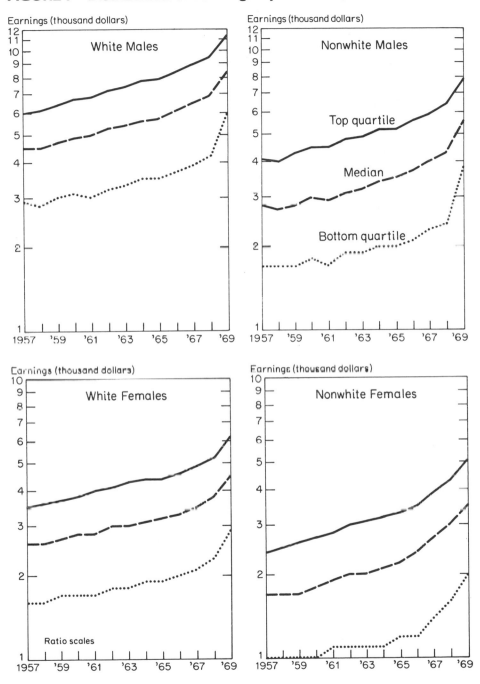

ages for the different race-sex groups, there is a significant decline in the amount of observed inequality for some groups. As might be expected, the greatest reduction in inequality appears for males, since for them the age profile rises and falls more steeply. For females, there is less reduction in inequality, and in fact, for nonwhite females of age 60 the dispersion is greater than the average for all groups combined. What Table 7 does suggest is that the differential observed in the average level of male and female earnings does not result from a highly unequal male distribution consisting of both lower-paid males and higher-paid males, contrasted with a cluster of females who tend to receive approximately the same earnings. In point of fact, female earnings by age are more unequal than male earnings. Male earnings do become more unequal with advancing age, but even at their most unequal point, they are more equal than those of females at any of the ages shown. This finding may well be attributable in part to a larger incidence of part-time work among females.

Although examination of the interquartile differences and the median levels of income does show the substantial differences in the size distribution of income for the different races and sexes, an actual comparison of the percentage of individuals in the different income size classes by race and sex provides a sharper contrast. This is done in Table 8. Twenty-four percent of white males had incomes over $10,000 in

TABLE 8 Percentage of Individuals in Earnings Size Classes

	Under $3,000	$3,000–$10,000	Over $10,000	Total
White males	20	56	24	100
White females	39	59	2	100
Nonwhite males	34	60	6	100
Nonwhite females	51	47	2	100

SOURCE: Based on Appendix Table A-3.

1968, whereas only 2 percent of white females were in this class. Nonwhite males do considerably better than white females, having 6 percent in the over $10,000 class, but the percentage of nonwhite females matched that of white females exactly at this income level. However, 51 percent of nonwhite females were found in the lowest income class, i.e., under $3,000.

The apparent stability of the size distribution of earnings hides the churning at the level of the individual wage earner, which has already been mentioned in connection with the examination of work history. This effect is summarized in Table 9 for race and sex groups for two different periods. In the recession period from 1957 to 1958, individuals who left employment, or suffered decreased or unchanged earnings, constituted approximately 50 percent of all workers, somewhat less for white males and females, and somewhat more for nonwhites. In contrast, in the period 1965–66, which was a period of upswing, between 60 and 65 percent of all individuals received increases, but even in this period the percentage with a decline or no change was appreciable, ranging from 25 to 30 percent over and above those who actually exited from employment. It should be recognized that the decreases in earnings are in most cases the result of individuals leaving employment during the course of the quarter,

TABLE 9 **Percentage Distribution of Employees by Change in Earnings, 1957–58 and 1965–66**

		Employed Both Years				
	Exits	With Decreases	No Change	With Increases	Entrants	Total
1957–58:						
White male	10	29	10	42	9	100
White female	17	21	9	36	17	100
Nonwhite male	15	30	9	34	12	100
Nonwhite female	19	19	14	29	19	100
1965–66:						
White male	7	21	6	56	10	100
White female	12	18	7	44	18	100
Nonwhite male	9	21	5	48	17	100
Nonwhite female	14	17	9	37	23	100

SOURCE: Based on Appendix Tables A-1 and A-2.

moving to a more part-time basis, or eliminating overtime. Some of the increase in earnings is due to a reversal of these factors. Whatever the cause, however, it is apparent from Table 9 that a substantial percentage of individuals is subject to earnings fluctuations due to the exits, decreases, increases, and entrances which take place.

The magnitude of the increases and decreases in earnings of individuals is, on the average, quite large. This is shown in Table 10, together with the percentage of employees in each year receiving increases and decreases.

The interesting aspect of these figures is the relative stability of both the average decrease in earnings and the average increase. While both tend to fluctuate, as would be expected, with economic conditions, the amount of fluctuation of either the average decreases or the average increases does not seem large relative to their average level, but the difference between them does fluctuate considerably. In the recession year of 1958, the average decline was 14 percent, whereas the average increase was 17 percent. In contrast, in 1967, the average decline fell to 10 percent, and the average increase rose to 20 percent. Perhaps even more important was the fact that only 52 percent of the individuals employed in both years received increases from 1957 to 1958, whereas 69 percent did so from 1966 to 1967. In other words, the net change in average earnings is the result of the level of decreases, the level of increases, and the relative number of employees receiving decreases and increases. If the analysis of wage behavior is to be meaningful, such structural characteristics as these must be explicitly built into the analysis; it cannot be based on the change in average earnings, assuming it to be representative of most employees, when in fact it is a net result of widely differing behavior. As has been pointed out, the LEED data do not permit an analysis of hours actually worked, so that it has not been possible to take this element into account

TABLE 10 Percentage of Employees with Decreases and Increases in Earnings and Percentage Change in Earnings, 1957–69

| | No Change or Decrease | | Increase | | Net Percent Change in Average Earnings |
	Percent of Employees	Percent Change in Earnings	Percent of Employees	Percent Change in Earnings	
1957–58	48	−14	52	17	1.0
1958–59	38	−14	62	19	6.6
1959–60	42	−12	58	19	5.4
1960–61	43	−14	57	18	2.9
1961–62	36	−11	64	19	6.9
1962–63	42	−12	58	17	4.1
1963–64	36	−11	64	18	6.2
1964–65	44	−11	56	18	3.8
1965–66	33	−11	67	20	7.5
1966–67	31	−10	69	20	8.0
1967–68	29	−12	71	19	8.2
1968–69	31	−12	69	20	8.4

SOURCE: Based on Appendix Table A-2.

in analyzing wage behavior. Nevertheless, it again seems apparent from the nature of the earnings distributions and their changes over time that variations in hours worked may be fully as important as the behavior of wage rates.

SUMMARY AND CONCLUSIONS

This study of the anatomy of earnings behavior has focused on four aspects: (1) age-earnings profiles and birth cohort earnings patterns; (2) sex and race differences in age profiles and earnings patterns; (3) work-history experience as related to age, sex, and race; and (4) the size distribution of earnings in terms of age, sex, and race, and its change over time.

The LEED data make it possible to trace both the shifts in age-earnings profiles over time and their relation to birth cohort patterns. For the period 1957 to 1969, each birth cohort enjoys a continual rise in average earnings over its lifetime. The shape of the age-earnings profile results from faster growth for younger generations than for older generations, each generation passing those older than itself and in turn being passed by still younger generations. In this way, the rise and fall observed in the age-earnings profile can be fully reconciled with ever-rising birth cohort earnings patterns.

The disaggregation of the age-earnings profiles and birth cohort patterns by race and sex reveals striking differences among the different groups. White males not only have substantially higher overall earnings, but their age-earnings profiles show a substantially faster rise to a peak and a greater subsequent decline to retirement age than is true for other groups. The age profile for nonwhite males is of similar shape, but it is substantially lower, and peaks earlier. White females, in contrast, have age-earnings profiles which decline slightly at the beginning of the childbearing ages, but subsequently continue to rise even during the period when the age-earnings profiles for both white and nonwhite males are declining, although white female earnings never attain even the nonwhite male level. The profile for nonwhite women does not reflect the childbearing decline observed for white females, but a decline does set in at approximately the same age as for nonwhite males. The level of the age-earnings profile for nonwhite females is lower than that of any other group.

Over time, age-earnings profiles have been shifting upward. In relative terms, the nonwhite profiles have shifted upward faster than the profiles for either white males or white females, thus narrowing the differential between the race groups. The age-earnings profile of white females, however, has shifted up more slowly than that of white males, thus causing the differential between white male earnings and white female earnings to widen.

The birth cohort earnings patterns for the different sex-race groups demonstrate that the differentials do result from differential rates of growth in earnings. After the early twenties, earnings of females grow at an appreciably lower rate than those of males. Nonwhite males grow at a slower rate than white males, but pass white females in the mid-twenties. Like the birth cohort earnings patterns for the population as a whole, the individual sex-race birth cohort patterns do not decline, except for brief periods in recessions; recessions tend to affect males and in particular nonwhite males more than females. This recession effect may well be due to greater involvement of males in direct production work, which entails layoffs in periods of declining output.

Male work history exhibits the expected pattern of a rising percentage of employment as youths enter the labor force, a period of steady high level employment, and subsequent slow decline as a result of mortality and eventual retirement. For white females, in the childbearing years the percentage employed is reduced, although even at the lowest point the percentage employed is three-fifths as high as at its earlier peak. After the childbearing years, the percentage of women employed continues to rise until the mid-fifties, a good ten years longer than for men. Nonwhite females do not follow the pattern of white females, but instead the percentage employed rises steadily up to the mid-fifties.

Behind the percentage employed figures, there are in all cohorts a rather large number of both exits and entrants. Since the LEED data are based on quarterly employer reports, an exit is an individual who is employed in the first quarter of one year but not in the first quarter of the following year. Similarly, an entrant is a person who was not employed in the first quarter of one year but who was employed in the first quarter of the subsequent year. These definitions, of course, understate the actual amount of in and out movement that goes on; it is possible to be unemployed for several months and still be considered employed in both periods if the period of unemployment does not contain a complete calendar quarter. Data on the percentage of employed individuals whose earnings increase or decrease from one year to the next provide additional evidence of the importance of such changes in employment. Not only is the percentage of individuals whose earnings decline between two periods large, but the absolute level of the average decrease and average increase in earnings between two periods is also quite large. The usually fairly small average change in earnings is the net result of much larger movements in exits and entrants from employment, and decreases and increases in earnings. Substantial fluctuations in earnings do occur even in periods when there is little apparent change in average earnings.

The size distribution of earnings moves upward in level over time, and, on the average, has become marginally more unequal. It is not true, however, that the differences in average income between males and females can be explained in terms of greater variation in male earnings. As measured by the interquartile difference in earnings in relation to the mean, the earnings of females in specific age groups vary more than those of males.

Deflation of current earnings by the Consumer Price Index does not alter the general conclusions, either for the year-to-year changes or for the whole period 1959–69. As would be expected, the deflated "real" changes in earnings are smaller than the current value changes, but since the same price deflator was used for all income levels and for all social and demographic groups, the structure of earnings behavior was unaffected by the deflation process.

The findings of this study have two important implications. First, demographic characteristics are central to an understanding of earnings differentials and the behavior of earnings over time. Second, work-history experience, its sensitivity to economic conditions, and its effect on earnings are important considerations for the analysis of policies related to income.

The importance of demographic factors for the determination of earnings has been generally recognized. A number of studies have adjusted age-sex-race groups for education, occupation, intelligence, skills, and other forms of human capital investment in an effort to explain, and in some cases to justify, the observed differentials. It may well be that cultural differences, differences in life-styles, differences in opportunities, and rational or irrational discrimination do account for the observed differences; it is not the function of this paper to discuss causality. Whatever the cause, however, it is important to recognize that some entire groups of individuals do receive less for their employment activities, and such differences are important in determining the distribution of income in our society.

The existence of substantial fluctuations in individual incomes from period to period is important because these irregularities do not necessarily reflect transitory elements. It has been popular for economists to concentrate on longer and longer time horizons, and to concern themselves with lifetime or permanent income. But for many members of the lower income classes it is not possible to shift resources easily from one time period to another. To be out of employment for a whole quarter may be quite serious for low-income individuals, and it is not possible for them to dip into savings to maintain consumption on a temporary basis. In point of fact, their major form of saving may be payments on installment debt, or in some cases on home mortgages. To the extent that such commitments are fixed in the short run, the individual may be forced, paradoxically, to curtail his current consumption in order to maintain his saving rate. The LEED data, of course, do not aggregate individuals into family units, and do not consider other sources of income such as transfer payments or income in kind. Where there are several wage earners in a family or other kinds of family income are available, the impact of the fluctuations in earnings on living standards may be less severe, but it seems reasonable that for families in the lower income groups it is quite substantial. Perhaps for lower income groups it would be more reasonable to think in terms of a current income hypothesis, which would suggest that what is received is what is spent, and that current living standards fluctuate directly with current income. In contrast, the permanent income hypothesis is a rich man's theory. Consumption can only be determined in terms of long-run income expectations and the pattern of life-cycle needs when the lack of correspondence between current income and outlay can be made up either by using existing assets or by borrowing against the expectation of future income. For the lower income groups, it is quite possible that next month's income is irrelevant, to say nothing of next year's.

NOTE: As indicated in the text, figures underlying most of the tables are to be found in the appendix, Tables A-1 through A-3. The appendix appears on microfiche and is to be found at the back of the book. Duplicate microfiche cards can be obtained from Microfiche Systems Corporation, 440 Park Avenue South, New York, N.Y. 10016.

4 | COMMENTS

Ahmad Al-Samarrie
Office of Management and Budget

Nancy and Richard Ruggles have long advocated a closer integration of microanalytic information with national income and other macrodata in order to gain more insights into the working of the economic system and to promote meaningful decision making by the major participants in the economy. Their article on the "Anatomy of Earnings" is a step in this direction.

It should be emphasized from the outset that the Ruggleses' paper is not intended to discuss causality, hence it is not based on a well-defined theoretical model. Its real contribution lies in organizing and analyzing an enormous body of detailed information on the economic and demographic characteristics of wage and salary earners and how they are related to the level and distribution of income within and among different groups over time. The underlying data base is the Social Security Administration's 1 percent LEED file. Included in this file are quarterly earnings data by age, sex, and color that cover a twelve-year period, 1957–69. The authors concentrate on the first quarter as an indication of annual earnings of covered workers. The first-quarter earnings are chosen presumably because they are not much affected by the payroll taxable limit (which has been rising over time) and because year-to-year changes in the first-quarter earnings are not biased by seasonal factors. Although the earnings generated from the LEED file are somewhat lower than those shown in the national income statistics (mainly because the LEED file does not cover most public employees or the self-employed), the two series seem to move fairly closely. Aside from coverage, the absence of information on occupation, education, marital status, or the number of hours worked by individuals is a limitation that has to be kept in mind when evaluating the results.

Four major areas are emphasized in the Ruggleses' paper: (a) the age and birth cohort earnings patterns of individuals, and their sensitivity to cylical fluctuations; (b) sex and color differences in the age and birth cohort earnings; (c) the work history of the various demographic groups, with emphasis on the entry into and exit from the labor force over their life cycle; and (d) the distribution of earnings by size, its relation to the demographic characteristics, and whether it changes significantly over time.

The authors reach many interesting conclusions, chief among which are the following:

1. Year-to-year changes in the age-earnings profile are affected by the pace of economic activity. This is reflected in the stationary or small earnings growth for all ages in the recession years of 1958 and 1961, and by the significant income gains in the second half of the 1960s, a period of rapid economic growth and rising employment. The level of economic activity seems also to have impacted the cohort earnings patterns. Workers who were born in 1911 and who entered the labor force around 1930 were found to have had much lower earnings potentials than those who were born in 1940. More significantly, recessions seem to affect the earnings of nonwhite males more adversely than those of other groups, perhaps because of their relatively heavy representation in durable manufacturing, an industry that tends to be hit by layoffs in periods of declining output.

2. Differences among the sex groups in the age-earnings profiles *narrowed* considerably over the 1957–69 period, *with nonwhite women's earnings showing the largest relative gain, followed by nonwhite males.* Incidentally, a similar conclusion was reached by Smith and Welch using the 1960

and 1970 censuses of population as a frame of reference. Ruggles and Ruggles also found that the earnings profiles of white women decline moderately in the early childbearing ages, but this phenomenon does not apply to nonwhite females, who may be forced to continue to work because of economic necessity.

3. There is substantial churning of individuals in and out of employment, and this has implications for earnings changes. Three generalizations appear relevant in this regard:

   a. A greater proportion of women than men enter and leave employment at all ages, especially the younger age groups. This, coupled with the relatively high incidence of part-time work among females, may partly explain why females' earnings by age are more unequal than male earnings. These could also be a factor in the observed differences in average income between males and females.

   b. *Nonwhites* have shown a greater tendency to change employers than white workers. This phenomenon, which holds especially true for nonwhite females, is perhaps another factor that may partly explain the reduced earnings gap between whites and nonwhites already alluded to.

   c. Year-to-year changes in total earnings are relatively small. These changes do, however, hide significantly large movements in specific components. In general, the loss in earnings which occurs when workers leave employment is largely offset by gain in earnings of entrants. Moreover, any decline in wages due to reduced overtime or a shift to part-time work tends to offset some of the gain in earnings that comes about through higher wage rates, longer weekly hours, and so forth. It is these net versus gross changes in earnings revealed by the microdata which give the paper under consideration special significance.

4. The authors found interesting things to say about the size distribution of earnings. There was, for example, a temporal increase in the inequality of the size distribution of earnings of various demographic groups with unchanged employers. Moreover, while the proportions of individuals who experience decreases and increases in their earnings change significantly from year to year, the average increase or decrease is relatively stable (Tables 9 and 10).

I only have a few comments, which I hope are relevant.

First, the *relative* size of the cohorts is not given explicit treatment by the Ruggleses. Other things remaining unchanged, if in one period there is a much greater influx of workers into the labor force than in another period (because of differences in birthrates), one would expect the earnings of the first group to grow much more slowly than those of the second group, at least during the first ten years of their working lives.

Second, one aspect of Figure 2 of the Ruggleses' paper is somewhat puzzling. Why should the 1911 cohort have a lower earnings potential than, say, the 1913 cohort, especially since members of the latter cohort entered the labor force at the trough of the depression of the 1930s? Does the relative size of the 1911 cohort explain its peculiar earnings pattern, reflecting perhaps a relatively large inflow of immigrants that year?

Third, the limit on the social security tax base, rising discontinuously from $4,200 in 1957 to $7,800 in 1969, puts an upper limit on the size of earnings included in the estimates of the first-quarter earnings at four times the tax base. This limitation introduced some small downward bias in the estimates of average annual earnings, but the bias is presumably concentrated in the white male group, ages 40 to 60. In the years during which the tax base was increased (by $600 in 1959, $1,800 in 1966, and $1,200 in 1968), some part of the reported increase in earnings for this group is a function only of the change in the tax base.

Fourth, Ruggles and Ruggles say little regarding the impact of earnings patterns of exit from or entry into *covered* employment. This aspect appears important for movements of military people (most of whom are young and black), especially during the Korean and Vietnam wars.

In conclusion, I would hope that efforts will be made to link the LEED file data with other socioeconomic data series available from the current population surveys, the 1970 census of population, and so on. These steps are necessary if we are to go into model building and policy simulation that link macro and micro aspects of the national economy.

Nancy Smith Barrett
The American University

In their discussion of sex differentials in age-earnings profiles, Ruggles and Ruggles observe that one reason for the flattening of the female earnings profile relative to males at age 24 is that the proportional withdrawal of women during the childbearing ages is greater for women with higher incomes than for women with lower incomes.

Another, and perhaps more important, reason why female age-earnings profiles are relatively flat is that women are not promoted into higher-paying jobs as they obtain seniority. Women are viewed as having a weaker labor force attachment than men and are usually not given the opportunity to acquire the type of on-the-job training requisite to rising along a career ladder.

Although labor force participation rates are higher for low-income women during the childbearing years, labor force *attachment* is stronger for higher-paid women. That is, such women interrupt their employment less frequently and for shorter periods of time. This can be seen from Table 2 of the Ruggles and Ruggles paper. The proportion of 24-year-old women entering and leaving the labor force in 1963 was much higher for the lower-income groups than for the higher-income groups.

Yet, despite the fact that the higher-income females drop out less frequently than others, their earnings profiles do not show any greater tendency to rise with age. A woman is perceived to have a weak labor force commitment whether or not she ever drops out. Even if she never marries, her earnings profile will be flatter than a comparably qualified male, because by the time her labor force commitment has been established (by her failure to marry), it is too late for her to acquire the necessary training for a position with a career ladder.

The segregation of women into sex-stereotyped occupations is one way of preventing women from improving their earnings as they age. However, even in male-dominated occupations, women hold a disproportionately small share of top-level positions. Clearly, the process is self-reinforcing. Women drop out because they hold boring and unchallenging jobs and see that they have nothing to gain from continuity in employment. Although the cultural values supportive of twenty-four-hour maternal care of preschool children are undoubtedly at work, the inverse relation between labor force attachment and earnings suggests that the nature of the employment experience is at fault as well. This behavior reinforces the employer's belief that women do not have a strong commitment to the job and, hence, the employer does not feel it is worthwhile to provide them with the on-the-job training requisite to career development.

The point to be made is that it is labor force attachment, not the participation rate of a cohort, that is most likely to affect its age-earnings profile. The fact that labor force attachment is stronger for higher-income women should produce a stronger upward pressure on overall age-earnings profiles in later years than if the reverse held true. Since this is not the case, one must conclude that traditional attitudes are more important in shaping an employer's expectations about the work commitment of female employees than differences in attitudes toward work of women themselves.

5

A. MYRICK FREEMAN III
Bowdoin College

The Incidence of the Costs of Controlling Automotive Air Pollution

I. INTRODUCTION

The automobile is a major source of air pollution in the United States. It is responsible for approximately two-thirds of all man-made emissions of carbon monoxide, and approximately half of the emissions of nitrogen oxides and hydrocarbons. In the Clean Air Act of 1970, Congress undertook a major revamping of federal policy toward air pollution control. Although there were major changes in the policy aimed at controlling emissions from stationary sources, these changes were over-shadowed by the new strategy regarding the automobile and its contribution to air pollution. For the first time, Congress itself specified emission standards to be met by all new cars produced in the 1975 and subsequent model years.

Specifically, the Clean Air Act required that all new cars produced for the 1975 and later model years meet emission standards (maximum emissions per vehicle mile) which were no more than 10 percent of the standards in effect when the law was passed. These standards were to

NOTE: This research has been supported by the Institute of Research for Poverty, University of Wisconsin—Madison. I am grateful to Tayler Bingham, Edwin H. Clark II, Robert Haveman, and William Shipman for comments and suggestions as the work progressed. I am also indebted to Nancy Dorfman for providing me with data from her work.

apply to emissions of carbon monoxide and hydrocarbons. A similar requirement was imposed on emissions of nitrogen oxides with the standard to be met in the 1976 model year. The law permitted the administrator of the Environmental Protection Agency (EPA) to grant a one-year delay in the deadline for meeting these standards if auto manufacturers requested the delay and showed that meeting the original deadline was not technically feasible. Manufacturers have requested and received one-year extensions of the 1975 deadline for carbon monoxide and hydrocarbons emissions and the 1976 deadline for nitrogen oxides.

The costs of meeting these standards will be substantial. EPA has estimated that design and equipment changes will increase the cost of new cars by between $200 and $300 over the 1970 models (Environmental Protection Agency, 1972). In addition, emission control devices decrease the fuel efficiency of new cars, resulting in an expected increase in fuel consumption of about 15 percent in comparison with the 1970 models. EPA estimates the total cost of installing emission control devices will be about $4 billion per year by 1976. Furthermore, annual operating and maintenance costs will be higher by 1976 by about $2.5 billion per year, and this figure will rise in subsequent years as the total number of cars equipped with emission control devices rises from year to year.[1]

The federal strategy for controlling automotive air pollution, as embodied in the Clean Air Act of 1970, raises several major issues which have become the focus of sharp debate in recent months. One issue concerns the technical feasibility of meeting the standards. In requesting an extension of the deadline, the auto companies argued that standards could not be met with existing technology.

A more fundamental issue is the effectiveness of the chosen strategy. The emission standards for automobiles were meant to contribute to the attainment of ambient air quality standards throughout the country. The Clean Air Act of 1970 requires that these ambient air quality standards be attained no later than 1977. Since the emission standards apply only to new cars starting with the 1975 model year (1976 with the extension), and since new car production replaces only about 10 percent of the total stock of cars each year, only about 10 to 20 percent of the cars being driven in 1977 will be meeting the emission control standards. For a number of cities, it appears that this reduction in emissions will not be sufficient to attain the ambient air quality standards (New York *Times*, 1973). These cities must find some supplementary means of reducing total automotive emissions if the ambient air quality standards are to be met by the deadline. In fact, some cities are faced with the problem that even after all the cars being driven in those urban areas are complying with the new emission standards, total emissions will still be too high, and ambient air quality standards will not be met.

As these problems become more visible, attention is being turned to alternative strategies toward the automobile, either as a replacement for, or as a supplement to, the emission standards approach. These alternatives would attempt to deal with one or more of the following problems:

1. The congressionally mandated emission standards control emissions per mile driven, but do not control or influence the number of miles driven.

2. The emission standards apply only to newly manufactured cars, so that the impact of the standards on total emissions depends on the rate at which present high-pollution vehicles are retired from the fleet and replaced by new low-pollution vehicles. Policy alternatives would consider controlling emissions from the existing fleet as well as from new cars.

3. Since many parts of the country do not presently have significant automotive air pollution problems, the present emission standards impose costs on car buyers in some areas for which there is little or no compensating benefit through reduction in air pollution damages. This is not only in some sense inequitable, but may represent a substantial resource misallocation.

In addition to the questions of technical feasibility and the effectiveness of the present strategy and possible alternatives, another issue being discussed is that of the income distribution effects, or incidence, of the costs of controlling automotive pollution. As society undertakes a significant reallocation of resources, such as represented by the move toward a cleaner environment, we should be concerned not only with the magnitude of costs and benefits, but also with questions involving who gains and who loses.

On the benefit side, there have been some preliminary attempts to determine the incidence of the damages due to air pollution. These studies suggest that lower-income families experience higher pollution levels and, therefore, are likely to benefit relatively more from pollution reduction (Freeman 1972; Zupan 1973).[2] However, these studies have been limited by the difficulty in placing dollar values on damages due to pollution or on benefits of pollution control.

Turning to the incidence of the costs of pollution control, economic theory, a priori reasoning, and some bits of evidence suggest that the costs of pollution control will be distributed in a regressive manner, i.e., that the cost per family will be a higher percentage of income for lower-income families (Freeman 1972). There are some data available to support this hypothesis. In a major study of the costs of air pollution control, EPA estimated the costs of meeting the present pollution control standards for the major classes of stationary sources of air pollution (Environmental Protection Agency 1972). These estimates of pollution control costs were then used to project likely price increases by industrial categories. An input-output model was used to trace through these price increases to twelve categories of personal consumption expenditures. Finally, for each personal consumption expenditure category, the relationship between family income and expenditure was determined from the 1961 Bureau of Labor Statistics, *Survey of Consumer Expenditures*. EPA concluded, "Since the percentage of income spent on food, tobacco, personal care, housing, household operation, and medical care generally declines with increases in family income, price increases in these categories would weigh most heavily on families in the lower income brackets" (Environmental Protection Agency 1972, p. 5-9). Since these are the largest categories of personal consumption expenditure, the net effect is likely to be a mildly regressive pattern of incidence.

EPA's study suggests, however, that automotive pollution control is a special case, and that these costs are distributed in a largely progressive pattern. The Agency estimated the total annual costs of achieving the automotive emission standards and allocated these costs to each income class according to the *Survey of Consumer Expenditures* data on expenditures for transportation. EPA concluded:

> Expenditures for transportation are largest for the middle income groups on a percentage basis; the lower 24 percent of families and the upper 2 percent of these groups spend about three-fifths and four-fifths respectively of the middle income group's percentage of transportation expenditures. Because transportation costs are projected to increase the most (4.3 percent) and because they are a significant share of all income groups' PCE, the differential impacts of the price increases by income groups tend to be dominated by the distribution of transportation expenditures. For this reason, the middle and upper income groups would probably be affected to a greater extent on a percentage basis than those families in the lower and the very highest income group (Environmental Protection Agency 1972, pp. 5-9, 5-10).

There are several reasons to be cautious about this conclusion, however. First, pollution control costs were allocated by income class according to estimates of total transportation expenditures by households. However, this total lumps together spending on purchases of both new and used cars, as well as operating expenses and spending on other modes of transport. The present strategy imposes costs directly only on new-car purchasers. A second reservation concerns the interrelationship between new- and used-car prices, and the possibility that the price mechanism may shift some part of the pollution control costs on to other than new-car buyers. Finally, there is the phenomenon of multi-car ownership by families and the large number of used cars owned by upper-income families. These all make it more difficult to draw inferences about the actual incidence of automotive pollution control costs from data on such a broad aggregate as transportation expenditures by income class.

More recently, Nancy Dorfman has completed a study of the distribution of the overall costs of federal air and water pollution control policies (Dorfman 1973). Considering both air and water pollution control together, and taking account of different possible assumptions about the incidence of taxes to finance the public share of costs, Dorfman found a more or less proportional incidence for 1972 but increasingly regressive patterns of incidence for 1976 and 1980. Her analysis of automotive pollution control costs was based on auto purchase and ownership data from the *Consumer Buying Indicators* (Department of Commerce). Actual costs for meeting 1972 automobile emissions standards and estimates of expected costs for 1976 and 1980 were distributed by income class on the assumption that used-car prices would adjust to changes in new-car prices so as to maintain the same relative prices and rates of price depreciation of cars of different ages. Costs per family were found to be approximately proportional to income over the lower- and middle-income range, but with the lowest income class (under $2,000 per year) bearing a much higher burden relative to income, and the cost relative to income declining for families with income over $15,000 per year. Dorfman's results are different from those reached in this study in that we find the pattern of incidence to be unambiguously regressive.

This paper has three major purposes. The first is to present an analysis of the distribution of automotive pollution control costs under the present strategy (the Clean Air Act of 1970). This estimate of incidence will be based on an explicit model of new-car and used car demand, prices, and user costs; and it will utilize data on the purchases and ownership of new and used cars according to income level. The second purpose is to consider the incidence of alternative strategies for controlling air pollution. Specifically, we shall investigate policy alternatives which will impose pollution control requirements on all owners of cars rather than only on new-car buyers. Alternative strategies will include costs which are imposed uniformly on all cars, costs which vary systematically with the age of the car, and costs which are related to car usage. The third purpose is to utilize the incidence data developed here to assess the target efficiency of proposals to mitigate the possible regressive impact of pollution control costs through subsidies.

The patterns of car ownership and purchase by income level are discussed in the next section. These data form the basis for the incidence analysis. In Section III, the concept of target efficiency is discussed. The analyses of the incidence of the present program and several alternative strategies are presented in Sections IV and V.

II. CAR OWNERSHIP AND PURCHASES BY INCOME

The conventional wisdom is that the rich own mostly new cars and purchase new cars while the poor buy used cars and own mostly older cars. While this picture of car ownership and purchase patterns by income is basically correct, it is an oversimplification which obscures more complex patterns of multiple car ownership and substantial purchases of used cars and ownership of older cars by upper-income multi-car families.

The Current Population Survey has gathered quarterly data on purchases of new and used automobiles by income class and ownership of automobiles broken down by model year of car and numbers of cars per family by income class as of July of each year. The Current Population Survey data are enumerated by household. The income concept is family income defined to include: money wages and salaries, net income from business or farm, dividends and interest, rent, and any other money income received by members of the household, before deductions for taxes, social security, and so forth.

It should be noted that the income measure used is a form of current income. Ideally, one would rather work with some measure of permanent income. For example, the real significance of an increase in the price of new cars for new car buyers with less than $3,000 per year current income will be less if a substantial portion of those buyers had permanent incomes which were well above $3,000 per year. In fact, it seems plausible that a significant number of car buyers, especially new-car buyers, in the lowest income class would be classified as "temporary poor" if their permanent incomes were known.

TABLE 1   Household Car Ownership by Number of Cars Owned, July 1971

| | | ———————Percent Owning——————— | | | |
Income Class	Number of Households (000)	One or More Cars	One Car	Two Cars	Three or More Cars
Under $3,000	10,700	43.6	38.0	5.1	0.5
$ 3,000–4,999	9,600	70.2	58.9	10.8	0.5
5,000–7,499	11,500	85.2	62.8	20.3	2.1
7,500–9,999	9,300	91.3	58.4	28.1	4.8
10,000–14,999	12,800	94.9	48.6	38.7	7.6
15,000 and over	8,700	96.6	33.9	47.9	14.8

SOURCE: U.S. Department of Commerce, Bureau of the Census, *Consumer Buying Indicators*, P-65, No. 40, May 1972.

With this in mind, let us first consider ownership by income class. Table 1 shows the percentage of households involved in car ownership, as well as a breakdown of the number of cars owned by each household. Over 90 percent of households with income over $7,500 own cars, and even in the $3,000 to $5,000 income class, 70 percent of households own at least one car. Multiple car ownership is a major characteristic of middle- and upper-income households. In fact, a majority of households with incomes over $10,000 own two or more cars.

Table 2 contains data on ownership of cars by households by model year or age of car. Since the survey was taken in July of 1971, the 1971 model cars are "new." As the last column of the table shows, the median age of cars declines with increasing family income. However, there are still substantial numbers of older cars owned by upper-income households.

In Table 3 this becomes more apparent. The table shows how cars of each vintage are distributed across income levels. The percentage of each age group owned by the lowest income class increases with age of car; but the percentage decreases with age for the highest income class. Nevertheless, while households with incomes over $10,000 represent only about 33 percent of all households, they own over 36 percent of all five-year-old and older automobiles.

Table 4 shows ownership patterns from a different perspective. For each income class, the table shows the percentage of households in that income class owning a car of a given vintage. For the $5,000 per year and over income classes, the rows sum to more than 100 percent because of multiple car ownership. The table confirms the fact that the rich own new cars and the poor own old cars. For example, barely 5 percent of households with under $5,000 a year income own a 1970 or 1971 model car, while close to 45 percent of $15,000 and over households are in this category. But, again, what is of interest is the lower right-hand corner of the table, and the substantial ownership of older cars by upper-income households. While only about 45 percent of the under $5,000 per year households own a car aged five years or older, over 60 percent of the households in the over $5,000 a year category own cars of this older vintage. With the exception of the highest income and oldest age category, not only do upper-income families own more new cars per family, but they own more old cars per family as well.

Data on car purchases by income level are consistent with the observed patterns of ownership. Table 5 shows household car purchases by income level for 1971. As expected, the percentage of households which purchased a new car in 1971 rises with income. But the percentage of households which purchased a used car also rises with income up to the $10,000 a year level.

TABLE 2 Household Car Ownership by Model Year, July 1971 (Thousands)

Income Class	Number of Households	Total Cars Owned	Cars per Household	Model Year						Median Age of Car
				1971	1970	1969	1968	1967	1966 and Earlier	
Under $5,000	20,300	13,200	.65	400	700	900	1,000	1,100	9,100	»4
$ 5,000–9,999	20,800	24,600	1.18	1,400	2,400	2,600	2,800	2,300	13,100	>4
10,000–14,999	12,800	19,000	1.48	1,500	2,400	2,500	2,300	2,000	8,300	14
15,000 and over	8,700	15,200	1.75	1,600	2,200	2,500	2,100	1,600	5,200	3
Not reported	2,200	2,300	1.05	200	200	300	200	200	1,200	>4
All households	64,800	74,300	1.15	5,100	7,900	8,600	8,400	7,300	37,000	4

SOURCE: U.S. Department of Commerce, Bureau of the Census, *Consumer Buying Indicators*, P-65, No. 40, May 1972.

TABLE 3 **Household Ownership of Cars by Model Year and Income Class, July 1971**

Age (years)	Model Year	Percentage of Cars of Given Age Owned by Income Class				
		Under $5,000	$5,000– 9,999	$10,000– 14,999	$15,000 and Over	Income Not Reported
0	1971	7.8	27.5	29.4	31.4	3.9
1	1970	8.9	30.4	30.4	27.8	2.5
2	1969	10.5	30.2	29.1	29.1	3.5
3	1968	11.9	33.3	27.4	25.0	2.4
4	1967	15.1	31.5	27.4	21.9	2.7
5 or older	1966 or before	24.6	35.4	22.4	14.1	3.2
	Percentage of Households in Income Class					
		31.3	32.9	19.8	13.4	3.4

SOURCE: U.S. Department of Commerce, Bureau of the Census, *Consumer Buying Indicators*, P-65, No. 40, May 1972.

TABLE 4 **Household Ownership of Cars by Model Year and Income Class, July 1971**

Household Income Level	Percent of Households Owning Car of Model Year					
	1971	1970	1969	1968	1967	1966 or Before
Under $5,000	2.0	3.4	4.4	4.9	5.4	44.8
$ 5,000–9,999	6.7	11.5	12.5	13.5	11.1	63.0
10,000–14,999	11.7	18.8	19.5	18.0	15.6	64.8
15,000 and over	18.4	25.3	28.7	24.1	18.4	59.8
Not reported	9.1	9.1	13.6	9.1	9.1	54.5
All households	7.9	12.2	13.3	13.0	11.3	57.1

SOURCE: U.S. Department of Commerce, Bureau of the Census, *Consumer Buying Indicators*, P-65, No. 40, May 1972.

TABLE 5 Household Car Purchases by Income Level, 1971 (Percent)

Income Class	Households Purchasing a Car	Households Purchasing a New Car	Households Purchasing a Used Car	Buyers Who Choose a New Car
Under $3,000	15.0	2.3	12.7	15.3
$ 3,000–4,999	24.5	5.6	18.9	22.9
5,000–7,499	34.5	10.3	24.2	29.9
7,500–9,999	38.5	11.4	27.1	29.8
10,000 and over	48.0	22.4	25.6	46.7
All households	34.9	12.6	22.3	36.1

SOURCE: U.S. Department of Commerce, Bureau of the Census, *Consumer Buying Indicators*, P-65, No. 43, December 1972.

III. TARGET EFFICIENCY

One reason for examining the incidence of automotive pollution control costs is that we (society) may decide that the pattern of incidence is inequitable; and we may wish to alter the pattern of incidence through some kind of subsidy scheme. Another reason for interest is that as the costs of meeting the 1976 automotive standards become more visible to consumers, and as costs of transportation controls and other policies necessary to meet ambient air quality standards in some areas become known, there may be considerable political reaction against the air pollution controls. It has been suggested that this kind of political backlash might be blunted by an appropriate program of subsidy. For example, A. Alan Post, the legislative analyst for the State of California, has said:

> Thus, if a disincentive or a direct regulatory action is to make the cost of essential transportation for low income workers and students prohibitively expensive, we will be confronted with the need to provide some form of exemption or subsidy for these people. Our experience to date has shown that disincentives or controls that make the cost of essential mobility prohibitive for any significant number of people are not politically acceptable (Post 1973, p. 9).

Also, the Environmental Quality Laboratory at the California Institute of Technology, in outlining their proposed strategies for meeting the air quality standards in the Los Angeles basin, included the following among their recommendations: "Mandatory installation of an evaporative control device on gasoline-powered 1966–69 vehicles . . . . Since this device is estimated to cost approximately $150 to purchase and install, some subsidy or cost sharing would be required" (Lees 1972, p. 23).

Subsidies of this sort are among several possible strategies for changing the distribution of income. Subsidies will have effects on resource allocation and economic efficiency which must be weighed when considering their use. However, our concern here is only with their evaluation in the context of redistributive or equity criteria. A number of criteria for judging income redistribution policies have been proposed and discussed in the literature. One such criterion has been proposed by Weisbrod—the target efficiency of the redistributive process (Weisbrod 1969).

Target efficiency refers to the extent to which the actual distribution of the benefits of some redistributive program coincides with the desired distribution of benefits. Where some target population has been identified as the desired beneficiary, one measure of target efficiency is the percentage of total program benefits which are delivered to the target population. This measure is termed "vertical efficiency."

"Horizontal efficiency" can be measured in two ways. The first is the percentage of members of the target group which actually receive benefits. Alternatively, where the redistributive program has the aim of meeting some target level of need (e.g., minimum income, full subsidy of specified costs), a second measure of horizontal efficiency is the dollar value of benefits received by the target group as a percentage of the total benefit *needs* of that target group.

Any subsidy of automotive pollution control costs for all households will have a lower vertical efficiency, the greater the percentage of the overall burden of pollution control costs actually borne by upper-income groups. A subsidy of pollution control costs for all households will have a virtually 100 percent horizontal efficiency in terms of coverage if the target class is defined as car-owning (or car-purchasing) households with income below some minimum. However, if the target group is defined to include all households with less than the minimum income, i.e., if the pollution control subsidy program is seen as part of a larger general income redistribution plan, the subsidy will have a relatively lower horizontal efficiency, since it will not provide benefits to non-car-owning households.

Because of our interest in equity considerations, and because of the possibility that subsidy proposals will be seriously discussed, we shall test the horizontal and vertical efficiencies of strategies to subsidize pollution control costs for automobiles. It will be assumed, for illustrative purposes, that the target group of desired beneficiaries consists of households with less than $5,000 income per year. This definition of the target group is dictated, in part, by the available data.

IV. MEETING THE 1976 NEW CAR STANDARDS

In this section, a user-cost model of the demand for cars is developed and used to analyze the relationships among prices and user costs for new and used cars. The model shows that when the price of new cars is increased; for example, because pollution control equipment is installed on new cars; there is an induced increase in both the prices and the user costs of used cars. The model is used to determine the magnitude and the incidence of these changes: (a) during the first year, when only new cars have pollution control equipment; and (b) at the end of the transition period, when the uncontrolled stock of cars has been fully replaced by cars meeting the 1976 standards. After this transition, the user costs of cars of all ages fully reflect the real resource cost of pollution control; and the incidence of these costs can be found by relating user cost as a function of age of car to the income of the owners. However, the model shows that during the transition period, changes in the prices of used cars without pollution control produce both capital gains and higher user costs to owners. The pattern of these pecuniary effects is also important for a full understanding of the impact on the distribution of income of introducing a pollution control program for new cars.

The empirical analysis uses 1971 as a base year. Car purchase and car ownership data for 1971 are combined with the projected incremental cost of moving from 1971 emission levels to the 1976 standards. The period of transition between 1971 and 1976 is ignored. In other words, the analysis is based on the assumption that new cars meeting the 1976 standards were available beginning with the 1972 model year.

This study, like many analyses of incidence or burden, does not attempt to take into account the effects of price changes on demand, or other second-order effects. Although changes in the relative prices of new and used cars are explicitly incorporated in the model, the empirical analysis assumes that consumers do not respond to these price changes by altering purchase patterns of new and used cars.[3]

A. The Costs of Control

There is considerable controversy over what will be the true costs of equipping 1976 model cars with the appropriate equipment to meet the emission standards. Auto manufacturers and oil companies in advertisements and public statements have cited figures far higher than those mentioned by independent sources and used by government officials in their analysis of the problem. Fortunately, since the concern of this study is with the relative burden of control costs among income classes, the accuracy of estimates of control costs per car is of only secondary importance. The estimates of control costs used here were published by EPA (Environmental Protection Agency 1972).

The 1971 model cars already must meet certain emission control standards. EPA estimates that the cost of meeting these standards amounts to $32.50 per car. EPA has identified three technological alternatives for achieving the 1976 emission control standards. The additional costs per car for manufacturing and installing additional devices and making certain design changes to reduce emissions below the 1971 level are estimated to range between $196.50 and $318.50. The auto manufacturers have committed themselves to the most costly of these alternatives. Therefore, it is assumed here that the manufacturing costs are increased by $320, and that this cost is fully passed on to consumers in the price of new cars.

EPA also estimates that emission control devices will reduce fuel efficiency, leading to increased operating costs. In addition there will be incremental maintenance costs associated with these devices. Increased fuel consumption costs are estimated at $24.70 per year, and maintenance costs are estimated to increase by $11.40—all at 1970 prices. The total increase in operating and maintenance costs is $36.10 per year.[4]

B. A Naive Model of Incidence

Before turning to the more sophisticated user-cost model, this section presents estimates of incidence based on the assumption that pollution control costs affect only new-car purchase prices, and the price increases are borne fully by the purchasers of new cars.

Two modifications of the data presented in earlier sections are utilized here. First, to take into account the increased operating and maintenance costs, this cost stream is discounted over a five-year period at 10 percent, and the present value is added to the equipment costs of pollution control. Hence it is assumed that the total impact of pollution control on new car purchasers is equal to $320 plus $135, or $455 per car. Second, since there is considerable variation in car-purchase behavior from year to year, both in aggregate and with respect to income levels, the three-year period 1970–72 was used to determine the average number of purchases per year per income level for both new and used cars.

Table 6 shows number of households, income per household, and percent purchasing new cars for each income class. The next column shows the costs per buyer ($455) as a percentage of family income for each income class. The impact of the pollution control costs is sharply regressive, with the implicit tax rate falling from 26.5 percent at the lowest income level to only 2.5 percent at the highest income level.

TABLE 6 The Incidence of the 1976 Standards, the Naive Model

Income Class	Number of Households (thousands)	Income per Household (dollars)	Percent Purchasing a New Car[a]	Cost per Buyer as a Percent of Family Income	Cost per Household as a Percent of Family Income
Under $3,000	10,800	1,714	2.6	26.5	.69
$ 3,000–4,999	9,425	3,964	5.3	11.5	.61
5,000–7,499	11,475	6,215	10.0	7.3	.73
7,500–9,999	9,475	8,696	12.4	5.2	.65
10,000 and over	21,600	18,444	21.3	2.5	.53

SOURCE: Calculated from U.S. Department of Commerce, Bureau of the Census, *Consumer Buying Indicators*, P-65 Series.
[a]Average for three years: 1970–72.

The final column shows average cost per household as a percentage of family income. In this case, the total costs incurred by members of an income class are averaged over all members of that class whether or not they purchased a car. This measure is not as useful for welfare purposes because it obscures the differences between the impact on those who purchase cars and those who do not. However, this is a widely used measure of incidence in other situations. Moreover, it will be useful in making comparisons with the incidence as determined by the user-cost approach taken below. The incidence per household is mildly regressive overall, but it shows some degree of progressivity in the lower- to middle-income range. In this respect, the results are similar to those of EPA cited in the introduction.

Suppose that some fraction of the purchase price were subsidized by the government. How efficient would this subsidy be in delivering benefits to the assumed target group of under $5,000 per year households? Approximately 10 percent of the total cost of pollution control devices on new cars would be borne by the target group. Hence the vertical efficiency of a subsidy of the purchase price would be only 10 percent, i.e., 10 percent of the total cost of the subsidy would go to the target group. If the purpose of the subsidy is to distribute benefits to all households of under $5,000 per year, the horizontal efficiency is also quite low. Only 3.9 percent of households in the target income class purchase new cars, thus horizontal efficiency is only 3.9 percent.

C. A User-Cost Approach

The basic postulate of the user-cost theory of the demand for capital goods is that the user's demand for a durable asset is derived from the flow of services provided by the good, and that it is the price of these services or rental cost of the durable, rather than its purchase price, which governs the demand to hold that asset for a given period of time.[5] For our purposes, user cost can be defined as the cost of owning an automobile for one year and is equal to the reduction in market value of the automobile during the year plus the implicit interest cost of capital tied up in car ownership

(1) $$c_{(i,t)} = P_{(i,t)} - P_{(i+1,t+1)} + rP_{(i,t)}$$

where $c_{(i,t)}$ is the user cost of an i-year-old car in year t, P represents market price, and r is the relevant interest rate or cost of capital.

The user-cost approach is valuable for at least three reasons. First, it permits the expression of the pollution control costs in annualized terms as an increase in user cost per year rather than as an increase in purchase price as in the naive model above. Second, the user-cost approach provides a method for expressing the total stock of used cars of all ages in terms of one-year-old equivalents.[6] And third, as will be shown below, the user-cost approach permits the development of a demand model for determining relative price effects and the way in which they alter the incidence of pollution control costs.

Let us first consider the pattern of incidence in the first year of the new pollution control program, i.e., when only new cars have pollution control. The introduction of pollution control requirements which raise the purchase price of new cars will have two kinds of effects which are partly offsetting in terms of incidence. First, because used cars are close substitutes for new cars, there will be an induced increase in the price of used cars. This results in a once-and-for-all capital gain for all present owners of used cars, i.e., cars of ages $i = 1, \ldots, n$. Second, the changes in purchase prices of new and used cars will result in increases in the user costs to all present car owners and to new-car purchasers. In addition, those who purchase new cars will experience higher operating and maintenance costs for their cars. The task now is to create a model expressing these effects, and to utilize available data and reasonable assumptions to estimate their magnitude by income class.

First, a model of new- and used-car demand is required to determine the magnitude and incidence of the capital gains resulting from the increase in the price of new cars. Abstracting from the effects of income and prices of all other goods, assume that in year t the quantity demanded of new cars, $D_{(0,t)}$, depends upon the purchase price of new cars, $P_{(0,t)}$, and the purchase price of one year used-car equivalents, $P_{(1,t)}$.[7] Further assume a constant elasticity relationship

(2) $D_{(0,t)} = P_{(0,t)}^a P_{(1,t)}^b$ $a < 0; b > 0$

In the used-car market, the stock of used cars is exogenously determined by past investment decisions. The price of used cars must be such as to make individuals willing to hold the existing stock. The used-car demand function takes the form

(3) $P_{(1,t)} = S_{(t)}^d P_{(0,t)}^f$ $d < 0; f > 0$

where the purchase price and stock of used cars are expressed in terms of one-year-old equivalents. To obtain the change in used-car purchase prices resulting from any autonomous change in new-car purchase prices, differentiate equation (3) with respect to new-car prices, or

(4) $\partial P_{(1,t)} / \partial P_{(0,t)} = f \dfrac{P_{(1,t)}}{P_{(0,t)}}$

This expression will be referred to as the price shifter, or "s".

A reasonable magnitude for s can be assumed on the basis of available empirical studies. Wykoff has estimated a form of equation 3 where the independent variables were user costs for new and used cars, rather than purchase prices. Although he concluded that "used-car prices remain largely unexplained," because of low $\bar{R}^2$ and low t-statistics, the elasticities calculated from the estimated coefficients seemed reasonable. The elasticity for the user cost of new cars was estimated to be .34 (Wykoff 1973, pp. 384–385). It can be shown that under some reasonable assumptions, including those made in equation 8 below, the elasticity (f) of used-car *price* with respect to new-car *price* will be of the same magnitude. Accordingly, it is assumed here that $f = 1/3$. Dorfman has gathered data on new- and used-car prices from published sources (Dorfman 1973). Her data showed that on a weighted average basis, the prices of one-year-old cars in 1973 were approximately 74 percent of new-car purchase prices. Combining these estimates, equation 4 shows that for every $4 increase in the purchase price of new cars, the price of one-year equivalent used cars can be expected to rise by $1, i.e., $s = 1/4$.

This model of price shifting and estimated values for s can be used to determine the capital gain for each used-car owner in the following way. The capital gain to the owner of a one-year-old equivalent used car is

(5) $g_{(1,t)} = s\, \Delta P_{(0,t)}$

Furthermore, if it can be assumed that the price structure for used cars remains constant, i.e., there are no changes in the relative prices of used cars of different ages, the capital gain for a car of age i is

(6) $\qquad g_{(i,t)} = s \, \Delta P_{(0,t)}(P_{(i,t)}/P_{(1,t)})$

The same price increases that produce capital gains for used-car owners also lead to increases in user costs for both used-car owners and new-car purchasers. The increase in user cost for a purchaser of a new car with pollution control is

(7) $\qquad \Delta c_{(0,t)} = (P'_{(0,t)} - P_{(0,t)}) - (P'_{(1,t+1)} - P_{(1,t+1)})$
$\qquad\qquad + r(P'_{(0,t)} - P_{(0,t)})$

where the primes indicate purchase prices of cars with pollution control. Assume that the rate of depreciation of purchase price for cars with pollution control is the same as has been observed for cars without pollution control. Then

(8) $\qquad P'_{(1,t+1)}/P'_{(0,t)} = P_{(1,t+1)}/P_{(0,t)} = h$

and by substitution

(9) $\qquad \Delta c_{(0,t)} = (1 - h + r) \, \Delta P_{(0,t)}$

This is the increase in the user cost to a buyer of a new car.[8]

To determine the changes in user costs imposed on owners of used cars, it is necessary to determine how user costs are affected by the changes in prices of used cars in the model above. Wykoff developed models of new- and used-car demands where user-cost variables replaced the price variables in the demand equation (Wykoff 1973). He found that the user-cost model explained new-car demand as well as a model based on purchase price variables. If this is the case, the price shifting model of equations 3 and 4 can be reformulated in terms of user cost and a shifter, s', can be derived

(3a) $\qquad c_{(1,t)} = S_{(t)}^{d'} c_{(0,t)}^{f'}$

and

(4a) $\qquad s' \equiv \partial c_{(1,t)}/\partial c_{(0,t)}$
$\qquad\qquad = f' \dfrac{c_{(1,t)}}{c_{(0,t)}}$

This permits the derivation of the changes in user costs for one-year-old used cars for any given increase in the price of new cars. The change in user cost is

(10) $\Delta c_{(1,t)} = s' \Delta c_{(0,t)}$

Wykoff has also analyzed how user costs for automobiles depreciated with age during the 1960s (Wykoff 1970). He found that after the first year of car life, user costs tended to decline at a constant rate such that

(11) $c_{(i,t)}/c_{(1,t)} = e^{-d(i-1)}$

Estimates of d, the constant depreciation rate, varied from .17 to .23 for standard and smaller models and were as high as .27 for expensive domestic cars. Accordingly, changes in user costs for older used cars are given by

(12) $\Delta c_{(i,t)} = s' \Delta c_{(0,t)} e^{-d(i-1)}$

The models of price changes, capital gains distribution, and changes in user costs are now complete. With assumptions as to the magnitudes of parameters, the models can be combined with data on purchase and ownership of cars to estimate the distribution of the cost of imposing pollution control standards during the first year.

The reasons for assuming $s = 1/4$ have been described above. The value for s' is also assumed to be 1/4.[9] On the basis of data from Dorfman (1973), the relative purchase price of one-year-old and new cars, h, is assumed to be equal to .74. The cost of capital, r, is assumed to be 10 percent. And finally, on the basis of data reported by Wykoff (1970), the rate of depreciation of user costs, d, is assumed to be equal to .2.

Assuming that pollution control requirements raised the price of new cars in 1972 by $320, the capital gains and user cost changes for owners of the existing stock of cars will be distributed among households as shown in Table 7. The holders of the existing stock of cars are made better off by the pollution control requirements, since the induced capital gain is roughly two and one-half times larger than the increase in user costs.[10] Although the net gain rises with income, the gain as a percentage of family income is highest for the lowest income class. The net gains are distributed in a progressive, or propoor, manner.[11]

It must be emphasized that the net gain shown in Table 7 is the result of a once-and-for-all capital gain experienced by used-car owners in the first year following the imposition of pollution controls on new cars. While user costs to used-car owners will continue to rise, there will be no further offsetting capital gains in subsequent years. Furthermore, the gain can only be realized by selling the car—either to purchase an older model or to forgo ownership altogether. If an individual retains his present car to the end of its useful life, the gain is just offset by an equal annual

TABLE 7 Incidence of the Capital Gains and User-Cost Changes for Used-Car Owners: the First Year

Income Class	Income per Household (dollars)	Capital Gain per Household (dollars)	Change in User Cost per Household (dollars)	Capital Gain as Percent of Family Income (percent)	Change in User Cost as Percent of Family Income (percent)	Net Change as Percent of Family Income (percent)
Under $5,000	2,674	+16.87	6.57	+.63	-.25	+.38
$ 5,000-9,999	7,473	+38.14	14.62	+.51	-.20	+.31
10,000-14,999	12,151	+53.91	20.52	+.44	-.17	+.27
15,000 and over	25,404	+70.71	26.75	-.28	-.11	+.17

SOURCE: Calculated from U.S. Department of Commerce, Bureau of the Census, *Consumer Buying Indicators*, P-65 Series.

equivalent flow of higher user costs. And if an individual trades in each year so as to maintain ownership at the same age level, the higher resale value of the original car is offset by a higher purchase price for the replacement.

The welfare significance of the capital gains should not be overemphasized. In terms of conventional indifference curve analysis, households experience both an increase in money income and an increase in the money price of one good such that the new budget line intersects the old one. Households could be better off, worse off, or indifferent depending on initial endowments and preferences.

In addition to the capital gains and changes in user costs of used cars, those who choose to purchase new cars will bear a burden in the form of higher user costs. Equation 9 was used to translate the change in purchase price into a change in user costs for new-car buyers. This increase in user costs was allocated by income class in accordance with the new-car purchase data summarized in Table 5. The increase in operating and maintenance costs of $36 per year was added to the increase in user charges calculated by equation 9. See Table 8. The pattern of incidence is

TABLE 8 The Incidence of User Costs for Buyers of New Cars

Income Class	Cost per Household[a] (dollars)	Cost per Household as a Percent of Family Income[a]
Under $3,000	3.90	.23
$ 3,000–4,999	7.95	.20
5,000–7,499	15.00	.24
7,500–9,999	18.60	.21
10,000 and over	31.95	.17

SOURCE: Calculated from U.S. Department of Commerce, Bureau of the Census, *Consumer Buying Indicators*, P-65 Series.
[a]Includes increased operating and maintenance costs of $36 per year per new car.

very similar to that of the naive purchase price model in Table 6. The incidence is approximately proportional up to the $10,000 income level. This is because although the burden per buyer is regressive, the proportion of households buying new cars declines as income falls.

Although the purchase data and car ownership data are tabulated on the basis of different income classifications, it is possible to merge the gain and cost data to get at least a rough idea of the overall incidence of the combined first-year gains to used-car owners and costs to new-car buyers. Because the stock of cars in existence at any point in time is far larger than the new-car purchases in a given year, the gains calculated in Table 7 outweigh the costs shown in Table 8. The net gains distributed by three broad income categories are as follows:

Income Class	As a Percentage of Family Income		
	Gain	Loss	Net
Under $5,000	+.38	−.21	+.17
$ 5,000–9,999	+.31	−.22	+.09
10,000 and over	+.22	−.17	+.05

The overall incidence is dominated by the gains to used-car owners. This offsets the proportional or slightly regressive distribution of user costs to new-car buyers; and the net result is a propoor distribution of gains. Both the gains and costs are lowest for the high-income group, but since the purchase of new cars is more skewed by income level than is the ownership of cars, the highest income group bears a relatively larger share of the costs than it receives of the gains.

We now turn to the structure of user costs in the new equilibrium, when the stock of cars has been replaced by newer vintage cars with pollution control. It is assumed that throughout the period of transition there were no further changes in pollution control requirements or costs. Thus the user cost of new cars is the same as that given by equation 9. Further, it is assumed that the structure of user costs by age is the same as that which prevailed before the introduction of pollution control, and which was investigated by Wykoff (1970). Wykoff found that the depreciation rate in the first year was substantially higher than in subsequent years. He found a two-step depreciation schedule which is described as follows

(13) $$c_{(1,t)}/c_{(0,t)} = e^{-d}$$

where $d \approx .35$, and

(14) $$c_{(i,t)}/c_{(1,t)} = e^{-d(i-1)}$$

where $i \geq 1$, $d \approx 2$.

Equations 13 and 14 were used to allocate user costs by income level on the assumption that the structure of ownership by age of car and income level was the same as that actually prevailing in 1971 and shown in Table 2. This allocation of costs is shown in Table 9.

There are several things to note about this distribution. First, the costs per household are substantially higher than those shown in Tables 6 through 8. In part, this is because there are no offsetting capital gains, and in part because by now all of the cars in the used-car stock have pollution control. Hence families cannot avoid the cost of pollution control in the

TABLE 9   The Incidence of User Costs, Used-Car Owners, All Cars Controlled

Income Level	Cost per Household (dollars)	Cost per Household as a Percent of Family Income
Under $5,000	43.17	1.61
$ 5,000–9,999	85.41	1.14
10,000–14,999	112.81	.93
15,000 and over	139.54	.55

SOURCE: Calculated from U.S. Department of Commerce, Bureau of the Census, *Consumer Buying Indicators*, P-65 Series.

long run by owning or purchasing a used car. Second, the incidence pattern is unambiguously regressive. The implicit tax rate on the under $5,000 per year income group is almost three times the tax rate on the $15,000 and over group.[12] In other words, when account is taken of the fact that ultimately all car-owning households will bear part of the costs of pollution control, the incidence pattern becomes much more regressive than when one investigates only the incidence of new-car purchase costs.

Again, the new-car purchase data can be merged with the user-cost data to obtain a rough picture of the incidence in the new equilibrium. See Table 10. Again, the overall pattern is regressive. However, the merging of the $15,000 and over income class with the $10,000–$15,000 class obscures the low implicit tax rate on the highest-income families.

TABLE 10   Overall Incidence, New and Used-Car Owners, All Cars Controlled

Income Class	Cost per Household (dollars)	Cost per Household as a Percent of Family Income
Under $5,000	48.94	1.83
$ 5,000–9,999	102.16	1.37
10,000 and over	155.73	.89

SOURCE: Calculated from U.S. Department of Commerce, Bureau of the Census, *Consumer Buying Indicators*, P-65 Series.

The total increase in user cost in the new equilibrium is $6,466 million per year. Of this amount, approximately $1,000 or 15 percent is borne by the under $5,000 per year income group. Hence the vertical efficiency of an across-the-board subsidization of user costs would be about 15 percent. Also, since only about 56 percent of households in the under $5,000 per year income group own cars, the horizontal efficiency of an across-the-board subsidy of user costs would be about 56 percent.

Alternatively, the subsidy could be directed at the purchase price of new cars. Since this subsidy would not cover the increased operating costs, it would have a slightly different distribution of its benefits than a full user-cost subsidy. However, the vertical efficiency of such a purchase price subsidy would not be substantially different from the 15 percent cited here.

V. THE INCIDENCE OF ALTERNATIVE CONTROL STRATEGIES

In the introduction, it was suggested that the present strategy directed at achieving pollution control standards for new cars produced after 1976 may not be the most appropriate. It will be approximately five years before normal replacement of the existing stock of cars results in the majority of cars on the road having been designed and manufactured to meet the 1976 standards. Furthermore, there are major unsolved problems concerning the durability and effectiveness of the technology which American manufacturers have apparently chosen to meet these standards. Finally, the federal standards do not take into account regional differences in the severity of the automotive air pollution problem. Some urban areas will probably have to take more severe action to control automotive emissions in order to meet the established ambient air quality standards (*New York Times* 1973; Lees 1972).

These factors have led some students of the problem to consider alternative control strategies which would be directed at controlling the emissions of all cars within the relevant jurisdiction. In this section, the incidence of the costs of three alternative strategies of this type are examined. In each case, the costs are purely hypothetical. No attempt has been made to relate costs to the achievement of actual air quality standards, nor was there any attempt made to utilize engineering data to determine a "realistic" cost. However, given the postulated hypothetical cost figures, the imputation of these costs among income groups appears valid. For other control schemes which have the same distributional impact but different total cost levels, the incidence patterns portrayed here would still be relevant, since the alternative programs would be proportional to those shown here.

Three kinds of control programs are considered:

1. Uniform control costs per car. It is assumed that every car on the road is required to install or retrofit the same emission control package, i.e., the increase in user costs is the same for all models and ages of cars.

2. Uniform emissions standards for all cars. It was assumed that all cars must meet the same emissions standards, but that the costs of meeting these standards was a rising function of age of car.

3. Costs related to use. The preceding strategies focus on emissions per mile, without attempting to control miles driven. A surcharge on gasoline purchases is one way of attempting to curtail automobile use as part of an overall air pollution control strategy.

A. Uniform Control Costs per Car

It was postulated that all cars would be required to incur the same level of control costs, and that the effect of these requirements would be to raise the user cost per car by $100 per year. The car ownership data were used to impute a control cost per owner and a control cost per household for each income level. The dollar amounts of these costs and costs as a percentage of family income are tabulated in Table 11.

TABLE 11   Incidence of Uniform Control Cost per Car

Income Class	Income per Household (dollars)	Control Cost per Owner		Control Cost per Household	
		Dollars	As a Percent of Family Income	Dollars	As a Percent of Family Income
Under $3,000	1,714	114	6.65	49.70	2.90
$ 3,000–4,999	3,964	117	2.95	82.00	2.07
5,000–7,499	6,215	129	2.08	109.70	1.77
7,500–9,999	8,696	141	1.62	129.20	1.49
10,000-14,999	12,151	157	1.29	148.79	1.22
15,000 and over	25,404	180	.71	174.10	.69

SOURCE: Calculated from U.S. Department of Commerce, Bureau of the Census, *Consumer Buying Indicators*, P-65 Series.

The pattern of incidence is highly regressive. For the under $3,000 income class, the implicit tax rate per car owner is more than nine times the corresponding tax rate on the highest income level. Even neglecting the under $3,000 per year class, which may include a high proportion of students and other voluntary temporary poor, the implicit tax rate per owner and per household is still more highly regressive than that found for the federal policy.

The vertical efficiency of an across-the-board subsidy of pollution control costs can be measured by the percentage of total control costs which is borne by the target group, i.e., the under $5,000 per year income class. Under the uniform control cost scheme, since the under $5,000 income class owns 18 percent of all cars owned by the household sector, it bears 18 percent of the total cost of the control imposed on the household sector. Hence, the vertical efficiency of an across-the-board subsidy scheme would be 18 percent. Since 56 percent of households in the under $5,000 per year income class own one or more cars, the horizontal efficiency of a subsidy scheme is 56 percent.

B. Control Costs Rise with Age of Car

For this section, it was postulated that the cost of controlling emissions for 1971 model cars resulted in an increase in user cost of $40 per car per year, and that user costs increased linearly with age to a level of $140 per year for 1966 and earlier model cars. This pattern of user cost results in a total cost of control per year approximately the same as the uniform control cost per car strategy analyzed above.

Table 12 contains control costs per household in dollar magnitude and as a percentage of family income. Again the pattern of incidence is regressive. However, this strategy does not impose absolutely larger costs on lower-income households, as one might have thought. This is because

TABLE 12   Incidence of Rising Control Costs with Age of Car

| Income Class | Control Cost per Household | |
	Dollars	As a Percent of Family Income
Under $5,000	80.59	3.01
$ 5,000–9,999	134.52	1.80
10,000–14,999	159.06	1.31
15,000 and over	175.40	.69

SOURCE: Calculated from U.S. Department of Commerce, Bureau of the Census, *Consumer Buying Indicators*, P-65 Series.

although low-income households tend to concentrate their ownership in the older age bracket, middle- and upper-income households own a larger number of the older vintage cars. The overall pattern of incidence is remarkably similar to that of the uniform control cost policy analyzed above. The implicit tax rate is slightly higher for the rising control cost strategy at the lowest income levels; but the tax rate is identical for both strategies at the highest-income class.

A subsidy plan which subsidizes the same percentage of control costs for all car owners would have a vertical efficiency of 20 percent. In other words, 20 percent of the subsidy would reach households in the $5,000 and under income class; and since 56 percent of the households in this income group own cars, the horizontal efficiency of such a subsidy program would be 56 percent.

An alternative subsidy scheme might cover only control costs for older vintage cars. For example, the subsidy might cover some fraction of the increase in user costs for 1967 and earlier vintage cars only. The vertical efficiency of that plan is somewhat higher, but is still a surprisingly low 24 percent. In other words, 76 percent of the benefits of such a subsidy would go outside the target income class. Moreover, of the 20.3 million households in the under $5,000 per year class, only 10.2 million or just over 50 percent would receive benefits from such a subsidy.

C. A Gasoline Tax

Gasoline purchase data by income class were available from the Brookings MERGE File for 1972.[13] A gasoline surtax was taken as representative of the several possible emissions control strategies directed at auto usage (miles driven) rather than auto ownership. A surtax of twenty cents per gallon was assumed in calculating Table 13; but the pattern of incidence would be the same for any strategy imposing costs on users in proportion to gasoline purchases.

Table 13 shows a pattern of incidence which is slightly progressive except at the extremes of the income distribution. The implicit tax rate rises from .84 percent for the $2,000–$3,999 per year class to 1.09 percent for the $15,000–$19,999 class. This contrasts with other control strategies analyzed here, all of which were regressive overall.

The data of Tables 11 and 13 are also relevant to the recent discussion of the distributional effects of alternative means of allocating scarce gasoline supplies. Allowing the price of gasoline to rise or imposing a surtax to control demand would not apparently have the regressive impact cited by opponents of price or tax policies. However, as Table 11 shows, the most commonly mentioned alternative, issuance of equal

TABLE 13 Incidence of Gasoline Surtax, Twenty Cents per Gallon

Income Class	Mean Income (dollars)	Tax Cost per Household Dollars	Tax Cost per Household As a Percent of Family Income
Under $2,000	1,062	13.72	1.29
$ 2,000–3,999	3,061	25.66	.84
4,000–5,999	5,000	41.44	.83
6,000–7,999	7,143	66.58	.93
8,000–9,999	9,000	90.12	1.00
10,000–14,999	12,000	128.60	1.07
15,000–19,999	17,500	190.28	1.09
20,000–25,999	22,250	236.16	1.06
26,000–49,999	33,684	305.16	.91
50,000 and over	95,484	296.16	.31

SOURCE: From data supplied by Nancy Dorfman from the Brookings MERGE File.

quantities of salable rationing coupons to each car owner, would have far more favorable distributional effects. The coupon scheme would involve a substantial transfer of income from the government (in the case of the surtax alternative) or oil producers (where the alternative was a price increase) to car owners, with the value of the transfer being a larger percentage of income for lower-income households.

VI. SUMMARY AND CONCLUSIONS

In this paper, we have developed a user-cost model of demand for new and used automobiles, and have used this model to trace out the effects of an increase in the price of new automobiles caused by the imposition of automotive emissions standards. In addition, we have compared the pattern of incidence that results from the present strategy with those which might result from alternative policies imposing requirements on all cars. EPA suggests that, relatively, the burden of the 1976 emissions standards will fall most heavily on middle-income groups. While this result is confirmed by the application of the naive model of new-car purchases, the more comprehensive user-cost model shows that the final result will be an unambiguously regressive distribution of the burden.

This conclusion is in contrast to Dorfman's finding of slight progressivity over the middle-income range (Dorfman 1973). It is difficult to pinpoint the reasons for our differences, but they appear to stem from different assumptions about the patterns of price changes for used cars, and different treatments of increased operating costs. Resolution of these differences probably requires more theoretical and empirical work to refine models of the structure of asset prices and rentals in the car market and the dynamics of the interaction between new- and used-car prices.

There are several limitations to the analysis presented here. First, there is considerable uncertainty as to what will be the costs of meeting the new-car standards by 1976. While most of the uncertainty regarding what technologies will be used has been resolved, there are still widely varying estimates as to the costs of utilizing these technologies. It is even difficult to reconcile estimates of control costs published by EPA at different times. Hence, all of the estimates of incidence presented here must be construed as indicating the *relative* distribution of the burden more accurately than the absolute levels of the burden.

Second, it should be noted that the incidence analysis assumes no changes in the patterns of automobile purchases and ownership in response to changes in the price of automobiles relative to other goods, or changes in the relative user costs of different models and vintages of automobiles. To the extent that consumers respond to changes in relative prices and user costs, the incidence patterns will be modified. Not only might the total quantity of automobiles demanded change, but there are likely to be changes in the model mix as well. This will be both because of changes in the relative prices of models and because of different own-price and cross-elasticities of demand among models and vintages. Also, the analysis abstracts from the possible effects of other forces such as rising fuel costs and rising costs of safety features, both of which are likely to compound the effects of pollution control requirements on the patterns of ownership and purchase.

Finally, the analysis considers only the effects of emission control costs borne directly by households as they purchase cars for private use. About 30 percent of each year's new-car production goes into commercial or governmental use. It is assumed that the emission control costs associated with these cars are passed on to consumers in a pattern similar to all other governmental and industrial pollution control costs.[14]

All of the strategies imposing direct control requirements on cars are regressive. The gasoline tax is the only exception revealed by our analysis, and that tax would be only slightly progressive through the middle-income range. The federal new-car strategy is substantially less regressive than the two alternative policies imposing requirements on all cars. With the federal strategy, after the transition the burden as a percentage of income for the under $5,000 group was about twice the burden on the over $10,000 group. However, for the two alternative strategies analyzed, the relative burden on the under $5,000 group was closer to three times the burden on the over $10,000 group. The analysis of target efficiency showed that the vertical efficiency of any across-the-board or general subsidy of pollution control costs would be quite low. The vertical efficiency of a subsidization of the costs of meeting the 1976 standards would direct only about 15 percent of its benefits to the under $5,000 per year income group. The vertical efficiencies of the uniform control costs and rising control costs with age strategies were 18 percent and 24 percent, respectively.

Finally, it is important to look specifically at the burdens placed upon households in the lowest income class by each of these strategies. In the first year, the 1976 new-car standards result in a net gain per household of approximately $10 for the under $5,000 per year class; and since only about 56 percent of the households in this income class own cars, this works out to a gain of approximately $18 per owner of a used car. On the other hand, each of the households in this income group purchasing a new car in the first year will experience an increase in user cost of approximately $170. While this would be a large burden relative to income, households in this situation could avoid, or at least reduce, the burden by retaining their old car or purchasing a used car rather than a new one.

After the effects of the new-car controls have been fully worked out, used-car owners in the under $5,000 class would be experiencing a $43 increase in user cost per household, or a $77 increase in user cost per owner. During the transition period between the first imposition of controls and the final equilibrium, the burden per household or per owner would be gradually rising to this level.

If control costs are imposed on all cars, the only way a low-income family can avoid the increase in user cost is to become a nonowner. The impact on low-income households could be substantial. As Table 11 showed, in the uniform control cost case, car owners in the under $3,000 per year income class had control costs of $114 per household or 6.65 percent of family income. The incidence patterns are roughly similar for the case of rising control costs with age of car.

Of major concern is the question of economic dependence on automotive transportation. If a control program prices a household out of the car market, will its members lose access to jobs? Morgan has reported some data on miles driven to work by income level (Morgan 1974). In general, as incomes per family rise, a greater percentage of family heads drive to work, and the average length of the trip rises. Over 40 percent of all families are not dependent on cars for travel to work (this includes families without a working head); and the percentage is almost 70 percent for the bottom two-fifths of the income scale. However, of those family heads who do drive at least ten miles to work and return, only about 30 percent report the availability of any public transportation alternative.

NOTES

1. These calculations do not take into account the rise in oil prices during 1974 associated with the Organization of Petroleum Exporting Countries (OPEC).
2. But for somewhat different results based on a different set of data and methods, see Gianessi, Peskin, and Wolff, Chapter 6, below.
3. For an analysis of the aggregate impact of meeting the 1976 standards which does consider changes in the pattern of purchases, see (Council on Environmental Quality 1972).
4. More recently, EPA has concluded that one catalyst replacement will be required during the first 50,000 miles of use. Catalyst replacement costs are estimated at between $50 and $155 per car (Environmental Protection Agency 1973, p. 4-8). These costs are not included in this study. Although this exclusion biases the estimated level of control cost, it does not materially affect the pattern of incidence of these costs.
5. Wykoff has developed the user-cost approach to create a model of the demand for automobiles. See (Wykoff 1970, 1973).
6. Briefly, the stock of used cars, measured in terms of one year old equivalents is given by

$$S_{(t)} = \sum_{i=1}^{n} S_{(i,t)}(c_{(i,t)}/c_{(1,t)})$$

   S_t is a weighted index, where the number of cars in each year group is weighted by the ratio of the user cost of cars of that age to the user cost of the one-year equivalent. The definition can be expanded to take into account different models of the same vintage. See (Wykoff 1973).
7. This is Wykoff's "superior good" model in which new cars are qualitatively different from used cars by virtue of their newness alone. He found that this model explained new-car purchases better than the alternative "stock adjustment" model which treats new cars simply as additions to the total stock of cars. See (Wykoff 1973).
8. In addition, new-car buyers incur increased operating and maintenance costs as described earlier. These are added to the change in user cost measured by equation 9.
9. Wykoff's best estimate of f' is .34. See (Wykoff 1973, pp. 384–385). He also estimates

$$c_{(1,t)}/c_{(0,t)} = e^{-\hat{d}}$$
$$= .7047$$

   where
$$\hat{d} = .35$$

   See (Wykoff 1970).
10. In actuality, this gain will be spread out over several years between 1972 and 1976 as emission standards gradually become more stringent and new-car prices gradually rise.
11. This surprising result that owners of used cars benefit in the first year from the imposition of pollution control is not particularly sensitive to the choice of values for the parameters and does not depend on s. The net gain to the owner of an i year old car is

$$g_{(i,t)} - \Delta c_{(i,t)} = s\,\Delta P_{(0,t)} \left\{ \frac{P_{(i,t)}}{P_{(1,t)}} - [(1+r-h)\,e^{-d(i-1)}] \right\}$$

   which will be greater than zero if

$$\frac{P_{(i,t)}}{P_{(1,t)}} > (1+r-h)\,e^{-d(i-1)}$$

and

$$s>0, \Delta P_{(0,t)}>0$$

The first inequality will hold for any reasonable set of values for the variables. The exponential term on the right side of this second equation is the ratio of user costs while the term on the left is the ratio of purchase prices. With the assumed values of r and h, the term in parentheses is substantially less than 1 (.36). Since the depreciation patterns for purchase price and user cost are likely to be similar, the inequality should hold in general.

12. As noted above, the data in the lowest income class may overstate the true degree of regressivity if it includes the "temporary poor," whose car purchases and ownership reflect a higher permanent income level.
13. I am indebted to Nancy Dorfman for making these data available to me. For some further interesting data on car use by income level, see (Morgan 1974).
14. See (Environmental Protection Agency 1972) and (Dorfman 1973).

REFERENCES

Council on Environmental Quality. *The Economic Impact of Pollution Control*. Washington, D.C., March, 1972.

Dorfman, Nancy S. "Who Bears the Cost of Pollution Control?: The Impact on the Distribution of Income of Financing Federally Required Pollution Control." Report prepared for the Council on Environmental Quality, August, 1973, processed.

Environmental Protection Agency. *The Economics of Clean Air—1972*. Washington, D.C., March, 1972.

―――. *The Cost of Clean Air—1973*. Washington, D.C., October, 1973.

Freeman, A. Myrick, III. "The Distribution of the Environment." In Allen V. Kneese and Blair T. Bower, eds., *Environmental Quality Analysis: Theory and Method in the Social Sciences*. Baltimore: Johns Hopkins Press, 1972.

Lees, Lester, et al. *Smog: A Report to the People*. Environmental Quality Laboratory, California Institute of Technology, 1972.

Morgan, James N. "Gasoline Price Inflation: Its Impact on Families at Different Income Levels." *Economic Outlook: U.S.A.* 1 (Spring 1974): 7–8.

New York Times. "Most Big Cities May Fail on '75 Clean Air Deadline." April 15, 1973.

Post, A. Alan. "Statement before Hearing Officer," Environmental Protection Agency, March 22, 1973.

U.S. Department of Commerce, Bureau of the Census. *Consumer Buying Indicators*. Series P-65. Washington, D.C.

Weisbrod, Burton A. "Collective Action and the Distribution of Income: A Conceptual Approach." In U.S. Congress, Joint Economic Committee, Subcommittee on Economy in Government, *The Analysis and Evaluation of Public Expenditures and the PPB System, A Compendium of Papers*. 91st Cong., 1st sess., 1969, pp. 177–197.

Wykoff, Frank C. "Capital Depreciation in the Postwar Period: Automobiles." *Review of Economics and Statistics* 52 (May 1970): 168–172.

―――. "A User Cost Approach to New Automobile Purchases." *Review of Economic Studies* 40 (July 1973): 377–390.

Zupan, Jeffrey. *The Distribution of Air Quality in the New York Region*. Washington, D.C.: Resources for the Future, Inc., 1973.

5 | COMMENTS

Frank W. Segel
Bureau of Economic Analysis

I. SUMMARY

A. Myrick Freeman's paper has three major purposes: (a) analysis of the distribution of automotive pollution control costs imposed by government regulations embodied in the Federal Clean Air Act of 1967 and Amendments of 1970; (b) analysis of the incidence of costs imposed by alternative strategies for controlling air pollution from private motor vehicles; (c) evaluation of the effectiveness of an across-the-board subsidy to neutralize the regressive impact of costs imposed by different strategies to control automotive pollution emissions. The paper is organized in four sections: patterns of car ownership and purchases, target efficiency measures, proposed user-cost model, and alternative strategies.

Patterns of Car Ownership and Purchases

The notion that the rich buy new cars and own mostly new cars while the poor buy used cars and own mostly used cars was tested against automobile purchase and ownership data enumerated in the July 1971 Current Population Survey. The data base of this study treats 1971 model cars as new. Examination of the household data that includes *purchases* of new and used cars by income class and *ownership* according to model of car and number owned per family indicated that upper-income households own a substantial inventory of cars older than the 1971 vintage. Table 3 shows that about 33 percent of all households have incomes over $10,000 but own over 36 percent of all automobiles that are five or more years old. Table 4 shows a similar pattern from a different perspective. It shows that 60 percent of the households reporting over $5,000 annual income own five-year-old and older cars, while only about 45 percent of households with annual incomes under $5,000 own cars in this vintage range.

Target Efficiency Measures

In this section, the possible need for a subsidy is introduced for two reasons: inequitable distributions of automotive pollution control costs may arise, and

---

NOTE: The views expressed are those of the discussant and do not purport to represent the views of the Environmental Studies Staff, the Bureau of Economic Analysis, or the U.S. Department of Commerce.

increased recognition that pollution control costs may be prohibitively high and thus may result in a reaction against such controls.

A subsidy, or cost sharing, of pollution control costs affects income distribution. Weisbrod (1969) proposed target efficiency of the redistributive process as a criterion for evaluation of income redistribution policies. Two measures of target efficiency were used in this paper. The first, "vertical efficiency," measures the percentage of total subsidy program benefits that are delivered to a predetermined target population. Coverage by a redistributive program is measured by "horizontal efficiency," which indicates the percentage of members of the target group that actually receive benefits.

As the incidence of pollution control costs upon upper-income groups increases, the vertical efficiency of an across-the-board subsidy of control costs decreases. The horizontal efficiency of such a subsidy is 100 percent if the target group is defined on the basis of car-owning (or car purchasing) households with a given level of annual income, and less than 100 percent if the target group includes all households in the given income category, those owning and those not owning automobiles.

The target group selected for this study is all households with yearly income less than $5,000.

Proposed User-Cost Model

A model based on annualized user costs is proposed for testing different strategies for meeting the 1976 new car antipollution standards. The present federal strategy of imposing emission controls only on new cars was analyzed first through a naive model of cost incidence and then through the user-cost model.

The assumptions of the naive model are that only new-car purchase prices are increased by pollution control costs and that these increases are borne fully by the buyers of new cars. It was estimated that the emission control device (presumably, a catalytic converter) elected by the automotive industry to meet 1976 standards will increase the price of new cars by $320 and increase associated annual operating and maintenance costs by $36. The operating and maintenance cost stream was discounted over a five-year period at a 10 percent discount rate to arrive at a total cost burden per new car of $455 present value. Application of this model to data on new-car purchases revealed an extremely regressive impact of control costs. Table 6 shows that the cost per buyer as a percentage of family income is 26.5 percent for incomes under $3,000 and 2.5 percent for income levels $10,000 and over. On the basis of costs per household, the result ranges from 0.69 percent to 0.53 percent. The naive model that is based on capital-cost increases on new cars yields a mildly regressive distribution of costs per household.

If the total cost were to be subsidized, the target group of under $5,000 per year households would receive only 10 percent of the total subsidy. In other words, the subsidy would have a vertical efficiency of 10 percent. Since only 3.9

percent of the target group buys new cars, this percentage represents the horizontal efficiency.

Freeman developed a "user-cost" model based on a model that Wykoff (1970) used to measure demand for automobiles. User costs are estimated on the basis of demand for, and purchase prices of, new and used cars.

Freeman states that the user-cost model has the advantages of measuring increases in annualized user costs in contrast to measuring increase in capital cost, measuring the total stock of used cars of all ages in terms of a one-year-old equivalent, and permitting development of a demand model to ascertain relative price effects on used cars.

A price-shifting factor was derived to measure the induced change in used-car purchase prices as a function of an autonomous change in new-car purchase prices. This induced change in used-car prices depends on the assumption that used cars are close substitutes for new cars. Further, used cars without pollution control can be assumed to be close substitutes for new cars with pollution control devices. It was estimated that a $4 increase in the purchase price of a new car generates an increase of $1 in the price of one-year-equivalent used cars. The analysis shows that this induced change results in a capital gain only in the first year of operation because of the price differential caused by pollution control devices. Further, used-car owners experience increases in user costs because of the same new-car purchase price increases that led to the capital gains. Increases in user costs for used cars are less than those for new cars. This difference is attributable to used cars not being perfect substitutes for new cars (Wykoff 1973). Increases in user costs to new- and used-car owners were augmented by associated increases in operating and maintenance costs.

The main thrust of this paper is an examination of the distribution of emission control costs resulting from the use of a user-cost model. This model was used to determine the pattern of incidence in the first year of the new pollution control program and in the subsequent equilibrium year, when the stock of noncontrolled cars has been completely replaced by emission-controlled cars.

In the first year, the user-cost model shows a net gain, or negative user cost, for new- and used-car owners because of the capital gain effect on used-car owners. This effect has a pro-poor distribution of 0.17 percent of family income for the target group, diminishing to an extreme of 0.05 percent for households in the $10,000 and over class.

After reaching a steady state wherein all cars are controlled, the user-cost model shows a regressive distribution ranging from 1.83 percent of family income of target households to 0.89 percent for households with $10,000 and over. If subsidized, the vertical efficiency is 15 percent and horizontal efficiency is 56 percent. Ownership patterns indicate that 56 percent of households with yearly incomes less than $5,000 own automobiles. It is assumed that purchase and ownership patterns are stable over the adjustment period.

Alternative Strategies

Two alternative strategies requiring control devices were examined. One involved uniform control costs per car through installation of the same emission control package across all cars. The other involved uniform emissions standards for all cars, where the cost of the emission control device increases with the age of the car in which it is to be installed.

The two alternatives were each regressive. Table 11 shows a range of 2.90 percent to 0.69 percent for uniform cost alternative. Table 12 shows a range of 3.01 percent to 0.69 percent for the uniform emission level alternative. If subsidized, their vertical efficiencies would be 18 to 20 percent, while their horizontal efficiencies would still be 56 percent.

In contrast to control strategies dependent upon automobile ownership, a third alternative based on automobile usage was examined. The third strategy is a tax on gasoline purchases that would impose pollution costs as a function of usage. This approach yields a slightly progressive distribution of the cost burden.

According to Freeman, the distribution of control costs shown by the naive model confirms EPA's suggestion that the burden of 1976 emission standards falls mostly on the middle-income group. In steady-state equilibrium, his user-cost model shows the federal strategy to be the least regressive relative to the other two approaches based on the use of an antipollution device.

II. CRITIQUE

Distributions of costs that would be imposed by the Federal Clean Air Act of 1967 and Amendments of 1970 and two alternative strategies for controlling automotive air pollutant emissions through control devices have been evaluated according to two criteria: (1) the impact of cost by income level (progressive, proportional, or regressive) and (2) the efficiency with which a particular strategy would distribute the benefits of an across-the-board subsidy aimed at lessening the cost impact.

No mention was made of the manner of financing any subsidization of a share of the purchase price of a new car with the antipollution device. Consequently, the impact of cost by income level was not compared against the tax increment by income level that would be imposed by the financing of the across-the-board subsidy. It is possible that the subsidy-financing tax burden may result in greater regressivity than the emission control cost burden.

Considering that the intent of a subsidy is to benefit a predetermined target group, it appears that a more direct mechanism can be used to reach a narrowly defined target group. The more appropriate target group should be only those households in a given income category that are actually affected by pollution control costs. Based on the car ownership patterns presented in the paper, only 56 percent of the households in the under $5,000 yearly income category comprise the appropriate target group. This group owns new and used cars. Further, this means-test constraint should not be limited to an income criterion but should include an appropriate wealth test. A wealth test should eliminate those for whom income is not an accurate measure of economic strength.

Because the proposed across-the-board subsidy does not conform to the vertical and horizontal tenets of an equitable system of taxation, it is proposed that only the affected target group should have their pollution control costs mitigated through the mechanism of a tax credit applicable to the federal income tax system. The suggested tax credit can be treated as equivalent to a negative income tax that is sufficient to neutralize the pollution control cost burden imposed on low-income households by government regulations. This approach assures 100 percent vertical target efficiency and 100 percent horizontal efficiency. That is, only the selected target group would benefit from a subsidy. An across-the-board subsidy is too diffused in its distributive effect to achieve a sharply focused stream of benefits that impinge only on the unduly burdened target group.

An important facet that has not been discussed is the effect of a subsidy upon the decision making of the automobile manufacturer. It was pointed out in the paper that the automobile industry has elected the most expensive of three possible methods to reduce emissions from an automobile engine to achieve 1976 government standards. No mention was made of alternative engine designs such as diesel, stratified-charge, Wankel, or electric designs. Because 1980 standards restrict permissible automobile emission to half of those that will be permitted in 1976, a long-run perspective should consider a least-cost solution possibility through manufacture of an engine that generates fewer pollutants. It is essential to compare a catalytic converter as an end-of-line method of abating air pollutants with a completely redesigned automobile engine as a change-in-propulsion-process method that generates fewer pollutants that have to be abated.

The latter approach requires the automobile manufacturer to assume more risk by investment in capital equipment necessary for production of less-pollutant-generating engines that would yield long-term benefits to society. Any subsidy of the difference in the new car purchase price resulting from pollution control devices would serve as an incentive to the manufacturer to be a risk averter by concentrating on the production of converters.

Changing the design of the engine to reduce generation of pollutants would probably lead to an increase in car prices relative to other goods and services, whereas a 100 percent subsidization of an end-of-line catalytic converter would tend to protect the prevailing car prices. In effect, such a subsidy benefits the seller of an automobile as well as the buyer. In the long run, the subsidy may lead to other than a least-cost method of reducing air pollutant emissions and would probably reduce the impact that relative price changes might have in reducing automobile use. Further, a subsidy applied to the catalytic-converter price differential still allows the manufacturer to obtain a profit through an administered pricing formula and to retain his share of the market.

It is paradoxical that price increases due to optional accessories such as air conditioners, power brakes, power steering, and power whatever are not viewed as undue burdens on the low-income household. The pressures of advertising and emulation have probably changed a relatively income-elastic demand for these accessories to a relatively inelastic demand. Higher automobile purchase prices in this case did not raise the subsidy issue. Even though government regulations will force the automotive industry to increase production costs owing to the installation of automobile pollution control devices, the effect on automobile supply and demand by the resulting increase in the purchase price and subsequent operating and maintenance costs of a new car should still be managed by the conventional market forces. People will either have to forgo other goods and services to own an expensive and an allegedly socially detrimental mode of transportation or make their preferences for improved mass transportation known to their legislative representatives.

Since the private automobile contributes over 50 percent by weight of all air pollution in the United States, the air pollution problem requires examination of the whole transportation system, not just one of its components. It is evident that a subsidy scheme aimed at neutralizing the burden of pollution control costs does not contribute to the reduction of demand for automobiles. Consideration of the alleged wasteful deployment of increasingly scarce resources to the production and use of the private car and all associated ancillary goods and services necessitates a careful study of the incidence of costs of pollution control and policies to lighten their burdens in the frame of reference of a total system, not a subsystem alone.

A minor matter that requires some comment is that of capital gains and user costs applicable to used-car owners. Their connection with a real benefit or burden to the used-car owner seems weak. Even if the assumption that an increase in the new-car purchase price will induce relative increase in the purchase prices of used cars is valid, there is no realized capital gain to a used-car owner until he sells. Furthermore, the individual seller of a used car has virtually no market power through which he could realize his potential capital gain. If a used-car owner trades his car for another more recent vintage used car, his capital gain from the "sale" aspect of the transaction is offset by the capital gain embodied in the price of the purchased used car. Only by selling without replacement can the owner of a used car realize the capital gain.

This reasoning leads to an interesting observation that increases in new-car purchase prices because of antipollution devices bestow capital gains upon the used-car dealer. That is, he obtains potential capital gains on his whole inventory of used cars and realizes these inventory gains as taxable ordinary income through sales.

A similar argument applies to the increased user cost for the used-car owner resulting from the upward change in the purchase prices of used cars. The real-cost burden is derivable only from the purchase of new cars with antipollution devices or from the installation of retrofit antipollution devices on all cars, new and used, as defined by the alternative strategies: that of uniform control costs per car and that of uniform emissions for all cars.

A real cost that some used-car owners are likely to face is that of increased fuel costs when new cars are equipped with a catalytic converter. Owners of pre-catalytic-converter cars equipped with high performance engines that operate more efficiently and economically with leaded gasoline will in all likelihood bear increased costs because the petroleum industry will shift more of its resources to the production of nonleaded gasoline. The nonleaded gasoline requirement by cars equipped with catalytic converters may very well shift the pricing structure of leaded as well as nonleaded gasoline upward.

6

LEONARD P.
GIANESSI
Resources for the Future

HENRY M.
PESKIN
Resources for the Future

EDWARD
WOLFF
National Bureau of
Economic Research

The Distributional Implications of National Air Pollution Damage Estimates

I. INTRODUCTION

Through the use of data from the 1970 U.S. Population Census, this paper attempts to distribute among the population estimates of national air pollution damages. It is impossible to proceed with such a task unless one is willing to make several assumptions, all of which can be criticized.

As a result, an unsympathetic reader, without too much effort, can discover twenty things wrong with the basic data. With a little imagination, he can convince himself that none of the assumptions is plausible. And, he might conclude that "garbage-in-garbage-out" would be the most fitting descriptor for this paper about pollution.

NOTE: The authors wish to acknowledge the helpful criticisms of Eugene Seskin and the assistance of Richard Ruggles. Financial support was provided by the National Science Foundation, grant SOC74-21391.

However, we feel that such a caustic view overlooks the fact that an estimation technique and not the data is the main focus of this paper. By discussing the distributional implications of a set of data that reflect our current state of knowledge, as poor as it is, we hope to demonstrate the advantages of what appears to be a promising direction for future research: the development and refinement of both aggregate and disaggregate economic measures as complements to one another.

In this analysis of the distributional implications of national estimates of air pollution damage we have, in effect, merged macrodata and microdata sets. We hope that the results are enticing enough to stimulate similar research efforts in this as well as other areas.

II. MAJOR ASSUMPTIONS

Our adjustments to incomes and income distributions require several assumptions. The most important of these will be discussed in this section. Other, less crucial assumptions are mentioned below in the section on methodology.

First, and perhaps most importantly, we are assuming that our basic data on the dollar values of national air pollution damages and on individuals' incomes are valid. Those familiar with the Census data base we are using—the Public Use Samples—are well aware of some of its limitations: the poor sampling of lower-income subpopulations, the failure to count as income in-kind transfers, the failure to include as income the value of a housewife's domestic services, and so on. Those with a knowledge of environmental data are even more aware of the difficulties associated with air pollution damage estimates. In principle, for our purposes, such estimates should measure the amount in dollars that the nation would be willing to pay in order to avoid the damages. However, in this instance, there is a wide gap between principle and practice. The actual data are a mixture of (some would say, wild) extrapolations of results from a handful of studies on health effects and property values, scraps of information on physical damage, and some pure guesses. This is not difficult to understand in view of the fact that the Environmental Protection Agency (EPA) has never made *official* estimates of the monetary damage for all air pollutants. While they did estimate the damage from stationary-source pollutants (especially particulates and sulfur oxides) in 1972,[1] they have not published any similar numbers since (as of this writing).

However, those familiar with the Census data and the environmental data are also aware that the limitations of both these data sets have not prevented their widespread use. In the Executive Office alone, the Council of Economic Advisers freely reports numbers from the Census data, while the Council on Environmental Quality has published damage estimates based on the environmental data.[2] Thus we are in good or, at least, official company when we assume their validity.

A second major assumption is that air quality and the damage associated with air quality at any point in time is highly correlated with the rate of emissions at that point in time. In addition, we assume that current conditions of air quality (as measured by emissions) are good indicators of the cumulative history of past conditions.

Our third major assumption is that over a suitably defined geographical area, the air is of constant quality and is confined to the area. This can be conceptualized if one thinks of each area as being covered by a plastic dome. In effect, this assumption treats air pollution as a pure public "bad" within an area and precludes the possibility of spillovers between adjacent regions.

These two assumptions, which fail to account for both meteorological and biological effects, are made out of necessity. In making them, we are following a frequent practice of blurring the distinction between emissions and ambient air quality. To do otherwise requires the development of comprehensive national air-diffusion models with extremely detailed data on point-source emissions, localized meteorological conditions, and geographical considerations, as well as data on residence times, decay functions, and the effects of cumulative exposures from various pollutants.

A fourth principal assumption is that an industry's emission level in an area is proportional to the industry's employment in the area. This assumption allows us to rely almost exclusively on the Public Use Samples for our basic data on regional effects, despite the fact that there is a considerable amount of data which would permit more precise estimates of local air pollutant emissions based on the size and practices of local establishments. The difficulty with this latter information is that it is not available nationally (and, in certain cases, where the number of establishments is few, the information may never be disclosed).[3]

Both the third and fourth assumptions suggest that the geographical areas chosen for analysis should be small enough to assure approximately uniform air quality, but large enough to assure a minimum of air spillovers and spillovers of people living in one area and working in another. A good compromise is found in the Census County Groups (which are similar to the Office of Business Economics [OBE] Economic Areas). In this analysis, these groups are subdivided into their Standard Metropolitan Statistical Area (SMSA) and non-SMSA components in order to reflect the greater air pollution damage expected in SMSA's as a result of the higher population densities and industrial activity.[4]

A fifth major assumption is that within any area, the value of a unit damage from air pollution is the same for each population unit living in the area. This assumption is probably not valid. As Baumol has noted, even if everyone's preferences for clean air and other goods were identical, under a "public bad" assumption, it is likely that wealthier individuals would place a higher value on a marginal unit of cleaner air than the less wealthy.[5] Thus, the distribution of damages between rich and poor would differ even if each suffered the same physical impacts. Our assumption implies that the distribution of damages is purely a function of the distribution of pollutants.

This assumption is necessary because we are using national damage totals as the starting point of our analysis. Essentially, we prorate the national totals to geographical areas and then we allocate an equal pro rata share of the area damage to each individual in the area. Since to some extent the national totals reflect the differential values placed on clean air by rich and poor,[6] our pro rata individual shares represent a weighted average of these differential values, the weights being the relative proportions of rich and poor in the national population.

There is another difficulty with this assumption. No *single* definition of a population unit is appropriate for calculating the pro rata share of an area's total damage. The national damage estimates that we are using represent a composite of damages to structures, human health, crops, general property, various materials, and so on. Thus, they are in some cases applicable to households alone, in other cases to individuals in households, and in still other cases to families. In this analysis, we assume that the distributional effects are primarily to individuals, and we believe that this assumption does not alter the general conclusions. Below, we shall suggest an approach for obtaining damage estimates that does not rely on national totals as a starting point and that does allow for both differences in the types of damages and in the incomes of people being affected.

Our final assumption is that within any geographical area, the total value of air pollution damage is proportional to the level of emissions. If, as many believe, damage is more than proportional to emissions, we are likely to understate the value of damage in those regions with very high emission levels.[7]

III. METHODOLOGY

The approach we use can be summarized in four major steps.

Pollution Generation

First, we estimated air pollution emissions in 1968 by two-digit Standard Industrial Classification (SIC) and industry Census classifications. This step relied on an extensive amount of data processing, which was undertaken in connection with a National Bureau project designed to expand national accounting systems by including the service flows from environmental assets.[8]

Dispensing with the estimation details, we can summarily describe the technique as an expansion and extension of published EPA estimates. These estimates cover fairly broad classifications by product and process, although neither type of classification is covered comprehensively. Therefore, it was necessary to disaggregate the EPA estimates, regroup them according to SIC classifications, and fill several gaps of missing information. For example, there was a need to fill the gap resulting from EPA's failure to report emissions of air pollutants from natural sources. The importance of this oversight can be seen if one realizes that the vast majority of particulates come from natural sources.[9]

National Damage Estimates

The second step was to estimate the damage value in 1970 dollars of the total 1968 emissions of the five principal types of air pollutants: sulfur oxides, particulates, carbon monoxide, nitrogen oxides, and hydrocarbons. As noted above, we did not estimate these values ourselves. Instead, we utilized two published sources. The first[10] relied heavily on several cross-section studies and estimated a total national damage of approximately $16.1 billion. However, the effects on health and property of carbon monoxide, hydrocarbons, and nitrogen oxides, the so-called mobile-source pollutants, were not estimated due to a lack of data.

This deficiency was partially corrected in the second source.[11] Babcock and Nagda used estimates of the relative "severities" of air pollutants to account more fully for the probable health and property damages associated with the mobile-source pollutants. As a result, the Babcock-Nagda computation raised the total damage value to $20.2 billion. The amount of damages associated with each pollutant is shown in Table 1.

The Babcock-Nagda procedure is not completely satisfactory, since the relative severities appear to rely almost entirely on EPA's air quality standards, which, in turn, rely heavily on EPA's estimates of the relative contributions of the pollutants to ill health.[12] Hence, the Babcock-Nagda nonhealth damage estimates for hydrocarbons and nitrogen oxides implicitly assume a close correlation between health effects and materials damage. In addition, it should be noted that the health effects which served as a basis for the severity rates were essentially "threshold" effects (i.e., the concentrations of pollutants for which adverse health effects are first observed in a controlled laboratory environment); and whether these "threshold" concentrations reflect actual health effects which can be translated into dollar terms is questionable.[13] There seems to be little consensus among the experts as to the relative severities of pollutants.

TABLE 1 **National Air Pollution Damage Estimates: 1968 (1970 dollars)**

Pollutant[a]	Tons $\times 10^6$	$\$ \times 10^6$
PM	141.3	5,878
SO_x	33.2	8,295
NO_x	20.6	3,062
HC	32.0	2,667
CO	100.1	250
Total		20,152

SOURCE: L. R. Babcock and M. L. Nagda, "Cost Effectiveness of Emission Control," *Journal of the Air Pollution Control Association* 23 (Mar. 1973): 1973–1979. The allocation of damages by pollutant was calculated by the present authors in connection with the National Bureau project mentioned above. U.S. Public Health Service, *Nationwide Inventory of Air Pollutant Emissions—1968* (Washington, D.C.: August 1970), and Midwest Research Institute, *Particulate Pollutant Systems Study*, Vol. I, *Mass Emissions* (Kansas City, Mo.: May 1971).

[a]PM = particulate matter; SO_x = sulfur dioxides; NO_x = nitrogen oxides; HC = hydrocarbons; and CO = carbon monoxide.

Had Babcock and Nagda used the severity ratios claimed by others, the estimated damages to property and health from the mobile-source pollutants would have differed substantially. Fortunately, however, the value associated with these damages accounts for only about 25 percent of the total estimated air pollution damages.

Calculation of Area Damages

Under our second and third major assumptions, the density of air pollutants is proportional to the emissions in an area and inversely related to the size of the area. However, the value of pollution damages depends not only on the density of air pollutants but also on the number of population units (families, households, persons) in the area.

The above considerations led us to the following formula for prorating a national damage estimate for the jth pollutant to the ith area

$$(1) \qquad D_{ij} \equiv \frac{D_j (P_i/A_i) T_{ij}}{\sum_i [(P_i/A_i) T_{ij}]}$$

where D_j is the national damage for pollutant j ($\equiv \sum_i D_{ij}$) in dollars; P_i is the number of population units in area i; A_i is the land area of i (hence, P_i/A_i is equal to the population density of area i); and T_{ij} is the emissions in tons of pollutant j in area i. The total damage in area i, D_i, is thus $\sum_j D_{ij}$.

Equation 1 suggests that for areas of equal size and emissions tonnage, the damage is less, the smaller the population; for areas of equal population and emissions tonnage, the damage is less, the larger the area; and for areas of equal population and size, the damage is less, the smaller the emissions tonnage.

The calculation of T_{ij} relies on our fourth major assumption relating employment to emissions. Generally, national emissions of an industry were prorated in proportion to the industry's employment in the area.[14] In particular, the vector of total national emissions for each industrial sector was divided by the sector's national employment. This yielded a vector of pollution emissions per employee for each sector. Then, by inspecting the Census Public Use records, the number of persons employed in a particular sector within each county group (broken down into its SMSA and non-SMSA components) was estimated. Multiplying the number of persons employed in a sector within an area by the vector of pollution emissions per employee yielded the estimate of the amount of each pollutant generated per area by each sector. Finally, by summing over all sectors having employees within the area, the area's total emissions of each pollutant, T_{ij}, were determined.

There were two exceptions to this procedure. First, the emissions in the household sector were calculated on the basis of automobile registrations and heating fuel consumption. Secondly, emissions from natural sources were allocated on the basis of acres of land by state that were subject to wind erosion[15] and acres of forests by state that were destroyed by wildfire.[16] The particulates from wind erosion were distributed in proportion to the relative size of the county groups, while the pollutants from forest fires were distributed to county groups on the basis of estimates of their relative forested areas.

Calculation of Per Capita Damages

The per capita damage in area i is defined as D_i/P_i. In terms of Equation 1, the formula for per capita damage is

$$(2) \qquad \frac{D_i}{P_i} = \frac{1}{P_i}\sum_j D_{ij} = \frac{1}{P_i}\sum_j \frac{D_j\left(\frac{P_i}{A_i}\right)T_{ij}}{\sum_i\left[\left(\frac{P_i}{A_i}\right)T_{ij}\right]} = \frac{1}{A_i}\sum_j \frac{D_j T_{ij}}{\sum_i\left[\left(\frac{P_i}{A_i}\right)T_{ij}\right]}$$

An examination of the derivatives of equation 2, taken with respect to A_i and P_i, indicates that per capita damages are more sensitive to the land area of i than to the population of i. Thus two regions with roughly the same emissions levels and population densities can have quite different per capita damages. The region with the smaller land area will have the greater per capita damage, reflecting the fact that under our "plastic dome" assumption, the pollutants are emitted to a smaller volume of atmosphere. However, it should be kept in mind that the assumption of no emissions spillovers is less valid the smaller the area. Therefore, a very high per capita damage estimate for a region with small land area is probably an overestimate for that region, while the per capita damage estimates for the neighboring regions are probably under-estimates.

Distributing Per Capita Damages

The final step was to distribute the per capita damage estimates to the population in order to investigate the impact on different income and racial groups. The tabulations summarizing these impacts were developed by associating with each Public Use record the per capita damage appropriate to the residence of the responding unit. For these tabulations, per capita incomes were defined as family incomes divided by the number of family members.

IV. RESULTS

The results will be presented in terms of their implications for the distribution of air pollution damages among regions and among individuals in different income and racial groups.

Regional Distributions

Per capita damages, damage levels, and emissions for each county group broken down by source of damage and by pollutant are displayed in the appendixes. Appendix I appears in print following the text of this paper. Appendixes II and III appear on microfiche at the back of the book. Part One of each appendix lists the county groups exclusive of their SMSA's, while Part Two lists the SMSA's. The area covered by both parts taken together includes the continental U.S., Alaska, and Hawaii.[17] An over-view of the first appendix is provided by Table 2 which lists the "worst"

TABLE 2   Ranking of Selected SMSA's and Non-SMSA's by Per Capita Damage in Dollars

	20 "Worst" SMSA's			20 "Best" SMSA's			20 "Best" Non-SMSA's	
1.	Jersey City, N.J.	888.41	1.	Binghamton, N.Y.-Pa.	9.90	1.	Montana	.84
2.	New York City, N.Y.	415.47	2.	Santa Barbara, Calif.	12.99	2.	W N.Dak.	1.56
3.	Erie, Pa.	348.28	3.	Bakersfield, Calif.	13.20	3.	NW Minn.-E N.Dak.	2.47
4.	Newark, N.J.	292.45	4.	Salinas-Monterey, Calif.	14.44	4.	N Kansas	2.65
5.	Paterson-Clifton, N.J.	253.88	5.	San Berradino, Calif.	15.56	5.	NW Texas	2.71
6.	Detroit, Mich.	242.61	6.	Duluth, Minn.-Wis.	16.13	6.	EC Calif.	3.22
7.	Chicago, Ill.	221.40	7.	Flint, Mich.	17.55	7.	SE S.Dak.-SE Minn.	3.30
8.	Cleveland, Ohio	214.69	8.	W. Palm Beach, Fla.	18.03	8.	SW Texas	3.31
9.	Providence, R.I.	205.21	9.	Utica-Rome, N.Y.	19.96	9.	SE Nebr.	3.59
10.	Philadelphia, Pa.	199.42	10.	Fresno, Calif.	21.71	10.	SE Colo.	3.70
11.	Gary-Hammond, Ind.	189.50	11.	Tucson, Ariz.	22.12	11.	C. Texas	3.86
12.	Los Angeles, Calif.	188.14	12.	Greenville, S.C.	22.15	12.	S. Dak.	3.88
13.	New Haven, Conn.	182.42	13.	Sacramento, Calif.	22.34	13.	S. Texas	4.30
14.	Pittsburgh, Pa.	179.01	14.	South Bend, Ind.	22.49	14.	SC Texas	5.10
15.	Salt Lake City, Utah	176.04	15.	Stockton, Calif.	23.65	15.	NW Fla.	5.31
16.	Milwaukee, Wis.	169.18	16.	Austin, Texas	24.57	16.	SW Okla.-NC Texas	6.27
17.	Boston, Mass.	154.77	17.	Las Vegas, Nev.	24.74	17.	W Ga.-E Ala.	6.28
18.	Bridgeport, Conn.	147.21	18.	Oklahoma City, Okla.	25.20	18.	NE Colo.	6.37
19.	Hartford, Conn.	135.44	19.	Honolulu, Hawaii	25.79	19.	NW Ohio	6.96
20.	Trenton, N.J.	134.65	20.	Rochester, N.Y.	25.81	20.	E Iowa-SW Wis.	6.97

SOURCE: See text.

(highest per capita damage) and "best" (lowest per capita damage) regions.

Perhaps the most significant feature of this appendix is the unevenness in the distribution of per capita air pollution damage across regions. While the national average is about $99 per person, it is at least twice as high in 10 SMSA's, and over four times as high in the two "worst" SMSA's. Clearly, the "worst" SMSA's are not typical of the nation as a whole. Of the 272 regions designated in the first appendix, 237 have damages less than $99 per person and 45 are under $10. In fact, of the national damage total of $20 billion, the 20 "worst" SMSA's account for 67 percent and the five "worst" for 31 percent.[18]

There are a few surprises in the results displayed in the appendixes and in Table 2. For example, Los Angeles's relative ranking is "in spite of," not "because of," the automobile. The contribution to per capita damage from the household sector in Los Angeles is a modest $30 or 16 percent of its total. This is largely due to the relatively low dollar damages that are assigned to the automobile's major pollutant, carbon monoxide.

Other peculiarities in the results can be better understood by studying the individual characteristics of the regions. Table 3 displays some of these characteristics for a few selected SMSA's. Note, for example, that Birmingham exceeds Erie in emissions tonnages for all pollutants and has only a slightly lower population density, yet it has only one-fifth of Erie's per capita damage. This result is a consequence of Erie's much smaller land area.

The effect of small land area is especially apparent with respect to Jersey City's $888 per capita damage estimate. Certainly this is an overestimate since much of the area's pollution probably spills over into Newark on the West, Paterson on the north, and the ocean on the east.[19] However, even when the Jersey City, Paterson, New York City, and Newark SMSA's were combined as one area in order to analyze this spillover effect, the combined per capita damage equaled $405, still exceeding all other SMSA's.

A comparison of Cleveland and San Francisco points out the importance of the composition of pollutants. The two SMSA's are roughly similar in population density, although Cleveland has a smaller land area. While this smaller land area partially explains Cleveland's higher per capita damage figure, another important factor is Cleveland's emissions of SO_x (even though its emissions of other pollutants are less than San Francisco's). The national damage estimates indicate that, per ton, SO_x is by far the most damaging pollutant.

An inspection of those areas with low damages reveals another feature of our results: the importance of the source of pollutants, especially

TABLE 3 Characteristics of Selected SMSA's

SMSA's	Land Area (square miles) (1)	Population (2)	Population Density (2)/(1)	Per Capita Damages (dollars)	Emissions (million tons/year)				
					PM	SO$_x$	CO	HC	NO$_x$
Birmingham	2,721	739,274	272	75.99	0.305	0.226	0.472	0.104	0.107
Los Angeles	4,069	7,036,463	1,730	188.14	0.926	0.734	2.732	1.002	0.514
Jersey City	47	609,266	12,851	888.41	0.024	0.055	0.160	0.056	0.036
San Francisco	2,478	3,109,519	1,254	126.00	0.373	0.245	1.426	0.580	0.219
Pittsburgh	3,049	2,401,245	788	179.01	0.542	0.748	1.668	0.350	0.338
Cleveland	1,519	2,064,194	1,359	214.69	0.216	0.489	0.855	0.347	0.203
New York	2,136	11,571,883	5,419	415.47	0.621	1.061	3.730	1.248	0.780
Erie	813	263,654	324	348.28	0.039	0.065	0.107	0.027	0.026
Bakersfield	8,152	329,162	40	13.20	0.279	0.028	0.203	0.074	0.037

SOURCE: See text.

TABLE 4   Total Pollution Damage to Regions by Source (Millions of dollars)

Region	Total (1)	Industry (2)	Household (3)	Nature (4)
New England	1,108.9	858.6	240.8	9.5
Middle Atlantic	8,696.4	6,305.0	2,362.7	28.6
South Atlantic	1,478.7	1,084.2	240.8	153.7
East South Central	605.0	439.4	49.1	116.5
West South Central	558.0	403.7	47.0	107.3
East North Central	4,493.7	3,740.4	590.1	163.2
West North Central	591.7	368.8	55.3	167.7
Mountain States	304.6	167.5	19.4	117.7
Pacific States	2,315.1	1,784.3	377.0	153.8
Total	20,152.1	15,151.9	3,982.1	1,018.0

SOURCE: See text.
NOTE: See the reference in footnote 17 for a map defining these regions.

natural sources. In many of the rural areas, nature is the dominating polluter.[20] The relative importance of pollution souces is summarized for broad regional classifications in Table 4. The proportionally stronger role for nature is apparent in the less industrialized regions.

Effect on Individuals

We now turn to the implications of our results as they relate to the distribution of air pollution damages among individuals classified by income and race.

Both Freeman, using data from the Kansas City, St. Louis, and Washington, D.C., SMSA's,[21] and Zupan, using data from the New York region,[22] have found evidence that poorer income groups are exposed to higher pollution levels. In contrast, our results, summarized in Table 5, do not support the hypothesis that air quality is distributed in a "prorich" manner. Of course, as a group the poor suffer more; but that is only because there are more of them. In per capita terms, we found that the greatest damage, as Baumol hypothesized, was suffered by high-income groups.

However, before concluding that the Freeman-Zupan results are inconsistent with ours, three differences in the studies should be emphasized. First, both Freeman and Zupan analyze air pollution differences *within* a smaller number of SMSA's. By design, such intra-SMSA differences are ruled out of our analysis. Had we used smaller geographical units, our results might have conformed more closely to

TABLE 5   Mean Per Capita Pollution Damage Incurred by Income Class

Income Class	Mean Pollution Damage	Percent of Persons in Income Class
$ 1,000 or less	$ 72.96	19.0
1,001–3,000	94.57	47.7
3,001–5,000	112.82	20.0
5,001–7,000	124.57	7.2
7,001–10,000	130.43	4.0
10,001–15,000	133.89	0.8
15,000 and above	142.76	1.2
Overall	99.29	100.00

SOURCE: See text.

theirs. Secondly, it is important to point out that our analysis, in contrast to Freeman and Zupan's, is geographically comprehensive, covering all SMSA's and non-SMSA's. Thus, account is taken of the fact that a significant number of poor live in rural regions that are relatively clean. Thirdly, it should be noted that Freeman's data are for 1960, while ours are for 1970. If air pollution has become more evenly distributed across and within SMSA's over the decade (perhaps as a result of air-cleanup programs), then the value of air pollution damages would have also become more evenly distributed between richer and poorer areas. In this connection, it is interesting to note that Zupan's analysis, using pollution data for 1970, evidenced a far weaker maldistribution to the poor than Freeman's analysis.

On one result, Freeman and ourselves agree. Nonwhites clearly suffer more damage than whites.[23] The relevant comparisons are shown in Table 6.

TABLE 6   Mean Per Capita Pollution Damage Incurred by Whites and Nonwhites

Race	Mean Pollution Damage	Mean Income	Percent of Persons
Whites	$ 97.55	$ 3,080.97	88.6
Nonwhites	115.67	1,823.22	11.4
Total	99.29	2,937.62	100.00

SOURCE: See text.

If air pollution damage is considered negative income, it is natural to investigate its effect on the income distribution. Given our previous findings that the rich seem to be suffering more damage than the poor, one would expect only a minor effect on the income distribution. In fact, the Gini coefficient for the distribution of personal incomes in 1970 was 0.421. After subtracting the per capita negative income attributed to air pollution damage, the Gini coefficient for the distribution rises to 0.434, indicating a slight tendency towards less equality of incomes.

Finally, we investigated the hypothesis—implicitly underlying Nordhaus and Tobin's use of income differentials to measure urban disamenities[24]—that higher income offsets air pollution damage. We looked at both the correlation between per capita income and per capita damage and the rank correlation between an area's mean income and its per capita damage. The first correlation was 0.34, indicating small but significant support for the hypothesis. However, the rank correlation, also small but significant, was −0.15, which, by itself, does not support the hypothesis. Both results taken together suggest that while there is a general tendency for higher incomes to parallel higher damages, there are probably many exceptions to the rule.

V. CONCLUSION

In at least two respects, the results of this study warrant further investigation because of their implications for policy. In the first place, if the rich suffer more than the poor from air pollution, then they have more to gain from cleanup programs. Thus, even without the equity consideration of how much different income groups *should* pay for a cleanup program, policymakers and politicians can take advantage of the fact that the rich should be *willing* to bear a proportionately larger tax burden, because it is in their own interest.

In the second place, if the geographical distribution of damages is as unequal as our results suggest, policymakers may wish to concentrate their antipollution activities in a similarly uneven manner. However, before EPA decides to "crack down" on Jersey City while neglecting Bakersfield, it should be recognized that our analysis looked only at the damages from air pollution and not at the opportunity costs of reducing those damages. Furthermore, it is possible that cleaning up only the very dirty areas engenders other distributional impacts that might be considered socially undesirable.

Given that a more thorough examination of the issues is needed, we can suggest three research efforts in increasing order of difficulty. First, the entire study should be replicated using newly available EPA data on pollution emissions. These data are not necessarily better than our emissions data, but their use would provide a measure of the sensitivity of our results to emissions levels.

Secondly, the implications of using smaller geographical areas should be investigated. At a minimum, the damage levels in Central Business Districts should be contrasted with the damage levels in non-Central Business Districts.

Thirdly, instead of national damage totals, a detailed microdata base should be used as the starting point of the analysis. Since microdata give important family and individual characteristics, it should be possible to assign a probable damage value to each microunit. For example, by using air pollution-health studies, an expected value of lost income due to increased morbidity and mortality from air pollution can be assigned to individual wage earners. This method of assigning air pollution damage will automatically account for the earner's position in the income distribution, and if he is at the higher end, he should be willing to pay more for cleaner air.

One by-product of this third effort would be the development of new and, hopefully, more accurate national damage totals. This line of research would further demonstrate that the development of aggregate and disaggregate economic measures are complementary activities.

NOTE: Appendix II, "Total Damage (in millions of dollars) from Pollutants, by County Group," and Appendix III, "Total Emission (in millions of tons), by County Group," appear on microfiche at the back of the book. Duplicate microfiche cards can be obtained from Microfiche Systems Corporation, 440 Park Avenue South, New York, N.Y. 10016.

TABLE A-1   Per Capita Damage (in Dollars) from Industrial, Household, and Natural Causes by County Group Part One: County Groups, Exclusive of Selected SMSA Components

County Group Code	County Groups	Total	Industry	Household	Nature
1	N Maine	7.41	1.08	0.58	5.75
2	S Maine	8.83	6.04	1.89	0.89
3	N Vermont, New Hampshire	11.09	9.78	1.31	0.0
4	S Vermont, Massachusetts, Rhode Island	51.45	39.75	10.59	1.11
5	S New Hampshire, Vermont, C Massachusetts, Connecticut	34.46	28.81	5.65	0.0
6	W Vermont, Massachusetts, E New York	12.55	8.14	1.62	2.79
7	N New York	12.35	8.09	1.53	2.72
8	W New York, NC Pennsylvania	16.98	9.98	1.22	5.78
9	W Pennsylvania, NE Ohio	26.39	24.37	2.03	0.0
10	C Pennsylvania	16.00	12.77	1.58	1.64
11	SC New York, NE Pennsylvania	10.05	8.62	1.43	0.0
12	E Pennsylvania	17.67	13.99	3.68	0.0
13	SE New York, N New Jersey, Connecticut	96.20	84.10	12.09	0.0
14	E Pennsylvania, C New Jersey	50.13	44.03	5.12	0.99
15	Mid Pennsylvania	18.48	15.60	2.88	0.0
16	Delaware, Maryland	16.30	13.18	1.88	1.24
17	W Virginia, N West Virginia	8.67	6.10	1.21	1.36
18	S Virginia	11.41	9.54	1.87	0.0
19	C Virginia	11.85	9.19	1.13	1.52
20	E North Carolina, S Virginia	7.16	5.97	1.19	0.0

County Group Code	County Groups	Total	Industry	Household	Nature
21	C North Carolina	10.88	7.53	2.29	1.06
22	SE North Carolina	11.56	7.11	1.80	2.64
23	NW North Carolina	11.73	9.87	1.85	0.0
24	S North Carolina	30.50	18.10	2.81	9.59
25	W North Carolina	25.88	7.62	1.65	16.60
26	W South Carolina	23.00	19.50	2.08	1.41
27	C South Carolina	24.73	9.48	1.07	14.18
28	N South Carolina	10.55	8.01	1.10	1.44
29	S South Carolina	12.05	4.85	0.61	6.58
30	E Georgia	9.95	5.57	0.83	3.55
31	N Florida	26.80	7.58	0.73	18.49
32	EC Florida	62.60	16.45	1.83	44.32
33	SW Florida	12.25	10.57	1.05	0.63
34	NW Florida	5.31	3.04	0.70	1.56
35	W Florida	10.43	5.83	1.44	3.15
36	SE Alabama	12.36	5.89	0.80	5.67
37	SW Georgia	11.65	8.21	0.66	2.78
38	C Georgia	10.37	6.39	0.88	3.10
39	W Georgia, E Alabama	6.28	4.96	1.32	0.0
40	N Georgia	29.20	17.24	1.10	10.86
41	C Alabama, E Mississippi	11.73	7.37	0.83	3.52
42	N Mississippi, W Tennessee, E Arkansas	9.23	6.05	0.66	2.51
43	N Alabama	20.03	18.79	1.24	0.0
44	SE Tennessee, NE Georgia	9.02	8.13	0.89	0.0
45	C Tennessee	16.86	12.09	1.16	3.61
46	E Tennessee	28.22	18.21	0.84	9.17
47	W Virginia	34.47	27.49	1.74	5.24
48	S West Virginia	21.31	15.88	0.96	4.47
49	C Kentucky	23.44	9.15	1.15	13.13
50	N Kentucky	24.88	10.83	1.12	12.94
51	W Kentucky, SW Indiana	14.16	11.03	1.16	1.97
52	WC Indiana	15.36	7.16	1.60	6.61
53	C Illinois	32.20	5.37	1.42	25.41
54	EC Illinois	41.34	5.60	1.86	33.88
55	NC Indiana	18.92	10.65	1.69	6.58

County Group Code	County Groups	Total	Industry	Household	Nature
56	C Indiana	25.48	20.80	2.01	2.66
57	EC Indiana	28.28	17.22	3.69	7.37
58	SW Ohio	15.07	8.30	1.60	5.16
59	WC Ohio	24.58	11.56	2.48	10.54
60	C Ohio	22.90	16.71	1.54	4.64
61	N West Virginia	19.05	17.84	1.21	0.0
62	SW Pennsylvania	37.91	35.50	2.41	0.0
63	NE Ohio	28.76	26.64	2.12	0.0
64	NW Ohio	6.96	5.03	1.93	0.0
65	N Ohio	20.09	17.98	2.11	0.0
66	E Michigan	23.29	20.13	3.16	0.0
67	NE Michigan	8.94	6.83	1.07	1.04
68	NW Michigan	7.97	5.58	1.08	1.32
69	SC Michigan	13.95	10.45	3.50	0.0
70	NE Indiana	13.52	11.99	1.53	0.0
71	SW Michigan, N Indiana	27.43	24.53	2.90	0.0
72	NE Illinois	19.97	18.38	1.59	0.0
73	NC Illinois	32.95	6.39	1.49	25.07
74	N Illinois, SE Iowa	37.48	7.91	1.27	28.30
75	E Iowa, SW Wisconsin	6.97	5.97	1.00	0.0
76	NC Illinois, SC Wisconsin	9.91	8.20	1.70	0.0
77	SE Wisconsin	12.98	9.48	1.93	1.57
78	NE Wisconsin	7.26	4.97	0.81	1.48
79	NC Wisconsin	14.59	10.99	0.77	2.83
80	NW Wisconsin	13.28	5.54	0.45	7.29
81	WC Wisconsin	9.84	6.08	1.00	2.76
82	Minnesota	9.81	4.76	0.67	4.37
83	NW Minnesota, E North Dakota	2.47	2.10	0.37	0.0
84	W North Dakota	1.56	1.42	0.13	0.0
85	Montana	0.84	0.77	0.07	0.0
86	South Dakota	3.88	1.37	0.12	2.39
87	SE South Dakota, SE Minnesota	3.30	1.92	0.51	0.87
88	Wyoming, W Nebraska	31.84	0.97	0.09	30.78
89	C Nebraska	22.84	1.46	0.17	21.22

TABLE A-1   Part One (continued)

County Group Code	County Groups	Total	Industry	Household	Nature
90	NE Nebraska, NW Iowa	20.02	2.15	0.41	17.47
91	NC Iowa	40.95	5.12	0.67	35.17
92	NW Iowa	37.62	4.24	0.93	32.44
93	S Iowa	25.89	4.36	0.78	20.75
94	SW Iowa	33.51	5.31	0.54	27.66
95	SE Nebraska	3.59	2.80	0.79	0.0
96	N Kansas	2.65	1.63	0.19	0.83
97	S Kansas	12.24	1.86	0.22	10.16
98	NW Missouri, NE Kansas	14.26	4.15	0.74	9.37
99	NC Missouri	26.80	4.83	0.62	21.35
100	WC Illinois	9.01	8.14	0.87	0.0
101	W Illinois, E Missouri	28.66	7.93	0.85	19.88
102	SE Missouri, SW Kentucky	8.17	7.47	0.70	0.0
103	S Missouri, SE Kansas	21.87	5.87	0.56	15.45
104	C Arkansas	13.61	7.22	0.45	5.94
105	WC Arkansas, EC Oklahoma	43.72	7.04	0.40	36.28
106	NE Oklahoma	39.60	12.56	0.87	26.17
107	Oklahoma	7.67	3.01	0.33	4.33
108	SW Oklahoma, NC Texas	6.27	2.06	0.49	3.72
109	NW Texas	2.71	1.13	0.15	1.43
110	WC Texas	8.26	2.69	0.42	5.14
111	SW Texas	3.31	1.10	0.16	2.06
112	C Texas	3.86	1.41	0.23	2.22
113	NE Texas	7.92	3.81	0.54	3.56
114	EC Texas	10.52	1.99	1.00	7.53
115	Mideast Texas	9.72	3.94	0.43	5.34
116	E Texas, NW Louisiana	10.40	6.60	0.58	3.22
117	NE Texas, SW Arkansas	14.59	6.35	0.43	7.82
118	E Louisiana	25.03	5.83	0.69	18.51
119	S Arkansas, WC Mississippi	12.22	6.75	0.46	5.02

TABLE A-1   Part One (concluded)

County Group Code	County Groups	Total	Industry	Household	Nature
120	Midwest Mississippi	31.21	6.45	0.43	24.33
121	EC Mississippi	28.47	7.74	0.53	20.20
122	SW Alabama, SE Mississippi	51.49	6.08	0.69	44.71
123	SE Louisiana, SW Mississippi	13.31	9.05	0.63	3.64
124	S Louisiana	9.38	7.63	0.99	0.75
125	SE Texas	11.55	4.86	0.59	6.11
126	SC Texas	5.10	2.49	0.20	2.41
127	S Texas	4.30	1.07	0.33	2.90
128	S New Mexico, W Texas	18.42	.80	0.07	17.55
129	N New Mexico	33.45	.98	0.09	32.38
130	SE Colorado	3.70	1.61	0.29	1.80
131	NE Colorado	6.37	1.78	0.18	4.42
132	W Colorado, SE Utah, SW Wyoming	15.90	1.56	0.10	14.23
133	W Idaho	12.55	1.77	0.15	10.63
134	W Montana, N Idaho	8.91	5.58	0.17	3.15
135	W Washington	16.11	15.29	0.82	0.0
136	SC Washington, NW Oregon	12.12	5.20	0.27	6.65
137	NW Oregon, SW Washington	20.06	10.70	0.58⁻	8.78
138	SW Oregon	14.23	5.71	0.35	8.17
139	SE Oregon, SW Idaho	9.29	1.44	0.14	7.71
140	Nevada, SW Utah	18.36	0.43	0.04	17.89
141	Arizona	19.94	1.06	0.08	18.80
142	SW California[a]	0.0	0.0	0.0	0.0
143	C California	17.19	9.33	0.31	7.55
144	EC California	3.22	2.60	0.62	0.0
145	Mideast California	10.07	9.45	0.62	0.0
146	N California	8.62	4.76	0.16	3.70
147	WC California	20.84	12.37	1.31	7.16
148	Alaska	7.06	0.07	0.02	6.97
149	Hawaii[a]	0.0	0.0	0.0	0.0

TABLE A-1 Per Capita Damage (in Dollars) from Industrial, Household, and Natural Causes by County Group Part Two: SMSA's

County Group Code	SMSA's	Total	Industry	Household	Nature
4	Boston, Massachusetts	154.77	116.56	37.10	1.11
4	Worcester, Massachusetts	64.88	50.98	12.78	1.11
4	Providence, Rhode Island	205.21	166.87	37.24	1.11
5	Hartford, Connecticut	135.44	103.04	32.40	0.0
5	New Haven, Connecticut	182.42	145.99	36.43	0.0
5	Springfield, Massachusetts– Connecticut	103.86	82.63	21.23	0.0
6	Albany, Troy, New York	35.50	23.47	9.23	2.79
7	Rochester, New York	25.81	14.18	8.91	2.72
7	Syracuse, New York	38.01	29.16	6.13	2.72
7	Utica–Rome, New York	19.96	14.21	3.03	2.72
8	Buffalo, New York	128.37	108.20	14.39	5.78
9	Erie, Pennsylvania	348.28	311.69	36.59	0.0
9	Youngstown–Warren, Ohio	89.73	80.85	8.88	0.0
11	Binghamton, New York– Pennsylvania	9.90	6.57	3.33	0.0
12	Wilkes-Barre– Hazleton, Pennsylvania	63.56	53.21	10.35	0.0
13	New York, New York	415.47	279.73	135.74	0.0
13	Bridgeport, Connecticut	147.21	109.15	38.06	0.0
13	Jersey City, New Jersey	888.41	569.67	318.74	0.0
13	Paterson–Clifton, New Jersey	253.88	162.30	91.58	0.0
13	Newark, New Jersey	292.45	218.06	74.40	0.0
14	Trenton, New Jersey	134.85	98.64	35.23	0.99
14	Philadelphia, Pennsylvania– New Jersey	199.42	166.74	31.69	0.99

County Group Code	SMSA's	Total	Industry	Household	Nature
14	Wilmington, Delaware– New Jersey– Maryland	78.60	66.83	10.79	0.99
14	Reading, Pennsylvania	71.99	62.31	8.70	0.99
14	Allentown, Pennsylvania– New Jersey	84.73	75.61	8.14	0.99
15	Harrisburg, Pennsylvania	33.91	27.27	6.65	0.0
15	Lancaster, Pennsylvania	67.40	58.66	8.74	0.0
15	York, Pennsylvania	46.93	41.13	5.79	0.0
16	Baltimore, Maryland	78.61	61.48	15.89	1.24
16	Washington, D.C.–Maryland– Virginia	105.81	77.92	26.66	1.24
19	Richmond, Virginia	82.84	72.14	9.17	1.52
20	Newport News–Hampton, Virginia	63.26	35.09	28.17	0.0
20	Norfolk–Portsmouth, Virginia	122.35	95.78	26.57	0.0
23	Greensboro–Salem, North Carolina	30.90	24.28	6.62	0.0
24	Charlotte, North Carolina	73.17	55.59	7.99	9.59
26	Greenville, South Carolina	22.15	15.38	5.36	1.41
27	Columbia, South Carolina	53.96	33.66	6.11	14.18
29	Augusta, Georgia– South Carolina	31.76	21.02	4.16	6.58
29	Charleston, South Carolina	26.35	16.77	3.01	6.58
31	Jacksonville, Florida	102.09	69.43	14.17	18.49
32	Orlando, Florida	84.74	33.23	7.18	44.32
33	Fort Lauderdale, Florida	56.31	46.82	8.86	0.63
33	Miami, Florida	59.20	48.24	10.32	0.63

TABLE A-1   Part Two (continued)

County Group Code	SMSA's	Total	Industry	Household	Nature
33	Tampa, St. Petersburg, Florida	97.05	82.57	13.85	0.63
33	West Palm Beach, Florida	18.03	14.32	3.08	0.63
40	Atlanta, Georgia	114.86	90.44	13.56	10.86
41	Birmingham, Alabama	75.99	68.22	4.24	3.52
42	Memphis, Tennessee–Arkansas	53.88	42.70	8.67	2.51
44	Chattanooga, Tennessee–Georgia	122.41	117.22	5.19	0.0
45	Nashville–Davidson, Tennessee	46.96	37.02	6.33	3.61
46	Knoxville, Tennessee	104.35	89.52	5.66	9.17
48	Huntington, West Virgina–Kentucky–Ohio	82.00	74.63	2.91	4.47
50	Louisville, Kentucky–Indiana	113.15	84.77	15.44	12.94
56	Indianapolis, Indiana	48.66	38.94	7.06	2.66
58	Cincinnati, Ohio–Kentucky Indiana	70.52	53.39	11.97	5.16
59	Dayton, Ohio	87.81	67.67	9.60	10.54
60	Columbus, Ohio	87.05	70.20	12.20	4.64
62	Johnstown, Pennsylvania	48.59	46.14	2.45	0.0
62	Pittsburgh, Pennsylvania	179.01	166.55	12.46	0.0
63	Akron, Ohio	90.71	77.02	13.69	0.0
63	Canton, Ohio	116.72	105.31	11.41	0.0
63	Cleveland, Ohio	214.69	192.27	22.42	0.0
63	Lorain–Elyria, Ohio	85.19	76.29	8.91	0.0
65	Toledo, Ohio–Michigan	90.04	81.02	9.02	0.0
66	Detroit, Michigan	242.61	206.14	36.47	0.0
66	Flint, Michigan	17.55	10.95	6.60	0.0
68	Grand Rapids, Michigan	55.53	46.46	7.75	1.32

County Group Code	SMSA's	Total	Industry	Household	Nature
69	Lansing, Michigan	37.23	31.89	5.33	0.0
70	Fort Wayne, Indiana	75.39	66.69	8.70	0.0
71	South Bend, Indiana	22.49	15.62	6.87	0.0
72	Chicago, Illinois	221.40	189.17	32.24	0.0
72	Gary–Hammond, Indiana	189.55	177.91	11.64	0.0
73	Peoria, Illinois	56.34	27.75	3.52	25.07
74	Davenport, Iowa–Illinois	69.73	37.60	3.83	28.30
76	Rockford, Illinois	33.65	27.13	6.52	0.0
77	Madison, Wisconsin	35.92	28.63	5.73	1.57
77	Milwaukee, Wisconsin	169.18	148.69	18.91	1.57
78	Appleton–Oshkosh, Wisconsin	38.94	32.90	4.57	1.48
80	Duluth, Minnesota–Wisconsin	16.13	7.94	0.90	7.29
82	Minneapolis, Minnesota	127.74	105.78	17.59	4.37
93	Des Moines, Iowa	81.39	51.16	9.48	20.75
94	Omaha, Nebraska–Iowa	67.46	33.74	6.17	27.66
97	Wichita, Kansas	30.57	17.70	2.72	10.16
98	Kansas City, Missouri–Kansas	83.76	67.04	7.34	9.37
101	St. Louis, Missouri–Illinois	98.44	69.08	9.48	19.88
104	Little Rock, Arkansas	63.78	54.08	3.76	5.94
106	Tulsa, Oklahoma	44.54	16.27	2.10	26.17
107	Oklahoma City, Oklahoma	25.20	15.30	5.56	4.33
113	Dallas, Texas	48.26	38.79	5.91	3.56
113	Forth Worth, Texas	48.75	36.96	8.22	3.56
115	Austin, Texas	24.57	12.82	6.41	5.34
116	Shreveport, Louisiana	32.62	26.90	2.51	3.22
120	Jackson, Mississippi	50.19	23.05	2.81	24.33
122	Mobile, Alabama	70.21	23.48	2.01	44.71
123	Baton Rouge, Louisiana	111.03	96:33	11.06	3.64

County Group Code	SMSA's	Total	Industry	Household	Nature
123	New Orleans, Louisiana	77.62	66.98	7.00	3.64
125	Beaumont–Orange, Texas	122.96	113.13	3.72	6.11
125	Houston, Texas	87.96	76.88	4.97	6.11
126	San Antonio, Texas	37.44	27.29	7.74	2.41
127	Corpus Christi, Texas	60.25	54.52	2.84	2.90
128	El Paso, Texas	55.75	33.11	5.09	17.55
129	Albuquerque, New Mexico	53.99	17.03	4.57	32.38
131	Denver, Colorado	39.33	28.85	6.05	4.42
132	Salt Lake City, Utah	176.04	153.15	8.66	14.23
134	Spokane, Washington	27.68	20.63	3.89	3.15
135	Seattle–Everett, Washington	44.10	36.49	7.62	0.0
135	Tacoma, Washington	56.43	49.47	6.96	0.0
137	Portland, Oregon–Washington	95.59	80.71	6.10	8.78
140	Las Vegas, Nevada	24.74	6.18	0.68	17.89
141	Phoenix, Arizona	33.91	13.34	1.77	18.80
141	Tucson, Arisona	22.12	2.66	0.66	18.80
142	San Diego, California	26.03	18.75	7.28	0.0
143	Los Angeles, California	188.14	150.72	29.87	7.55
143	Anaheim, California	118.80	80.13	31.12	7.55
143	Bakersfield, California	13.20	5.00	0.65	7.55
143	Fresno, California	21.71	13.04	1.12	7.55
143	Oxnard–Ventura, California	40.04	28.96	3.53	7.55
143	San Bernardino, California	15.56	7.26	0.75	7.55
143	Santa Barbara, California	12.99	3.51	1.92	7.55
144	Stockton, California	23.65	20.02	3.63	0.0
145	Sacramento, California	22.34	18.41	3.93	0.0
147	Salinas–Monterey, California	14.44	5.43	1.85	7.16
147	San Francisco, California	126.00	97.63	21.21	7.16

TABLE A-1   Part Two (concluded)

County Group Code	SMSA's	Total	Industry	Household	Nature
147	San Jose, California	50.24	28.83	14.25	7.16
149	Honolulu, Hawaii	25.79	15.61	2.26	7.91
	National Total	99.29	74.65	19.62	5.02

[a]There are no non-SMSA components.

NOTES

1. *The Economics of Clean Air*, Annual Report of the Administrator of the Environmental Protection Agency, Senate Document No. 92-67; 92nd Congress, 2nd Session, March 1972. The damage estimates therein are based on Larry B. Barrett and Thomas E. Waddell, "The Cost of Air Pollution Damages: A Status Report," Appendix I–J in the Final Report of the Ad Hoc Committee on the Cumulative Regulatory Effects on the Cost of Automotive Transportation, Office of Science and Technology, February 28, 1972. A revision of the Barrett and Waddell estimates will be published shortly.

2. For example, see *Environmental Quality*, The Second Annual Report of the Council on Environmental Quality (Washington, D.C.: August 1971), p. 107.

3. Recently, a completely new source of regional data on emissions has become available, EPA's National Emissions Data System. These data are derived by applying EPA's pollution emission factors to state estimates of industrial activity and automobile usage. Unfortunately, this information is so new that we have not been able to exploit it for the present analysis.

4. The specific rules for allocating employment (and thus emissions) between the SMSA and non-SMSA components of a County Group are as follows: If a person both works and lives in an SMSA or works and lives outside an SMSA, employment is allocated by place of residence. If he lives in an SMSA but works outside an SMSA, employment is allocated to the non-SMSA component of the County Group. If he lives outside an SMSA but works in an SMSA, employment is allocated proportionally to total employment among all the SMSA components in the County Group. (If a person lives in a County Group with no SMSA's but works in an SMSA, he is excluded from the sample. Approximately 0.8 percent of all cases fell into this category.)

5. William J. Baumol, "Environmental Protection and Income Distribution," in Harold M. Hochman and George Peterson, eds., *Redistribution Through Public Choice* (New York: Columbia University Press, 1975).

6. This is true if health damages are measured by forgone earnings.

7. Depending on the shape of the true emissions-damage relationship, we also may be overstating the damage in regions with very low emissions levels. Since it turns out that our damage estimates for these regions are already very low, we do not feel that this latter problem is very serious.

8. A large amount of detailed documentation supporting the emissions estimates is available through direct communication with the authors.

9. Efforts of reworking and expanding the EPA estimates required a detailed review of more than one hundred technical studies on the generation of air pollutants.
10. Barrett and Waddell, *Cost of Air Pollution Damages.*
11. L. R. Babcock and M. L. Nagda, "Cost Effectiveness of Emission Control," *Journal of the Air Pollution Control Association* 23 (Mar. 1973): 1973–1979.
12. L. R. Babcock and M. L. Nagda, Letter to the Editor, *Journal of the Air Pollution Control Association* 22 (Sept. 1972): 727–728.
13. For a discussion of the merits of using laboratory experiments to infer the human health effects of air pollutants, see L. Lave and E. Seskin, *Air Pollution and Human Health* (Baltimore: Johns Hopkins University Press, forthcoming).
14. See footnote 4 for the employment allocation rules.
15. U.S. Department of Agriculture, *Basic Statistics—National Inventory of Soil and Water Conservation Needs, 1967* (Washington, D.C.: Jan. 1971).
16. U.S. Department of Agriculture, *Wildfire Statistics* (Washington, D.C.: Aug. 1973).
17. For a map showing county group and SMSA boundaries, see U.S. Department of Commerce, *Areas Defined on County Group Public Use Samples*, Form BC-81.
18. It is interesting to note that the 20 "worst" SMSA's account for 26 percent of the U.S. population, while the five "worst" account for 8 percent of the population.
19. The amount of the overestimate is somewhat offset since, as noted above, our assumption of a proportional emissions-damage relationship tends to *underestimate* the damages in heavily polluted areas such as Jersey City.
20. Indeed, we may be greatly underestimating the total impact of natural sources. Lack of data has precluded estimates of natural emissions of biologically produced NO_x, which on a worldwide basis ten times exceeds man-made emissions. See Environmental Protection Agency, *Air Quality Criteria for Nitrogen Oxides* (Washington, D.C.. January 1971), p. 3-1.
21. A. Myrick Freeman, III, "Distribution of Environmental Quality," in Allen V. Kneese and Blair T. Bower, eds., *Environmental Quality Analysis* (Baltimore: Johns Hopkins University Press, 1972).
22. Jeffrey M. Zupan, *The Distribution of Air Quality in the New York Region* (Baltimore: Johns Hopkins University Press, 1973). Zupan defines the New York region as "a 31-county tri-state area centered on Manhattan."
23. Zupan, relying on IRS data for his incomes, did not report any racial distributions.
24. William Nordhaus and James Tobin, "Is Growth Obsolete?" *Economic Growth*, Fiftieth Anniversary Colloquium V (New York: National Bureau of Economic Research, 1972).

6 | COMMENTS

Nancy Dorfman
Economic Consultant

The purpose of the paper under discussion is to advance our understanding of the way in which damages from air pollution, and in turn the benefits from cleaning it up, are likely to be distributed nationwide with respect to per capita income, race, and geographical location. Before summarizing the paper, let me emphasize why I feel that the issue is one of particular importance from the point of view of federal policy. The environmental program which has been legislated by Congress differs from the great majority of federal programs in two fundamental respects. First, the benefits, unlike those that can be presumed to flow from national defense, medical research, and similar efforts, cannot be construed as serving members of the community at large in more or less equal proportions, nor are they aimed at specific, identifiable target groups such as the poor, the elderly, or farmers. The beneficiaries are as yet not well defined. Second, the burden of support for the program does not follow the conventional pattern of federal financing, since virtually none of it flows from the federal treasury. While the distribution of the costs of programs which are financed through the federal tax system can be assumed, in general, to reflect some sort of public consensus regarding what constitutes a desirable degree of equity, the distribution of the burden of meeting federal air pollution standards is only beginning to be understood. It appears at the moment that it will look more like a consumption tax than the progressive federal tax structure. In launching what is to become a continuing and expensive under-national taking of this sort, it is not sufficient to evaluate it from the point of view national costs and benefits without some attention to its distributional consequences.

Efforts to appraise the distribution of the costs of the program have already yielded some promising insights. Further investigation is called for, but both the conceptual framework and the empirical basis for such studies are already well advanced. Although estimates of total costs leave much to be desired at the present time, we have, at least, a pretty good idea of what it is that we are trying to measure. Analyzing the benefits of the program presents a challenge of a different order. To date, most economists have hesitated to wrestle with such delicate issues as how to place values on human life and health or on the amenities of clean air. Their reluctance has demonstrated an uncharacteristic humility, but it has left the field to policymakers who, though they cannot afford such modesty, may be even less well equipped to deal with the issues. Decisions are, in fact, being, and will continue to be, made regarding permissible standards of environmental quality and, unless economists come to grips with the problem of measuring benefits and their distribution, such decisions are likely to be made on grounds that are not only inadequate but possibly totally irrelevant. The present study helps to underscore some of the hurdles that will have to be overcome before economists can offer policymakers much good advice in this area.

The specific task which the authors set themselves was to prorate some rather widely used estimates of the annual dollar cost of nationwide damages from five major air pollutants among all SMSA's and county groups exclusive of SMSA's in the United States, to convert the prorated damages within each area to a per capita basis and then to evaluate them with respect to income and race of area residents. The final product purports to be a nationwide distribution of the cost of pollution damages by income, race, and geographical area.

Estimates of nationwide dollar damages were prorated to individual areas on the basis of indexes which the authors developed of the proportion of total national damages due to each pollutant that occurred in each area in 1970. Their indexes were arrived at in the following ways.

First, for industrial pollution, the total volume of emissions of each pollutant was estimated by two-digit Standard Industrial Classification (SIC) categories, using what the authors describe as an "expansion and extension" of published Environmental Protection Agency (EPA) industry estimates. The resulting vectors of emissions for each industry were divided by industry employment to yield a set of vectors of emissions per employee by industry. The latter were in turn multiplied by industry employment in each area to derive total emissions by area. Emissions due to households in each area were estimated separately on the basis of automobile registrations and home fuel consumption. Natural source emissions were calculated on the basis of total acreage and forested areas within each location.

The authors recognized that damages from pollution depend not only on the volume of emissions but on population within an area as well, so that, in arriving at their indexes of area damages, they multiplied total area emissions by local population density. This product was in turn divided by the sum of such products for all areas in the United States to derive an index of the relative share of total national damages from each pollutant by area. Pollution indexes were then divided by local population estimates to arrive at the final set of area indexes of per capita damages from each pollutant. These were, in turn, multiplied by the national dollar damage totals per pollutant, to achieve measures of per capita dollar damages by area. Lastly, damage estimates were summed across pollutants to arrive at the final measures of total per capita damages by area.

The authors were now in a position to evaluate their estimates of per capita pollution damages in relation to income and race of residents of each area. From a conversation with two of the authors, I understand that income and race of a sample of residents from each area were established from the Census of Use file, permitting them to build up a nationwide distribution of per capita damages by income, race, and location.

With respect to race, they found blacks, on the average, to suffer about 25 percent greater pollution damages than whites. Geographically, the distribution showed a high degree of variance, as might have been expected. By income, damages appear to fall more heavily on the rich than on the poor, but the correlation between per capita income and per capita damages was only .35, while the rank correlation was −.15. Let us now examine more closely the method by which these distributions were arrived at.

The authors were careful to spell out the succession of assumptions which underlie their estimates. The list bears repeating: (1) Air quality within an area is highly correlated with the rate of emissions. (2) Damages are highly correlated with the level of air quality. (3) Emissions from an industry within an area are proportional to local employment in that industry. (4) Damages from emissions which emanate from an area are confined to that area. (5) Air quality is constant throughout an area. (6) Within any area, the value of a unit of damage is the same for each population unit. (7) Estimates of national damages from pollutants are valid.

The authors are more comfortable with most of these assumptions than I am, but, in view of the need for some basis for conjecture in this area and the obstacles that line the path to it, I am prepared to live with the first four for the time being. Acceptance of the last three, however, calls for a suspension of critical judgment which I am not yet ready to grant.

Ignoring, for the moment, the values that different members of the population are likely to place on damages from pollution, the assumption that all individuals within an area suffer equal exposure to pollution is contrary to the limited information which we have. The authors themselves cite two independent studies of pollution exposure within metropolitan areas which indicate its distribution by income to be just the reverse of what they found nationwide. Specifically, both Freeman and Zupan found the poor to be subject to significantly higher concentrations than the rich within four major urban areas. Although the number of areas studied was limited, given what is known about the tendency for the poor to congregate in central cities, there is reason to believe that replications would confirm these results in other urban areas. Had the present authors limited themselves to establishing between-area differentials in concentration of various pollutants, their results might have presented an interesting counterpoise to those of the earlier studies. But, unfortunately, any insights along these lines have been thoroughly beclouded by their procedure in assigning values to damages from each pollutant which they then summed across pollutants.

If the damages from separate pollutants are to be totaled, rather than examined separately, then, in order to assess even the relative distribution of damages by income class, it is essential, at the very least, that relative values assigned to units of damages from different pollutants be correctly measured. In other words, their "weights" in the total must approximately conform to the relative costs they impose. The authors assigned values to damages from individual pollutants on the basis of a set of rather widely publicized estimates of total national damages attributable to each pollutant in 1968, which they updated to 1970. Let us consider how these national damage estimates were arrived at in the first place. They come from two separate sources. The estimates of total national damages from sulfates and particulates are based on a much-cited survey by Barrett and Waddell of a number of independent cross-sectional studies of losses of property, life, and health due to air pollution. For each pollutant, Barrett and Waddell added the damages caused to health and mortality, materials, residential property values, and vegetation. It would appear, to begin with, that they became involved in a certain amount of double counting when they added to their estimates of damages to residential property values the damages to health and mortality. If homeowners place any value at all on the health aspects of clean air, it ought to be reflected in property values.

But what of the valuation of damages to life and health themselves? These are based on Lave and Seskin's estimates of the savings that a 50 percent reduction in nationwide air pollution would effect in terms of reductions in days of work lost due to ill health and early mortality, and in the cost of treatment and prevention of illness. Days of work lost are valued in terms of average earnings of those actually in the labor force, thereby excluding housewives, the retired, and children.

Lave and Seskin have made pathbreaking contributions to our knowledge of the association between morbidity and air pollution rates, but it is difficult to regard their valuation of losses as other than an act of desperation. It is all too easy to find fault with specific details of the method: the numerous omissions, as well as the insensitivity to the specific incidence of morbidity from air pollution among individual groups, for example the elderly and the poor, whose earnings differ from the average, not to mention the absence of any attention at all to the cost of pain and anguish. However, my major quarrel is with the basic premise that the collective willingness to pay for an increase in health and longevity has much of anything to do with its effect on gross national product. The question at issue is how much, altogether, would individuals be willing to pay for marginal increments in the community's average expectation of life and health? I doubt that most persons, if asked, would weigh very heavily the anticipated effect on either their own or the nation's gross value of product. Judging from the apparent unwillingness of most persons to insure themselves or their families fully against loss of earnings due to death or ill health, I infer that most of us prefer to assume some risk in this respect. On the other hand, few of us would happily go to our graves or succumb to chronic bronchitis merely by virtue of having our lifetime earnings insured.

So much for the valuation of damages from sulfates and particulates. For estimates of damages from mobile-source emissions, the authors relied on a second study by Babcock and Nagda with which I am not familiar. According to the present authors, the bases of these estimates are even more questionable than those of stationary sources and, furthermore, only damages to health and materials are allowed for. Mobile-source emissions, as it happens, are not known to cause severe damage to health or materials, although their effect on the amenities can sometimes be devastating. The lack of attention to these effects shows up in an anomaly, which the present authors allude to, in the damage estimates for the city of Los Angeles. Per capita estimates of damages in that community due to mobile-source emissions turn out to be only 7 dollars per year, while damages from other sources amount to 201 dollars per year. It is difficult to know what to make of area damage totals whose components are so capriciously weighted.

Even were we to accept the national damage estimates as a basis for valuing total costs of emissions, the question of differential willingness to pay would remain when it comes to distributing such costs by income class. The authors have assumed an equal willingness to pay among all individuals in the country per unit of pollution exposure. This implies that an individual's willingness to pay is not influenced by his ability to pay and that damages sustained by an individual are independent of his earnings or of the value of his property. The latter postulate violates, of course, the premise on which the national damage estimates are based. The authors take cognizance of this shortcoming as far as the within-area distribution of damages is concerned but make no effort to adjust for differential damages due to income variances either within or between areas.

The authors of the paper are not, of course, responsible for the unsatisfactory state of the art of measuring pollution damages. In adopting the existing estimates, even if only as a common denominator to permit them to cumulate damages from a variety of sources, they have, however, left themselves open to criticism, not the least of which is that they have lent credence to the estimates. However, more to the point, in assigning the implied dollar weights to damages from various pollutants, they have camouflaged what might otherwise have been a useful set of estimates of the distribution, by income and other variables, of average per capita exposure to specific pollutants among a comprehensive list of geographical sectors of the country. Such estimates could not, in themselves, have provided an adequate basis for determining the income distribution of pollution exposure nationwide because of the neglect of within-area differentials, but they would have provided some information about the between-area distribution to contrast with what is already known about the distribution within certain areas. In the attempt to push their results beyond what the present state of knowledge justifies, ground has been lost rather than gained.

I should like to recommend that the authors report their distributions in terms of the volume of emissions of specific pollutants rather than in terms of cumulative dollar damages. For purposes of policy making, the cumulation of damages across pollutants is, in any event, a mixed blessing. The abatement effort is, after all, not one, but a collection of programs. All sources of pollution need not be attacked in the same degree, nor is the distribution of the burden of abatement costs the same for all sources. Mobile sources of emissions, for example, present a rather different regulatory problem than do stationary sources. The burden, as well as the benefits, in abating the former tends to be concentrated within the geographical area from which they emanate, unlike the situation which prevails regarding industrial pollution. From the point of view of examining tradeoffs, aggregation destroys valuable evidence in this case.

Finally, some thought ought to be given to whether the passage of a federal pollution control act does not, in itself, suggest that the benefits from abatement are regarded by the public as accruing not solely to the local residents who breathe the air. Some, at least, ought perhaps to be treated as external to the specific locality.

7

JAMES P.
SMITH
The Rand Corporation

and

FINIS R.
WELCH
University of California
at Los Angeles and
the Rand Corporation

Black/White Male Earnings and Employment: 1960-70

I. INTRODUCTION

Our goal in this paper is to examine several aspects of relative black/white male earnings between 1960 and 1970, using the 1960 and 1970 One-in-100 Samples of the United States Census of Population.[1]

There is absolutely no question that relative earnings of black Americans increased during the decade. There are, however, real questions about root causes of this change. Before summarizing our interpretations of the evidence, we should note that although by historical standards the gain of the sixties is truly prodigious, the absolute magnitude of the change is not overwhelming. In 1959, the average weekly earnings of employed black men came to 57 percent of the amount earned by

NOTE: We should like to thank Orley Ashenfelter, of Princeton University, and Rodney Smith, of the Rand staff, for their comments on an early draft. We are grateful as well to research assistants Frank Berger, Richard Buddin, Anthony Casesse, Ann Dukes, and Iva Maclennan. The research was supported by a contract from the U.S. Department of Labor to the Rand Corporation, and by a grant from the Ford Foundation to the National Bureau of Economic Research. James P. Smith's work on the present report began while he was a research associate at the National Bureau of Economic Research.

employed white men. The ratio had increased to 64 percent by 1969—i.e., about 16 percent of the wage differential was bridged during the decade.

In accounting for growth in black/white wage ratios between 1960 and 1970, the evidence is, first, that younger, more recent cohorts of blacks gained more than older cohorts. Second, within experience classes, rising schooling levels and migration have contributed to the relative increases in black earnings. But the bulk of our evidence is that most of the gain of the sixties was broad-based. We did not find that gains were confined either to the highly schooled or to those employed by the governmental sector.

Our descriptions of occupation and industry of employment also indicate that the gains accruing throughout the sixties were very broadly based. There was marked black/white convergence of occupational distributions during the period, with the most pronounced change being realized by those blacks we estimate to have entered the work force between 1960 and 1970.

Similarly, for the same group, we found—especially for those who had attended college—that employment is moving from the traditional governmental to the private sector. It also seems that there are quite strong geographical patterns to changing black/white earnings ratios, with stronger gains registered in the South and North Central regions than in the Northeast and West.

Finally, in comparing earnings distributions, we find that there is more variance among black men than among white men. This is true both of observed weekly wages and annual earnings and of our predictions of them based on least-squares regressions. Annual earnings variance is dominated by variance in weeks worked. But location of residence and years of schooling also play an important role.

II. THE 1960s: THE HISTORICAL SETTING

Although our analysis in this paper relies on the 1960 and 1970 censuses, we think it is important first to place that decade in historical perspective. In many ways, the 1960s represented a sharp departure from the previous pattern of relative black/white incomes. It has also been claimed that the data available for the 1970s already indicate that the relative economic position of blacks has started to deteriorate from the position achieved in the late sixties. It is our view that isolating the underlying causes of the improvement during the sixties enables us to better assess whether the

1960s constituted a temporary aberration or whether the gains registered during that decade bode well for changes during the 1970s.

The paucity of good income data by race before 1940 is well known. Apparently, the best available statistics are those contained in the decennial United States Census Reports. These reports give a color breakdown of the occupations of individuals for each Census year since 1890. Gary Becker in his famous work on the economics of discrimination used income weights from the 1940 Census to construct a time series index of the relative occupational position of blacks.[2] Becker concluded that the fifty-year period from 1890 to 1940 was best characterized as one in which the relative economic position of blacks remained remarkably stable. He stated more tentatively that the 1940s were a decade in which the black/white mean ratio finally began to rise. This latter finding was confirmed in a more detailed and careful study of this period by James Gwartney.[3] Gwartney found that the nonwhite/white income ratio rose on average by 12 percent within regions during the 1940s.

Beginning in 1947, annual data for annual incomes are available in the Current Population Reports. Table 1 gives ratios of median incomes of nonwhite to white *families* for each year from 1947 to 1974.[4] Although the post-World War II era is characterized by a definite upward drift in the relative income of blacks, there were sharp cyclic swings. The picture is not of a smooth trend in relative black incomes; rather, the evidence is of a relatively small trend factor imposed on an unstable, cyclically sensitive, series. From 1947 into the mid-1950s, the ratio increased from .51 to .56. There followed a slight downward movement which continued into the early 1960s. Black/white incomes began to climb again after 1963 with a jump between 1965 and 1966 and a steady rise between 1966 and 1970. The dramatic increase between 1965 and 1966 is often used as evidence that the civil rights laws that just preceded this (1964–65) played a large causative role in accounting for the recent improvement in the earnings of blacks. However, year to year changes in the series are often quite irregular, and we think that this inference is not warranted on the basis of this evidence alone. For example, there are two other points (1951–52 and 1958–59) where the increase in the black/white ratio is about as large as the 1965–66 change. In those years, there was, of course, no comparable legislation. This issue of the effect of this legislation is obviously important and we admittedly cannot adequately address it with cross-sectional data for only two years. However, our empirical evidence does cast some doubt on the role of this legislation. First, we are able to attribute the rise in the ratio to factors (schooling, migration) that move more continuously over the period. Second, our single attempt to measure the influence of the governmental sector indicated that its effect was probably small.

TABLE 1   Ratio of Median Income of Black and White Families

Year	Ratio: Black and Other Races to White	Black to White
1974	0.62	0.58
1973	0.60	0.58
1972	0.62	0.59
1971	0.63	0.60
1970	0.64	0.61
1969	0.63	0.61
1968	0.63	0.60
1967	0.62	0.59
1966	0.60	0.58
1965	0.55	0.54
1964	0.56	0.54
1963	0.53	(NA)
1962	0.53	(NA)
1961	0.53	(NA)
1960	0.55	(NA)
1959	0.54	0.52
1958	0.51	(NA)
1957	0.54	(NA)
1956	0.53	(NA)
1955	0.55	(NA)
1954	0.56	(NA)
1953	0.56	(NA)
1952	0.57	(NA)
1951	0.53	(NA)
1950	0.54	(NA)
1949	0.51	(NA)
1947	0.51	(NA)

SOURCE: U.S. Department of Commerce, Social and Economic Statistics Administration, Bureau of the Census.

NOTE: NA = not available. The ratio of black to white median family income first became available from this survey in 1964.

After 1970, and especially if the 1974 data are ignored, black/white relative wages began once again to decline. It is this most recent downturn that has ignited the pessimism about the prospects for the future.

A more detailed representation of the recent period is given in Table 2 which lists ratios of black/white income for males, females, and families

TABLE 2 Relative Black/White Median Income for All Persons 14 Years and Older

Year	Males ——— All Workers	Full-Year Workers	Females ——— All Workers	Full-Year Workers	Family Income
1974	.61	.70	.90	.91	.58
1973	.60	.67	.90	.85	.58
1972	.61	.68	.93	.86	.59
1971	.60	.68	.88	.88	.60
1970	.59	.68	.91	.82	.61
1969	.58	.68	.84	.80	.61
1968	.59	.67	.79	.76	.60
1967	.57	.64	.78	.74	.59

SOURCE: Current Population Reports, Series P-60.

from 1967 to 1974. The general picture is a sharp rise in the late sixties followed by reasonably constant ratio during the seventies. In the last few years, there apparently was a slowdown in the rate of improvement for blacks. However, in view of the recessionary state of the economy, this slowdown may not contradict our predictions of continued improvement. Business cycle downturns typically reduce black relative wages, so much so, in fact, that the relatively constant ratio of black to white male income, in spite of the current recession, can be taken as evidence that longer-run forces are nullifying downward pressures. For example, a more optimistic view emerges in the relative wages of full-year workers (Table 2), where, presumably, the business cycle factors are better controlled.

At best, the patterns exhibited in Tables 1 and 2 are difficult to interpret. Not only are they confounded by business cycles, but they fail to correct for geographic location, age, schooling, and so on, factors which our analysis of the Census data shows are important determinants of the relative earnings position of blacks. We find little in the published tables now available for the recent past that seriously alters our confidence in the conclusions we derive based on the 1960–70 comparisons. Although our study will deal exclusively with racial comparisons of males, brief mention should be made of the pattern of relative female wages by race. Both over the more recent period and over the entire postwar period, the gains achieved by black males relative to white males are small compared to those achieved by black women relative to white women.

III. BLACK/WHITE WAGE RATIOS: THE 1960 AND 1970 CENSUSES

Table 3 illustrates the black/white ratios found in the U.S. Census. From among those persons described, we analyze data for only those males with earnings in the two years in question, 1959 and 1969. Self-employed men are excluded, as are men with more than 40 years of imputed work experience. Also excluded are those whose work experience is negative, when calculated as current age minus age of leaving school.[5]

Numbers reported are ratios of averages,[6] i.e., they are average black earnings or weekly wages relative to appropriate averages for whites. The first column gives the black/white wage ratio for six experience classes in 1970. The second column contains the same ratios for 1960, but this column is pushed down by two rows. Thus, the first entry, .510, is black/white earnings for the 1–5-year experience cell in 1960; this cell had 11–15 years of experience by 1970. The trend within an experience cell as a new cohort enters can be read up the diagonal; the within-cohort life cycle trends are illustrated across a row.

A number of patterns are apparent. First, the large earnings differentials that existed in 1960 were partly eroded between 1960 and 1970, but, as of 1970, differences remained large. Second, black/white earnings ratios are highest for those we estimate as having entered the labor market during the sixties, and they are higher for those entering between 1965 and 1970 than for 1960–65 entrants. Among cohorts who were in the labor market in 1960, with the exception of college graduates, we find that by 1970 the relative position of blacks had improved only slightly over 1960 levels. But, among the cohorts whose work experience predates 1960, the pattern exhibited for post-1960 entrants continues to hold: namely, that in comparison to whites, younger cohorts—more recent entrants into the labor market—fare better than their earlier counterparts.

Third, the gains that occurred between 1960 and 1970 are broadly based. With one exception, earnings ratios were higher in 1970 for every cohort than in 1960.[7] This wage growth was fairly uniformly distributed across experience and education cells for white males. This apparent growth neutrality for whites contrasts sharply with the patterns emerging among blacks, where the extent of the gain is positively related to

TABLE 3 Black/White Earnings Ratios for Cohorts in 1960 and 1970

Cohort Experience as of 1970 (Years Out of School)	Average Annual Earnings		Average Weekly Earnings		
	1970	1960	1970	1960	1970/60
I. All School Completion Levels					
1–5	.653	–	.702	–	–
6–10	.648	–	.677	–	–
11–15	.621	.510	.641	.568	.073
16–20	.601	.529	.618	.573	.045
21–30	.594	.545	.616	.585	.031
31–40	.604	.540	.620	.574	.046
II. Elementary School Graduates (8 Years Completed)					
1–5	.835	–	.865	–	–
6–10	.779	–	.802	–	–
11–15	.708	.673	.737	.703	.034
16–20	.710	.688	.717	.713	.004
21–30	.749	.671	.763	.708	.055
31–40	.721	.719	.740	.741	–.001
III. High School Graduates (12 Years Completed)					
1–5	.775	–	.806	–	–
6–10	.769	–	.791	–	–
11–15	.729	.654	.749	.714	.035
16–20	.731	.676	.750	.714	.036
21–30	.678	.655	.698	.685	.013
31–40	.675	.623	.690	.648	.042
IV. College Graduates (16 Years Completed)					
1–5	.716	–	.775	–	–
6–10	.647	–	.692	–	–
11–15	.662	.618	.688	.655	.033
16–20	.654	.559	.675	.582	.093
21–30	.519	.446	.557	.470	.087
31–40	.504	.389	.522	.421	.101

education level. The most spectacular improvement is undoubtedly that of college-educated blacks, although the less skilled also gained relative to whites. Some of the decline in growth rates by experience class in the complete black sample is due to shifting weights toward the less educated in the older experience groups. The decline in relative black/white wages as education increases becomes somewhat attenuated by 1970, for the older experience groups.

An obvious source of gain between 1960 and 1970 is the improvement in the general level of economic activity that occurred during this period. The U.S. aggregate average unemployment rate, 5.5 percent in 1959, had fallen to 3.5 percent by 1969. The penalties imposed by business contractions are not uniform over education, age, or racial groups, and as business conditions improved over the decade, black earnings would have increased relative to white. Since it is widely acknowledged that the principal cyclical setbacks occur in employment levels rather than in wage structures, the weekly wage comparisons in Table 3 are probably less contaminated by the business cycle than are annual income comparisons.[8] The gains reported by blacks are smaller in the wage than in the annual earning comparisons.

Although there is a presumption in the literature known to us that wage rates are quite insensitive to cyclic vagaries, the empirical basis for this presumption is unclear. A careful analysis of wage flexibility under cyclic fluctuations could go far in relieving our concern that the relative wage gains we document are merely a by-product of improving market conditions.[9] A number of the patterns we find seem to us inconsistent with a purely business-cycle explanation. Other researchers have provided convincing evidence that during recessionary periods those most adversely affected are the less skilled (schooled),[10] yet we find that those blacks who gained most in comparison to whites had the most schooling. Secondly, the change in the real characteristics of people (i.e., schooling or location) observed during the decade would, in the absence of any business-cycle trends, have led to an improvement in the relative income position of blacks. It may be that part of the story of gain in relative black earnings during the sixties is one of business cycles, but there seems to be considerable room for the operation of other factors.

Cohort, Life Cycle, and Calendar Year Effects

One feature common to all cross-sectional comparisons of black/white earnings differences is that younger blacks fare better in comparison to whites than their older counterparts. This fact, in and of itself, is consistent with extreme life cycle or cohort views (and, with a variety of intermediate views) that have very different implications for the future course of black/white differentials. Early theories of labor market discrimination tended toward a life-cycle explanation, holding that on-the-job black earnings increase less rapidly with work experience than white earnings. These theories of "secondary" labor markets view labor markets as stratified with some groups of workers being less upwardly mobile over their careers than others.

More recent comparisons have contrasted cross-sectional profiles taken at different points in time. If anything, these contrasts tend to support the extreme alternative to the life-cycle view, which is that differences in the cross-section are indicative of cohort differences. For example, in Table 3 the evidence of gains between 1960 and 1970 for blacks relative to whites suggests that given individuals were relatively unaffected. In contrast to the life-cycle view that predicts declining relative black wages between 1960 and 1970 within cohorts as workers aged ten years, the evidence is that wage ratios either remained constant or increased slightly. The aggregate gain stems mainly from changes in composition.

The extreme life-cycle view offers no basis for predictions of future patterns of wage differentials. The cohort view, on the other hand, does provide a basis for predictions if the future course of differences among cohorts conforms to the past. Suppose the evidence of the 1960–70 Census contrasts between cohorts is maintained in examination of the more recent data, the natural extension is to ask why cohort experiences seem so different over time.

There are a number of competing explanations to be scrutinized. These include questions of effects of modern antidiscriminatory legislation, trends in school quality and student achievement, as well as the possibility of secular trends in (front-end) market discrimination per se. But, whatever the explanation, any potential to understand secular forces rests exclusively on an ability to distinguish secular trends from life-cycle and cyclical forces operating in the cross section.

In general, cross-sectional data cannot easily decompose relationships that arise simply from maturation and those that are the result of a person of a particular age being the recipient of a variety of experiences that are unique to his generation. Each individual in a cross section is a member of a distinct cohort at one point on his life-cycle path. If between-cohort effects are important, the data must be adjusted before one has "pure" life-cycle elements. For example, the large secular increases in labor force participation rates for married women suggest that cohort effects could seriously contaminate cross-sectional labor supply studies. Similarly, improvement in school quality or home environment probably has led to a secular increase in the human capital stock of successive generations and thus affects observed cross-sectional wage earnings profiles. Although cohort or generational effects are recognized as important sources of bias in cross-sectional data, most investigators assume simply that empirically observed links between age and earning capacity are only the results of education and the associated skill acquisition process. By comparing cross sections at different points in time, the potential of distinguishing between those effects is established. For example, Welch [16] found that within each of two cross sections (1960 Census and Survey of Economic Opportunity [SEO]), the income gain associated with an added year of schooling was lower for older workers. But, since these workers were older, they had attended schools in periods in which schools were themselves different, and had entered the labor market when the market afforded different opportunities. By comparing persons of the same cohort (i.e., persons who had gone to similar schools and entered the labor market at similar times) between these cross sections, drawn seven years apart, Welch found little evidence of attenuation over the life cycle in the return to schooling. Evidently, the attenuation observed within each data set referred only to vintage or cohort effects, not to maturation per se.

Comparisons of successive cross sections give potential insight into distinctions between experience and cohort effects, but these comparisons are themselves confounded by calendar year effects. The problem is that conditions of labor demand vary through time. If several cohorts could be observed throughout their careers under constant labor market conditions, vintage and experience effects could more easily be distinguished. But labor markets do not remain stable and prices (wage rates) reflect the market conditions associated with the calendar year in which exchanges occur. Because of the identity that calendar year equals vintage plus years in the labor market, it is never possible to separately identify calendar year, experience, and vintage effects from time series observations of cross sections without explicit parameterization of these effects. But, although the need for explicit parameterization is recognized because several cross sections are observed simultaneously, and because some geographic detail is available to permit analysis of differences between markets at a point in time, the constraints imposed by explicit parameterization are less bothersome than they would be with less data. For example, Rosen [12] has demonstrated that if one is willing to pursue the theoretical implications of life-cycle human capital models in detail, then cohort and life-cycle effects are identified in a single cross section—this, despite the one-to-one correspondence between age and cohort.

First, observe relative wage changes within cohorts. For those who had entered the work force prior to 1960, black relative wages did not fall between 1960 and 1970.[11] In either cross section (reading down a column), black/white wage ratios clearly deteriorate as experience increases or vintage is older, and the rate of decline is more pronounced at higher levels of school completion. But the within-cohort changes between 1960 and 1970 are the mirror image of patterns exhibited in the cross section. Not only did the relative position of blacks improve as they added ten years of work experience, but this improvement was greatest at higher schooling levels. There are at least two extreme views for reconciling differences between cross-section and time-change patterns. One is that calendar year effects overwhelm the inherent tendencies exhibited in the cross sections. A strong increase in demand for black relative to white labor, coupled with an increased demand for more schooled labor, has this capability. In this view, unless the changes in demand patterns are persistent, more accurate projections of future changes should rely upon cross-sectional patterns. The other view is that changes within cohorts will persist and that the cross-sectional comparisons are dominated by vintage effects.

Table 4 rearranges the data of relative weekly wages to facilitate vintage comparisons. In Table 4, the row comparisons hold work experience constant and allow cohorts to change. The observed pattern is one of persistent cohort improvement in black/white earnings ratios with relatively larger gains accruing to more schooled workers. The data reported in Tables 3 and 4 are not consistent with either a pure life-cycle or a vintage hypothesis. The pure life-cycle explanation predicts that black/white earnings ratios will decline throughout the work career.[12] Between 1960 and 1970 they clearly did not. The simplest vintage model would describe black/white wage ratios as functions only of cohort—of time of entry into the job market. Other factors influencing income that vary after a cohort enters the market would be race neutral so that variation in them would not affect wage ratios. If vintage effects reflect secular change, either through rising relative quality of black labor or declining front-end labor market discrimination, then younger, more recent cohorts of blacks would fare better in comparison to whites than older cohorts, but the differences existing within a given cohort in 1960 would persist to 1970.

As far as career performance is concerned, it is difficult to conceive of relatively simple theories based either upon labor market discrimination or upon investments in skills acquired on the job that predict the observed patterns of increases within cohorts in relative black earnings.[13] Because of this, calendar year effects, i.e., changes in labor markets, emerge as a likely candidate for explaining the observed increases within cohorts. We attribute the rising wages between cohorts to differential vintage effects that favor black males. Our "best guess" for rationalizing the proskill bias in rising black/white wage ratios within cohorts is that most of the explanation lies in improving school quality. There is evidence that nominal attributes such as days attended, school retardation rates, teacher educational levels, and teacher salaries have been improving

TABLE 4   Black/White Ratios of Average Weekly Earnings by Years of Work Experience, 1960 and 1970

Years of Work Experience	Average Weekly Earnings		
	1970	1960	1970/60

I. All School Completion Levels

Years of Work Experience	1970	1960	1970/60
1–5	.702	.568	.134
6–10	.677	.573	.104
11–15	.641	.581	.060
16–20	.618	.587	.031
21–30	.616	.574	.042
31–40	.620	.574	.046

II. Elementary School Graduates (8 Years Completed)

Years of Work Experience	1970	1960	1970/60
1–5	.865	.703	.162
6–10	.802	.713	.089
11–15	.737	.724	.013
16–20	.717	.696	.021
21–30	.763	.741	.022
31–40	.740	.710	.030

III. High School Graduates (12 Years Completed)

Years of Work Experience	1970	1960	1970/60
1–5	.806	.714	.092
6–10	.791	.714	.077
11–15	.749	.682	.067
16–20	.750	.690	.060
21–30	.698	.648	.050
31–40	.690	.590	.100

IV. College Graduates (16 Years Completed)

Years of Work Experience	1970	1960	1970/60
1–5	.775	.655	.120
6–10	.692	.582	.110
11–15	.688	.582	.106
16–20	.675	.517	.158
21–30	.667	.421	.136
31–40	.522	.422	.100

throughout most of this century for black students relative to whites. (See Welch [17].) Possibly more importantly, black students have been switching to integrated, traditionally white-dominated, schools—especially colleges.

IV. ACCOUNTING FOR BLACK/WHITE INCOME DIFFERENTIALS

To sort through the impact of various factors on earnings comparisons, we have estimated regression equations separately for blacks and whites in 1960 and 1970. Our objective is to identify the most important structural differences in black and white wage equations and to account, insofar as possible, for wage differentials, based upon both observed characteristics and parameter differences. Individuals are partitioned according to our estimate of years of work experience. The independent or explanatory variables fall into four groups: (1) school completion; (2) geographic location; (3) government employment; and (4) years of work experience.

There are two variables for school completed. The first ranges from 0 to 12 and indicates years of elementary and secondary schooling. The second measures years of postsecondary schooling. If a person reports a positive number of years of college, the grade-school variable is set equal to 12. This "spline" function is linearly segmented to permit slope coefficients in the partial relation between (log) wages and years of schooling to differ between the first 12 and succeeding years, but the linear segments are constrained to join at 12 years. This specification allowing for nonlinearities in the returns to schooling is useful, since it enables us to discover non-skill-neutral effects of governmental antidiscriminatory policies or improving school quality. Tests of equality for the two coefficients within experience classes show that equality can be rejected in most cases.[14]

Geographic location includes yes/no binary variables indicating residence for the South, North Central and West regions. The omitted (base) class is the Northeastern region. Dummy variables are included if the individual resides in a standard metropolitan statistical area (SMSA) and if the residence is within a central city of the SMSA, so that the omitted class refers to residents of nonmetropolitan areas. A variable is also included indicating years in current residence, to approximate recency of migration.

A number of variables are added indicating whether the individual is an employee of the federal government and whether he works in an industry that is regulated by the federal government.[15] For those who neither work for the federal government nor work in industries regulated by the federal government, two additional variables are added. One represents purchases by the federal government as a fraction of value-added originating in the industry. The other is similarly defined for purchases of state and local governments. With these variables, we attempt to identify wage effects of governmental efforts to enforce antidiscriminatory legislation.

If black relative wages are affected by either working for, or being regulated by, the federal government or are correlated with the government's share of industry product, an argument that this legislation had an effect would seem stronger. Our presumption is that the federal government can have the most immediate and direct impact upon those firms most dependent on it.

The remaining class of variables describes a quadratic in years of work experience. Although regressions are computed within experience classes, these variables are included to allow for correlations within class between wages and work experience. The estimated equations take the form

(1) $$y = x'b_0 + d_1 x' \delta_1 + d_2 x' \delta_2 + d_1 d_2 x' \delta_{12} + u$$

where

$$d_1 = \begin{cases} 1 \text{ if black} \\ 0 \text{ otherwise} \end{cases}$$

and

$$d_2 = \begin{cases} 1 \text{ if } 1960 \\ 0 \text{ otherwise} \end{cases}$$

The dependent variable, y, is the logarithm (base e) of the weekly wage in constant Consumer Price Index (CPI) dollars; x represents a vector of the individual's characteristics as described in the above list of explanatory variables; b_0, δ_1, δ_2 and δ_{12} are the associated parameter vectors; and u is the omnipresent residual. Parameter vectors for individual groups in each year are

$$1970 \begin{cases} \text{white } b_0 \\ \text{black } b_0 + \delta_1 \end{cases} \qquad 1960 \begin{cases} \text{white } b_0 + \delta_2 \\ \text{black } b_0 + \delta_1 + \delta_2 + \delta_{12} \end{cases}$$

In this form, δ_1 summarizes parameter race effects and is simply the difference between black and white parameters in 1970. Similarly, δ_2 describes year effects and is the difference between 1960 and 1970 parameters for whites. The interaction effect δ_{12} allows the year differences in parameters to vary by race or, equivalently, it allows race differences to vary by year. This fully interactive model yields exactly the same ordinary least-squares (OLS) regression coefficients as would be obtained from the four separate race-by-year regressions. It does, however, give slightly different test statistics since in this pooled form the estimate of residual variance (σ_u^2) is based on the sum of the residual quadratics over the four groups, instead of being estimated separately for each group.[16] The advantage of this specification is that it simplifies tests of linear hypotheses for race and year coefficient differences.

Estimates of equation 1 appear in Appendix Table A-2. Although the statistics are interdependent, so that sequential tests risk incorrect inference, it is clear from inspection of the t-statistics for estimates of the parameters δ_1, δ_2 and δ_{12} that the fully interactive specification of equation 1 is too general in the sense that it allows for parameter differences that apparently do not exist. It is, of course, true that by imposing parameter equality either between races, between years, or both, estimation efficiency is gained.[17] The impression that estimates based on equation 1 are not efficient is strengthened when they are used to "account" for black/white earnings differentials. Too often we find a prediction of a small but statistically "significant" effect (of, as an example, increasing black earnings relative to whites resulting from declining differences in schooling) numerically swamped by a statistically "insignificant" effect (of, say, numerically large but insignificant year differences in schooling coefficients).

Several of the variables suppressed in the constrained estimates are statistically significant in the fully interactive model.[18] But in no case is a variable suppressed nor is race, year, or race-year interaction suppressed when its effect estimated in the fully interactive model is significant in more than two of the six experience classes. Even though the imposed constraints (among the six experience classes, there are 186 coefficients deleted from the fully interactive specification) delete variables that in the main appear insignificant in the fully interactive model, the joint test for significance clearly rejects the null hypothesis.[19] Although the computed F-statistics for the classes are not large by conventional standards (ranging from 1.2 to 2.6), the number of observations is simply too large to permit acceptance of the implied null hypotheses. This problem of an inability to reject hypotheses is common to large samples and has resulted in a number of attempts to weaken test criteria.[20] For our purposes, we note only that the constrained estimators are more efficient and whatever biases they imply are simply biases that we feel are necessary to clarify our estimates of factors contributing to increasing black/white ratios.

Results

The summary of our results and imposed coefficient constraints (suppressed variables) is:

1. Education—The Returns to Schooling

Income differences associated with schooling may vary by school level, an individual's cohort or vintage, his position in the life cycle, the general state of the economy, and perhaps even personal characteristics, like one's race or sex. It is important that evidence of the underlying nature of observed variation be provided since implications of the several potential sources of variance differ dramatically, not only for purposes of describing the likely course of future black/white wage comparisons, but for educational policy as well. For example, the well known cross-sectional deterioration of the returns to schooling with increasing age may be a life-cycle phenomenon that results from a negative correlation between the proportion of income devoted to two types of investment (schooling and on-the-job training) or it may reflect improvement in the schooling quality and home environments of new, more recent cohorts.

For the grade-school variables, the full interactive estimates suggest statistically "significant"[21] race interaction for all six experience classes, with returns to grade school for blacks being lower than for whites. Based on our estimates, the marginal returns to postsecondary schooling are actually higher for blacks in the 1–5-year experience interval. We find no statistically significant difference by race in the college returns in the other experience intervals. If school systems are not an effective means of increasing black incomes, it is clear that the problem lies at the elementary and secondary levels.

Both the unconstrained and constrained estimates of returns to grade schooling show a clear life-cycle pattern, with schooling being a less important discriminator of earnings for older, more experienced workers. In contrast, the estimated returns to college also indicate a declining life-cycle profile, but most of the change occurs between the 1–5 and 6–10 classes, and thereafter the descent is slow relative to the changing returns observed for grade schooling. We consider this an important finding and worth additional research. A number of hypotheses are consistent with this. Quite probably the skills acquired in college are more complementary with job experience than are skills acquired in grade school. Rates of obsolescence of knowledge could differ by skill level with less rapid rates at higher skill levels.[22]

Concentrating on the coefficients that measure secular movements, we found no trend in the returns to grade school for either race between 1960 and 1970. The full interaction estimates of wage returns to college indicate year interaction, with returns lower in 1960 than in 1970 in all classes. The associated t-ratios exceed 2.0 in absolute value in three experience intervals. This rise in returns to college in 1970 may be surprising to many. It was thought that the middle sixties could have been a critical turning point in the market for educated people. The comparatively well-educated postwar baby-boom cohorts were beginning in the last half of the decade to enter the labor market. This historically unique large increase in the relative supply of educated men combined with some factors reducing the relative demand for skilled labor could have begun the long-awaited decline in the returns to schooling. Using the Census data, this decline in the skill differential had not occurred by 1970. Based on results in the fully interactive model, we impose the following constraints: for grade-school coefficients, all year and race-year interactions are suppressed; for college coefficients, all race-year interactions and all race interactions except the 1–5 experience group are suppressed.

This last finding serves as a benchmark for an important paper by Richard Freeman [4] whose observations are from the published summary tables from the CPS. He claims that by the mid-seventies career paths for college graduates were substantially depressed relative to the past (notably, 1969). His point is illustrated in Table 5. Clearly, on the basis of these published tables, returns to recent college graduates have declined. Although Freeman argues that this observed change is (1) severe and (2) permanent, there is reason for skepticism. Freeman's analysis is restricted to the 1967–73 period and uses only the boundary years for calculations of change. Clearly, using these two years maximizes the decline in the relative income of college graduates. If, for example, 1967 is used as the base, the overall decline is much less pronounced. In fact, with an exception for the youngest age group, there is little evidence of any change at all.

The fact that cyclical factors may explain declining relative earnings of the young is added reason for skepticism about the permanency of "the declining economic value of higher education." It is generally argued that cyclical downturns offer a relative advantage to more skilled workers. This argument is founded on the presumption of "quasi fixity" or specificity of training on the job being positively correlated with levels of schooling. If it is, the argument goes that the more skilled workers will be stockpiled or hoarded by firms during periods of reduced labor demand with an eye toward recouping any short-run losses during future expansionary periods. The empirical basis for this argument (see Oi [10] and Rosen [11]) is strong, and if it is correct, its counterpart is that if a firm is in the process of hoarding, i.e., underutilizing, its skilled manpower, it surely will not be simultaneously hiring new (young) skilled laborers.

If the theory predicts that skilled workers with job seniority are less vulnerable to cyclic vagaries than others, it must also predict that new entrants to the skilled work force are more vulnerable than others. The large influx of college graduates that coincided with the recent cyclical

TABLE 5 Recent Returns to Education: Mean Income Ratios

Age	1967 HI/EL[a]	1967 C/HI[b]	1969 HI/EL	1969 C/HI	1971 HI/EL	1971 C/HI	1973 HI/EL	1973 C/HI
	Year-Round Full-Time Workers							
Male:								
All Races								
25–34	1.34	1.32	1.22	1.39	1.33	1.29	1.30	1.23
35–44	1.38	1.50	1.38	1.54	1.32	1.50	1.21	1.48
45–54	1.31	1.50	1.32	1.65	1.30	1.64	1.37	1.56
55–64	1.26	1.49	1.32	1.66	1.36	1.48	1.27	1.61
65+	1.12	1.72	1.25	1.42	1.31	–	1.32	1.37
25+	1.27	1.44	1.29	1.53	1.28	1.46	1.24	1.40
Female:								
All Races								
25–34	1.40	1.36	1.45	1.42	1.42	1.38	–	1.34
35–44	1.27	1.64	1.29	1.31	1.31	1.54	1.31	1.49
45–54	1.20	1.48	1.25	1.43	1.35	1.45	1.27	1.37
55–64	1.30	1.40	1.35	1.50	1.38	1.56	1.33	1.39
65+	1.43	–	1.27	–	1.44	–	–	–
25+	1.26	1.46	1.28	1.40	1.34	1.44	1.26	1.36
	All Workers							
Male:								
All Races								
25–34	1.38	1.33	1.24	1.33	1.42	1.27	1.37	1.19
35–44	1.37	1.54	1.41	1.87	1.36	1.55	1.27	1.52
45–54	1.35	1.53	1.36	1.64	1.36	1.66	1.37	1.56
55–64	1.33	1.55	1.39	1.68	1.43	1.59	1.36	1.57
65+	1.34	1.76	1.46	1.58	1.44	1.64	1.36	1.69
25+	1.47	1.47	1.52	1.50	1.53	1.48	1.49	1.41
Female:								
All Races								
25–34	1.22	1.42	1.32	1.54	1.40	1.51	1.35	1.45
35–44	1.30	1.47	1.26	1.37	1.26	1.47	1.33	1.35
45–54	1.33	1.54	1.41	1.54	1.44	1.54	1.45	1.45
55–64	1.51	1.58	1.58	1.69	1.57	1.71	1.58	1.66
65+	1.61	1.90	1.70	1.45	1.49	1.55	1.47	1.43
25+	1.58	1.51	1.60	1.50	1.61	1.50	1.60	1.42

[a]HI/EL is the ratio of high school to elementary.
[b]C/HI is the ratio of college graduates to high school.

downturn seems to have met a predictable fate. Whether their reduced relative wage will persist is uncertain, but the recent experience is a dubious basis for extreme pessimism.

The available evidence is that schooling, especially college, offers earned rates of return to recent cohorts of blacks that are comparable with those earned by whites. This appears not to have been true of earlier cohorts of blacks for whom returns to schooling were sharply lower.

The improved prospects of schooling as a vehicle for increasing black income has had its consequences on school enrollment rates. According to Table 6A there has been a remarkable upsurge since 1965 in school attendance for blacks at both the preelementary and postsecondary levels. College enrollments increased 55 percent, while enrollment rates for whites rose by only 15 percent between 1965 and 1974. Perhaps the most dramatic evidence of this shift is illustrated in Table 6B. During the 1970–74 period, the proportion of black males enrolled in college rose from 16 to 20 percent, while the corresponding proportion for white males fell from 34 to 28 percent.

The historical record suggests that convergent schooling levels have been an important source of increasing income parity for blacks. Whether this is in fact true, requires accurate estimates of the effects of schooling on earnings. Whether schooling will continue to be an important avenue of social and economic mobility depends very much on the future course of the income returns to schooling. If the economic value of higher education is falling, it is important that this evidence be presented. Evidence which "goes the other way" is equally important. This evidence cannot be obtained from summary tabulations without corrections for confounding factors. To interpret the recent experience, it is especially

TABLE 6A   Percent Enrolled in School by Age: 1965, 1970, and 1974

Age	Black			White		
	1965	1970	1974	1965	1970	1974
3 and 4 years	12[a]	23	29	10	20	29
5 years	59	72	87	72	81	90
6 to 15 years	99	99	99	99	99	99
16 and 17 years	84	86	87	88	91	88
18 and 19 years	40	40	44	47	49	43
20 to 24 years	9	14	17	20	23	22

SOURCE: U.S. Department of Commerce, Social and Economic Statistics Administration, Bureau of the Census.
[a]Includes persons of "other" races.

TABLE 6B   College Enrollment of Persons 18 to 24 Years Old by Sex: 1970 and 1974 (In thousands)

Sex and College Enrollment	——Black——		——White——	
	1970	1974	1970	1974
	Both Sexes			
Total persons, 18 to 24 years	2,692	3,105	19,608	22,141
Number enrolled in college	416	555	5,305	5,589
Percent of total	15	18	27	25
	Male			
Total persons, 18 to 24 years	1,220	1,396	9,053	10,722
Number enrolled in college	192	280	3,096	3,035
Percent of total	16	20	34	28
	Female			
Total persons, 18 to 24 years	1,471	1,709	10,555	11,419
Number enrolled in college	225	277	2,209	2,555
Percent of total	15	16	21	22

SOURCE: U.S. Department of Commerce, Social and Economic Statistics Administration, Bureau of the Census.

important that evidence be obtained of interdependencies between age profiles of income returns to schooling and general levels of economic activity.

2. Geographic Location

Even after adjusting for education, experience, and government employment, regional differences in black/white earnings persist. The South is distinguished by low wages for both blacks and whites. Further, compared to the Northeast, black/white earnings ratios are consistently lower in the South. In 1970, white male wages are 8 to 13 percent lower, while black wages in the South range from 15 to 30 percent below those for blacks in the Northeast. These black/white Southern wage ratios decline rapidly with experience. As we mentioned earlier, declining wage ratios with experience can be attributed either to cohort or life-cycle factors, and the South may differ from the rest of the country in both. Although we rejected year interaction for all experience classes, race-year interaction existed for the three classes with up to 15 years of experience. An interpretation that appeals to us is that there are differential vintage effects favoring black Southern males for the post-World War II labor market entrants. An alternative explanation is that the presumably more intense discrimination in the South against blacks takes the form of restricting blacks from occupations that have rising career wage profiles.

Disparities among the other three regions excluding the South are less pronounced. In the North Central region, for all classes with at least 10 years of experience, blacks and whites receive wages 3 to 5 percent higher than the Northeast benchmark. For these experience classes, the increase is independent of race and year, so that in our constrained estimates we suppress all race, year, and race-year interaction. In the North Central region, for workers with less than ten years experience, black wages were higher in 1970 than for blacks in the Northeast, but no white wage differentials existed between those two regions. Apparently, black/white earnings ratios increased in both the South and North Central regions relative to other areas. For these less experienced North Central workers, the main coefficient and year interaction is suppressed, but race and race-year interaction is permitted. The main coefficient for the West is suppressed for those with more than 15 years of experience. The estimates suggest that earnings of all persons in the West fell from 1.4 to 10 percent between 1960 and 1970, relative to wages in other regions.

3. Government Employment

After adjusting for schooling, experience, and location, employees of the federal government in 1970 have higher wages than others—a differential of 5 to 16 percent for whites and 15 to 30 percent for blacks. This premium for blacks over whites represented a 10 percent decline from an even higher differential in 1960. In fact, the black/white wage ratio did not change for federal employees between 1960 and 1970. The decline relative to the private sector simply notes the approximately 10 percent increase that occurred in the private sector. The variable for direct employment by the federal government is retained with race and race-year interaction, but year interaction is omitted.

Employees of regulated industries earn 8 to 16 percent more than those in the rest of the private sector. Employment in industries regulated by the federal government is included without race, year, or race-year interaction. Between 1960 and 1970, black employment shares of these industries increased, so that regulated industries contributed slightly to rising earnings ratios. The regression coefficients for the shares of industrial products purchased by the government are very large. They predict for whites that earnings in this form of indirect government employment exceed those of the private sector by one-third to one-half. Since we have similar results for another independently drawn sample,[23] we feel that the estimate cannot be reasonably construed as resulting either from purely random fluctuations or from peculiarities of these samples. Instead, we think they signal real industrial wage differences. We will not speculate here about causes of these differentials, but will note that we feel that industrial wage differentials represent a fruitful area of research about which too little is currently known.

Wage differentials between white employees of federal contractors and those in the private sector are also large, as are the estimated discrepancies in black/white wage ratios between this and other sectors. Where whites fare well, blacks appear to do even better. This, of course, is what we would expect from "affirmative action." The rub is that in these industries implied black/white earnings ratios fall at an average annual rate of 3 to 6 percent per year relative to the private sector (which was rising at about 1 percent per year). We cannot think of a simple and suitable explanation for this decline. Federal shares of industry value added is retained with year interaction being suppressed. All interaction is suppressed for state and local governments' shares of industry product.

4. Experience

All interaction is suppressed for the variables indicating years of work experience and its square.

Accounting for Black/White Earnings Differentials

In this section, we present our attempts to account for the black/white wage ratio as it existed in 1970, and for changes in the ratio between 1960 and 1970. Groups are specified separately by race, year, and work experience. For each (the logarithm of) weekly wages is taken as a linear function of the schooling, location, government employment, and experience variables described earlier so that (the logarithm of) the black/white wage ratio is the difference in the linear expressions and (the logarithm of) the change in the ratio is the difference in differences. For the ratio, R, we have

(2) $\ln R = y_1 - y_2 = x_1'\beta_1 - x_2'\beta_2 + u_1 - u_2$

and

(3) $\Delta \ln R = (y_1 - y_2) - (y_3 - y_4) = (x_1'\beta_1 - x_2'\beta_2)$

$- (x_3'\beta_3 - x_4'\beta_4) + (u_1 - u_2) - (u_3 - u_4)$

where x refers to characteristics affecting earnings with associated parameter vectors β. The subscripts are: 1 = blacks, 1970; 2 = whites, 1970; 3 = blacks, 1960; and 4 = whites, 1960. We are concerned with averages and assume that the x's refer to mean vectors for the respective groups. The estimated equations include intercepts, so that estimates are forced through the geometric mean for each group. Henceforth, we refer to OLS regression parameter estimates rather than their conceptual counterparts and omit reference to residual means, which are constrained to zero. In comparing equation 1 to equations 2 and 3 note that

$$b_0 = \beta_2$$
$$\delta_1 = \beta_1 - \beta_2$$
$$\delta_2 = \beta_4 - \beta_2$$
$$\delta_{12} = (\beta_3 - \beta_1) - \delta_2$$

Accordingly, equation 2 is rewritten as:

(2.i) $\ln \bar{R} - (x_1' - x_2')b_0$

(2.ii) $+ x_1 \delta_1$

where the first term on the right-hand side is the main effect of black/white mean characteristic differences, weighted by white parameter values, and the second term (2.ii) adjusts for race parameter interaction.[24] Equation 3 is rewritten as

(3.i) $\Delta \ln \bar{R} = [(x_1 - x_2)' - (x_3 - x_4)']b_0$

(3.ii) $+ (x_1 - x_3)' \delta_1$

(3.iii) $- (x_3 - x_4)' \delta_2$

(3.iv) $- x_3' \delta_{12}$

where the main effects of 1960–70 changes in characteristic differences, evaluated at 1970 white parameter values, is measured by the first term. The second adjusts for race interaction, the third for year interaction, and the fourth for race-year interaction.

In this form, note that the intercept race-year interaction coefficient estimates (with opposite sign) the growth in the black/white wage ratio not explained by changes in characteristics included as explanatory variables. This unexplained residual represents our estimate of skill-neutral relative racial vintage effects. One can only speculate, as we shall, about the factors contributing to the black relative income growth contained in the intercept. It is important, however, that if vintage effects exist, they are obvious candidates for time-related shifts in the intercepts of these wage-determining equations.

Similarly, notice that the year interaction intercept coefficient estimates time-related shifts in real wages of whites. Our estimates among the six experience classes show average annual growth for wages of whites ranging from 2.3 to 2.8 percent. We think these numbers agree with consensus estimates of real wage changes over the period. Similarly, we estimate that neutral wage growth for blacks exceeded that of whites by average annual differentials ranging from 0.62 to 1.08 percent. These estimates are summarized in Table 7, which also contains observed average annual increments in annual earnings and weekly wages for whites and for black/white ratios.

TABLE 7 Observed Growth in Earnings and Black/White Ratios with Residuals from Regression Accounting for Change, 1960–70

Average Annual Percentage Change	Years of Work Experience					
	1–5	6–10	11–15	16–20	21–30	31–40
Annual Earnings (Observed Increase)						
Whites	3.00	2.78	2.99	3.06	3.21	3.15
Black/White Ratio	2.67	2.25	1.75	1.29	1.09	1.09
Weekly Wages (Observed Increase)						
Whites	2.49	2.41	2.66	2.76	2.74	2.64
Black/White Ratio	2.25	1.73	1.06	0.75	0.70	0.68
Weekly Wages (Accounting Residual—Standard Errors in Parentheses)						
Whites	2.81	2.60	2.41	2.30	2.53	2.57
	(.23)	(.19)	(.18)	(.18)	(.13)	(.15)
Black/White Ratio	0.96	0.62	0.75	1.08	0.81	1.02
	(.39)	(.31)	(.24)	(.20)	(.15)	(.18)

Table 8 summarizes the spline function estimates of returns to grade school and college. These coefficients are given special attention because differences in school completion levels seem an important source of black/white wage differentials and because growth in black schooling levels relative to whites appears to be an important source of growth in relative black earnings. Locational effects seem even more important than schooling in the accounting, but the pattern of change vis-à-vis location seems more a result of black/white coefficient differences and of time-related changes in coefficients than a gain due to migration per se. In any case, black/white earning differentials exist in all regions, and the

TABLE 8   Regression Coefficients for Years of Schooling by Work Experience Classes (*t*-statistics in parentheses)

Years of Experience	White, 1970	Interaction		
		Race	Year	Race-Year
Fully Interactive Model: Grade Schooling Coefficients				
1–5	.138	−.046	.012	−.005
	(18.9)	(4.8)	(1.1)	(0.3)
6–10	.107	−.015	−.012	−.011
	(21.4)	(2.3)	(1.7)	(1.2)
11–15	.067	−.013	.004	−.004
	(14.6)	(2.3)	(0.7)	(0.6)
16–20	.061	−.016	−.002	−.004
	(13.9)	(2.8)	(0.4)	(0.6)
21–30	.058	−.028	.001	.001
	(19.9)	(7.3)	(0.3)	(0.1)
31–40	.047	−.019	.007	−.011
	(15.3)	(4.6)	(1.5)	(1.9)
Fully Interactive Model: College Coefficients				
1–5	.123	.039	−.024	−.006
	(25.0)	(3.8)	(3.1)	(0.3)
6–10	.088	.012	−.008	.008
	(20.9)	(1.4)	(1.2)	(0.6)
11–15	.090	.007	−.011	−.011
	(21.9)	(0.9)	(1.6)	(0.9)
16–20	.088	−.001	−.020	−.013
	(19.6)	(0.1)	(2.8)	(0.9)
21–30	.076	.009	−.004	−.021
	(20.2)	(1.2)	(0.6)	(1.7)
31–40	.074	.001	−.025	−.002
	(13.3)	(0.1)	(2.6)	(0.1)
Constrained Estimates: Grade Schooling Coefficients				
1–5	.143	−.046	–	–
	(27.6)	(6.9)		
6–10	.101	−.018	–	–
	(28.3)	(4.0)		
11–15	.069	−.015	–	–
	(22.7)	(4.0)		
16–20	.062	−.019	–	–
	(22.1)	(5.2)		
21–30	.058	−.027	–	–
	(29.4)	(10.7)		

TABLE 8 (concluded)

| Years of Experience | White, 1970 | Interaction | | |
		Race	Year	Race-Year
Constrained Estimates: Grade Schooling Coefficients				
31–40	.049	−.023	–	–
	(22.5)	(8.3)		
Constrained Estimates: College Coefficients				
1–5	.124	.034	−.024	–
	(26.9)	(4.2)	(3.8)	
6–10	.093	–	−.011	–
	(26.0)		(2.0)	
11–15	.092	–	−.013	–
	(27.0)		(2.5)	
16–20	.088	–	.023	–
	(23.8)		(4.0)	
21–30	.077	–	−.008	–
	(24.4)		(1.5)	
31–40	.074	–	−.024	–
	(15.2)		(2.9)	

income potential to migration is limited. In contrast, patterns of schooling coefficients and of changing race differences in schooling levels suggest that schooling continues to offer real potential for black income growth.

Table 9 summarizes our regression estimates of factors contributing to black/white earnings differentials as of 1970. In all cases, schooling accounts for a much larger part of the black/white earnings differential than does location, government employment, or work experience. Except for the first experience class, the schooling effect is approximately equally divided between the main effect of lower average completion levels and the effect of lower schooling coefficients. For example, in the class with 1 to 5 years of work experience, the coefficient, −.174, for the main effect of schooling differences indicates that when weighted by schooling coefficients for whites, the black/white difference in average schooling is large enough to predict black wages (approximately) 17.4 percent below whites. The −.49 is an adjustment for the lower returns blacks gain for schooling. This rather large racial interaction effect in 1970 must be considered quite tentative, since we have found it sensitive to model specification.[25] For the other experience intervals, the race interaction term reflects a lower return to black elementary and secondary schooling.

TABLE 9   Black/White Weekly Wage Ratios: Observed Ratios with Regression Accounting for Differentials, 1970

Variable	Main Effects	Race Interaction	Total
Class I: 1–5 Years of Work Experience[a]			
Accounting summary:			
Years of schooling	−.175	−.491	−.666
Geographic location	−.052	.077	.025
Government employment (direct; regulated and supply industries)	−.011	.013	.002
Experience correction	.010	–	.010
Total	−.228	−.401	−.629
Residual = .204			
Class II: 6 10 Years of Work Experience[b]			
Accounting summary:			
Schooling	−.137	−.186	−.323
Location	−.039	.031	−.008
Government	−.010	.005	−.005
Experience	.003	–	.003
Total	−.183	−.150	−.333
Residual = −.107			
Class III: 11–15 Years of Work Experience[c]			
Accounting summary:			
Schooling	−.123	−.154	−.277
Location	−.037	−.008	−.045
Government	−.011	.008	−.003
Experience	.001	–	.001
Total	−.170	−.154	−.324
Residual = −.137			
Class IV: 16–20 Years of Work Experience[d]			
Accounting summary:			
Schooling	−.127	−.185	−.312
Location	−.038	−.027	−.065
Government	−.009	.019	.010
Experience	.000	–	.000
Total	−.174	−.193	−.367
Residual = −.123			

TABLE 9 **(concluded)**

Variable	Main Effects	Race Interaction	Total
Class V: 21–30 Years of Work Experience[e]			
Accounting summary:			
Schooling	−.131	−.242	−.373
Location	−.029	−.068	−.097
Government	−.008	.020	.012
Experience	.000	–	.000
Total	−.168	−.290	−.458
Residual = −.046			
Class VI: 31–40 Years of Work Experience[f]			
Accounting summary:			
Schooling	−.139	−.178	−.317
Location	−.033	−.049	−.082
Government	−.006	.030	.024
Experience	−.001	–	−.001
Total	−.179	−.197	−.376
Residual = −.137			

[a]Log (base e) of observed weekly wage ratio = −.422
[b]Log (base e) of observed weekly wage ratio = −.439
[c]Log (base e) of observed weekly wage ratio = −.481
[d]Log (base e) of observed weekly wage ratio = −.491
[e]Log (base e) of observed weekly wage ratio = −.503
[f]Log (base e) of observed weekly wage ratio = −.512

Three characteristics—Southern, central city, and metropolitan resident—dominate the geographic location accounting in explaining black/white 1970 wage ratios. The Southern black wages are the single most important locational source of low black relative wages. We find that Southern residence reduces the black/white wage ratio from 3 to 13 percent. This differential grows monotonically with experience and reflects primarily differential coefficients rather than characteristics. The central city variables increase relative black wages by approximately 6 percent. The negative effect of fewer blacks living in central cities is overwhelmed by the positive differential favoring blacks. The metropolitan variable leads to a 2 to 3 percent reduction in the relative black wage. The net effect of all the locational variables is small in the first two experience intervals. In the 11+ experience groups, black wages range from 4 to 9 percent lower because of their locational distribution. The detrimental effect of predominantly Southern residence is simply much more pronounced for older workers.

The systematic earnings determinants with adjustments for race coefficient interaction predict a black/white wage ratio below the one actually observed for those with 1 to 5 years of experience. The discrepancy between predicted and observed ratios is absorbed by intercept-race interaction denoted as the residual in Table 9. For all other experience classes the intercept interaction term is negative, so that the regressions underaccount for black/white wage differences, i.e., relative to whites blacks earn less on the average than predicted by the regression equations.

Table 10 contains our summary accounting for 1960–70 changes in wage ratios. Here, patterns are confounded by interaction. The main effects, those based on changes in characteristic differences (at 1970 white coefficient values) consistently predict rapidly rising wage ratios, with schooling playing the leading role. Thereafter, the lower coefficients on black grade schooling and the 1970 increase in returns to college (where black/white completion differentials are large) take their toll. The most rapid increases in schooling occurred in the earlier decades of this century, but these are still sizable increases, especially for blacks.[26]

Surprisingly, vintage effects—time-based coefficient changes—are evident only for the income returns to college. Considerable data (Welch [15], [16], [17]) exist to suggest that the nominal characteristics of schools which are presumably indicative of "quality" have progressed steadily for whites and even more rapidly for blacks. There is in fact no strong a priori reason to assume that increased quality of schooling will necessarily alter the semilogarithmic coefficients of wages on schooling. First, under stationary labor market conditions, the model of investment in human capital presented by Yoram Ben-Porath [3] clearly makes this point. Second, as markets adjust in response to increased skills associated with increased schooling quality, the returns to education may decline. Finally, the firm-specific theories of investments in human capital on the job and the associated quasi-fixity hypotheses[27] all predict countercyclic movements in returns to schooling, and it is at least within the realm of imagination that the relatively "tighter" labor markets of 1969 in comparison to those of 1959 nullified longer-term tendencies.

Nonetheless, full skill-neutrality of vintage effects derived from secular improvement in quality of schooling is not intuitively obvious and we—at least one of us, who is on record as predicting the opposite result [16]—are surprised by these estimates, at least for grade-school coefficients. Estimates for college do show time-related increases in returns that are not easily explained without reference to vintage hypotheses or to changing patterns of colleges attended by blacks.

Locational effects for those with the least experience are dominated by race-year interaction—a result of rising black earnings ratios in the South

TABLE 10 Average Annual Percentage Increase in Black/White Weekly Wage Ratios, 1960–70: Accounting According to Regression Estimates by Work Experience Class

| | Main | Interaction Effects | | | |
Variable	Effects	Race	Year	Race × Year	Total
Class I: 1–5 Years of Work Experience[a]					
Accounting summary:					
Years of schooling	.91	−.40	−.22	–	.29
Geographic location	−.00	.11	−.02	1.02	1.11
Experience correction	.03	–	–	–	.03
Subtotal	.94	−.29	−.24	1.02	1.43
Government employment (direct; regulated and supply industries)	.12	.03	–	−.31	−.16
Total	1.06	−.26	−.24	.71	1.27
Residual = .96					
Class II: 6–10 Years of Work Experience[b]					
Accounting summary:					
Schooling	.76	−.19	−.07	–	.50
Location	.10	.12	.05	.50	.77
Experience	.01	–	–	–	.01
Subtotal	.87	−.07	−.02	.50	1.28
Government	.05	−.01	–	−.21	−.17
Total	.92	−.08	−.02	.29	1.11
Residual = .62					
Class III: 11–15 Years of Work Experience[c]					
Accounting summary:					
Schooling	.40	−.20	−.07	–	.13
Location	.03	.10	.05	.23	.41
Experience	.01	–	–	–	.01
Subtotal	.44	−.10	−.02	.23	.55
Government	−.01	−.01	–	−.23	−.25
Total	.43	−.11	−.02	.00	.30
Residual = .75					
Class IV: 16–20 Years of Work Experience[d]					
Accounting summary:					
Schooling	.23	−.26	−.09	–	−.12
Location	.04	.14	−.04	–	.14

TABLE 10 (concluded)

		Interaction Effects			
Variable	Main Effects	Race	Year	Race × Year	Total
Experience	−.00	–	–	–	−.00
Subtotal	.27	−.12	−.13	.00	.02
Government	−.00	.00	–	−.33	−.33
Total	.27	−.12	−.13	−.33	−.31
Residual = 1.08					

Class V: 21–30 Years of Work Experience[e]

Accounting summary:					
Schooling	.46	−.45	−.03	–	−.02
Location	.06	.18	.00	–	.24
Experience	.00	–	–	–	.00
Subtotal	.52	.27	.03	.00	.22
Government	−.02	.02	–	−.34	−.34
Total	.50	−.25	−.03	−.34	−.12
Residual = .81					

Class VI: 31–40 Years of Work Experience[f]

Accounting summary:					
Schooling	.13	−.34	−.05	–	−.26
Location	.05	.15	−.00	–	.20
Experience	−.01	–	–	–	−.01
Subtotal	.17	−.19	−.05	.00	−.07
Government	.01	.03	–	−.30	−.26
Total	.18	−.16	−.05	−.30	−.33
Residual = 1.02					

[a]Observed increase = 2.25
[b]Observed increase = 1.73
[c]Observed increase = 1.06
[d]Observed increase = 0.75
[e]Observed increase = 0.70
[f]Observed increase = 0.68

and North Central regions between 1960 and 1970—and are dominated by the South, where most blacks live. For whites, there was a net migration out of the central city and into the metropolitan areas and the South, but these were so small relative to black migration that almost all the net change in relative wages is caused by black migration and changing coefficients.[28]

Table 11 summarizes these coefficients, which are our "other things equal" estimates of increases in the earnings ratio observed between 1960 and 1970 in the South and North Central regions, relative to the Northeastern base.

TABLE 11 Race and Race-Year Interaction Coefficients for the South and North Central Regions (*t*-statistics in parentheses)[a]

Years of Experience	——— South ———		—— North Central ——	
	Race	Race-year	Race	Race-Year
1–5	−.017	.152	.075	.082
	(0.5)	(3.6)	(2.4)	(1.7)
6–10	−.097	.045	.141	.123
	(3.7)	(1.4)	(5.6)	(3.2)
11–15	−.158	.044	–	–
	(6.9)	(1.7)	–	–

[a]The sign of the race-year interaction is from the form described in equation 1. (Race-region interaction coefficients are included for reference.)

Between 1960 and 1970 our estimate is that the black/white wage ratio in the South increased by 15.2 percent for those entering the labor market in 1965–69, in comparison to the wage experienced in 1959 by those who entered between 1955 and 1959. The insignificant race interaction for the South suggests that the 15.6 percent rise for those with 1 to 5 years of experience essentially nullified the historically low relative earnings of blacks in the South. For those with 6 to 10 years of experience, there is evidence of growth during the decade, but the 1970 differential is 10 percent below that of the Northeast and Western regions. The black/white wage ratio also appears to have increased in North Central areas during the sixties for younger workers, so that by 1970 black relative earnings are higher there than in other regions. The year interaction effects described in Table 11 reflect a wage decline in the West relative to other regions that apparently occurred during the sixties. In most cases reduction in wages in the West effectively increased the national black/white earnings ratio, which shows only that a larger proportion of whites than blacks live in the West.

In sum, our accounting results for systematic determinants of changes in black/white wage ratios are:

1. Geographic location has the largest and most favorable effect of factors examined here. Locational effects are dominated by

changed earnings ratios within regions, and migration seems of secondary importance.

2. Schooling's role is ambiguous. Black and white completion levels are converging, but returns to grade schooling are less for blacks than whites. For the first three experience classes, with 15 or fewer years of experience, the effect of converging levels is dominant and schooling seems an important source of growth in relative black income. For those with more than 15 years of experience, changed patterns of school completion between the 1960 and 1970 cohorts result in predictions of falling relative wages for blacks. Black schooling gains, as measured by increases in number of years completed, exceed those of whites, but because of differences in returns, the value of the increased schooling of whites (as a proportion of wages) exceeds the estimated value of the schooling of blacks.

V. THE ROLE OF GOVERNMENT: A SUMMARY

There is by now a time-honored tradition in empirical analysis of treating discrimination as a residual: if an income difference exists and cannot be explained by age or schooling, it is "discrimination." It is regrettable that a concept that warrants as much attention as discrimination must be relegated to the "everything else" file in empirical research. Although no real solution is in sight, the advent of affirmative action does offer some interesting possibilities.

Throughout this analysis, we have tried to identify government's role in changing black/white earnings ratios, and were unable to find much of an effect. In the introduction, we noted that Census data are not well suited for this purpose. The data are adequate if one is interested only in the direct effects on those employed by the federal government or in regulated industries, because industry of employment is known. The problems arise in trying to identify effects of government on employment and wages in the private sector. The only method at our disposal was an indirect one—to focus on industries which supply products to governments. Executive Orders Nos. 11246 and 11375 required that large-scale federal contractors comply with the 1964 legislation (or at least supply evidence of why their attempts to comply have failed) or risk losing their contracts. While it is true that interested parties have legal recourse against any firm in violation of civil rights legislation, we felt that the implied threat of pressures on government contractors for "affirmative action" gave us our best chance to observe effects of this legislation.

Adjusting for schooling, experience, and location, white federal employees earn 5 to 8 percent more than other white workers, and this differential doubles late in the work career. In 1970, the premium for blacks was 10 to 15 percent greater than for whites, but this 1970 premium for blacks represented a 10 percent drop from that of 1960. In fact, the black/white wage ratio did not change for federal employees between 1960 and 1970. The decline relative to the private sector simply reflects the approximately 10 percent increase that occurred in the private sector.

In our samples, the fraction of all workers employed by the federal government declined slightly between 1960 and 1970. Although blacks are more likely than whites to be federal employees, the proportion of blacks so employed is falling relative to whites, and the drop is most pronounced for younger workers.

Employees of regulated industries earn 10 to 12 percent more than those in the unregulated private sector. Between 1960 and 1970, black employment shares of these industries increased, so that regulated industries contributed to rising earnings ratios. Earnings in indirect government employment exceed those of the unregulated private sector by one-third to one-half.

We expected large wage differentials between white employees of federal contractors and those in the unregulated sector. Where whites fare well, blacks appear to do even better, conforming to our intuition of the effects of "affirmative action." The rub is that in these industries implied black/white earnings ratios fall at an average annual rate of 3 to 6 percent per year relative to the unregulated private sector (which was rising at about 1 percent per year). The accounting results suggest that none of the government employment variables has an appreciable effect, although the estimated impact of indirect government employment is negative and dominates effects estimated for direct employment (also negative) and for employment in regulated industries (positive).

The Census data indicate that effects of affirmative action during the sixties were probably small. Yet, these data are far from ideal, and we were unable to perform more exacting tests. For example, we did not know whether an individual was employed by a large-scale government contractor. If so, how large was it? (There should be scale economies, since prosecution of a large employer affects more employees.) Is it unionized and what is the union's attitude toward affirmative action? Is it growing, i.e., would increasing the proportion of minority employees require explicit displacement of others? And, most importantly, how dependent is the firm on sales to governments? This final question includes both the government's share of sales and the alternatives available to the firm if the government were not to purchase its product. That is, we expect that defense contractors are much more dependent on governments than are, say, shoe manufacturers, independent of the fraction of a firm's output of shoes the government happens to buy. The judgment on affirmative action will remain in doubt until these questions are answered.

VI. EARNINGS INEQUALITY

Up to this point, we have concentrated on differences in mean earnings and have ignored other attributes of the full earnings distributions. In this section, we deal only with the distribution of market earnings, and are ignoring all nonlabor income. Although this limits any welfare statements one may care to make, this restriction was necessary for empirical and theoretical reasons. It is well known that nonearnings income is inaccurately reported in the Census, so that other data sets are better suited for a study of total income inequality. Moreover, the determinants of earnings are conceptually distinct from the factors causing dispersion in asset income. The incentives to save, inter-generational transfers of wealth, and the distribution of government transfer payments are crucial for nonlabor income. Ignoring this income probably leads to an underestimation of total income at both the lower and upper tails of the income distribution—the lower tail because of government transfers, the upper tail because of nonhuman wealth income. Also, the sample is restricted to non-self-employed males. Including the self-employed would increase inequality and impart a more positive skew to the distribution.

If earnings dispersion were similar for blacks and whites, and if dispersion in 1960 were equal to that of 1970, then an analysis of means would fully describe all changes. Yet, using some conventional statistics, Gini coefficients (Appendix Table A-3) or standard deviations of log earnings (Figure 1), black males' earnings are clearly less evenly distributed than whites' earnings. In fact, earnings of blacks are so much more dispersed than whites' earnings that variance among blacks exceeds total earnings variance even when the total is defined to take black/white differences in means into account.[29]

Lorenz curves for earnings in 1960 and 1970, shown as Figures 2A and 2B, offer a more complete characterization of the two distributions.[30] Although the black curves typically lie outside the ones for whites, indicating greater inequality, they cross in the upper right corner, showing less positive skewness in black distributions. We suspect that it is this concentration of income in the upper 10 percent for whites and a corresponding high proportion of low-income blacks that leads to many of the popular conceptions about racial differences in income inequality.

FIGURE 1 **Standard Deviations of Log (Base *e*) Earnings by Age and Race for 1960 and 1970**

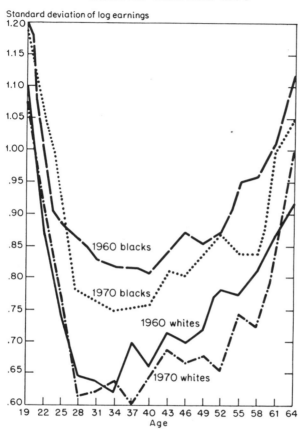

Standard deviation of log earnings

The crossing of the Lorenz curves means that a unique ranking of inequality by race is not possible. At some parts of the distribution (low and middle income), there exists more relative dispersion for blacks. In the top tail of the distribution, the relative dispersion of white earnings is greater. Those summary measures which weight the bottom tail of the distribution more heavily (i.e., log variances) will tend to rank blacks over whites in inequality. Other measures (e.g., coefficients of variation) could produce the opposite result. Since it has been used frequently by others, we use log variances of earnings as our measure of inequality.

To contrast earnings variance with differences in means, we present indexes of the degree of overlap in the black and white densities in Table 12. These indexes give proportions of blacks whose earnings exceed

FIGURE 2A Lorenz Curves for Black and White Earnings, 1960

Cumulative percent of earnings

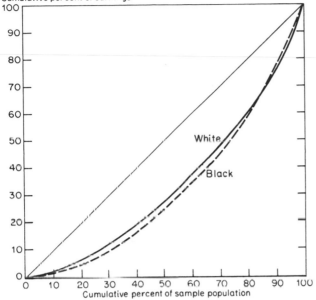

FIGURE 2B Lorenz Curves for Black and White Earnings, 1970

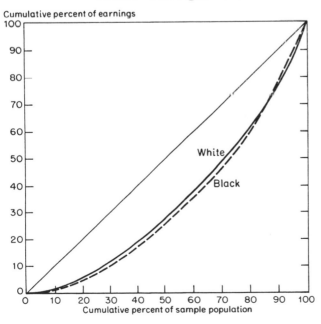

TABLE 12 Proportions of Blacks with Earnings Greater Than Geometric Mean Earnings of Whites and Proportions of Whites with Earnings Less Than Geometric Means of Blacks, by Work Experience: 1970 and 1960

Years of Experience	1970		1960	
	Blacks Exceeding White Geometric Mean	Whites Falling Short of Black Geometric Mean	Blacks Exceeding White Geometric Mean	Whites Falling Short of Black Geometric Mean
I. Annual Earnings				
1–5	.342	.187	.265	.150
6–10	.261	.139	.184	.111
11–15	.193	.110	.161	.089
16–20	.190	.133	.141	.098
21–30	.187	.109	.174	.102
31–40	.219	.124	.194	.122
II. Weekly Wages				
1–5	.366	.200	.234	.143
6–10	.269	.139	.185	.108
11–15	.203	.127	.147	.093
16–20	.181	.123	.147	.093
21–30	.199	.127	.156	.108
31–40	.189	.124	.190	.115

geometric means for whites and, similarly, proportions of whites whose earnings fall short of geometric means for blacks. If logarithmic earnings are symmetrically distributed, geometric means are also median earnings. In this case, our indexes of distributional overlap measure the proportion of blacks with earnings greater than that of the "average" white and the proportion of whites with earnings less than that of the "average" black.[31] The increased overlap observed in 1970 suggests that the story told by the convergence in means is not negated by movements in other parts of the distribution (i.e., the decline in variance). Indeed, the increased congruency of black and white earnings distributions exhibited in 1970 as compared to 1960 is additional evidence that the gains achieved by blacks are shared by a sizable fraction of the black population. The observation that in 1970 at least one-third of the blacks with 1–5 years of experience had earnings (measured in terms of annual earnings or weekly wages) in excess of earnings of the average white is a basis for at least guarded optimism.

A complete explanation of the greater inequality in black earnings is beyond the scope of this report, but we can point to some reasons. Recall that in the estimated earnings equation, the dependent variable is the logarithm of the weekly wage, defined as earnings last year divided by weeks worked last year. Our estimates, therefore, are precisely those that would result if the dependent variable were (the log of) earnings, and (the log of) weeks worked were introduced as an explanatory variable whose coefficient is constrained to unity.[32]

Assume then that equation 1 is written for the individual group with annual earnings as the dependent variable and with weeks worked included as an independent variable with unit coefficient

(1') $\ln y = x'\beta_i + u$

Variance (in $\ln y$) explained by the estimated equation is

(4) $\sigma^2_{\ln y,i} = b'_i V_i(x) b_i$

where b_i refers to the estimated parameter vector for the ith group and $V_i(x)$ is the associated variance-covariance matrix of characteristics. Consider the following partitioning of the vector of characteristics in equation 1'

(5) $x' = \{x'_1, x'_2, x'_3, x'_4, x'_5\}$

with

x'_1 = schooling (years of grade school, years of college);

x'_2 = location (North Central, South West, metropolitan, central city, years in current residence);

x'_3 = government employment (federal employee, employee of regulated industry, federal share of industry, state and local governments' share of industry);

x'_4 = experience (years of experience, years of experience squared).

and,

x'_5 = weeks worked (log of weeks worked).

Omitting the subscript, i, for the group, the part of earnings variance attributed to the jth set of explanatory variables is:

(4.i) $\sigma^2_{\ln y, V(x_j)} = b'_j V(x_j) b_j$

where b_j describes the parameter partition conforming to x_j, and $V(x_j)$ is the diagonal block in $V(x)$ describing the variance of x_j. Similarly,

(4.ii) $\sigma^2_{\ln y, C(x_j, x_k)} = 2b'_j C(x_j, x_k) b_k$

where b_j and b_k refer to x_j and x_k, and $C(x_j, x_k)$ is the covariance of x_j, x_k, so that (4.ii) is that part of explained variance attributable to covariance between x_j and x_k.

Results of this variance accounting appear in Table A-4. The two most salient patterns—the U-shaped career variance profiles and the higher variances for blacks than whites—hold for both predicted earnings or wage variance and for the estimated residual variances. The variances in log weeks worked have the same U-shaped age or experience profiles as log earnings. However, in preliminary analysis we find that more complete control of employment factors tends to eliminate the U-shaped character of earnings variances and produce instead continuously rising variance profiles.[33] If eventually confirmed, this would be a disturbing finding because nonmonotonic patterns are more powerful in discriminating among alternative hypotheses about sources of income inequality over life cycles. For example, Mincer [9] uses U-shaped variances to refute the stochastic and sorting theories of income distribution. The common theme of the chance or sorting models is that (proportionate) differences among individuals will emerge and persist, producing rising dispersion in income. Human capital theory can rationalize the initial decline in variances as reflecting a weak correlation between earnings capacity and the proportion of earnings invested.

In our measures of explained variance, the partial effect of weeks worked accounts for roughly one-half of all earnings variance.[34] With the business-cycle improvement between the decades, the relative role played by employment declined for both races but at a more rapid rate for blacks. We also investigated the distribution of weekly hours. Except for a slight increase at the youngest ages, average weekly hours remained essentially unchanged between the decades, with whites working about two more hours per week than blacks. The variance in weekly hours declined for black males but showed no trend for whites.[35]

Because each separately increases earnings, the positive correlation between education and weeks worked is another cause of earnings dispersion. Essentially, an elastic labor supply function blesses the same individuals with high wages and hours and spreads out the distribution of income. Because the schooling coefficients and the covariance between education and weeks worked decline, this interaction has its primary influence in the earlier experience intervals. Moreover, it usually has a slightly larger effect among whites and thus does not help explain race differences.[36]

Depending upon one's view of the underlying cause of hours variation, it may be preferable, especially for welfare statements, to partition that part of total earnings dispersion due to hours worked. If the hours decision is voluntary, reflecting the leisure choice of individuals, hours variance should be eliminated so that it does not confound the more fundamental inequality in earnings potential. A preferred measure of the variation in earnings potential would be weekly or hourly wages.

Alternatively, if the principal reason for the larger variance among blacks is that they are subjected with greater frequency to random shocks or spells of unemployment, then at least some of the hours effects should be included to measure the distribution of well-being. But in any case, so long as leisure time has value, earnings fluctuations resulting from fluctuations in time worked should not be viewed as equivalent to variance associated with wage differentials.

Even though employment instability is an obvious cause of inequality, it is important to note that the interracial differences are not due solely to such employment factors. Using the variance in either log weekly or hourly wages as our measure of inequality, the dispersion among blacks still far exceeds that of whites.

For all but the most recent cohorts, schooling is more unequally distributed among black males. There exists a clear secular trend for both races toward less dispersion in schooling and a narrowing of the differentials in variance between races. Combined with estimates of similar average returns to education within experience classes, this larger variance in black schooling would imply more black earnings inequality. However, proportionate variation in human capital as measured only by years of schooling completed accounts for little of the *difference* in inequality. The variance attributed to schooling declines as one increases the experience interval. The lower schooling variances in 1970 also lead to a reduction in inequality for both races.

The regional distribution of blacks, combined with the larger variance in black earnings between geographical units, is a dominant element explaining the higher inequality among blacks. The larger contribution of these regional characteristics in the older experience intervals reflects the widening between-region variance in black/white wages. Part of schooling's contribution to explained variance is captured via covariance between schooling and geographic location. This only summarizes what we have long known: average school completion levels are higher where wages are high. Because of stratification by experience, experience per se plays only a small role within each of the groups. Similarly, government employment is relatively unimportant, accounting for about 10 percent of explained weekly wage variance.

Two cross sections do not provide enough time-series points to analyze secular trends in income inequality. The business-cycle improvement during the decade, by contracting relative wage and employment levels, would alone force one to qualify any statements concerning long-term trends. For those aged 18 to 65, log variances in weekly or yearly earnings rose for white men but remained relatively constant for black men between 1960 and 1970. The lower between-race variance in 1970 was not sufficient to prevent aggregate inequality from rising.[37] For both races, the total variance is dominated by the within-age-cell variances. Seventy percent of the aggregate white variance consists of within-age-cell variance. This reflects less a steeply graduated age earnings profile for whites. Between-age-cell variance is lower for blacks both absolutely and as a proportion of total variance. During the sixties, within-age-cell variance fell, so the overall rise is due to the larger between-age variances and changing age weights. Using Gini coefficients or log variances, inequality increased at the younger ages for both races. After age 30, earnings inequality decreased within age groups. By and large, an identical pattern emerges by experience, except that there is no change in inequality during the earliest intervals for blacks.

Secular trends in inequality frequently reflect the delayed consequences of past birthrates as differences in birthrates among cohorts transform the observed age distributions. Because of the sharply inverted U-shaped characteristic of within-age-cell variances, aggregate inequality will be most sensitive to any changes in the weights given to younger or older age groups. Such changes did occur between 1960 and 1970 and they caused measured inequality to rise. In Table 9, the observed earnings inequality for each sample is contrasted with those that would result with age distributions of the other samples. Table 13 shows the effect of the distribution of men by age on earnings inequality.[38]

TABLE 13   The Effect of the Distribution of Men by Age on Earnings Inequality

Age Weights	Variance in Log Earnings			
	1960 Whites	1960 Blacks	1970 Whites	1970 Blacks
1960 whites	.7267	.9374	.7405	.8658
1960 blacks	–	.9353	–	.8656
1970 whites	–	–	.8126	.9223
1970 blacks	–	–	–	.9326
Uniform	.7656	.9762	.7823	.9087
Actual within age cell	.5755	.8100	.5524	.7656

Undoubtedly, the most fundamental change involved the replacement of the cohorts of the 1930s by those born in the 1940s. The 21–30 age group in 1960 consisted of individuals born during the depression when birthrates were low. These cohorts constituted the 31–40 age group in 1970 and we note a sharp decline in the relative weight assigned to the 31–40 group in 1970. The increased density of the 21–30 age interval in 1970 is, of course, a consequence of the high birthrates of the 1940s.

Compared to the 1960 age distribution, the oldest ages also received larger weight in 1970.

The larger weights given to the younger and older groups in 1970 are a factor leading to increased inequality for both races. If the 1960 age weights were maintained in 1970, the variance in log earnings would have been reduced by .07 for both races. It is interesting that the divergence in age from a uniform distribution reduced inequality in 1960 but increased it in 1970.

In contrast to the recent experience, future changes in age distributions will probably reduce aggregate measures of inequality. By the 1980 Census, the impact of the low birthrates in the late 1950s will be felt. Later still, the subsequent birthrate decline observed during the 1960s will further contribute to a lowering of measured income inequality by reducing the population share of high-earnings-variance young people. Differences between races in existing age distributions explain only a negligible amount of the race difference in earnings inequality.

Table 14 controls for the distribution of men by education level. As education levels rose between the decades, weights given to the lower

TABLE 14 **The Effect of the Distribution of Men by Age and Education on Earnings Inequality**

Age and Education Weights	Variance in Log Earnings			
	1960 Whites	1960 Blacks	1970 Whites	1970 Blacks
1960 whites	.7267	.9397	.7458	–
1960 blacks	–	.9353	.7759	.8942
1970 whites	–	–	.8126	.8951
1970 blacks	–	–	–	.9326

education groups fell. Because marginal variances by education levels differ, aggregate variances change with altered weights. Empirically, the within-education-group variances are negatively ranked with education at the younger and middle ages, but there is a tendency for this ranking to reverse at older ages.[39] The earlier ranking dominates, so that as education levels increase, average within-cell variances decline. Partly offsetting this is an increase in between-age-cell variances that occurs when education levels rise and the aggregate age earnings profile becomes steeper. If blacks in either 1960 or 1970 had the white education weights, blacks' inequality would have fallen, but only slightly. This relatively small net effect results from a reduction in the within-cell variance of .05 to .06 not being completely offset by a rise in between-cell variances. Blacks' inequality would have been 4 percent higher in 1970 if the 1960 black education weights had been maintained. There was no net change for whites over time as the reduction in within-cell variance is offset by higher between-cell variance.

Little is known about the causes of the difference in marginal variances by education levels. Some of it (especially the high variances for less educated males at young ages) is caused by larger employment instability. Variation in schooling quality at different schooling levels and ability variation among people completing that level are other explanations.

Because of popular emphasis on between-race differences, there is a tendency to neglect the vast disparities that exist within a race. But blacks apparently live in a world in which the pie, albeit a smaller one, is distributed in a quite uneven manner. In Table A-5 we have listed three conventional indicators of the economic well-being of blacks and whites—years of schooling, health status, and quality of schooling. Not surprisingly, the average levels are lower for blacks. But, *the absolute and proportionate variances are higher for blacks*. Human capital appears to be distributed more unequally among blacks.

The Census data obviously give a very incomplete explanation for the greater dispersion in black income. We would like to free ourselves from these data constraints and speculate about some of the root causes of these differences, but that is a project for another day.

VII. OCCUPATIONAL AND INDUSTRIAL CLASSIFICATIONS

Important changes in occupational and industrial distributions by race appear to have been in process by 1970. There are always elements of ambiguity in any occupational or industrial classification, so that our results can only be viewed as suggestive. Yet, comparisons of this sort offer the potential for an insight into the dynamics of race differences in economic success that cannot be obtained by reference to earnings alone. Suppose, for example, that the income gains documented in the earlier sections had been achieved alongside increasing black-white occupational disparity (segregation) and that blacks were increasingly concentrated in public sectors of the economy, whereas whites were moving toward private sectors. In what sense would we be willing to argue that we are moving toward racial parity? Would we be as sanguine about the viability of income gains achieved in this manner as we would in a situation in which black and white income, schooling, occupational, and industrial distributions were increasingly congruent?

The occupational and industrial classes we use are not standard. The occupational classes are deliberately specified to highlight race differences. Subject to a "manageable" number of classes, we combined the more narrowly defined Census groups with an eye to preserving as much between-group wage variance as possible. These combinations were also designed to retain most of the race differences exhibited in narrower Census classes in 1960. This procedure permits a simple summary of race differences, while preserving the opportunity to observe changes in occupational congruency between 1960 and 1970.

Table 15 presents 1970 occupational distributions according to ten classes, separately for blacks who were in the labor market by 1960, for

TABLE 15   Estimated Permanent Occupational Distributions in 1970 (Percent)

Occupation	Blacks in Labor Market by 1960 (1)	Blacks Entering 1960–69 (2)	All Whites (3)
Professors, scientists, artists	2.1	5.2	9.6
Service professionals	1.9	2.1	3.5
Managers	2.7	8.4	13.9
Skilled clerical and sales	1.2	5.4	7.3
Mechanics, foremen	11.1	12.3	19.4
Craftsmen, apprentices	5.0	10.7	5.6
Low clerical and sales	8.4	9.0	9.5
Operatives	30.9	31.5	19.4
Laborers, service workers	35.3	14.8	10.3
Unknown	1.4	0.6	1.5

NOTE: Index of Distributional Congruency
| (1) × (2) | (1) × (3) | (2) × (3) |
| .875 | .722 | .901 |

black entrants between 1960 and 1969, and for all whites. In recognition of life-cycle changes in occupational status, the observed distributions for the first two experience classes have been revised. In examining cohort changes for whites between 1960 and 1970, there is evidence of considerable occupational change for persons with up to 5 years' experience in 1960.[40] There was less dramatic evidence of 1960–70 change for those with 6–10 years of experience in 1960, and little change for those with more than 10 years' work experience. From this, we infer that although occupational change is often part of the work career, the bulk of this change occurs in the first few years after entering the labor market. To allow for this career-related change, observed occupational distributions for the two cohorts (experience classes 1–5 and 6–10) entering during the sixties are modified according to 1960–70 changes in occupation observed for the corresponding cohorts a decade earlier. This adjustment is given for the jth cohort by

$$f^*_{ij,70} \propto f_{ij,70}(f_{ij+2,70}/f_{ij,60})$$

where the index, i, indicates occupation, f^* is the adjusted, and f the observed, proportions of workers in the respective classes.

From Table 15, it is clear that the occupational distribution of blacks entering the labor market in the sixties is sharply different from that of earlier entrants. We computed an index of congruency to contrast the occupational distributions in 1970 of blacks who entered the labor market before 1960 to all whites and to blacks who entered the labor force between 1960 and 1969. Finally, we compared white to black entrants during the sixties. The index of congruency between the ith and jth groups is defined as

$$I_{ij} = \sum_l f_{il} f_{jl} \Big/ \frac{\sum (f_{il}^2 + f_{jl}^2)}{2}$$

where l indexes the occupation and f refers to proportions such that

$$\sum_l f_{il} = \sum_l f_{jl} = 1$$

This index is bounded by 0 (no overlap in distributions) and 1 (complete congruency) and is a first cousin to a simple correlation coefficient. The main difference is that the denominator is an arithmetic, rather than a geometric, mean.

This index for pre-1960 black entrants and all whites is 0.722. It is 0.875 for pre- and post-1960 black entrants and rises to 0.901 for the comparison of post-1960 blacks to whites. With this measure as our standard, the occupational distribution of black entrants during the sixties is more similar to the distribution of whites than it is to other blacks. We view this as important supplementary evidence of the extent of the gain in relative economic status of blacks realized during the sixties. Table 16 provides black/white indexes of occupational congruency within schooling and experience classes for 1960 and 1970. It further documents the improvement between cohorts exhibited in the earlier wage and earnings comparisons.

TABLE 16 Indexes of Black/White Occupational Congruency by Schooling and Labor Market Experience, 1960 and 1970

Experience in 1970	Years of Schooling Completed							
	—8–11—		—12—		—13–15—		—16+—	
	1970	1960	1970	1960	1970	1960	1970	1960
1–5	.979	–	.896	–	.874	–	.910	–
6–10	.925	–	.895	–	.816	–	.841	–
11–15	.893	.863	.815	.818	.753	.746	.844	.705
16–20	.873	.822	.803	.748	.738	.726	.827	.764
21–25	.871	.819	.774	.755	.735	.714	.832	.850
26–35	.864	.789	.793	.739	.693	.623	.779	.719

Our industrial classes are selected to highlight the potential role of government in eliminating race differences in wages and employment. Accordingly, there are two categories for direct governmental employment—one for the federal government and another for state and local governments. An additional two categories refer to aggregates of industries regulated by federal and by state and local governments. Finally, there are two classes that we hope measure indirect governmental employment. Assignment to indirect governmental employment represents an attempt to identify the role of governments as consumers of products of private industries. Unfortunately, we do not have data indicating if an individual works for a firm with government contracts and if this represents an important part of the firm's business. We do, however, have access to data showing government acquisitions by industry, and we converted these purchases into shares of the respective industry's value added.

When we observe an individual who is not directly employed by a government and does not work in a regulated industry, a random number is drawn from a 0–1 uniform density. If that number is less than the federal share of the industry's product, the worker is dubbed "indirect federal employee."[41] If the random number lies between the federal and the aggregate governmental share, the worker is an indirect state and local government employee. Otherwise, he "works" in the private (private-private?) sector. This assignment scheme is biased and conservative in the sense that black/white changes between 1960 and 1970 are understated. In defense, we note only that we have no clear alternative. We consider it likely that antidiscriminatory legislation is more easily enforced among firms most dependent on governments for sales. Based on variation among industries in government revenue shares, we attempt

TABLE 17 Estimated Employment Distributions by Industry for 1960 and 1970

Employer	No College			Some College		
		1970: Entered Labor Force			1970: Entered Labor Force	
	1960: All	Before 1960	1960–69	1960: All	Before 1960	1960–69
I. Blacks						
Private	71.2	64.7	64.4	56.7	59.2	62.4
Federal government						
Direct	4.0	4.0	3.2	15.9	12.5	7.7
Indirect	4.4	4.8	5.4	3.9	5.5	6.3
Regulated	4.2	4.7	3.9	3.3	3.2	3.5
State & local govt.						
Direct	1.1	1.7	1.4	5.6	5.0	5.0
Indirect	3.9	3.7	3.0	2.1	2.2	2.4
Regulated	1.6	2.2	2.0	1.8	2.4	2.3
Unknown	9.6	14.2	16.7	10.7	10.0	10.4
II. Whites						
Private	69.6	67.0	67.4	69.7	69.7	70.4
Federal government						
Direct	2.9	3.1	2.0	5.0	5.2	3.5
Indirect	6.0	6.5	6.4	7.8	7.2	7.2
Regulated	6.4	6.3	5.5	4.2	4.2	4.1
State & local govt.						
Direct	2.3	2.9	2.6	3.4	3.1	3.1
Indirect	4.1	4.1	4.1	3.0	3.3	3.5
Regulated	2.1	2.3	1.6	1.6	1.5	1.5
Unknown	6.6	7.8	10.4	5.5	5.8	6.7
III. Black Relative to White Shares						
Private	1.02	.96	.96	.81	.85	.89
Federal government						
Direct	1.38	1.29	1.60	3.18	2.40	2.20
Indirect	.73	.74	.84	.50	.76	.88
Regulated	.66	.75	.71	.78	.76	.85
State & local govt.						
Direct	.48	.59	.54	1.65	1.61	1.61
Indirect	.95	.90	.73	.70	.67	.68
Regulated	.76	.96	1.25	1.12	1.60	1.53
Unknown	1.45	1.82	1.60	1.94	1.72	1.55

to estimate age and schooling distributions by race among employees of firms whose product is produced for governments, in contrast to age-schooling employment distributions among firms whose product is produced for use in the private sector.

Table 17 summarizes our information of changes in industrial distributions. Employment shares by industrial group are given for blacks (panel I), whites (panel II) and for blacks relative to whites (panel III) as of 1960, and in 1970 for pre- and post-1960 entrants separately for those who had no more than twelve years of schooling and for the combined 13–15 and 16+ classes. The most notable change occurred for those who had some college education. The relative black share dropped sharply between 1960 and 1970 in direct federal employment (where 16 percent of all blacks who had attended college were employed in 1960, in comparison to 5 percent of whites). The most pronounced increase in employment shares of blacks who had attended college between 1960 and 1970 was in the private-private and the indirect federal sectors. The drop in direct federal employment shares for blacks accompanied a (somewhat less pronounced) drop for whites and suggests that at least for those who have attended college, the federal government is less of a "growth industry" than many would imagine. The increase in the private sector employment of blacks who have attended college would seem to be reason for optimism, although the more-than-proportionate increase in that part of the private sector whose product is purchased by the federal government suggests that this change may have been associated, in part, with some "arm twisting."

VIII. CONCLUSION

There are many ways of slicing up data, but whatever one's angle of vision, the improvement in the relative income of black males during the 1960s is impressive. Equally eye-catching is the universal sharing of these gains across experience and schooling classes. Those whose relative position improved most are more likely to be the most educated and the more recent entrants into the labor market.

We feel the data summarized offer a mildly optimistic picture for black relative wages. First, the most pronounced gains in earnings ratios are associated with increased schooling levels, and black school completion continues to rise relative to white levels. Second, younger cohorts fare better than their older peers. Whatever the cause of the inter-cohort differentials exhibited in 1970, if the experience of the sixties is a basis for prediction, wage ratios within cohorts will not decline as time passes, at least, not by very much.

Viewed from the historical perspective of relatively constant or deteriorating black/white wages, the experience of the sixties is encouraging. It is still important to note that although the patterns of gains found between 1960 and 1970 suggest that earnings will rise for blacks relative to whites, the rate of increase is likely to be slow. Among those who were in the work force in both years, 1960 and 1970, black relative earnings increased from 0.57 to 0.62. The aggregate ratio in 1970 is roughly 0.64 when the higher earnings of new entrants are taken into account.

If the most optimistic view is taken and the relative wage of new black entrants changes by the same amount (11.8 percent) in each new decade as it did between 1960 and 1970, and if the within-cohort growth continues at 0.04, we shall have to wait until the Census of 2000 before parity for new entrants is achieved. Full racial parity would take another 40 years, so that few of us will be alive to see it. Since the improvement in the 1960s was exaggerated by the business-cycle gains, racial income equality will probably take a good deal longer and could easily be partly nullified by a two or three percentage point increase in the unemployment rate.

Many have argued that the rise in black/white wage ratios over the sixties is the effect of enforced compliance to fair employment legislation of what is popularly known as affirmative action. While this issue is not addressed directly, we have compiled some indirect evidence that the economic impact of this legislation is probably overrated. Based on our work, the largest gains in black/white wage ratios have occurred in industries least vulnerable to federal or local government "arm twisting."

APPENDIX

TABLE A-1 Proportion with Zero Earnings

Years of Experience	White 1960: Education Group				Black 1960: Education Group			
	8	12	16	All	8	12	16	All
1–5	.179	.030	.021	.058	.273	.101	.046	.186
6–10	.083	.013	.007	.029	.120	.066	.009	.109
11–15	.022	.015	.005	.025	.099	.065	.039	.084
16–20	.033	.099	.008	.027	.109	.052	–	.088
21–30	.038	.018	.015	.032	.097	.069˙	.036	.087
31–40	.053	.051	.105	.059	.112	.087	.105	.111

TABLE A-2 Regression Results for Combined Samples of Black and White Males in 1960 and 1970, by Years of Work Experience[a]

	1 to 5 Years		6 to 10 Years		11 to 15 Years		16 to 20 Years		21 to 30 Years		31 to 40 Years	
Interaction	Full Inter-action	Con-strained Estimates	Full Inter-action	Con-strained Estimates	Full Inter-action	Con-strained Estimates	Full Inter-action	Con-strained Estimates	Full Inter-action	Con-strained Estimates	Full Inter-action	Con-strained Estimates
I. Schooling												
A. Grade school	.1376 (18.86)	.1434 (27.56)	.1075 (21.38)	.1006 (28.34)	.0566 (14.58)	.0687 (22.69)	.0614 (13.91)	.0623 (22.10)	.0578 (19.89)	.0585 (29.35)	.0466 (15.26)	.0495 (22.45)
Race	−.0457 (4.79)	−.0460 (6.91)	−.0148 (2.29)	−.0176 (3.96)	−.0134 (2.28)	−.0151 (3.96)	−.0164 (2.84)	−.0187 (5.24)	−.0279 (7.29)	−.0269 (10.65)	−.0188 (4.65)	−.0234 (8.28)
Year	.0115 (1.10)	—	−.0119 (1.65)	—	.0044 (.71)	—	.0021 (.36)	—	.0013 (.32)	—	.0066 (1.46)	—
Race-year	−.0045 (.34)	—	−.0113 (1.23)	—	−.0045 (.56)	—	−.0042 (.55)	—	.0007 (.13)	—	−.0115 (1.95)	—
B. College	.1225 (24.98)	.1237 (28.87)	.0880 (20.86)	.0927 (26.01)	.0901 (21.88)	.0920 (26.96)	.0882 (19.58)	.0881 (23.81)	.0757 (20.23)	.0773 (24.39)	.0744 (13.27)	.0744 (15.25)
Race	.0390 (3.84)	.0336 (4.25)	.0117 (1.42)	—	.0070 (.89)	—	−.0007 (.09)	—	.0089 (1.17)	—	.0006 (.05)	—
Year	−.0241 (3.13)	−.0243 (3.75)	−.0078 (1.18)	−.0107 (1.99)	−.0108 (1.64)	−.0135 (2.56)	−.0200 (2.79)	−.0233 (3.97)	−.0038 (.64)	−.0076 (1.51)	−.0254 (2.59)	−.0244 (2.94)
Race-year	−.0055 (.34)	—	−.0079 (.62)	—	−.0112 (.89)	—	−.0126 (.91)	—	−.0210 (1.69)	—	−.0018 (.08)	—
II. Location												
A. North Central	−.0223 (.82)	—	.0212 (.93)	—	.0068 (.31)	.0307 (2.56)	.0150 (.66)	.0366 (3.23)	.0376 (2.27)	.0510 (5.90)	.0350 (1.82)	.0474 (4.57)
Race	−.1064 (2.50)	.0744 (2.44)	.1299 (3.69)	.1410 (5.56)	.0360 (1.05)	—	.0055 (.16)	—	.0060 (.23)	—	.0127 (.41)	—
Year	.0412 (1.01)	—	−.0018 (.05)	—	.0370 (1.18)	—	.0174 (.56)	—	.0343 (1.46)	—	−.0115 (.41)	—

TABLE A-2 (continued)

II. Location (continued)

Interaction	1 to 5 Years		6 to 10 Years		11 to 15 Years		16 to 20 Years		21 to 30 Years		31 to 40 Years	
	Full Inter-action	Con-strained Estimates	Full Inter-action	Con-strained Estimates	Full Inter-action	Con-strained Estimates	Full Inter-action	Con-strained Estimates	Full Inter-action	Con-strained Estimates	Full Inter-action	Con-strained Estimates
Race-year	-.1308 (1.96)	-.0821 (1.66)	-.1281 (2.44)	-.1234 (3.20)	-.0530 (1.08)	—	.0446 (.92)	—	-.0291 (.78)	—	.0551 (1.22)	—
B. South												
Race	-.1454 (5.31)	-.1323 (7.71)	-.1226 (5.27)	-.1290 (8.88)	-.0921 (4.08)	-.0837 (5.48)	-.1257 (5.33)	-.0826 (5.59)	-.0733 (4.29)	-.0915 (8.24)	-.1089 (5.42)	-.1026 (7.63)
Year	-.0178 (.44)	-.0169 (.54)	-.0897 (2.65)	-.0970 (3.70)	-.1553 (4.77)	-.1580 (6.86)	-.1768 (5.20)	-.2008 (10.16)	-.2249 (8.94)	-.2110 (14.04)	-.1777 (5.89)	-.1985 (11.00)
	.0170 (.41)	—	.0063 (.18)	—	.0121 (.37)	—	.0685 (2.08)	—	-.0345 (1.39)	—	-.0020 (.07)	—
Race-year	-.1289 (2.02)	-.1521 (3.62)	-.0602 (1.17)	-.0453 (1.37)	-.0365 (.77)	-.0440 (1.69)	-.0096 (.20)	—	.0171 (.47)	—	-.0226 (.51)	—
C. West												
Race	-.0693 (2.32)	-.0441 (2.01)	-.0677 (2.61)	-.0651 (3.46)	-.0568 (2.30)	-.0369 (1.95)	-.0186 (.72)	—	.0117 (.61)	—	-.0082 (.36)	—
	.0454 (.86)	—	.0406 (.92)	—	.0369 (.85)	—	.0066 (.15)	—	-.0307 (.90)	—	-.0374 (.89)	—
Year	.0802 (1.71)	.0423 (1.23)	.0896 (2.33)	.0780 (2.77)	.1359 (3.75)	-.0988 (3.77)	.0278 (.77)	.0138 (.72)	.0293 (1.05)	.0461 (2.96)	.0552 (1.63)	.0516 (2.67)
Race-year	-.0619 (.72)	—	-.0229 (.34)	—	-.0875 (1.35)	—	.0444 (.70)	—	.0521 (1.04)	—	.0500 (.81)	—
D. Metropolitan	.0357 (1.60)	.0192 (.96)	.1092 (5.80)	.0966 (5.76)	.1698 (9.21)	.1387 (8.52)	.1728 (8.96)	.1467 (8.87)	.1850 (13.09)	.1693 (13.79)	.2185 (13.07)	.1905 (13.11)
Race	-.0211 (.56)	.0013 (.04)	-.0477 (1.44)	-.0161 (.65)	-.1175 (3.69)	-.0449 (1.95)	-.0735 (2.19)	-.0313 (1.35)	-.0950 (3.90)	-.0702 (4.00)	-.0750 (2.64)	-.0385 (1.86)
Year	.1293 (3.71)	.1663 (6.79)	.0524 (1.83)	.0755 (3.72)	-.0060 (.22)	.0566 (2.96)	.0263 (.96)	.0823 (4.44)	.0367 (1.76)	.0669 (4.81)	.0410 (1.62)	.1048 (6.43)

Table (rotated). Coefficients with absolute t-statistics in parentheses below each coefficient. Dashes (—) indicate empty cells.

Variable	(1)	(2)	(3)	(4)	(5)	(6)	(7)	(8)	(9)	(10)	(11)	(12)
Race-year	.0330 (.54)	—	.0663 (1.33)	—	.1473 (3.19)	—	.0861 (1.85)	—	.0489 (1.39)	—	.0843 (2.02)	—
E. Central city	-.0379 (1.65)	-.0555 (3.14)	-.0765 (3.79)	-.0686 (4.59)	-.0322 (4.57)	-.0942 (6.53)	-.0999 (4.81)	-.0946 (6.58)	-.0460 (3.07)	-.0576 (5.31)	-.0554 (3.20)	-.0478 (3.70)
Race	.0517 (1.46)	.1138 (4.09)	.0976 (3.18)	.0982 (4.25)	.1518 (5.07)	.1629 (7.53)	.1042 (3.37)	.1437 (6.56)	.1204 (5.31)	.1382 (8.38)	.1376 (5.15)	.1411 (7.18)
Year	-.0390 (1.08)	—	.0160 (.53)	—	-.0312 (.34)	—	.0160 (.55)	—	-.0253 (1.16)	—	.0183 (.70)	—
Race-year	.1705 (2.96)	—	.0094 (.20)	—	.0191 (.44)	—	.0731 (1.65)	—	.0411 (1.24)	—	.0102 (.26)	—
F. Years in current residence	-.0158 (9.48)	-.0112 (12.54)	-.0072 (4.40)	-.0083 (9.95)	-.0037 (2.35)	-.0039 (5.03)	-.0003 (.19)	—	.0002 (.20)	—	-.0006 (.67)	—
Race	.0064 (2.72)	—	-.0034 (1.52)	—	-.0005 (.22)	—	-.0001 (.08)	—	-.0010 (.82)	—	.0027 (2.21)	—
Year	.0041 (1.61)	—	.0000 (.01)	—	-.0004 (.20)	—	-.0005 (.32)	—	.0005 (.37)	—	.0036 (2.91)	—
Race-year	-.0010 (.28)	—	.0034 (1.01)	—	.0011 (.37)	—	.0013 (.64)	—	.0033 (1.85)	—	-.0020 (1.09)	—

III. Government Employment

Variable	(1)	(2)	(3)	(4)	(5)	(6)	(7)	(8)	(9)	(10)	(11)	(12)
A. Federal employee	.1037 (1.59)	.0522 (1.09)	.0865 (1.77)	.0755 (2.14)	.0737 (1.65)	.0829 (2.64)	.0523 (1.20)	.0612 (2.11)	.0838 (3.04)	.0666 (3.24)	.1596 (4.53)	.1584 (5.76)
Race	.0234 (.28)	.0663 (.93)	.0717 (1.08)	.1054 (1.86)	.0957 (1.58)	.0950 (1.86)	.1648 (2.83)	.1489 (3.15)	.1561 (4.01)	.1681 (4.96)	.1188 (2.39)	.1211 (2.75)
Year	-.1035 (1.07)	—	-.0124 (.18)	—	.0235 (.37)	—	.0180 (.31)	—	-.0392 (.94)	—	-.0115 (.20)	—
Race-year	.2034 (1.63)	.1120 (1.43)	.1020 (1.08)	.0559 (.90)	.0795 (.94)	.0920 (1.68)	.0433 (.55)	.0818 (1.60)	.1192 (2.04)	.0929 (2.31)	.0676 (.85)	.0581 (1.07)
B. Industry regulated by federal govt.[b]	.1534 (3.34)	.1694 (6.09)	.1218 (3.46)	.1394 (6.63)	.0949 (2.82)	.0870 (4.66)	.1354 (3.95)	.1191 (6.54)	.1211 (4.93)	.1148 (8.45)	.1631 (5.37)	.1447 (9.06)
Race	.0619 (.88)	—	-.0238 (.42)	—	-.0209 (.40)	—	-.0790 (1.44)	—	-.0455 (1.13)	—	-.1329 (2.90)	—
Year	-.0277 (.38)	—	.0135 (.25)	—	-.0162 (.34)	—	.0202 (.43)	—	.0044 (.12)	—	-.0198 (.46)	—
Race-year	.0350 (.28)	—	.1476 (1.65)	—	.0460 (.59)	—	.0166 (.22)	—	.0441 (.79)	—	.2157 (3.35)	—

TABLE A-2 (concluded)

	1 to 5 Years — Full Interaction	1 to 5 Years — Constrained Estimates	6 to 10 Years — Full Interaction	6 to 10 Years — Constrained Estimates	11 to 15 Years — Full Interaction	11 to 15 Years — Constrained Estimates	16 to 20 Years — Full Interaction	16 to 20 Years — Constrained Estimates	21 to 30 Years — Full Interaction	21 to 30 Years — Constrained Estimates	31 to 40 Years — Full Interaction	31 to 40 Years — Constrained Estimates
Interaction												
III. Government Employment (concluded)												
C. Federal share of industry product[c]	.3629 (4.97)	.4073 (7.17)	.2050 (3.14)	.2997 (6.53)	.2712 (4.29)	.3177 (7.29)	.1976 (3.06)	.2560 (5.88)	.2356 (5.03)	.2833 (8.33)	.2501 (4.54)	.3212 (7.53)
Race	.2424 (2.10)	.1754 (1.67)	.0962 (.94)	.0042 (.05)	.1410 (1.34)	.0622 (.67)	.2222 (2.11)	.1658 (1.79)	.2284 (2.68)	.1619 (2.10)	.5248 (5.05)	.4282 (4.48)
Year	.1029 (.88)	–	.1836 (1.99)	–	.0829 (.95)	–	.1111 (1.27)	–	.1014 (1.49)	–	.1862 (2.13)	–
Race-year	.4814 (2.18)	.6549 (3.63)	.2343 (1.36)	.4012 (2.85)	.1863 (1.22)	.3202 (2.64)	.3757 (2.48)	.4916 (4.08)	.3866 (3.06)	.5269 (5.12)	.2446 (1.53)	.5261 (4.10)
D. State and local govt. share of industry product[c]	.5973 (4.52)	.5188 (6.87)	.5938 (5.52)	.4210 (7.08)	.5440 (5.52)	.4423 (8.22)	.4030 (3.99)	.3760 (7.19)	.5004 (6.38)	.3938 (9.80)	.3874 (4.22)	.3583 (7.54)
Race	-.2275 (1.09)	–	-.3636 (2.18)	–	-.3717 (2.42)	–	.0660 (.43)	–	-.0867 (.76)	–	.0351 (.26)	–
Year	-.2227 (1.14)	–	-.1792 (1.13)	–	-.1039 (.71)	–	-.0387 (.27)	–	.2129 (1.90)	–	-.0856 (.65)	–
Race-year	.6024 (1.94)	–	.3398 (1.41)	–	.4918 (2.26)	–	-.1323 (.63)	–	.1675 (1.04)	–	.0004 (.00)	–
IV. Experience												
A. Years	.2361 (6.69)	.1871 (9.43)	.2111 (2.66)	.1020 (2.40)	.0522 (.42)	.0593 (.91)	-.0348 (.19)	.1104 (1.22)	-.0713 (1.64)	-.0140 (.62)	.0585 (.82)	-.0344 (.92)
Race	-.0390 (.75)	–	-.1465 (1.27)	–	-.2202 (1.20)	–	.1290 (.49)	–	.0479 (.75)	–	-.1553 (1.49)	–
Year	-.0366 (.68)	–	-.1357 (1.16)	–	.0975 (.54)	–	.0082 (.03)	–	.0953 (1.53)	–	-.0817 (.82)	–

Race-year	-.0916 (1.13)	.1117 (.65)	—	—	.2813 (1.07)	.3172 (.87)	—	-.0484 (.53)	—	.0911 (.61)	—
B. Years squared	-.0220 (3.80)	-.0156 (4.86)	-.0040 (1.52)	-.0015 (.61)	-.0002 (.26)	.0013 (.25)	-.0029 (1.15)	.0014 (1.65)	.0002 (.56)	-.0009 (.92)	.0004 (.77)
Race	.0048 (.56)	—	—	—	.0084 (1.19)	-.0038 (.53)	—	-.0010 (.82)	—	.0022 (1.52)	—
Year	.0035 (.40)	—	—	—	-.0038 (.56)	-.0004 (.06)	—	-.0018 (1.52)	—	.0012 (.81)	—
Race-year	.0152 (1.16)	-.0075 (.70)	—	—	-.0105 (1.04)	-.0086 (.85)	—	.0009 (.52)	—	-.0014 (.66)	—
V. Intercept											
Intercept	2.6091 (25.20)	2.5998 (40.13)	3.2324 (18.91)	3.7070 (8.75)	3.7615 (4.47)	4.5404 (2.91)	3.2696 (4.01)	5.2380 (9.29)	4.5490 (15.85)	3.5146 (2.60)	5.0960 (7.70)
Race	.2661 (2.03)	.2043 (2.59)	-.1072 (1.97)	-.1571 (3.40)	1.5076 (1.11)	-1.1697 (.50)	-.1227 (2.84)	-.5516 (.68)	-.0463 (1.54)	2.4904 (1.36)	-.1371 (4.23)
Year	-.3411 (2.41)	-.2818 (12.08)	-.2600 (13.65)	-.2418 (13.45)	-.8809 (.75)	-.2770 (.12)	-.2308 (13.12)	-1.4538 (1.85)	-.2535 (19.28)	1.0677 (.58)	-.2574 (16.66)
Race-year	-.0393 (.21)	-.0962 (2.47)	-.0620 (2.02)	-.0754 (3.16)	-1.5944 (1.18)	-3.0981 (.95)	-.1078 (5.52)	.4737 (.41)	-.0815 (5.44)	-1.5005 (.57)	-.1015 (5.73)
R^2	.36	.36	.39	.39	.39	.38	.38	.36	.35	.34	.33
Variance of estimate	.5096	.5105	.3428	.2965	.2964	.2955	.2957	.3232	.3234	.3641	.3649
Degrees of freedom	17,613	17,641	17,442	16,722	16,722	16,752	16,609	31,254	31,287	24,899	24,932

NOTE: Observations are of individuals. The dependent variable is log, base e, of weekly wages.

[a] These are estimates of equation 1 in the text.

[b] Industries regulated by the federal government include railroads and railway express service, trucking service, water transportation, air transportation, radio broadcasting and television, telephone (wire and radio), and telegraph and miscellaneous communication services.

[c] The government share of the industry product is the ratio of government purchases from the industry to value added originating in the industry. Data for these calculations were obtained from BLS Bulletin 1972; resultant shares are available on request from the authors.

TABLE A-3   Gini Coefficients—Male Earnings

Samples	All	Ages 18–25	26–35	36–45	46–55	56–65
1960 whites	.360	.445	.268	.296	.338	.437
1960 blacks	.435	.556	.370	.363	.392	.506
1960 combined	.423	.513	.346	.363	.399	.495
1970 whites	.376	.477	.276	.288	.325	.434
1970 blacks	.440	.570	.344	.357	.386	.493
1970 combined	.424	.528	.321	.347	.381	.477
Zero Earners Excluded						
1960 whites	.324	.388	.251	.280	.315	.347
1960 blacks	.353	.434	.314	.312	.329	.365
1960 combined	.367	.422	.310	.333	.358	.388
1970 whites	.323	.419	.248	.270	.293	.327
1970 blacks	.346	.441	.285	.302	.313	.343
1970 combined	.359	.432	.283	.312	.332	.359

TABLE A-4 **Explained Variance Summary**
(σ^2 = variance in annual earnings; σ_1^2 = explained variance in annual earnings; σ_2^2 = explained variance in weekly wages)

	Whites 1970				Whites 1960			
	(1)	(2)	(3)	(4)	(1)	(2)	(3)	(4)

I. Experience Class, 1–5 Years

$\sigma^2 = .773; \sigma_1^2 = .273; \sigma_2^2 = .773$ $\sigma^2 = .857; \sigma_1^2 = .393; \sigma_2^2 = .110$

	(1)	(2)	(3)	(4)	(1)	(2)	(3)	(4)
Schooling (1)	.040	.004	.003	.035	.054	.010	.003	.064
Location (2)		.008	.000	.007		.016	.001	.016
Government employment (3)			.006	.002			.006	.004
Weeks worked (4)				.138				.187

II. Experience Class, 6–10 Years

$\sigma^2 = .481; \sigma_1^2 = .129; \sigma_2^2 = .048$ $\sigma^2 = .533; \sigma_1^2 = .193; \sigma_2^2 = .063$

	(1)	(2)	(3)	(4)	(1)	(2)	(3)	(4)
Schooling (1)	.030	.003	.001	.018	.036	.006	.002	.029
Location (2)		.007	.000	.002		.012	.001	.005
Government employment (3)			.004	.000			.004	.001
Weeks worked (4)				.058				.093

III. Experience Class, 11–15 Years

$\sigma^2 = .370; \sigma_1^2 = .070; \sigma_2^2 = .031$ $\sigma^2 = .397; \sigma_1^2 = .126; \sigma_2^2 = .044$

	(1)	(2)	(3)	(4)	(1)	(2)	(3)	(4)
Schooling (1)	.016	.002	.001	.005	.022	.005	.001	.013
Location (2)		.007	.000	.001		.012	.001	.002
Government employment (3)			.004	−.000			.004	−.001
Weeks worked (4)				.034				.067

IV. Experience Class, 16–20 Years

$\sigma^2 = .419; \sigma_1^2 = .077; \sigma_2^2 = .030$ $\sigma^2 = .389; \sigma_1^2 = .125; \sigma_2^2 = .044$

	(1)	(2)	(3)	(4)	(1)	(2)	(3)	(4)
Schooling (1)	.016	.003	.000	.007	.021	.006	.000	.011
Location (2)		.008	.000	.002		.013	.001	.003
Government employment (3)			.003	−.001			.003	−.000
Weeks worked (4)				.039				.066

V. Experience Class, 21–30 Years

$\sigma^2 = .413; \sigma_1^2 = .083; \sigma_2^2 = .034$ $\sigma^2 = .463; \sigma_1^2 = .149; \sigma_2^2 = .047$

	(1)	(2)	(3)	(4)	(1)	(2)	(3)	(4)
Schooling (1)	.017	.003	.000	.006	.020	.007	−.000	.013
Location (2)		.010	.000	.002		.016	.000	.004
Government employment (3)			.003	−.001			.003	−.001
Weeks worked (4)				.043				.085

VI. Experience Class, 31–40 Years

$\sigma^2 = .422; \sigma_1^2 = .110; \sigma_2^2 = .038$ $\sigma^2 = .535; \sigma_1^2 = .177; \sigma_2^2 = .053$

	(1)	(2)	(3)	(4)	(1)	(2)	(3)	(4)
Schooling (1)	.016	.004	.001	.005	.016	.007	−.000	.012
Location (2)		.012	.000	.003		.024	.001	.007
Government employment (3)			.010	.002			.018	−.001
Weeks worked (4)				.064				.105

TABLE A-4 (concluded)

	Blacks 1970				Blacks 1960			
	(1)	(2)	(3)	(4)	(1)	(2)	(3)	(4)

I. Experience Class, 1–5 Years

$\sigma^2 = 1.130;\ \sigma_1^2 = .430;\ \sigma_2^2 = .090$ (Blacks 1970) $\qquad \sigma^2 = 1.187;\ \sigma_1^2 = .591;\ \sigma_2^2 = .206$ (Blacks 1960)

	(1)	(2)	(3)	(4)	(1)	(2)	(3)	(4)
Schooling (1)	.030	.008	.003	.041	.056	.041	.009	.037
Location (2)		.020	.001	.012		.060	.009	.005
Government employment (3)			.008	.005			.015	.001
Weeks worked (4)				.268				.327

II. Experience Class, 6–10 Years

$\sigma^2 = .730;\ \sigma_1^2 = .256;\ \sigma_2^2 = .094$ $\qquad \sigma^2 = .819;\ \sigma_1^2 = .398;\ \sigma_2^2 = .150$

	(1)	(2)	(3)	(4)	(1)	(2)	(3)	(4)
Schooling (1)	.036	.014	.003	.021	.051	.036	.007	.023
Location (2)		.034	−.000	.003		.043	.005	.013
Government employment (3)			.004	.001			.008	.001
Weeks worked (4)				.135				.207

III. Experience Class, 11–15 Years

$\sigma^2 = .551;\ \sigma_1^2 = .148;\ \sigma_2^2 = .064$ $\qquad \sigma^2 = .695;\ \sigma_1^2 = .314;\ \sigma_2^2 = .117$

	(1)	(2)	(3)	(4)	(1)	(2)	(3)	(4)
Schooling (1)	.018	.010	.002	.006	.025	.023	.005	.011
Location (2)		.028	.000	.002		.048	.005	.002
Government employment (3)			.004	−.000			.010	.002
Weeks worked (4)				.077				.181

IV. Experience Class, 16–20 Years

$\sigma^2 = .536;\ \sigma_1^2 = .149;\ \sigma_2^2 = .069$ $\qquad \sigma^2 = .608;\ \sigma_1^2 = .273;\ \sigma_2^2 = .116$

	(1)	(2)	(3)	(4)	(1)	(2)	(3)	(4)
Schooling (1)	.013	.011	.002	.004	.019	.022	.004	.010
Location (2)		.036	.001	.003		.051	.007	.005
Government employment (3)			.006	−.000			.013	.002
Weeks worked (4)				.074				.140

V. Experience Class, 21–30 Years

$\sigma^2 = .555;\ \sigma_1^2 = .163;\ \sigma_2^2 = .073$ $\qquad \sigma^2 = .648;\ \sigma_1^2 = .286;\ \sigma_2^2 = .108$

	(1)	(2)	(3)	(4)	(1)	(2)	(3)	(4)
Schooling (1)	.009	.012	.002	.003	.011	.017	.003	.008
Location (2)		.043	.002	.003		.057	.007	.001
Government employment (3)			.006	.001			.014	.001
Weeks worked (4)				.083				.168

VI. Experience Class, 31–40 Years

$\sigma^2 = .632;\ \sigma_1^2 = .192;\ \sigma_2^2 = .088$ $\qquad \sigma^2 = .734;\ \sigma_1^2 = .322;\ \sigma_2^2 = .131$

	(1)	(2)	(3)	(4)	(1)	(2)	(3)	(4)
Schooling (1)	.007	.012	.002	.004	.007	.016	.002	.006
Location (2)		.053	.003	.005		.077	.011	.009
Government employment (3)			.010	.002			.018	−.001
Weeks worked (4)				.093				.176

NOTE: In the first experience class, experience accounts for 2.9 to 6.5 percent of explained variance, and the covariance between experience and weeks worked accounts for 2.5 to 3.8 percent. In other classes, experience within intervals accounted for little wage variation.

TABLE A-5   Measures of Variation in Alternative Indicators of Well-Being

Measure	Schooling[a] Experience Group					
	1–5	6–10	11–15	16–20	21–30	31–40
Variance 1960 blacks	7.056	10.86	11.7	12.50	13.62	12.7
Variance 1960 whites	7.475	9.29	9.71	9.67	10.19	10.0
Coefficient of variation 1960 blacks	.2070	.2774	.3052	.3322	.3937	.440
Coefficient of variation 1960 whites	.1889	.2180	.2326	.2399	.2585	.285

Measure	Health Status[b] Blacks	Whites
c.v. Proportion in good health	.7895	.7106
c.v. Length of latest health limitation	.8231	.6098

Characteristic	Selected 12-Grade School Characteristics[c]			
	Blacks		Whites	
	Mean	S.D.	Mean	S.D.
Teachers' experience	11.66	3.21	10.72	3.10
Quality of teachers' college	6.74	.103	.741	.046
Teachers' verbal ability	21.2	2.56	23.1	1.48
Teachers' salary (dollars)	6464.8	1494	6745.6	1210
Pupil/teacher ratio	25.8	12.1	23.1	8.65
Days in session	179.9	4.14	179.4	4.03
Attendance (percent)	91.4	3.67	94.3	2.38
Library volumes per student	4.65	3.99	5.65	4.01

[a]U.S. Census.
[b]1966 Survey of Economic Opportunity data. For derivation, see James P. Smith, "Life Cycle Allocation of Time in a Family Context," Ph.D. dissertation, University of Chicago, 1972.
[c]James S. Coleman et al., *Equality of Educational Opportunity*, OE 38001, U.S. Office of Education, 1966.

NOTES

1. This paper is in part a compilation of two earlier papers: "Black/White Wage Ratios: 1960–1970" and "Inequality: Race Differences in the Distribution of Earnings." It contains a good deal of additional supporting evidence and a shorter version was issued as a final report to the Department of Labor by the Rand Corporation. (See R-1666, June 1975.)
2. See his *Economics of Discrimination*, page 140. Becker simply used income by occupation data in 1940 to weight the occupations. Therefore, a secular increase in his index would imply that blacks were moving more rapidly than whites into occupations that had high wages in 1940.
3. See James Gwartney [5].
4. Before 1965, the Current Population Survey (CPS) did not provide a black/white income ratio. Because other nonwhites have higher incomes than blacks do, the nonwhite to white income ratio exceeds the ratio of black to white incomes. Fortunately, for an analysis of secular trends the two ratios appear to move together. Therefore, the ratio of nonwhite to white income provides an accurate picture of the long-term trends in black/white income ratios.
5. As assumed from Table 3:

SCHOOL LEAVING AGE

Schooling level (years)	0–7	8	9–11	12	13–15	16	17 and above
Age	14	16	18	20	23	25	28

6. Weekly wages are earnings last year divided by weeks worked last year. The average weekly wage used here is total earnings of all persons divided by total weeks worked, i.e., individual earnings per week are weighted by weeks worked.
7. The sole exception is for weekly wages of elementary school graduates for the cohort with 31 to 40 years of work experience in 1970.
8. We have also excluded males with zero earnings from this study. Table A-1 of the Appendix describes the left-out group.
9. In particular, the recently available 1-in-100 Public Use Samples contain state of residence identification, so that these data on wages and weeks worked can be merged with other sources which indicate state-specific levels of economic activity.
10. Available evidence of the distribution of cyclic effects refers to employment rather than wages (see Kosters and Welch [8] and Kalachek [7]). Yet it is hard to conceive of a "theory" of wage flexibility that predicts negative correlation between employment and wage changes.
11. A number of "secondary labor market" hypotheses have been put forward to describe earnings and job progress over working careers. The presumption underlying these theories is that some jobs, those dubbed "secondary," are dead-end, with little prospect for career progress in wages and job status, while other jobs facilitate upward mobility. Persons who seem likely candidates for secondary careers are disproportionately black and less schooled. The observed relative wage performance of blacks during the sixties is not consistent with these theories.
12. A life-cycle argument has been suggested in Jacob Mincer's work [9]. The observed convergence in relative wages by skill level could be rationalized in Mincer's human capital model by a negative correlation between initial postschool earning capacity and the proportion of time spent in job-related investment activities.
13. One interesting possibility is that job markets are less discriminatory than schools, so that, relative to whites, blacks have a comparative advantage in acquiring skills on the job rather than in school.

14. Degrees of freedom in each of the regressions are large, so that the normal approximation can be used. In the 24 regressions (6 experience classes, 2 races, and 2 years) the absolute value of the computed t-statistic exceeds 1.96 in 19 of 24 cases, with the largest calculated value being 7.2 for blacks in 1970 with 21–30 years of experience. Exceptions include: (1) blacks 1970, 6–10 years of experience ($|t| = 0.6$); (2) whites 1960, 6–10 years ($|t| = 1.8$); (3) whites 1960, 16–20 years ($|t| = 1.5$); (4) whites 1960, 31–40 years ($|t| = 0.4$); and (5) blacks 1960, 31–40 years ($|t| = 1.4$).

15. In preliminary analysis a variable was also included to indicate whether an individual was an employee of state and local government, and this variable was permitted to interact with the one denoting Southern residence. No consistent pattern emerged, and the variable for employment by state and local governments was deleted in subsequent estimates.

16. If Q_i is the sum of squared residuals for the ith group and df_i is the associated degrees of freedom, then the estimate of residual variance within group is $S_i^2 = Q_i/df_i$ and for the pooled sample it is $S^2 = \Sigma Q_i/\Sigma df_i$.

17. The potential loss is the bias entailed by incorrect constraints.

18. Of the 186 coefficients deleted in constrained estimation, 12 have associated t-statistics exceeding 2.0 (in absolute value) computed from the fully interactive equations.

19. The computed F-statistics are:

Experience class = 1–5 6–10 11–15 16–20 21–30 31–40
F = 1.95 1.92 1.18 1.36 1.51 2.61

Degrees of freedom = 28; 17,613 29; 17,413 30; 16,722
33; 16,576 33; 31,254 33; 24,899

The associated (0.01) critical value F(30; ∞) = 1.69.

20. See in particular references [10] and [11].

21. By statistical "significance" we use the arbitrary rule that a coefficient is significant if its associated t-statistic is 2.0 or more. Henceforth, the term significant is not placed in quotation marks, but comments about significance should be taken with a grain of salt.

22. For an attempt to disentangle these hypotheses, see Rosen [11].

23. The sample is the 1966 Survey of Economic Opportunity; see Welch [15] and [16].

24. The relative weight given to characteristic differences and coefficient differences is somewhat arbitrary. Characteristic differences could just as easily have been weighted by black coefficients if coefficient differences were weighted by white characteristics. This would have reduced the size of the first term relative to the second.

25. For example, if we simply entered years of schooling as our independent variable, the main effect in the 1–5 experience interval would remain essentially unchanged, but the race interaction would be cut by one-third, and the total schooling effect cut by one-half.

26. The following table gives the rise in education between 1960 and 1970 within experience classes:

CHANGE IN EDUCATION LEVEL BETWEEN 1960 AND 1970 WITHIN EXPERIENCE CLASS

Sample	1–5	6–10	11–15	16–20	21–30	31–40
Blacks	.72	1.1	1.51	1.60	1.87	1.52
Whites	.35	.35	.76	1.02	.98	1.22

27. See the papers by Becker [1], Oi [10], and Rosen [11].
28. The migration pattern is illustrated as:

MIGRATION PATTERNS OF BLACKS
(Change between 1960 and 1970 in the proportion of blacks living in these areas)

Areas	Experience Groups					
	1–5	6–10	11–15	16–20	21–30	31–40
Metropolitan region	.0541	.0665	.0454	.0405	.0521	.0406
Central city	.0493	.0650	.0426	.0354	.0477	.0446
South	−.0498	−.0719	−.0395	−.0204	−.0630	−.0459

29. Total earnings variance,

$$\sigma^2 = f\sigma_1^2 + (1-f)\sigma_2^2 + f(1-f)(\bar{y}_1 - \bar{y}_2)^2$$

where σ^2 is earnings variance among blacks, σ_2^2 is earnings variance among whites, f is the proportion of blacks in the population, and $\bar{y}_1$ and $\bar{y}_2$ refer to mean earnings for blacks and whites, respectively. Our statement about earnings inequality for blacks refers to the logarithm of earnings and is a statement that $\sigma_1^2 > \sigma^2$.

30. The Gini coefficients were computed for the 1960 Census with $100 intervals until $10,000 and $1,000 intervals between $10,000 and $25,000. The midpoints of these intervals were used and the open-ended interval was assigned a value of $40,000. For the 1970 Census, $100 intervals were used and the open-ended category of $50,000 and above was assigned $65,000.

31. In each case the base within groups is 0.5, i.e., approximately 50 percent of whites' earnings exceed the white geometric mean.

32. That is, we have imposed the constraint that annual earnings be proportionate to weeks worked.

33. Hourly wage rates are appropriate because of the absence of direct employment variation. Unfortunately, the Census does not provide direct measures of hourly rates. An hourly wage could be computed by dividing previous year's earnings by annual hours worked, but employment variation would be reintroduced through the back door. In some preliminary work on the SEO, which has better measures of hourly rates, variances in log hourly wages were upward sloping.

34. Note that the constraint of a unit coefficient for (log) weeks worked implies that the variance of weeks worked is that part of total earnings variance attributed to weeks worked when all other factors are held constant.

35. The surveying for the 1970 Census occurred during Good Friday week. Unfortunately, we do not know if people answered the weekly hours question with their normal work week or excluded the holiday. One hopeful sign that this may not be as serious a problem as many of us had feared is that in examining the variance among age groups, the patterns were about as smooth in 1970 as they were in 1960.

36. The effect was also larger in 1960 than 1970, presumably reflecting the more elastic labor supply functions in recession years.

37. Due no doubt to the aggregate variance being heavily weighted by the white sample.

38. Single-year age cells from ages 18–65 were used in Table 13. The total variance σ_T^2 may be expressed as

$$\sigma_T^2 = \sum_{i=1}^{N} P_i(\sigma_i^2 + d_i^2)$$

where P_i is the proportion of people in age cell i, σ_i^2 is the within-cell variance, and d_i is the difference between the within-cell mean and the overall mean. Table 9 results from varying the P_i and adjusting the between-cell variances to reflect the new overall mean. For Table 10, 7 education cells were used: 0–7, 8, 9–11, 12, 13–15, 16, and 17+ years of schooling completed.

39. For a thorough and illuminating investigation of these within-cell variances, see Jacob Mincer's *Schooling, Experience, and Earnings* [9].
40. The extent of the change declines as schooling level rises.
41. In the regression analysis, federal and state and local governments' shares of industry products are entered directly, as explanatory variables. This distinction between the two imputation techniques is important. It must be true that government shares of products of individual firms vary considerably within industrial classes. Consider the random assignment procedure used here under the assumption that by 1970 federal contractors responding to pressure for affirmative-action recruiting, within a given industry, are more likely to employ blacks than are other firms in the industry. Our procedure assumes that the government's share of the industry's product is the probability that a black working in a given industry is an indirect federal employee—a clear understatement. Further, the amount of the understatement depends upon the average governmental share and the bias should decline as the governmental share rises. Not only are these imputations biased, but estimates of change between 1960 and 1970 are also biased. If clustering of blacks in firms with government contracts is more common in 1970 than in 1960—and it should be as a consequence of the 1964 legislation and the executive orders that followed—then changes over the decade are understated.

   In the regression analyses, provisions for race interaction on coefficients for government employment have the potential to compensate for these biases. Assume, for simplicity, that firms specialize by selling either all or none of their product to the government. Assume further that wages in firms with governmental sales exceed those of other firms by a given fraction which may or may not depend on race. For whites, the excess of the mean wage in an industry relative to wages in firms with no governmental sales will be proportionate to the government's share of the industry's product—assuming that labor/output ratios are constant. If blacks are clustered in firms with sales to the government, then their average wage within the industry will exceed that of whites, and this clustering effect will be reflected in the race interaction coefficient.

REFERENCES

1. Becker, Gary. *Human Capital.* New York: National Bureau of Economic Research, 1964.
2. ———. *Economics of Discrimination.* 2d ed. Chicago and London: University of Chicago Press, 1971.
3. Ben-Porath, Yoram. "The Production of Human Capital and the Life Cycle of Earnings." *Journal of Political Economy* 75 (July/Aug. 1967): 352–365.
4. Freeman, Richard. "The Declining Economic Value of Education." Processed, 1975.
5. Gwartney, James. "Changes in the Nonwhite/White Income Ratios 1939–1967." *American Economic Review* 60 (Dec. 1970): 872–883.
6. Hanoch, Giora. "Hours and Weeks in the Theory of Labor Supply." The Rand Corporation, R-1787-HEW (in preparation).

7. Kalachek, E. "Determinants of Teenage Employment." *Journal of Human Resources* (Winter 1969): 3–21.
8. Kosters, Marvin, and Welch, Finis. "The Effects of Minimum Wages on the Distribution of Changes in Aggregate Employment." *American Economic Review* (June 1972): 323–332.
9. Mincer, Jacob. *Schooling, Experience, and Earnings.* New York: National Bureau of Economic Research, 1974.
10. Oi, Walter. "Labor as a Quasi-Fixed Factor." *Journal of Political Economy* 70 (Oct. 1962): 538–555.
11. Rosen, Sherwin. "Short-Run Employment Variation on Class I Railroads in the United States, 1947–1963." *Econometrica* 36 (July/Oct. 1968): 511–529.
12. ———. "Toward a Theory of Life Cycle Earnings." Processed, 1975.
13. Toro-Vizcarrondo, Carlos, and Wallace, T. Dudley. "A Test of the Mean Square Error Criterion for Restrictions in Linear Regressions." *Journal of American Statistical Association* 63 (June 1968): 558–572.
14. Wallace, T. Dudley. "Weaker Criteria and Tests for Linear Restrictions in Regressions." *Econometrica* 40 (July 1972): 689–698.
15. Welch, Finis. "Labor Market Discrimination: An Interpretation of Income Differences in the Rural South." *Journal of Political Economy* 75 (June 1967): 225–240.
16. ———. "Black-White Returns to Schooling." *American Economic Review* 63 (Dec. 1973): 893–907.
17. ———. "Education and Racial Discrimination." In Orley Ashenfelter and Albert Rees, eds. *Discrimination in Labor Markets.* Princeton: Princeton University Press, 1973.

7 | COMMENTS

Orley Ashenfelter
Princeton University

The Smith–Welch paper represents an enormous amount of data collection and analysis. The results are clearly and faithfully reported, even when they do not seem to support the (perhaps vested) interests (of at least one) of the authors. I cannot imagine a different organization of the data that would be likely to change the results appreciably. In consequence, those who are interested in the subject of racial differences in economic success owe a considerable debt to the authors of this paper. Nevertheless, there is an important sense in which I believe the paper is largely a failure.

Surely the most important part of the paper is the attempt in the second section to provide an accounting, or explanation, of why the ratio of black to white male earnings increased over the period 1959 to 1969. In principle, this could be done very successfully if we could first verify empirically that the effect of a unit of a characteristic (such as schooling) on earnings was the same for both black and white groups in both 1960 and 1970. Changes in the average characteristics of the black and white populations could then provide an unambiguous accounting of the sources of relative earnings growth, with any residual decrease in discrimination affecting the constant terms in the regressions. As it turns out, the effects of the characteristics of workers on their earnings are neither the same by race group or over time. This introduces considerable ambiguity into the accounting process. As can be seen from Table 6, for example, the accounting process based on observed characteristics produces predictions of declines in the relative incomes of blacks in the three highest experience classes, but increases in the three lower experience classes. Since there were actually increases in the relative earnings of blacks in all experience classes, objective characteristics are supposed to have helped boost the relative earnings of younger blacks but to have kept relative earnings from going up even faster among older blacks. And this is true even though the single most important objective characteristic, the schooling gap, was narrowing in each experience class. The upshot is that the "residual," or component of growth in the relative earnings of blacks not accounted for by objective characteristics, is large and almost identical in every experience class. Thus, we have failed to "explain" the cause of the increase in the relative earnings of black males.

It is natural to attribute this large residual to a general decline in labor market discrimination during the 1960s. Before doing so, however, it would be useful to have at least some direct evidence that nondiscrimination was a factor of importance. One way to do this is to search for larger increases in the relative earnings of black workers in the sectors of the economy where it might plausibly be argued that antidiscrimination forces would be greater. The authors have tried to do just this, though, as they admit, the Census of Population provides only very crude data for this purpose. In particular, they have examined the change in the relative earnings of black male workers in sectors which they estimate to have been affected directly or indirectly by the government, on the presumption that government may have been an independent force in the reduction of labor market discrimination. There are now several studies using microeconomic data of a different kind that find, as do the authors, little impact that can be attributed directly to government action.[1]

Where does this leave us? In my view, it leaves us with a very considerable puzzle. To amplify this, Table 1 contains annual data on the relative wage and salary earnings of black men and women through the most recent year available. These data from the Current Population Survey reports are for year-round, full-time workers and thus provide some control, though not as much as would be desirable, on cyclical changes in annual working hours. These aggregate data are not entirely comparable to the aggregates that Smith and Welch use, but they do suggest to me an increase in the relative earnings of black males sometime during the 1960s comparable to the magnitude that Smith and Welch observe. These data also suggest to me that the relative earnings of black males were very stable until around the mid-1960s and that most of the increase that did take place may have been completed by the early 1970s, though it will take

TABLE 1 Ratios of Nonwhite to White Median Wage and Salary Earnings for Year-Round, Full-Time Workers,[a] 1955–73

	Men	Women
1955	.64	.57
1956	.62	.55
1957	.63	.60
1958	.65	.62
1959	.61	.66
1960	.67	.70
1961	.66	.67
1962	.63	.63
1963	.65	.64
1964	.66	.69
1965	.64	.71
1966	.63	.71
1967	.68	.77
1968	.69	.78
1969	.69	.82
1970	.70	.85
1971	.71	.90
1972	.70	.87
1973	.72	.88

SOURCE: Various reports from the *Current Population Surveys*. For details see Ashenfelter [1].
[a]A year-round, full-time worker is defined as a worker who worked 50-52 weeks per year and 35 or more hours per week.

considerably more experience before this can be confirmed. Perhaps more important, the relative earnings data for black women suggest that there will be no easy resolution of the puzzle. For these data show continuous upward progress in the relative earnings of black women until the early 1970s. Thus, attributing the increase in the relative earnings of black males to post-1964 Civil Rights activities requires an explanation for the considerable steady progress of the relative earnings of black women in the period before 1964. On the other hand, attributing the steady increase in the relative earnings of black women to the gradual relative increase in their skills (as measured, say, by schooling) requires an explanation of why the gradual relative increase in the skills (as measured again, say, by schooling) of black men had so little effect on their relative earnings before the mid-1960s.

In sum, this subject clearly will require considerably more effort before we have a clear empirical picture based on a convincing causal foundation. Smith and Welch have helped to provide a part of this foundation.

NOTE

1. See Ashenfelter and Heckman [2] and Goldstein and Smith [3].

REFERENCES

1. Ashenfelter, Orley. "Changes in Labor Market Discrimination Over Time." *The Journal of Human Resources* 5 (Fall 1970): 403–430.
2. Ashenfelter, Orley, and Heckman, James. "Measuring the Effect of an Anti-Discrimination Program." In Orley Ashenfelter and James Blum, eds., *Evaluating the Labor Market Effect of Social Programs* [Princeton: Industrial Relations Section, Princeton University, 1976].
3. Goldstein, Morris, and Smith, Robert S. "The Estimated Impact of Antidiscrimination Laws Aimed at Federal Contractors." *Industrial and Labor Relations Review* (forthcoming).

Alvin Mickens

New York University

The paper by Finis Welch and James P. Smith represents an impressive effort in manipulating and analyzing data from the latest decennial Census. The study will surely be of great value in providing new angles of vision for analyzing the relative progress of blacks and will add fresh material to the growing controversy over the extent and permanence of the apparent improvement in the relative economic status of blacks by experience cohorts.

The Smith and Welch findings of black experience-cohort gains relative to whites' parallel Richard Freeman's results of black progress (Brookings Papers on Economic Activity, 1: 1973) analyzed from the age-cohort approach. Both find that there have been remarkable gains for black male and female workers, when measured by the more recent age/experience cohorts. Both the Freeman study and the Smith-Welch paper reach conclusions which challenge the conventional view that there has been little improvement in black economic status relative to whites in terms of relative incomes and life-cycle labor market activity, especially when cyclical factors are carefully accounted for. I do not so much want to carry a brief for the standard view as to cite some critical limitations to which, I believe, the Smith-Welch paper fails to give adequate consideration. These factors, in my view, mainly center around black interregional migration, southern black progress, and overall economic activity.

First, recent studies, including a paper by Wayne Vroman, have shown that the gains in relative income for black males, even in the prosperous decade of the 1960s, were pretty much confined to the South and were barely evident in the Northeast and North Central regions. Smith and Welch, too, note that the third most significant argument "explaining" a major part of the relative earnings gain is black migration out of the South and the improvement in earnings of resident southern blacks. Since the major strides in educational improvements occurred mainly among resident southern blacks, I suspect that a certain amount of intercorrelation here captured some of the importance of the southern-resident and regional variables the authors employ. In fact, Smith and Welch do show that estimated gains by blacks were reinforced by interregional and metropolitan migration of the black population.

When Smith and Welch consider the black/white cohort earnings ratios shown in Tables 3A and 3B, they do not, of course, adequately account for the peculiar effects of the southern region. Nor do they properly caution that 1969 was an incomparably better year than 1959 for overall economic activity. Moreover, the prolonged expansion from 1961 to 1969 exceeded any experienced in the postwar period and contrasts dramatically to the stop-and-go, generally stagnant 1950s. Thus, 1960s labor market entrants could surely be expected to make spectacular gains relative to 1950s labor market entrants.

It has been repeatedly documented that (1) the status of black workers improves relative to whites during expansions, and declines relative to whites during contractions, and (2) recent evidence suggests that occupational mobility and earnings/educational differentials, however measured, are highly elastic with respect to cyclical activity. In this connection, one might also mention that the speed and duration of expansion also affect black employment opportunities.

In spite of the strong emphasis attributed to education and schooling quality as accounting for the narrowing of the black-white differentials for the 1960s labor market entrants, Smith and Welch were not able to isolate fully the pervasive effects of the prolonged labor market tightness experienced in that decade from the operation of other determinants purporting to measure separately cohort life-cycle effects, although their employment variables do adjust for some of the expansionist impact.

The specter that haunts these cross-sectional approaches, which are "snap-shots" of cohort gains at points in time, and which are in sharp contrast to the minimal relative progress of blacks documented in time series, is a reconciliation problem perhaps similar to that of time series versus cross-section surveys in aggregate consumption studies.

Since the relative gains for the black earnings profiles in 1970 seemed to have been registered so widely for practically all the experience cohorts, one might seek out an argument more compelling than schooling quality or "vintage": and that is the very distinct possibility that the 1960s expansion, like the 1940–48 period, achieved a dramatic one-time gain in black-white earnings ratios, and overall probably had a more equalizing impact than previous expansions.

This contention also applies to the occupational-industrial analysis in the paper. While the 1960s black entrants to the labor force may be approaching greater occupational congruency with whites, available data from another angle of vision using an occupational dissimilarity index approach show that the concentration of black workers in just three occupations (operatives, laborers, and private households) still accounts for over 40 percent of the black labor force, with little overall change since 1957. Less than 21 percent of white workers are concentrated in these jobs.

I suggest, moreover, that the pattern of gains in earnings for various experience cohorts may not square uniformly with the Welch-Smith interpretation of major gains for the latest experience cohorts when we compare cohort gains within occupations.

For example, in professional groups for both sexes, the gains in relative incomes are shown to be at least as large for many of the 1950s entrants as they were for the 1960s entrants.

If our major argument is that education improvement, in isolation from cyclical factors, accounts for the gain in relative incomes for more recent black experience cohorts, we might look at black progress in occupations ranging from ones considered more sensitive to cyclical factors to those considered less sensitive. A category I regard as "less sensitive" is the professional-technical group. My own estimates indicate that the black proportion of total employment in this group increased more during 1957–63 than during 1963–69, and the same was nearly true for managers and proprietors.

Finally, I want to note some areas to which the cross-sectional approach employed by Smith and Welch gives inadequate attention. One is the much higher unemployment of black high school graduates relative to white high school dropouts. In every year for which data are available, some 12 to 18 black graduates are jobless for every 10 white school dropouts. No such pattern exists between white graduates and dropouts. Second, labor force participation rates for black males have been experiencing a dramatic decline, a trend that shows up even for men under 45. If anything, this trend accelerated in the latter 1960s (the reference point where the most recent experience cohort of blacks show dramatic relative gains). Also, if we look at those occupations in which the bulk of the black labor force is crowded—operatives, laborers, household workers, and sales clerical—we find that real earnings have held constant since 1967.

How are we to reconcile the hopeful "light at the end of the tunnel" emerging from cross-sectional studies of this type with the persistent gloomy results revealed in the dark tunnel of time-series studies? Perhaps longitudinal approaches made possible from Continuous Work History Samples of the Social Security Administration—once this file overcomes problems of incomplete coverage and can account for utilization continuity—may offer the way for overcoming the dissonance of opposite signs portrayed in relative black economic progress emerging from time-series and cross-sectional data.

In the meantime, I feel that more promising avenues for future research in these areas point in the direction of analysis of labor market segmentation and barriers to mobility among submarkets.

By using an index of occupational congruency Welch and Smith manage to bias upward the estimated improvement in the distribution of blacks, since they compare unweighted flows of recent black job market entrants to "stocks" of the distribution of occupationally classified whites. Such an index could be expected to exhibit more "congruency" if the (most recent) distributional flows of blacks into occupations are considered better educated and trained than previous whites—or blacks—already classified in existing jobs in 1960.

If they had compared the flows (1960–70) of new black occupational entrants to flows of new white occupational entrants for the same period and then asked:

How long will it take for blacks in a given occupation to approach parity with whites? I surmise that the answer that would emerge would put the estimate far enough into the distant long run so that, as Keynes might say, we might all be dead!

A more appropriate index for gauging this kind of progress would be one of occupational dissimilarity. Ron Oaxaca's paper, using such an index, showed no improvements when occupational comparisons of black-white, male-female were made over the years 1958–71.

I trust that we do not have to wait for 1980 or 1984, to determine whether or not the gains that seem to impress the authors, are real.

I am convinced that if the 1970s repeat the 1950s pattern of "stagflation" and low overall economic growth, many of the touted gains registered for the 1970 cohorts will probably erode and the black-white earnings differential can be expected to remain relatively constant.

8

RONALD L. OAXACA
University of Arizona

The Persistence of Male-Female Earnings Differentials

With the passage of the 1963 Federal Equal Pay Act and the 1964 Civil Rights Act, it was hoped that the earnings differentials between the races and the sexes would be substantially reduced. In the case of the male-female earnings differential, it is clear that the high expectations of the federal legislation have yet to be realized. It has been ten years since the passage of the Civil Rights Act; yet the earnings gap between the sexes remains sizable.

This paper examines some of the factors responsible for the continued existence of sizable earnings differentials between the sexes. In and of itself, the existence of an earnings differential is not necessarily indicative of the extent of labor market discrimination. The crucial question is: What proportion of the observed differential is attributable to discrimination and what proportion is justifiable on some generally accepted grounds of equity. Looked at in this way, it is clear that the success or failure of legislation in reducing discrimination cannot be measured by changes in the gross earnings differential alone. Therefore, our analysis will focus on estimated changes in the proportion of the gross male-female earnings differential that result from discriminatory practices in the labor market.

NOTE: This research was supported in part by a grant from the Research Council of the University of Massachusetts at Amherst. The author gratefully acknowledges helpful comments by Ronald G. Ehrenberg and David Shapiro, the support of Albert Chevin who made available computer programs which substantially facilitated the processing of the Census Public Use Samples, and the research assistance of Richard Kahn.

The outline of the paper is as follows: the underlying analytical model is developed in Section I; the empirical results are presented and discussed in Section II; Section III is a summary and conclusion; and the appendix contains supplementary regressions.

I. ANALYTICAL FRAMEWORK

The Economics of Discrimination

In the Becker model of discrimination, economic agents assert their propensities to discriminate against a given group of workers by acting as if the net cost of dealing with the group is greater than the direct money cost involved [Becker 1971]. For example, employers apply a psychic markup to the nominal wage that would be given to workers whom they have a distaste for hiring. Similarly, consumers apply a psychic markup to the price of a product or service which is produced or sold by workers whom they would prefer to avoid dealing with. In the case of workers, some may psychologically discount the wage they would receive from working with members of a group whom they would prefer to avoid. The extent of an economic agent's propensity to discriminate is measured by the percentage markup or discount applied to members of certain demographic groups. This percentage markup or discount is called the discrimination coefficient, and it measures the psychic costs incurred in dealing with workers from these groups.

Unless men and women are virtually identical with respect to the determinants of earnings, the magnitude of the gross earnings differential tells us little about the extent of discrimination in the labor market. This is because sex differences in the characteristics which determine earnings would generate sex differences in earnings even in the absence of discriminatory employment practices. Of course, such differences in the determinants of earnings reflect societal discrimination in terms of social conditioning from cradle to grave and unequal access to educational and vocational opportunities. In this sense, any difference in earnings would reflect discrimination in a larger context; however, we are interested here in discrimination that stems from the labor market. Thus, personal characteristics are taken as given. The overall effects of labor market discrimination can be measured by the market discrimination coefficient (D), which is defined to be the proportionate difference between the actual male/female earnings ratio and the ratio in the absence of discrimination. In terms of natural logarithms

(1) $\ln (D + 1) = \ln (Y_m / Y_f) - \ln (Y_m^0 / Y_f^0)$

where Y_m and Y_f are the observed full-time earnings of men and women, respectively, and Y_m^0 and Y_f^0 are their respective full-time earnings in the absence of discrimination. According to Becker, the market discrimination coefficient will depend on such factors as the degree of substitutability between male and female workers, market structure, returns to scale, the relative supply of female workers, the average discrimination coefficient, and the dispersion in individual discrimination coefficients.

Suppose the production function can be characterized as $Z = F[L, K]$ and $L = \alpha_m L_m + \alpha_f L_f$ where Z represents output, L represents the labor input, K is vector of other inputs, and α_m and α_f are the efficiency parameters of male (L_m) and female (L_f) labor, respectively. The marginal products of men and women are denoted by MP_m and MP_f, respectively. Thus,

$$MP_m / MP_f = \alpha_m / \alpha_f$$

In the absence of discrimination, cost minimization brings about

$$Y_m^0 / Y_f^0 = \alpha_m / \alpha_f$$

but in a discriminating labor market, net cost minimization implies

(2) $Y_m / Y_f = (D + 1)(\alpha_m / \alpha_f)$

Let the observed gross male-female earnings differential (G) be defined by

(3) $G + 1 = Y_m / Y_f$

Now substituting (3) in (2) and taking logs of both sides we have

(4) $\ln (G + 1) = \ln (D + 1) + \ln (\alpha_m / \alpha_f)$

which is merely a rearrangement of equation 1. According to equation 4, the gross differential (in logs) can be separated into the effects of discrimination and the effects of male/female productivity differences. In the special case of perfect substitutes ($\alpha_m = \alpha_f$), any observed differences in earnings would be totally the result of labor market discrimination.

Cross-Section Model

The methodology employed in this section is derived from the author's previous study of male-female wage differentials [Oaxaca 1973]. The purpose of a cross-section analysis is to estimate the market discrimination coefficient at a point in time. Estimates of the effects of discrimination can be made for two cross sections, 1960 and 1970, and then compared.

We wish to specify and estimate a functional relationship between earnings and various socioeconomic variables: $Y = f(X_1, \ldots, X_k)$; where Y represents earnings, and the X's represent socioeconomic determinants of earnings. A commonly accepted functional form for the earnings relationship is that of the semilog specification which can be justified on the basis of human capital theory [Becker 1966]. Thus,

$$\ln(Y) = \Sigma_k \beta_k X_k$$

where β_k is the percentage effect on earnings from a change in X_k, other things held constant. Given a cross section of male and female workers, we can specify the corresponding statistical models as

(5) $\ln(Y_{jm}) = \sum_k \beta_{mk} X_{jmk} + \mu_{jm5} \qquad j = 1, \ldots, N_m$

(6) $\ln(Y_{jf}) = \sum_k \beta_{fk} X_{ifk} + \mu_{if6} \qquad j = 1, \ldots, N_f$

where m and f index men and women, respectively; N_m and N_f are the number of men and women, respectively; j indexes the jth worker in each group; k indexes the kth variable; and μ_{jm5} and μ_{jf6} are the error terms.

We shall assume that in a nondiscriminatory labor market, the parameters in (5) and (6) would be identical for men and women, i.e., in the absence of discrimination, men and women would face a common earnings structure. Accordingly, differences between the sexes in personal characteristics provide the basis for a justifiable earnings differential; whereas male-female differences in the parameters provide the basis for measuring the degree of labor market discrimination. Since we have no way of knowing what the common earnings structure would be in the absence of discrimination, we are forced to make some assumption about this. We shall assume that the male earnings structure given by (5) would be the common earnings relationship that would apply to both men and women in the absence of discrimination. If sex discrimination against women exists, this assumption asserts that the currently observed average earnings of men is exactly what we should observe in the absence of discrimination, but the observed average earnings of women is below what they would receive in a nondiscriminating labor market. We could have assumed, instead, that the female earnings relationship given by (6) is the common earnings structure that would apply in the absence of discrimination. This assumption implies that the currently observed average earnings of women would be equal to their average earnings in the absence of discrimination; however, in this instance, discrimination against women would manifest itself as a situation in which men received, on the average, higher earnings than they would be entitled to in a nondiscriminating labor market.

Our assumption that the male earnings relationships would be the prevailing earnings structure in the absence of discrimination is not an entirely arbitrary assumption. The intents of the 1963 Federal Equal Pay Act and the 1964 Civil Rights Act were not to correct earnings disparities by lowering the earnings of white or male workers, but rather to bring about compliance with the goal of equal employment opportunity by increasing the earnings of affected minority and female workers. Consequently, the achievement of equal employment opportunity would most likely produce a common earnings structure more closely resembling the current male earnings relationship.

By a well-known property of ordinary-least-squares regression we have the following relationships:

$$\ln(\bar{Y}_m) = \sum_k \hat{\beta}_{mk} \bar{X}_{mk}$$

$$\ln(\bar{Y}_f) = \sum_k \hat{\beta}_{fk} \bar{X}_{fk}$$

where $\bar{Y}_m$ and Y_f are the geometric mean earnings of men and women, respectively; $\bar{X}_{mk}$ and $\bar{X}_{fk}$ are the average values of the kth variable for men and women, respectively; and $\hat{\beta}_{mk}$ and $\hat{\beta}_{fk}$ are the corresponding estimated coefficients. The gross earnings differential is calculated as

(7) $$\ln(G+1) = \ln(\bar{Y}_m) - \ln(\bar{Y}_f)$$

Under our assumption about the common earnings relationship, we have

(8) $$\ln(\hat{Y}_m^0) = \sum_k \hat{\beta}_{mk} \bar{X}_{mk} - \ln(\bar{Y}_m)$$

(9) $$\ln(\hat{Y}_f^0) = \sum_k \hat{\beta}_{mk} \bar{X}_{fk}$$

where $\hat{Y}_m^0$ and $\hat{Y}_f^0$ are the respective estimated earnings of men and women in the absence of discrimination. If we substitute equations 7, 8, and 9 into the formula for the market discrimination coefficient given by (1), it can be shown that

(10) $$\ln(\hat{D}+1) = \ln(\hat{Y}_f^0) - \ln(\bar{Y}_f) = \sum_k \Delta\hat{\beta}_k \bar{X}_{fk}$$

where $\Delta\hat{\beta}_k = \hat{\beta}_{mk} - \hat{\beta}_{fk}$, and $\hat{D}$ = the estimated market discrimination coefficient. The relative productivity of men is estimated from equations 8 and 9 as

(11) $$\ln(\hat{\alpha}_m/\hat{\alpha}_f) = \ln(\hat{Y}_m^0/\hat{Y}_f^0) = \sum_k \hat{\beta}_{mk} \Delta\bar{X}_k$$

where

$$\Delta\bar{X}_k = \bar{X}_{mk} - \bar{X}_{fk}$$

The decomposition of the gross earnings differential into the effects of discrimination and the effects of productivity differences is accomplished through the substitution of equations 10 and 11 into equation 4:

$$\ln (G+1) = \ln (\hat{D}+1) + \ln (\hat{\alpha}_m/\hat{\alpha}_f) = \sum_k \Delta\hat{\beta}_k \bar{X}_{fk} + \sum_k \hat{\beta}_{mk} \Delta\bar{X}_k$$

The statistical significance of male-female differences in the estimated coefficients can be directly estimated by combining equations 5 and 6 into a single pooled regression in which the male observations are identified by a sex dummy variable:

$$\ln (Y_j) = \sum_k (\Delta\beta_k X_{jk} M_j + \beta_{fk} X_{jk}) + \mu_j \qquad j = 1, \ldots, N_f + N_m$$

where $M_j = 1$ if the worker is male and $=0$ otherwise.

The test for the overall structural difference between the male and female earnings relationships given by (5) and (6), respectively, is equivalent to a joint test of significance corresponding to the $\Delta\beta_k$'s.[1]

Annual rates of change in gross earnings differentials, discrimination, and relative productivity can be estimated from appropriate comparisons between 1960 and 1970 Census cross-section results. Let $\Delta \ln (G+1) = \ln (G+1)_{70} - \ln (G+1)_{60}$ and similarly for $\Delta \ln (D+1)$ and $\Delta \ln (Y_m^0/Y_f^0)$.[2] We then have

$$g = \partial \ln (G+1)/\partial t = \Delta \ln (G+1)/10$$

$$d = \partial \ln (D+1)/\partial t = \Delta \ln (D+1)/10$$

$$m - f = \partial \ln (Y_m^0/Y_f^0)/\partial t = \Delta \ln (Y_m^0/Y_f^0)/10$$

so that $g = d + m - f$: where $g =$ the annual percentage rate of change in the male/female earnings ratio; $d =$ the annual percentage rate of change in the male/female earnings ratio attributable to changes in discrimination; and $m - f =$ the annual percentage rate of change in the male/female earnings ratio attributable to change in relative productivity or labor quality (m and $f =$ the rates of growth of male and female labor quality, respectively).

Time-Series Model

By comparing cross-section results from widely spaced periods in time, we hope to be able to make some judgment about trends in discrimination and relative productivity. The inferences drawn about trends derived from comparisons between two Census years implicitly assume either that cyclical conditions were the same in the two periods or that changes in discrimination are unaffected by the business cycle. This is an important consideration because what is believed to be a trend may in reality be a transitory phenomenon reflecting different cyclical conditions in the periods covered by the Census data. Consequently, a time-series approach will be pursued in a manner similar to that followed by Orley Ashenfelter in his study of changes in racial discrimination over time [Ashenfelter 1970].

The time-series analog of equation 2 is given by

(12) $Y_m(t)/Y_f(t) = [D(t)+1][\alpha_m(t)/\alpha_f(t)]$

Suppose that the market discrimination coefficient has constant, trend, and cyclical components. One specification could be

(13) $D(t)+1 = \exp[C_0 + dt + a_1 V(t)]$

where d is the percentage change in the male/female earnings ratio attributable to changes in discrimination; and $V(t)$ is a cyclical aggregate demand variable. In periods of tight labor markets, the cost of employment discrimination rises due to a general shortage of labor. Also, any worker resistance to equal employment opportunities for women may become less acute in periods of relative prosperity. A reasonable cyclical indicator is given by the unemployment rate of white males 35–44. Accordingly, we would expect $a_1 > 0$. Allowing for exponential growth in marginal productivities, we have

(14) $\alpha_m(t)/\alpha_f(t) = [\alpha_{0m} \exp(mt)]/[\alpha_{0f} \exp(ft)]$

where m and f are the growth rates of male and female labor productivities, respectively. Ideally, it would be preferable to use wage rates rather than earnings in examining discrimination in rates of pay; however, time-series wage data are not disaggregated according to sex. The use of earnings data for year-round full-time workers is an effort to circumvent the lack of wage-rate data. Unfortunately, there still remains the problem that even among year-round full-time workers, men and women do not typically work the same number of hours. It has been estimated that men in this category may work as many as 10 percent more hours during a year than women [Council of Economic Advisers (CEA) 1973]. As an attempt to capture variations in relative hours worked, we introduce the ratio of the female unemployment rate, $U_f(t)$, to the male unemployment rate, $U_m(t)$, as a proxy for the relative use of female labor. If we now substitute equations 13 and 14 into 12, take logs of both sides, and add the labor utilization term and a disturbance term, we arrive at the operational representation of equation 4:

(15) $\ln[G(t)+1] = C + gt + a_1 V(t) + a_2[U_f(t)/U_m(t)] + \mu_{15}(t)$

where $g = d + m - f$.

Given our estimate of the adjusted growth rate of the male/female earnings ratio (g), we could estimate the percentage change attributable to discrimination if we had some independent estimate of the growth rate in the relative labor quality of males ($m - f$). Following Ashenfelter, we define the following index of labor quality:

$$Q_j(t) = \sum_s P_{sj}(t) Y_s, \qquad j = m, f$$

where $Q_j(t)$ is the labor quality index; P_{sj} is the proportion of workers in the jth sex group with s years of schooling; and Y_s is the earnings attributable to s years of schooling in some base period. Although the labor quality index for men should be constructed using male earnings, the choice of earnings figures for women is not so obvious. If we believe that male-female earnings differences within given schooling categories are solely the result of discrimination, it would be proper to use the male earnings figures to construct the female labor quality index. On the other hand, if we believe that sex differences in earnings within given schooling categories are solely the result of lower quality schooling for women, then it would be proper to use the earnings figures for women in the construction of their labor quality index. One could argue that women specialize in subject matters that raise their productivity in the home rather than in the market sector. Even here, a question arises as to what extent such specialization is a response to anticipated discrimination in the labor market. We thus arrive at one index for men and two alternative indexes for women:

$$Q_m(t) = \sum_s P_{sm}(t) Y_{sm}$$

$$Q'_f(t) = \sum_s P_{sf}(t) Y_{sm}$$

$$Q''_f(t) = \sum_s P_{sf}(t) Y_{sf}$$

Assuming that the labor quality indexes grow exponentially, we can posit the following time-series relationship:

$$\ln [Q_m(t)/Q_f(t)] = C_0 + (m - f)t + \mu(t)$$

Given $\hat{g}$ and $(\hat{m} - \hat{f})$, it is then possible to obtain $\hat{d}$.

According to Becker, the market discrimination coefficient can be expected to increase with increases in the relative supply of female workers, the average propensity to discriminate, and the variance of individual discrimination coefficients. Thus, for example, an increase in the female proportion of the labor force would widen the male-female earnings differential, even though there were no changes in the propensity to discriminate. This could occur because the increased proportion of women must partly be absorbed by firms with discrimination coefficients above the former equilibrium market discrimination coefficient. Consequently, women would have to accept a lower relative wage which then raises the equilibrium market discrimination coefficient. Since the nonwhite proportion of the labor force has been fairly constant, Ashenfelter was able to ignore the relative supply factor in his analysis of race earnings differentials [Ashenfelter 1970]. Furthermore, the assumption of a nonshifting, perfectly inelastic nonwhite relative supply curve allowed him to interpret equation 15 as a relative demand curve. Thus, changes in the race earnings differential could be attributed solely to changes in relative demand. Unfortunately, this assumption is not tenable in the case of sex discrimination because the relative supply of females has been rising steadily. Therefore, equation 15 is interpreted as a reduced-form equation. In a structural relative demand equation, we would expect a positive relationship between the male-female earnings differential and the relative supply of women. This implies that our estimate of the change in the earnings differential, attributable to discrimination, $\hat{d}$, measures the combined effects of changes in relative female labor supply and changes in the expected value and variance of individual discrimination coefficients.

The most important source of the overall earnings differential between the sexes is probably their differing occupational distributions, as opposed to unequal pay for equal work. It is currently a matter of debate whether and to what extent the different occupational distributions are the results of labor market discrimination and to what extent different job preferences are responsible. Promising research is being conducted by psychologists studying whether there really are sex and race differences in motivation, aspirations, and expectations about career fulfillment [Gurin 1974] and [Laws 1974]. Such research provides the psychological and sociological backdrops for different occupational attachments and labor-supply elasticities. For the present, we confine ourselves to trends in occupational distributions and short-run cyclical determinants of occupational distributions. The time-series relationship is specified as

$$O_{ij}(t) = b_{0ij} + b_{1ij}t + b_{2ij}V(t) + \mu_{ij}(t)$$

where i denotes the ith occupational category, j denotes male or female, O_{ij} is the percent of the jth group's labor force who are in the ith occupation, t is the time-trend variable, $V(t)$ is the cyclical demand variable (the unemployment rate of white males aged 35–44), and $\mu_{ij}(t)$ is the disturbance term. The changes in male-female differences in occupational distribution can be directly estimated by

$$\Delta O_i(t) = \Delta b_{0i} + \Delta b_{1i}t + \Delta b_{2i}V(t) + \mu_i(t)$$

where

$$\Delta O_i(t) = O_{im}(t) - O_{if}(t), \; \Delta b_{1i} = b_{1im} - b_{1if}, \text{ and } \Delta b_{2i} = b_{2im} - b_{2if}.$$

It is clear that the effects of changes in occupational distributions on the male-female earnings differential depend on male-female earnings differentials within occupations. To see this explicitly, let us consider the following identity:

(16) $\quad \ln(Y_m/Y_f) \equiv \sum_i \ln(Y_{im})O_{im} - \sum_i \ln(Y_{if})O_{if}$

where all earnings are geometric means, and O_{im} and O_{if} are the proportions of the male and all female labor forces in occupation i, respectively. Next, let $\ln(G_i + 1) = \ln(Y_{im}) - \ln(Y_{if})$, where G_i is the male-female earnings differential in the ith occupation. Now substitute for $\ln(Y_{if})$ in (16) the expression given by $\ln(Y_{if}) = \ln(Y_{im}) - \ln(G_i + 1)$. After collecting terms we have

(17) $\quad \ln(Y_m/Y_f) = \sum_i [\ln(Y_{im})\Delta O_i + \ln(G_i + 1)O_{if}]$

Differentiating both sides of (17) with respect to time yields

(18) $\quad \dfrac{\partial \ln(Y_m/Y_f)}{\partial t} = \sum_i \left[\ln(Y_{im})\Delta b_{1i} + \dfrac{\dot{Y}_{im}}{Y_{im}}\Delta O_i + \ln(G_i + 1)b_{1if} + g_i O_{if} \right]$

Thus, the contribution of each occupation to changes in the overall male/female earnings ratio can be estimated from equation 18.

Overall occupational dissimilarity between the sexes can be measured by means of an index used by the Council of Economic Advisers in their recent report on the economic role of women [CEA 1973]. For purposes of examining continuous movements in occupational dissimilarity, we compute the value of the index for each year as

$$I(t) = \tfrac{1}{2}\sum_i |\Delta O_i(t)|$$

where $I(t)$ is the index of occupational dissimilarity and $|\Delta O_i(t)|$ is the absolute value of the difference between the percentage of men in the ith occupation at time t and the percentage of women in occupation i at time t. If men and women were equally concentrated across all occupations, the index would equal zero. On the other hand, if each occupation were either all male or all female, the value of the index would equal one hundred. Intermediate values of the index indicate varying degrees of occupational dissimilarity. In order to detect trend and cyclical changes in occupational dissimilarity between the sexes, regressions of the following type are estimated: $I(t) = b_0 + b_1 t + b_2 V(t) + \mu(t)$.

II. EMPIRICAL RESULTS

Cross Section

The data for the cross-section analysis are urban worker subsamples drawn from the 1/1000 Public Use Samples of the 1960 and 1970 censuses. Of the variety of 1/1000 samples available from the 1970 Census, the 15 percent Neighborhood Characteristics sample was used in this study. Our analysis is confined to those who worked 50–52 weeks in the year preceding the Census year, who resided inside urban areas, and who were either government or private wage and salary workers. The gross differential in (geometric) mean earnings for whites rose from 79 percent in 1959 to 84 percent in 1969, while for blacks it declined from 95 percent to 60 percent over the same period.[2]

The earnings regressions corresponding to equations 5 and 6 are reported in Tables A-1 and A-2 in the appendix. We are more directly concerned with the resulting (log) decomposition of the sex earnings differentials into the effects of sex differences in the estimated coefficients and sex differences in the mean values of the independent variables. The former provides the basis for estimating the discrimination coefficient and the latter yields an estimate of labor quality or productivity differentials. These decompositions are reported in sum and also separately by independent variable in Tables 1 and 2. For each year there are two sets of decompositions: one set is based on earnings regressions which control for government employment, occupation, and industry, whereas the other set is based on earnings regressions which omit these variables. By not controlling for these variables, we hope to capture the effects of employment barriers on measured discrimination. Certainly, it is not implausible to argue that employment barriers have a larger impact on the overall earnings disparities between the sexes than do instances of unequal pay for equal work.

In Tables 1 and 2 the sum of the numbers in the columns headed by $\Delta\hat{\beta} \cdot \bar{X}_f$ is an estimate of the differential attributable to discrimination, $\ln(\hat{D}+1)$. The sum of the numbers in the columns headed by $\hat{\beta}_m \cdot \Delta\bar{X}$ is an estimate of the differential attributable to differences in personal characteristics. These sums and their components are expressed as percentages of the gross differential in logs.[3] As expected, the estimated effects of discrimination are always larger when calculated from the regressions that do not control for government, occupation, and industry. This result is more pronounced in 1960 and for blacks. As can be seen from Table 1, the estimated effects of sex discrimination among whites increased from 1960 to 1970 under both decompositions. Furthermore, the gross logarithmic earnings differential increased by less than the

TABLE 1   Decomposition of the Earnings Differential for Whites

	$\Delta\hat{\beta} \cdot \bar{X}_f$	Percent of $\ln(G+1)_{60}$	$\hat{\beta}_m \cdot \Delta\bar{X}$	Percent of $\ln(G+1)_{60}$	$\Delta\hat{\beta} \cdot \bar{X}_f$	Percent of $\ln(G+1)_{60}$	$\hat{\beta}_m \cdot \Delta\bar{X}$	Percent of $\ln(G+1)_{60}$
			A. 1960: $\ln(G+1)_{60} = 0.5818$					
Experience	0.0248	4.3	0.0037	0.6	0.0428	7.4	0.0039	0.7
Education	0.1490	25.6	0.0044	0.8	0.0883	15.2	0.0061	1.0
Region	0.0010	0.2	0.0009	0.2	0.0005	0.1	0.0010	0.2
City size	0.0484	8.3	0.0065	1.1	0.0628	10.8	0.0079	1.4
Marital status	−0.0995	−17.1	0.0665	11.4	−0.1066	−18.3	0.0792	13.6
Children	0.0460	7.9	0.0000	0.0	0.0591	10.2	0.0000	0.0
Part-time	0.0137	2.4	0.0286	4.9	0.0270	4.6	0.0316	5.4
Recent move	−0.0091	−1.6	−0.0004	−0.1	−0.0064	−1.1	−0.0003	−0.1
Government	−0.0272	−4.7	−0.0002	−0.0				
Occupation	−0.2374	−40.8	0.0755	13.0				
Industry	−0.0245	−4.2	0.0560	9.6				
Constant	0.4528	77.8	0.0000	0.0	0.2796	48.1	0.0000	0.0
	0.3380	58.1	0.2415	41.5	0.4471	77.0	0.1294	22.2

TABLE 1 (concluded)

	$\Delta\hat{\beta} \cdot \bar{X}_f$	Percent of ln(G+1)₇₀	$\hat{\beta}_m \cdot \Delta\bar{X}$	Percent of ln(G+1)₇₀	$\Delta\hat{\beta} \cdot \bar{X}_f$	Percent of ln(G+1)₇₀	$\hat{\beta}_m \cdot \Delta\bar{X}$	Percent of ln(G+1)₇₀
			B. 1970:	ln(G+1)₇₀ = 0.6131				
Experience	0.0356	5.8	0.0009	0.1	0.0686	11.2	0.0004	0.1
Education	0.1474	24.0	0.0157	2.6	0.0112	1.8	0.0203	3.3
Region	0.0068	1.1	0.0003	0.0	0.0190	3.1	0.0003	0.0
City size	0.0527	8.6	0.0034	0.6	0.0556	10.7	0.0045	0.7
Marital status	−0.1233	−20.1	0.0663	10.8	−0.1388	−22.6	0.0766	12.5
Children	0.0334	5.4	0.0000	0.0	0.0429	7.0	0.0000	0.0
Part-time	0.0205	3.3	0.0252	4.1	0.0312	5.1	0.0270	4.4
Recent move	−0.0039	−0.6	−0.0004	−0.1	−0.0080	−1.3	−0.0014	−0.2
Government	−0.0399	−6.5	−0.0039	−0.6				
Occupation	−0.2354	−38.4	0.0694	11.3				
Industry	0.0235	3.8	0.0446	7.3				
Constant	0.4741	77.3	0.0000	0.0	0.3943	64.3	0.0000	0.0
	0.3915	63.7	0.2215	36.1	0.4860	79.3	0.1277	20.8

SOURCE: The figures in this table are derived from earnings regressions corresponding to year-round urban workers from the U.S. Census 1/1000 Public Use Samples of 1960 and 1970. The Neighborhood Characteristics 15 percent sample was the particular 1/1000 sample used for the 1970 regressions.

TABLE 2 Decomposition of the Earnings Differential for Blacks

	$\Delta\hat\beta \cdot \bar{X}_f$	Percent of $\ln(G+1)_{60}$	$\hat\beta_m \cdot \Delta\bar{X}$	Percent of $\ln(G+1)_{60}$	$\Delta\hat\beta \cdot \bar{X}_f$	Percent of $\ln(G+1)_{60}$	$\hat\beta_m \cdot \Delta\bar{X}$	Percent of $\ln(G+1)_{60}$
			A. 1960: $\ln(G+1)_{60} = 0.6684$					
Experience	0.2738	41.0	0.0039	0.6	0.4499	67.3	0.0041	0.6
Education	0.1275	19.1	-0.0126	-1.9	-0.1001	-15.0	-0.0164	-2.5
Region	0.0253	3.8	0.0152	2.3	0.0036	0.5	0.0183	2.7
City size	0.0253	3.8	0.0078	1.2	0.0571	8.5	0.0077	1.2
Marital status	-0.0616	-9.2	0.0208	3.1	-0.0549	-8.2	0.0356	5.3
Children	0.0130	1.9	0.0000	0.0	0.0096	1.4	0.0000	0.0
Part-time	0.0440	6.6	0.0476	7.1	0.0718	10.7	0.0498	7.5
Recent move	-0.0030	-0.4	-0.0006	-0.1	0.0118	1.8	-0.0005	-0.1
Government	-0.0186	-2.8	0.0046	0.7				
Occupation	-0.0676	-10.1	0.0833	12.5				
Industry	0.0488	7.3	0.1074	16.1				
Constant	-0.0132	-2.0	0.0000	0.0	0.1174	17.6	0.0000	0.0
	0.3937	59.0	0.2774	41.6	0.5662	84.6	0.0986	14.7

TABLE 2 (concluded)

	$\Delta\hat{\beta}\cdot\bar{X}_f$	Percent of $\ln(G+1)_{70}$	B. 1970: $\ln(G+1)_{70} = 0.4699$					
			$\hat{\beta}_m\cdot\Delta\bar{X}$	Percent of $\ln(G+1)_{70}$	$\Delta\hat{e}\cdot\bar{X}_f$	Percent of $\ln(G+1)_{70}$	$\hat{\beta}_m\cdot\Delta\bar{X}$	Percent of $\ln(G+1)_{70}$
Experience	0.0916	19.5	0.0103	2.2	0.0911	19.4	0.0096	2.0
Education	-0.0917	-19.5	-0.0234	-5.0	-0.4830	-102.8	-0.0311	-6.6
Region	-0.0307	-6.5	0.0027	0.5	-0.0522	-11.1	0.0029	0.6
City size	0.0105	2.2	0.0001	0.0	0.0092	2.0	0.0002	0.0
Marital status	-0.1290	-27.5	0.0326	6.9	-0.1199	-25.5	0.0422	9.0
Children	0.0408	8.7	0.0000	0.0	0.0501	10.7	0.0000	0.0
Part-time	0.0006	0.1	0.0101	2.1	0.0143	3.0	0.0125	2.7
Recent move	-0.0012	-0.3	0.0011	0.2	-0.0009	-0.2	0.0013	0.3
Government	-0.0404	-8.6	-0.0001	0.0				
Occupation	0.0739	15.7	0.0173	3.7				
Industry	-0.0894	-19.0	0.0920	19.6				
Constant	0.4961	105.6	0.0000	0.0	0.9235	196.5	0.0000	0.0
	0.3311	70.4	0.1427	30.3	0.4322	92.0	0.0376	8.0

SOURCE: See Table 1.

increase in measured discrimination. This means that an increase in the relative productivity of white women, as evaluated in terms of the white male earnings regressions in each year, prevented the gross earnings gap from widening more than it actually did. Table 2 indicates that discrimination among blacks diminished over the decade, but by less than the reduction in the gross earnings differential (in logs). This implies that the decrease in the gross earnings differential between black men and black women would not have been as large if it were not for the rise in the relative productivity of black women. The information in Tables 1 and 2 can be used to estimate annual percentage rates of change in the male/female earnings ratio, discrimination, and relative productivity. These calculations have been made and are later presented and compared with time-series estimates.

An important aspect of labor market discrimination against women is the impact of government on sex earnings differentials. Our cross-section analysis sheds some light on the impact of government employment on male/female relative earnings. It is evident from the decomposition of the gross earnings differential that government employment reduces the average earnings of all men relative to the average earnings of all women in the labor market when compared with the male/female earnings ratio in the nongovernment sector. This occurs because the male-female earnings differential is less in government than nongovernment employment and because a larger proportion of female workers than male workers are employed by government. This narrowing of the overall earnings differential increased from 1960 to 1970 for both blacks and whites. The earnings regressions presented in the appendix to this paper reveal that between 1960 and 1970 the earnings advantage of government over nongovernment employment declined for all four race/sex groups. In the case of white men, earnings were actually lower in government as compared with nongovernment employment; furthermore, this discrepancy widened over the decade. This, of course, does not contradict the increased importance over the decade of government employment as a factor tending to narrow the male/female earnings ratio: the decrease in the earnings advantage of government over nongovernment employment was less for women than for men. These findings are consistent with the hypothesis that public sector employment is less discriminatory than employment in the private sector.

Before turning to the time-series results, a few comments are in order concerning the effects of childbearing on the earnings differential between men and women workers. Because the common earnings structure in the absence of discrimination is assumed to be the male earnings structure, the effects of childbearing must necessarily show up entirely as a contribution to the estimated effects of differences in coefficients. These effects have been included in our estimates of the discrimination coefficient.[4] One could argue that the wage effects of childbearing reflect discrimination in terms of access to positions offering on-the-job training and in terms of forced leave or quitting. An equally plausible argument against including the effects of childbearing in our estimates of discrimination is that childbearing reflects voluntary household decisions regarding the allocation of time between market and nonmarket work. If we were to accept this argument, then our estimates of the discrimination coefficient in each year would be lowered; however, the direction of change in the estimated discrimination coefficients between 1960 and 1970 would not be affected. In the case of white women, the increment in measured discrimination would rise because the effects of children on the sex earnings differential declined between 1960 and 1970. In the case of black women, the reduction in measured discrimination would be larger because the effects of children on the sex earnings differential increased over the Census decade.

Time Series

As has been previously stated, the advantage of the time-series analysis is that it may shed some light on the effects of cyclical movements on the male/female earnings ratio. Furthermore, yearly changes in magnitudes such as the sex earnings ratio and occupational distribution are directly estimated by time-series regressions. The time-series data are in the form of published averages and differ somewhat in concept from the Census microdata. Although some effort has been made to achieve comparability between the cross-section and time-series data, the remaining differences should be borne in mind when comparing the empirical findings.

The time-series earnings data are the median earnings of year-round full-time workers. The trends in gross differentials in median earnings were estimated from regressions of the type specified in equation 15. Variations on this specification were also estimated and the results are reported in Table 3. It is evident that the gross male-female earnings differential widened among whites and narrowed among nonwhites over the period 1955–71. The results also seem to suggest that sex earnings differentials move countercyclically as evidenced by the positive coefficients corresponding to the unemployment rate of white males 35–44; however, these coefficients are never statistically significant at the levels adopted in this study. Gross differentials widened with increases in the ratio of female/male unemployment, but this variable is statistically significant only for nonwhites.

TABLE 3 Estimated Reduced-Form Equations for Male-Female Earnings Differentials (1955–71)

Dependent Variable: ln $(Y_m/Y_t)^a$	Whites				Nonwhites			
Constant	0.3121†	0.3106†	0.3329†	0.4041†	0.1569	0.1701	0.1927	0.1947
	(0.0809)	(0.0735)	(0.0694)	(0.0516)	(0.1953)	(0.1823)	(0.1829)	(0.1857)
D(1966–71)		−0.0017				−0.0044		−0.0076
		(0.0009)				(0.0023)		(0.0088)
Time	0.0046†	0.0064†	0.0070†	0.0147†	−0.0207†	−0.0160†	−0.0153†	
	(0.0011)	(0.0013)	(0.0013)	(0.0021)	(0.0037)	(0.0044)	(0.0046)	
D · time		−0.132 × 10⁻³*	−0.132 × 10⁻³*					
		(0.054 × 10⁻³)	(0.054 × 10⁻³)					
Time squared				−0.524 × 10⁻³†			−0.286 × 10⁻³	−0.696 × 10⁻³
				(0.106 × 10⁻³)			(0.164 × 10⁻³)	(0.430 × 10⁻³)
Unemployment rate of white males 35–44[b]	0.0186	0.0154	0.0134	0.0035	0.0512	0.0410	0.0398	0.0388
	(0.0097)	(0.0090)	(0.0085)	(0.0065)	(0.0277)	(0.0265)	(0.0266)	(0.0273)
Ratio of female/male unemployment rates[b]	0.0828	0.0848	0.0683	0.0151	0.3146*	0.3084*	0.2845*	0.2694
	(0.0481)	(0.0437)	(0.0414)	(0.0317)	(0.1349)	(0.1258)	(0.1266)	(0.1302)
$\bar{R}^2$	0.80	0.84	0.86	0.93	0.77	0.80	0.80	0.79
Durbin-Watson	1.30	2.00	2.06	2.21	1.27	1.84	1.72	1.44

NOTE: Standard errors appear in parentheses.

*Significant at the 0.05 level in a two-tailed test.

†Significant at the 0.01 level in a two-tailed test.

[a]The median wage and salary earnings correspond to year-round full-time workers, i.e., those who work 50–52 weeks per year and 35 or more hours per week. These data were taken from various issues of the *Current Population Reports*, Series P-60, Consumer Income, U.S. Bureau of the Census.

[b]The unemployment statistics refer to the civilian noninstitutional population 16 years and older. These data were taken from the *Manpower Report of the President*, March 1973, pp. 148–149.

It is reasonable to suppose that sufficient time has elapsed since the passage of the 1963 Federal Equal Pay Act and the passage of the 1964 Civil Rights Act to detect any significant impact such legislation may have had on sex differentials in earnings. Are earnings differentials by sex any smaller than they would have been had there been no such legislation? Most likely, there would be no immediate impact of such legislation due to normal lags in the effective implementation of the laws.

To test for differences in the sex earnings ratios in the period following the federal legislation, a dummy variable representing the period 1966–71 was entered in the reduced-form equations for male-female earnings differentials. For both whites and nonwhites, the estimated coefficient was negative but not statistically significant. As an alternative specification, the dummy variable for the period 1966–71 was interacted with the time-trend variable. The estimated coefficient on the interaction term was negative for both whites and nonwhites but statistically significant only for whites; nevertheless, the negative effect was extremely small, indicating that after 1966 the white male/white female earnings ratio grew at a rate 0.01 percent per annum less than the pre-1966 rate. To pursue the possibility that the rate of change of the male/female earnings ratio was not constant over the perod 1955–71, a time-squared term was entered in the reduced-form equation.[5] Both the linear and quadratic terms of the time variable are statistically significant only for whites, and the corresponding coefficients imply that the log of the white male/white female earnings ratio attained a maximum in 1968 and began declining thereafter. In other words, the growth rate of the earnings ratio was positive but declining prior to 1968, and was negative after this period.

In order to estimate the rate of change in the sex earnings ratio attributable to changes in discrimination, we require independent estimates of changes in relative productivity. These latter estimates were obtained from equations in which the log of the ratio of male/female labor quality indexes was regressed on a time trend. In the case of whites, a quadratic specification of the time variable was also estimated. These regressions are presented in Table 4. The estimated annual percentage change in the male/female earnings ratio that can be attributed to changes in labor market discrimination ($\hat{d}$) is calculated as the difference between the gross annual percentage change in the earnings ratio ($\hat{g}$) and the annual percentage change in relative labor quality ($\hat{m} - \hat{f}$). The estimates of these parameters are first calculated from the regressions that include just the linear time-trend variable. These estimates are presented in Table 5 along with their counterparts derived from the cross-section results given in Tables 1 and 2. Despite the differences in data sources and methods, there is a broad consistency between the cross-section and

TABLE 4 Estimated Growth Rates of Relative Labor Quality (1952–71)

Group	Dependent Variable[a]	Constant	Time	Time Squared	$\bar{R}^2$
Whites	$\ln (Q_{wm}/Q'_{wf})$	−0.0314* (0.0029)	0.0021* (0.0002)		0.92
		−0.0382* (0.0019)	0.3949×10^{-2}* (0.0352×10^{-2})	-0.0085×10^{-2}* (0.0016×10^{-2})	0.98
	$\ln (Q_{wm}/Q''_{wf})$	0.5805* (0.0029)	0.0020* (0.0002)		0.91
		0.5738* (0.0020)	0.3779×10^{-2}* (0.0371×10^{-2})	-0.0083×10^{-2}* (0.0017×10^{-2})	0.98
Nonwhites	$\ln (Q_{nm}/Q_{nf})$	−0.0524* (0.0060)	0.0011* (0.0004)		0.40

NOTE: Standard errors appear in parentheses.
*Significant at the 0.01 level in a two-tailed test.
[a]The dependent variables are the natural logarithms of the ratio of the male labor quality index to the female labor quality index. The quality index for a given group in a given year is calculated by summing over the white male earnings in a given schooling category in 1959 weighted by the proportion of the group who fall in the particular schooling category in the given year. For white females the indexes Q'_{wf} and Q''_{wf} are calculated using white male and white female earnings, respectively. The earnings data correspond to individuals who worked 40 or more weeks in 1959 and were obtained from a special tabulation of the 1/1000 sample from the 1960 Census. These tabulations were kindly made available by Orley Ashenfelter. The schooling categories are as follows: less than 5 years, 5–8 years, 9–11 years, 12 years, 13–15 years, and 16 years or more. The data corresponding to the proportion of workers in these categories are reported for 1952, 1959, 1962, and 1964–71. They are available from the *Manpower Report of the President*, March 1973, Table B9, p. 177. Because of discontinuities in the data, Durbin-Watson statistics are not reported.

time-series results. Both show an annual percentage increase in the male/female earnings ratio among whites and a decrease among nonwhites. The estimated rate varies from 0.3 percent to 0.5 percent a year for whites and from −2.0 percent to −2.1 percent a year for nonwhites. Large differences in estimates occur with respect to $\hat{d}$ and $\hat{m} - \hat{f}$. This is to be expected in view of the crude nature of the labor quality index calculated from the time-series data available. Educational distribution alone is an extremely narrow basis on which to gauge changes in relative labor quality. In this regard, the Census microdata are clearly superior, because they provide detailed information on several different components of overall labor quality. Because the educational distribution of male workers has been improving over the years vis-à-vis female workers, it is not surprising that the time-series construction shows a rise in male relative to female labor quality. The tendency is to bias downward the estimated rate of change in the sex earnings ratio attributable to discrimination. In spite of this, discrimination is estimated to have increased among whites and to have fallen among nonwhites.[6] The cross-section estimates reveal a decrease in male/female relative labor

TABLE 5 Derived Rates of Change from Cross Sections and Time Series

	—g—	—d—		—$m - f$—	
Whites					
Cross section	0.0031[a]	0.0053[b]	0.0036[c]	−0.0022[b]	−0.0005[c]
Time series	0.0046[d]	0.0025[e]	0.0026[f]	0.0021[e]	0.0020[f]
Nonwhites					
Cross section	−0.0198[a]	−0.0063[b]	−0.0136[c]	−0.0135[b]	−0.0062[c]
Time series	−0.0207[d]	−0.0218[e]		0.0011[e]	

[a] $g = [\ln (G+1)_{70} - \ln (G+1)_{60}]/10$.

[b] $d = [\ln (\hat{D}+1)_{70} - \ln (\hat{D}+1)_{60}]/10$

and

$$m - f = g - d$$

where

$$\ln (\hat{D} + 1) = \sum_k \Delta\hat{\beta}_k \bar{X}_{fk} + [\ln (G+1) - \ln (\hat{G}+1)]/2$$

These calculations are based on the cross-section Census earnings regressions that control for government, occupation, and industry.

[c] d and $m - f$ are derived as in footnote b except that the underlying regressions do not control for government, occupation, and industry.

[d] $g = \partial \ln [G+1]/\partial t$ estimated from the time-series male/female relative earnings regressions in which t enters in linear form.

[e] $d = g - (m - f)$; where $m - f = \partial \ln (Q_m/Q_f)/\partial t$ estimated from the time-series relative labor quality regressions which used white male earnings as weights and in which time enters in linear form.

[f] d and $m - f$ are derived as in footnote e except that the underlying relative labor quality regressions used white female earnings as weights.

quality for both whites and nonwhites. They also reveal an increase in discrimination among whites larger than the time-series estimates, and they show a decrease in discrimination among nonwhites smaller than the time-series estimates.[7]

Returning to the question of the impact of legislation on the male/female earnings ratio, we note that the quadratic specification of the time variable in the relative earnings and relative labor quality equations permit the treatment of $\hat{g}$ and $\hat{d}$ as functions of time. Let

$$g(t) = \partial \ln [Y_m/Y_f]/\partial t = a_1 + 2a_2 t$$
$$m(t) - f(t) = \partial \ln [Q_m/Q_f]/\partial t = b_1 + 2b_2 t'$$
$$d(t) = g(t) - [m(t) - f(t)] = a_1 - b_1 + 2(a_2 t - b_2 t')$$

where a_1, b_1, $a_1 - b_1 > 0$ and a_2, b_2, $a_2 - b_2 < 0$. Since the relative earnings regressions are estimated over the period 1955–71 and the relative labor quality regressions extend over the period 1952–71, we have the relationship $t' = t + 3$. Substituting for t' we have $d(t) = a_1 - b_1 - 6b_2 + 2(a_2 - b_2)t$. To calculate the year in which the sex earnings ratio attains a maximum as a result of discrimination, set $d(t)$ equal to zero and solve for t: $\hat{t} = (a_1 - b_1 - 6b_2)/2(b_2 - a_2)$. These computations were performed for whites. Using the translation $T = 1954 + t$, the results suggest that discrimination began to diminish in 1966.[8]

The evidence seems to suggest a small but discernible reversal in the trend toward increases in the white-male–white-female earnings differential at about the same time we would have expected government policy to start taking effect. The problems with interpreting these results as indicative of the effects of government policy are formally the same as those problems encountered in the Phillips curve literature on the effectiveness of wage-price guideposts. We may only be observing the net effect of many factors which are not otherwise accounted for by the regression in the particular period under study. Yet as slim as the evidence is that government policy was responsible for damping or reversing the growth in the sex earnings differential for whites, the results do point to a small reduction in discrimination for whatever reasons.

Turning now to male-female occupational changes over time, Table 6 presents the estimated effects of trend and cyclical factors on male-female differences in occupational distribution for eight occupational categories.[9] First examining the results for whites, we find that statistically significant trends in male-female differences in occupational concentration occurred in favor of men in the following occupations: professional & technical, and managerial, officials, and proprietors. On the other hand, statistically significant trends in white male-female differences in occupational concentration occurred in favor of greater relative female concentration in the following occupations: clerical & sales, and farming. Cyclical factors exerted no statistically significant independent influence on male-female differences in occupational concentration except for the laborers category. In this occupation, loose labor markets lead to increases in male concentration over female concentration. In the case of nonwhites, we find statistically significant trends in the concentration of male employment over the concentration of female employment among the following occupations: managerial, officials, & proprietors; craftsmen; and service & private household workers. Statistically significant trends in nonwhite male-female occupational concentration differences indicate a trend toward greater relative representation of nonwhite females among clerical & sales workers and laborers. In periods of loose labor markets, male concentration increases over female concentration among professional and technical workers and decreases among craftsmen. The estimated coefficients of the unemployment rate of white males 35–44 were not statistically significant in the remaining occupations.

TABLE 6 Estimated Equations for Changes in Sex Differences in Occupational Distribution (1958–71) (Dependent variable: Percent of total male employment in a given occupation minus percent of total female employment in the occupation[a])

Occupation	Whites					Nonwhites				
	Constant	Time	Unemployment Rate of White Males 35–44[b]	$\bar{R}^2$	Durbin-Watson	Constant	Time	Unemployment Rate of White Males 35–44[b]	$\bar{R}^2$	Durbin-Watson
Professional & technical	−0.9790 (0.4638)	0.0764* (0.0253)	−0.2085 (0.1133)	0.78	1.66	−3.1990† (0.4662)	−0.0252 (0.0254)	0.2954† (0.1139)	0.65	1.75
Managerial, officials, & proprietors	8.6062† (0.4542)	0.1125† (0.0248)	0.0593 (0.1109)	0.74	1.86	0.0102 (0.4126)	0.1821† (0.0225)	0.1821 (0.1007)	0.89	1.15
Clerical & sales	−28.8499† (1.0829)	−0.2229† (0.0590)	0.5459 (0.2645)	0.84	1.89	2.8764 (1.8642)	−1.1711† (0.1016)	−0.5570 (0.4553)	0.95	1.04
Craftsmen	19.4761† (0.5529)	0.0359 (0.0301)	−0.2116 (0.1350)	0.50	1.42	10.0941† (0.7328)	0.2974† (0.0399)	−0.5931† (0.1790)	0.95	2.04
Operative	3.8552† (0.5996)	0.0445 (0.0327)	0.0231 (0.1464)	0.10	1.77	10.7835† (1.2715)	0.0514 (0.0693)	−0.2101 (0.3106)	0.13	1.27
Laborers	5.2462† (0.4826)	−0.0127 (0.0263)	0.2753* (0.1179)	0.53	1.15	24.5461† (1.4435)	−0.6087† (0.0787)	−0.0062 (0.3526)	0.91	1.30
Service & private household	−12.9273† (1.2967)	0.1087 (0.0707)	−0.3981 (0.3167)	0.51	2.15	−50.6768† (3.3311)	1.3584† (0.1816)	1.1797 (0.8136)	0.88	0.68
Farming	6.0177† (1.2718)	−0.1635* (0.0693)	−0.1670 (0.3106)	0.35	0.95	5.5264 (2.5749)	−0.0772 (0.1404)	−0.3044 (0.6289)	−0.15	1.08

NOTE: Standard errors appear in parentheses.
* Significant at the 0.05 level in a two-tailed test.
† Significant at the 0.01 level in a two-tailed test.
[a] Data on occupational distribution were annual averages and were taken from *Current Population Reports* Series, **P**-50, Labor Force Characteristics, U.S. Bureau of the Census, for 1958–59, and from *Employment and Earnings and Monthly Report on the Labor Force*, Bureau of Labor Statistics, for 1960–71.
[b] Refer to footnote b in Table 3.

As has been discussed earlier, we can directly measure overall occupational similarity/dissimilarity through the use of a single index. The regressions relating this index to the time trend and cyclical variables are reported in Table 7. As the results show, there was no movement in

TABLE 7   Estimated Equations for Occupational Dissimilarity (1958–71)
(dependent variable: index of occupational dissimilarity[a])

Group	Constant	Time	Unemployment Rate of White Males 35–44[b]	$\bar{R}^2$	Durbin-Watson
Whites	43.0401*	0.0279	0.132×10^{-3}	−0.04	1.88
	(0.6261)	(0.0341)	(0.1529)		
Nonwhites	51.5426*	−0.1751	−1.0637	0.12	1.23
	(2.2250)	(0.1213)	(0.5434)		

NOTE: Standard errors appear in parentheses.
*Significant at the 0.01 level in a two-tailed test.
[a]The index of occupational standing is calculated as one-half the sum of the absolute values of the difference between the percentages of males and females in each occupation. For the source of the occupational data used in the construction of the index refer to footnote a in Table 6.
[b]Refer to footnote b in Table 3.

the index for either whites or nonwhites over the period 1958–71. Since broad occupational categories were used, these findings do not rule out the possibility of changes in occupational dissimilarity occurring among more disaggregated classifications. The CEA index based on more disaggregated data was calculated as 62.9 in 1960 and 59.8 in 1970 for whites and nonwhites combined [CEA 1973]. This slight movement toward occupational similarity represents a reduction of 3.1 percentage points over a ten-year period, or an average reduction of only 0.3 percentage points a year. Thus, the use of more detailed data does not alter the conclusion that little progress has been made in the area of sex differences in occupational distribution.

It has been shown earlier that the effects of changes in occupational distributions on the overall male-female earnings differential depend on the earnings differentials within occupations. Unfortunately, yearly occupational earnings data are not available for each race/sex group separately. Such data are, however, available in Census years. Consequently, the data from our urban worker subsamples are used to calculate occupational effects on changes in relative earnings in accordance with equation 18. These estimated effects are shown in Table 8. Changes

TABLE 8 Effects of Occupational Developments on the Annual Rate of Change in the Overall Male/Female Earnings Ratio[a]

Group	Professional and Technical	Managers, Officials, and Proprietors	Clerical and Sales	Craftsmen	Operatives	Laborers	Services and Private Household	Farming[b]	$\sum_i \left[\dfrac{\partial \ln (Y_m/Y_f)}{\partial t}\right]_i$
Whites	0.0076	0.0138	−0.0276	0.0105	0.0053	0.0007	0.0028	−0.0099	0.0032
Nonwhites	−0.0031	0.0156	−0.0932	0.0292	0.0086	−0.0394	0.0655	−0.0045	−0.0213

[a]The effect of the ith occupation on the annual percentage change in the overall sex earning ratio is calculated from equation 18 as

$$\left[\frac{\partial \ln (Y_m/Y_f)}{\partial t}\right]_i = \ln (Y_{im}^{59}) \Delta \hat{b}_{1i} + \frac{Y_{im}}{Y_{im}} \Delta \hat{O}_i^{59} + \ln (G_i^{59}+1) \hat{b}_{1if} + g_i \hat{O}_{if}^{59}$$

$\Delta \hat{b}_{1if}$, $\hat{b}_{1if}$, $\Delta \hat{O}_i^{59}$, and $\hat{O}_{if}^{59}$ are derived from the occupational regressions in Tables 6 and A-3. $(\dot{Y}_{im}/Y_{im}) = \ln Y_{im}^{69} - \ln Y_{im}^{59})/10$, and $g_i = [\ln (G_i^{69}+1) - \ln (G_i^{59}+1)]/10$. The occupational earnings data are from the urban worker subsamples of the 1960 and 1970 1/1000 Census Public Use Samples.

[b]Since the urban worker subsample in 1959 contained only one white woman and no black women in farming, the geometric mean earnings of female laborers in 1959 were used in lieu of farm earnings to calculate the partial effect of farmings.

within the clerical & sales occupation tended to substantially narrow the overall sex earnings differential for whites, while the managerial and craftsmen occupations contributed substantially to a widening of the differential. In the case of nonwhites, the clerical & sales and laborer occupations contributed significantly to a narrowing of the differential. The managerial, craftsmen, and services & private household occupations contributed to a substantial widening of the earnings gap among nonwhites. Because of the hybrid nature of these estimates, their sums do not exactly equal either the cross-section or time-series annual rate of growth in the male/female earnings ratio.

III. CONCLUDING REMARKS

From the middle of the 1950s to the beginning of the 1970s the male-female earnings differential for year-round workers increased among whites and decreased among blacks. Both the cross-section and time-series analyses point to an increase in sex discrimination among whites and a reduction in sex discrimination among blacks as the factors responsible for the trends observed in their respective gross earnings differentials. During this period there occurred little or no movement toward occupational similarity between men and women in either racial group.

Government has been shown to have some narrowing effect on earnings differentials. Government employment has had the effect of reducing the economy-wide male-female earnings differential below the private sector differential. That is to say, the male-female earnings differential would be larger in the absence of public-sector employment. There is also some suggestion that legislation may also have had an effect on the sex earnings differential. This is especially true for whites. Over the entire period of 1955 through 1971 there was, on the average, an increase in the earnings differential due to discrimination; however, the rate of increase was not constant. Starting around 1966, the adjusted growth rate of the male-female earnings differential among whites diminished or perhaps even became negative due to reductions in discrimination. Government policy stemming from the 1963 Federal Equal Pay Act and the 1964 Civil Rights Act may have been responsible for the downturn in the steady growth in the earnings differential due to discrimination. Although the adjusted white-male/white-female earnings ratios were smaller after 1966 than what would have been predicted on the basis of pre-1966 relationships, the effects were fairly small.

We have seen that sex earnings differentials rise during periods of loose labor markets and fall during periods of tight labor markets. This supports the expectation that efforts toward greater equal employment opportunity will enjoy more success during periods of relative prosperity. At such times, there is a maximum of flexibility for making needed changes in employment practices where women and minorities are concerned. In this regard, it is interesting to note that the unemployment rate of white males aged 35–44 averaged 1.9 percent over the period 1966–71 as compared with 3.0 percent over the period 1955–65. Any efforts toward promoting equal employment opportunities during 1966–71 surely benefited from coincidence with full employment.

There are certain nagging problems with the residual approach to measuring discrimination. Space limitations permit only brief mention of these problems, but they do merit careful attention by students of the economics of discrimination. We have assumed that a common earnings structure would exist in the absence of discrimination. It can be argued, however, that specialization within households could lead to different earnings structures for men and women even in the absence of discrimination. This has implications for sex differences in the acquisition of on-the-job training and occupational choice. It is extremely difficult to give any precise information about the allocation of time within households that would exist if there were no sex discrimination in the market sector.

Clearly, the legislative intent of the 1964 Civil Rights Act was to go beyond the narrow definition of discrimination inherent in the 1963 Equal Pay Act, which prohibited unequal pay for equal work. It is debatable whether the wider view of discrimination is adequately reflected by earnings regressions that control for broad occupational categories. One could argue that adjusted earnings differentials within broad occupational groupings mainly reflect discriminatory employment practices, whereas, sex differences in broad occupational affiliation mainly reflect voluntary labor supply decisions explainable in terms of a household life cycle maximization model. It is the author's contention that the traditional occupational choices of women have been in large part conditioned by the rational expectation of labor market discrimination. Therefore, the estimates of discrimination obtained from the inclusion and exclusion of occupation, industry, and government employment are best viewed for policy purposes as lower and upper bounds to measured discrimination.

Although the residual approach to measuring discrimination avoids the difficult questions regarding the interactions of social and political institutions in determining sex roles, the approach does possess a certain operational practicality. The objective is to arrive at a set of regression control variables that reasonably reflect legislative intent with regard to implied definitions of unlawful discrimination. The residual approach allows us to measure discrimination in accordance with legislative intent and to gauge progress in terms of this standard. It is obvious that there has been a growing impatience over the race and sex earnings differentials that have long persisted in our society. While there is a genuine scholarly interest in researching the formation of these roles, public policy toward discrimination has not awaited, and should not await, the definitive treatment of the subect.

APPENDIX

Background regressions which are used in the construction of Tables 1, 2, and 8 in the main text are reported in this appendix. The cross-section earnings regressions are reported in Tables A-1 and A-2, and the estimated equations for changes in occupational distribution are given in Table A-3.

A brief explanation will be given of the procedures used in connection with the cross-section earnings regressions. As is stated in the text, the cross-section data are drawn from the 1960 and 1970 Census 1/1000 Public Use Samples. In 1960, there was only one type of Public Use Sample available, but in 1970 there were six subcategories to choose from. For this study, the 1970 Neighborhood Characteristics 15 percent sample was used. Our data refer to those who worked 50–52 weeks in the year prior to the year in which the Census was conducted, who also resided inside urban areas, and who also were either government or private wage and salary workers.

Those familiar with Census data know that the Bureau of the Census establishes cutoff levels beyond which household and individual incomes are not reported. The cutoffs and their associated open intervals were $25,000 in 1960 and $50,000 in 1970. The problem confronting the researcher is what income should be assigned to individuals whose incomes are reported to lie somewhere in these open-ended intervals. A commonly accepted practice, and one which is followed in this study, is to estimate the upper tail of the income distribution as a Pareto distribution. From the Pareto distribution we can estimate the mean income of the above $25,000 or $50,000 class.

Assume that the Pareto density function describes the distribution of income above some level of income Y_0:

$$n(y) = \alpha Y_0^\alpha y^{-(1+\alpha)} \qquad \text{for } Y_0 < y < \infty$$
$$n(y) = 0 \qquad \text{for } y \leq y_0$$

where $\alpha > 1$.

TABLE A-1 Census Earnings Regressions for Whites

Dependent Variable: ln (earnings)	1960				1970			
	Male		Female		Male		Female	
	Equation 1	Equation 2	Equation 1	Equation 2	Equation 1	Equation 2	Equation 1	Equation 2
EXP	0.0224†	0.0241†	0.0224†	0.0253†	0.0263†	0.0310†	0.0256†	0.0284†
	(0.0010)	(0.0011)	(0.0015)	(0.0016)	(0.0010)	(0.0010)	(0.0016)	(0.0017)
$EXP^2/10$	-0.0031†	-0.0033†	-0.0034†	-0.0042†	-0.0038†	-0.0043†	-0.0039†	-0.0044†
	(0.0002)	(0.0002)	(0.0003)	(0.0003)	(0.0002)	(0.0002)	(0.0003)	(0.0003)
EDUC	0.0390†	0.0537†	0.0258†	0.0459†	0.0564†	0.0732†	0.0438†	0.0722†
	(0.0015)	(0.0014)	(0.0028)	(0.0027)	(0.0018)	(0.0015)	(0.0033)	(0.0029)
NEAST	0.0201	0.0109	0.0383*	0.0358	0.0318†	0.0435†	0.0542†	0.0583†
	(0.0114)	(0.0119)	(0.0180)	(0.0194)	(0.0121)	(0.0124)	(0.0193)	(0.0201)
NCENT	0.0862†	0.0848†	0.0546†	0.0409*	0.0676†	0.0841†	0.0186	0.0028
	(0.0116)	(0.0121)	(0.0186)	(0.0201)	(0.0122)	(0.0124)	(0.0195)	(0.0204)
WEST	0.0773†	0.0605†	0.0844†	0.0753†	0.0227	0.0096	0.0190	-0.0011
	(0.0129)	(0.0136)	(0.0204)	(0.0222)	(0.0129)	(0.0134)	(0.0210)	(0.0220)
U499	-0.0599†	-0.0614†	-0.1292†	-0.1561†	-0.0956†	-0.0964†	-0.1447†	-0.1572†
	(0.0109)	(0.0115)	(0.0164)	(0.0179)	(0.0127)	(0.0132)	(0.0195)	(0.0205)
UR499	-0.0232	-0.0162	-0.1056†	-0.1337†	-0.0378*	-0.0393*	-0.1370†	-0.1624†
	(0.0145)	(0.0153)	(0.0247)	(0.0268)	(0.0151)	(0.0156)	(0.0253)	(0.0265)
UR500	0.0888†	0.1083†	-0.0083	-0.0118	0.0570†	0.0786†	-0.0336*	-0.0360*
	(0.0093)	(0.0098)	(0.0151)	(0.0164)	(0.0102)	(0.0106)	(0.0161)	(0.0169)
SINGLE	-0.2900†	-0.3385†	-0.0189	-0.0385*	-0.4050†	-0.4722†	-0.0215	-0.0329
	(0.0132)	(0.0138)	(0.0169)	(0.0184)	(0.0139)	(0.0143)	(0.0191)	(0.0201)
DS	-0.0935†	-0.1377†	0.0146	-0.0271	-0.1360†	-0.1646†	0.0238	0.0177
	(0.0226)	(0.0238)	(0.0207)	(0.0226)	(0.0208)	(0.0216)	(0.0211)	(0.0222)
WID	-0.1768†	-0.1999†	-0.0145	-0.0440	-0.1493†	-0.1596†	-0.0017	-0.0150
	(0.0331)	(0.0350)	(0.0226)	(0.0247)	(0.0406)	(0.0422)	(0.0254)	(0.0267)

TABLE A-1 (continued)

Dependent Variable: ln (earnings)	1960				1970			
	Male		Female		Male		Female	
	Equation 1	Equation 2	Equation 1	Equation 2	Equation 1	Equation 2	Equation 1	Equation 2
CHILD	-0.2741† (0.0148)		-0.0415† (0.0049)	-0.0533† (0.0053)	-0.2575† (0.0166)		-0.0235† (0.0049)	-0.0302† (0.0051)
PARTIME		-0.3024† (0.0156)	-0.3494† (0.0164)	-0.4509† (0.0176)		-0.2762† (0.0171)	-0.3781† (0.0184)	-0.4600† (0.0190)
MOVE	0.0124 (0.0108)	-0.0103 (0.0113)	0.0519† (0.0183)	0.0349 (0.0200)	-0.0051 (0.0110)	-0.0209 (0.0112)	0.0218 (0.0198)	0.0339 (0.0208)
GOVT	-0.0360 (0.0190)		0.1793† (0.0280)		-0.1084† (0.0157)		0.1470† (0.0255)	
PROF	0.1158† (0.0188)		0.3669† (0.0369)		0.1355† (0.0192)		0.3960† (0.0372)	
MANAGE	0.2994† (0.0179)		0.4047† (0.0396)		0.2480† (0.0186)		0.4286† (0.0428)	
CLER	-0.1199† (0.0185)		0.2021† (0.0295)		-0.1102† (0.0202)		0.1937† (0.0308)	
CRAFT	-0.0146 (0.0173)		0.1821† (0.0550)		0.0090 (0.0181)		0.2910† (0.0546)	
OPER	-0.1327† (0.0175)		0.0689* (0.0346)		-0.0778† (0.0190)		0.1217† (0.0386)	
PRIV	-0.9112† (0.2291)		-0.6654† (0.0624)		-0.9597† (0.2305)		-0.5995† (0.0862)	
SERV	-0.2031† (0.0226)		-0.0622 (0.0348)		-0.1372† (0.0231)		-0.0540 (0.0356)	
LABOR	-0.1963† (0.0253)		-0.2058 (0.1095)		-0.2356† (0.0258)		-0.0124 (0.0746)	

	(1)	(2)	(3)	(4)
FARM	-0.4458† (0.1197)	-0.7368 (0.4867)	-0.4672† (0.1341)	-0.3817 (0.2713)
NOCC	-0.0179 (0.0346)	0.1126 (0.0604)		
AG	-0.0081 (0.0853)	0.2878 (0.1631)	0.1569 (0.0937)	-0.0255 (0.1778)
MINE	0.1676† (0.0596)	0.4882† (0.1287)	0.2518† (0.0538)	0.4337† (0.1215)
CON	0.2240† (0.0218)	0.0692 (0.0576)	0.2997† (0.0218)	0.3302† (0.0627)
DURMAN	0.2396† (0.0153)	0.2912† (0.0268)	0.2722† (0.0160)	0.2659† (0.0290)
NONDUR	0.2175† (0.0163)	0.2060* (0.0266)	0.2131† (0.0180)	0.1713† (0.0301)
TRANS	0.2094† (0.0173)	0.2824† (0.0304)	0.2699† (0.0184)	0.2894† (0.0336)
WTRADE	0.1837† (0.0202)	0.2116† (0.0365)	0.2222† (0.0203)	0.2146† (0.0380)
FINANCE	0.1113† (0.0211)	0.1419† (0.0269)	0.2114† (0.0221)	0.2021† (0.0275)
BUSREP	0.0941† (0.0263)	0.1317† (0.0445)	0.1199† (0.0261)	0.1607† (0.0430)
PERSER	-0.0696* (0.0334)	0.0080 (0.0401)	-0.0699 (0.0385)	-0.0853* (0.0414)
REC	0.0799 (0.0502)	0.0630 (0.0709)	0.1010* (0.0502)	0.0298 (0.0822)
PROFSER	-0.0423 (0.0225)	0.0010 (0.0270)	0.1168† (0.0208)	0.0709† (0.0258)
PUBADM	0.1860† (0.0266)	0.1118† (0.0422)	0.3448† (0.0238)	0.2049† (0.0421)

TABLE A-1 (concluded)

Dependent Variable: ln (earnings)	1960				1970			
	Male		Female		Male		Female	
	Equation 1	Equation 2	Equation 1	Equation 2	Equation 1	Equation 2	Equation 1	Equation 2
NOIND	0.1127† (0.0376)		0.1877† (0.0610)					
CONSTANT	7.7381	7.6938	7.2853	7.4142	7.8670	7.8042	7.3929	7.4099
S.E.E.	0.4522	0.4786	0.4576	0.5016	0.5556	0.5775	0.6098	0.6422
R^2	0.32	0.24	0.37	0.24	0.33	0.27	0.26	0.18
NOBS	13,996	13,996	5,650	5,650	17,746	17,746	8,293	8,293

SOURCE: U.S. Census 1/1000 Public Use Samples of 1960 and 1970. The Neighborhood Characteristics, 15 percent sample was the particular sample 1/1000 sample used for the 1970 regressions.

NOTE: Standard errors appear in parentheses. The difference between Equation 1 and Equation 2 is that Equation 2 does not control for government employment, occupation, or industry.

*Significant at the 0.05 level in a two-tailed test.
†Significant at the 0.01 level in a two-tailed test.

TABLE A-2 Census Earnings Regressions for Blacks

Dependent Variable: ln (earnings)	1960 Male		1960 Female		1970 Male		1970 Female	
	Equation 1	Equation 2	Equation 1	Equation 2	Equation 1	Equation 2	Equation 1	Equation 2
EXP	0.0260†	0.0297†	0.0106	0.0021	0.0325†	0.0325†	0.0271†	0.0288†
	(0.0036)	(0.0037)	(0.0059)	(0.0062)	(0.0040)	(0.0040)	(0.0054)	(0.0055)
EXP²/10	-0.0038†	-0.0044†	-0.0025*	-0.0016	-0.0047†	-0.0048†	-0.0043†	-0.0049†
	(0.0006)	(0.0006)	(0.0010)	(0.0011)	(0.0007)	(0.0007)	(0.0010)	(0.0010)
EDUC	0.0209†	0.0271†	0.0074	0.0376†	0.0320†	0.0425†	0.0405†	0.0871†
	(0.0043)	(0.0041)	(0.0083)	(0.0084)	(0.0064)	(0.0059)	(0.0096)	(0.0089)
NEAST	0.1670†	0.0959†	0.1835†	0.2673†	0.0553	0.0610	0.2107†	0.2618†
	(0.0357)	(0.0367)	(0.0604)	(0.0631)	(0.0435)	(0.0440)	(0.0541)	(0.0557)
NCENT	0.2418†	0.2923†	0.1403*	0.2095†	0.2120†	0.2321†	0.1506†	0.1923†
	(0.0352)	(0.0357)	(0.0597)	(0.0636)	(0.0431)	(0.0426)	(0.0548)	(0.0566)
WEST	0.2731†	0.3162†	0.1754	0.2580	0.1613†	0.1592†	0.1898*	0.2241†
	(0.0533)	(0.0550)	(0.0927)	(0.0989)	(0.0555)	(0.0603)	(0.0751)	(0.0789)
U499	-0.1152†	-0.1300†	-0.2470†	-0.3794†	-0.1252†	-0.1384†	-0.0956	-0.1168*
	(0.0349)	(0.0361)	(0.0585)	(0.0624)	(0.0452)	(0.0458)	(0.0570)	(0.0596)
UR499	-0.3979†	-0.3906†	-0.2810*	-0.3089*	0.0582	0.0068	-0.1639	-0.1295
	(0.1017)	(0.1050)	(0.1267)	(0.1362)	(0.0910)	(0.0904)	(0.1132)	(0.1191)
UR500	0.0191	-0.0030	0.0129	-0.0621	-0.0036	0.0168	-0.0697	-0.0456
	(0.0440)	(0.0456)	(0.0795)	(0.0856)	(0.0477)	(0.0484)	(0.0613)	(0.0645)
SINGLE	-0.2183†	-0.2500†	-0.0482	-0.1092	-0.3325†	-0.3824†	0.0315	0.0031
	(0.0430)	(0.0447)	(0.0719)	(0.0776)	(0.0491)	(0.0494)	(0.0612)	(0.0645)
DS	-0.0117	-0.0478	0.0332	0.0024	-0.0670	-0.1059	0.0917	0.0332
	(0.0465)	(0.0482)	(0.0572)	(0.0615)	(0.0546)	(0.0555)	(0.0516)	(0.0541)
WID	-0.1030	-0.1761*	0.0729	-0.0245	-0.1778	-0.2153	0.0586	-0.0692
	(0.0856)	(0.0886)	(0.0729)	(0.0782)	(0.1107)	(0.1129)	(0.0773)	(0.0806)

TABLE A-2 (continued)

Dependent Variable: ln (earnings)	1960				1970			
	Male		Female		Male		Female	
	Equation 1	Equation 2	Equation 1	Equation 2	Equation 1	Equation 2	Equation 1	Equation 2
CHILD			-0.0083 (0.0122)	-0.0062 (0.0129)			-0.0196* (0.0097)	-0.0241* (0.0102)
PARTIME	-0.2860† (0.0400)	-0.2993† (0.0414)	-0.4362† (0.0508)	-0.5445† (0.0539)	-0.1258* (0.0613)	-0.1565* (0.0620)	-0.1296* (0.0569)	-0.2469† (0.0588)
MOVE	-0.0535 (0.0474)	-0.0475 (0.0491)	-0.0146 (0.0878)	-0.1985* (0.0928)	0.0370 (0.0507)	0.0419 (0.0507)	0.0492 (0.0680)	0.0512 (0.0588)
GOVT	0.0776 (0.0510)		0.1988* (0.1010)		-0.0084 (0.0538)		0.1499* (0.0638)	
PROF	0.0758 (0.1364)		0.3076 (0.2279)		0.2602* (0.1139)		0.2872 (0.1535)	
MANAGE	0.0477 (0.1656)		0.1143 (0.3587)		0.2824* (0.1249)		0.2164 (0.1961)	
CLER	0.0086 (0.1193)		0.3035 (0.2085)		0.0144 (0.0989)		-0.0073 (0.1389)	
CRAFT	-0.0036 (0.1176)		-0.1594 (0.3003)		0.0524 (0.0973)		-0.1950 (0.2094)	
OPER	-0.0106 (0.1139)		0.0357 (0.2166)		-0.0239 (0.0943)		-0.0995 (0.1507)	
PRIV	-0.3197 (0.2349)		-0.2672 (0.2202)		-0.2065 (0.4331)		-0.6454† (0.1675)	
SERV	-0.1367 (0.1144)		-0.0925 (0.1973)		-0.1556 (0.0943)		-0.1740 (0.1390)	

	(1)	(2)	(3)	(4)
LABOR	-0.0961 (0.1162)	0.3793 (0.3465)	-0.1437 (0.0978)	0.0463 (0.2237)
FARM	-0.5651 (0.4311)		-0.9071* (0.4595)	0.5971 (0.8580)
NOCC	0.0376 (0.1373)	-0.1266 (0.2843)		
AG	0.1090 (0.3431)		-0.0164 (0.3637)	-0.4323 (0.7392)
MINE	0.2018 (0.4783)		-0.0326 (0.3259)	-0.0814 (0.7314)
CON	0.2281† (0.0755)	0.0137 (0.6271)	0.2049* (0.0860)	0.5193 (0.2960)
DURMAN	0.3661† (0.0506)	0.4443† (0.1646)	0.2310† (0.0645)	0.2979† (0.1133)
NONDUR	0.3007† (0.0537)	0.1841 (0.1365)	0.1707* (0.0726)	0.1913 (0.1103)
TRANS	0.2340† (0.0569)	0.2070 (0.2342)	0.1861† (0.0719)	0.2611* (0.1275)
WTRADE	0.2526† (0.0824)	0.1447 (0.2945)	0.0465 (0.0907)	0.2684 (0.1860)
FINANCE	-0.0262 (0.0843)	-0.0276 (0.1582)	0.0542 (0.0970)	-0.0506 (0.1107)
BUSREP	-0.0591 (0.0942)	-0.2281 (0.2298)	0.0280 (0.1017)	-0.0303 (0.1505)
PERSER	-0.0481 (0.0716)	-0.1158 (0.1146)	-0.1633 (0.1094)	0.0210 (0.1057)
REC	-0.1631 (0.1345)	0.2221 (0.3620)	-0.7850† (0.2222)	0.5806* (0.2833)
PROPSER	0.2074† (0.0731)	0.1001 (0.0986)	0.0215 (0.0817)	0.1476 (0.0832)

TABLE A-2 (concluded)

Dependent Variable: ln (earnings)	1960				1970			
	Male		Female		Male		Female	
	Equation 1	Equation 2	Equation 1	Equation 2	Equation 1	Equation 2	Equation 1	Equation 2
PUBADM	0.2565†		0.2030		0.2527†		0.2799*	
	(0.0754)		(0.1573)		(0.0857)		(0.1152)	
NOIND	0.1158		0.2105					
	(0.0960)		(0.2266)					
CONSTANT	7.3907	7.4536	7.4039	7.3362	7.7694	7.7791	7.2733	6.8556
S.E.E.	0.4755	0.5003	0.6043	0.6598	0.7116	0.7296	0.7231	0.7682
R^2	0.33	0.24	0.44	0.31	0.19	0.14	0.28	0.17
NOBS	1,374	1,374	768	768	1,981	1,981	1,315	1,315

SOURCE: See Table A-1.
NOTE: Standard errors appear in parentheses. The difference between Equation 1 and Equation 2 is that Equation 2 does not control for government employment, occupation, or industry.
*Significant at the 0.05 level in a two-tailed test.
†Significant at the 0.01 level in a two-tailed test.

TABLE A-3 **Estimated Equations for Changes in Occupational Distribution (1958–71)**
(Dependent variable: percent employment in a given occupation[a])

Occupation	Constant	Time	Unemployment Rate of White Males 35–44[b]	$\bar{R}^2$	Durbin-Watson
		A. White Males			
Professional and technical	11.3643† (0.5480)	0.2736† (0.0299)	−0.2278 (0.1338)	0.95	0.94
Managerial, officials, and proprietors	13.2259† (0.7473)	0.1093* (0.0407)	0.2450 (0.1825)	0.32	1.74
Clerical and sales	13.6593† (0.4492)	−0.0416 (0.0245)	−0.0124 (0.1097)	0.23	1.83
Craftsmen	20.3804† (0.5230)	0.0574 (0.0285)	−0.1986 (0.1277)	0.64	1.33
Operatives	22.9887† (0.5801)	−0.1853† (0.0316)	−0.9266† (0.1417)	0.77	1.42
Laborers	5.2030† (0.5441)	0.0180 (0.0297)	0.3614† (0.1329)	0.44	1.10
Service and private household	4.3243† (0.7091)	0.1155* (0.0387)	0.3495 (0.1732)	0.35	2.27
Farming	9.1708† (0.2923)	−0.3609† (0.0159)	0.3567† (0.0714)	0.99	1.69
		B. White Females			
Professional and technical	12.3432† (0.4514)	0.1972† (0.0246)	−0.0193 (0.1102)	0.92	1.72
Managerial, officials, and proprietors	4.6197† (0.4684)	−0.0033 (0.0255)	0.1856 (0.1144)	0.27	1.74
Clerical and sales	42.5092† (0.9368)	0.1812† (0.0511)	−0.5583* (0.2288)	0.84	1.72
Craftsmen	0.9042† (0.1285)	0.0215* (0.0070)	0.0130 (0.0314)	0.54	1.76
Operatives	19.1335† (0.3786)	−0.2298† (0.0206)	−0.9497† (0.0925)	0.91	1.77
Laborers	−0.0432 (0.1748)	0.0306† (0.0095)	0.0861 (0.0427)	0.40	2.20
Service and private household	17.2516† (0.0984)	0.0068 (0.0599)	0.7475* (0.2683)	0.53	1.46
Farming	3.1531* (0.4126)	−0.1974* (0.0770)	0.5238 (0.3450)	0.71	0.97

TABLE A-3 (concluded)

C. Nonwhite Males

Occupation	Constant	Time	$\bar{R}^2$	Durbin-Watson
Professional and technical	2.5417† (0.3678)	0.3769† (0.0201)	0.98	2.12
Managerial, officials, and proprietors	0.6109 (0.5462)	0.2406† (0.0298)	0.86	1.78
Clerical and sales	5.8846† (0.9903)	0.2473† (0.0540)	0.77	1.27
Craftsmen	10.3353† (0.7423)	0.3378† (0.0405)	0.95	1.96
Operatives	26.9486† (1.0229)	0.2436† (0.0558)	0.92	2.02
Laborers	24.7543† (1.5901)	−0.5894† (0.0867)	0.90	1.26
Service and private household	15.7325† (2.0518)	−0.0622 (0.1119)	−0.14	0.75
Farming	13.3805† (1.1225)	−0.8018† (0.0612)	0.98	1.98

D. Nonwhite Females

Occupation	Constant	Time	Unemployment Rate of White Males 35–44[b]	$\bar{R}^2$	Durbin-Watson
Professional and technical	5.7407† (0.6636)	0.4021† (0.0362)	−0.2782 (0.1621)	0.96	1.64
Managerial, officials, and proprietors	0.6007 (0.4320)	0.0586* (0.0236)	0.2362* (0.1055)	0.26	1.84
Clerical and sales	3.0082 (2.2699)	1.4183† (0.1237)	0.6044 (0.5544)	0.95	0.61
Craftsmen	0.2413 (0.1560)	0.0404† (0.0085)	0.0509 (0.0381)	0.71	2.32
Operatives	16.1651† (1.7777)	0.1921 (0.0969)	−0.9050 (0.4342)	0.70	0.87
Laborers	0.2082 (0.2760)	0.0194 (0.0150)	0.1528* (0.0674)	0.21	2.76
Service and private household	66.4093† (5.1175)	−1.4205† (0.2790)	−1.2912 (1.2499)	0.76	0.54
Farming	7.8541* (3.1927)	−0.7245† (0.1740)	1.3951 (0.7797)	0.84	1.21

*Significant at the 0.05 level in a two-tailed test.
†Significant at the 0.01 level in a two-tailed test.
[a]Refer to footnote a in Table 6 of the text.
[b]Refer to footnote b in Table 3 of the text.

The cumulative distribution is given by

$$N(y) = \int_{Y_0}^{y} n(v)\,dv = 1 - Y_0^{\alpha} y^{-\alpha}$$

where $N(y)$ is the proportion of workers earning incomes less than or equal to y. Let $G(y)$ be the proportion of workers earning incomes greater than y, then

$$G(y) = 1 - N(y) = Y_0^{\alpha} y^{-\alpha}$$

or in terms of logs,

$$\ln G(y) = \alpha \ln (Y_0) - \alpha \ln (y)$$

Let $G(Y_1)$ and $G(Y_2)$ be the proportion of workers earning incomes greater than Y_1 and Y_2, respectively. By substituting these pairs of values into the equation for $\ln G(y)$ and solving for α, we obtain

$$\hat{\alpha} = -\ln |G(Y_1)/G(Y_2)|/\ln (Y_1/Y_2)$$

We have for 1960 $Y_1 = \$15,000$ and $Y_2 = \$25,000$, but for 1970 $Y_1 = \$35,000$ and $Y_2 = \$50,000$.

The average income of those earning above $Y_2 (\bar{Y}_h)$ is calculated as the conditional mean of y for $y \geq Y_2$:

$$\bar{Y}_h = E(Y|y \geq Y_2) = \int_{y_2}^{\infty} yn(y)\,dy \bigg/ \int_{y_2}^{\infty} n(y)\,dy = \frac{\hat{\alpha}}{\hat{\alpha} - 1} Y_2$$

where $Y_2 = \$25,000$ and $\$50,000$ for 1960 and 1970, respectively. Values of $\bar{Y}_h$ were estimated in each year for the combined sample of all four race/sex groups. Each worker whose income was reported in the open-ended interval was assigned an income of $\bar{Y}_h$. For the independent variables, these workers were assigned the mean values corresponding to the members of their particular race/sex group whose incomes were in the open-ended interval.

The independent variables used in the earnings regressions are briefly defined here. EXP = potential experience calculated as age − education − 6 years. EDUC = years of schooling completed. NEAST, NCENT, and WEST are regional dummy variables representing the Northeast, Northcentral, and West, respectively. The South is the regional reference group. U499, UR499, and UR500 are urban city size dummy variables representing residence in a central city located in an urban area of 50,000–499,999, residence in the remainder of an urban area 50,000–499,999, and residence in the remainder of an urban area of 500,000 or greater. Residence in a central city located in an urban area of 500,000 or greater is the city size reference group. SINGLE, DS, and

WID are marital status dummy variables representing never married, divorced or separated, and widowed. Married workers form the marital status reference group. CHILD = the number of children born to the female worker. PARTIME is a dummy variable which identifies individuals who worked less than thirty-five hours during the week prior to the Census week. MOVE is a dummy variable which identifies individuals who have changed county, state, or national residence since the age of eighteen during the previous five years. GOVT is a dummy variable which identifies government workers. The occupational dummy variables are defined as follows: PROF = professional, technical, and kindred workers; MANAGE = managers and administrators, except farm; CLER = clerical and kindred workers; CRAFT = craftsmen and kindred workers; OPER = operatives (including transport equipment operatives); PRIV = private household workers; SERV = service workers; LABOR = laborers, except farm; FARM = farmers, farm managers, farm laborers, and farm foremen; and NOCC = no occupation reported. Sales workers form the occupational reference group. The industry dummy variables are as follows: AG = agriculture, forestry, forestry, and fisheries; MINE = mining; CON = construction; DURMAN = manufacturing, durable goods; NONDUR = manufacturing, nondurable goods; TRANS = transportation, communications, and utilities and sanitary services; WTRADE = wholesale trade; FINANCE = finance, insurance, and real estate; BUSREP = business and repair services; PERSER = personal services; REC = entertainment and recreation services; PROFSER = professional and related services; PUBADM = public administration; and NOIND = industry not reported. Retail trade workers form the industry reference group.

NOTES

1. Computer delays and difficulties precluded carrying out these tests. For additional information on these testing procedures see [Oaxaca 1974].
2. The earnings data from the 1960 and 1970 censuses correspond to 1959 and 1969, respectively.
3. Because of rounding-off errors, these mutually exhaustive decompositions do not, in general, add up to the exact value of the gross differential in logs.
4. Had we instead assumed the female earnings structure to be the common earnings structure, the effects of childbearing would have shown up entirely as the effects of differences in the mean values of the independent variables, e.g., as a source of earnings differentials attributable to worker productivity differences.
5. This specification was suggested to the author by Andrea Beller.

6. The time-series estimates of d along with their associated standard errors are given below.

Whites		Nonwhites
0.0025*	0.0026*	−0.0218†
(0.0011)	(0.0011)	(0.0037)

*Significant at the 0.05 level in a two-tailed test.
†Significant at the 0.01 level in a two-tailed test.

7. To handle the discrepancies from rounding-off errors in the cross-section decompositions, the difference between the actual and calculated gross differentials in logs was apportioned equally between the measures of discrimination and productivity differences reported in Tables 1 and 2.
8. The results also predict that the male/female labor quality ratio for whites should peak in 1974.
9. The separate occupational regressions are reported by race and sex in Table A-3 of the appendix.

REFERENCES

Ashenfelter, Orley. "Changes in Labor Market Discrimination Over Time." *Journal of Human Resources* 5, no. 4 (Fall 1970).

Ashenfelter, Orley, and Rees, Albert, eds. *Discrimination in Labor Markets.* Princeton: Princeton University Press, 1973.

Becker, Gary S. *The Economics of Discrimination.* Chicago: University of Chicago Press, 1971.

Becker, Gary S., and Chiswick, Barry R. "Education and the Distribution of Earnings." *American Economic Review* 56, no. 2 (May 1966).

Bergmann, B. R., and Adelman, I. "The 1973 Report of the President's Council of Economic Advisors: The Economic Role of Women." *American Economic Review* 63, no. 4 (Sept. 1973).

Blinder, Alan S. "Wage Discrimination: Reduced Form and Structural Estimates." *Journal of Human Resources* 8, no. 4 (Fall 1973).

Bronfenbrenner, Martin. *Income Distribution Theory.* Chicago: Aldine-Atherton, 1971.

Council of Economic Advisors. *Economic Report of the President.* Washington, D.C.: Government Printing Office, 1973.

Fuchs, Victor R. "Differences in Hourly Earnings Between Men and Women." *Monthly Labor Review* 94, no. 5 (May 1971).

———. "Short-Run and Long-Run Prospects for Female Earnings." NBER Working paper No. 20, December 1973.

Gurin, Patricia. "Research Requirements for Employment Discrimination." Paper presented to the Research Workshop on Equal Employment Opportunity, Alfred P. Sloan School of Management, M.I.T., January 1974.

Hurd, M. D. "Changes in Wage Rates Between 1959 and 1967." *Review of Economics and Statistics* 53, no. 2 (May 1971).

Johnson, Thomas. "Returns from Investment in Human Capital." *American Economic Review* 60, no. 4 (Sept. 1970).

Laws, Judith Long. "Psychological Factors in Women's Work Motivation." Paper presented to the Research Workshop on Equal Employment Opportunity, Alfred P. Sloan School of Management, M.I.T., January 1974.

Malkiel, B. G., and Malkiel, J. A. "Male-Female Pay Differentials in Professional Employment." *American Economic Review* 63, no. 4 (Sept. 1973).

Oaxaca, Ronald L. "Male-Female Wage Differentials in Urban Labor Markets." *International Economic Review* 14, no. 3 (Oct. 1973).

———. "Another Look at Tests of Equality Between Sets of Coefficients in Two Linear Regressions." *American Economist* 18, no. 1 (Spring 1974).

Polachek, Solomon W. "Differences in Expected Post-School Investment as a Determinant of Market Wage Differentials." Paper presented to the Research Workshop on Equal Employment Opportunity, Alfred P. Sloan School of Management, M.I.T., January 1974.

8 ‖ COMMENTS

Nancy Smith Barrett
American University

Ronald Oaxaca has applied a previously developed methodology to analyze trends in male-female earnings differentials in the period 1955–71.[1] The approach is an attempt to sort out the effect of discrimination from other factors that might account for the earnings gap and to test hypotheses about changes in sex discrimination since 1955.

Oaxaca concludes from his analysis that for white year-round, full-time workers, the male-female differential in median earnings (adjusted for hours worked) increased by 15 percent from 1955 to 1971 with about 55 percent of this attributable to increased discrimination and the rest due to the relative increase in an index of male to female labor quality. He found a small rate of decline in the rate of increase in discrimination after 1965 which he suggests may be related to more favorable government policies toward women reflected in the 1963 Federal Equal Pay Act and the 1964 Civil Rights Act.

For nonwhite year-round, full-time workers, Oaxaca found a significant decline in the male-female earnings differential, from 73 percent in 1955 to 33 percent in 1971 and concludes that practically all of this gain for black women represented a decline in sex discrimination. He makes the interesting, and I believe accurate, suggestion that this decline in the black sex differential not attributable to differences in labor quality was more likely due to black women gaining access to jobs formerly held by white women than their penetration of male occupations. If this is true, it is, of course, inappropriate to refer to the effect as a decline in sex discrimination per se, but instead it should be attributed to differential rates of change of racial discrimination by sex.

Oaxaca found very little change in male-female occupational structure over the period. Employment of women relative to men increased most rapidly in the sales and clerical fields that were already traditionally dominated by women, supporting the view that the relative deterioration of female wages during a period of rapid influx into the labor force is due to crowding into occupations where their wages are low because of their exclusion from other kinds of work.[2] White females lost representation relative to white males in the Professional and Technical, Managerial, and Officials and Proprietors categories, suggesting that efforts to penetrate higher status occupations have not been successful. Oaxaca also found that the sex earnings gap falls in tight labor markets, suggesting that prosperity promotes equality and recession fosters discrimination.

The tone of Oaxaca's conclusions is hedgingly optimistic. We still have sex discrimination, particularly among whites, but its rate of increase is on the decline. And black women are faring much better relative to black men, albeit at the expense of white women. And if we can regain prosperity and full employment we can expect even more success.

Oaxaca's paper addresses an extremely important issue, particularly in view of an explicitly stated governmental policy to reduce discrimination in the United States. Unfortunately, I cannot concur with the author's optimistic interpretation of the trends.

My objections are concerned with both his methodology and interpretation. I have always been uneasy about studies that treat discrimination as an un-explained residual, since we have available a number of hypotheses about the way discrimination is transmitted that are certainly susceptible to empirical testing. But if we can ignore that issue—and let me say parenthetically that I think it is extremely dangerous to let this research be disseminated outside of econometric conferences with the label "discrimination" applied to the unex-plained residual—we must, at least, be sure that we have accounted for all the factors that might have been responsible for changes in the sex earning gap before we draw conclusions about trends in discrimination. This isn't to say everything must be included—but the important things must be.

To use an index of years of schooling as a measure of labor quality and then to use this index as the sole source of nondiscriminatory wage change (other than hours worked) may be permissible for a study of black-white earnings differen-tials, a la Ashenfelter,[3] but its extension to an analysis of sex discrimination is not warranted. Oaxaca observes that a major difference between race and sex factors is that female labor force participation has increased sharply relative to that of men, whereas this has not been the case for blacks relative to whites. What Oaxaca does not observe is that the age composition of the female labor force has also undergone a radical change over the period, particularly for white women, with an important shift occuring around 1965 that increased the relative participation of women under 25. We are all aware that the age profiles of male-female earnings, particularly for whites, are not very far apart until around age 25 and then widen rapidly until age 55 when they begin to close again. There are a number of reasons for this, involving barriers to the acquisition of human capital and to managerial jobs for women, but I do not have time to explore these issues here. The point is that these discrepancies in the age-profiles of the male-female earnings rates, together with a shift in the age composition of new labor force entrants around 1965, can more than account for the so-called decline in the rate of increase in discrimination Oaxaca observes when his data are not adjusted for age.

Table 1 shows the percent change in labor force participation rates for white women over the period 1955–71, and for the subperiods 1955–65 and 1966–71.

TABLE 1 **Percentage Change in Labor Force Participation Rates of White Females by Age, 1955–71**

Period	Age								
	16+	16–17	18–19	20–24	25–34	35–44	45–54	55–64	65+
1955–71	23.5	21.7	5.8	26.4	32.9	25.8	25.8	33.6	−11.4
1955–65	10.4	−4.0	−2.7	7.4	10.7	11.0	16.9	26.7	−7.6
1966–71	11.8	26.8	8.7	17.7	20.1	13.3	7.6	5.5	−4.1
Female/male earnings ratio (1966)	.57	.87	.87	.68	.55	.48	.50	.55	.62

SOURCE: Labor Force Participation Rates: U.S. Department of Labor, *Manpower Report of the President*, 1973. Earnings Ratio: Isabel V. Sawhill, "The Economics of Discrimination Against Women: Some New Findings," *Journal of Human Resources* 8 (Summer 1973), pp. 383–395. Estimated from the *Current Population Survey*, 1966.

In the earlier period, the growth in participation for young women was considerably below the average for all women, with the highest rates of entry coming in the age group with the largest male-female earnings gap. Since 1966–71 the rate of entry is much higher for young women, who experience much less discrimination with respect to earnings. However, and this is extremely important, just because these young women have higher earnings relative to men than older women, there is no evidence that they will not face exactly the same sort of wage discrimination for the same reasons when they get older. Hall and others have suggested that older black workers as a group have relatively low earnings because of a "vintage effect," that is, they have less education than younger workers.[4] This implies that the improved earnings position of younger black workers represents a real gain due to a decline in discrimination in educational opportunity. But educational opportunities have not changed significantly for women over the period and lower wages for older women undoubtedly reflect their inability or unwillingness to acquire human capital or to attain managerial status that would increase their earnings profile as they age. This means that an increase in overall female earnings as a result of a reduction in the average age of the female work force does not imply that discrimination has declined or that any individual woman has a higher expected lifetime earnings stream than before, even though a different interpretation could be made for blacks. It may well be that consciousness-raising has produced an incentive for younger women to penetrate male occupations, but there is not evidence of this and Oaxaca's occupational results do not suggest such a trend.

In Table 2, I show some crude estimates of the impact of changes in the age structure of the female labor force that would have occurred if there had been no change in the male-female earnings ratio by age. ER is the female-male earnings ratio by age for full-time workers computed from the Current Population Survey in 1966 and adjusted for hours worked. Over the entire 1955–71 period, for white females, changes in their age distribution alone should have *increased* the overall ER by .61 percent per year. In the earlier period, 1955–65, the potential annual rate of increase was .41 percent, while in 1966–71 it was 1.2 percent! Now these estimates are admittedly crude and the use of 1966 earnings data was arbitrary. However, Fuchs has shown that there is not much difference in the age profiles of the sex earnings ratios between 1960 and 1970.[5] On the other hand, there is likely to be some interaction in the labor quality index that would reduce the absolute marginal impact of the age effect.

Apart from the implications for the absolute changes in sex discrimination (that now will increase by the amount of the potential increase in ER associated with changing age composition) what is most interesting is the huge difference in this effect before and after 1965. Not only has the rate of increase in the wage gap attributable to discrimination increased by about .6 percent more per year overall than Oaxaca estimates (less any interaction with the labor quality index), but the rate of increase in discrimination would increase substantially (by .8 percent per year) after 1965 rather than decrease. Not only is all the slowdown Oaxaca observes explained by the changing age distribution of the female labor force, but it is more than accounted for and by a large margin, indicating an increase rather than decline in the *rate of increase* of discrimination. The influx of young men into the labor force since the deescalation in Vietnam has undoutedly worked in the same direction, but I have not tried to estimate that effect.

Table 3 shows similar computations for black females. Changing age distribution had very little effect on their earnings relative to black males, except after 1965 when a changing age composition had the potential effect of increasing the female-male earnings ratio by .9 percent per year. This implies that after 1965, Oaxaca overstated the amount of reduction in sex discrimination (if one can properly call it that) in the black labor force.

Not only does Oaxaca fail to correct for age, but the assumptions he makes about his labor quality index may also bias his results. For instance, in order to obtain the result that the rate of discrimination declined after 1965 he had to assume that the male and female labor quality indexes grew at a constant rate. Since his entire paper was concerned with trend analysis, I am puzzled that he did not test for a nonlinear trend in the labor quality indexes also. Since there is, for all practical purposes, a finite limit to the amount of formal education one receives (statistically it is the 16+ category), then labor quality cannot grow indefinitely. More than likely, the relative educational gains of white males is a once and for all phenomenon. Furthermore, as Oaxaca observes, if labor quality

TABLE 2 **Estimated Effect of Changing Age Composition of the White Female Labor Force on the Female/Male Earnings Ratio, 1955–71**

Age (Group i)	Change in Labor Force of Age Group (Thousands) (1)	Change in (LF); Relative to Overall Change in Labor Force (2)	$\dfrac{ER_i}{ER}$ (3)	(2) × (3) (4)
1955–71	(Average Annual Rate of Change 0.61 Percent)			
16+	10,103	1.00	1.00	
16–17	634	0.063	1.534	.097
18–19	783	0.078	1.534	.120
20–24	2,285	0.226	1.199	.271
25–34	1,422	0.141	0.970	.137
35–44	952	0.094	0.846	.080
45–54	2,160	0.214	0.881	.189
55–64	1,631	0.161	0.970	.156
65+	236	0.023	1.093	.025
				Σ = 1.073
1955–65	(Average Annual Rate of Change 0.41 Percent)			
16+	4,870	1.00	1.00	
16–17	286	0.059	1.534	.091
18–19	439	0.090	1.534	.138
20–24	773	0.159	1.199	.191
25–34	22	0.005	0.970	.005
35–44	745	0.153	0.846	.129
45–54	1,378	0.283	0.881	.249
55–64	1,046	0.215	0.970	.209
65+	159	0.033	1.093	.036
				Σ = 1.047
1966–71	(Average Annual Rate of Change 1.2 Percent)			
16+	4,287	1.00	1.00	
16–17	266	0.062	1.534	.095
18–19	119	0.028	1.534	.043
20–24	1,299	0.303	1.199	.363
25–34	1,236	0.288	0.970	.279
35–44	189	0.044	0.846	.037
45–54	633	0.148	0.881	.130
55–64	454	0.106	0.970	.103
65+	91	0.021	1.093	.023
				Σ = 1.074

SOURCE: See Table 1.

TABLE 3 **Estimated Effect of Changing Age Composition of the Black Female Labor Force on the Female/Male Earnings Ratio, 1955–71**

Age (Group i)	Change in Labor Force of Age Group (Thousands) (1)	Change in (LF)$_i$ Relative to Overall Change in Labor Force (2)	$\dfrac{ER_i}{ER}$ (3)	(2) × (3) (4)
1955–71 (Average Annual Rate of Change 0.15 Percent)				
16+	1,439	1.00	1.00	
16–17	57	0.040	1.29	.052
18–19	95	0.066	1.25	.083
20–24	342	0.238	1.12	.267
25–34	259	0.180	1.02	.184
35–44	198	0.138	0.917	.127
45–54	256	0.178	0.899	.160
55–64	194	0.135	0.951	.128
65+	41	0.028	1.07	.030
				$\Sigma = \overline{1.029}$
1955–65 (Average Annual Rate of Change 0.0 Percent)				
16+	801	1.00	1.00	
16–17	27	0.034	1.29	.044
18–19	37	0.046	1.25	.057
20–24	147	0.184	1.12	.206
25–34	55	0.069	1.02	.070
35–44	171	0.213	0.917	.195
45–54	181	0.226	0.899	.203
55–64	148	0.185	0.951	.176
65+	36	0.045	1.07	.048
				$\Sigma = \overline{1.000}$
1966–71 (Average Annual Rate of Change 0.9 Percent)				
16+	505	1.00	1.00	
16–17	12	0.024	1.29	.031
18–19	24	0.048	1.25	.060
20–24	183	0.362	1.12	.405
25–34	188	0.372	1.02	.379
35–44	8	0.016	0.917	.015
45–54	53	0.105	0.899	.094
55–64	35	0.069	0.951	.066
65+	2	0.004	1.07	.004
				$\Sigma = \overline{1.055}$

SOURCE: See Table 1.

is related to experience as well as to education, then the growing attachment of females to the labor force ought to raise relative female labor quality. If these factors were taken into account, male labor quality relative to female labor quality would not have increased at a constant rate over the period and the earnings gap attributable to discrimination would have been greater. Furthermore, if the rate of relative gains of men slowed later in the period, then the decline in the rate of growth of discrimination cited by Oaxaca would not have been observed.

In general, I find it very difficult to be optimistic about trends in sex discrimination when so little progress seems to be made in reducing occupational segregation by sex. We all know that instances of unequal pay for equal work are rare and that the Equal Pay Act of 1963 merely ratified existing practice. The Civil Rights Act of 1964 was more specifically addressed to the issue of occupational discrimination, but the evidence is that women are losing rather than gaining representation in high status occupations.

There are other problems. The paper fails to address the consequences of inability of many women to get full-time work. The interpretation of the cyclical results also has to be viewed with caution. My own work, for instance, has shown female unemployment to rise relative to men's in tight labor markets,[6] suggesting that prosperity does not unequivocally improve the labor force status of women.

Most of my remarks have been addressed to sex differentials among whites, in part because discrimination on the basis of sex seems to be more of a problem and a growing problem within that group. However, while I have less quarrel with the data for sex differences between blacks, I have difficulty accepting the interpretation that sex discrimination per se is any less present. Black women are not penetrating male occupations; racial discrimination is simply less severe among women. Undoubtedly this is because no women—black or white—gain much from seniority. Hierarchical relationships in female employment are less prevalent and black women and white women are systematically excluded (voluntarily or involuntarily) from acquiring human capital and attaining managerial positions. To the extent that black women drop out of the labor force less frequently than white women, they may even have an advantage. It is disturbing indeed if this equalization among women is cited as a triumph for racial equality and as a sign of lessening of racial discrimination. There are simply fewer channels through which racial discrimination can be transmitted among females than among males. And my own personal opinion is that women workers have less of a Beckerian taste for discrimination[7] in general, in part because they feel less threatened by the encroachment of racial minorities on their jobs or pay standards.

Despite these reservations about the interpretation of the experience of the 1960s, for a number of reasons I, personally, see some grounds for optimism about the future relative income position of women. First and foremost are the social changes and the growing awareness of young women that sex roles based on outdated needs and institutions need not limit their labor force experience to being a nurse, secretary, domestic worker, saleslady, or elementary school teacher. I think young women are growing increasingly to expect a more or less continuous labor force commitment and that the men they live with will, in turn, see that these trends are to their advantage as well. Most of the evidence that I have seen suggests that if progress is being made along these lines it is at a snail's pace. The ideology of the women's movement has developed much faster than its practical implications. But to evaluate these prospects in a rigorous and scientific way, as opposed to an impressionistic one, one needs an underlying theoretical rationale for discrimination on which to base a structural model. For instance, one approach suggests that women as a group will only attain equality with men if they penetrate male occupations at an early age, stay in the labor force, and acquire human capital and assume managerial responsibilities conducive to substantial growth of their wages over the life cycle. In other words, occupational choices of *young* women may be the key to forecasting the future age-earnings profile of all female workers. The empirical analogue to this model would be to examine changes in the sex composition of the various occupational categories by age group to determine whether or not the observed tendency of the female-dominated occupations to absorb most of the increases in the female labor force is due to the choices of young women or instead to those of older women whose career horizons may be more limited. The implications for the future course of male-female wage differentials may be much more interesting than any simple extrapolation in the trend of some unexplained residual—labeled "discrimination" only for want of a better word, and perhaps to elicit some emotional reaction. Such pure empiricism can only run up against some of the problems I have described. Again, I applaud the effort to measure discrimination and to ascertain whether or not it is waning. But to design effective social policy to eliminate discrimination, one must develop a theoretical explanation, not just a chart of its course.

NOTES

1. Oaxaca's paper extends the methodology developed by Gary S. Becker in *The Economics of Discrimination* (Chicago: University of Chicago Press, 1957) and applied by Orley Ashenfelter in "Changes in Labor Market Discrimination over Time," *The Journal of Human Resources* 5 (Fall 1970), pp. 403–430, to analyze racial discrimination.
2. This hypothesis is suggested by Barbara Bergmann in "The Effect on White Incomes of Discrimination in Employment," *Journal of Political Economy* 74 (March-April 1971), pp. 294–313.
3. Ashenfelter, "Changes in Labor Market Discrimination."
4. See Robert E. Hall's discussion of a paper by Richard B. Freeman, "Changes in the Labor Market for Black Americans," *Brookings Papers on Economic Activity* (1973: 1), p. 126.
5. Victor R. Fuchs, "Short-Run and Long-Run Prospects for Female Earnings," presented at the Annual Meeting of the American Economic Association, December, 1973.
6. Nancy S. Barrett and Richard D. Morgenstern, "Why Do Blacks and Women Have High Unemployment Rates?" *The Journal of Human Resources* 9 (Fall 1974), pp. 452–462.
7. Becker, *The Economics of Discrimination.*

Alvin Mickens

New York University

Oaxaca's paper represents an enormously innovative and up-to-date measurement of the discrimination component in the earnings differential between women and men. He also provides a useful framework for tracking its changing behavior over time.

Oaxaca adapts a discrimination model measuring the adjusted growth rate of male-female earnings differences, with a cyclical measure of labor market tightness, and time as the main arguments accounting for changes in the behavior differential. The gross earnings differential provides a residual which, when adjusted by an index employed to account for male-female labor quality differences, purports to "explain" the amount of the widening pay differential between men and women over the 1957–71 period attributable to discrimination.

The same determinants, i.e., a cyclical component and time trend, are also arguments in the differential changes in male-female occupational distribution over time and in measuring the effects of changes in occupational distribution on the gross male-female earnings differential.

Oaxaca finds that the gross male-female earnings differential rose 15 percentage points, from 55 percent in 1955 to 70 percent by 1971, and his results estimate that more than one-half of the differential was due to sex discrimination, with the discrimination component on the increase up to 1966. He finds that a reduction in discrimination from 1966 onward probably operated to check further widening in the earnings gap after 1968.

He estimates that part of the slowdown in the widening pay gap may have been caused by the lagged impact of federal equal pay legislation (1963), and the 1964 Civil Rights Act, but notes that the legislation's enforcement machinery operated concurrently with other factors (e.g., labor market tightness and the military draft) which were probably far more significant.

At any rate, Oaxaca's own results suggest that Equal Employment Opportunity Commision and equal pay enforcement effects were minimal in this respect. On the whole, Oaxaca's findings are impressive. His estimate (of over 50 percent) certainly exceeds a different one recently made for the Council of Economic Advisers, which claimed that only about 20 percent of the pay difference between men and women was due to sex bias.

This is the more remarkable since Oaxaca's index of relative labor productivity is constructed in a manner that fails to account adequately for recent shifts in the labor market behavior of women in terms of their labor force participation and attachment, and in the rising proportion of the total U.S. labor force comprised of women (from 30 percent in 1950 to 41 percent in 1973).

Now, during this period males gained on females in terms of school years completed, but male labor force participation and the proportion of men in the labor force have declined since 1960, whereas, for females, dramatic rises occurred in both these statistics. Oaxaca's index therefore overstates the importance of male labor productivity changes relative to females and correspondingly probably underestimates the amount of the male-female pay differential properly ascribable to discrimination.

This point concerning the rising importance of female labor in the U.S. economy deserves further elaboration, since it has crucial implications for the future of female job segregation and unemployment. Neoclassical theories regarding women's "weak" attachment to the labor market are founded on nothing much stronger than outmoded sexist notions of women's "proper" social role. They satisfy what Galbraith terms a "convenient social virtue" of facilitating growing household consumption. Whether or not one can accept this view, it is significant that almost every projection made in recent years regarding labor force growth has been consistently understated, usually by the amount of the substantial underestimate in the growth of the female labor force.

Now, given the growing segregation of women in jobs predominantly "female," such as elementary and secondary school teacher and clerical worker, combined with the inflationary surge certain to "push" more women out of the home and into the labor market, unless male labor force participation declines more drastically, relative unemployment for women can be expected to move sharply upward in the coming years. This may lead to further widening in the amount of the male-female differential due to discrimination, because the additional women entrants must be absorbed in jobs more restrictive in terms of sex bias and must try to get hired by employers with higher than average "discrimination coefficients." One possible counter to forestall this outcome would be a more determined federal enforcement against, and monitoring of, sexist labor market practices.

A final point, Oaxaca offers two alternative interpretations of the reduction in the nonwhite male-female earnings differential—a marked contrast to the white relationship. One is greater relative reduction in sex discrimination against nonwhite females relative to a reduction in racial discrimination against nonwhite males. The other interpretation, which he feels to be the more likely, and which I would like to underscore, is that while nonwhite females have not really invaded traditionally nonwhite male jobs, they have probably been relatively more successful in "nailing down" a larger share of traditional white female jobs (e.g., clerical and health workers).

Moreover, given the unaccountable decline in the black male labor force participation, the stronger labor force attachment of black women relative to white women, and finally the persistence of black male segregation in jobs such as nonfarm laborers and operatives—employment highly sensitive to the level of aggregate activity—it is hardly surprising that the diminution of the male-female pay differential has been more marked among nonwhites.

Oaxaca mentions the sort of "chicken or egg" dispute among economists as to the extent to which differing sex occupational distributions are due to job market bias, and the extent to which they may be ascribed to differing job preferences between men and women. He points to some "promising" research conducted by psychologists testing whether there are "real" differences by sex as to motivations, aspirations, and expectations regarding career fulfillment. I, for one, am not too hopeful that any illuminating result will emerge from such findings. Labor market sex bias operates, on the one hand, directly to constrict female job opportunities, while generating, on the other hand, intricate feedback which conditions female job and career aspirations, expectations, and motivations from adolescence to old age. I know of no generally acceptable econometric technique which could adequately model these joint tendencies.

9

GREG DUNCAN
University of Michigan

Labor Market Discrimination and Nonpecuniary Work Rewards

I. INTRODUCTION

While wage and salary income is the most important payment that an individual receives from his job, it is not the only one. Fringe benefits such as paid vacation, sick days, insurance plans, and the like are provided by most employers. Their importance is not insignificant—a recent survey has shown that these benefits amounted to about one-quarter of total payroll outlays.[1] Beyond these pecuniary benefits are the more difficult to quantify "nonpecuniary" benefits, such as job security, freedom to accept or reject overtime work, flexibility of the job assignment, and healthy and safe working conditions. These nonmonetary rewards are components of total earnings, since it is reasonable to think of workers as being willing to give up a job with higher income for one with more of these nonmonetary benefits. Additional but more ambiguous benefits can be included if one adopts the more normative viewpoint that work should be meaningful and challenging to the worker. Job autonomy and variety are examples of these benefits.

NOTE: The author is a graduate student at the University of Michigan. This paper has benefited considerably from comments by several members of the Economic Behavior Program of the Institute for Social Research. Charles Cowan did most of the computer work. He also suggested the technique of dividing payment differences into between and within occupation effects.

355

It is not at all obvious that income from a job approximates the total of all pecuniary and nonpecuniary payments. Jobs involving self-employment, for example, have traditionally been the way in which workers may opt for higher nonpecuniary payments, often at the expense of monetary reward. In understanding issues relating to job earnings, then, it is important to measure and analyze nonmoney work payments.

In this paper, I investigate two issues related to the correspondence between pecuniary and nonpecuniary work payments. The first concerns labor market discrimination. Many studies have attempted to document earnings differentials by race and sex. Of the more recent ones, Oaxaca[2] uses data from the 1967 Survey of Economic Opportunity and finds that average wages of women are about half those of men. Differences in individual characteristics between the sexes are found to account for about half of these wage differences. Cohen[3] also studies sex differences and attempts to adjust for fringe benefits and personal and institutional characteristics. He finds a residual annual income difference of about $2,500. Estimates of black-white differentials are somewhat smaller than those between sexes. Gwartney,[4] for example, finds that after adjusting for differences in education, scholastic achievement, age, region, and city size, nonwhite median income is about 80 percent of white male income.

Some authors attribute a substantial portion of the wage differentials to the occupational distribution of women and blacks. These groups are seen to be excluded from certain occupations and are overrepresented in others; as a result they earn lower incomes than they would if their occupational distribution were identical to that of white men. Another part of the earnings differential is due to discrimination *within* a particular occupation—that is, among the workers in a certain occupation, blacks and women may earn less than equally qualified white men. Until now, empirical studies have used a pecuniary work payment measure, such as annual income or hourly wage, to measure the effects of discrimination. Looking at the extent to which blacks and women differ from white men in nonpecuniary payments will provide a more complete look at labor market discrimination. Expanding the earnings concept to include the nonmoney payments may either increase or decrease the estimated prevalence of discrimination. Cohen, for example, reports that women are less likely to report unhealthy working conditions on their jobs. The number of fringe benefits available to women, moreover, is considerably less than those available to men. To the extent that nonpecuniary payments compensate for income differentials, discrimination is overstated by a simple income measure. If nonmoney benefits reinforce differences in income, discrimination is understated.

The second issue under investigation here is the extent to which labor income determinants, such as education and labor market experience, affect nonpecuniary work payments. Estimates of the importance of these human capital investments for labor incomes have been the subject of numerous studies. Their importance in determining "psychic income," much of which consists of nonpecuniary job payments, is usually asserted but not substantiated for lack of data. Some of these data, however, are now available and they will be examined in this paper.

II. THE DATA

The data used here come from the 1972–73 Quality of Employment Survey, which was conducted by the Survey Research Center for the Employment Standards Administration and the National Institute for Occupational Safety and Health. Interviews were taken early in 1973, using a national probability sample of about 1,500 employed persons 16 years of age or older who worked for pay 20 hours a week or more.[5] Some of the purposes of the survey were to describe and assess work-related problems, to associate working conditions with various indicators of workers' well-being, and to develop efficient measures of job satisfaction.

Income information comes from direct questions on the subject. The various nonpecuniary payments analyzed in this paper come from questions about the various working conditions that each individual experiences. The actual benefits used will be described in detail below. Briefly, they fall into three groups. The first is the set of fringe benefits that jobs make available to workers. The second group is composed of three job characteristics that are unambiguous "benefits" to the vast majority of workers. These are (1) whether job conditions are healthy and safe, (2) the extent to which the worker has control over overtime hours, and (3) employment stability throughout the year. A final set of benefits is an index of the extent to which the worker makes decisions on his job and has work with variety, interest, and meaning to him.

III. THE THEORETICAL MODEL

Each worker brings to the labor market a certain mix of training, aptitude, and demographic characteristics that determines, first, the occupations that are available to him and, second, given the occupation, the level of income and nonpecuniary payments that he will receive. Different occupations offer different combinations of the two types of payments. The self-employed occupations, for example, typically pay higher nonpecuniary rewards relative to income. The relationships between income, nonmoney payments, occupation, and earnings determinants are shown in Figure 1.

FIGURE 1 Income and Nonpecuniary Payments for Three Occupations and Three Earnings Capacity Groups

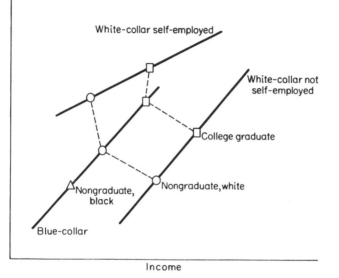

Nonpecuniary payments

White-collar self-employed

White-collar not self-employed

College graduate

Nongraduate, white

Nongraduate, black

Blue-collar

Income

Suppose that there are only three occupations: white-collar self-employed, white-collar not self-employed, and blue-collar. The white-collar occupation with self-employment has a higher mix of the non-money payments relative to income than the white-collar not self-employed occupation, and both of these tend to have higher levels of both money and nonmoney rewards than the blue-collar occupation. Further, suppose that a person's ability to choose an occupation is determined by three combinations of education and race: those who have graduated from college (regardless of race) have the highest earnings capacity, nongraduate blacks have the lowest, and nongraduate whites are in between these groups. Figure 1 shows how individuals in these groups are able to earn combinations of income and nonpecuniary payments. College graduates are able to choose among all three occupations. Typically, their choice will be between the two white-collar occupations. The self-employment white-collar occupation offers higher non-pecuniary payments to the graduate but at the expense of a lower annual income. The occupation actually chosen will depend upon the individual's relative preferences for the money and nonmoney aspects of work. The nongraduate whites may also choose among the three occupations but they will be unable to earn as much as the graduates in any of them. For these nongraduates, the self-employment white-collar occupation offers the highest nonpecuniary payments and the lowest income; the white-collar occupation without self-employment pays the nongraduate whites the highest income and lowest nonpecuniary payments, while blue-collar work lies between these other two occupations. Blacks without a college degree are excluded from white-collar occupations altogether and are able to obtain only blue-collar employment. Furthermore, within the blue-collar occupations, they are discriminated against and are paid both fewer pecuniary *and* nonpecuniary payments for their blue-collar work.

The above discussion suggests that several factors must be taken into account when earnings differences for various race and sex subgroups are investigated. First, both the pecuniary and nonpecuniary components of total earnings must be included. Individuals earning low incomes may be compensated by higher nonpecuniary payments, so that simple income differentials may overstate the total earnings differentials. Second, it will be necessary to control for some of the training and skill differences of individuals, so that earnings differentials are not falsely attributed to race or sex when, in fact, they are due to training differences. Third, it is necessary to distinguish the extent to which payment differences result from occupational choice as opposed to within-occupation differentials. In Figure 1, it was seen that blacks earned less than similarly qualified whites, because they were excluded from white-collar occupations (that is, the payments varied by race between occupations). They also earned less within the blue-collar occupation to which they had been restricted (i.e., payments differed *within* an occupation). These effects from both between and within occupations need to be distinguished.

IV. THE EMPIRICAL MODEL

Monetary and nonmonetary work-payment differentials will be investigated with a series of multiple regressions of each of the payment variables on a common set of explanatory variables. To control for training differences, the regressions will include years of formal education and labor market experience. The latter variable is ascertained directly from the question "How many years in total have you worked for pay since you were 16 years old?" To account for the expected nonlinear experience-earnings profile, the square of years of experience is also included as a separate predictor.[6] Income and nonpecuniary payment differentials by race and sex will be investigated through the inclusion of three dummy variables in the regression: (i) whether white female, (ii) whether black female, and (iii) whether black male. Coefficients on these variables will show the extent to which these subgroups differ in their payments from the group of white men. Since the various dependent variables are scaled in different ways, each is standardized so that the coefficients on the independent variables refer to the fraction of a standard deviation of the payment variable which is associated with a one-unit change in the particular independent variable.

In sum, the basic equation which will be used to predict the set of various payment variables is:

$$\text{Payment} = a + b_1(\text{Education}) + b_2(\text{Experience}) + b_3(\text{Experience})^2$$
$$+ b_4(\text{Whether white female}) + b_5(\text{Whether black male})$$
$$+ b_6(\text{Whether black female}) + u$$

This functional form is not identical to the ones used in some other wage studies, because it fails to allow the coefficients on the education and experience variable to differ among the race-sex subgroups. Reported coefficients on these variables will thus be a weighted average of coefficients among the groups.

To account for the within and between occupation variations in the payments, two additional regressions will be run. The first will explain the pecuniary or nonpecuniary payment which results from occupational choice. Each individual is assigned the mean payment level of his occupation, and then the set of mean payments for all individuals is predicted by the education, experience, and race-sex dummy variables listed above. The coefficient on a race-sex variable, say for white females, will show the payment differential between white women and equally educated and experienced white men that is due to the fact that white women are concentrated in different occupations than men. The estimated coefficient on education will reflect the extent to which education affects the payment by placing individuals in occupations with different payment levels. These will be called the *between occupation* effects.

The second additional regression will explain *within occupation* payment effects. These effects are calculated by subtracting each individual's payment from his mean occupation payment. These differences are then predicted by the same independent variables used in the other two regressions.[7]

The success of this between/within-occupation division in actually quantifying the extent to which the explanatory variables operate through occupational choice itself, rather than within occupations, is dependent upon several factors. First, the occupational classification must be sufficiently broad to include enough individuals so that average pecuniary and nonpecuniary payments for each occupation are meaningful. On the other hand, each occupation must be homogeneous enough so that within occupation differentials are not actually differences between two similar but distant occupations.

A ten-category occupation classification will be used for the empirical section of this study. It is given in Table 1. Sample sizes for the black male

TABLE 1 Occupational Classification with Numbers of Observations from Various Race-Sex Groups[a]

Occupation	White Males	White Females	Black Males	Black Females	Total
Professional and technical	134	70	4	4	212
Managers and administrators	179	31	5	4	219
Sales	44	21	2	1	68
Clerical	54	131	5	20	210
Craftsmen	179	10	7	2	198
Operatives, except transport	114	58	13	12	197
Transport equipment operatives	44	2	8	0	54
Laborers	49	3	8	1	61
Farmers and farm managers	34	1	1	0	36
Service workers	58	72	12	18	160
Total	889	399	65	62	1,415

[a]Calculated from the 1972–73 Quality of Employment Survey.

and black female groups are rather small and, as a consequence, considerably more confidence can be placed in estimated effects for white women than for these other groups. It should be noted that the various race-sex groups differ considerably in their distributions across occupations. Relative to white men, women are much less likely to be in managerial and administrative occupations or to be craftsmen. (See Table 1.) They are overrepresented in the clerical and service categories. Small sample sizes do not permit confident statements about the distribution of blacks across occupations, but the pattern of underrepresentation in higher status occupations has been confirmed in other studies using much larger samples.

The occupational division of effects also depends upon the assumption that within occupation effects are similar across occupations. That is, deviations from the mean payment in one occupation are related to the same things that lead to deviations in other occupations. A more complete study of the problem would examine each occupation separately for an explanation of the within occupation variability in payments. Our sample size does not permit this and our results must be interpreted with this in mind. We seek an estimate of the order of magnitude of between/within occupation effects of the various payment predictors.

V. RESULTS

Income

Annual labor income is the most studied of all payment variables; results for it will be presented first. Data on this variable come from the question "How much does your income from your job figure out to be a year, before taxes and other deductions are made?"[8] The distribution of income by occupation is presented in Table 2. The pattern is a familiar

TABLE 2 Annual Labor Income, by Occupation[a]

Occupation	Mean Income	Number of Observations
Professional and technical	$11,808	212
Managers and administrators	14,000	219
Sales	12,408	68
Clerical	6,788	210
Craftsmen	9,926	198
Operatives, except transport	7,641	197
Transport equipment operatives	9,789	54
Laborers	6,988	61
Farmers and farm managers	12,561	36
Service workers	5,555	160
Total	$9,629	1,415

NOTE: Standard deviation = $6,611.
[a]Calculated from the 1972–73 Quality of Employment Survey.

one. Professionals and managers earn the highest incomes, laborers earn the least, with the remaining occupations falling in between.

How this income variable (when standardized) relates to the race-sex dummy variables, education, and experience is presented in Table 3.

TABLE 3 Regression Coefficients for Earnings Predictors with Annual Labor Income the Dependent Variable[a]

Predictor	Dependent Variable: Annual Income (Standardized)		
	Total Effect	Between Occupation Effect	Within Occupation Effect
White female	−.69†	−.23†	−.46†
Black male	−.13	−.17†	.04
Black female	−.75†	−.35†	−.40†
Education	.10†	.05†	.05†
Experience	.07†	.02†	.04†
(Experience)^2	−.001†	−.0003†	−.0007†
R^2	.30	.24	.15
N − 1,415			

†Coefficient is statistically different from zero at the 1 percent probability level.
[a]Calculated from the 1972–73 Quality of Employment Survey.

Since the dependent variable is standardized, coefficients are the estimated fraction of a standard deviation in income which is associated with a unit change in the independent variables. For example, the −.69 coefficient in the "total effects" column for white females means that when education and experience are taken into account, white women earn about two-thirds of a standard deviation of income less than white men. Since income's standard deviation is $6,611, this amounts to a difference in level of payments of $4,561. The .10 coefficient on education is interpreted similarly: each additional year of education is associated with a one-tenth of a standard deviation (or about $661) increase in annual income. Estimated coefficients which are statistically different from zero at the 5 percent probability level are denoted with a single asterisk, those at the 1 percent level have a dagger.

White women earn about $4,500 less than white men with similar education and experience. This difference can be divided into income differences due to the distribution of white women across occupations and to differences within each of the occupational classifications. This division is given in the second and third columns of Table 3. It is seen that about one-third of the income difference of white women can be attributed to the fact that they prefer, or are crowded into, lower-paying occupations and the remaining two-thirds is the result of payment differences within occupations. The size of this estimated male-female income differential is somewhat larger than that found in other studies. Part of this discrepancy is due to the inclusion of part-time workers (i.e., those working between 20 and 35 hours per week), many of whom are women. When annual income is divided by average number of hours worked per week and then standardized and regressed on this same set of explanatory variables, the coefficient for white females drops from $-.69$ to $-.51$. The coefficient on black females is similarly reduced from $-.75$ to $-.62$. The division of these coefficients into within and between occupation effects is quite similar to that given in Table 3. Other factors contributing to the discrepancy may be absence of control for institutional characteristics (e.g., union membership) and personal characteristics (e.g., marital status and health problems).

Income differentials between black and white men are much smaller than the male-female differences. The total estimated income gap between black and white men with the same distributions of education and experience is a little more than one-tenth of a standard deviation (or $860). Examination of the between and within occupation division of this effect reveals that it is entirely attributable to the fact that blacks are in lower-paying occupations than whites.

Income differences for black women are similar to, and slightly larger than, those of white women. This difference is divided equally into within and between occupation effects.

It is also instructive to examine the ways in which education and experience pay off in labor income. An additional year of education is associated with a tenth of a standard unit increase in income. Half of this increase is due to the fact that additional education makes higher-paying occupations more accessible; the other half is due to income differentials by education *within* the various occupations.

Labor force experience also results in higher income. The significant coefficients on experience and (experience)^2 imply a parabolic experience-income profile. As one might expect, most of the payoff to experience comes from within a particular occupation. A smaller part comes from the fact that different occupations are associated with differences in average experience levels for workers in them. These experience levels by occupation are given in Table 4. Jobs with the lowest mean experience levels are in the lower status blue- and white-collar occupations.

In sum, large income differences exist between white men and similarly qualified women. Black men also earn less but the differential is not nearly as great for them. The male-female difference is due partly to

TABLE 4   Average Years of Labor Force Experience, by
Occupation[a]

Occupation	Average Years of Experience	Number of Observations
Professional and technical	17.9	212
Managers and administrators	22.1	219
Sales	19.7	68
Clerical	15.8	210
Craftsmen	19.6	198
Operatives, except transport	19.0	197
Transport equipment operatives	21.1	54
Laborers	15.2	61
Farmers and farm managers	27.8	36
Service workers	18.3	160
Total	19.0	1,415

NOTE: Standard deviation = 12.9.
[a]Calculated from the 1972–73 Quality of Employment Survey.

the prevalence of females in lower-paying occupations and partly to
pay differences within the given occupations. We shall turn now to an
examination of other types of work payments to see if this income
differential accurately reflects the total pecuniary and nonpecuniary
differences. The extent to which the race-sex groups earn higher nonmonetary benefits than white males means that income differences
overstate total earnings differences. To the extent that they earn fewer of
these nonpecuniary payments, differences will be understated.

Fringe Benefits

Fringe benefits have in recent years become a very important earnings
component. The Quality of Employment Survey asked respondents
whether any of the following fringe benefits were made available on their
jobs:
1. Vacation days with full pay
2. Full pay sick days
3. Medical insurance for off-the-job illness or injury
4. Life insurance for off-the-job death
5. Retirement program
6. Training program to improve skills
7. Profit sharing

8. Stock options
9. Free or discounted meals
10. Free or discounted merchandise

The value of each of the fringe benefits will vary by firm, occupation, and wage rate. Rather than attempt to assign a value to each benefit, they are combined into an additive index.[9] The payment score for each worker is simply the number of the various benefits that he reports available on his job. The distribution of scores by occupation is given in Table 5. With the exception of the predominantly self-employed occupation of managers and farmers, occupations rank in average number of fringe benefits roughly by status.

TABLE 5 Average Number of Fringe Benefits Available, by Occupation[a]

Occupation	Mean Number of Benefits	Number of Observations
Professional and technical	5.1	212
Managers and administrators	3.6	219
Sales	4.2	68
Clerical	5.4	210
Craftsmen	4.3	198
Operatives, except transport	4.3	197
Transport equipment operatives	4.2	54
Laborers	3.3	61
Farmers and farm managers	0	36
Service workers	3.6	160
Total	4.3	1,415

NOTE: Standard deviation = 2.6.
[a]Calculated from the 1972–73 Quality of Employment Survey.

The ways in which the number of fringe benefits relate to the race-sex subgroups, education, and experience are presented in Table 6. Without taking into account the occupational choice, none of the race-sex subgroups significantly differ from white males in total number of fringe benefits available. Both of the human capital variables, however, have a significant effect in number of fringe benefits, although their estimated importance is about half as great as their effect on labor income.

When the between and within occupation effects for the race-sex sub-groups are estimated, some fascinating results emerge. While the overall number of fringe benefits available to women did not differ from those available to similarly qualified men, this result appears to be the

TABLE 6 Regression Coefficients for Earnings Predictors with Number of Fringe Benefits the Dependent Variable[a]

Predictor	Dependent Variable: Fringe Benefits (Standardized)		
	Total Effect	Between Occupation Effect	Within Occupation Effect
White female	.07	.20†	−.13†
Black male	.06	.06	−.00
Black female	−.00	.16†	−.16
Education	.06†	.02†	.03†
Experience	.02*	.00	.02*
(Experience)^2	−.0004†	−.00003	−.0004†
R^2	.04	.11	.03
N = 1,415			

*Coefficient is statistically different from zero at the 5 percent probability level.
†Coefficient is statistically different from zero at the 1 percent probability level.
[a]Calculated from the 1972–73 Quality of Employment Survey.

sum of two significant effects which cancel each other out. Women earn significantly more fringe benefits because they are in occupations where a larger average number of benefits are made available. Much of this effect comes from the underrepresentation of women in the self-employed occupations which provide few fringe benefits. *Within* the various occupations, however, women receive significantly fewer fringe benefits than men of similar education and experience. These two opposing effects offset one another.

Healthy and Safe Working Conditions

The health and safety of work was ascertained in the question "Does your job at any time expose you to what you feel are physical dangers or unhealthy conditions?" Responses are less precisely measured than those given for the income and fringe benefit variables because conditions that are unhealthy and unsafe to one worker may not be evaluated as such by another. Those responding affirmatively to the question were given a score of zero, all others were scored one. Higher values for the variable thus indicate greater health and safety benefits.

The proportion of workers reporting healthy and safe working conditions in each of the occupational classifications is shown in Table 7. It is somewhat surprising that almost half of the entire work force feel that their work exposes them to dangerous and unhealthy conditions and that

TABLE 7 Proportion of Individuals Reporting Healthy and Safe Working Conditions, by Occupation[a]

Occupation	Proportion Healthy and Safe Conditions	Number of Observations
Professional and technical	.64	212
Managers and administrators	.69	219
Sales	.71	68
Clerical	.81	210
Craftsmen	.36	198
Operatives, except transport	.39	197
Transport equipment operatives	.33	54
Laborers	.38	61
Farmers and farm managers	.17	36
Service workers	.58	160
Total	.56	1,415

NOTE: Standard deviation = .50.
[a]Calculated from the 1972–73 Quality of Employment Survey.

in no occupation does this proportion fall much below 20 percent. As might be expected, white-collar occupations are considerably healthier and safer than blue-collar ones, with farmers and farm managers at the very bottom.

Regression results appear in Table 8 and show that each of the race-sex subgroup scores significantly *higher* on this nonpecuniary payment available than do white men.[10] For women, the positive difference is due mostly to holding jobs in safer occupations. Some of the effect, however, is attributable to their obtaining safer and healthier jobs within the various occupations. The finding that black men report somewhat safer and healthier jobs than white men is somewht puzzling. None of the differences are due to their distribution across occupations; all result from reports of safer jobs within the occupations. It could be that blacks are less inclined to conceive of or report their job as unhealthy or dangerous. Since the number of blacks is small, the mean scores on this variable across occupations would not be affected very much, while all the bias would show up as within occupation effects. Lacking any proof of this bias, however, we must accept the possibility that income deficits for black males may be compensated for by healthier and safer conditions.

Of the education and experience variables, only the former has a significant effect. Looking across the other columns of Table 8, one sees that education pays off in healthier and safer jobs by placing individuals in healthier and safer occupations.

TABLE 8 Regression Coefficients for Earnings Predictors with Whether Healthy and Safe Working Conditions the Dependent Variable[a]

| Predictor | Total Effect | Dependent Variable: Whether Healthy and Safe Conditions (Standardized) | |
		Between Occupation Effect	Within Occupation Effect
White female	.44†	.26†	.18†
Black male	.28*	.03	.26†
Black female	.31*	.23†	.08
Education	.05†	.04†	.01
Experience	.006	.006†	.000
(Experience)^2	−.00003	−.00008	.00004
R^2	.06	.24	.01
N − 1,415			

*Coefficient is statistically different from zero at the 5 percent probability level.
†Coefficient is statistically different from zero at the 1 percent probability level.
[a]Calculated from the 1972–73 Quality of Employment Survey.

Control over Overtime Hours

One desirable job characteristic is that the worker himself be able to choose whether or not he should work overtime hours and not be penalized in any way if he refuses the overtime work. Over three-quarters of the respondents gave some kind of definition of overtime work on their job—ranging from working more than so many hours per day or week to working before or after certain hours or on days that are not normal work days. For those who gave a definition of overtime work, questions were then asked about who determines whether the worker will put in the work. For jobs in which the overtime hours are set by the employer or supervisor, workers were further questioned as to whether they could refuse to work overtime without being penalized in any way. From this sequence of questions, the variable "control overtime hours" was constructed as follows:

The variable equals: 3 if no definition of overtime on job or if decision on overtime hours is mostly up to the respondent

2 if decision on overtime hours is up to employer but the respondent can refuse them without penalty

1 if decision on overtime hours is up to employer and respondent would be penalized if he refused to do the overtime work.

The mean scores on this payment variable by occupation are given in Table 9. Workers in high status and high self-employment occupations report the greatest freedom in setting overtime hours; operatives and laborers report the least.

TABLE 9 Mean Score on "Control Overtime Hours" Payment Variable, by Occupation[a]

Occupation	Average Score on Control Overtime Hours Variable	Number of Observations
Professional and technical	2.70	212
Managers and administrators	2.79	219
Sales	2.75	68
Clerical	2.26	210
Craftsmen	2.22	198
Operatives, except transport	2.02	197
Transport equipment operatives	2.31	54
Laborers	2.03	61
Farmers and farm managers	3.00	36
Service workers	2.32	160
Total	2.41	1,415

NOTE: Standard deviation = .72.
[a]Calculated from the 1972–73 Quality of Employment Survey.

When education and experience levels are accounted for (Table 10), women and blacks report less control over overtime hours than white men, although these differences are often small and statistically insignificant. White women differ the least, and all of this differential can be attributed to their placement in occupations with less control over hours. Black women have one-quarter of a standard deviation less control over overtime than white males. This difference can be divided equally into the between and within occupation effects. Black men fall between the two female subgroups in their control of overtime work; nearly all of this difference stems from their overrepresentation in occupations characterized by less control.

While these race-sex differences are rather small and only sporadically significant, the importance of education and labor force experience is much larger and quite significant. Both education and experience appear

TABLE 10 Regression Coefficients for Earnings Predictors with "Control Overtime Hours" the Dependent Variable[a]

Predictor	Total Effect	Dependent Variable: Control Overtime Hours (Standardized)	
		Between Occupation Effect	Within Occupation Effect
White female	−.02	−.04*	.02
Black male	−.14	−.10*	−.04
Black female	−.25*	−.13†	−.11
Education	.07†	.06†	.007
Experience	.02†	.01†	.008
(Experience)²	−.0003*	−.0001†	−.0001
R^2	.05	.23	.003
N = 1,415			

*Coefficient is statistically different from zero at the 5 percent probability level.
†Coefficient is statistically different from zero at the 1 percent probability level.
[a]Calculated from the 1972–73 Quality of Employment Survey.

to allow individuals to choose occupations with a greater amount of control over overtime hours.

Employment Stability

Jobs which provide stable employment throughout the year are generally thought to be more desirable than seasonal jobs or jobs with frequent layoffs. The importance of this characteristic is greatest for main earners within families and least for casual labor force participants. To the extent that the respondent selection was restricted to those who worked more than 20 hours in the week prior to the interview and the interviewing was conducted during the early months of the year (and thus excluded Christmas and summer vacation workers), most of those for whom employment stability would not be a problem were excluded from this analysis. The employment stability variable was constructed from the following question: "Do you think of your job as one where you have regular steady work throughout the year, is it seasonal, are there frequent layoffs, or what?" Those responding that their jobs were seasonal or had frequent layoffs were scored zero, all others received a value of one. The distribution of responses across the occupational classification is given in Table 11. Employment stability thus defined is not a serious problem to

TABLE 11   Proportion of Workers Reporting Stable Employment, by Occupation[a]

Occupation	Proportion Reporting Stable Employment	Number of Observations
Professional and technical	.95	212
Managers and administrators	.94	219
Sales	.93	68
Clerical	.98	210
Craftsmen	.83	198
Operatives, except transport	.91	197
Transport equipment operatives	.87	54
Laborers	.74	61
Farmers and farm managers	.94	36
Service workers	.91	160
Total	.91	1,415

NOTE: Standard deviation = .28.
[a]Calculated from the 1972–73 Quality of Employment Survey.

most of the work force: more than 9 of every 10 workers report that their jobs provide this nonpecuniary payment. This is particularly true of those in white-collar occupations. Craftsmen and laborers are the most likely to experience seasonal work or frequent layoffs.

Regression results presented in Table 12 reveal significant differences among the race-sex groups in reported employment stability only for white women. They enjoy *more* stable work than white men and this is entirely the result of their absence from occupations which fail to provide steady employment. Coefficients for black men and women are not statistically significant.

Both education and experience are associated with jobs that provide steady employment. The payoff of education is mostly the result of its allowing entrance into more stable occupations. For labor force experience, however, the within occupation effect is much larger than that between occupations.

Job Autonomy

Apart from the reasonably unambiguous nonpecuniary payments already discussed, there are job characteristics which develop the individual by allowing him to participate in the decisions that affect his work, challenge

TABLE 12   Regression Coefficients for Earnings Predictors with Employment Stability the Dependent Variable[a]

Predictor	Total Effect	Dependent Variable: Employment Stability (Standardized)	
		Between Occupation Effect	Within Occupation Effect
White female	.13†	.16†	−.03
Black male	.13	−.00	.13
Black female	−.08	.14	−.22
Education	.04†	.03†	.01
Experience	.02†	.004†	.015†
(Experience)^2	−.0003*	−.00003	−.00024
R^2	.02	.24	.01
N = 1,415			

*Coefficient is statistically different from zero at the 5 percent probability level.
†Coefficient is statistically different from zero at the 1 percent probability level
[a]Calculated from the 1972–73 Quality of Employment Survey.

his creativity, or simply give him varied and interesting tasks. These characteristics are less ambiguous than the other payment variables. Some individuals may not care about those characteristics and therefore would not forgo a higher paying job for one in which these characteristics were present.

An index of job autonomy and variety was constructed from questions about the extent to which an individual's job was associated with the following characteristics:

1. Requires the learning of new things
2. Allows freedom as to how work is done
3. Allows decision making
4. Requires creativity
5. Allows varied work
6. Avoids repetition
7. Allows taking part in decisions
8. Helps keep the respondent informed
9. Helps the respondent to understand the kind of person he really is

Responses to each of these questions were translated into a four-point scale. The score equaled 4 if the job required "a lot" of that characteristic, 3 if it was somewhat related to the characteristic, 2 if the association between job and characteristic was "a little," and 1 if the characteristic was "not at all" a part of the job. An empirical investigation of these components revealed that although there are a considerable variety of concepts, none offset any other and so a simple additive index of them could be formed. The resultant variable consists of the sum of the nine variables, each of which ranges from 1 to 4.

Average job autonomy scores for the different occupations are presented in Table 13. Not surprisingly, farmers report the most autonomous and varied work, followed closely by professionals, managers and salespersons. Craftsmen report job autonomy equal to the overall mean, and the remaining occupations score below average autonomy.

TABLE 13   Mean Job Autonomy Index, by Occupation[a]

Occupation	Mean Job Autonomy Index	Number of Observations
Professional and technical	29.8	212
Managers and administrators	29.7	219
Sales	28.4	68
Clerical	24.4	210
Craftsmen	26.4	198
Operatives, except transport	21.6	197
Transport equipment operatives	23.5	54
Laborers	23.1	61
Farmers and farm managers	31.2	36
Service workers	25.6	160
Total	26.4	1,415

NOTE: Standard deviation = 5.5.
[a]Calculated from the 1972–73 Quality of Employment Survey.

Regression results (in Table 14) show that all of these race-sex groups report significantly less job autonomy than do white males with similar education and experience. The deficit is largest for blacks—both black men and women score about one-third of a standard deviation less on job autonomy. A look across the columns of Table 14 shows that about half of the total deficit for black males is attributable to the fact that they work in occupations with less autonomy and the remaining half is due to their obtaining less autonomous jobs *within* the occupations. For black females, the between occupation effect is greater than that from within the occupations.

The autonomy deficit for white women is not as great as that for blacks, although it is large enough to be statistically significant. Most of it comes from the occupational distribution of the white women.

TABLE 14 Regression Coefficients for Earnings Predictors with Job Autonomy the Dependent Variable[a]

Predictor	Total Effect	Dependent Variable: Job Autonomy (Standardized)	
		Between Occupation Effect	Within Occupation Effect
White female	−.18†	−.11†	−.06
Black male	−.35†	−.17†	−.19
Black female	−.35†	−.22†	−.12
Education	.10†	.08†	.02†
Experience	.04†	.02†	.03†
(Experience)²	−.0006†	−.0002†	−.0004†
R^2	.16	.25	.03
N = 1,415			

†Coefficient is statistically different from zero at the 1 percent probability level.
[a]Calculated from the 1972–73 Quality of Employment Survey.

The importance of education in allowing individuals to choose autonomous jobs is as great as its importance in determining income. But while the effect of education on income was equally divided into the between and within occupation effects, its effect on job autonomy comes mostly from placing individuals in occupations with greater autonomy. A smaller, but still significant, within occupation effect for education is shown in Table 14.

Labor force experience also has an important association with job autonomy, half of which comes from between occupation effect, the remaining half from within occupations.

VI. SUMMARY AND CONCLUSIONS

This paper has looked beyond the well-documented pecuniary work payment differentials between white men and similarly qualified women and blacks to see whether other desirable work characteristics compensate or reinforce these income differences. Some compensating work payments were observed. Relative to white men with the same amount of education and labor force experience, women and black men report safer and healthier working conditions. Further, white women responded that their jobs provided significantly greater employment stability.

Differences in some job characteristics were seen to exacerbate the observed income differentials. Members of all three race-sex subgroups reported considerably less autonomy and variety in their work than did white males with the same amounts of education and experience. Control of overtime hours was significantly less for black females.

One way in which labor market discrimination against population subgroups operates is by crowding their members into certain occupations and preventing their entry into others. The resulting differences in the distribution of the labor force across occupations accounts for most of the observed payment differences. Some additional differentials show up *within* the various occupations: women earn significantly less income than similarly qualified white men within the occupations; they also have jobs which provide fewer fringe benefits. A compensating payment difference within occupations for women is healthier and safer working conditions.

The net result of these compensating and reinforcing nonpecuniary payment differentials on the estimated total labor market discrimination will depend upon the ways in which these various payments combine into a measure of total earnings. If characteristics such as control over overtime hours and variety are considered to be more important than the others, then the large income differences between white men and the race-sex subgroups (in particular women) will underestimate total discrimination. If, on the other hand, the payments of healthy and safe working conditions and employment stability receive much more weight than the others, the income differentials will overstate the extent of discrimination.[11] However, given the huge income gap between white men and the other groups and relatively small differences in the nonpecuniary characteristics, it would be difficult to argue that the latter compensate for the former. Regardless of how one chooses to define earnings, differentials in those earnings between the sexes and races are pervasive in the labor market.

NOTES

1. *Fringe Benefits, 1971* (Washington, D.C.: Economic Analysis and Study Group, Chamber of Commerce, 1972).
2. Oaxaca, Ronald, "Male-Female Wage Differentials in Urban Labor Markets," *International Economic Review*, Vol. 14, No. 3, Oct. 1973.
3. Cohen, Malcolm S., "Sex Differences in Compensation," *Journal of Human Resources*, Vol. 6, Fall 1971.
4. Gwartney, James, "Discrimination and Income Differentials," *American Economic Review*, Vol. 60, No. 3, June 1970.

5. Since the distribution and importance of fringe benefits to full-time workers may differ from those working less than full time, I have replicated much of the analysis of this paper for those working at least 35 hours per week. Results are quite similar and are presented in "Nonpecuniary Work Rewards: Implications for Studies of Earnings Functions, Discrimination, and Labor Union Effects" (Ph.D. diss., University of Michigan, 1974). Significant differences will be noted at appropriate places in this paper.

6. These variables comprise the standard human capital earnings function given by Jacob Mincer in *Schooling, Experience, and Earnings* (New York: National Bureau of Economic Research, 1974).

7. This technique was used to explain between and within industry differentials in investment behavior of firms by Robert Eisner in "A Permanent Income Theory for Investment: Some Empirical Explorations," *The American Economic Review*, Vol. 57, No. 3, June 1967.

   One desirable property of the division of the total effects of the predictors into between and within occupation effects is that the coefficients estimating these latter effects will always add up to the total effect. This is because the two "subeffects" are uncorrelated with one another.

8. Respondents unable to estimate their annual income were asked how often they received work payments (e.g., weekly, monthly) and how much they typically received per pay period. These numbers were then converted into annual equivalents.

9. It is possible to obtain a crude valuation of fringe benefits by assigning the fraction of payroll that firms report allocating to the various fringe benefits. This information is gathered annually on a sample of firms by the Chamber of Commerce. When this valuation is applied to the respondents of the Quality of Employment Survey who worked more than 35 hours per week, it is found that there is little difference in the occupational distribution of fringe benefits (see Table 5) but substantial changes in the extent to which the various race-sex subgroups differ from white males in the receipt of fringe benefits (Table 6). The .07, .06, and −.00 coefficients for white females, black males, and black females respectively, become .19, .06, and .16. The white female coefficient is large enough to be significant at the 1 percent probability level. Thus when part-time workers are excluded from the analysis and fringe benefits are valued with outside data, women receive more fringe benefits than white men. When fringe benefits are combined with income to obtain a more comprehensive earnings measure, however, it is found that the impact of fringe benefits on total earnings differences between the races and sexes is quite small.

10. All of the assumptions necessary for ordinary least squares regression are not met for this dependent variable and several of those which follow. Here, the payment variable is confined to taking on only the values of zero and one, thus producing a heteroscedastic error term. Estimated coefficients will, as a result, be unbiased but inefficient.

11. Combining pecuniary and nonpecuniary payments into a single earnings measure is a difficult and rather arbitrary process. In my dissertation, I combine the two kinds of payment in two ways—1. with a Cobb-Douglas utility function that weights each of the nonpecuniary measures equally (job autonomy is omitted) and also gives the entire set of nonpecuniary measures a weight equal to that on the pecuniary earnings measure; and 2. with coefficients obtained from a regression of a linear combination of the pecuniary and nonpecuniary measures on education, experience, and the square of years of experience. When the race-sex earnings differences using these earnings measures are compared to differences using wage rate with and without fringe benefits for the sample of quality-of-employment respondents who worked 35 hours or more

per week, one obtains the following coefficients (and standard errors in parentheses):

Race-Sex Subgroup	Wage Rate	Earnings Measure (Standardized)		
		Wage Rate and Fringe Benefits	Cobb-Douglas Utility Index of Wage, Fringe and Nonpecuniary Benefits	Regression Index of Wage, Fringe and Nonpecuniary Benefits
White female	−.57	−.56	−.44	−.32
	(.05)	(.05)	(.05)	(.06)
Black male	.08	.09	.06	.11
	(.12)	(.12)	(.12)	(.13)
Black female	−.62	−.62	−.59	−.55
	(.12)	(.12)	(.12)	(.12)

SOURCE: 1972–73 Quality of Employment Survey.
NOTE: Other variables included in the regression: education experience, (experience)^2, job tenure, whether a nervous condition limits the type of work respondent could do.

Thus, when more comprehensive earnings measures are used, it is found that earnings differences between white men and white women are considerably (although certainly not completely) reduced and that compensating benefits are *not* found for either black females or black males.

10

WILLIAM R. JOHNSON
University of Virginia

Uncertainty and the Distribution of Earnings

LINKS BETWEEN UNCERTAINTY THEORY AND THE DISTRIBUTION OF INCOME

The language of uncertainty theory is familiar to the student of the distribution of income. The same functions which are used by probability theorists to describe outcomes of stochastic events are also used to describe the observed distribution of income or earnings; the normal, the log-normal, and the Pareto distributions are the most familiar examples. It is not necessarily true, however, that the use of these functions to describe the distribution of income implies that income itself is a stochastic variable whose behavior is subject to laws of chance like a roulette wheel. Indeed, many theories of the distribution of income employ functions usually associated with probability densities to describe deterministic models of the distribution of income. Lydall (1968), for example, proposes an entirely deterministic model of income distribution at the upper tail of the distribution which yields the Pareto function. Others have attempted to construct theories which transform symmetrically distributed abilities into the asymmetric, skewed pattern of observed incomes. The hallmark of these theories is that, given an individual's characteristics, his income is entirely determined except possibly for some small error term.

NOTE: The author is a graduate student at the University of Virginia.

While deterministic models of the income distribution borrow the mathematical functions of probability theory, stochastic theories make income itself, to some extent, a chance event or a stochastic variable. The form of the income distribution in these models depends in part on the probability density function of the stochastic elements of income. One such stochastic theory of the income distribution is that of Champernowne (1953), in which income this period depends on income last period in a probabilistic way. Champernowne shows that this Markovian process can ultimately yield a Paretian distribution of incomes, regardless of the initial distribution of income. These results were extended by Mandelbrot (1961).

Milton Friedman has also advanced a stochastic model of income determination (1953). In this case, however, it is not time-dependent stochastic processes which are the key to the model but the year-to-year variation of transitory income around permanent income, which was later to play a central role in Friedman's theory of the consumption function. Friedman was probably overly impressed with the annual variation in incomes as a result of his earlier studies of the income of professionals in independent practice, a group whose incomes probably vary more than the average (Friedman and Kuznets, 1945). The apparent great uncertainty of annual incomes led Friedman to emphasize the fact that the inequality of annual incomes is greater than the inequality of permanent lifetime incomes and, by extension, the distribution of utility. Friedman went farther than this in his discussion of uncertainty; he brought out the role of risk in the choice of occupation. That is, some individuals choose occupations in which the dispersion of incomes is greater than in other occupations. Chance would govern their permanent incomes as well as annual incomes. However, by emphasizing the role of choice as well as chance in the process (since an individual selects among different lines of work), Friedman again cautioned against interpreting income inequality as reflecting inequality of, in this case, expected utility. In part, the distribution of income is unequal because some individuals make risky choices and earn income with varying degrees of success.

Recent empirical studies are beginning to echo Friedman's appeal to uncertainty in explaining income inequality. Jencks (1972), especially, finds that none of the familiar determinants of earnings—demographic characteristics, family background, schooling, cognitive ability—explain more than a small fraction of the observed inequality of income in the United States. Jencks ascribes some of the unexplained variance to random factors: "In general, we think that luck has far more influence on income than successful people admit" (1972, p. 227). Although Jencks's results are open to serious question because of his peculiar model and the heterogeneity of his data sources, his inability to explain much of the dispersion in earnings has been duplicated by other studies. Recent work using microdata files has failed to explain more than a small fraction of the total variance in individual earnings. For example, Taubman and Wales's recent work with the extremely rich Thorndike-Hagan file of veterans emphasizes the failure of deterministic models to explain much income inequality (Taubman and Wales, 1973). Their earnings function, which included not only traditional demographic variables, but also extensive measures of ability taken from armed forces test results, and family background variables, had R^2's of around .10. Recent work by Paul Taubman (reported in this volume) extends the Taubman-Wales results and raises the explained variance of earnings to more than 40 percent. Hall (1973) estimated wage equations for race-sex groups from Survey of Economic Opportunity data and found standard errors of estimate for his equations of nearly forty cents per hour. These results indicate that earnings are hard to predict; there seems to be a good deal of indeterminacy in earnings.

Taubman and Wales performed an experiment which sheds light on the structure of uncertainty in earnings. In their estimate of 1969 earnings, they used as an explanatory variable the error from their equation estimating earnings in 1955 for the individual. In this way, any permanent, yet unobserved, explanation of earnings in 1955 would help to explain earnings in 1969. Interestingly, the inclusion of these residuals raised the R^2 from .10 to .33, indicating that these permanent unobserved factors account for close to one-quarter of the variance in incomes (Taubman and Wales, 1973, p. 37). As for the rest of the variance in incomes, Taubman and Wales concluded that "... two-thirds of the variation in earnings in any year represents either random events such as luck, and/or changes in underlying characteristics" (1973, p. 38).

TYPES OF UNCERTAINTY IN INCOMES

Uncertainty not only plays a role in several theories of the distribution of income, but it appears that empirical estimates confirm the existence of a large amount of uncertainty or unexplained variance in the estimation of earnings. To the extent that uncertainty plays a role in the determination of earnings, the probability density functions of the stochastic terms of the earnings function determine, in part, the shape of the distribution of earnings. The stochastic elements in earnings are of two basic types. The first is the year-to-year variability in earnings which led Friedman to distinguish between observed income and permanent income. The importance of this short-run variability has been discounted by Thurow who says: "The distribution of lifetime incomes probably looks very similar to the distribution of annual incomes" (1969, p. 108). There is, however, another facet of uncertainty which transcends the year-to-year variations—unexplained permanent dispersion in incomes. The permanent uncertainty is clearly one key to the inequality of lifetime incomes among individuals and is, therefore, the focus of this paper.

CAUSES OF UNEXPLAINED PERMANENT DISPERSION IN EARNINGS

What accounts for this unexplained permanent variation in earnings? Certainly, some of the explanation rests with actual differences in individuals which are not, or cannot be, observed by the statistician. Although the Taubman and Wales data encompassed a broad range of explanatory variables, there are undoubtedly unmeasured differences in personality, motivation, and ability which create real differences in individual productivities. In this case, apparent uncertainty in incomes is due not to stochastic variables in the earnings function but to unobserved differences in characteristics. That is, firms pay wages which reflect marginal products and recognize differences in productivity among individuals; however, outside observers cannot recognize or measure all of the factors which affect an individual's productivity. These unobserved components clearly look like earnings uncertainty to the outside observer and they may be just as uncertain a priori to the individual himself. A person may not be aware, in advance, of all of the factors which affect his productivity and, to this extent, unobserved components are uncertain to him, too.

Another source of differences in earnings of observationally equivalent persons are compensating wage differentials for nonmonetary aspects of jobs. In other words, part of earnings may be payments for job characteristics rather than for personal characteristics. Lucas in an empirical investigation of job characteristics finds rather perverse results; many characteristics of jobs which are usually considered to be unpleasant are rewarded negatively rather than positively ceteris paribus (Thurow and Lucas, 1972). Greg Duncan (in this volume) studies the impact of fringe benefits in reducing wage differentials.

A third reason for unexplained differences in earnings is one which has been emphasized recently in another context—costly information and imperfect markets. This rubric embraces two principal hindrances to perfectly competitive labor markets—first, the institutional forces of unions and industrial structure which prevent the achievement of perfect competition; and second, the costs of acquiring information both for the worker and for his (potential) employer, and the related costs of mobility between occupations and geographic locations. To the extent that information is imperfect and mobility is costly, then differences in earnings of persons with exactly the same productivity will not be eliminated. An estimated earnings function would not be able to explain all the variance in earnings even if we could measure every characteristic which affects an individual's productivity.

THIS PAPER

The dispersion of permanent lifetime incomes among observationally equivalent persons can be ascribed either to unobserved differences in personal characteristics which affect an individual's productivity or to imperfections in labor markets which allow equally productive individuals to be paid different amounts. The subject of this paper is not the cause of uncertainty in earnings but rather the effect of uncertainty on the wage structure itself. The principal focus is on differences in uncertainty across occupations: Is there a tradeoff between risk and return in occupational earnings? The importance of this question as regards the distribution of income is at least twofold. First, if average earnings are higher in occupations which have greater unexplained variance in earnings (and therefore less certain earnings to the potential entrant to the occupation), then the market is compensating for uncertainty, and the distribution of expected utility is likely to be less unequal than the distribution of observed incomes. Second, the positive correlation of dispersion with average earnings provides an explanation for the observed skewness in the distribution of labor incomes.

In the rest of this paper, the tradeoff between risk and return in the labor market is estimated, using data from the 1970 Census. In order to estimate uncertainty, an earnings function is specified. Because many significant variables cannot be observed, estimates of uncertainty are necessarily biased. The effect of this bias on the results is considered. Results for different demographic groups indicate that the risk-return relation exists and seems to be related to the degree of occupational immobility in the demographic group.

A SIMPLE MODEL OF EARNINGS

Consider a simple linear model of permanent, lifetime earnings. Intertemporal variation of earnings is not important here, only the dispersion of earnings across individuals. Let

(1) $Y_{ij} = \alpha_i + \beta_i Z_j + \delta_i A_j + \tilde{X}_{ij}$

where

   Y_{ij} is the permanent earnings of individual j in occupation i;
   α_i is a parameter (scalar);
   Z_j is a vector of observed characteristics of individual j;
   A_j is a vector of unobserved characteristics of individual j;
   β_i, δ_i are parameter vectors conformable to Z_j, A_j; and
   $\tilde{X}_{ij}$ is the stochastic element of earnings for individual j in occupation i.

Assume that $\tilde{X}_{ij}$ is distributed identically for all individuals in occupation i, although clearly the value $\tilde{X}_{ij}$ takes on may be different for each person. The expected value of $\tilde{X}_{ij}$ is zero. An individual's earnings in occupation i are determined by his characteristics, Z_j and A_j, the reward occupation i puts on these characteristics, and a chance element, $\tilde{X}_{ij}$. This stochastic term is permanent for the individual—his one draw from the distribution determines his earnings in the occupation forever.

In an econometric earnings function, both A_j and $\tilde{X}_{ij}$ are pushed into the error term of the equation. They must be separated, at least conceptually, because the unobserved characteristics, A_j, may be known by the individual choosing an occupation, whereas $\tilde{X}_{ij}$ cannot be known, by definition. Inability to observe A_j will introduce bias into the estimates of uncertainty; unexplained variance in earnings for individuals with the same Z_j could arise from either $\tilde{X}_{ij}$ or differences in A_j.

Given the earnings function of (1), an individual is assumed to maximize his lifetime expected utility by choosing the appropriate occupation. For an individual with a given set of attributes, Z_j and A_j, the choice is made on the basis of the α_i, β_i, δ_i, and the distribution of $\tilde{X}_{ij}$ for each occupation. Clearly, no person actually knows α_i, β_i, and δ_i; what they may know is mean earnings in occupation i for individuals with similar characteristics, and an impression of the dispersion of earnings around the mean. In fact, Freeman (1971) finds that college students are quite well informed about the pattern of earnings in various occupations. By maximizing expected utility in choosing an occupation, persons will be basing their choice both on mean earnings and the uncertainty, or dispersion, of earnings. Analogous to financial theory, equilibrium in the labor market should involve a tradeoff between risk and return across occupations for given demographic groups. Occupations with a great deal of uncertainty must offer greater than average wages in order to entice entrants. One of the key assumptions here is the lack of mobility between occupations. To the extent that individuals move between occupations, the risk-return relationship is mitigated; a person who fares poorly in one occupation will move to another. In reality, given the costs of mobility (including the training costs for the new occupation), there is an optimal pattern of occupational "search," similar to the job search process described by Mortensen (1970). It suffices to assert that the more mobility between occupations, the weaker the relationship between risk and return.

THE DATA

Earnings distributions for full-time workers broken down by race, age, sex, education and occupation are given in the 1970 Census. Each distribution gives the dispersion of full-time earnings for individuals in a given age, sex, race, and education group for a particular occupation. By comparing mean earnings and dispersion across occupations, *within* a given demographic group, the contribution of Z_j to earnings does not have to be explicitly estimated. For the time being, we assume that all individuals in a particular demographic group (same Z's) have the same unobserved characteristics, A_j. I shall later investigate the bias introduced into our estimates by such an assumption.

FUNCTIONAL FORM

In order to specify a functional form for estimation, both a utility function and a distribution function for $\tilde{X}_{ij}$ must be postulated. The traditional use of mean and variance is not necessarily appropriate; recent work in the theory of uncertainty shows that the mean-variance criteria can be inconsistent with the expected utility hypothesis (see Feldstein [1969]). A convenient hypothesis is that earnings and the stochastic term follow a log-normal distribution, whereas the utility function is of the constant relative risk aversion type. Then, expected utility can be expressed as a linear function of the log of the mean of income and the variance (see Weiss [1972]). On the other hand, if earnings are normally distributed, then utility can be written as a simple function of mean and variance. In this study, many different functional forms were tried.

Since the distribution data come grouped into rather large income classes, the data were fitted to both the normal and the log-normal distributions in order to estimate parameters of the earnings distributions.[1] Otherwise, the error in estimating variances directly from grouped data would be large, especially with the open-ended highest income bracket. Then, the estimated parameters of these normal and log-normal approximations were used to estimate risk-return relationships. The dependent variable in each estimated equation was either the mean earnings in the occupation for the particular demographic group, as computed by the Census Bureau, or the log of that mean.

RESULTS

The results cannot be easily summarized. No one specification was clearly superior for all 36 demographic groups (2 race groups, 3 age groups and 6 education groups). Neither the normal nor the log-normal approximation to the distribution of earnings was clearly superior for all demographic groups, by a chi-squared test of goodness of fit, so both were used. For every demographic group, the estimated coefficient on the dispersion variable, the standard deviation of earnings, was positive. Even when the coefficient of variation was used as the dispersion variable, the results were positive when earnings were fitted to the log-normal distribution. As an example of the results, Table 1 gives the results for all demographic groups for one of the estimated equations. Results for blacks were less definite because earnings distributions were available for fewer occupations.

Because the estimated coefficient on the dispersion variable was positive in virtually every case, it appears that one can say with a fair degree of assurance that uncertainty is compensated to some degree in the labor market. However, at least two caveats should be appended to this assertion. First, the measure of uncertainty used, dispersion of 1969 full-time earnings, does not necessarily represent the permanent dispersion of earnings. To the extent that annual earnings fluctuate around permanent earnings, this measure of dispersion overstates the permanent dispersion in earnings. Only a longitudinal sample could reveal the extent of transitory variation in incomes. Friedman and Kuznets's data for independent professional incomes are probably not representative (Friedman and Kuznets, 1945). A second qualification to the results is that the risk of unemployment seems to exert a negative influence on relative occupational earnings in many of the samples. This influence is measured by the variable FULLEMP, which is high when the risk of unemployment or part-time work is low. Thus, the market does *not* seem to compensate for the risk of unemployment undertaken in a given occupation, a relationship Hall (1970) has suggested for geographic areas.[2] Because we have used cross-sectional data from a generally low unemployment year (1969), we have certainly not measured adequately the effect of *cyclical* unemployment on average occupational earnings.

TABLE 1 **Regression Results: Effect of Earnings Dispersion on Mean Earnings across Occupations for Various Demographic Groups**
(Dependent variable: mean occupational earnings; *t*-ratios in parentheses)

Educ.	N	FULLEMP[a]	GRWTH[b]	Standard Deviation[c]	Constant	R^2 Adj.
			Regression Coefficients			
			Male Whites, Aged 25–34			
0–8	55	6,299	9.856	.7141	−1,016	.254
		(1.344)	(2.003)	(3.397)	(.2233)	
9–11	84	3,100	8.348	.3708	4,163	.178
		(1.364)	(3.007)	(3.007)	(1.843)	
12	101	−1,633	8.625	1.048	7,110	.245
		(.470)	(3.734)	(4.365)	(1.962)	
13–15	100	18,357	7.728	.6269	−10,273	.400
		(6.985)	(3.184)	(3.768)	(3.902)	
16	90	11,829	7.409	.5332	−2,695	.133
		(2.863)	(1.856)	(1.943)	(.6864)	
17+	73	201	3.908	1.111	6,733	.156
		(2.857)	(.8189)	(3.847)	(4.989)	
			Male Whites, Aged 35–54			
0–8	83	8,601	12.05	.6224	−1,945	.293
		(2.893)	(3.076)	(3.151)	(.6711)	
9–11	96	14,792	12.969	1.144	−8,590	.309
		(2.361)	(3.117)	(4.631)	(1.3471)	
12	107	14,523	14.95	1.689	−9,970	.535
		(3.158)	(4.507)	(8.261)	(2.267)	
13–15	103	28,681	14.108	1.837	−23,722	.708
		(5.317)	(4.643)	(12.04)	(4.606)	
16	94	331.5	11.085	1.923	4,086	.573
		(5.075)	(2.489)	(10.615)	(4.450)	
17+	79	569.2	4.856	2.044	4,452	.533
		(7.322)	(.661)	(8.814)	(3.132)	
			Male Whites, Aged 55–65			
0–8	77	1,634	20.07	.3981	5,268	.238
		(.8418)	(4.278)	(1.580)	(2.662)	
9–11	83	3,344	21.79	.4137	4,236	.268
		(1.691)	(4.672)	(1.990)	(2.073)	
12	95	283.6	25.55	1.462	4,104	.422
		(3.656)	(4.206)	(7.217)	(4.705)	

TABLE 1 (continued)

Educ.	N	FULLEMP[a]	GRWTH[b]	Standard Deviation[c]	Constant	R^2Adj.
			Regression Coefficients			
		Male Whites, Aged 55–65 (continued)				
13–15	86	18,509	18.93	1.110	−11,713	.482
		(3.880)	(3.829)	(5.734)	(2.518)	
16	71	264	20.74	1.706	5,391	.378
		(4.123)	(2.950)	(6.261)	(3.690)	
17+	56	35,984	10.951	.861	−22,858	.250
		(2.106)	(1.044)	(3.043)	(1.431)	
		Male Blacks, Aged 25–34				
0–8	19	−31.71	15.50	.2187	4,403	.589
		(1.3203)	(2.828)	(2.196)	(13.55)	
9–11	24	.748	18.795	.511	4,348	.727
		(.0211)	(6.345)	(1.950)	(5.609)	
12	30	7,174	7.120	.755	−2,267	.383
		(1.532)	(1.857)	(2.377)	(9.518)	
13–15	23	6,867	4.671	−.148	1,517	–
		(.986)	(.922)	(.2753)	(.2443)	
16	11	−6,818	1.949	.952	12,294	–
		(.798)	(.1332)	(.9377)	(1.692)	
17+	6	23,333	−12.30	−.1138	−9,508	–
		(.728)	(.423)	(.051)	(.2704)	
		Male Blacks, Aged 35–54				
0–8	25	5,665	14.84	.297	−890	.288
		(1.232)	(2.609)	(1.549)	(.207)	
9–11	28	8,975	17.36	−.007	−2,006	.322
		(1.687)	(2.504)	(.0369)	(.422)	
12	34	26,451	11.428	.1225	−18,254	.558
		(4.385)	(2.204)	(.8717)	(3.165)	
13–15	26	28.23	7.184	.1208	7,533	–
		(.205)	(1.105)	(.340)	(5.883)	
16	15	278.9	9.179	1.372	3,939	.615
		(4.952)	(.945)	(3.237)	(2.448)	
17+	10	40,331	−2.363	2.512	37,565	–
		(2.231)	(.2337)	(6.728)	(2.393)	
		Male Blacks, Aged 55–64				
0–8	19	6,037	6.696	.5212	−1,873	.463
		(1.828)	(1.075)	(2.967)	(.602)	

TABLE 1 (concluded)

Educ.	N	Regression Coefficients FULLEMP[a]	GRWTH[b]	Standard Deviation[c]	Constant	R^2 Adj.
9–11	20	−6,824 (1.828)	6.125 (1.075)	.908 (2.967)	9,981 (.602)	.735
12	15	−2,814 (.373)	−3.889 (.493)	.560 (1.590)	8,180 (1.110)	–
13–15	8	2,840 (.193)	−.306 (.030)	1.745 (2.560)	−842 (.054)	.458

SOURCE: 1970 Census of Population PC(2)-8B, *Earnings by Occupation and Education.*
[a]FULLEMP is the ratio of average earnings of all workers to average earnings of full-year workers. A high figure indicates little part-time work or unemployment.
[b]GRWTH is the rate of growth of the occupation from 1960 to 1970.
[c]Standard deviation is the standard deviation of earnings, under the normal approximation.

An indication of the economic significance of the results displayed in Table 1 is given in Table 2, which presents the dollar impact on mean wages of a change in the dispersion variable of one standard deviation. Clearly, not only are the results statistically significant, but they are also economically significant, with dollar effects ranging from $277 to $4,124.

UNCERTAINTY AND IMMOBILITY

As mentioned above, the risk-return tradeoff should have a steeper slope, the less mobility there is between occupations. When persons are locked into their choices of occupations, then there is no opportunity for an ex post equalizing movement between occupations. Dispersion in earnings can exist under such circumstances. If, on the other hand, mobility is perfect between occupations, then there should be no differences in earnings among occupations which do not stem from differences in individual characteristics or nonpecuniary factors. Another way to see this is to consider that with perfect mobility, there is no penalty for choosing a highly risky occupation, because one can leave costlessly if one's luck is bad.

Interestingly, the data do support a tentative conclusion that immobility may be related to the strength of the tradeoff between risk and return. Figure 1 presents data on mobility between broad occupational classes—broader, in fact, than the units of observation for the risk-return equations. The data are grouped to correspond most closely with the

TABLE 2   Dollar Effects of Mean Occupational Earnings of a One Standard Deviation Change in the Dispersion Variable: Equation Reported in Table 1, White Males

Education	Effect on Mean Occupational Earnings
Age 25–34	
0–8	$ 519
9–11	277
12	567
13–15	443
16	423
17+	1,208
Age 35–54	
0–8	544
9–11	927
12	1,480
13–15	1,974
16	2,722
17+	4,124
Age 55–65	
0–8	327
9–11	414
12	2,184
13–15	1,373
16	3,106
17+	2,029

groupings of our estimated equations. As expected, immobility rises sharply from the 20–34 to the 35–49 age group and slightly beyond that. Immobility also rises with education in the two older age groups, while it tends to fall with education in the lowest age group. It is well to caution that these results may be peculiar because of the breadth of occupational classes involved in the definition of mobility.

In Figure 2, the estimated coefficients on the dispersion term (standard deviation of earnings) are plotted for the equation whose complete results appear in Table 1. In fact, the coefficients seem to behave quite like the measures of immobility in Figure 1. For the middle age group, effect of dispersion increases with education; for the younger age group,

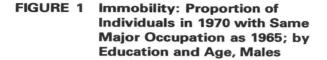

FIGURE 1 **Immobility: Proportion of Individuals in 1970 with Same Major Occupation as 1965; by Education and Age, Males**

SOURCE: 1970 Census.

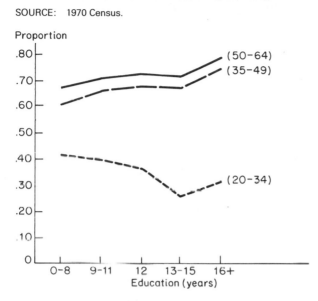

FIGURE 2 **Regression Coefficients: Dispersion Term (Standard Deviation, Normal Approximation) by Education and Age; White Males**

SOURCE: Table 1.

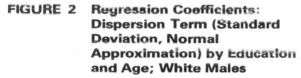

there is not such a clear pattern. While it is probably incorrect to make too much of this similarity, the evidence does point both to a positive relationship between risk and return in the labor market and to an association of the goodness of fit or strength of this relationship and occupational immobility. The robustness of these conclusions is underscored by the large number of demographic groups and functional forms used in making the estimates.

THE PROBLEM OF OMITTED VARIABLES

So far, the observed association between the dispersion of earnings and mean earnings across occupations, but within demographic groups, has been attributed to the tradeoff between risk and return in the labor market. In this section of the paper, another explanation for these results is considered—the omission of ability as a variable.

The bias introduced by the omission of A_j or ability from the estimates causes two kinds of error: first, the measured dispersion of the random term, $\tilde{X}_{ij}$, for an occupation includes the dispersion of A_j in addition to the true dispersion of $\tilde{X}_{ij}$; second, the effect of differences in mean ability across occupations is omitted from the equation explaining differences in mean earnings across occupations. In the mean-variance framework (to make the analysis easier), assume that the "true" relationship for a given demographic group is

(2) $\qquad Y_i = K + \gamma(\text{var }\tilde{X})_i + \beta A_i$

or

$\qquad \hat{Y}_i = Y_i - \beta A_i = K + \gamma(\text{var }\tilde{X})_i$

where

$\qquad Y_i$ is mean earnings in occupation i;

$\qquad (\text{var }\tilde{X})_i$ is the variance of "true" $\tilde{X}$ in occupation i;

$\qquad A_i$ is the mean ability of individuals in occupation i; and

$\qquad K$, γ, and β are parameters.

The coefficient γ is the payment for risk which we are trying to estimate. Note that we initially assume that occupations reward ability identically, that β is the same for all i.

Instead of estimating this "true" relation, we estimate

(3) $\qquad Y_i = k + g[\text{est (var }\tilde{X})_i]$

where est (var $\tilde{X})_i$ is the measured variance of earnings within occupation *i.* The purpose of this analysis is to discover the extent to which the estimated parameters, k and g, differ from the true parameters, K and γ. The measured variance of earnings, est $(\text{var } \tilde{X})_i$, can be written

(4) $$\text{est } (\text{var } \tilde{X})_i = (\text{var } Y)_i = (\text{var } \tilde{X})_i + \beta^2 (\text{var } A)_i$$

where $(\text{var } A)_i$ is the variance of A within occupation i and $\tilde{X}_{ij}$ is independent of A. Considering only large-sample properties of the estimate,

$$\text{plim } g = \frac{\text{cov } [(Y_i), \text{est } (\text{var } \tilde{X})_i]}{(\text{var } Y_i)}$$

$$= \frac{\text{cov } [(\hat{Y}_i + \beta A_i), (\text{var } \tilde{X})_i + \beta^2 (\text{var } A)_i]}{(\text{var } \hat{Y}_i) + \beta^2 (\text{var } A_i) + \beta \text{ cov } (\hat{Y}_i, A_i)}$$

Thus

(5) $$\text{plim } g = \gamma \frac{\text{var } \hat{Y}_i}{\text{var } \hat{Y}_i + \beta^2 (\text{var } A_i)}$$

$$+ \frac{\beta \text{ cov } [A_i, (\text{var } \tilde{X})_i] + \beta^2 \text{ cov } [\hat{Y}_i, (\text{var } A)_i] + \beta^3 \text{ cov } [A_i, (\text{var } A)_i]}{(\text{var } \hat{Y}_i) + \beta^2 (\text{var } A_i)}$$

If abilities are randomly distributed among occupations, then all the covariance terms will be zero in the probability limit, and var A_i, the variance of average ability across occupations, is zero. In this case, there is no bias because plim $g = \gamma$. In fact, these are reasonable assumptions, given the assumptions of the model (there is no reason to expect any particular pattern of abilities across occupations if β is the same for each occupation), so that in the probability limit, abilities should be identically distributed across occupations.

If, on the other hand, β differs from occupation to occupation, then (5) becomes

(6) $$\text{plim } g = \gamma \frac{\text{var } \hat{Y}_i}{\text{var } \hat{Y}_i + \text{var } \beta_i A_i}$$

$$+ \frac{\text{cov } [\beta_i A_i, (\text{var } \tilde{X})_i] + \text{cov } [\hat{Y}_i, \beta_i^2 (\text{var } A)_i] + \text{cov } [\beta_i A_i, \beta_i^2 (\text{var } A)_i]}{\text{var } \hat{Y}_i + \text{var } \beta_i A_i}$$

Again, the first and second covariance terms are zero in the probability limit, but the third will be positive even if A_i and $(\text{var } A)_i$ are not correlated because β_i is positive. Thus, (6) becomes

(7) $$\text{plim } g = \gamma \frac{\text{var } \hat{Y}_i}{\text{var } \hat{Y}_i + \text{var } \beta_i A_i} + \frac{\text{cov } [\beta_i A_i, \beta_i^2 (\text{var } A)_i]}{\text{var } \hat{Y}_i + \text{var } \beta_i A_i}$$

If individuals do not know their abilities and are therefore choosing occupations regardless of β_i, then there may again be random assortment of abilities to occupations. In this case, A_i and $(\text{var } A)_i$ will again be constant, in the probability limit, across occupations. Thus, var $\beta_i A_i$ will equal A_i var $\beta_i > 0$ and $\text{cov}[\beta_i A_i, \beta_i^2 \text{ var }(A)_i]$ will depend on cov (β_i, β_i^2). The net distortionary effect will be indeterminate because var $(\beta_i A_i)$ decreases g while cov $[\beta_i A_i, \beta_i^2 (\text{var } A)_i]$ increases the estimate.

Curiously, if individuals do know their abilities and β_i, the distortion becomes less positive. In this case, high ability individuals will choose occupations which reward ability highly, so that cov $(\beta_i, A_i) > 0$, and therefore, var $(\beta_i A_i) > A_i$ var $(\beta_i) > 0$. The denominator of the first term of (7) is larger and the bias becomes less positive. In fact, if the covariance term in (7) were zero, then the estimate g would underestimate γ. In fact, however, cov $[\beta_i A_i, \beta_i^2 (\text{var } A)_i]$ will be positive even if A_i and $(\text{var } A)_i$ are constant over i, because β_i is positively correlated with β_i^2.

Although there is no evidence on β_i, there is some evidence that cov $[A_i, (\text{var } A)_i]$ may be negative. Data gathered during World War II which matched civilian occupations of military men with scores on armed forces tests show that, as expected, people in higher status or higher income occupations tend to perform better on tests (Harrell and Harrell, 1945). However, the variance of ability within an occupation, as measured by test scores, tends to decrease as the average ability of the occupation increases. This result may be explained by the assumption of a minimum level of ability which differs from occupation to occupation. Occupations with higher standards will have higher average abilities and, because a smaller range of abilities is acceptable, a smaller ability variance. Under these circumstances, cov $[\beta_i A_i, \beta_i^2 (\text{var } A)_i]$ will be smaller than it would be if A_i and $(\text{var } A)_i$ were the same for all i, but still may be either positive or negative. Thus, one cannot say for sure whether it will be overestimated or underestimated, but at least there is no definite positive bias.

CONCLUSION

In this paper, a stochastic model of earnings was used to derive estimable relations between risk and return in the labor market. The estimates reveal a systematic positive effect of earnings dispersion on average earnings. This result holds up for many different demographic groups, and for both the normal and log-normal approximations to the distribution of earnings. Furthermore, the estimated coefficients for the dispersion term are larger for demographic groups which are less mobile between occupations, conforming to theoretical expectations. Finally, the omission of certain key variables, while a problem, may not be a serious source of bias in the estimates.

There are two implications of these findings for the distribution of income. First, since the market compensates for risk, in the form of earnings uncertainty, the distribution of expected utility is less unequal than the distribution of incomes. However, the reverse is true if the risk of unemployment is considered. Second, if the variance of earnings around an occupational mean is positively related to the occupational mean, then there is a "real" explanation for the rightward skewness in the distribution of earnings. Consider the third moment of the distribution, a traditional measure of skewness

$$S = \sum_i \sum_j (Y_{ij} - \bar{Y})^3$$

where, as before, i indexes occupations, j indexes individuals. If earnings within an occupation are not skewed around the occupational mean, and the means themselves are not skewed around the population mean, then

$$S = 2 \sum_i (\text{var } Y)_i (\bar{Y}_i - \bar{Y})$$

where $(\text{var } Y)_i$ is the variance of earnings within occupation i and $\bar{Y}$ is the population mean. Clearly, the size of S depends on the positive correlation between $(\text{var } Y)_i$ and $\bar{Y}_i$.

NOTES

1. The normal and log normal approximations were based on a procedure in Aitchison and Brown (1957).
2. Another variable, GRWTH, the percentage change in employment in the occupation, 1960–70, was a proxy for changing demand. As expected, its coefficients were positive and significant. The age-earnings profiles were tried as variables but were not significant.

REFERENCES

Aitchison, J., and Brown, J. A. C. *The Lognormal Distribution.* Cambridge: Cambridge University Press, 1957.

Champernowne, D. G. "A Model of Income Distribution," *Economic Journal* 68 (June 1953).

Feldstein, M. "Mean-Variance Analysis in the Theory of Liquidity Preference and Portfolio Selection." *Review of Economic Studies* 36 (Jan. 1969).

Freeman, R. *The Market for College-Trained Manpower.* Cambridge, Mass.: Harvard University Press, 1971.

Friedman, M. "Choice, Chance, and the Personal Distribution of Earnings." *Journal of Political Economy* 61 (Aug. 1953).

————. *A Theory of the Consumption Function.* Princeton: Princeton University Press for NBER, 1957.

Friedman, M., and Kuznets, Simon. *Income from Independent Professional Practice.* New York: NBER, 1945.

Hall, R. "Why Is the Unemployment Rate so High at Full Employment?" *Brookings Papers on Economic Activity*, 3:1970.

————. "Wages, Income and Hours of Work in the U.S. Labor Force." In Glen Cain and Harold Watts, eds., *Income Maintenance and Labor Supply.* New York: Academic Press, 1973.

Harrell, T., and Harrell, M. "Army General Classification Test Scores for Civilian Occupations." *Educational and Psychological Measurements* 5 (Autumn 1945).

Jencks, C. *Inequality.* New York: Basic Books, 1972.

Lydall, H. *The Structure of Earnings.* Oxford: Clarendon Press, 1968.

Mandelbrot, B. "Stable Paretian Random Functions and the Multiplicative Variation of Income." *Econometrica* 29 (Oct. 1961).

Mortensen, D. "Job Search, the Duration of Unemployment, and the Phillips Curve." *American Economic Review* 60 (Dec. 1970).

Taubman, P., and Wales, T. "Higher Education, Mental Ability and Screening." *Journal of Political Economy* 81 (Jan./Feb. 1973).

Thurow, L. *Poverty and Discrimination.* Washington, D.C.: Brookings Institution, 1969.

Thurow, L., and Lucas, R. E. B. *The American Distribution of Income: A Structural Problem.* Joint Economic Committee, Mar. 1972.

Weiss, Y. "The Risk Element in Occupational and Educational Choices." *Journal of Political Economy* 80 (Nov./Dec. 1972).

11

THOMAS
OSMAN
University of Wisconsin

The Role of Intergenerational Wealth Transfers in the Distribution of Wealth over the Life Cycle: A Preliminary Analysis

While studies of the distribution of personal nonhuman wealth in the United States have been few,[1] those studies available have consistently shown a high degree of inequality in the distribution of wealth.[2] The most recent complete study of the U.S. wealth distribution, a 1962 Federal Reserve survey,[3] measured a Gini coefficient of inequality in the distribution of personal wealth among consumer units to be .76 (this compares with a Gini coefficient of .43 for the distribution of income in the same year).[4] This study indicated that the top 1/2 of 1 percent of U.S. consumer units owned 22 percent of the personal wealth, the top 2.5 percent wealth-owning consumer units owned 43 percent of the personal wealth, while the net worth of the bottom 10 percent of U.S. consumer units was negative. (See Table 1.)

Together with a concentration of wealth among a relatively few persons among the population as a whole, there is a concentration of

NOTE: The author is a graduate student at the University of Wisconsin-Madison.

TABLE 1 Distribution of Wealth: December 31, 1962

Wealth	Consumer Units (Millions)	Percentage Distribution Consumer Units	Wealth
Total	57.9	100	100
Negative	1.0	2	a
Zero	4.7	8	a
$1 to $999	9.0	16	a
1,000 to 4,999	10.8	19	2
5,000 to 9,999	9.1	16	5
10,000 to 24,999	13.3	23	18
25,000 to 49,999	6.2	11	18
50,000 to 99,999	2.5	4	14
100,000 to 199,999	0.7	1	8
200,000 to 499,999	0.5	1	13
500,000 and over	0.2	a	22

SOURCE: Dorothy S. Projector and Gertrude S. Weiss, *Survey of Financial Characteristics of Consumers*, Board of Governors of the Federal Reserve System, August 1966, Tables A-2, p. 98; A-16, p. 136; A-36, p. 151.

NOTE: Sums of tabulated figures in this section may not equal totals because of rounding.

a Less than ½ of 1 percent.

wealth by age group; the consumer units headed by a person 35 or younger in 1962 owned 7 percent of the personal wealth, yet constituted 22 percent of the nation's consumer units. In contrast, those consumer units headed by a person aged 55 or older constituted 35 percent of the nation's population, but owned 56 percent of the personal wealth.[5] Moreover, while there is a concentration of total wealth among the older age cohorts, the degree of wealth ownership inequality *within* a given age cohort as measured by the Gini coefficient is relatively consistent, with Gini coefficients for the age cohorts ranging from .83 to .70.[6]

While age and differing wealth accumulation functions have been employed to explain inter-age cohort wealth differences, the role of inter-generational wealth transfers in wealth distribution inequality over the life cycle has been largely ignored.[7] In this paper, I examine the possible role of inter-generational wealth transfers in explaining the constant inequality of wealth distribution observed for all cohorts during the life cycle.

The importance of inter-generational wealth transfers in wealth inequality can be approached by considering what the distribution of wealth would be like in a hypothetical society in which all inter-generational physical wealth transfers were forbidden. In such a society, the life-cycle accumulation of wealth of an individual or family unit would start from a very low level early in the life cycle, would accumulate, peak at a period before retirement, and wealth stocks would be consumed during retirement until death (Figure 1). The total wealth of a family unit

FIGURE 1   Accumulation of Wealth for Individuals/Family Units in a Society with No Inter-generational Wealth Transfers

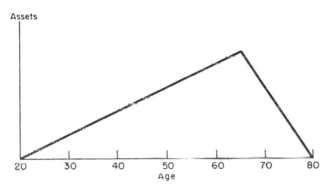

Assets

Age

SOURCE: A. B. Atkinson, "The Distribution of Wealth and the Individual Life Cycle," *Oxford Economic Papers* 23 (July 1971): 239–254.

or individual could be reduced to a function of savings, return on savings, and age; in equation form, this wealth relationship may be expressed as

$$[\{[S_1(1+R_1)+S_2](1+R_2)\}+S_N]1+R_N \ldots$$

where

S is the net saving of the unit in a given year;
R is the rate of return on the savings; and
N is the number of years that the unit has been saving.

In such a hypothetical society, while inequalities in the distribution of physical wealth would not disappear, such inequalities that did exist would be due to age, differing savings rates, and differing rates of return on savings, rather than inter-generational wealth transfers.[8]

In such a society, it would be expected that as a given cohort of the population aged, the inequality in the distribution of wealth *within* a given cohort would *increase*, as the impact of age and differing wealth accumulation rates within the cohort took effect. Inequality in the distribution of wealth within a given age cohort would be expected to be greatest in the older cohorts, where the life-cycle factors would have had the longest time to make an impact, and least in the youngest cohorts. Wealth in such a hypothetical society would be concentrated in the control of the aged, with the younger cohorts of the population having little of the society's total wealth. Finally, the average amount of wealth owned by units within each cohort would increase until retirement, and then be drawn down.[9]

THE U.S. WEALTH DISTRIBUTION

Contemporary America's wealth distribution agrees with the general distribution that would result in such a hypothetical society in that the nation's wealth is concentrated in the hands of the aged,[10] and in that the average asset holdings per consumer unit increase with age.[11]

Where the U.S. differs from the hypothetical society with no inter-generational wealth transfers is in the degree of wealth ownership inequality *within* the various age cohorts; instead of wealth inequality increasing within the cohort as the cohort aged, as in our hypothetical society, the degree of wealth ownership inequality, as measured by the Gini coefficient, remains relatively fixed over the life cycle. What accounts for the high degree of inequality in wealth ownership observed for the younger age cohorts? The issue I wish to explore is: What is the role of inter-generational wealth transfers in explaining the constant high degree of inequality of U.S. wealth ownership observed throughout the life cycle.[12]

METHODS OF U.S. INTER-GENERATIONAL WEALTH TRANSFER

Inter-generational wealth transfer occurs both during the life of both parties in the transfer process, and at the death of one. The three main methods of wealth transfer available are trust funds, transfers by the processes of direct inheritance, and transfers through gifts given while the donor is still alive.

While very little information exists on the importance of inter-generational wealth transfers in the U.S. distribution of wealth, a recent analysis of the information contained in the 1962 Federal Reserve Survey provides some information on trusts and direct inheritances in the form of estates in probate.[13] The analysis breaks down wealth holding by type of asset form, and by age group for individuals; Table 2 shows what

TABLE 2 **Importance of Trusts and Estates in Probate as a Percentage of the Total Wealth Owned by the Age Cohort, Individuals, 1962**

Age Cohort	Percentage of Total Wealth of the Cohort Held in the Form of Trusts and Estates	Percentage of the Total Personal Wealth in 1962 Owned by the Various Age Cohorts
0–25	8.69	1.6
25–34	21.68	8.7
35–44	5.87	17.9
45–54	1.18	23.2
55–64	1.66	25.1
64+	.56	23.5
		100

SOURCE: Table V-4, Tables V-13 to V-20; in Appendix 5, "The Distribution of Assets Among Individuals of Different Age and Wealth," in Raymond W. Goldsmith, ed., *Institutional Investors and Corporate Stock*, pp. 394–427 (New York: NBER, 1973).

percentage of personal U.S. wealth in 1962 was owned by which age cohort, and what percentage of the total assets of each age cohort was in the form of trust funds and estates in probate.[14]

From Table 2, it appears that inter-generational wealth transfers in the form of trusts and estates in probate are an important asset source for the youngest age cohorts; after the age of 45, trusts and estates in probate are a minor asset source. This table indicates that inter-generational wealth transfers could be a factor in explaining the high degree of wealth-ownership inequality observed in the younger age cohorts.

TRUST FUNDS

Data for 1972 indicated that in that year minimum gross transfers by the inheritance process totaled 38.8 billion dollars, while in 1970 trust funds earned 7.5 billion dollars in income.[15] Total funds held in personal trusts in 1968 were estimated to be 138 billion dollars, and have been growing rapidly.[16] From the individual analysis of the 1962 Federal Reserve Survey data, it appears that the device of trust funds is an important factor in explaining the high degree of inequality in the distribution of wealth observed among the younger age cohorts.

Moreover, trust fund assets are highly concentrated. In 1969, the top 1/2 of 1 percent of U.S. wealth-holding adults owned 85 percent of the value of *all* trust fund assets, and 92 percent of the value of trust funds were owned by the top 1 percent of the U.S. adult wealth holders.[17] Trust assets appear to be an important asset source for very wealthy young persons.[18]

Table 3 summarizes the 1962 data on trust funds as an asset source for individuals. From this table, it appears that trust funds are a minor asset source for almost all individuals in all age cohorts possessing less than $200,000 in assets. However, for those individuals under the age of 44, and with more than $200,000 in assets, it appears that trust funds are an important asset source.[19]

TABLE 3 Percentage of Assets Held in the Form of Trusts of Individuals in 1962 by Age and Asset Level

Asset Level	Age					
	0–25	25–34	35–44	44–55	55–64	64+
$30,000 to $60,000	3.38	1.8	a	a	1.05	–
60,000 to 100,000	18.14	–	a	a	–	1.0
100,000 to 200,000	–	–	a	–	1.75	a
200,000 to 500,000	30.76	8.78	3.62	.005	.032	2.11
500,000 to 1,000,000	13.71	13.60	81.76	2.09	a	a
1,000,000+	b	93.68	12.07	2.65	5.24	1.48
Percentage of all assets of all age and wealth levels in the form of trusts	5.02	18.2	5.9	.071	1.29	a

SOURCE: Tables V-13 to V-20, pp. 413–428, in Appendix 5, "The Distribution of Assets Among Individuals of Different Age and Wealth," in Raymond W. Goldsmith, ed., *Institutional Investors and Corporate Stock* (New York: NBER, 1973).
aLess than 1 percent.
bSee note 18, end of text.

After age 44, trust fund assets become a relatively insignificant asset form for all wealth levels, with no more than 5.25 percent of the assets of any post age 44 cohort being held in the form of trust funds, with trust assets relative to total assets declining with age for all asset classes.[20]

Further information on the importance of trust funds as an asset source for individual wealth holders with assets of greater than $200,000 is in data on the distribution of assets of all individuals in 1962. While trusts were only 3.3 percent of the assets of all individuals, they constituted 13.7 percent of all assets of those individuals with between $500,000 and $1,000,000 in assets, and 13.5 percent of the assets of millionaires and multimillionaires.[21] Moreover, a special Treasury study[22] of 1957 and

1959 estate tax returns revealed that, taken as a class, between 54 and 56 percent of the millionaires created one or more trusts contingent upon their death, and that trust formation increased steadily with the size of the millionaires' assets; while between 51 and 53 percent of the millionaires with $1,000,000 in assets created trusts, 64 to 77 percent of the millionaires with assets of $10,000,000 or more created trusts.[23]

The amount of the trusts created in the estate as a percentage of the total estate after taxes increased steadily with wealth level, with those millionaires with more than $10,000,000 in assets placing nearly a *third* of their total assets in trust.[24] Furthermore, trust usage increased with the size of the estate among *all* top wealth holders; for estates of between $100,000 and $300,000, only 13–16 percent of the estates created trusts, but 54–56 percent of the millionaires' estates created trusts.[25]

As over 80 percent of the trusts studied in the 1957 and 1959 estate returns expired within one generation,[26] with the majority of the trust fund assets going to members of the decedent's family, trust funds can be viewed as an important method of inter-generational wealth transfer.[27]

DIRECT INHERITANCE

While trusts are an important means of inter-generational wealth transfer, direct inheritance, as measured by annual absolute amounts, is more important. Survey data for the American population as a whole has indicated that inheritance is a minor source of assets; some 80 percent of the U.S. population claims never to have inherited *any* assets, and only 1 percent of the population as a whole admits to having inherited assets of $25,000 or more.[28] Such data have led scholars to discount the role of inheritance in the distribution of wealth and income.[29]

Most inheritances are apparently received late in life;[30] while only 8 percent of spending units have inherited by the age of 25, over 40 percent of the spending units aged 75 or older have inherited.[31] For those few that inherit more than $25,000, the largest increase in inheritance comes in the age cohort 55–64, indicating an inter-generational transmission of wealth late in the life cycle.

While the largest inheritors (those receiving inheritances of $100,000 or more) are concentrated in the older age cohorts (ages 45 to 64),[32] this tells nothing of the relative importance of inheritance to the top wealth-holding classes.

Some information is available from an analysis of the 1962 Federal Reserve Board study of individual asset holdings;[33] the asset class labeled "estates in probate" gives a direct measure of some of the inter-generational wealth transfers via inheritance occurring in that particular year.[34]

The analysis of the 1962 data revealed that for all individuals under the age of 25, estates in probate made up only 3.6 percent of the total wealth but comprised 56.87 percent of the wealth of individuals with assets of between $30,000 and $60,000, and 15.7 percent of the assets of individuals with assets of between $500,000 and $1,000,000 in this age group.

For all individuals aged 25 to 34, estates in probate totaled 3.56 percent of the total wealth but comprised 59 percent of the wealth of individuals in this age class with assets of between $200,000 and $500,000.

After age 35, estates in probate are 1 percent or less of the asset forms of individuals, except for those aged 44–55 with between $60,000 and $100,000 in assets; estates in probate were 3 percent of the assets of this class.[35]

From this data, it appears that direct inheritance, as measured by the asset form "estates in probate," is of greater importance as an asset source for wealthy individuals under the age of 35 than for other persons.

The apparent conflict between the 1962 survey data and the surveys on inheritance as to when in the life cycle most inheritances are received can be resolved, inasmuch as for the older cohorts, the relative importance of inheritance is less, because these persons usually already have substantial assets; hence, an asset class such as "estates in probate," while large in absolute terms for the older cohorts, will be smaller in relative terms. It is for this reason that inheritance earlier in the life cycle is a relatively more important source of assets for the younger cohorts.

Support for the contention that inheritance is an important source of assets for top wealth holders comes from survey data in Table 4. From this table, it appears that inherited assets are of little importance for the 97.5 percent of the population with assets of less than $100,000. No more than 24 percent of the consumer units in any asset class below $100,000 would admit to any inheritance, and 12 percent was the highest number in any asset class below the $100,000 asset level that would admit to having inherited a "substantial" share of their current assets.

However, when one examines the data on inheritance relating to the 2.5 percent of U.S. wealth-holding consumer units that own 43 percent of the nation's wealth, it becomes apparent that inheritance plays an increasingly larger role in explaining the assets of a consumer unit as the wealth of the consumer unit increases.

While 22 percent of the consumer units with assets of $100,000 to $199,000 admit to having inherited a "substantial" portion of their current assets, 34 percent of the top wealth-holding class (assets,

TABLE 4 **Inherited Assets in Relation to Total Assets,**
December 31, 1962
(Percentage distribution of consumer units)

			Inherited Assets			
				Portion of Total Assets		
Group Characteristic	All Units	None	Some	Small	Sub-stan-tial	Not Ascer-tained
All units	100	83	16	12	5	a
Size of wealth:						
$ 1–$999	100	95	5	5	a	a
1,000–4,999	100	87	12	9	4	a
5,000–9,999	100	82	18	12	6	a
10,000–24,999	100	77	23	17	6	a
25,000–49,999	100	75	24	16	9	a
50,000–99,999	100	74	24	12	12	2
100,000–199,999	100	46	54	32	22	a
200,000–499,999	100	59	41	28	13	a
500,000 and over	100	39	59	24	34	2
1962 income:						
$ 0–$2,999	100	84	16	10	6	a
3,000–4,999	100	88	12	9	3	a
5,000–7,499	100	84	16	12	4	a
7,500–9,999	100	80	20	14	5	a
10,000–14,999	100	84	16	11	5	a
15,000–24,999	100	73	27	21	6	a
25,000–49,999	100	58	42	34	8	a
50,000–99,999	100	71	26	12	14	3
100,000 and over	100	31	66	9	57	2
Age of head:						
Under 35	100	91	9	8	1	a
35–44	100	87	13	9	3	a
45–54	100	83	17	12	4	a
55–64	100	75	24	17	7	1
65 and over	100	79	21	12	9	a

SOURCE: D. S. Projector and G. S. Weiss, *Survey of Financial Characteristics of Consumers*, Table A-32, p. 148 (Washington, D.C.: Board of Governors of the Federal Reserve System, 1966).
aLess than ½ of 1 percent.

$500,000+) state that a substantial portion of their assets came from inheritance, and 59 percent of this wealth-holding class admits to having inherited at least *some* portion of their current assets.[36]

A crude quantitative measure of the importance of inter-generational wealth transfers in the distribution of wealth at various stages of the life cycle, and by asset level, can be established by combining the 1962 data for individuals of the share of assets held in the form of trusts and the share of assets held in the form of estates in probate. These two asset forms, for all individuals in all age and asset classes, constitute 4.11 percent of all asset value in 1962.[37] However, for the top wealth-holding individuals, inter-generational wealth transfers, only a portion of which are measured by the data on assets in trust and estates in probate, are given below in Table 5 for 1962.

TABLE 5 Percentage of Assets Held in the Form of Trusts and Estates of Individuals in 1962 by Age and Asset Level

Asset Level	Age Cohort					
	0–25	25–34	35–44	44–55	55–64	64+
$30,000 to $59,999	59.87	1.8	—	3.65	1.1	—
60,000 to 99,999	18.0	—	—	—	—	—
100,000 to 199,999	—	—	1.8	—	2.2	—
200,000 to 499,999	30.76	68.23	3.6	—	1.1	2.1
500,000 to 999,999	29.4	13.6	81.92	2.31	2.3	—
1,000,000+	—	93.97[a]	12.0	4.1	6.0	1.4

SOURCE: Tables V-13 to V-20, pp. 413–428 in Appendix 5, "The Distribution of Assets Among Individuals of Different Age and Wealth," in Raymond W. Goldsmith, ed., *Institutional Investors and Corporate Stock* (New York: NBER, 1973).
[a]See note 18, end of text.

From this incomplete evidence, inter-generational wealth transfers in the form of trusts and estates appear to be an important source of assets for those wealth holders with wealth of over $200,000—in particular, for young top wealth holders. The inference from Table 5 is that without the existence of these inter-generational wealth transfers, the distribution of wealth in the cohorts under age 45 would be more equal than it is now.

INTER-VIVOS GIFTS

While most inter-generational wealth transfers apparently still occur at the death of one of the generations involved, the possibility exists for large-scale undetected inter-generational wealth transfers in the form of gifts to occur while the donor is still alive. Through such lifetime giving, large amounts of wealth can be transferred between generations, enabling wealth inequality to persist and develop anew in younger age cohorts.

Federal law only requires that a gift tax return be filed if the giver of the gift gives one individual more than $3,000 in gifts in any one year; a donor of gifts could give less than $3,000 each to as many persons as he desired and not be required to file a federal gift tax return.[38] These exemptions would enable large-scale gift giving over long periods of time to go undetected by federal data on gifts.

For example, if a man with five children gave each child $3,000 per year over a thirty-year period, each child would have received $90,000 in gifts, and the father would have given away $450,000. Under federal law, his wife could also give away to each child $3,000 per year, per child (a total of $450,000). In addition to the $3,000 annual tax-free gifts each parent could give to their children, each parent could also give away up to a total of $30,000 to a single child or to the children, in various amounts, additional, tax-free, once in the parents' lifetimes.[39] The end result would be a total of $960,000 transferred from parents to children, and *no* federal gift or inheritance taxes paid on this transfer of wealth.

What little and incomplete data on inter-vivos gifts exists indicates that lifetime gift giving is growing, and is potentially a very important method of inter-generational wealth transference.

Data for 1965 indicated that some 3.9 billion dollars in lifetime gifts were large enough to be required to file federal gift tax returns.[40] Between 1963 and 1966, total amount of lifetime gifts subject to the gift-tax filing requirement increased 49.5 percent and the number of returns increased 31.6 percent. If these trends have continued since 1965, the total amount of gifts subject to the federal gift-tax filing requirement would total over eight billion dollars by the early 1970s.[41]

Of the 3.9 billion dollars in gifts in 1965 subject to the federal gift-tax filing requirements, 3.1 billion, or over 75 percent, went to donees other than spouses or charities; hence this 3.1 billion dollar total gives some idea of the minimum amount involved in the annual inter-generational transfer of wealth via lifetime giving.[42]

Moreover, the 1965 gift tax data indicate that large sums were being transferred by means of lifetime gift giving to individuals other than spouses of the donors. In 1965, 536 donors gave gifts of $500,000 or more (238 giving gifts of more than $1,000,000), and 3,684 gave gifts of between $100,000 and $500,000. The possibilities of the giving of such large amounts of wealth resulting in the formation of a new generation of top wealth holders is obvious; several such years of large-scale gift giving would result in the donee being in the top 1 percent of U.S. wealth holders.[43]

Additional information on the transfer of wealth via lifetime gift giving comes from a special Treasury study matching estate and gift tax returns of individual taxpayers in 1957 and 1959. This study showed that as the size of the gross estate increased, the percentage of decedents in that estate class who had made lifetime gifts rose steadily. While only 10 percent of the owners of estates of $300,000 or less had given away gifts some time during their lifetimes, 52 percent of all millionaires had, and 92 per cent of those millionaires with wealth of over 10 million dollars had some time during their lives made gifts.[44]

Duration of lifetime giving followed the same general pattern as the frequency of lifetime giving; as asset levels increased, the longer the period of time that the decedent had been engaged in lifetime giving.[45]

However, the 1957–59 Treasury study indicated that at least for those two years, lifetime gifts were a small amount relative to the total value of the decedent's estate. Gifts totaled only 2.7 percent of the total value of the estates in the $300,000 asset level, and rose to only 7.5 percent of the estate value in the millionaire class.[46] This indicates that while substantial tax advantages exist in the giving of gifts during life, as compared to leaving the same amount of money at death (gift tax rates are only 75 percent of the comparable federal estate tax rates) inter-vivos gift giving was a relatively infrequent method of wealth transfer as recently as the late 1950s. However, the 1965 federal gift tax data indicate a rapid rise in lifetime giving, such that a considerable amount could be being transferred via lifetime gift giving at the present time.

CONCLUSIONS

This paper began by examining the possible role of inter-generational wealth transfers in explaining the high and persistent degree of inequality in wealth ownership measured over the life cycle. From the data analyzed, it appears that inter-generational wealth transfers in the form of trusts and inheritances are a relatively more important asset source for younger persons (in particular those pre age 45 cohorts) and an especially important asset source for young top wealth holders (wealth holders younger than age 45 with more than $200,000 in assets). It appears that without inter-generational wealth transfers, the assets of young top wealth holders under age 45 might be severely reduced. To the extent that the concentration of assets in the control of young top wealth holders is a source of the high degree of inequality in wealth ownership observed in the under age 45 cohorts, the elimination or reduction of inter-generational wealth transfers would apparently work to reduce the observed inequality in the distribution of wealth among the young.

The best studies available on the national distribution of wealth in 1860 indicate that in that year, the top 3 percent of U.S. wealth-holding families owned 45 percent of the nation's wealth;[47] in 1962 the top 2.5 percent of U.S. wealth-holding consumer units were estimated to own 43 percent of the U.S. private wealth. The role of inter-generational wealth transfers in explaining the high degree of wealth inequality from genera-tion to generation has been rejected by numerous scholars because of the apparent lack of quantitative importance of these transfers to the assets of the general population. From the data presented in this paper, it appears that inter-generational wealth transfers are not an important asset source for 97.5 percent of the population; however, for the top 2.5 percent of U.S. consumer units, who own 43 percent of the nation's wealth, they appear to be an important asset source, and an important possible reason for the persistent inequality in the distribution of wealth observed from generation to generation.

NOTES

1. Recent studies on the distribution of personal wealth in the United States have included: R. J. Lampman, *The Share of Top Wealthholders in National Wealth: 1922–1956* (Princeton: Princeton University Press, 1962); Staunton K. Calvert and James D. Smith, "Estimating the Wealth of Top Wealthholders from Estates Tax Returns," *Proceedings of the Business and Economics Statistics Section: American Statistical Association Annual Meeting*, September 1964; D. S. Projector and G. S. Weiss, *Survey of Financial Characteristics of Consumers* (Washington, D.C.: Board of Governors of the Federal Reserve System, 1966); James D. Smith and Stephen D. Franklain, "The Concentration of Personal Wealth, 1922–1969," *Papers and Proceedings of the American Economic Association*, May 1974, pp. 162–167.

2. All of the above studies found a concentration of wealth ownership in the control of a small percentage of the population. Lampman found that the top 1 percent of wealth-holding adults owned 26.1 percent of personal wealth in 1953; Smith dis-covered that the top 1 percent of adults owned 26.7 percent in 1958; the Federal Reserve study indicated that the top $\frac{1}{2}$ of 1 percent of U.S. consumer units owned 22 percent of the nation's wealth; and Smith for 1969 has found that the share of the top 1 percent of wealth-holding adults was 23.8 percent.

3. Projector and Weiss, *Survey of Financial Characteristics*. A "consumer unit" in the survey was defined to consist of families and unrelated individuals as defined by the Census. See Projector and Weiss, p. 49.

4. Ibid., p. 30.

5. Ibid., Table 2, p. 12.

6. James Smith, Stephen D. Franklain, Douglas A. Wion, *Financial Concentration in the United States*, Urban Institute Paper #1208-2 (Washington, D.C.: Urban Institute, June 1975), pp. 11–13.

7. The possible role of inter-generational wealth transfers in the lifetime distribution of wealth was first brought to my attention by an article by A. B. Atkinson, "The Distribution of Wealth and the Individual Life Cycle," *Oxford Economic Papers* 23 (July 1971): 239–254.

8. Ibid., pp. 240–242.

9. Assuming that the wealth could be liquidated and then consumed as income in retirement. Ibid., pp. 240–242.

10. Projector and Weiss, *Survey of Financial Characteristics*, Table 2, p. 12.

11. See Martin David, "Increased Taxation with Increased Acceptability—A Discussion of Net Worth Taxation as a Federal Revenue Alternative," Table 6, Figure 1, *Journal of Finance* 28 (May 1973): 490–491.

12. See Smith, Franklain, and Wion, *Financial Concentration in the U.S.*, pp. 11–13.

13. John Bossons, "The Distribution of Assets Among Individuals of Different Age and Wealth," Appendix 5 of *Institutional Investors and Corporate Stock*, Raymond W. Goldsmith, ed. (New York: NBER, 1973).

14. The information asked in the 1962 survey in regard to trust fund ownership was to determine the ownership rights to the *body* of the trust, not to the income alone. If the consumer unit only had rights to the income from the trust fund, it was not to count the trust fund assets among its assets. Projector and Weiss, *Survey of Financial Characteristics*, p. 77. The asset class "estates in probate" was the beneficial interest of the consumer units in estates still in the process of probate, and whose final distribution of assets at the time of the survey had not occurred. Projector and Weiss, p. 66.

15. Data on amounts transferred by the inheritance process from *Statistics of Income 1972: Estate Tax Returns*, U.S. Treasury Department, Internal Revenue Service Publication 764 (Washington, D.C.: U.S. Government Printing Office, 1975), pp. 2, 6. Data on the income of trust funds from *Statistics of Income, 1970: Fiduciary Income Tax Returns*, U.S. Treasury Department, Internal Revenue Service Publication 808 (Washington, D.C.: U.S. Government Printing Office, 1973), p. 4. The income figure for the trusts is the total income reported, before a deduction for deficit, for most of the personal trusts in the United States. Ibid., p. 1.

16. In 1960 personal trust funds administered by banks and trust companies totaled $71.9 billion; in 1965, they totaled $115 billion; by 1968, these trust funds had grown to $138 billion. Table 5-12, p. 244, in Goldsmith, ed., *Institutional Investors and Corporate Stock*.

17. Smith and Franklain, "The Concentration of Personal Wealth, 1922–1969," *Papers and Proceedings of the American Economic Association*, May 1974. Trusts can be divided into two forms: those trusts created while the grantor of the trust was living (inter-vivos trusts) and those trusts created by the terms of the grantor's will after the grantor's death (testamentary trusts). As the 1962 survey asked consumer units to include only those trusts in which the consumer unit had a right to the assets of the trust (see note 14), the type of the trust is not of particular importance.

18. Bossons, "The Distribution of Assets," Table V-14, pp. 415–416. The figure of 93 percent of the assets of millionaires aged 25 to 34 being in trust funds is probably a statistical error. While the 1962 Federal Reserve Board study highly oversampled the top wealth holders for asset information relative to their share of the population as a whole, the data on *young* top wealth holders in the survey sample is small, because of their infrequency. For example, while there were 245 consumer units with wealth of over $500,000 sampled, there were only 8 of these consumer units with wealth of this size with a head under the age of 35 in the sample. The sample data are much more reliable for those consumer units with a head aged 35 or older. Because of this small sample size among *young* top wealth holders (i.e., only 16 units with assets of

$100,000 or more and with a head under the age of 35 were in the sample), the under age 35 data for those with assets of $50,000 or more should be studied with caution. The absence of millionaires in the under age 25 class does not mean that they do not exist; rather, they were not detected in the sample. For data on the actual sample size by various classes, see Table A-35 in Projector and Weiss, *Survey of Financial Characteristics*.

19. My own opinion is that most millionaires under the age of 35 (in particular those under the age of 25) are millionaires by inter-generational wealth transfers. Support for this thesis comes from Bossons, "The Distribution of Assets," Table V-4, p. 403, in which he breaks out the assets of millionaires. From this table, the amount of assets of millionaires (25 billion) is stable in the 25 to 35 age class, and in the 35 to 44 age class, but then more than doubles to over 63 billion in the age 45 to 54 class. This doubling indicates to me the "arrival" of the so called self-made millionaires later in the life cycle.

20. Bossons, "The Distribution of Assets," Tables V-16 to V-19, pp. 419–425.

21. Ibid., Table V-19, pp. 425–426.

22. Reported in C. S. Shoup, *Federal Estate and Gift Taxes* (Washington, D.C.: Brookings Institution, 1966), pp. 137–227.

23. Ibid., Table B-1, p. 155.

24. Ibid.

25. Ibid., p. 156, Table B-2.

26. Data from the 1957 and 1959 Treasury Study of Trusts formed in top wealth holders' estates indicate that 90 percent of the trusts by number formed in estates of $60,000 to $300,000 in size expired after one generation, 90 percent of the trusts by number formed by estates of size $300,000 to $1,000,000 expired within one generation, and 85 percent of the trusts formed in the estates of over $1,000,000 expired within one generation. (Figures found by adding the percentages of those trusts that skipped one generation and those trusts in which the spouse of the trust founder was the sole life tenant. Shoup, *Federal Estate and Gift Taxes*, Table B-6, p. 161.)

27. Data from the 1957 and 1959 estate tax returns studied by the Treasury indicated that 73.4 percent of the trusts established by all estates studied by number were "family trusts" in that the body or corpora will eventually pass outright to the children, grandchildren, or great-grandchildren, or spouse of the settlor. Gerald R. Jantscher, *Trusts and Estate Taxation* (Washington, D.C.: Brookings Institution, 1967), computed from Table V-7, p. 95. By total amount of the trust bequest, some 71 percent of the total amount left in trust bequests by the decedents in 1957 and 1959 were left in the so called "family trusts," the body of trust that would pass eventually to the children, grandchildren, great-grandchildren of the settler. Jantscher, computed from data in V-19, p. 126

28. See Table A-32, p. 148 in Projector and Weiss, *Survey of Financial Characteristics*, Table 7-4, p. 89 in J. M. Morgan, M. H. David, W. J. Cohen, and H. E. Brazer, *Income and Welfare in the United States* (New York: Macmillan, 1962); Table 15, p. 64, in John B. Lansing and John Sonquist, "A Cohort Analysis of Changes in the Distribution of Wealth," in Lee Soltow, ed., *Six Papers on the Size Distribution of Wealth and Income* (New York: NBER, 1969).

29. Herman Miller of the U.S. Census Bureau in his book, *Rich Man, Poor Man* (New York: Thomas Crowell, 1971) discounts the role of inheritance in the distribution of wealth, pp. 156–158. Christopher Jencks in his study of the relationship between education and income concluded that inheritance was of little importance in the overall distribution of income. Christopher Jencks and Associates, *Inequality: A Reassessment of the Effect of Family and Schooling in America* (New York: Basic Books, Inc., 1972), pp. 212–214.

30. Josiah Wedgwood in his classic study of inheritance (*The Economics of Inheritance* [London: George Routledge and Sons, 1929]) determined from a search of probate records that 90 percent of the estates he studied were inherited before the age of 55, and 66 percent between the ages of 35 and 54 (pp. 174–175). Survey data on inheritance indicate that the majority of inheritances occur between the ages of 35 and 65. Given the present trend to longer life-spans of the parents due to medical advances, it seems possible that the time of inheritance in the life cycle today is later that when Wedgwood did his study. Assume that the parent has children between the ages of 25 and 35, and that he lives to age 65 to 70. That would make his children ages 35 to 45 when they receive their inheritances. Much inheritance appears to be an occurrence of the later stage of the life cycle.

31. Lansing and Sonquist, "A Cohort Analysis of Changes," Table 16, p. 65.

32. Ibid., Table 15, p. 64.

33. Bossons, "The Distribution of Assets," Tables V-13 to V-19, pp. 413–425.

34. "Estates in probate" can be viewed as inheritance in the process of being distributed to the heirs; see also note 14. The estates may be in the process of probate for several years or a longer period of time.

35. Bossons, "The Distribution of Assets," Tables V-13 to V-19, pp. 413–425.

36. See Table 4.

37. Bossons, "The Distribution of Assets," Table V-19, p. 425.

38. *Statistics of Income, 1965: Fiduciary, Gift and Estate Tax Returns*, U.S. Treasury Department, Internal Revenue Service (Washington, D.C.: U.S. Government Printing Office, 1967), p. 41. The assumption is that these are gifts of present interest, not future interest.

39. The $30,000 figure is the federal gift-tax individual lifetime donor exclusion. The $30,000 amount may be given to a single person, free of gift taxes, or be split among several persons, free of gift taxes, as long as the total amount of the gifts given under this exclusion total $30,000 or less per donor.

40. Data on gifts for 1965 are for only those gifts not made either to spouses or to charities; data from *Statistics of Income: 1965 Fiduciary, Gift and Estate Tax Returns*, Tables 7 and 8, pp. 53–54.

41. The $8 billion figure assumes that lifetime gifts in absolute amounts continue to grow at the 15 percent annual rate of growth set between 1963 and 1966.

42. Some of the gifts could be intragenerational wealth transfers (i.e., brother to sister of the same age) as well as inter-generational wealth transfers (i.e., parents to children).

43. The top 1 percent of U.S. adults in net worth in 1969 had a net worth of at least $200,000. Net gifts of $100,000 for two years would be sufficient to place the donee in the top 1 percent of U.S. adult wealth holders. Data on minimum net worth from Smith, "The Distribution of Financial Assets," Table 1.

44. Shoup, *Federal Estate and Gift Taxes*, Table C-3, p. 182.

45. Ibid., Table C-10, p. 192.

46. Ibid., Table C-3, p. 182.

47. Robert E. Gallman, "Trends in the Size Distribution of Wealth in the Nineteenth Century: Some Speculations," in Soltow, ed., *Six Papers on the Size Distribution of Wealth and Income*.

9, 10, 11 ‖ COMMENTS

W. Lee Hansen

University of Wisconsin-Madison

I want to commend the Conference Program Committee for adding this Student Papers Session. The importance of stimulating and recognizing graduate student research through a session like this cannot be overemphasized. Equally important, students are given a firsthand look at how professional economists interact and test new ideas through their research and participation in conferences such as this. I hope that the Session can become a regular part of future Conference programs.

I am honored to have been selected to discuss the three student papers. My intention is to discuss them one by one, focusing largely on how the papers might be extended through future work by the authors.

GREG DUNCAN

Greg Duncan comes at the subject of income distribution in a way different from the earlier papers at this Conference.[1] His concern lies in identifying and measuring the nonpecuniary elements of compensation and, specifically, in determining how these nonpecuniary rewards might affect estimates of labor market discrimination against females and blacks. All too often we pay only lip service to the nonmonetary elements of work compensation, focusing instead on the readily measured and available money earnings variable. Yet as readers of Adam Smith know, these elements must be an integral part of any analysis of labor markets and of income distribution. In the past, economists have been thwarted by an absence of data. But fortunately, the University of Michigan Survey Research Center has taken on the task of gathering much data of use to economists, including, recently, information not previously available for individuals on the nonpecuniary elements of compensation. Thus, we have an opportunity to learn whether the nonmoney components of wages are distributed in such a way as to shift the relative "full income" position of different race and sex groups.

The finding that nonpecuniary factors are not in the aggregate distributed in the same way as income comes as no real surprise, given the way in which they are measured. Nor is it too surprising that these factors differ by occupations, so that, say, for women, the advantages derived from certain benefits associated with the pattern of occupational attachment are offset because, within these

---

NOTE: Student papers consist of the contributions of Greg Duncan, William R. Johnson, and Thomas Osman.

Comments on Duncan, Johnson, and Osman (Chaps. 9, 10 and 11) ‖ **413**

occupations, women receive fewer of these benefits than do men of comparable backgrounds. And finally, the fact that the somewhat more favorable flow of these various benefits accrues to females and blacks is still not sufficient to upset the notion that these two groups suffer from substantial labor market discrimination.

To nail down these conclusions, we really need to know more about a number of things which are not touched upon in the paper. For one thing, it is possible that the greater part-time attachment of women to the labor force affects these results. It seems possible that for regular full-time workers the differences in these assorted benefits would be smaller than reported here; part-time workers, whether male or female, probably confront different compensation packages.

The results obtained may also be affected because no money values have been placed on the various nonpecuniary benefits. For fringe benefits this could be done rather easily; instead of simply adding up the number of a rather mixed bag of benefits received by individuals, it should be possible to assign dollar values on these benefits. Even though the resulting estimates might be rough, they would permit an approximation to "full" income. By then entering full income into the initial regression as the dependent variable, we would be in a position to compare these new results with those in Duncan's Table 6, and thus be better able to assess the extent to which our more usual estimates of the effects of labor market discrimination are biased. However, because the value of most of the fringe benefits will be proportional to money income, we would not expect any dramatic shifts to result except inasmuch as different occupations have different patterns of fringe benefits.

For other items, such as "control over overtime hours" and "job autonomy," one might simply assign arbitrary money values which would then further expand the measure of full income. These items would probably have to be valued relative to average money income in an occupation, given the fact that all occupations are being compared in the analysis. Because there might be disagreement about the value of these items, it would be well to experiment with a range of values and thereby determine the sensitivity of the results. Finally, the employment stability aspect might be treated along the lines suggested by Johnson in his paper.

To summarize, this paper is a highly useful first effort to expand the scope of that all-important income variable to include both pecuniary and nonpecuniary rewards. This should help us add to our knowledge of the dimensions of labor market discrimination and permit us to learn more about the distribution of full income.[2]

WILLIAM R. JOHNSON

William R. Johnson's paper is an impressive piece of work, attempting as it does to explore the systematic forces making for long-run differences in earnings levels among occupational groups. In addition to a careful review of what we know about the subject of uncertainty, he proposes a theoretical model of earnings, estimates it, and comments on the results. Age groups are used to get at the lifetime aspects of the problem, and some of the variance is effectively controlled by stratifying for level of educational attainment. The two major results seem plausible.

Uncertainty, as reflected by the dispersion variable, is compensated for by higher average earnings. However, this is not the case when the risk of unemployment is greater. Whether the effect of the risk of unemployment is already captured in earnings is not fully clear, however. Perhaps the use of wage-rate data, hourly or weekly earnings, would permit a more appropriate test for this latter hypothesis. In any case, the results in Table 2 were a bit perplexing. While I would expect a one standard deviation change in the dispersion variable to have a larger absolute effect on mean earnings for each successively higher educational group, and likewise for the prime age groups (35–54 versus 25–34 and 55–64), it is not clear whether the relative effects move in the same direction, as I would expect they should; listing the mean earnings for each occupational group would easily resolve this point.

The second set of results pertaining to the association between risk return and mobility is also consistent with the author's hypothesis. The results are weaker, however, and one might also question them on the grounds that a different set of occupational groups is used; hence, the empirical base for the two tests is not comparable. It would be useful to redo the tests using similar data, to the extent that this is possible.

Several additional comments might be made. One concerns the stability of the risk-return relationship. Would one obtain the same results for 1960 or for some other year? Only by knowing this can we consider accepting the hypothesis, for the model posits a world in which an individual's future is largely determined by his initial level of earnings, given the stability of the forces underlying what is called uncertainty. (I cannot help but comment here on the Ruggles and Ruggles finding that the cohort of new workers entering the labor market in the early 1930s seemed to have suffered a permanent impairment of its earnings, relative to those individuals in the immediately preceding and succeeding cohorts. I have noticed a similar phenomenon for engineers who obtained their degrees in the early 1930s.) Another comment concerns the stability of the relationship when longitudinal data are examined. It would be useful to test the model with such data, e.g., the Parnes data or the Michigan Longitudinal Panel. Still another comment concerns the risk-return and occupational immobility. Here, the direction of causality is not clear. Should we not expect the proportion of individuals remaining in an occupation in some subsequent period to be positively related to the risk-return situation in some initial given year? This would reflect the fact that those already there prefer to remain in the occupation to take advantage of their bounty. But what this implies about the proportion of new entrants coming into an occupation is much less clear. Would we expect the proportion to be larger or smaller?

A minor point. On the problem of omitted variables, Johnson suggests an interesting approach in getting at the ability factor. But rather than relying for empirical support on an old study from 1945, a study whose results can be questioned because the preservice occupations may have borne little or no relationship to postservice occupations, it might be better to build on more recent data such as the Thorndike-Hagen sample or the National Opinion Research Center (NORC) sample.

Finally, more thought should be given to the use of the term uncertainty to describe the various forces leading to persistent earnings differences. As used here, the term embraces far too much, taking into account those factors which reflect permanent uncertainty. In this sense it is like that old term "technical change" which covers a multitude of things we know little about. Let us hope that we can do a better job of isolating these factors now grouped under uncertainty as longitudinal data become available to us. Maybe there is uncertainty arising from not knowing on what earnings track a person will find himself, but once the choice of a job is made, that uncertainty is forever dispelled.

TOM OSMAN

Tom Osman has done an interesting job in his effort to throw more light on the relative constancy of wealth inequality across age cohorts. Both the Lansing-Sonquist study for the United States and the Atkinson Study for the United Kingdom indicate that wealth inequality varies little across age cohorts; the Survey of Financial Characteristics of Consumers (SFCC)–Projector data indicate the same thing. Osman finds this puzzling and properly so, for any reasonable life-cycle model of earnings and savings would appear to predict a widening of wealth inequality as cohorts age. Although others have suggested that inter-generational wealth transfers are responsible for the higher than expected extent of wealth inequality for the younger age cohorts, Osman attempts to document this suspicion by drawing upon a variety of secondary data which he weaves together in a highly effective way. He demonstrates with the scanty data available that recorded large-scale inter-generational transfers, via trust, inheritance, and inter-vivos gifts are inversely related to the age of the cohort, i.e., they flow most heavily to the younger cohorts, and that, not unexpectedly, larger proportions of total assets of younger cohorts are held by those with already high levels of assets, i.e., transfer wealth is most highly concentrated for the younger cohorts. Osman's conclusions that these transfers are "important" cannot be disputed. On the other hand, there may be more to the story, as I should like to suggest.

I calculated Gini coefficients for his age cohort data—from the Projector data as tabulated by Bossons—and find that total asset Gini coefficients were .686 for the 25–34 cohort, .703 for the 35–44 cohort, and .716 for the 45–54 cohort. This is a slight but virtually insignificant upward drift, which differs from Lansing and Sonquist, in whose work no trend was apparent. If the Gini coefficients are recalculated after excluding wealth in trusts, they fall to .620, .696, and .713, respectively, as would be expected. Of course, the trusts are recorded trusts—others may have already expired and thus escape detection. Hence, the true Gini coefficients would be lowered below the recalculated figures I have just provided. By exactly how much they would fall cannot be known with certainty in the absence of a new data source or some ingenious effort to purge the asset data of previous transfers via trusts. Perhaps this could be done in at least some crude way, although the sample size will severely limit what can be done. On another front, it might be possible to look at the asset distribution for those who have received inheritances. Unfortunately, we shall probably not be satisfied with whatever we find because of the slender data base at our disposal.

Earlier, I mentioned that there might be more to the story. Assume that a life-cycle earnings-savings model would lead to a widening of wealth inequality for successive age cohorts. But now incorporate inter-generational wealth transfers into the model, such that inequality for younger age cohorts increases substantially, along the lines described by Osman. Since there seems to be no reason to assume that the younger cohorts will be less able than other cohorts to expand their augmented wealth over time, the effect of inter-generational transfers will simply be to raise the intercept of the Gini slope across cohorts. Thus, inequality would still be expected to increase with age.

The data, however, do not indicate this to be the case. Moreover, the magazine *Fortune* tells us about the continuous emergence of new self-made millionaires. What this suggests, then, is the old familiar story, of considerable "churning" in the wealth distribution over the life cycle. Some units move up into the top of the wealth distribution and others move down, but on balance there appears to be more downward than upward movement, notwithstanding our expectations.

Where does this leave us? Clearly we need to know more about the inter generational transfer of material and financial wealth, not to mention human wealth. The extent to which young people vault to the top must be established. But we shall gain illumination only as we are able to trace out the extent of shifting individual fortunes over the life cycle. And if it is true that most fortunes are depleted almost as fast as they are generated, that is, in two or three generations, as my comments suggest may be the case, then the implications for analysis of economic power relationships may be somewhat different from what is often suggested by analysts of the power structure.

In any case, this is a fascinating subject. I commend Tom Osman for arousing my curiosity with his extremely useful paper.

NOTES

1. It should be mentioned that this paper reflects the author's early work on what is now a completed dissertation. This dissertation was awarded the John Parker Prize here at the University of Michigan. Many of the suggestions I make have already been incorporated into the completed dissertation, a copy of which can be obtained through University Microfilms.

2. As was pointed out by several participants in the Conference, nobody knows exactly what labor market discrimination is and to what extent the remaining differences in income (after correction for known factors making for differences) between males and females and whites and blacks reflect discrimination.

12

PAUL J.
TAUBMAN
University of Pennsylvania
and National Bureau of
Economic Research

Schooling, Ability, Nonpecuniary Rewards, Socioeconomic Background, and the Lifetime Distribution of Earnings

I. INTRODUCTION

All individuals or families do not receive the same income or earnings. This inequality, the most indisputable fact about the distribution of income, has been found in capitalist and socialist economies, in democratic and dictatorial countries, and in biblical through modern times. There are other characteristics of the income distribution that are nearly as well documented for modern countries. For example, the distribution is not

NOTE: Reprinted by permission of North-Holland Publishing Company from *Sources of Inequality of Earnings*, Amsterdam, 1975. This research was supported by National Science Foundation grant GS-31334 to the NBER. The paper grew out of earlier work done jointly with Terence Wales, to whom an intellectual debt is owed, both in general and for specific comments on earlier drafts.

symmetrical but has a longer right-hand tail, and both average income and its variance generally increase with education and age.[1]

Economists have constructed various theories that purport to explain the income distribution. Some aspects of these theories have been tested against empirical observations.[2] This study will extend the range of such tests. In addition, we will generate some new facts that a complete theory should be able to explain.

The Personal Distribution of Earnings

Personal income is equal to the sum of labor earnings, returns to capital, and transfer payments. The distribution of transfer payments and of returns to financial capital will not be examined in this study. We shall focus primarily on earnings from work, to which the introductory statements on inequality also apply.

Most theoretical and related empirical work on the distribution of earnings falls into the "human capital" or "stochastic" theory categories, or constitutes some blend thereof. The human capital model assumes that people are paid a wage equal to their (real) marginal product. This wage varies over individuals because of differences in inherited or acquired skill levels. The stochastic theories assume that an individual's earnings over time depend on the cumulative history of random events.

Many of the models that economists have proposed to explain some or all of the features of the earnings distribution are presented in Section II. Some problems with these theories are also given in this section along with some testable hypotheses. Section III contains a description of how the NBER-TH sample was obtained and the major characteristics of the sample. The main regressions on which this study is based are given in Appendix A. In Section IV we discuss the effects of particular coefficients, grouped into categories, in the regressions for earnings reported on separate surveys conducted in 1955 and 1969. The categories in order of appearance are: education, mental ability, family background, work experience, compensating adjustments for nonpecuniary rewards, and finally, business assets.

In Section V we examine the extent to which the distribution of variables in each of these categories are the causes of variance, skewness and kurtosis. This section also examines the Lorenz curves for 1955 and 1969, and the stability of these curves. The stability of an individual's position in the overall distribution is examined in Section VI. This section also tests certain aspects of the human capital and stochastic theory models. Section VII contains conclusions.

II. SUPPLY AND DEMAND FOR LABOR

A traditional method of analyzing labor markets is via supply and demand curves. Suppose for the moment that all people are homogeneous with respect to skills that determine earnings. Assume that with a given quantity of capital and other factors of production, the marginal product of labor decreases as the number of employees increases. In a competitive labor market (with no on-the-job training), employers will hire that number of workers at which the marginal product is equal to the real wage rate, W/P (for convenience we shall set P at 1 and henceforth speak of wages only). The supply of labor will depend on the real wage rate and an equilibrium will be found where the supply and demand curves intersect.

In our example, an equilibrium wage rate of W_0 will clear the market and everyone who works the same hours will earn the same amount. This conclusion, which is not valid, depends crucially on the assumption that each person has the same skills. This study is based on the proposition that many different skills—inherited and acquired—help determine earnings. It is fairly easy, however, to incorporate many of the skills into the above analysis *if what is known as an "efficiency units" model is valid.* Suppose individual one, who has a particular complex of skills, is designated as the "standard" person. Let capacity be designated as C. As long as C_j/C_1 *always* equals b_j, we can state that the jth person is equivalent to h_j standard workers.

Since the employer would be indifferent to hiring person 1 at a wage of, say, W_0 or person j at a wage of $b_j W_0$, the demand curve can be redrawn in standard worker units. The supply curve can also be drawn in efficiency units as $\Sigma_j b_j Q_j$ where Q_j is the quantity of labor the jth person would offer at a particular standardized wage rate. In this efficiency model, a person who is 110 percent of standard capacity will always receive a wage 110 percent of the standard wage, but the equilibrium level of the standard wage will vary with the supply and demand curves.

An important set of questions that relate to this model are: What particular skills determine capacity? Are these skills inherited or acquired? Is the quantity of acquired skills consistent with the amount economists would define as optimum? Before considering these questions, however, we will examine briefly a model in which relative capacity, C_j/C_1, is not fixed but varies.

The world of work is subdivided into many different occupations, which are associated with different tasks and levels of responsibility. For example, the *Dictionary of Occupational Titles* differentiates thousands of occupations, some of which require physical strength; some, mental ability; and some, combinations of particular skills. A person's relative capacity may remain constant within an occupation but vary over occupations.[3] Thus, a person's observed relative capacity would depend on the occupation he worked in, which, in turn, would depend in part on the occupational wage structure. Though this model is complicated, in principle it is still possible to formulate and solve it as a general equilibrium model, in which individuals choose that occupation which yields them the highest income or utility.[4] One particularly important feature of this occupation-skill model is that some skills may not be at all useful in some occupations.[5]

Now let us return to the simpler efficiency units model. At the end of our previous discussion of this model we raised certain questions about what skills determine earnings or capacity. At a general level, we can classify those skills as cognitive, affective, physical, and psychological. Cognitive skills include learned facts and information, as well as recall and decision-making abilities. Affective skills include leadership and social behavior. Physical skills include strength, coordination, and dexterity, while psychological skills include extroversion, reaction to stress, and degree of neuroticism.

At this stage of our knowledge, we hardly know which particular skills determine earnings or capacity, since no sample contains reliable measures of all feasible skills and few samples contain direct measures of even a representative skill from each of the categories mentioned.[6] However, several studies have shown that certain aspects of intelligence and of leadership are valid. See Taubman-Wales (1974), Griliches and Mason (1972), Wise (1972), and Featherman (1971).

Suppose, however, that we have measurements on an exhaustive list of skills for each individual. We could then estimate an earnings equation such as

(1) $Y = aX_1 + bX_2, \ldots, cX_m + u$

where Y is earnings, $X_1, \ldots, X_m$ are the M measures of skill, and u is a random error representing "luck" or institutional phenomena.[7]

Each coefficient in the equation indicates the effect on earnings of increasing the associated X by one unit. It is worth noting that the coefficients may not be stable over time. For example, suppose there is a big increase in the supply of any X. In the efficiency units model, this will lead to shifts in the supply curve (in efficiency units) and a decrease in the standard wage rate, which, in turn, would decrease all coefficients proportionately. In more complex models, the effect on the coefficients of an increased supply in any one skill level depends on the individual supply and demand elasticities for each skill as well as on cross elasticities of demand. But in general the coefficients will not change proportionately.[8]

While estimation of equation 1 with many skills would represent a major achievement, our task would not be over, since we would then want to know what determines the level of each X or what policies could affect the distribution of earnings.

Inherited and Acquired Skills

The level of any skill or attribute a person possesses at any point in time is determined by his genetic endowments and by his environment.[9] As we are using the term environment, it includes all postconception events that influence the individual. Thus, it encompasses formal and informal training for all the skills discussed earlier, prenatal diet, expenditures on health which determine whether skills can be used, and random events. A huge literature has been devoted to assessing the relative importance of nature and nurture for particular skills and attributes.[10] As we come closer to estimating equation 1, this literature will become more important in economics, but at the current time it does not seem necessary to summarize it.

Since we have neither measured all the possible skills nor know their nature-nuture combination, we shall not estimate equation 1. We shall, however, make use of a modified procedure. Suppose each of the X_j's is represented as a function of genetics and environment. If, for example,

$$(2) \qquad X_{ji} = c_i G_i + d_i N_i$$

where G is genetic endowments, N is environment, and i is the individual, we can then rewrite equation 1 as

$$(3) \qquad Y_i = \Sigma_j a_j c_j G_i + \Sigma_j a_j d_j N_j = e_i G_i + f_i N_i$$

Equation 3 represents progress primarily because we do have measures of several aspects of environment.

Training

People learn or increase their skill levels in many ways, with some methods better for some skills than for others. However, some of the most important "training" institutions are the family, the peer group, the school, the military, and the job.

The family can affect the child's cognitive, affective, physiological, and psychological development by a variety of subtle and obvious means including: the behavior and attitudes of parents and siblings; material and nonmaterial goods and services provided to the child; love and affection; and degree of permissiveness in rearing. While it would be most useful and convincing if we could incorporate measures of parental behavior, love, material goods, and so on, in our equations, we do not have such information and are reduced to using proxies.

There are several difficulties in interpreting the coefficients of a proxy. A proxy, by definition, is assumed to be correlated with the true but unobserved variable. But the proxy may be insignificant, because it is too crude a measure, i.e., has too low a correlation with the true variable. Alternatively, the proxy may be correlated with several true variables whose separate effects we may be interested in. For example, father's education may be related to his earnings, his methods of child rearing and certain genetic (and thus partially inheritable) abilities.[11] Fortunately, if several proxies are used, it can be shown that each proxy will tend to reflect the underlying variable with which it is most highly correlated.[12]

We shall use proxy variables such as family income and wealth, religion, urban or rural residence, and parents' education and occupation, which are all often available and often made use of. We shall supplement this list with other proxies that we think are related to child-rearing techniques and family atmosphere.

The peer group can also affect the amount of schooling a person acquires and can directly affect all broad skill categories through its attitudes and reward structure, but the only available information which might be related to peer-group effects is a question on how the individual spent his time while growing up.

Both sociologists and economists have incorporated formal schooling into the earnings equation. It must be emphasized that schooling can affect cognitive, affective, physiological, and psychological skills though there is no reliable information on which of these changes determine earnings.[13] The most common though obviously very crude measure of education is years of schooling. However, following the lead of Solmon and Wachtel (1975), who used the same sample, we shall also incorporate certain measures of college quality.[14]

While all the people in our sample worked, the amount and type of work and of learning on the job has varied by individual and can affect earnings. Indeed, a major innovation in the earnings distribution literature is Mincer's theory of investment in on-the-job training, which is described below in more detail. For the most part, we measure this by years on civilian jobs, but we also examine the effects of military service and of time spent in one occupation on earnings in another.

Taste for Risk and Nonpecuniary Rewards

The models we have been examinining explain earnings by differences in skills. It is possible, however, to explain some features of the earnings distribution by differences in tastes toward work or nonpecuniary returns from work. Friedman (1957), for example, has suggested that skewness arises because while most persons are risk averse, some people are risk lovers.[15] Those in the latter group may initially choose an occupation in which there is a small chance of a very high income. Since success is not won overnight, eventually we observe some of these who succeed, and over time the average earnings of the winners grow more than those of persons who were risk averse.[16]

Friedman's model is closely aligned with that of von Neumann-Morgenstern, in which a person bases his decisions on the expected value of the utility of a set of outcomes, defined as $\Sigma P_i U(Aj)$, where P_i is the probability of the A_i event occurring and $U(Aj)$ is its utility. Suppose A_1 equals $\bar{B}$. Then it can be shown that if a person has diminishing marginal utility, he will attach more utility to, and choose, A. In other words, he is averse to risk. Alternatively, if his marginal utility exhibited increasing returns, he would be a risk lover and choose B in the above example.

While, in principle, it is possible to conduct controlled experiments in which people choose between various alternatives to determine an individual's utility function and degree of risk aversion, we do not have that option. Instead, we shall use questions dealing with preferences for employment versus self-employment and with the desire for job security to estimate crudely the amount of earnings people have been willing to forgo for safety.

The reduction in average earnings of the risk averse can be thought of as a nonpecuniary reward, called peace of mind, received by those who dislike risk. There can be many other positive and negative nonpecuniary rewards attached to jobs. Those rewards are important in our study of the determinants of the earnings distribution because nonpecuniary rewards can induce offsetting changes in monetary rewards.[17] The choice between pecuniary and nonpecuniary rewards can be treated in the general framework of utility maximization.[18]

There are also substantial problems in quantifying the tradeoffs between monetary and nonmonetary returns. The two major difficulties are determining which of all possible nonpecuniary returns are relevant and measuring differences in preferences. However, since the data set that we are using has measures of only a few possible nonpecuniary rewards, we have not had to choose. Our measures are crude and relate primarily to whether a particular reward was operative at a time of occupational choice. The many problems associated with these measures are discussed in Chapters 8 and 9 in Taubman (1975).

III. THE NBER SAMPLE

In this study, our empirical work will be based primarily on the 5,100 men in the NBER-TH sample.[19] The sample was drawn from a group of some 75,000 men who during 1943 volunteered to enter the Army Air Force's pilot, bombardier, and navigator training program. The people in this group obviously had to meet the health and physical requirements to be in the Army. Also, according to Thorndike and Hagen (TH), to enter this program, "a man first had to be single, be between the ages of 18 and 26, pass a fairly rigorous physical examination, and pass a screening aptitude test, the Aviation Cadet Qualifying Examination. This examination was primarily a scholastic aptitude test, though perhaps with a slightly technical and mechanical slant. The qualifying score on the screening test was set at a level that could be reached by approximately half the high school graduates, the country over."[20] The men who qualified and volunteered for the program were then given a battery of some seventeen tests which measure various types of mental and physical skills. These test scores as well as certain biographical information on hobbies and family background determined which of the men were accepted for the Air Cadet program.

Thorndike and Hagen (TH) decided in 1955 to draw a sample of 17,000 men who had taken a given battery of tests between July and December 1943. Beginning in late 1955 and throughout 1956, TH received responses from some 10,000 civilians and 2,000 men still in the military. The questionnaire that they used, which is to be found in *Sources of Inequality of Earnings*,[21] contains, among other things, an earnings occupation history from World War II to the date of the questionnaire.[22]

In 1968, Taubman and Wales (TW) contacted Thorndike and learned that he had retained a printout of the test scores, earnings, and a few other items for 9,700 people who were civilians in 1955, and also the completed questionnaires for about 8,600 of these men. With the concurrence of the Air Force, Thorndike kindly agreed to make available all of this information, as well as the address list as of 1956.

It was recognized almost immediately that it would be possible to update addresses via army serial numbers and the V.A.'s life insurance and claims file.[23] Thus, John Meyer and F. Thomas Juster of the

National Bureau of Economic Research (NBER) quickly agreed to conduct another interview using Bureau funds. This questionnaire, which is to be found in *Sources of Inequality,* was eventually answered in 1969 and early 1970 by some 5,100 out of about 7,500 people for whom correct addresses were available.[24] TW initially used the detailed information on education, ability, family background, and personal characteristics from the two surveys (for about 80 percent of the men) to examine the rate of return to education and the use of education as a screening (signaling) device.

The respondents had been promised summaries of the results of the questionnaire. When mailing these summaries in 1971, the NBER included a short questionnaire to try to resolve some of the puzzles raised by TW and others. Some 3,000 people responded to this one mailing. When funding was received from the National Science Foundation (NSF) for this project, another large questionnaire dealing with more aspects of family background and other matters was sent out and was returned by 4,474 people.[25] These last two questionnaires are also to be found in *Sources of Inequality.*

TH found little in the way of response bias in 1955. Taubman and Wales have shown that in 1969 the mentally more able and more educated were more likely to respond. However, TW also showed that there was no significant difference in the 1955 earnings equations between those who did and those who did not respond in 1969; thus, the data can be used for structural analysis.[26]

Sample Characteristics

The qualifications needed to be a potential member of this sample guarantee that the NBER-TH sample will not be representative of the U.S. male population of the same age. About one-quarter of the men fall into each of the categories of high school graduate, some college, bachelor's degree, and at least some graduate work.[27] Also, a person had to be in the top one-half of the I.Q. distribution to enter this program and the average ability level has been heightened by the aforementioned response bias.

The average age in 1943 was 21, with three-quarters of the men aged 19 to 22. At least in 1943, the program's qualifications assure us that its men were, on the average, in better mental and physical health than the U.S. male population aged 18 to 26. Given that these men volunteered to train for flight duty, it seems likely that they are less risk averse than the population as a whole, which may be a partial explanation of the high percentage of people who are self-employed in 1969.[28] We do not know how many nonwhites, if any, are in the sample, though the education and test aptitude qualifications suggest to us that whites probably make up 99 percent of the group.[29]

In her dissertation, Wolfe (1973) has compared this sample and the corresponding U.S. age cohort of white males for a number of characteristics. She finds a higher percentage of Jews and a smaller percentage of Catholics in this sample. The men in this sample have fathers with above-average education (and occupational status) and fathers-in-law with even higher educational attainment. Also, the people in this sample have above-average earnings in each year studied, even if the comparison is made with white males of the same education and age, with the differentials greater at a later age and at lower levels of education.

It is of some interest to compare the earnings inequality in this sample with that of the random sample of white males aged 45 to 59 (in 1966) studied by Kohen, Parnes and Shea (1975). They find, for example, that the share of total family income received in 1968 by the bottom 25, 50, 75, and 95 percent is 14, 35, 62, and 89 percent, respectively. In the NBER-TH's sample each of the corresponding figures is smaller by 5 to 6 percentage points. Thus, despite having a more restricted range in mental ability, education, and risk aversion, the NBER-TH sample has more inequality in family income than a nationwide cohort of about the same age. This result may be due to the heavier concentration of self-employed men in NBER-TH or to the heavier concentration of people in the NBER-TH in the right-hand tail of the earnings distribution.

Clearly the sample is not representative of the U.S. population, and in the case of education and I.Q., does not have any members representative of a large portion of the population. Moreover, some of the dimensions in which it is nonrandom will be shown to be related to earnings. The nonrepresentativeness and truncation of some variables will mean that the distribution of earnings should not correspond to that for the U.S. population. Still, the sample can be thought of as a random stratified sample in which the weights for various strata do not correspond to the population weights.[30] *It is well known that such unequal weighting will not cause the coefficients estimated from the data to be biased.* Thus, we can use this sample to study the effects of education, ability, and so on, on various aspects of inequality. We cannot, however, extrapolate the results to those levels of education and ability not included in our sample. And as noted above, measures of inequality such as variance should not be the same as in the population. However, such inequality measures calculated *within* education and ability groups or the changes in the measures over time may apply to the population.

IV. A SUMMARY OF THE DETERMINANTS OF EARNINGS AT VARIOUS POINTS OF TIME

In this section we shall summarize the results of the earnings equations for 1955 and 1969, presented in the appendix, by comparing the relative importance of coefficients of various variables. It is important to realize that we are discussing partial regression coefficients in which all other variables in the equations in the appendix have been held constant.

Several measures of importance can be used. In this section we shall be concerned primarily with those related to the range and to the variance in earnings. Later we will consider issues connected with skewness and kurtosis. An obvious measure of importance is the R^2 or the amount of the variance explained by the set of variables. Of course the R^2 in our sample may not generalize to the U.S. population because our sample is truncated in education and ability and is drawn more heavily from some strata than others. Since we do not know all respects in which this sample differs from the U.S. population nor how to extrapolate the results to the truncated portion of the population, we shall not try to calculate a weighted R^2. Many of these problems are less severe when we compare total or partial R^2's for the same people but in different years.

The variance explained by a set of independent variables combines two elements—the predicted value of the dependent variables, Y_i, as compared to the mean of Y, and the number of times each Y_i occurs. An alternative measure of importance is the difference in the average level of earnings, $Y_1 - Y_2$, caused by a set of variables. This range measure is related to the $Y_i - \bar{Y}$ portion of the variance but does not indicate how many people are at each Y_i.[31]

For ease of exposition, we shall discuss the 1955 and 1969 results for one variable at a time. Unless otherwise noted, these results are drawn from equations in which many other variables have been included. The variables which have been held constant include: education, mathematical ability, various measures of socioeconomic background of the respondent and of his wife, information on self-employment and on teaching, a crude measure of risk preference, age and work experience, health, hours worked, marital status, and attitudes toward nonpecuniary rewards. While we have included many variables, we never explain more than 45 percent of the variance in earnings. The coefficients of any included variables will be biased if correlated with any omitted variable which determines earnings.[32]

Because of computer capacity limitations, we were forced to drop some variables which were consistently nonsignificant in preliminary runs. Table A-3 in Appendix A lists all of the variables that we tried but which were not significant in our earnings equation. In the equations presented, all the variables are either significant in one or more years or were significant in either the next to the last runs or in the Taubman-Wales equations from which this analysis commenced. When we cite coefficients for variables not in the last equation, the numbers are taken from the most complete versions of the final equations in which the variables appeared.

Formal Education

Formal schooling can affect physical, cognitive, psychological, and affective skills.[33] It would greatly increase our understanding of what schooling does if we could identify the particular skills that affect earnings and measure the change in all skills produced by schooling. However, since we do not have such measures or even know what the appropriate skills are, we shall have to be satisfied with crude measures of quantity and quality of schooling.

We represent quantity by level of education obtained. We use dummy variables for various responses. Earnings in 1969 generally increase with education.[34] However, despite our having included variables to hold constant nonpecuniary rewards, including those associated with precollege teaching, risk preference, and self-employment, those with just a bachelor's degree earn more than those with some graduate work. As shown in Table 1, the *increase* in earnings from education for the average high school graduate ranges from 8 percent for some college to 82 percent for non-self-employed M.D.'s, with bachelor's degree holders receiving 20 percent more.[35] (We have standardized by the average non-self-employed high school graduate's earnings of $10,300.)

In 1955, the same general pattern emerges, except that the effects of education are uniformly smaller and are not always statistically significant. For example, obtaining a bachelor's degree or some college would add 11 and 5 percent more to the $6,000 (1958 prices) received by the average non-self-employed high school graduate. *However, our self-employment variables are only measured in 1969. The resulting measurement error has probably caused us to overstate the relative returns to education of the not-self-employed in 1955.*[36]

The total effect of education may be understated if one of the mechanisms by which education alters earnings is measured after the completion of education and is also included in our equations. One such route would be the occupation the person was in. The variables on occupation we have used in these equations are teacher, self-employed businessman, professional, and business assets. The teacher variable is included because we felt that teachers receive more nonpecuniary

TABLE 1 The Increase in Earnings from Education in 1955 and 1969

Level of Schooling	Percentage Increase from Education[a]		Number of Observations as of 1955[b]	Number of Observations as of 1969[b]
	1955, Average Age 33	1969, Average Age 47		
Some college	5	8	1,145	1,162
Bachelor's	11	20	1,415	1,332
Some graduate	8	18	220	250
Master's	6	29	336	419
Ph.D.	13	43	238	298
LL.B.[c]	6	53	140	140
M.D.[c]	71	82	48	48

NOTE: The variables in the equation which have been held constant include: education, mathematical ability, various measures of socioeconomic background of the respondent and of his wife; information on self-employment and on teaching; a crude measure of risk preference, age and work experience, health, hours worked, marital status, and attitudes toward nonpecuniary rewards.

[a] Calculated for the average high school graduate, not self-employed, who attended the quality of college of the average person with just some college.

[b] In the high school category, there were 1,246 observations in 1955 and 1,139 in 1969.

[c] In this equation this variable was also included in Ph.D. group. Moreover, these are salaried people only.

rewards as a substitute for earnings than are received in other occupations.[27] The various self-employment measures are designed to eliminate all of the return on financial capital included in the earnings estimate; rewards for bearing the extra risk of entrepreneurship; and perhaps unmeasured attributes that lead to being a successful business-man. However, it is possible that these measures have incorporated some of the influences of education. For example, education's affect on prior earnings could conceivably explain much of the difference in the accumulation in business assets; however, crude analysis suggests that such effects of education would be small. Moreover, if the self-employment variables were not included, the bachelor's, some college, and master's coefficients would all be *smaller* because the self-employed are more concentrated at the lower education levels.

It is also possible that a person's tastes for nonpecuniary rewards or risk bearing are partially formed by education. The inclusion of the so-called nonpecuniary variables caused the some college and bachelor's level coefficients to decrease and the graduate level coefficients to increase in both years.

College Quality

As a crude measure of college quality, we have included for each person's undergraduate school the Gourman Index (of Academic Quality).[38] In 1969, we find that attendance at a school that ranked 100 points (the standard deviation) higher in the index is associated with a $450 increase in earnings. After our usual standardizing, the effect of the 100 point difference in college quality of $4\frac{1}{2}$ percent is about half the size of the effect of obtaining some college. In 1955, a 100 point increase in undergraduate-school quality leads to a $140 increase in earnings or $2\frac{1}{4}$ percent after standardization. Once again this is about half the size of the coefficient on the some college variable.[39]

The quality index used is obviously not the only one possible but we have not studied this problem in detail since it is the focus of the work of Wales (1973) and especially of Solmon (1973).

Mental Ability

In TW it was found that the seventeen tests taken by the people in 1943 contained at least four factors, but only the first factor, which was denoted mathematical ability but which probably correlates well with a standard I.Q. measure, was a significant determinant of earnings.[40]

In both 1969 and 1955 we tested for an interaction between mental ability and all other variables by computing separate equations within each ability fifth. Using analysis of covariance, we could not reject the hypothesis that the effects of all variables, including education, were independent of the level of ability in each year.

In both 1955 and 1969, as shown in Table 2, the coefficients on two of the top four fifths are significant. These coefficients are not sensitive to the inclusion of the self-employment-related variables.[41] The effects of each fifth increase in ability add a greater percentage to earnings in 1969 than in 1955, with the differences more pronounced in the top two ability fifths.

The numbers in Table 2 can be compared directly with those in Table 1. Thus the average difference in earnings between those in the top and bottom fifths of ability (14 percent and 19 percent in the two years) exceeds the effect of obtaining a bachelor's degree in 1955 and is nearly as large in 1969.

A person's test scores generally depend on his innate ability, the quality and quantity of pretest schooling, and differences in other aspects of "environment." Often we would like to know what portion of test scores (and associated earnings) are due to genetics and to environment. Suppose that the measures of religion, parents' and own educational attainment, occupation, income, and so forth, included in our earnings

| Ability Level | Percentage Change in Earnings from Ability (Bottom Fifth to the Fifth Shown)[a] | | Number of Observations[b] |
	1955, Average Age 33	1969, Average Age 47	
2nd fifth	5[c]	5[c]	848
3rd fifth	5[c]	7[c]	925
4th fifth	9	14	972
Top fifth	14	19	1,047

NOTE: The variables in the equation which have been held constant include: education, mathematical ability, various measures of socioeconomic background of the respondent and of his wife; information on self-employment and on teaching; a crude measure of risk preference, age and work experience, health, hours worked, marital status, and attitudes toward non-pecuniary rewards.

[a]The dollar difference is divided by the not self-employed high school graduate's average earnings.
[b]In the bottom fifth there were 808 observations.
[c]Not significant at the 5 percent level.

are the only environmental differences that determine test scores. Ability coefficients in the earnings equations would then be net of the environmental influences.[42] Of course, if other aspects of environment affect test scores, the ability coefficient will still be a mixture. Taubman and Wales, who examined the genetic/environmental problem, conclude that in the *tests we are using* most of the variation in scores is due to genetic differences (or other nonmeasured dimensions of environment). This finding in no way tells us innate ability is more important than learned knowledge, since we have not examined the effects of various types of learned knowledge on earnings.

Since the sample includes only the top half of the I.Q. distribution, it seems safe to conclude that ability is a more important direct determinant of the range of earnings than education for those who are at least high school graduates. Even when self-employment information is not used, the same conclusions are reached, though the differences are smaller.

Family Background

An individual's "socioeconomic background" can determine earnings for a variety of reasons, including being a proxy for: genetic endowments;

TABLE 3   Increase in 1955 and 1969 Earnings Associated with Various Socioeconomic Measures

Socioeconomic Measures	Percentage Increase in Earnings from Differences in Various SES Characteristics[a]		Number of Observations
	1955, Average Age 33	1969, Average Age 47	
Father's education			
Attended high school	6[b]	7[b]	1,409
Attended college	4[b]	5[b]	770
Father's occupation			
Business owner	2[b]	5[b]	1,699
Teacher	1[b]	−8[b]	360
Mother's education			
Attended high school	3[b]	3[b]	1,671
Attended college	2[b]	4[b]	685
Family never moved before high school graduation	−1[b]	−5[b]	1,452
Jewish	33	40	239
Protestant	−3[b]	−9	2,910
Religious school several times per week	−9	−11	236
Never went to religious school	−.1[b]	−3[b]	1,509
Biog[c] 2nd fifth and biog 3rd fifth	4	5	1,795
Biog 4th fifth and biog top fifth	11	8[b]	1,893
Father-in-law's education (per year)	1	1	e
Mother-in-law high school or college	−1[b]	6	2,294
Private elementary school	4[b]	27[b]	21
Private high school	25	29	99
Time spent on sports[d]	4[b]	10	e
Time spent on chores[d]	−3[b]	−10	e
Time spent on hobbies[d]	3[b]	−6[b]	e
Time spent on part-time job[d]	5	11	e

Notes to Table 3:

NOTE: The variables in this equation which have been held constant include: education, mathematical ability, various measures of socioeconomic background of the respondent and of his wife; information on self-employment and on teaching; a crude measure of risk preference, age and work experience, health, hours worked, marital status, and attitudes toward nonpecuniary rewards.

The omitted categories can be found by subtracting the included ones from 4,600.

^aThe dollar difference is divided by earnings of the average, non-self-employed high school graduate.
^bNot significant at the 5 percent level.
^cBiog is a weighted average of information on activities, education, preferences, and family background which was formed by Thorndike and Hagen from data collected by the military in 1943.
^dDifference between spent most time and hardly any time.
^eContinuous variables.

differences in "training" which increase cognitive, affective or physical skills; nonmonetary tastes; and business contacts, pull, and nepotism.

The measures of family background we have analyzed include: father's education and occupation; mother's education and labor force participation; wife's education and her parents' education and occupation; various data related to family income, wealth, and city size while respondent was growing up; how the respondent spent his time while growing up, age at entering school, and religious preferences.[43] The results are given in Table 3.

In TW, the two measures of socioeconomic status (SES) used were father's education and the so-called biography variable. This biography variable is based on the respondent's family income and education, his hobbies, sports and interests, and his pretest education and grades as reported in 1943.[44]

It was, of course, a bit frustrating that a variable made up of so many disparate items with unknown contributions determined earnings. Thus, we are happy to report that inclusion of information collected in 1969 and 1972 similar to that collected in 1943 has substantially reduced the size of the biography coefficient, but the top two-fifths are still significant and the coefficients are monotonic. It is interesting to note that the big shift in the 1969 and 1955 coefficients occurred only after we included information on attitudes toward nonpecuniary rewards and a proxy for family wealth, implying that these are the components in the biography variable that influenced earnings. The differences between the top two-fifths and bottom fifth are 11 percent and 8 percent in 1955 and 1969. This is one of the few variables that has a smaller percentage effect in 1969.

In this study, father's education is insignificant both in 1969 and in 1955. Part of the reduction of significance of this variable occurs when the *father is an owner* variable is introduced. However, the reduction in size and significance of the coefficient is primarily associated with the introduction of the respondent's business assets variables. Since this variable is not often used in other studies, there is a suggestion that father's education is a proxy for family wealth and business ownership.[45]

There are other SES variables which are significant. Perhaps the most interesting of the new measures are the Jewish and Protestant variables.[46] Compared to Catholics (as well as to atheists, agnostics, and others, who all earn about the same amount in the various years), Jews received from 33 to 40 percent more earnings than the average high school graduate and Protestants from 3 to 9 percent less.[47] The reader is reminded that these differences are net of the influence of education (including M.D.), mental ability, self-employment, and various other personal attributes and family SES dimensions.[48]

At least for the generation being discussed, it seems likely that those who are Jewish had more of a taste for acquiring knowledge, and as shown in Taubman (1975) achieved more education and went to better schools, given ability and other SES measures.[49] Hence, for given levels of schooling and mental ability in 1943, Jews may have acquired more knowledge useful in earning a living. Given the evidence in Taubman (1975), I would suggest that religious upbringing affects motivation and other psychological skills. We cannot, however, rule out the possibility that some unmeasured, genetically determined characteristics are related to religion. Unfortunately, since we do not know what unmeasured attributes are important determinants of earnings, we cannot usefully examine the genetics literature to see what if any differences exist by religion.[50]

The idea that the extent of religious commitment or the differing environment in families of various religions can mold the individual receives some further support in the sample. That is, we find that those who remembered attending religious classes (not parochial school) several times a week earn 9 to 11 percent less than those who attended once or twice, whereas those who did not attend earn 1 to 4 percent less. Since the latter group would not have come from "typical" families of the 1920s and 1930s, it seems possible that the variable represents attitudes toward material success.

Another set of variables which reflect both the type of family and affective, physical, cognitive, and psychological attitudes that can be formed by the family and the peer group are contained in the question (asked in 1972): "Indicate how you spent your time while growing up."[51] The categories examined were sports, hobbies, chores, part-time job, reading, and other. The last two groups were never significant and will not be discussed here except to note that reading is related to the ability measure and educational attainment. The remaining categories were significant in 1969 but only part-time job was significant in 1955.

The difference in earnings of those who spent practically no time and those who spent the most time on part-time jobs is 5 percent and 11 percent in 1955 and 1969, with the working group earning more. It seems likely that the latter group came from poor families and needed money for themselves and/or valued financial success greatly. These men would be willing to work hard and apparently have succeeded, with success being cumulative over time.[52] In 1955 and 1969 those who spent much time on sports while growing up earn 4 percent and 10 percent more than those who spent practically no time on sports. Several explanations for this result are available. First, activity in sports may show up in later life as better physical fitness, and as shown below, healthiness is related to earnings. (In this explanation, 1955 has a smaller impact because of less health deterioration at that age.) Second, most sports involve both a competitive and cooperative structure which are also found in many work situations. That is, a boy's play is training for a man's work. Third, activity in sports may be indicative of energy and aggressiveness that pay off in the business world.[53] Finally, there is some indication in Thorndike and Hagen that in 1955 sports distinguishes company presidents and vice-presidents from treasurers. This suggests that sports in the 1920s and 1930s was an indicator of family wealth and availability of leisure time, or an indicator of attitudes such as risk taking.

The hobby variable has practically no effect in 1955 but in 1969 those who spent the most time on hobbies received 6 percent less, which is significant at the 10 percent level in the final equation. The most obvious explanation for this finding is that many, though not all, hobbies represented the opposite of sports and the effects should be reversed.

The last and perhaps most difficult of these to explain is the chore result. Those who spent much time on chores earn 3 percent and 10 percent less in 1955 and 1969 with the former not significant. Initially, we had expected chores to be a proxy for "willingness to take on responsibility" and to have a positive effect. Morton, however, argues that families who insist on their children doing chores are lower middle class and are very interested in conformity. He further argues that these families will produce "tame" individuals who make the ideal bureaucrat and who receive less earnings than people in riskier jobs (see below). We might add that Morton only refers to one piece of empirical evidence, which, he acknowledges, is not very compelling.

As might be expected, time spent on chores and on a part-time job are positively correlated ($R^2 = .13$) but the differences in emphasis of paid and family work apparently reflect different types of environment and different types of men.

Thus far, we have included SES measures which are strongly related to family upbringing and taste formation. Parental income or wealth can also influence a child's earnings by being used to purchase goods that produce marketable skills, by being a proxy for nepotism, or by being a proxy for genetically determined skills.

One possible proxy for family income is father's education, which, as we have already indicated, is not significant once business assets are included in the equation. Another possible proxy is father's occupation but this also does not explain directly much of the differences in earnings, with the other variables held constant.[54]

Two extremely important determinants of earnings are type of elementary school and type of high school attended. The coefficient on private elementary school is positive but not significant, probably because 22 of the 29 people who went to private elementary school went to private high school. Thus the elementary school coefficient only measures the extra earnings above private high school. Those who attended both private elementary and private high school in 1955 earn 29 percent more than those who always went to public schools. In 1969, those who went to private elementary and private high school earn 56 percent more than those who did not go to private school.

Our explanation for this result is that those who went to private elementary schools in the 1920s came from very wealthy families who provide a good home environment and/or genes, or who used pull to aid their sons. The pull argument seems to be the most likely, since the variable is primarily a proxy for large amounts of wealth.[55]

We are still left with the need to explain the change in the coefficient between 1955 and 1969. We would argue that a screening, sorting explanation is relevant, since even if nepotism is involved, one wants to see how good the person under consideration is before giving him an important job; of course, a person can probably become vice-president more quickly if his father owns the company.

Another interesting finding in our equations that suggests nepotism is that *father-in-law's education*, measured continuously in years, is a significant determinant of the respondent's *earnings* in both 1955 and 1969.[56] A primary explanation of these results is that business and social contacts provided by the father-in-law are important. But there can be other explanations. For example, daughters from good social backgrounds may have the necessary graces—not learned in school—which help to promote their husbands. Alternatively, women with successful fathers may be able to spot and marry men with those characteristics that made for their father's success or push their husbands into achieving success.

Interestingly, mother-in-law's education also is positively related to earnings in 1969, with the high school variable somewhat greater than the college variable, though the two are combined in the final equation. This finding makes it less likely that women are marrying men who are like their fathers and suggests nepotism.

Thus far, we have been concerned with the effects of individual aspects of SES on earnings. Except for religion, none of these has an impact as large as ability or education on the range of earnings in 1955 or 1969. However, it is possible for a person to fall into the top or the bottom category of all SES measures. Using the significant coefficients only, the average difference in earnings for such "extremists" would total about $14,000 or 140 percent of our average earnings in 1969, and $5,500 or 90 percent in 1955, and far exceed the direct effect of ability or education on earnings.[57]

The other dimensions of SES that we have tried but have found to be insignificant, perhaps because of their crudeness, include: whether the respondent was the youngest or oldest sibling, additional crude proxies for family wealth based on type of house; the labor force status of the respondent's mother when the respondent was less than 5 and less than 14 years old; being reared on a farm; size of city or town he grew up in; the region of the country in which raised; and age at time of entry into school.

To conclude this section, we should like to discuss several objections that have been raised concerning the SES variables and that might also apply to some of the taste and other variables still to be discussed. One set of objections is that the variables used have multiple interpretations and have not been validated as measures of the phenomena that we ascribe to them. Our defenses against this set of objections are: that when many proxies are used, each one tends to represent the one or several forces it correlates with most closely; that since we do not yet know what dimensions of SES affect earnings nor have a theory to guide us, it is important to use the empirical information at hand to suggest variables which should be validated; that a form of validation is replication, which has been performed successfully in the 1955 and 1969 equations and in Taubman (1975) for education, ability, and net worth variables.

Another set of objections is that, perhaps, because of the absence of a well-specified theory, we have tried many variables and may only be observing chance correlations. This argument suggests that 5 percent of the SES variables might be significant due to chance, but we have found more like 40 percent significant. More importantly, none of the variables not significant in 1969 are significant in 1955 and nearly all of the variables significant in 1969 are also significant in 1955.[58] The R^2 between earnings in the two years does not exceed .2; thus, the probability of finding coefficients significant at the 5 percent level in both years does not exceed one-third of 1 percent.

Maturation and Work Experience

A well-known and documented result is that (real) earnings increase with age till at least age 40. While we do not have data for all ages, the results for 1955 and 1969 in Table 4 certainly are in accord with this finding. The

TABLE 4 Age, Experience, and Hours Worked

Coefficients on:	1955	1969
Age	.08	−.11
Year of first full-time job	−.11	−.15
Hours worked, first job, 1969	−.01[a]	.07
Hours worked, second job, 1969	−.03	−.12
Weeks lost due to illness, 1969	−.03[a]	−.18

NOTE: The variables in this equation which have been held constant include: education, mathematical ability, various measures of socioeconomic background of the respondent and of his wife; information on self-employment and on teaching; a crude measure of risk preference, age and work experience, health, hours worked, marital status, and attitudes toward nonpecuniary rewards.

[a]Not significant at the 5 percent level.

general explanations for the upward sloping age-earnings profiles are (1) as people age, mental and physical maturation increase those skills that determine earnings, (2) work experience and learning by doing increase earnings-related skills, (3) people are promoted on the basis of performance on the job and/or seniority, and (4) beyond a certain age senescence sets in or skills depreciate.[59]

Without distinguishing, for the moment, type of work experience, time on the job can be represented as $TJ = (\text{age} - \text{year of first job} - H)$, where H represents such things as time not working because of illness, unemployment, and departures from the normal period of time to complete a given level of schooling. If maturation is important, then age should have a separate effect from TJ.

Both age and year of first job (at the 6 percent level) are significant in 1969, but apparently senescence or depreciation has set in, since age in Table 4 is negative. In 1955, the separate age effect is nearly zero. The year-of-first-job coefficient can be treated as the negative of the experience coefficient. Thus, contrary to most findings, the absolute value of the experience coefficient is greater later in life, even though we have deflated by the Consumer Price Index. However, between 1955 and 1969, the effect of years experience has only risen about 50 percent, which is less than the percentage increase in average earnings of non-self-employed high school graduates or people with any other education level. That experience is more important than maturity in 1955 is not surprising given the evidence in Mincer (1974). It is somewhat surprising to find large senescence effects in 1969, since the discussion in Bloom (1964) suggests little changes in intelligence and certain other skills before age 50, and since weeks lost through illness have been held constant.[60] However, the results may also be due to discrimination on account of age for those who were fired in 1968 or 1969.

To try to refine the work-experience measure, we included information on military service after initial discharge, and type of work experience. We find that the additional military-experience data do not explain earnings, perhaps because military experience is a good substitute for civilian experience, or because, contrary to the above, experience on the job is not important. In Taubman (1975) we find that the earlier people enter into high-paying occupations, the more they earn in 1969 and that some 1955 jobs are better preparation than others, depending on one's 1969 occupation. These results suggest that some training is not general and that some people were in the wrong jobs in 1955 if they wanted to maximize their lifetime earnings.[61]

Earnings depend on hourly wage rates and hours worked. Unless there is a backward-bending supply curve of labor, higher wage rates will lead to greater hours worked and more earnings.[62] In 1969, each additional hour per week on the first job adds $70 to annual earnings.[63] If we use an average hourly wage rate per week of $350, we would estimate σ in the footnote as about -1.2. Each additional hour on the second job is associated with a $120 decrease in earnings, apparently because some of those people with low wage rates want higher material standards. Thus, both results, which rely on perhaps erroneous estimates of hours, suggest that the supply curve has some backward-bending sections.

Despite the fact that the hours data refer to 1969, we included them in 1955. The hours on second job are still significantly negative, while the hours on first job have become negative and insignificant. It appears that moonlighters work hard over long periods of time, since hours on second job is negatively related to recalled estimates of initial earnings and to the probability of the wife's working in 1968.

Weeks lost through illness in 1969 has a negative impact on 1969 and 1955 findings but only the 1969 coefficient is significant. The $180 a week lost would indicate a $9,000 a year job if the figures exclude paid sick leave, but we have no way of knowing if this is how the question was interpreted. Incidentally, this variable caused the self-assessed healthiness variable used by TW to become insignificant.

Nonpecuniary Rewards

There are monetary and nonmonetary rewards from a job. Since we expect people to base their job-choice decisions on the total of pecuniary and nonpecuniary rewards, those occupations which pay heavily in a nonpecuniary form should have a compensatory change in wage payments. We do not have available measures of the nonpecuniary aspects of various occupations, which we shall assume to be occupation specific, but equally accessible to all; however, we do have some crude information related to the preference of individuals on specific nonmonetary aspects of a job. For example, the respondents were asked, "Assuming that you thought that the financial possibilities were about the same, would you prefer to work for yourself or for somebody else or no preference?"[64] In 1955, those who preferred to be salaried earn 6 percent less than the

TABLE 5 Nonpecuniary Tradeoffs with Earnings, Relative to Salary of Average High School Graduate (Percentage of earnings for several variables[a])

	1955	1969	Number of Observations
Prefer to be salaried	−6	−10	962
Teacher	−10	−18	256
Reasons for taking 1972 occupation field when started:[b]			
Prospects of future financial success	−9	−17	1,200
Chance for independent work	5[c]	11	1,519
Person-to-person contact	−2[c]	1[c]	
Chance to help others	8	8	2,090
Represented a challenge	−13	−10	784
Job security	8	13	1,415
Free time	−1[c]	−2[c]	

NOTE: The variables in this equation which have been held constant include: education, mathematical ability, various measures of socioeconomic background of the respondent and of his wife; information on self-employment and on teaching; a crude measure of risk preference, age and work experience, health, hours worked, marital status, and attitudes toward nonpecuniary rewards.
[a]The dollar differences are divided by the earnings of the average non-self-employed high school graduate.
[b]Each coefficient refers to a "no" answer; hence, "yes" and the "no responses" are the omitted groups.
[c]Not significant at the 5 percent level.

average (non-self-employed) high school graduate (see Table 5). In 1969, the people who preferred to be salaried earn 11 percent less. It is important to realize that these results are from equations which hold constant being self-employed and amount of business assets.

We are interpreting the answer to the question as indicating risk preference, and that following the expected utility approach, risk averters give up some average earnings to reduce dispersion. Is this a reasonable interpretation? Taubman (1975) discusses in some detail how this variable could correspond to an economist's definition of risk aversion. We conclude there that in a formal sense, if respondents thought like economists, the question would distinguish between risk averters and risk lovers. In a less formal sense, people may simply be responding to their belief that a particular occupation is risky. This question was asked in 1969. It is possible that people who failed in their work now choose the salaried answer because of their failure. However, in Taubman (1975), Chapter 8, we show that this variable is not related to a (self-reported) measure of the difference between actual and expected financial success. However, an alternative explanation of the question might be that those who value being their own boss would earn less, especially since those who prefer independence in working do earn less (see below). While the results do not support the "being your own boss" explanation, this may mean that this explanation does not dominate the risk interpretation in this sample. While the results do not prove the risk interpretation result, there is, however, some evidence that bears on this issue which tends to corroborate it. As discussed in Taubman (1975) Chapters 8 and 9, this same variable determines schooling, the amount of business assets, and returns to capital in a manner consistent with risk preference. Finally, it is also worth reporting that the variable is significant and has the same sign in nearly all within-occupation equations. Moreover, in her dissertation, Wolfe has found that those who prefer to be salaried have less children for a given income, i.e., appear to be less willing to risk having children.[65]

Another set of questions asked in 1972 was, "As best as you can remember, what factors influenced your decision to enter the occupational field you are in at the present time? Check yes or no to each of the following and indicate factors that were of special importance."[66] In our equations, the dummy variable for each factor used was set at one if the respondent answered "no."

In 1969, the salary, person-to-person contact, and free-time variables were not significant in preliminary runs though salary nearly was. The other variables indicate that those who were not worried about future financial success receive 17 percent less than those who were worried (or didn't answer),[67] those not interested in independent work earn 10 percent more, those who wanted to help others earn 8 percent less, those who wanted to have a challenge earn 17 percent more, and those interested in job security receive 13 percent less earnings.[68] In 1955, when many of the people were in different jobs and even in different occupations, nearly all of the same variables are significant, and all the signs on the variables significant in 1969 are the same, though the magnitude is always less than in 1969.

Intuitively, all of these results seem quite plausible, and each one is internally consistent with the others. However, there is still the question of whether these variables are related to nonpecuniary preferences. This issue is discussed in detail in Taubman (1975), where it is concluded that the variables are probably related to preferences. This conclusion is in part based on the findings in Chapters 8 and 9 that the variables have effects consistent with the above interpretation in other equations. Moreover, the introduction of these variables has a big impact primarily on the various graduate education variables, which seems quite reasonable, since we often think that Ph.D.'s and other graduate students choose nonpecuniary rewards, such as independence in work or helping others.[69]

The basic threads running through these findings are that people who are willing to work hard on difficult or risky projects will end up with substantially more earnings, while those who are more interested in the intrinsic rewards of the job will receive less. While this is hardly a startling conclusion, we know of no other study which has been able to obtain significant impacts after holding constant such things as education and ability. Moreover, the consistency of findings between 1955 and 1969 suggests that the 1972 survey responses are not ex post rationalizations, and this is confirmed by the finding in Chapter 8 that responses to these variables are not a function of ex ante/ex post differences in monetary success.

The tradeoffs of earnings with nonpecuniary returns is quite large. Excluding the teacher dummy, which is discussed below, but including all the other significant coefficients in Table 5, we find that the difference in earnings due to various nonpecuniary preferences could be as high as 55 percent or $5,500 in 1969, and 40 percent or $2,500 in 1955, which are greater than all education effects except that for M.D.

The last nonpecuniary-related variable that we have used is that of being a precollege teacher. We find that such people earn 10 percent and 18 percent less in 1955 and 1969. The premium paid to be a teacher is even larger before the nonpecuniary variables are introduced, which seems reasonable. We cannot, however, rule out the possibility that teachers earn less because they are less able.

Business Assets

The respondents were asked for their "earnings," without definition of the concept. However, we would expect the self-employed to report their net income from their business, since most people would find it difficult to separate earnings derived from labor from those derived from capital. To try to hold constant the returns from capital, we have included a dummy variable for self-employed businessman, another dummy for self-employed professional, and most importantly, a continuous variable on amount of business assets.[70] All of these variables were measured only in 1969. The extra measurement error involved in using these variables in 1955 undoubtedly affects the comparability of our answers and our R^2, though comparison of 1955 and 1969 equations, which only use data available in both years, indicates that general conclusions on R^2 are not affected. We shall interpret the coefficients on the business-asset variable as the rate of return on financial capital invested in business.[71]

In 1969, the coefficient on the business-asset variable, which is an estimate of the before-tax rate of return, is .12. Such a figure is not unlike the .7 to .10 estimates usually found in studies such as Kravis (1962).[72] The dummy variable for self-employed businessman is still significant, though assets and hours worked are included in the 1969 equations, and equals 10 percent of the standardized base. The self-employed professionals, who may not have much in the way of financial investments, receive 31 percent more than the non-self-employed professionals (though the denominator is too low, since, for comparability, we have divided by the average earnings of high school graduates).

In 1955, the coefficient on 1969 business assets is still highly significant (a t of 11) at .03 even though the growth of assets must not have been uniform during the period, and some people must have changed their self-employment/salaried status. Probably because of the increased measurement error involved in using the 1969 asset and hours variables in 1955, the 1969 self-employment businessman dummy is as important in 1955 as in 1969. On the other hand, the 1969 self-employed professional dummy is not significant, presumably because many of these people were salaried in 1955 and had not had a chance to display their true worth to their employers.

Conclusion

The many and varied comparisons made in this section lead to several important conclusions. First, the effects of nearly all variables change during a person's life cycle and, in general, display a profile that increases with age. Second, the profiles are steeper for the education variables than for most other variables, though as shown in more detail below, the steepest profile is for those who attended private elementary school. Third, even after holding constant a wide variety of variables, we still find that education leads to large and statistically significant differences in earnings. These differences, however, are relatively small in comparison with those arising from the conglomeration of family background, attitudes, and nonpecuniary preferences and are no larger than the differences which are the result of ability. While we shall return to the topic below, it is also important to realize that a large portion of the differences in annual earnings is due to unmeasured variables and random events.

V. INEQUALITY: EXTENT AND CAUSES

In this, as in most samples, the distribution of earnings is skewed to the right.[73] Since most people *assume* that something called "ability" or capacity is normally distributed, much attention has been paid to the question of why earnings exhibit a skewed distribution.[74] Becker (1964) and Mincer (1970) have demonstrated that such distributions can be generated by "acquired" human capital models. Mandelbrot (1962) explains skewness solely in terms of many different inherited skills. Champernowe (1953), Aitchison and Brown (1957), and others have shown that stochastic processes that operate continuously can generate skewed distributions.[75] In Friedman's model (1953), skewness arises from behavior toward risk rather than from differences in abilities.

Inequality in Earnings

The inequality in earnings can be measured in several ways.[76] One important measure is the Lorenz curve, which indicates the percent of total earnings received by the top X percent. The Lorenz curves for 1955 and 1969 are presented in Figure 1. Also drawn in that figure is a diagonal which is the Lorenz curve that would be observed if each person had the same earnings. In all years studied, earnings are not distributed equally and are below the diagonal.

All summary measures of relative inequality of two Lorenz curves will yield the same ranking *provided* the two curves do not intersect.[77] Conversely, if the curves intersect, there are always some measures that would disagree on whether curve 1 or 2 is more unequal. Since earnings do not follow any well known distribution, we have used the nonparametric Kolmogorov-Smirnov test (KS) to determine if the difference in the

FIGURE 1 Cumulative Earnings Distributions, 1955 and 1969, Percentage of Total Earnings Held by the Bottom X Percent

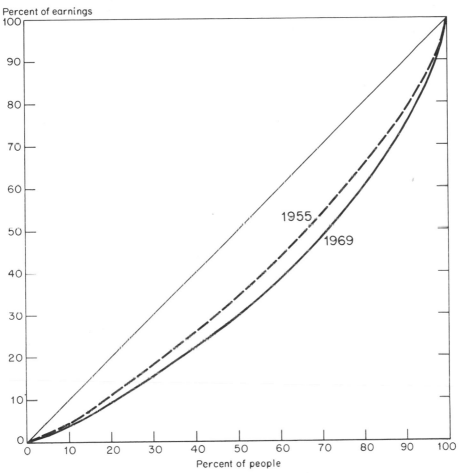

Percent of earnings

Percent of people

Lorenz curves is statistically significant. Results of the KS test indicate that the 1969 curve is statistically different from (more unequal than) the 1955 curve.

We also have examined the Lorenz curves for various education and mental ability groups.[78] In either 1955 or 1969, the Lorenz curves for any two mutually exclusive groups, such as high school and some college, were never significantly different at the 5 percent level though many were at the 10 percent level. For any particular group, the 1969 curve was always beneath the corresponding 1955 curve and the maximum differences which range from 6 to 10 percentage points were always significant at the 5 percent level. Thus, there is little difference in inequality in earnings between various education and ability groups in any year but in each case there is more inequality in 1969 than in 1955.

From Variance to Kurtosis

Thus far we have indicated that earnings inequality has varied from year to year. For many purposes, however, it is necessary to ask how particular features of the distribution have changed over time and to what extent these features and their change are the consequence of the distribution of education, mental ability, and so on. A quantifiable and at times decomposable description of a distribution can be obtained from various "moments" of the distribution.[79] The first four moments measure the mean, variance, skewness, and kurtosis of the distribution.

In 1969, in Table 6, our standard deviation, σ, is \$9.4.[80] In some types of labor markets, we would expect σ to increase when average earnings did. For these cases a standardized measure is provided by the coefficient of variation, σ/mean, which is about two-thirds in 1969.

Several measures of symmetry have been proposed in the literature. To avoid reranking the observations as we hold constant education and other sets of variables, we shall use the third moment standardized by the second to eliminate scale effects. A distribution is skewed to the right when this measure is positive, as is our 1969 estimate of 3.0. At the 5 percent level, we can reject the null hypothesis that the population is normally distributed, which is symmetric, using a test developed by Fisher.

Kurtosis measures the frequency of observations in the tail or near the mean of the distribution. We use the fourth moment divided (standardized) by the second. From this ratio we subtract 3 which is the expected value of the kurtosis in a normal distribution. Larger values such as our 12 indicate that there are too many observations in the tails or too few near the mean as compared with the normal curve.

In 1955, the mean earnings are \$7,300 (in 1958 dollars). The standard deviation is \$3.8 thousand and the coefficient of variation is about 1/2. Our skewness and kurtosis estimates are 5.4 and 62.0 respectively, neither of which would be in accord with the null hypothesis that the distribution is normal. Thus in both 1955 and 1969, the distribution of earnings is skewed to the right and has larger numbers of people in the tails.

Given the differences between our sample and the U.S. population, the results on the various inequality measures in any one year have restricted interest until we control for education, ability, and so forth. But the changes during the 14 years are of substantial interest—especially since such data are not generally available over such a time span and so late in the life cycle.

TABLE 6 Sources of Inequality in 1969 and 1955

	Standard Error	Skewness	Kurtosis
1969			
Y	9.42	3.05	13.90
$Y - Y_1$	7.75	2.76	14.75
$Y - Y_2$	9.11	3.22	15.27
$Y - Y_3$	9.33	3.11	14.31
$Y - Y_4$	8.63	2.82	13.39
$Y - Y_5$	9.20	3.12	14.61
$Y - Y_6$	9.33	3.05	13.91
$Y - Y_7$	9.06	3.11	14.78
$Y - Y_8$	9.37	3.01	13.71
1955			
Y	3.81	5.35	61.99
$Y - Y_1$	3.41	5.56	78.24
$Y - Y_2$	3.74	5.47	65.09
$Y - Y_3$	3.78	5.41	62.88
$Y - Y_4$	3.65	5.40	68.50
$Y - Y_5$	3.74	5.46	64.29
$Y - Y_6$	3.80	5.32	62.34
$Y - Y_7$	3.69	5.42	65.12
$Y - Y_8$	3.80	5.33	61.99

NOTE: The Y_1 through Y_8 series are based on equations in Table A.1 in Appendix A

Y_1 = all variables.
Y_2 = education coefficients, including M.D. and LL.B., and the Gourman rating.
Y_3 = mental ability variables.
Y_4 = business assets, and the self-employed businessmen and professional dummies.
Y_5 = prefer to be salaried and the 4 other nonpecuniary variables.
Y_6 = age, year of first job, hours worked, hours on second job.
Y_7 = time spent, private schools, in-law, biography, religion, size of current town, never-move variables.
Y_8 = teacher, no response in 1972, weeks lost from illness, age entered school, religious school attendance, and weight variables.

Between 1955 and 1969, the mean earnings in constant dollars grew by about 100 percent. Since the standard deviation increased by a greater amount than the mean, the coefficients of variation increased by 27 percent.[81] The changes in the skewness and kurtosis measures are both negative. Thus, contrary to the usual interpretation of stochastic theories, the distribution is becoming *less* asymmetric and less deviant from a normal curve as the people age (though the 1969 curve is far from a normal curve).[82]

Sources of Variance, Skewness and Inequality

Our sample is, of course, better educated, mentally more able, probably less risk averse, and more limited in age than the population. Since all these characteristics affect earnings and have a distribution different from that in the population, there is no reason to expect to find that the distribution of earnings is the same as that in the population. Despite this, we can still use the sample to study some problems of interest. For example, suppose the true equation *in the population* is

(1) $\qquad Y_i = X_i a + u_i$

where X_i is a vector of (measured) independent variables, a is the associated vector of coefficients and u_i are errors arising from random events and unmeasured variables. Because our distribution of the X's differs from the population, we have an unequally weighted stratified sample.[83] As long as the u's are distributed the same as in the population, we can study the distribution of $Y - Xa = u$ to determine what the population distribution would be if everyone has the same education and ability, and if wage rates did not change.

In examining the sources of various aspects of inequality, several things must be noted. First, since the equation's coefficients are selected so as to minimize the variance of the residuals with no attention given to the skewness or kurtosis, the results (on sources) are less reliable for these latter two measures than for the variance.[84] Second, despite this caveat, the effects of the X's on skewness and kurtosis might be larger than those on variance.[85]

Table 6 contains estimates for 1969 of the standard error, skewness, and kurtosis with the latter two standardized by the standard error raised to the appropriate power.[86] This standardization is appropriate, since we are primarily interested in the question of whether the distribution would be normal or would be much less skewed if ability, and so forth, were the same for everyone. But variables which reduce the residuals will also reduce u^3 or u^4; thus, the resulting series could be as skewed though $\Sigma(Y_i - \bar{Y})^3$ would be smaller.

We present the estimates for earnings (Y) and residual earnings, $(Y - X^*a)$, where X^*a refers to a subset or all of the variables used in the equations in Table A-1. If we had estimated an equation with just X^*, generally we would have obtained different estimates of these coefficients. But since such coefficients would be biased estimates of the true parameters, it was felt that it was better to use the estimates from the comprehensive equation.[87]

Using the most comprehensive equation available, the standard error of the residual earnings is reduced by about 18 percent to $7.8 in row 2 of

Table 6. The remaining rows in the table, identified at the bottom, indicate the effects of various sets of variables. For purposes of reference, Y_2 will be called education, Y_3 mental ability, Y_4 self-employment, Y_5 nonpecuniary tradeoffs, Y_6 work-related experiences, Y_7 socioeconomic standing, and Y_8 miscellany. The reduction in the standard errors indicates the partial R's—ignoring sign—of these variables but because reductions in variance depend upon the covariance of the independent variable, the effects of the individual rows are not additive.[88]

The self-employment data reduces the standard error, σ, by 8 percent, with business assets being the most important single variable. The SES variables reduce σ by 5 percent. The quantity and quality of education variables (including M.D. and LL.B.) reduce σ by less than 4 percent and all other sets of variables have even smaller impacts on σ.

In the sample, the standardized skewness measure is 3.05. As shown in the $Y - Y_1$ row, the full set of variables reduces the skewness by 10 percent to 2.76.[89] Thus, even if education, ability, SES, business assets, and so on, were equal for all individuals, the earnings distribution would be about 90 percent, as skewed as originally, once we adjust for the reduction in variance from holding each of these items constant.

Interestingly, when education, ability, and the nonpecuniary tradeoffs are individually held constant, the *standardized* skewness measure *increases* between 1 and 5 percent. On the other hand, the self-employment variables *reduce* the relative skewness by 7 percent and the miscellaneous variables in Y_8 reduce skewness by 1 percent.

Thus, we can conclude that if everyone in the sample had the same education or ability or nonpecuniary preferences, the earnings distribution would have slightly more skewness.[90] We can also conclude that differences in self-employment (size of business assets and being self-employed) have contributed greatly to the existing skewness in the distribution in this sample.

Now let us examine kurtosis. In the sample the standardized kurtosis measure had a value of 13.9 which is far from, and significantly different from, the zero expected in the normal distribution.[91] The standardized kurtosis measure based on the residuals from equation 2 is increased by 6 percent. Looking at the other rows, we find that only holding constant self-employment and the miscellany in Y_8 has led to a reduction in relative kurtosis. Even with self-employment held constant, the distribution of earnings would exhibit kurtosis. On the other hand, the elimination of education differences leads to a big increase in kurtosis. This suggests that education pushes more people away from the mean and makes for a smoother transition to the tails, whose existence is not related to education.

1955

Our analysis of the source of inequality in 1955 earnings distributions is handicapped by the fact that several of our most important variables—including the self-employment ones—are measured only in 1969 and must have changed between 1955 and 1969. Nevertheless, let us examine the same statistics on inequality. As shown in Table 6, the standard error of earnings in 1955 is $3.8 (thousands of 1958 dollars). Since the 1955 equation has a smaller R^2, the standard error of $Y - Y_1$ has only been reduced by 10 percent. The standard error of earnings is reduced by about $1\frac{1}{2}$ to 3 percent by each of education, ability, risk preference, and nonpecuniary variables, work experience, SES and the miscellany in Y_8, but the self-employment variables reduce the standard deviation by 4 percent.

The 1955 skewness measure is 5.3, which is much greater than in 1969. Examining the various rows, we find that holding constant any subset (except work experience and the miscellany) of the whole set of the characteristics in equation 2 *increases* relative skewness.[92]

Much the same pattern appears on kurtosis. The residuals from the full or any partial set of variables (except the miscellany) have greater standardized kurtosis than in the original earnings data and this kurtosis is greater in 1955 than in 1969.

Pattern by Education Level

Since we have eliminated the average difference in earnings for people with different amounts of education and ability, the above analysis essentially analyzes the *between cell* contribution of education and ability, to inequality. For several purposes it is important to study inequality *within* various education and ability cells. As shown in Table 7, in 1955 the standard error is lowest for those with only a high school education, at the peak for those who started or completed college, and intermediate for those with more formal education than a bachelor's degree.[93] The relative skewness and kurtosis measures increase sharply from high school through a bachelor's degree, then fall to their lowest level for those with at least some graduate work. In each education group, neither earnings nor the log of earnings are distributed normally.

In 1969, it is still true that the earnings distribution is neither normal nor log-normal. In other respects, the pattern is much different from 1955. While high school graduates still have the lowest standard error, graduate students (including M.D.'s and LL.B.'s) have the highest. The

TABLE 7 Effects of Various Sets of Variables on Inequality by Four Levels of Education, in 1955 and 1969

	1955			1969		
	Standard Error	Skewness	Kurtosis	Standard Error	Skewness	Kurtosis
High school						
Y	2.81	2.87	13.68	7.12	3.59	21.36
$Y - Y_1$	2.50	1.97	9.79	5.74	2.68	17.50
$Y - Y_2$	2.82	2.84	13.50	7.12	3.61	21.50
$Y - Y_3$	2.80	2.89	13.97	7.07	3.61	21.62
$Y - Y_4$[a]	2.64	2.34	10.74	6.28	3.18	19.41
$Y - Y_5$	2.73	2.79	13.26	6.84	3.56	21.64
$Y - Y_6$	2.80	2.79	13.10	7.07	3.60	21.68
$Y - Y_7$	2.75	2.82	14.04	6.84	3.47	20.39
$Y - Y_8$	2.82	2.80	13.48	7.13	3.52	21.37
Some college						
Y	4.30	5.37	51.00	9.79	3.29	15.20
$Y - Y_1$	3.87	5.25	53.81	8.32	2.87	15.45
$Y - Y_2$	4.29	5.30	51.17	9.72	3.30	15.32
$Y - Y_3$	4.30	5.38	50.98	9.75	3.29	15.30
$Y - Y_4$	4.14	5.33	52.67	9.02	3.09	15.58
$Y - Y_5$	4.25	5.45	52.48	9.58	3.36	15.96
$Y - Y_6$	4.29	5.39	51.45	9.72	3.28	15.12
$Y - Y_7$	4.13	5.30	51.18	9.37	3.23	15.36
$Y - Y_8$	4.30	5.30	50.21	9.76	3.23	14.84
Bachelor's degree						
Y	4.25	6.30	77.92	9.64	2.81	11.50
$Y - Y_1$	3.93	6.94	99.70	8.38	2.57	11.35
$Y - Y_2$	4.23	6.36	79.06	9.58	2.85	11.80
$Y - Y_3$	4.22	6.34	78.52	9.60	2.85	11.76
$Y - Y_4$	4.13	6.41	85.69	9.02	2.48	9.69
$Y - Y_5$	4.19	6.40	79.79	9.50	2.85	11.85
$Y - Y_6$	4.22	6.40	80.63	9.50	2.84	12.76
$Y - Y_7$	4.15	6.53	83.65	9.35	2.90	12.60
$Y - Y_8$	4.26	6.32	78.25	9.58	2.78	11.28
Graduate work						
Y	3.33	2.53	10.29	10.02	2.96	12.73
$Y - Y_1$	2.89	1.56	8.08	8.19	2.65	13.63
$Y - Y_2$	3.12	2.21	9.35	9.55	3.16	14.54
$Y - Y_3$	3.29	2.60	10.84	9.93	3.00	13.02
$Y - Y_4$	3.14	2.33	9.55	9.08	2.79	12.74
$Y - Y_5$	3.27	2.62	11.03	9.79	3.05	13.53
$Y - Y_6$	3.32	2.53	10.30	9.85	2.97	12.85
$Y - Y_7$	3.32	2.50	10.77	9.80	3.01	13.49
$Y - Y_8$	3.27	2.47	10.01	9.83	2.97	13.04

NOTE: For definitions, see Table 6.

[a]While this row should repeat the row for Y, there is a small recorded change since a few people whom we treat as not having attended college went for less than a semester and have a Gorman rating.

skewness and kurtosis measures are greatest for high school graduates and then decrease through the bachelor's level, followed by a slight increase at the graduate level. The major change in the high school category between 1955 and 1969 requires comment. We suggest that the above average growth in the standard error and the large absolute and comparative increase in the skewness and kurtosis measures occur because even the talented or lucky individual among high school graduates finds that it takes longer to get to the top. Thus, in 1955, these people would not be so far out in the right-hand tail as they are in 1969. Perhaps because of a different distribution of talent among the more educated, because of credentialism based on education, or because of nepotism, this same phenomenon does not occur in other education classes.

More light can be shed on these and other issues by examining the distribution of the residuals in each education class. Since we are not able to find significant differences in the coefficients by ability or education level, we can use the same sets of coefficients that we employed previously in making these calculations.

Consider first the 1955 results in Table 7. At each education level, the standard error declines by about 10 per cent, with the self-employment variables ($Y - Y_4$) generally responsible for the largest reduction in the standard error and the SES($Y - Y_7$) and nonpecuniary tradeoffs ($Y - Y_5$) variables nearly as important.

In all but the bachelor's group, holding the self-employment variable constant causes a reduction in the relative skewness measure. The opposite is true in Table 6 for the total sample. It seems likely that this difference is due to the use of a separate standardization factor in each education level or, in other words, the total sample combines within education distributions which have different parameters. In the high school and graduate level, kurtosis decreases when self-employment is held constant, while the opposite is true at the other two education levels. No other set of characteristics has a large impact on skewness or kurtosis in 1955 at more than one education level.

In 1969, the picture is more varied. The standard error of $Y - Y_1$ is nearly identical for all but the high school category, which remains the lowest, and much of the difference in skewness and, to a lesser extent, kurtosis, disappears. At each education level, holding constant the self-employment variable substantially reduces the standard error and the relative skewness and the estimates of relative kurtosis of the high school and bachelor's degree categories. Once again SES and nonpecuniary variables play an important secondary role in determining the standard error but have little effect on skewness and kurtosis.

Mental Ability

Since very little information has ever been presented about the distribution of earnings by mental ability, it is appropriate to repeat the above analysis by the five ability levels. Table 8 contains the distribution statistics for earnings for each ability fifth. In 1955, the standard error is lowest for the bottom fifth and highest for the top. The middle fifth, however, has a lower standard error and coefficient of variation than the group on either side. (Since the standard error of the log of earnings does not vary with ability, the above results may be due to a few extreme observations—as is also suggested by the skewness and kurtosis measure.) Both skewness and kurtosis follow the same pattern, with highest values in the top fifth; however, none of the earnings distributions within an ability cell are normal or log-normal.

In 1969, the standard deviation follows the same pattern as in 1955 (though the top fifth has the lowest coefficient of variation). Skewness and kurtosis are substantially lower in the top two-fifths than in the lowest three-fifths; however, none of the distributions are normal or log-normal.

TABLE 8   **Effects of Various Sets of Variables on Inequality by Five Ability Levels, in 1955 and 1969**

| | ——— 1955 ——— | | | ——— 1969 ——— | | |
Ability Fifth	Standard Error	Skewness	Kurtosis	Standard Error	Skewness	Kurtosis
Bottom fifth						
Y	2.91	2.92	14.79	7.81	3.39	17.89
$Y - Y_1$	2.67	1.90	9.54	6.71	2.98	20.23
$Y - Y_2$	2.88	2.89	14.96	7.60	3.55	19.83
$Y - Y_4$	2.83	2.45	12.36	7.24	3.29	20.36
$Y - Y_5$	2.85	2.94	15.27	7.61	3.45	18.49
$Y - Y_6$	2.91	2.81	13.84	7.76	3.40	17.96
$Y - Y_7$	2.83	2.64	12.60	7.68	3.25	17.48
$Y - Y_8$	2.91	2.86	14.67	7.75	3.26	17.02
2nd fifth						
Y	3.90	5.39	49.39	9.14	3.50	17.95
$Y - Y_1$	3.53	5.41	56.95	7.52	2.98	17.57
$Y - Y_2$	3.86	5.41	50.26	8.89	3.55	18.28
$Y - Y_4$	3.78	5.37	52.09	8.38	3.16	17.11
$Y - Y_5$	3.83	5.47	50.96	8.89	3.55	18.66
$Y - Y_6$	3.88	5.44	50.47	9.07	3.47	17.83
$Y - Y_7$	3.76	5.31	49.88	8.86	3.56	19.15
$Y - Y_8$	3.89	5.36	49.29	9.04	3.44	17.61

TABLE 8   (concluded)

Ability Fifth	1955 Standard Error	1955 Skewness	1955 Kurtosis	1969 Standard Error	1969 Skewness	1969 Kurtosis
3rd fifth						
Y	3.32	3.02	13.73	9.06	3.36	16.44
$Y - Y_1$	2.86	2.20	9.98	7.52	2.95	16.64
$Y - Y_2$	3.22	2.89	13.11	8.81	3.50	17.87
$Y - Y_4$	3.07	2.67	11.89	8.16	3.05	15.37
$Y - Y_5$	3.25	3.07	14.28	8.84	3.44	17.32
$Y - Y_6$	3.32	2.94	13.32	8.97	3.37	16.65
$Y - Y_7$	3.27	2.99	13.93	8.79	3.44	17.48
$Y - Y_8$	3.30	2.98	13.46	9.05	3.31	16.16
4th fifth						
Y	3.82	3.80	23.84	9.66	2.77	11.42
$Y - Y_1$	3.40	3.66	25.99	7.76	2.66	13.56
$Y - Y_2$	3.75	3.89	25.00	9.39	2.95	12.73
$Y - Y_4$	3.63	3.65	23.43	8.75	2.66	11.86
$Y - Y_5$	3.74	3.87	24.71	9.42	2.81	11.93
$Y - Y_6$	3.81	3.76	23.74	9.53	2.77	11.61
$Y - Y_7$	3.70	3.87	25.24	9.19	2.84	12.18
$Y - Y_8$	3.83	3.78	23.83	9.59	2.71	11.12
5th fifth						
Y	4.50	7.27	95.12	10.26	2.77	11.29
$Y - Y_1$	4.17	7.77	114.43	8.81	2.45	10.41
$Y - Y_2$	4.47	7.33	96.74	10.00	2.89	12.16
$Y - Y_4$	4.36	7.51	104.38	9.55	2.49	9.69
$Y - Y_5$	4.45	7.33	96.34	10.12	2.83	11.85
$Y - Y_6$	4.48	7.31	96.70	10.15	2.75	11.15
$Y - Y_7$	4.39	7.41	99.69	9.85	2.82	11.93
$Y - Y_8$	4.49	7.26	95.45	10.21	2.78	11.46

NOTE: See Table 6 for definitions. $Y - Y_3$ is omitted since Y_3 contains only the ability variables.

Table 8 also presents the inequality pattern by ability level once other variables have been held constant. As we have consistently found in dealing with 1955, the self-employment variables cause the biggest reduction in the standard error in most ability fifths, with the SES and nonpecuniary tradeoffs contributions almost as large. In the 1969 data, holding self-employment constant substantially reduces the standard error and skewness.

At first glance, the inequality pattern seems confusing. For example, when comparing the education results, we find high school to be (about) the lowest on skewness and kurtosis in 1955 but the highest in 1969. A similar reversal occurs in the ability results.

A sorting uncertainty model can be used to explain these reversals and other results contained in Tables 6 and 7. The basis of this model is that it is difficult to measure in advance a person's capacity to perform in various jobs. Firms also do not use piece pay rates perhaps because of difficulty in measuring one person's productivity and of interdependencies within production lines or hierarchical structures. Firms, therefore, initially assign people to particular jobs on the basis of certain "objective" criteria, such as education, marital status, and military record, and certain "subjective" criteria such as performance at an interview.[94] In addition, appointment may be based on discrimination, as evidenced by race, gender, or parental pull.

Since firms know that the above criteria or signals are fallible, they continuously monitor performance on the job to base decisions on which to fire, to retain, and to promote. Average initial earnings may be fairly uniform when studied by objective criteria, because of morale problems associated with different pay for the same position and because at low-level jobs a person has little chance to use initiative or display productivity outside of a narrow range.[95] People with more potential capacity perform better, are promoted faster, and have a higher growth rate in earnings. However, promotions occur somewhat randomly, because the particular vacancies a person is qualified for occur irregularly, because a person's talent may not be recognized at once if he "blooms" late, and because family connections or nepotism results in faster promotions for equally qualified persons.[96]

Now, how does this model, with some other considerations, explain the previous findings? First, high school graduates have less objective credentials and probably less parental pull than the more educated, and they start at lower rungs in the career ladder. By 1955, the high school graduates have made some progress, but they have not yet made it to those positions, such as manager or successful business owner, where salaries are very high.[97] Thus in 1955, high school graduates have a smaller standard error, skewness, and kurtosis than those with some college and a bachelor's degree, because some in the latter two groups have received promotions to very responsible positions. By 1969, when the men are about forty-seven years old, firms have sorted out people by capacity; thus the talented high school graduate has received his promotions and is at or near his potential capacity at age forty-seven. However, the distribution of talent in the high school group is different from that in the other groups, with relatively few such talented people among the less educated. This difference arises for several reasons. For example, the more talented partly inherit their capacity from successful parents, who encourage them to get more education. Second, some sources of their capacity (such as drive and creativity) may lead to academic leanings and scholarships. Third, for most people, education may be a necessary ingredient in the formation of capacity.

Now, how do we explain the ability results? A plausible argument can be made that the mental ability measure we use is correlated with other types of cognitive and, to a lesser extent, noncognitive skills. Following the lines of the above argument, we would expect skewness and kurtosis for the less able to be relatively low in 1955 and high in 1969. Comparing the bottom and top fifths, we find this to be the case. However, Table 8 also indicates very large values of skewness and kurtosis in the second fifth in 1955 and an extremely large increase for the top fifth.

While we can construct a plausible explanation of the changes in inequality measure on the basis of a sorting uncertainty model, other theories are also consistent with the results. For example, Mincer (1970) has shown that in his theory

$$\frac{\sigma^2(YP)}{\sigma^2(Yj)} - 1 = \frac{r^2\sigma^2(C_T)}{\sigma^2(E_S)} + \frac{2r\rho\sigma(C_T)}{\sigma(E_S)}$$

where

$\sigma^2(YP)$ is the variance in peak earnings;
$\sigma^2(Yj)$ is the variance in earnings in the overtaking year;
r is the rate of return on postschool investment;
$\sigma^2(C_T)$ is the variance in the sum of postschool investment;
$\sigma^2(E_S)$ is the variance in initial postschool earnings capacity; and
ρ is the correlation between dollar investments in schooling and post-school investment.

We shall discuss the issue in more detail later, but it is approximately true that 1955 corresponds to the overtaking year (in any event, $\sigma^2(Yt)$ will increase with t if ρ is positive). Thus Mincer's interpretation of the faster growth in σ between 1955 and 1969 for high school graduates is that either ρ or $\sigma(C_T)/\sigma(E_S)$ is greater for these people.

Skewness in Mincer's model arises primarily from the correlations between the means and variances of earnings (within education cells). However, under the same assumptions as above we can express the nonstandardized skewness as

$$\frac{\sigma^3(YP)}{\sigma^3(Yj)} - 1 = 3\rho_1 r\frac{\sigma(C_T)}{\sigma(E_S)} + 3\rho_2 r^2\frac{\sigma^2(C_T)}{\sigma^2(E_S)} + \frac{r^3\sigma^3(C_T)}{\sigma^3(E_S)}$$

where ρ_1 and ρ_2 are the correlations between E_s^2 and C_T and E_S and C_T^2 respectively. Generally speaking, ρ_1 and ρ_2 will have the same sign as ρ; hence, $\sigma^3(YP)$ would certainly exceed $\sigma^3(Yj)$ if $\sigma^3(C_T)$ and $\sigma^3(E_S)$ have the same sign. The theory would also suggest that the faster the growth in variance within educational levels, the faster the growth in skewness, provided the last term is about the same at all education levels. This is borne out in our sample. The findings are not inconsistent with Mincer's model and indeed can not be made so since $\sigma^3(C_T)$ can vary by education level.

VI. INDIVIDUAL STABILITY IN THE EARNINGS DISTRIBUTION

While many of our findings are based on variables not previously used in studies of earnings, in principle the same phenomena could be examined for different cohorts in Census-type samples. The longitudinal data in our sample also permit us to extend our understanding of the dynamic evolution of the earnings distribution and to analyze the relationship of annual to lifetime earnings by examining the stability of an individual's position in the earnings distribution over time.

The empirical facts on stability and change over a long time span are very valuable in themselves, since the distribution of lifetime earnings is more important for many purposes than that of any one year's earnings. But equally important, these facts allow us to test, and thus have a chance to reject, certain earnings' distribution theories, as described below.

Individual Stability and Change in the Earnings Distribution

To examine individual stability in the distribution, we have calculated the "transition probability matrix" for the people who reported earnings in both 1955 and 1969. Table 9 indicates the percentage of people who ended up in any tenth of the 1969 earnings distribution from any given tenth in the 1955 distribution.[98] For example, of the people with the lowest 10 percent of the earnings in 1955, in 1969, 39 percent were still at the bottom, an additional 30 percent could be found between the 10 percent and 30 percent percentiles, and less than 9 percent have moved up into the top 30 percent of the distribution. As a simple (ordinal) measure of stability we can use the average percentile position, which has risen from 5 percent to 26 percent by 1969.

Percentile in 1955	Number in 1955	Percentile in 1969 (Percent of Row Sum)			
		Bottom 10%	10 < 20	20 < 30	30 < 40
Bottom 10%	412	38.7	19.1	10.6	6.5
10 < 20	484	15.2	21.7	16.5	11.4
20 < 30	368	16.4	20.4	14.4	10.6
30 < 40	358	8.9	12.6	16.2	18.1
40 < 50	516	5.4	13.0	13.2	14.8
50 < 60	586	4.9	10.0	7.3	13.9
60 < 70	353	3.1	7.1	3.7	6.8
70 < 80	565	3.0	2.5	3.5	6.1
80 < 90	500	1.2	3.2	2.8	4.0
Top 10%	462	1.7	1.5	0.8	1.3
Number, 1969	4,607	451	492	397	428

For contrast, consider the people in the top 10 percent in 1955. In 1969 44 percent were still in the top 10 percent, an additional 35 percent were in the next 20 percent of the distribution, and only 4 percent had fallen below the thirtieth percentile. The average percentile position had fallen from 95 percent to 80 percent in 1969.

In the other tenths in 1955, people tend to be close to their starting position with, for example, from 39 percent to 64 percent of the people falling within the same or neighboring tenths of the distribution. Not more than 30 percent of the people in the row lie above the seventieth percentile in 1969 until we reach the 60–70 percent interval in 1955, while at least 30 percent of the row fall below the thirtieth percentile in 1969 until we reach the 50–60 percent interval in 1955. The average percentile standing in 1969 for each tenth in 1955 rises continuously; but, on the average, people who were in the bottom 40 percent in 1955 have a higher percentile standing in 1969, while the reverse is true for those in the top 60 percent in 1955.[99]

As shown in Table 10, between 1955 and 1969 about 1 percent of the people suffered a decline in nominal earnings; and 15 percent had a growth of less than 75 percent.[100] For almost 50 percent of the sample, earnings grew between 75 percent and 175 percent while for 3 percent of the sample, earnings grew in excess of 500 percent. Using individual

——— Percentile in 1969 (Percent of Row Sum) ———						Average Percentile in 1969
40 < 50	50 < 60	60 < 70	70 < 80	80 < 90	90 < 100	
5.6	6.5	3.9	2.7	3.4	2.6	25.7
10.8	8.9	4.1	2.3	2.0	1.6	29.2
10.0	9.3	7.1	4.8	4.5	1.9	34.6
15.6	11.1	6.7	6.4	2.5	1.7	38.7
16.5	15.2	9.9	7.8	3.1	1.4	42.8
14.6	13.9	11.9	11.1	7.5	4.2	46.9
14.8	16.7	15.3	17.3	11.8	3.3	57.0
11.1	14.0	17.2	17.7	16.1	8.9	62.8
3.8	11.2	9.8	19.0	26.0	19.0	71.3
3.9	6.9	4.5	10.0	25.5	43.7	80.1
491	520	428	470	501	416	

NOTE: The cutoff points by tenths for 1955 are: $4,068, $4,788, $5,028, $5,388, $6,000, $6,468, $7,188, $8,028, $8,798. The cutoff points by tenths for 1969 are: $8,899, $10,000, $12,000, $15,000, $16,510, $19,000, $23,000, $30,000.

observations, the average percentage change is 175 percent and the average annual compound growth rate between 1955 and 1969 is 4.7 percent which, over 14 years, is equivalent to an increase of about 90 percent. (There is no reason to prefer one measure to the other.)

Of the people who were in the second tenth of earnings in 1955, 1 percent had a decrease in (nominal) earnings. Nearly 16 percent (the mode) had a gain between 125 percent and 150 percent, while 8.5 percent had a growth in excess of 300 percent. The average growth rate in earnings in this tenth is 176 percent.

Of the people in the eightieth to ninetieth percentile in 1955, nearly 5 percent had a decrease in their nominal earnings. The mode is in the 75 percent to 100 percent interval, and 14.5 percent had a growth rate in excess of 300 percent. The mean growth rate in the next to bottom and the next to top rows are identical; but there are more people in both tails of the distribution in the eightieth to ninetieth percentile, and the two distributions are significantly different at the 5 percent level (KS test).

In all but the two extreme rows, the mean growth in earnings only ranges from 151 percent to 176 percent and the compound rates range from .045 to .051. However, those whose earnings placed them in the top

TABLE 10 Distribution of Growth Rate in Earnings 1955 to 1969 by Earnings Percentile in 1955: Whole Sample[a]

Growth Rate (= 1969 Income Less 1955 Income/1955 Income)

1955 Percentile	<0	0 < .25	.25 < .50	.50 < .75	.75 < 1.00	1.00 < 1.25	1.25 < 1.50	1.50 < 1.75
0 < 10	.000	.007	.010	.046	.077	.116	.082	.100
10 < 20	.002	.010	.006	.056	.126	.152	.157	.118
20 < 30	.000	.005	.035	.070	.138	.177	.087	.130
30 < 40	.000	.000	.039	.064	.128	.131	.193	.103
40 < 50	.002	.006	.043	.094	.090	.173	.093	.125
50 < 60	.000	.000	.026	.099	.141	.178	.152	.105
60 < 70	.006	.020	.059	.057	.105	.150	.142	.096
70 < 80	.004	.030	.044	.087	.119	.143	.103	.127
80 < 90	.010	.048	.062	.068	.118	.114	.098	.092
90 < 100	.086	.043	.110	.087	.089	.087	.089	.100
Total	.011	.018	.045	.076	.110	.145	.115	.113

70 percent to 90 percent in 1955 have distributions which are significantly different (KS test, 5 percent level) with more people in both tails than those in the bottom 10 percent to 50 percent. In the bottom tenth, the mean change is 267 percent with a heavy concentration in the right-hand tail. In the top tenth, the mean change is only 143 percent; and there is a heavy concentration in the left-hand tail.

Distribution of Growth Rates by Education Level

Tables 11 through 14 show the growth rate distributions for each of four education levels. Since, in these tables, cutoff points for the tenths are those for the entire sample, we may compare the corresponding rows. In the tenth to twentieth percentile, about 68 percent, 57 percent, 45 percent, and 36 percent of people with high school, some college, a bachelor's degree, and at least some graduate training had earnings increases no greater than 150 percent. The average growth in earnings increases with education for people with the same earnings in 1955. Despite the relatively small sample sizes within each of these 1955 percentiles, the KS test rejects the hypothesis that the cumulative

								Mean
								Compound
						Mean	Annual
							Growth	Growth
1.75<	2.00<	2.25<	2.50<	2.75<	3.00<		Rate	Rate
2.00	2.25	2.50	2.75	3.00	5.00	>5.00		

──────── Growth Rate (= 1969 Income Less 1955 Income/1955 Income) ────────

1.75< 2.00	2.00< 2.25	2.25< 2.50	2.50< 2.75	2.75< 3.00	3.00< 5.00	>5.00	Mean Growth Rate	Mean Compound Annual Growth Rate
.107	.070	.075	.043	.036	.135	.092	.2675	.68
.101	.076	.037	.050	.023	.064	.021	.1759	.51
.065	.082	.030	.026	.041	.081	.030	.1806	.46
.123	.050	.039	.031	.036	.042	.017	.1671	.48
.075	.063	.053	.025	.020	.057	.019	.1550	.46
.089	.068	.037	.031	.010	.037	.026	.1715	.45
.105	.102	.023	.031	.031	.059	.018	.1610	.46
.087	.051	.053	.021	.028	.071	.032	.1702	.45
.082	.062	.032	.052	.024	.106	.030	.1760	.47
.065	.041	.039	.030	.024	.089	.022	.1425	.36
.089	.066	.044	.034	.027	.076	.030	.1757	.47

[a]Those with zero earnings in either year are excluded.

distribution of, say, the second and ninth rows are the same in each education level.

For any one educational level, the results are similar to those given for the whole sample in Table 2. That is, except for the top and bottom row, the mean percentage change is independent of the earnings percentile in 1955.[101] The people at the bottom in 1955 have the highest growth rate, while those at the top in 1955 have the lowest growth rate (except for the high school category). Within each education level, those with high earnings in 1955 tend to have distributions with a greater percentage of people in both tails than people with low incomes. Despite the relatively few observations within these tables, the differences in the distribution by row are significant. Thus, we can conclude that results in Table 10 do not occur because high school graduates are more concentrated in the lower percentiles in 1955.

In the appendix, we present several equations in which the dependent variable is $(Y69 - Y55)/Y55$. (The reader who wishes to examine the determinants of $Y69 - Y55$ can do so by subtracting the 1955 regression from the 1969 one.) The first equation contains all the variables used in the final equation for 1955 and 1969, while the second adds $Y55$.

TABLE 11 Growth Rate in Earnings 1955 to 1969 by Earnings Percentile in 1955: High School Graduates

Growth Rate (= 1969 Income Less 1955 Income/1955 Income)

1955 Percentile	<0	0 < .25	.25 < .50	.50 < .75	.75 < 1.00	1.00 < 1.25	1.25 < 1.50	1.50 < 1.75
0 < 10	.000	.006	.012	.093	.086	.154	.105	.117
10 < 20	.000	.012	.012	.093	.216	.234	.191	.100
20 < 30	.000	.000	.091	.091	.190	.223	.074	.140
30 < 40	.000	.000	.086	.140	.194	.172	.151	.065
40 < 50	.000	.005	.116	.152	.152	.223	.076	.112
50 < 60	.000	.000	.024	.167	.190	.286	.095	.143
60 < 70	.000	.016	.078	.109	.172	.234	.109	.016
70 < 80	.012	.049	.074	.210	.222	.136	.049	.049
80 < 90	.032	.063	.168	.131	.116	.074	.063	.074
90 < 100	.120	.040	.173	.067	.080	.067	.080	.120
Total	.012	.016	.080	.122	.159	.184	.103	.098

TABLE 12 Growth Rate in Earnings 1955 to 1969 by Earnings Percentile in 1955: Some College

Growth Rate (= 1969 Income Less 1955 Income/1955 Income)

1955 Percentile	<0	0 < .25	.25 < .50	.50 < .75	.75 < 1.00	1.00 < 1.25	1.25 < 1.50	1.50 < 1.75
0 < 10	.000	.000	.010	.040	.102	.163	.061	.112
10 < 20	.008	.000	.008	.076	.114	.152	.167	.106
20 < 30	.000	.009	.009	.072	.153	.198	.090	.108
30 < 40	.000	.000	.042	.073	.125	.188	.208	.104
40 < 50	.000	.009	.050	.161	.120	.190	.046	.143
50 < 60	.000	.000	.040	.140	.180	.100	.160	.100
60 < 70	.000	.045	.112	.067	.123	.202	.135	.045
70 < 80	.007	.067	.081	.101	.135	.121	.128	.095
80 < 90	.000	.066	.041	.082	.131	.139	.106	.082
90 < 100	.081	.060	.081	.126	.104	.096	.067	.067
Total	.011	.022	.049	.099	.126	.158	.108	.101

1.75< 2.00	2.00 < 2.25	2.25 < 2.50	2.50 < 2.75	2.75 < 3.00	3.00 < 5.00	>5.00	Mean Growth Rate	Mean Compound Annual Growth Rate
.130	.043	.062	.049	.025	.067	.049	1.875	.056
.068	.031	.006	.012	.019	.006	.000	1.246	.037
.033	.033	.017	.000	.025	.066	.017	1.559	.037
.075	.032	.011	.032	.043	.000	.000	1.234	.041
.049	.031	.031	.013	.005	.022	.013	1.260	.036
.000	.024	.024	.024	.024	.000	.000	1.238	.034
.078	.047	.031	.000	.031	.078	.000	1.377	.038
.062	.037	.012	.012	.000	.037	.037	1.354	.034
.032	.053	.000	.074	.021	.095	.000	1.307	.029
.053	.040	.067	.013	.027	.027	.027	1.199	.033
.063	.037	.027	.023	.020	.039	.016	1.386	.034

NOTE: Items in this table are fractions of row sum except the last two columns.

1.75 < 2.00	2.00 < 2.25	2.25 < 2.50	2.50 < 2.75	2.75 < 3.00	3.00 < 5.00	>5.00	Mean Growth Rate	Mean Compound Annual Growth Rate
.092	.071	.061	.030	.051	.133	.082	2.675	.069
.083	.076	.030	.045	.023	.076	.038	1.759	.051
.063	.108	.036	.036	.027	.072	.018	1.800	.049
.146	.031	.042	.010	.010	.000	.010	1.671	.045
.074	.065	.032	.037	.018	.051	.005	1.550	.042
.080	.060	.020	.000	.020	.080	.020	1.715	.040
.067	.067	.011	.022	.034	.034	.034	1.617	.043
.054	.034	.067	.014	.034	.054	.007	1.702	.037
.090	.032	.024	.041	.041	.090	.033	1.700	.041
.074	.059	.037	.022	.022	.089	.015	1.495	.031
.081	.061	.032	.029	.028	.067	.024	1.611	.043

NOTE: Items in this table are fractions of row sum except the last two columns.

TABLE 13   Growth Rate in Earnings 1955 to 1969 by Earnings Percentile in 1955: Bachelor's Degree

Growth Rate (= 1969 Income Less 1955 Income/1955 Income)

1955 Percentile	<0	0 < .25	.25 < .50	.50 < .75	.75 < 1.00	1.00 < 1.25	1.25 < 1.50	1.50 < 1.75
0 < 10	.000	.015	.015	.015	.105	.045	.060	.075
10 < 20	.000	.011	.000	.011	.066	.120	.099	.120
20 < 30	.000	.016	.000	.078	.094	.125	.063	.172
30 < 40	.000	.000	.000	.032	.138	.053	.213	.138
40 < 50	.004	.011	.011	.044	.063	.170	.159	.144
50 < 60	.000	.000	.016	.063	.143	.222	.111	.079
60 < 70	.008	.008	.031	.039	.086	.094	.180	.117
70 < 80	.000	.010	.019	.058	.082	.159	.087	.192
80 < 90	.011	.040	.038	.048	.136	.115	.107	.079
90 < 100	.072	.039	.112	.086	.065	.112	.112	.119
Total	.012	.017	.029	.050	.091	.126	.125	.130

TABLE 14   Growth Rate in Earnings 1955 to 1969 by Earnings Percentile in 1955: Graduate Training

Growth Rate (= 1969 Income Less 1955 Income/1955 Income)

1955 Percentile	<0	0 < .25	.25 < .50	.50 < .75	.75 < 1.00	1.00 < 1.25	1.25 < 1.50	1.50 < 1.75
0 < 10	.000	.012	.000	.000	.012	.047	.082	.071
10 < 20	.000	.020	.000	.010	.051	.051	.141	.162
20 < 30	.000	.000	.014	.028	.069	.111	.125	.111
30 < 40	.000	.000	.027	.000	.040	.107	.200	.107
40 < 50	.005	.000	.010	.055	.050	.155	.100	.130
50 < 60	.000	.000	.028	.028	.028	.083	.278	.111
60 < 70	.014	.014	.028	.028	.056	.111	.111	.194
70 < 80	.000	.008	.023	.039	.094	.148	.133	.109
80 < 90	.000	.028	.019	.009	.075	.123	.104	.142
90 < 100	.080	.030	.100	.050	.110	.080	.090	.100
Total	.010	.011	.024	.029	.061	.110	.123	.124

			Growth Rate (= 1969 Income Less 1955 Income/1955 Income)					
1.75< 2.00	2.00< 2.25	2.25< 2.50	2.50< 2.75	2.75< 3.00	3.00< 5.00	>5.00	Mean Growth Rate	Mean Compound Annual Growth Rate
.119	.105	.105	.015	.045	.164	.120	3.087	.075
.176	.099	.088	.066	.000	.179	.015	2.044	.059
.094	.063	.047	.047	.063	.109	.030	1.938	.057
.106	.096	.043	.043	.043	.074	.021	1.934	.053
.096	.077	.074	.022	.019	.067	.037	1.754	.053
.143	.079	.048	.048	.000	.016	.032	1.926	.050
.141	.164	.016	.023	.008	.078	.008	1.718	.048
.101	.043	.067	.029	.019	.082	.053	1.923	.053
.085	.073	.068	.040	.011	.102	.034	1.794	.049
.066	.033	.033	.026	.026	.105	.007	1.413	.037
.106	.078	.059	.033	.021	.089	.034	1.877	.050

NOTE: Items in this table are fractions of row sums except the last two columns.

			Growth Rate (= 1969 Income Less 1955 Income/1955 Income)					
1.75 < 2.00	2.00 < 2.25	2.25 < 2.50	2.50 < 2.75	2.75< 3.00	3.00 < 5.00	>5.00	Mean Growth Rate	Mean Compound Annual Growth Rate
.071	.094	.094	.071	.035	.247	.165	2.147	.095
.111	.131	.051	.101	.051	.080	.040	2.176	.063
.097	.139	.028	.042	.069	.097	.069	2.275	.053
.173	.040	.067	.040	.053	.120	.027	2.085	.060
.100	.095	.085	.035	.050	.110	.020	1.766	.057
.111	.111	.056	.056	.000	.056	.056	2.214	.055
.111	.083	.042	.083	.070	.042	.014	1.827	.054
.117	.094	.039	.023	.055	.094	.023	1.879	.050
.113	.094	.009	.066	.028	.142	.047	2.173	.055
.060	.030	.030	.060	.020	.110	.050	1.702	.044
.105	.090	.052	.054	.045	.113	.046	2.191	.057

NOTE: Items in this table are fractions of row sums except the last two columns.

We shall concentrate first on the second equation, which contains $Y55$ and which has an R^2 of .20. The inclusion of $Y55$ in our equation means that we have held constant all the other systematic determinants of Y and its percentage change, including luck and $K55 - I55$ where $K55$ is the stock of investment in on-the-job training and $I55$ is the investment in that year.[102] But the coefficients on the other variables in this equation represent the effect of each variable on the growth rate, net of the effects passed on through $Y55$.[103]

The higher a person's 1955 earnings are, the slower his growth rate rate will be. The coefficient of $-.09$ is highly significant with a t value of 19. As just explained, the coefficient on the earnings variable represents the effect of all the unmeasured variables. Results presented later suggest that one of the important unmeasured variables is luck. The on-the-job training variable, $K55 - I55$, may also be important though tests of the theory presented below tend to conflict with Mincer's theory.

Previous research based on cross-section data has shown that age earnings profiles tend to be steeper for the more educated. Using the same people at different points of time, we also find that the average growth rate increases continuously with education (except for some graduate), with most of the difference from high school graduates being statistically significant. The coefficients on the education variables are larger than most of the other coefficients although attending private elementary school is the single largest coefficient.

While the average growth rate increases monotonically with ability, none of these coefficients are significant at the 5 percent level. There are, however, several interesting variables which have significant and large effects. For example, those who are Jewish have a growth rate 21 percentage points above that of Catholics. Those who attended private elementary school have a growth rate 80 percent higher than those who did not. Also, mother-in-law's and father-in-law's education are both significant and positive.

Of the time spent on youth variables, sports and part-time jobs have significant positive effects, while chores have a significant negative effect. The nonpecuniary variables are significant with the exception of helping others and job security, which is significant at the 6 percent level. Those not interested in future financial prospects, nor in challenging work, have a slower growth rate, which is also true for those interested in independence in their work. The people who prefer to be salaried have a 10 percentage point slower growth rate.

The age variable has a negative coefficient implying a concave earnings function. The positive sign on the year of the first job also implies concavity but this coefficient is only significant at the 7 percent level.

Those who were self-employed in 1969 have a faster growth in earnings. Increased hours on the first job in 1969 also lead to a faster growth rate, but the opposite is true for hours on the second job.[104] Those who moved interregionally after 1955 have a faster growth rate, as do those who lived in bigger cities in 1969. Good health in 1969, as reflected in weeks lost from illness and weight, are associated with higher growth rates.

We have reestimated the equations, dropping the variables that pertain exclusively to 1969. The general results are unchanged.

The equations clearly indicate that there are important systematic elements in the distribution of growth rates from 1955 to 1969. Is there an underlying structure that explains which of the determinants of earnings in 1955 and 1969 are also significant in the growth-rate equations? In Mincer's theory, differential growth rates reflect differential investments in on-the-job training (OJT). Thus, the more educated, those whose in-laws have high education, those who attended private elementary school, those who do not want to be self-employed, those who do not want to be independent, those not interested in future financial success, and those who are Jewish, all invest more than the omitted categories. Mincer may be right, but one still wonders why these groups are different.

An alternative explanation is that because of uncertainty, people have to demonstrate their competence on the job, which determines how quickly they ascend their career ladders. There are different career ladders with different characteristics. Some careers are relatively safe, but as a consequence have both a relatively low ceiling on earnings and a narrow distribution of outcomes. Other careers have higher earnings ceilings but more risk. Because people are relatively risk averse, the latter careers have higher average earnings. The difference in earnings between ladders is greater for older persons because the sorting process takes place *sequentially* over time, and people only gradually reach the upper parts of the hierarchy.

This explanation, which can be applied easily to the risk-preference and other nonpecuniary variables, can also explain why the other variables are significant. For example, the in-law and private school variables can be interpreted as proxies for nepotism. In an uncertain world, a nepotistic system can function by a person's being given a secure job and then, only if he has the ability, being promoted (though his promotions may come faster for equal ability). Since there are pay scales within a firm, even the owner's son will only receive very high earnings if he holds an important job. We have argued earlier that the religious variable is associated with drive and hard work, but such effort may only pay off cumulatively. Finally, the education findings reflect the types of career ladders chosen by the more educated. Very few of our college graduates worked at any job but owner/manager, salesman, or professional. Their choice may have been based on opportunities or preferences, but in any event, these can be the careers within which sorting is important and ceiling earnings are high.[105]

Test of Predictions of Some Earnings Distribution Theories

We begin the discussion with the stochastic theories.[106] In these models initial earnings depend on an individual's capacity, but the change in earnings depends on luck. Let the earnings of the ith individual in year t be represented by Y_{it} and the random event by e_{it} which is assumed to be independent of Y_{it-1}. The stochastic theories can be written as

(1) $\qquad Y_{it} = Y_{it-1} + e_{it} = Y_{io} + \sum_{j=0}^{N} e_{it-j}$

(1a) $\qquad \ln Y_{it} = \ln Y_{it-1} + e_{it} = \ln Y_{io} + \sum_{j=0}^{N} e_{it-j}$

The variance of Y_t can be expressed as

(2) $\qquad \sigma^2_{Y_t} = \sigma^2_{Y_o} + \sum \sigma^2_{e_{t-j}} + 2\sum \sigma_{Y_o e_{t-j}} + 2\sum_{j>k} \sigma_{e_{t-j} e_{t-k}}$

There is a similar expression for $\sigma^2_{\ln Y}$.

An important case arises if the e's are serially independent. Then after a long enough passage of time, the distribution of Y_t will depend solely on the distribution of e_t, the last two terms in (2) will be zero, and σ^2_{YT} will increase each year by the addition of σ^2_{et}. Thus, this version of the stochastic theory predicts that the variance of earnings will increase continuously with age. Since the theories assume that e_t is distributed independently of Y_{it-1} and its systematic determinants, σ^2_e should be homoscedastic over the different education levels and other X's.

Some stochastic models assume that Y_{io} is determined by education, and so on, and then luck determines ΔY. Here the correlations of education, and so on, with Y should decline over time, since the variance of Y_t increases while that of Y_o is constant.[107] Moreover, a hypothesis of stochastic models is that e_{it} should be distributed independently of Y_{it-1} or Y_{io}.

How do these predictions compare with our findings? As shown in Tables 6, 7, and 8 the standard error of earnings and its log increased between 1955 and 1969 in the whole sample and in each of the education and ability groups. However, contrary to predictions of the model, the errors display heteroscedasticity in both years with respect to both education and mental ability.

The stochastic theories require that the difference or the percentage change in earnings be independent of $Y55$. But Table 10 indicates that the mean growth in earnings is different at the highest and lowest level of 1955 earnings.[108] The difference in mean growth rates might be attributable to transitory effects that do not become impounded into a person's earnings base, but such an explanation is not in accord with the model's Markovian assumptions. As is evident from the pattern of the percentage changes, and as has been confirmed by direct calculations, the *average difference* in earnings increases with the level of $Y55$.

Education, ability, family background, nonpecuniary preferences, and other characteristics yield an R^2 about 4 points higher in 1969 than in 1955, even when we exclude the information such as business assets which pertain directly to 1969. This is contrary to the model's prediction.

All in all, the particular version of the stochastic model that we are testing does not seem to fit the data well. Of course, other versions that make different assumptions about either the pattern of serial correlations or the relationship of the e's and the determinants of Y_o could be in accord with the facts. See, for example, Kalecki (1945). However, I have yet to see a version of the stochastic theory that can be made consistent with all the findings presented above, unless the sorting model described below is thought of as a stochastic model.

Investment in On-the-Job Training Models

Next, let us consider the investment in on-the-job training theory as presented by Mincer (1970). His model can be thought of in the following terms. Suppose skills learned on the job increase a person's marginal productivity to many employers. If an employee who receives general on-the-job training is legally free to accept any job offer at any time, after finishing his training he will be paid a wage equal to his new, higher marginal product (in a competitive market). Next, suppose occupation A gives no general training and will pay a person the same wage rate throughout his lifetime, but occupation B involves general training and has a rising age/earnings profile for an individual. A rational person would choose the occupation whose earnings stream has the larger present discounted value. But Mincer argues that with free entry into both occupations, the present value of the two earnings streams will be equalized. Since a person will receive a real wage equal to his marginal product after training, he must be paid less than his marginal product while being trained.

Mincer expresses his theory as

(3) $$Y_{it} = Y_i^* + r \sum_{j=0}^{t} [\lambda_{ij} Y_j] - \lambda_{it} Y_t$$

where Y^* (which depends on schooling, ability, and so forth) is the constant earnings of a person who never invests on the job, λ is the fraction of earnings invested or k_t/Y_t, r is the rate of return on investments in on-the-job training, and Y is observed earnings. Mincer assumes that investments are a monotonically decreasing function of age. The change in earnings, $Y_{t+1} - Y_t$, can be written as $rk_{t+1} - (k_{t+1} - k_t)$ which certainly will be positive if k decreases with age.

Mincer introduces several concepts to help analyze the path of earnings in 3. One concept is that there is some peak level of earnings, Y_p, at which $\lambda_{it} = 0$. Another important concept is the overtaking point, which is designated as the year in which $r \sum \lambda_{it} Y_t$ equals $\lambda_t Y_t$ or when $Y_t = Y^*$. Let us write $\sum \lambda_{it} Y_t$ as K_t and $\lambda_t Y_t$ as I_t.

At the peak earnings period, the variance in earnings will be

(4) $$\sigma_{Y_p}^2 = \sigma_{Y^*}^2 + r^2 \sigma_{K_t}^2 + 2r\rho_{Y^*K_p} \sigma_{Y^*} \sigma K_p$$

where ρ_{YK} is the correlation between Y and K. While at the overtaking point, which we designated as j

(5) $$\sigma_{Y_j}^2 = \sigma_{Y^*}^2$$

In equation 4, the variance over individuals in observed earnings depends on the variance of Y^*, the variance of investments in OJT and the correlation between Y^* and K. At the overtaking point, $rK_t - I_t$ and the variance in observed earnings equals the variance in Y^*. If r and ρ are nonnegative, Mincer's model indicates that the variance in earnings should increase from the overtaking to the peak year. Also, since individual variation in investment in OJT is not measured, the contribution of the measured variables to observed earnings should be greater in the overtaking year.[109]

The above conclusions are conditional on the sign of ρ. We can also derive other tests which also depend on the sign of ρ, or in which ρ does not enter. Suppose we rank individuals by earnings in the overtaking period (1955) and calculate mean earnings in both 1955 and 1969 for people within the bottom tenth, second tenth, . . . , top tenth *in 1955*. Then, using equation 3, we can calculate that the mean change in a cell is

(6) $$\bar{Y}_p - \bar{Y}_j = r\bar{K}_p$$

(if r is the same for all).

Now, if $\bar{K}_p$ and $\bar{Y}^*$ are not correlated, the expected value of $r\bar{K}$ should be the same for each cell. If, however, $\bar{K}_p$ is positively correlated with Y^*, the $r\bar{K}$ will increase with $\bar{Y}_j$. But the correlation of Y^* and $\bar{K}_p$ is the "between cell" estimate of ρ. The model, of course, could be expressed in terms of $\ln Y$ in which case (5) can be approximated by $(\bar{Y}_p - \bar{Y}_j)/\bar{Y}_j$.

It may be helpful to view this problem in another way. If the distribution of K_p is independent of Y^*, then, when examined at the overtaking point, Mincer's theory yields the same testable hypothesis on growth rates as the stochastic theory, expressed in equation 1a. Mincer's model, however, yields different predictions when growth rates are calculated from a year that is not the overtaking point. We can see this best if we specify the on-the-job training investment function. Mincer in his analysis often assumes that the individual's investment paths are exponential as in equation 7

(7) $\lambda_{it} = A_i e^{-b_i t}, 0 < A_i < 1, b_i > 0$

The implications of this investment equation, which are derived in Taubman (1975), will be summarized here. Mincer usually restricts b_i to be the same for all individuals while letting A_i vary. In this case, the length of the overtaking period is the same for all A_i although the actual overtaking year will vary for people of the same age because of differences in time spent in school and, perhaps, in military service. Mincer's model, therefore, predicts that those with the higher A_i will always have higher growth rates in earnings.

If we knew A_i for each person, we could test the theory directly. We can, of course, calculate the average earnings that a person with a given set of measurable skills would receive. But the difference between an individual's actual earnings and this average would also include the effects of other unmeasured skills, and so on.

Suppose, however, in a year prior to the overtaking period, we were to order people by observed earnings and then calculate average earnings within each of successive tenths in the distribution. For each individual $Y_i - \bar{Y}$ would be equal to $(rK_t - I_t) + Y^*$, where these last terms are calculated about their mean values. A person can fall into the lowest tenth of the distribution for a variety of reasons.[110] If one thinks of drawings from distributions of $(rK - I)$ and of Y^*, the average value of each of these variables must be negative in the lowest decile of observed earnings. Similar analysis indicates that the average of $rK - I$ will increase monotonically with average earnings. Note that no mention was made of any correlation between $(rK - I)$ and Y^*. Positive or negative correlation would affect the average levels of $(rK - I)$ and Y^* in each tenth, but would not affect the statements about the qualitative pattern of the change in the average as earnings increase.

Since grouping by average earnings separates people by average level of $(rK - I)$, it is possible to determine whether those who have been investing more in preovertaking years and for whom $(rK - I)$ is smaller, are the ones with the greater increase in earnings. Similarly, if b varies in equation 6, those who invest more will have a higher growth rate in earnings.

According to Mincer, the overtaking point occurs in no more than $1/r$ years of work experience or probably less than a decade. In 1955, in the NBER-TH sample, the length of time in the civilian post-World War II labor market is 8 to 10 years for most high school graduates, 7 to 9 years for most of those with some graduate work, and 5 to 8 years for those with one or more degrees.[111] As a first approximation, let us assume that everyone was at the overtaking point in 1955. It also appears that 1969 corresponds to the peak earnings period. (This conclusion is based on the age distribution of 45 to 52 and on comparisons between the 1969 and recalled 1968 earnings data.)

Earlier, we observed that Mincer's model predicts an increase in the variance in observed earnings from overtaking to peak period, for positive (and for small negative) values of ρ. The variance does increase in the whole sample and in every education and ability group for Y and for $\ln Y$. The model also predicts that the R^2 explained by the measured variable should decrease with age, which is contrary to our results, even excluding several important variables measured only in 1969.

Our results also provide additional information on ρ. In Mincer's theory, coefficients on all skills other than those produced by OJT would remain constant if OJT did not change, and the change in coefficients occurs only because of differentials in average investment in OJT. The $Y69-Y55$ coefficients can be obtained by subtracting the two comparable equations.[112] Nearly every variable that has a positive effect on $Y69$ or $Y55$ has a positive effect on the change in earnings; i.e., ρ would be positive for all of these variables. Similarly, the growth rate equations reveal a number of variables which have positive and significant effects on earnings, and which are positively related to the level of earnings.

The material on the distribution of growth rates reveals a different picture. The average growth rate in the whole sample or in the education subgroups indicates that ρ is zero over much of the range but negative if the highest and lowest values of $Y55$ are included. Negative values of ρ can be consistent with growth in the variance, but such a finding seems strange, given the above discussion of ρ from regression results, and, especially, since those tables do not hold constant the variables with a positive ρ.

Until now we have assumed that everyone was at the overtaking point in 1955. However, because the more educated have worked fewer years and because individuals follow different investment paths, this assumption is unlikely to hold for *all* individuals. Mincer often specifies in his investment function that bi is equal to $\bar{b}$ for all persons. For this investment function, the overtaking period is the same for people with the *same education* (who begin work in the same year). But the distribution of growth rates within education groups, Tables 11 through 14, exhibits the same pattern of results as above, even if we standardize for differences in age and time on the job. Thus, if on the average, we are at, or before, the overtaking point within each education group, ρ in the ln form would be negative or zero.

There is another possibility to consider. Suppose that contrary to Mincer, the b's differ; but on the average, people in all educational levels were at the overtaking point in 1955. At every education level, there will be a dispersion of b's about $\bar{b}$. Since earnings increase with education, on the average, people with high education but low earnings in 1955 must be investing more than people with less education and the same earnings. But those people with less education and high earnings in 1955 must be investing less than the more educated. Thus, at each level of 1955 earnings, the mean growth rate should increase with education as is found in Tables 11 through 14. But the same argument would suggest that *within an education class*, those with smaller earnings in 1955 must on the average have been investing more than those with larger earnings, and that the mean growth rates should be inversely related to $Y55$.[113] Yet in Tables 11 through 14 the mean growth rates are constant, except for the very top and bottom tenths, again suggesting negative or zero correlations.

It is possible that high school graduates are beyond the overtaking point, whereas those with one or more degrees have not yet reached the overtaking point. For those people not yet at the overtaking point, those investing more in 1955 should have the higher growth rate. Thus, the correlation between mean growth rates and 1955 earnings level should be positive for high school graduates and negative for college graduates. But once the top and bottom fifths are eliminated, there is no correlation at any education level in the average growth rates and a slight negative correlation at any education level in the compound growth rates.

The classification by observed percentiles in 1955 may be affecting the test of Mincer's theory since his formulation does not deny that an individual's earnings in a year may be affected by random events. Suppose such events are transitory so that, ignoring the job investments, $Y_t = \bar{Y} + e_t$. Then as in Friedman (1957), we would expect the top and bottom tenth of 1955 earnings to include a larger proportion of those with large positive and negative e's. But with transitory events uncorrelated over fourteen years, we would also expect those at the top in 1955, because of large positive e's, to have low growth rates, and so on. Replacing the observed fraction of people in the top tenth in the left-hand cell with the overall sample percentage, the average growth rate becomes about 1.8, while a comparable adjustment for the right-hand cell for the bottom tenth reduces its average growth rate to about 2.2. This implies a U-shaped pattern of average growth rates. However, if transitory events are found in varying amounts throughout the distribution, Friedman's analysis would suggest that the estimates of ρ would be biased towards zero or that the true ρ would be more negative.

The essence of Mincer's argument is that labor markets function well. There are several reasons why our data might cause us to reject the investment hypothesis, though Mincer's theory might be a partial explanation of earnings and the labor market. By 1955, the market might have adjusted for *expected* wage changes that were *not* realized. However, if forecasts are generally incorrect, it is difficult to consider how investment models can ever be verified with either cross-section or time-series samples; or more importantly, how such samples can be analyzed within the context of equilibrium investment models.

Second, Mincer's formulation only applies to general on-the-job training. We presented some evidence earlier that suggests that nongeneral training is important. No one has yet analyzed the implications of firm-specific training on earnings profiles although some arrangements must lead to rising profiles. However, we suspect that there is too much uncertainty and lack of information, and too many barriers to competition to permit markets to function well.

Sorting Uncertainty and Hierarchy Models

Suppose that employers are uncertain about a person's productivity, because performance depends on many skills, some of which are difficult to test for in advance. The firm could let a person fill any job and use a piecework system to pay him. But on most jobs, a piecework system is not used because of the difficulty in measuring an individual's output and because of the possibility of negative outputs associated with bad decisions. An alternative procedure is to learn by observing. In this model, firms initially place an individual in a job which is an entry position for one or more career paths. Then, firms make successive decisions to fire, retain, or promote, on the basis of both the observed and required competency in the particular position held.

Ross has recently analyzed such a model, in which firms, who use an expected discounted profit criteria, acquire information by sampling on initial and subsequent assignments. In his model, he assumes that an individual's skill level remains constant. But the solution of this model indicates that on the average, earnings will rise with time on the job, even though skills are not being created on the job.[114]

Without more information, it does not appear possible to specify the optimal assignment path. Instead, we shall postulate a partial adjustment model that is built up of several elements. The peak earnings a person can earn can be represented as

(8) $\quad Y^* = f(x)$

where x is a vector of inherited and acquired skills. Progress along a career path can be represented as

(9) $\quad Y_T^N = Y^* \dfrac{b}{T} t \text{ for } t < T, 0 > b$

Actual earnings in any year depend on random events and on performance versus normal performance

(10) $\quad Y_t = \alpha Y_T^N + (1-\alpha) Y_{t-1} + u_t, 0 < \alpha < 1$

If b is the same along all ladders, then the coefficients of the X's should change proportionately over time. However, there is every reason to believe that some career ladders are steeper than others or that b varies. Similarly, α can also vary by occupation.

While this model has certain similarities with the previous two, it yields some different predictions. Consider first the R^2 between Y and X. As in the stochastic models, if u_t are distributed independently, the variance of u will increase with t. To determine the change in R^2 as people age, we must examine the variance of the independent variables times their coefficient in comparison with the growth of the variance of

$$\sum_{j=0}^{t} \alpha^j u_{t-j}$$

Since in our empirical work, we generally do not include Y_{t-1}, the estimated coefficients on the X's will be those implied by equation 9. This equation can be written as Xd_t. In our equations the variance of the X's is a constant as the people age, but the coefficients, and thus their contribution to the variance of Xd_t, alter. It is possible, therefore, for the R^2 to increase or decrease as people age. As just noted, when the u's are independent, this model postulates a growth in the residual variance in Y. The model also indicates that σ_y^2 will grow as people age, as long as the d's have the same sign and increase with time.

Next let us consider the change in earnings as people age. From equation 10 we see that

(11) $dY_t/dt = \alpha b Y^*[1/(T-t)]^2 + (1-\alpha)dY_{t-1}/dt$

which for most purposes we can treat as $b[Y^*/(T-t)]$. As noted earlier, b probably varies by career ladder or occupation. In general, we would expect people who work in jobs such as manager and professionals to have the highest b. Because the x's help determine the occupation a person is in, we would expect that those x's which determine Y^* would influence b in the same direction.

Over a fourteen-year period $(1-\alpha)^j dY_{t-1}$ can be treated as close to zero except for large dY_{t-1}.[115] Thus, ignoring the last term in (9), dY_t should be positively related to Y^* and Y^N in 1955. It can be shown that the percentage change in Y should be independent of the 1955 value of Y. However, the larger dY_{t-1} terms, which cannot be ignored, will be more concentrated among those with the highest and lowest 1955 earnings. Since the model indicates that Y_t will grow faster the more Y^N exceeds Y_{t-1}, those with very low earnings would grow fastest over a fourteen-year period.

Alternatively, the model could be expressed in terms of ln Y in place of Y. The only major difference in the above analysis is that the percentage change of earnings from the equivalent of (9) would be dependent on b and could vary by education, and other factors.

None of these predictions are contradicted by the results given in previous chapters and used in the tests of the other theories. But since the theory is not tightly specified, especially in comparison with Mincer's, these tests are relatively weak. A more definitive test of this theory and Mincer's could be made if more years of earnings were available, since the dynamic implications vary for those. But such tests await more and better data.

VII. CONCLUSIONS AND QUESTIONS

Empirical Results

In our regressions, we have found a number of significant variables, many of which have never been examined before. Nearly all of these variables have the same sign in equations explaining earnings in widely separate years and also have what we consider to be consistent signs in equations explaining educational attainment, test scores, and assets.

In the earnings equations, we find that educational quantity and quality, mental ability, business assets, certain aspects of family background (discussed below), preferences towards risk and towards nonmonetary aspects of a job, locational information, hours of work, health, and work experience and age are significant determinants of earnings. Among this list of items are several, which, to my knowledge, have never been found significant in earnings equations, partly because they have never been studied. But the empirical results are in accord with economic and social science theory. For example, economists and others have long recognized that people can trade off earnings for nonpecuniary rewards; but previously information on what nonpecuniary rewards are traded off with earnings and the importance of such rewards were not available.

Our family background variables are much different from those in most other studies. For example, parents', or especially fathers', education and occupation are often used as the major index of SES. Although we started off using these variables, we found that they became insignificant, especially when business assets were held constant. This suggests to us that education and occupation act primarily as proxies for financial and business inheritance, perhaps tinged with nepotism, and not for home training. (Since parental education is associated with the educational attainment and test scores of respondents, we are only speaking of direct effects on earnings.)

While the traditional SES variables are not significant, we have found others that seem to be related to the types of family life and child-rearing processes that people have in mind when they talk of training and taste formation. For example, we find that Jews earn significantly more than, and Protestants significantly less than, Catholics (and the few atheists and agnostics). Other studies have found that Jews of this and surrounding generations have more drive and motivation for financial success. Others, in small samples, have found that some Catholic groups—such as German or French—do better than the average Protestant. Given the education cutoff, in our sample and the cohort involved, it seems likely that we have drawn Catholics from the above-average earnings group.

Another aspect of religious upbringing that affects earnings is frequency of attendance at religious (not parochial) school, with those attending most often earning the least, and those never attending earning the most. The ones who attended more than twice a week are probably certain subgroups of Catholics and more Orthodox Jews. This variable may help to distinguish those less interested in the material aspects of life.

The nonattendees are more difficult to explain although nonattendance in the 1920s or early 1930s may represent a very atypical family.

We also find that those who attend private elementary school and high school earn about $5,000 a year more in 1969. While there are a number of explanations for this result, the one that appeals to us is that these people come from very wealthy families who use pull to advance their sons.

We also find that those who spent their time differently on various activities while growing up earn different amounts. The explanations for these findings include indication of respondents' tastes and attitudes as well as certain types of family rearing. For example, we argued that respondents who remembered spending time on chores came from families that are interested in conformity and produce people who enter into bureaucracies and safe jobs.

The more educated earn more although the graduate coefficients are not always higher than the bachelor's coefficients.[116] The effects of education increase with age, and the age/earnings profiles are steeper for education than for most other variables. However, in this sample, which is stratified differently from the population and which has a truncated distribution of education and ability, the (average) range in earnings arising from education are dwarfed by the range arising from the combination of SES variables, or of tradeoffs for nonpecuniary rewards, and are only of the same magnitude as the range associated with mental ability.

Mental ability has a continuous direct effect on earnings (as well as indirect effects through educational attainment). The age/earnings profile slope upward with only a tendency for the more able to have significantly steeper profiles.

Risk premiums and nonpecuniary tradeoffs are also a greater percentage of earnings as people age. Given the crudeness of measures (zero, one dummies), it is not surprising that variables such as job security and a preference to be salaried, both of which are related to risk avoidance, have separate effects. Combining these different variables and others such as chores and SES proxies into categories, the impression conveyed is that those who take safe, unchallenging, and conventional jobs fall progressively further behind in earnings. That is, the high-paying jobs are at the top of certain career ladders and cannot be reached by people on other ladders.

Time on the job is important especially early in a person's career, but experience in some types of work is more transferable than in other types. However, people generally do best when they do not switch occupations. It also appears that hours worked is an important determinant of earnings (though the data are only available for 1969). However, there are a large group of men who moonlight because their earnings are low.

Business assets, as measured in 1969, are one of the most important variables in our equation, by itself explaining 10 percent of the variance in earnings. The coefficient is .12 in 1969, which is not extremely high on a before-tax basis.

We have also calculated the same equations within various occupations. Since many of the above variables are related to occupational choice, coefficients tend to be smaller and are significant less often. But we do find clear evidence that some skills and attributes are more important in some occupations than others. For example, intelligence is more important for the self-employed. Moreover, the self-employed, who have more control over their work environment, have larger coefficients on the various nonpecuniary measures.

We can explain more of the variance in earnings in 1969 than in 1955, even when we restrict our attention to variables equally accurate in both years (i.e., when we ignore business assets, and so on). Second, the truncated education variable has a partial R^2 of about .05, though some of the effects of education may be impounded in the nonpecuniary and other variables. The biggest partial R^2 in each year is attached to the 1969 business-asset variable. This result probably does not generalize to the population, since we have a high proportion of self-employed, and several with large amounts of business assets. The SES variables (including all the time-spent variables) and the nonpecuniary variables (including a preference to be salaried) each explain about 3 percent of the variance in the two years.

Most of the variables have little or no effect on our relative skewness and kurtosis measures. However, business assets, attending private elementary and high school, the nonpecuniary variables, and the time spent all reduce skewness and kurtosis sharply in 1969.

Methodology

Perhaps the simplest way to describe the methodological advances we have made is that many phenomena, skills, and attitudes that economists, sociologists, biographers, and others have hypothesized as being related to earnings, can be represented or captured by simple questions that can be included in mail surveys. It seems likely that more systematic efforts would allow us to incorporate many other skills, attitudes, and preferences, or to refine existing measures.

Relationship of Theory to Empirical Work

At the beginning of this paper, there was a discussion of various theories, hypotheses, and ideas that have been advanced to explain various features of the distribution of earnings. Our empirical results do shed some light on the validity and importance of many of these. For example, Friedman suggested that skewness arose because of differences in risk preferences. The variables which are related to risk preferences include the preference to be salaried item, the entered occupation because of job-security item, and the time spent on chores item.[117] In each year, we find that those wanting to avoid risk earn significantly less, and that the differential grows with age and is a greater percentage of average earnings (of high school graduates) as people age.

Avoidance of risk can be considered one type of nonpecuniary reward. We find that tastes toward other types of nonmonetary returns also show up as a reduction in earnings—presumably through the type of occupation in which a person chooses to work. We find that those who want interesting work, or to help others, or who are not interested in future financial success earn less, and that these differentials increase with age. But these variables do not contribute to skewness and kurtosis.

We also find evidence that those who are willing to work hard or have drive or concern for financial success receive greater earnings. These conclusions are based on the effects of religion, part-time job while growing up, and entrance in occupation because it (work) was challenging. These variables have larger effects over time.

These last several sets of results also suggest that models which emphasize that training and taste formation (on earnings-related aspects) occur in the family, religious institutions, and within peer groups have a large grain of truth to them. However, the lack of significance of parental education and occupation suggest that education is too crude an indicator of the differences in upbringing.

Many people have argued that a good portion of earnings differentials arise because of family pull. While we have no variable which is an unambiguous measure of nepotism, we have several which lend themselves to that interpretation. This, for example, is the simplest explanation of the in-laws education results, and of why the inclusion of business assets wipes out the father's education coefficients. Nepotism and/or inheritance of controlling interest in a business seem to be likely explanations of why the 22 people who went to private elementary and high school earn on average up to 50 percent more than people who went to public or parochial school.

Some theories such as the one that goes under the general title of human capital are more general in nature. To the extent that the human capital model means that people can improve their earnings capacity by expending time and resources on schooling or informal training, we find strong support in our analyses. The education coefficients are significant and large. Certain types of family environment and childhood activities are also significant. But the human capital model often is presented as one in which people invest rationally, i.e., invest to the point where the rate of return on the last dollar equals the cost of capital. This proposition is very difficult to test, because many of the returns to education are of a nonmonetary variety, have not been examined in this study, and are not easy to convert into monetary equivalents.

Mincer, in a brilliant series of pieces, has demonstrated that if all on-the-job training is general, if all returns to such training are in monetary terms, and if the market functions as a competitive market would, then the human capital model would predict at what age earnings profiles would rise with age for investors; and that the more investment, the steeper the profile. His model also predicts that the labor market adjusts occupational wages so that the present discounted value of lifetime earnings would be the same (to marginal choosers) in relevant occupations. In its most general form, this theory is a tautology with, for example, the amount invested in a year adjusting to make equations into identities. But with restrictions the theory can be tested. We have performed certain tests. We find evidence that is at variance with the Mincer model unless certain correlations are postulated. We also find some evidence that skills learned in one occupation may not be as transferable to another occupation as homegrown skills. This suggests that all training is not general.

We have also examined stochastic models. Since these can be represented as difference equations or Markov chains, it is also true that these models can be used to explain any age profile of variance of earnings as well as generating skewed models. But the most common stochastic models assume that errors are uncorrelated. We find several pieces of evidence at variance with this view. For example, the percentage change in earnings from 1955 to 1969 is not independent of 1955 earnings level, and the R^2 of the systematic elements increases over time although the stochastic model implies a decrease.

The sorting-uncertainty model, which we believe in, receives some support from these findings. In part, this support is in the growth in importance of the effects of education and ability, since these determine potential earnings. Additional support comes from the growth in the differentials associated with drive, risk aversion, willingness to work hard, and so forth, as summarized above. That is, these subjective measures are best displayed on the job. The differential of 1955 experience on 1969 earnings would be consistent with this model.

Problems and Extensions

Several different types of problem remain. First, our interpretation of many of the new variables that we have used may be wrong. It would be very useful for someone else, perhaps a psychologist or sociologist, to test, validate, and improve our measures of risk aversion, eleemosynary behavior, and so on. Second, we have spent very little time examining interactions which may be very important and whose omission may be biasing some of our results. Third, we have not related our various cross-section periods to macro time-series development. Fourth, the results are only generated within an atypical sample of a cohort, which in turn may be atypical because of war experience and because of the Depression, and because the economy and society are much altered now. Thus, many of our findings must be subject to replication in other groups before being accepted as not false. Finally, we have not made much progress on the nature/nurture or genetic/environment explanations of the distribution. Hopefully, progress on this issue will be forthcoming soon.

APPENDIX: REGRESSIONS

TABLE A-1 Earnings Equations for 1955 and 1969

Independent Variables	—1955 Earnings—		—1969 Earnings—	
	Coefficient	t-value	Coefficient	t-value
Education				
Some college	−.21	1.0*	−1.10	2.0
Bachelor's	.13	.6*	.16	.3*
Some graduate work	−.05	.2*	−.01	.0*
Master's	−.15	.5*	1.15	1.6*
Ph.D. + LL.B. + M.D.	.22	.5*	2.52	2.6
LL.B.	−.38	.8*	1.12	1.1
M.D.	3.49	5.3	4.13	2.9
Ability				
2nd fifth	.28	1.6	.54	1.4*
3rd fifth	.31	1.9*	.71	1.9*
4th fifth	.56	3.3	1.40	3.7
5th fifth (top)	.82	4.8	1.98	5.1
Biography				
2nd fifth ⎫ 3rd fifth ⎭	.21	1.5*	.56	1.7*

TABLE A-1 (continued)

Independent Variables	—1955 Earnings—		—1969 Earnings—	
	Coefficient	t-value	Coefficient	t-value
4th fifth 5th fifth	.66	4.5	.80	2.4
Father H.S.				
Father college				
Religion				
Jewish	2.00	7.7	4.13	7.0
Protestant	−.15	1.3*	−.93	3.6
Attended religious school				
often	−.51	2.0	−1.14	2.0
Attended religious school				
never	−.01	.1*	−.33	1.2*
Father-in-law H.S.+	.05	3.0	.10	2.7
Mother-in-law H.S.+	−.01	.1*	.57	2.1
Time spent on sports	.06	1.7*	.26	2.9
Time spent on chores	−.05	1.3*	−.27	2.8
Time spent on hobbies	.04	1.0*	−.15	1.7*
Time spent on part-time				
job	.07	2.1	.29	3.8
Never moved before H.S.	−.06	.5*	−.43	1.7*
Attended private high				
school	1.49	3.9	2.80	3.3
Attended private elementary				
school	.23	.3*	2.98	1.6*
Factors which influenced entering				
occupation				
Future financial prospects				
(No = 1)	−.54	4.2	−1.77	6.0
Independence (No = 1)	.27	2.1	1.19	4.1
Challenging work (No = 1)	−.76	5.0	−1.70	4.9
Help others (No = 1)	.48	3.8	.86	3.0
Job security (No = 1)	.48	4.0	1.41	5.2
Prefers to be salaried	−.37	2.9	−1.00	3.4
Other assets (own business,				
real estate), 1969	.03	11.5	.12	20.4
Self-employed businessman,				
1969	.72	4.4	1.09	2.9
Self-employed professional,				
1969	.45	1.7*	3.30	5.5
Teacher, pre-college	−.61	2.4	−1.86	3.1
Hours on main job, 1969			.07	4.7
Hours on second job, 1969	−.03	3.3	−.12	5.2

TABLE A-1 (concluded)

Independent Variables	—1955 Earnings—		—1969 Earnings—	
	Coefficient	t-value	Coefficient	t-value
Weeks lost from illness, 1969	−.03	1.6*	−.18	3.8
Mobile 1955 to 1969	.08	2.7	.33	5.1
Age	.08	3.3	−.11	1.9*
Year of first job	−.11	5.1	−.15	3.1
Current residence in town of 50,000 to 1,000,000	.46	3.6	1.09	3.7
Current residence in city in excess of 1,000,000	.92	5.1	2.89	7.0
College quality (Gourman rating)	.0014	3.5	.0044	4.3
Weight, 1969 (100's of lbs.)	6.68	2.7	24.73	4.4
Weight-squared, 1969	−1.69	2.5	−6.45	4.2
Dummy for nonresponse in 1972	1.23	3.9	2.54	3.6
Constant	−.97	.3*	−7.74	1.2*
R^2	.19		.32	
Standard error	3.43		7.80	
Degrees of freedom	4,548		4,547	

*Not significant at the 5 percent level.

TABLE A-2 Earnings Equations ($(Y69 - Y55)/Y55$)

Independent Variables	Equation 1		Equation 2		Equation 3		Equation 4	
	Coefficient	t-value	Coefficient	t-value	Coefficient	t-value	Coefficient	t-value
Education								
Some college	.040	.8*	.070	1.5*	.082	1.7*	.116	2.4
Bachelor's	.143	2.8	.214	4.4	.187	3.6	.245	4.8
Some graduate work	.122	1.5*	.173	2.2	.142	1.7*	.180	2.2
Master's	.362	4.8	.393	5.4	.332	4.6	.338	4.8
Ph.D. + LL.B. + M.D.	.487	4.0	.543	4.6	.491	4.1	.511	4.4
LL.B.	.191	1.3*	.176	1.2*	.464	3.1	.493	3.4
M.D.	.793	3.9	1.114	5.6	1.357	6.8	1.676	8.5
Ability								
2nd fifth	−.009	.2*	.016	.3*	.013	.2*	.038	.7*
3rd fifth	−.006	.1*	.024	.5*	−.003	.1*	.021	.4*
4th fifth	.013	.2*	.063	1.2*	.020	.4*	.061	1.1*
5th fifth (top)	.018	.3*	.098	1.8*	.036	.6*	.098	1.8*
Biography								
2nd fifth ⎤ 3rd fifth ⎦	.008	.2*	.039	.8*	.016	.3*	.039	.8*
4th fifth ⎤ 5th fifth ⎦	−.080	1.6*	−.035	.7*	−.063	1.3*	−.028	.6*
Religion								
Jewish	.037	.4*	.215	2.7	.203	2.4	.376	4.5*
Protestant	−.036	1.0*	−.049	1.4*	−.023	.6*	−.031	.8*
Attended religious school often	−.009	.1*	−.056	.7*	−.032	.4*	−.071	.9*
Attended religious school never	−.037	1.0*	−.042	1.2*	−.035	.9*	−.037	1.0*
Father-in-law H.S.+								
Mother-in-law H.S.+	.075	2.0	.077	2.1	.106	2.7	.113	2.9
Time spent on sports	.014	1.1*	.020	1.6*	.006	.5*	.009	.7*

TABLE A-2 (concluded)

Independent Variables	Equation 1 Coefficient	Equation 1 t-value	Equation 2 Coefficient	Equation 2 t-value	Equation 3 Coefficient	Equation 3 t-value	Equation 4 Coefficient	Equation 4 t-value
Time spent on chores	−.030	2.1	−.032	2.4	−.024	1.7*	−.027	2.0
Time spent on hobbies	−.010	.8*	−.006	.6*	−.016	1.3*	−.014	1.1*
Time spent on part-time job	.017	1.6*	.024	2.3	.016	1.5*	.021	1.9*
Never moved before H.S.	−.012	.3*	−.018	.5*	−.009	.2*	−.013	.4*
Attended private high school	.005	1.5*	−.001	.4*	.114	.9*	.629	2.4
Attended private elementary school	.720	2.9	.790	3.3	.622	2.3	.236	1.9*
Factors which influenced entering occupation								
Future financial prospects (No = 1)	−.137	3.3	−.188	4.7	−.203	4.8	−.261	6.3
Independence (No = 1)	.065	1.6*	.078	2.0	−.039	.9	−.049	1.2*
Challenging work (No = 1)	−.060	1.5*	−.084	2.1	−.052	1.2*	−.069	1.7*
Help others (No = 1)	.019	.5*	.052	1.4*	−.049	1.2*	.083	2.1
Job security (No = 1)	.021	.6*	.069	1.9*	.091	2.3	.139	3.6
Prefers to be salaried	−.066	1.6*	−.102	2.5	−.167	3.9	−.215	5.2
Other assets (own business, real estate), 1969	.005	1.5*	.013	4.4				
Self-employed businessman, 1969	.405	4.7	.443	5.4				
Self-employed professional, 1969	.080	1.5*	.146	2.8				
Teacher, pre-college, 1969	−.080	.9*	−.126	1.5*				
Hours on main job, 1969	.011	5.5	.010	5.2				
Hours on second job, 1969	−.007	2.0	−.010	3.1				
Weeks lost from illness, 1969	−.017	2.6	−.020	3.1	−.018	2.7	−.020	3.1
Mobile 1955 to 1969	.028	3.1	.036	4.1	.022	2.4	.026	2.9
Age	−.029	3.7	−.022	2.9	−.027	3.3	−.021	2.7
Year of first job	.021	3.0	.012	1.8*	.016	2.3	.009	1.3*

	(1)		(2)		(3)		(4)	
Current residence in town of 50,000 to 1,000,000	.060	1.4	.105	2.6				
Current residence in city in excess of 1,000,000	.211	3.6	.297	5.2				
College quality (Gourman rating)								
Weight, 1969 (100's of lbs.)	1.114	1.4*	1.684	2.2	1.083	1.3*	1.509	1.9*
Weight-squared, 1969	-.288	1.3*	-.430	2.0	-.271	1.2*	.376	1.7*
Dummy for nonresponse in 1972	.040	.4*	.156	1.6	-.055	.6*	-.009	.1*
Entered school age 7+	-.074	.8*	-.116	1.3*	-.077	.8*	-.108	1.2*
Y55			-.089	19.1			-.067	14.4
Constant	-.424	.5*	-.494	.6*	.344	.4*	.332	.4*
R^2	.135		.200		.084		.124	
Standard error	1.109		1.067		1.142		1.117	
Degrees of freedom	4,547		4,546		4,555		4,554	

*Not significant at the 5 percent level.

TABLE A-3 Variables Insignificant in 1969 and 1955 Earnings Equations

Mother's education
Father's education
Single, marital status
Father owner-manager
Father professional
Mother's work status
Had own room as child
High school health
Rank in military
Raised by grandparents
Raised on farm
Number of moves within neighborhood when growing up
Type of house grew up in
Time spent reading
Why entered present job:
  Salary or pay offered
  Personal contacts
  Provided a lot of free time
Retirement information
Military service after World War II
Length of service in military
Being the youngest and oldest child
Present health condition
Voting habits: frequency of participation in local, state, and national elections
Political self-concept: degree of conservativeness or liberalness
Opinion on extent of freedom of youth
Opinion on people's concern with financial security
Opinion on rate of racial integration in last 10 years
For the items listed below, how does your total work experience to date compare with
  what you expected when you first started?
  Requirement for independent judgment
  Responsibility
  Prospects for advancement
To what degree does success in your work depend on
  Your own performance
  Having the right connections
  Being able to get along with people
  Being lucky or unlucky
  Having a college diploma
  Working hard
Do you enjoy your work?
Based on your own personal experience, what do you think high schools and colleges
  should concentrate on?
  Basic skills

TABLE A-3 (concluded)

General knowledge
Career preparation
Activities
Social awareness

NOTES

1. For international comparisons see Lydall (1968). For the U.S., see Miller (1966).
2. See, for example, Mincer (1970).
3. Even this need not be true. For example, different types of skills may be more or less important depending on the types of machinery used.
4. Tinbergen (1959) has formulated this type of model and Reder has examined some features of such a model though he uses somewhat different terminology. Indeed, the usual general equilibrium models state that each individual is a separate factor of production because he has his own bundle of skills.
5. Suppose, for example, the only two occupations are manager and manual worker and that intelligence received such a high wage in managerial work that all people with an I.Q. above 110 are managers. Assume also that physical strength is of no importance as a manager, but that among manual workers strength increases capacity while I.Q. does not. Finally, assume that all those with I.Q.'s greater than 110 have above average strength (though the correlation is not perfect). Then, for people with I.Q.'s above 110, variations in strength would not affect earnings, while for those with lower I.Q.'s and less strength, only variations in strength would affect earnings. Thus, in this example, each skill is redundant in one occupation and only a portion of the distribution of each skill determines earnings. This analysis, of course, suggests that it may be necessary to examine earnings functions within occupations and that in the whole sample the effect of a skill may have upper and lower limits.
6. Indeed, for some possible skills, appropriate measures have not yet been designed. Perhaps the Terman sample (1959) contains the most information, but it is small and limited to people with I.Q.'s (as children) of 140 and over. The Project Talent (1964) and to a lesser extent the Little-Sewell (1958) samples have more skill information for the period when their respondents were in elementary and high school, but currently little in the way of earnings data, since the people graduated from high school no earlier than 1958.
7. As equation 1 is written, all skills have an independent, linear effect. This representation was chosen for simplicity. Interactions between skills should be not assumed away in empirical work, especially because Roy (1950) has demonstrated that if skills affect earnings multiplicatively, symmetric skill distributions yield asymmetric earnings distributions—an important feature of the observed distribution. See also Mandelbrot (1962).
8. There is one other special case to note. It is possible that only skill differences relative to the average matter, e.g., the brightest lawyer may receive twice as much per case as the average lawyer. If all lawyers received more training and increased their legal

skills X percent, none might receive more earnings. However, the effect on earnings of legal brightness between lawyers should be given by the coefficients in (1).

9. The genetic effect can be both direct and indirect. For example, a person's knowledge level can depend on innate ability and on educational attainment, which is partly determined by innate ability.

10. See for example Jinks and Fulker (1970), Burt (1971), Cavelli-Sforza (1971), or Mittler (1971).

11. See Kagan (1971) for the last. Some of the former are discussed in Sewell and Shah (1967).

12. See Crockett (1960).

13. For evidence on some noncognitive effects as well as the mechanism by which education causes these changes see Simon and Ellison (1973).

14. A problem with many of these measures is that they seem more related to cognitive development than to the other skills. However, certain information on type and size of college may be related to noncognitive changes.

15. Alternatively, he has also suggested that people are risk averse to small changes but are willing to gamble to achieve major gains.

16. There is no corresponding group of people with large losses because, as Lebergett (1959) points out, the inept (risk lover) generally cannot raise as much financial capital as the successful risk lover. Lebergett, in fact, presents some evidence that for the non-self-employed the earnings distribution is nearly symmetric—though, of course, this need not follow from the above model, since there are some risky salaried occupations such as that of stockbroker.

17. For example, reasoning from personal introspection, some economists have thus explained the low earnings (and rate of return on educational investment) for Ph.D.'s and theologians.

18. It is possible, however, that tastes or the parameters of the utility function are partly determined by family background or by education, in which case the extra earnings attributed to, say, education are inadequate as a measure of the total returns to education if tastes are also included in the equation. See, for example, McConnell in Clark et al. (1972).

19. Much of the descriptive material is drawn from Taubman and Wales (1974), Chapter 4; and from B. Wolfe's dissertation (1973).

20. Thorndike and Hagen (1959), pp. 8 and 9.

21. Taubman (1975).

22. It is important to note that because of their vocational emphasis, much care and attention was paid to assigning occupation codes. See their description on pp. 90–107.

23. The V.A. graciously provided new addresses at no charge. Additional updates were obtained by checking phone books of the city of the last known address.

24. Initially, we had felt that 2,500 responses would have qualified this survey as a success.

25. The NSF funds also enabled the NBER to extract more information from the TH questionnaire, including the details on the job and earnings history.

26. For the post-1969 questionnaires we have adopted the practice of including a "no response" dummy variable. Since this tends to be significant over time the more successful are continuing to respond more.

27. This is a much better level of education than among World War II veterans—even if we restrict ourselves to high school graduates. See Miller (1960).

28. The high percentage may also be due to the availability of V.A.-guaranteed loans, better financial position of parents and in-laws, or business competence.

29. However, several of the highest ranking black Air Force generals in 1972 were in the Air Cadet program in World War II.

30. The reader is reminded that TW rejected the hypothesis of a success bias over and above the response bias by education and ability level.

31. However, the range and variance only indicate the direct effect of a variable. There can also be indirect effects; for example, parental income can determine educational attainment.

32. Formally, if the true equation is $Y = X\alpha + Z\delta + u$, where u is a random variable, the expected value of the ordinary least-squares estimate of δ obtained when Z is omitted is: $E(a) = \delta + E(X^1X)^{-1}XZ\delta = \alpha + \beta\delta$. β is equal to the coefficient in $Z = X\beta$. The bias is $\beta\delta$ which is zero only if β or δ is zero.

33. See, e.g., Simon and Ellison (1973) or McConnell in Clark et al. (1972) for some evidence on the noncognitive developments.

34. These calculations assume that all post-high-school graduates attend a college of the average quality of people who had only had some college. The quantity effects are slightly larger when quality is omitted, but never by more than $200.

35. If self-employment variables were not included, the increases would be: 14 percent for some college; 28 percent for bachelor's; 80 percent for LL.B.; and 110 percent for M.D. These increases are less than those given in TW, primarily because of the introduction of self-employment variables, though the graduate level coefficients were much smaller before we introduced some variables related to nonpecuniary returns. Essentially, the same percentage increases are obtained from equations using the log of earnings. If we adopt Mincer's 1973 model, these percentage changes divided by the associated number of years of education beyond high school are an estimate of the rate of return from education which is less than 6 percent at all education levels.

36. When the self-employment information is omitted, the 1955 differentials are: some college 11 percent; bachelor's degree 14 percent; LL.B. 14 percent and M.D. 82 percent, which are very close to those given in TW.

37. However, the variable could mean that on some unmeasured aspect of ability, teachers are less able.

38. This is described in more detail in Chapter 4 in Taubman (1975). Because the index is scaled arbitrarily, we initially included it and its square in the equations. Since these two terms together are never significant and do not explain more of the variance of earnings than the linear term, we use only the linear term.

39. The introduction of the quality variable causes a 5 percent to 10 percent reduction in the coefficients of the Jewish, year of first job, attendance at private high school, and attendance at private elementary school variables, as well as a 10 percent increase in the precollege-teacher dummy in 1969 and smaller changes in 1955. The quality index may still be acting as a proxy for unmeasured attributes but we would hope that it in part measures the extra value added imparted by better schools.

40. No attempt was made here to reinvestigate the usefulness of the other factors. Since we convert the test score data into dummy variables for the different fifths of the factor score distribution, we are assuming that post-test-taking events (not otherwise measured) do not change the fifths of the ability distribution a person would belong to in each of the particular years studied.

41. Since people had to be in the top half of the Air Cadet General Test (ACGT) to be able to volunteer for the program, these fifths are more like tenths.

42. If this is true, equation is $Y = a$ (innate ability) $+ bX$, but we estimate $Y = a^*$ (innate ability $+ cX) + b^*X$, then our least-squares estimate of a^* and b^* are identical for those for a and $b - ac$.

43. The weights of this index are based on how well the items predicted success in pilot and navigator school. This is a wider list than that used in most previous studies, and some of the variables require justification as SES measures. Almost all of these variables are significant in both 1969 and 1955. Several of the variables have been used at one time or another by others; see, for example, Blau and Duncan (1967) and Sewell and Shah (1967).

44. The original items, which were collected by the military, are not extant though much information has been re-collected in 1969 and 1972.

45. This also suggests that the business asset variable reflects inheritances or nepotism rather than the cumulative effect of education, arising out of extra earnings.

46. In 1969 the respondents were asked to indicate their religious preference by checking one of Protestant, Catholic, Jewish, None, Other. It is possible that different answers would have been obtained if "the religion you were raised in" was asked. Compared to the U.S. white population, the NBER-TH had 1.7 percent more of both Jews and Others and 5 percent fewer Catholics. However, the differences from white males in the particular cohorts who were at least high school graduates would probably be smaller.

47. If self-employment and M.D. are not held constant, Jews earn even more. The asset variable is measured imperfectly, but it is difficult to attribute a difference of $4,000 a year to this.

48. In a study of college graduates of the first half of the century, Hunt (1963) also found similar qualitative results. Also using the same basic data source, Haveman and West (1952) found that being Jewish was the most important determinant of earnings of people who graduated from college in the first half of this century. Featherman (1971) also found Jews to earn more and some Catholics, such as French, to earn more than the average Protestants. Both the Hunt and Featherman studies hold constant education and mental ability as well as other variables.

49. For example, Eckland (1965) finds that for given test scores and social class, Jews go to higher quality institutions of learning. This would indicate either higher tastes for education, more motivation and drive, or lower costs relative to returns. He also finds that certain ethnic groups of Catholics do better than the average Protestants. Given the education cutoff in the Air Force program, it seems likely that our Catholics come largely from these successful ethnic groups.

50. We also cannot rule out the possibility that the Jews and other non-Protestants are a more select group of their respective populations. However, given the nature of the Air Force work they volunteered for, it might be argued that those who volunteered could include more people who wanted to gain revenge on Germany or quickly inflict destruction in large doses. However, the revenge motive would seem to suggest that Jews and, to a lesser extent, Catholics would be a more random (less select) group of their religious compatriots with respect to the characteristics that determine earnings.

51. 1 is for practically no time spent and 5 is for the most time spent.

52. If we are right about the type of families that these men came from, we would expect them to have a high rate of time preference, and less access to capital early in their lives; thus, we would find it hard to interpret the growth in earning over time as an investment theory, as in Mincer.

53. Related to this last viewpoint is the idea that people who play sports may be more able to make decisions quickly. If intellectualism is taken as evidence of the opposite personality, it is interesting that the Phi Beta Kappa's among top management earn substantially less than other people. See the Taubman-Wales (1974) appendix using the Lewellen data.

54. There are, however, several caveats that must be attached to this conclusion. First, father's occupation (and resulting income) has an indirect effect on earnings through the amount of schooling the respondent receives. Second, and more importantly, father being an owner is significant when the self-employment variables are not included. Third, in 1968 the father's occupation and education have a much greater impact on the range in family *income* than on earnings of the *head*. This suggests that income inequality is perpetuated through generations directly through financial inheritance (including business assets) and indirectly through educational attainment. The biography variable also includes some parental wealth indicators, though it is not clear what aspects of the variable determine earnings.

55. Indeed, when we include a crude measure of net worth in our equations, the private school variables become insignificant and much smaller. Since private schooling is both different from public schooling and more costly to the respondent's parents, it might be argued that these results are due to quality differentials. But if this argument is accepted, it is difficult to explain why in Taubman (1975) neither type of private school is significantly related to our ability measure, which contains some learned knowledge.

56. Dummy variables for father-in-law's occupation and spouse's education are not significant.

57. This only includes items in Table 3. Business assets and some other variables may be partly determined by SES.

58. The ones not significant had small coefficients in both years (though smaller in 1955), but we explain more of the earnings variance in 1969. Since $(X'X)$ is nearly the same in the two years, the variance of the coefficients relative to the size of the coefficients is smaller in 1969. Presumably, similar reasoning explains why some of the education coefficients are not significant in 1955.

59. It is also possible that age is a proxy for particular cohorts. While most people in the survey are within 7 years of one another, the youngest people did not begin work till after serving in the military, whereas many of the older people began work before World War II.

60. Also, we have not included those with zero earnings, which would include those (if any) retired or unemployed for mental or physical health reasons.

61. The ranking of occupations is about the same in all years; hence, if you are going to be a manager in 1969, you should choose to be one earlier if you have the option.

62. Earnings $= WH$. $\partial \text{Earnings}/\partial W = H(1+\sigma)$ where $\sigma = W\,\partial H/H\,\partial W$. While this is the usual way of viewing the problem, our equations relate Earnings to H. $\partial \text{Earnings}/\partial H = W(1+1/\sigma)$. With backward-bending supply curves, σ might be negative.

63. Part of this earnings increase represents the substitution of material goods for leisure. Unfortunately, the hours data, which were only collected in 1969, do not mesh perfectly with the earnings data, since the earnings in 1969 are those on main job only, while we have separate estimates for hours on first and second job. However, the 1968 earnings data, which include second job, give similar results, so that this caveat need not be important.

64. An additional question was asked in which "about the same" was replaced with "slightly favorable if you worked for yourself." This second question was never significant given the first, but the first question always yielded significant coefficients in the earnings equations of various years.

65. These examples all assume that risk preference is a trait which is exhibited in all activities. This assumption may be wrong. For example, some college professors may be risk lovers in the field of ideas but risk averters in other matters.

66. The factors examined were: salary offered, prospects of eventual financial success, chance to do interesting work, chance for independent work, chance for a lot of person-to-person contact, chance to help others, represented a challenge, job security, and provided a lot of free time. We did not examine type of training in school, type of training in military, personal contacts, or always liked that kind of work.

67. The denominator, as usual, is the earnings of the average non-self-employed high school graduate. If the current salary variable answer is included, the coefficient is 10 percent.

68. For those who want to try to replicate these findings in other studies, it is important to note that several of the variables, e.g., independence, and helping others, were not significant by themselves but became significant after the financial prospects variable was added to the equation.

69. For a few of these variables, the answers may represent an individual's recognition of his own limitations. For example, those who like to help others may not have the aggressiveness to be successful managers. In such a case, the variable represents skills that determine earnings.

70. It also includes nonresidential real estate and other nonspecified items. The variable is crude, since people were only asked to check one of eight categories including "don't have" and "over $80,000."

71. This interpretation, however, may be wrong for several reasons. Consider the results obtained from regressing a person's earnings which equal wage income plus returns from capital (assuming that education, etc., is held constant by sample design). That is, we regress $W + rk = cK$. The expected value of c would be equal to $E\Sigma(w + rK)(K)/\Sigma K^2 = r + \Sigma(wK/K^2)$. If wage income and business assets are not correlated (linearly) the coefficient on K will be an unbiased estimate of the returns from capital, but if people with more capital also have higher wage rates (education, etc., constant) then c is biased upwards as an estimate of r.

72. Also, the asset variable must be measured with error, since people only checked categories into which their assets fell, and because the data were taken from an item in which real estate holdings could be included with the business assets. Christensen (1970) has argued that because unincorporated businesses do not have to pay the corporate income tax, a 7 percent to 10 percent return is consistent with the 15 percent before-tax return made by corporations.

73. See Lydall (1968) or Kravis (1962) for surveys of other samples. Lebergett (1959) suggests that among males working full time who are not self-employed, the earnings distribution in 1959 approaches normality. For some purposes, however, the self-employed and unemployed should be included in the earnings distribution.

74. There is little direct evidence on the distribution of capacity. I.Q. scores, for example, are generally *scored* so as to be normally distributed.

75. For an excellent summary of all these models, see Mincer (1970).

76. See Atkinson (1970), Mincer (1970), Kravis (1962).

77. See Atkinson (1970).

78. The education and ability groups are those defined above.

79. We shall assume that the expected values of the first four moments can be estimated from the actual value. This need not be true. For example, if the distribution were Pareto, the expected value of the variance would be infinite though a number could be obtained from the data.

80. To insure comparability with the regression results, and to save on costs, the 1955 and 1969 statistics are based on the approximately 4,600 people who reported earnings in both years.

81. One skewed distribution that has been used to describe the earnings distribution is the log-normal. The skewness and kurtosis results for the log of earnings in Table 6 are not consistent with the null hypothesis that earnings in 1955 and 1969 are distributed in log-normal fashion. Given our earlier results on (nonintersecting) Lorenz curves and Atkinson's theorems, the coefficients of variation and the standard error, which are measures of inequality, must increase.

82. Careful analysis of nationwide random samples has generally resulted in the conclusion that the earnings do not follow the log-normal distribution for high levels of income, but probably because of the restricted distribution of education, mental ability, and age in our sample, the deviations from the log-normal case (on a chart not shown) are greater and occur over a wider range of earnings in this sample.

83. It is well known that such samples yield unbiased estimates of the a's. Thus we can use the equations we have developed to examine the effect of the various X's on earnings for the range of each X in the sample.

84. Since most of our variables are "zero, one" dummies, our coefficients are estimates of the mean in various cells. Provided our model specifications—including interaction and homoscedasticity—are correct, the residuals represent the distribution within various cells and can be used to study skewness and kurtosis.

85. For example, suppose that the variable being considered is a "zero, one" dummy variable, Z. The "ones" in the Z variable could all be located just so that eliminating the effect of Z would eliminate completely any (nonnormal) kurtosis in the earnings distribution. Since most of our variables have been transformed into dummy variables, the effects of, say, schooling depend on the distribution of people by education level and their coefficients.

86. See Kendall and Stuart (1961).

87. However, part of the effects of, say, education may be appearing in other coefficients whose variables are partially determined by education.

88. All the moments in Table 3 are calculated about the mean that applies to each row

89. The reduction in $\Sigma(u_i^3)$ is about 50 percent.

90. This increase is partly due to the distribution of people in each category, e.g., nearly rectangular over the education groups and in the ability and SES instances, and partly to the pattern of the coefficients.

91. We have already subtracted 3 which is the value if the distribution is normal. The unstandardized measure of kurtosis, Σu_i^4, would decline substantially, but even with the initial variance, the distribution would not be normal.

92. The major difference between the 1969 and 1955 results for the self-employment variables may well be due to the measurement problem, i.e., some in the right-hand tail in 1955 are no longer self-employed in 1969, while some with large business holdings in 1969 were not yet self-employed.

93. There are from 950 to 1,330 people in each cell.

94. The criteria used may vary depending on supply of the "best" groups relative to total demand.

95. There can still be a wide variance within, say, education groups, because initial position obtained may depend on nepotism, being at the right place at the right time, or because of the importance of subjective criteria.

96. Wise (1972) has examined the effects of such a system on the variance of earnings, using a Markov model.

97. Pay does not increase linearly with position. See Lydall (1968). For some specific evidence on corporate executives see Taubman-Wales (1974), Chapter 8, Appendix L.

98. There are not exactly 10 percent of the sample in each row or column for two reasons. First the dividing points were found for all respondents with nonzero earnings in the sample, while some individuals were not included in this table, primarily because they did not report earnings in both years. Secondly, in a few instances, a large number of people reported earnings equal to the dividing point. While we could randomly allocate people to each adjoining class to fill it, it was simpler and not misleading to place people in only one class.

99. Some of this difference may reflect attenuation, since those in the bottom tenth cannot fall but can rise in 1969, etc. In all but one comparison, the Kolmogorov-Smirnov (KS) test would reject the hypothesis that each row is distributed the same as its adjacent rows.

100. In this section we use nominal earnings rather than the constant dollar ones used earlier. This change is made because the determination of the cutoff points was done, early on, in current dollars. Deflation would not change the pattern or conclusions.

101. There is, however, a tendency in each of the tables for the average compound growth rate to decrease with 1955 earnings, partly because of the wider variance in growth rates at the higher 1955 percentiles.

102. We have expressed the on-the-job training variable in this way to be in accord with Mincer's model, as explained below.

103. It can be demonstrated that if we compare the estimates of $Y = Xd + Ze$ and $Y = Xf + (Z + Xb)g$ that our estimates of g and e would be identical, while the estimate of f would equal that of $d - bg$.

104. This may be because the 1969 earnings are only for the main job, while the 1955 earnings may include all jobs. However, this variable seems to represent those people with low wage rates who work hard. Thus it may represent some of the same forces in 1955.

105. Even if this alternative explanation is accepted, Mincer's theory may be correct in a formal sense. Lifetime earnings within career ladders can be adjusted so that they are the same net of risk premiums and nonpecuniary rewards. But even here, the increase in earnings need not be due to on-the-job training but could solely reflect the firm's learning by observation, although a combination of the two learning mechanisms seems more likely.

106. See Mincer (1970) for an interesting survey and analysis of these theories. The original work in this area is due to Aitchison and Brown (1957), Champernowne (1953), Rutherford (1955), and Mandelbrot (1962). Various assumptions about the distribution of the e's and about the validity of equations (1) or (1a) can lead to a normal, log-normal, Pareto, or other distributions.

107. The stochastic-processes theories also provide no explanation of why age earnings profiles slope upward or why the steepness of the profiles varies with education.

108. Those with high earnings in 1955 also have distributions with fatter tails for which the theory offers no explanation.

109. Unless the individual variation in OJT is perfectly correlated with some measured variables.

110. Y^* may be very negative and $(rK_t - I_t)$ not a large enough positive number to offset Y^*. Second, both terms may be moderately negative; and third, $rK_t - I_t$ may be a large negative and Y^* not large enough positive to offset it.

111. About half of the high school graduates and one-third of the some-college group began work before 1942.

112. However, since 10 percent of the people received more education after 1955, the education variables are a bit different.

113. This tends to happen in the compound growth rates but the differences are not significant.

114. Of course, a person may exercise only certain skills when he reaches particular rungs on the ladder. But in this model the person always had the skill, and it was not created on the job.
115. For example, if $\alpha = .1$, $(1 - \alpha)^{14}$ is less than .2.
116. The inclusion of various nonpecuniary and attitude variables generally raises the coefficients on graduate education.
117. Our argument is that the people came from homes that bred conformity.

REFERENCES

Aitchison, J., and Brown, J. A. *The Lognormal Distribution.* Boston: Cambridge University Press, 1957.

Arrow, K., and Lind, R. "Uncertainty and Evaluation of Public Investment Decisions." *American Economic Review* 60 (June 1970): 364–378.

Atkinson, A. B. "On the Measurement of Inequality." *Journal of Economic Theory* 2 (Sept. 1970): 244–263.

Becker, G. *Human Capital.* New York: Columbia University Press, 1964.

———. "Human Capital and the Personal Distribution of Income: An Analytical Approach." Woytinsky Lecture No. 1, University of Michigan, Ann Arbor, 1967.

Blau, P., and Duncan, O. D. *The American Occupational Structure.* New York: John Wiley & Sons, 1967.

Bloom, B. S. *Stability and Change in Human Characteristics.* New York: John Wiley & Sons, 1964.

Burt, C. "Quantitative Genetics in Psychology." *British Journal of Mathematical and Statistical Psychology* 24 (May 1971): 1–21.

Cavalli-Sforza, L. L., and Bodmer, W. F. *The Genetics of Human Population.* San Francisco: W. H. Freeman & Co., 1971.

Champernowe, D. G. "A Model of Income Distribution." *Economic Journal* 63 (June 1953): 318–351.

Christensen, L. "Tax Policy and Investment Expenditures in a Model of General Equilibrium." *American Economic Review* 60 (May 1970): 18–22.

Clark, B., et al. *Students and Colleges: Interaction and Change.* Center for Research and Development in Higher Education, University of California at Berkeley, 1972.

Crockett, J. "Technical Note." In I. Friend and R. Jones, eds., *Consumption and Savings,* Vol. 2. Philadelphia: University of Pennsylvania Press, 1960.

Eckland, B. "Academic Ability, Higher Education and Occupational Mobility." *American Sociological Review* 30 (Oct. 1965): 735–746.

Featherman, D. "The Socioeconomic Achievement of White Religo-Ethnic Subgroups: Social and Psychological Explanations." *American Sociological Review* 36 (Apr. 1971): 207–222.

Friedman, M. *A Theory of the Consumption Function.* Princeton: Princeton University Press, 1957.

———. "Choice, Chance and the Personal Distribution of Income." *Journal of Political Economy* 61 (Aug. 1953): 277–290.

Griliches, Z., and Mason, W. "Education, Income and Ability." *Journal of Political Economy* 80 (May-June 1972): S74–S103.

Havemann, E., and West, P. *They Went to College: The College Graduate in America Today.* New York: Harcourt, Brace, 1952.

Hunt, S. J. "Income Determinants for College Graduates and the Return to Educational Investment." *Yale Economic Essays* 3 (Fall 1963): 305–357.

Jinks, J. L., and Fulker, D. W. "Comparison of the Biometrical, Genetical, Mava and Classical Approaches to the Analysis of Human Behavior." *Psychological Bulletin* 73 (May 1970): 311–349.

Kagan, J., and Tulkin, S. "Social Class Differences in Child Rearing during the First Year." In H. R. Schaffer, ed., *The Origins of Human Social Relations.* New York: Academic Press, 1971.

Kalecki, M. "On the Gibrat Distribution." *Econometrica* 13 (Apr. 1945): 161–170.

Kendall, M. G., and Stuart, A. *The Advanced Theory of Statistics.* London: Griffin Press, 1961.

Kohen, A., Parnes, H., and Shea, J. "Income Instability Among Young and Middle-Aged Men." In James D. Smith, ed., *The Personal Distribution of Income and Wealth.* New York: NBER, 1975.

Kravis, I. "Relative Income Shares in Fact and Theory." *American Economic Review* 49 (Dec. 1959): 917–949.

————. *The Structure of Income: Some Quantitative Essays.* Philadelphia: University of Pennsylvania Press, 1962.

Lebergott, S. "The Shape of the Income Distribution." *American Economic Review* 49 (June 1959): 328–347.

Little, J. *A State-Wide Inquiry into Decisions of Youth About Education beyond High School.* Madison: University of Wisconsin Press, 1958.

Lydall, H. *The Structure of Earnings.* Oxford: Clarendon Press, 1968.

Mandelbrot, B. "Paretian Distributions and Income Maximization." *Quarterly Journal of Economics* 76 (Feb. 1962): 57–85.

Merton, R. *Social Theory and Social Structure.* Glencoe, Ill.: Free Press, 1949.

Miller, H. *Income Distribution in the United States, 1960.* Bureau of the Census Monograph. Washington, D.C., 1966.

————. "Annual and Lifetime Income in Relation to Education: 1939 to 1959." *American Economic Review* 50 (Dec. 1960): 962–986.

Mincer, J. "The Distribution of Labor Incomes: A Survey with Special References to the Human Capital Approach." *Journal of Economic Literature* 3 (Mar. 1970): 1–26.

————. *Schooling, Experience and Earnings.* New York: NBER, 1974.

Mittler, P. *The Study of Twins.* Middlesex, England: Penguin Books, 1971.

Project Talent. *The American High School Student.* Comparative Research Project No. 635, University of Pittsburgh, 1964.

Reder, M. "A Partial Survey of the Theory of Income Size Distribution." In L. Soltow, ed., *Six Papers on the Size Distribution of Wealth and Income.* New York, NBER, 1969.

Roy, A. D. "The Distribution of Earnings and of Individual Output." *Economic Journal* 60 (Sept. 1950): 489–505.

Rutherford, R. S. G. "Income Distribution: A New Model." *Econometrica* 23 (July 1955): 277–294.

Sewell, W. H., and Shah, V. P. "Socioeconomic Status, Intelligence, and the Attainment of Higher Education." *Sociology of Education* 40 (Winter 1967): 1–23.

Simon, B., and Ellison, A. "Does College Make a Person Healthy and Wise?" In L. Solmon and P. Taubman, eds., *Does College Matter?* New York: Academic Press, 1973.

Solmon, L. "The Definition and Impact of College Quality." NBER Working Paper No. 7, 1973.

Solmon, L., and Wachtel, P. "The Effects on Income of Type of College Attended." *Sociology of Education* 48 (Winter 1974): 75–90.

Spence, M. "Market Signalling." Discussion Paper No. 4, Public Policy Program, Kennedy School of Government, Harvard University, 1972.

Taubman, P. J. *Sources of Inequality of Earnings.* Amsterdam: North-Holland, 1975.

Taubman, P. J., and Wales, T. *Higher Education and Earnings: College as an Investment and a Screening Device.* New York: McGraw-Hill for the Carnegie Commission on Higher Education and the National Bureau of Economic Research, 1974.

Terman, L., and Oden, M. *The Gifted Group at Mid-Life: Thirty-Five Years' Follow-Up of the Superior Child.* Genetic Studies of Genius, Vol. 5. Stanford: Stanford University Press, 1959.

Thorndike, R., and Hagen, E. *Ten Thousand Careers.* New York: John Wiley & Sons, 1959.

Tinbergen, J. "On the Theory of Income Distribution." In *Selected Papers.* Amsterdam: North-Holland, 1959.

Wales, T. "The Effect of College Quality on Earnings: Some Empirical Results." *Journal of Human Resources* 8 (Summer 1973): 306–317.

Wise, D. "Academic Achievement and Job Performance: Earnings and Promotions." Ph.D. dissertation, University of California at Berkeley, 1972.

Wolfe, B. "A Socioeconomic Analysis of Family Building Behavior." Ph.D. diss., University of Pennsylvania, 1973.

12 | COMMENTS

James Morgan
University of Michigan

In an era of burgeoning interest in microeconomic data and analysis, and an exploding supply of data, the NBER-Thorndike data set clearly has an important place. It starts, of course, with a selected group who: (a) applied during 1943 for an Army Air Force pilot, bombardier, and navigator training program, (b) passed a screening test, (c) took a battery of tests after preliminary acceptance, and replied to a mail questionnaire in 1955.[1] And the 1969 follow-up further selected those: (a) with good addresses, and who (b) were willing to return a much more comprehensive questionnaire (5,100 of them). Still smaller subsets provided further information in 1971 and 1972 (3,000, 4,474). If we described them as brighter, physically tougher, risk taking, probably more successful than average, and still alive and cooperative, we should not be far off.

Second, we need to keep in mind that things are measured at different points in time. Taubman carefully points this out during the paper, but one must always worry about the extent to which reports in 1972 about why one chose an occupation twenty years earlier may be affected by how successful one was in that occupation.

The analysis is really four analyses, one of earnings levels in 1955 and 1969, one of the distribution (inequality, variance, skewness, and kurtosis), one of the trends between 1955 and 1969 in individual incomes, and one of the possibility of testing of certain theories about reasons for inequality. It is not easy to summarize all this.

EARNINGS LEVELS

First, earnings levels: With such a rich body of data, and with no single theory to serve as guide (no theory in some areas, and competing theories in others), the author is justified in doing some ransacking. He does it by a sequence of regressions, eliminating things that do not seem to matter, even in multiple regression analyses simultaneously with the obvious other variables, as, for example, education.

What mattered? Education of course, and in a nonmonotonic way—as we have usually found in out analyses. *Finishing* something like high school or college is what matters. (Perhaps credential effects are more important than we admit?)

Occupation matters, and reduces the apparent importance of education when it is introduced. The quality of the college matters. And a mental ability test matters, even in the regression with education, and without any apparent interaction with educaton. Family background matters, but it seems to be more a matter of wealth than father's education. The Jews, and to a lesser degree Catholics, do better, even controlling for education (including a dummy variable for M.D. degrees). And some reports on how time was spent when growing up seem to matter, part-time jobs and sports positively, hobbies and chores negatively. Going to a private high school pays off, as do the education of father-in-law and mother-in-law, a result interpreted as nepotism. (I have another interpretation.) Among the things that did not matter were birth order, growing up on a farm, region, and so on.

Business assets have a powerful effect on the respondents "earnings," but may only reflect the difficulty in separating labor earnings from a return on capital in one's own business. A larger proportion than average of these people were self-employed.

And of course, age and work hours affect earnings.

Interesting comparisons and reassuring confirmations come from doing this analysis for both 1955 and 1969, even though some of the variables were only measured in 1969, and a few only later in 1972 (reasons for occupational selection). Such confirmation is at least a partial substitute for searching half the data and assessing a final model on the other half.

Finally, some attitudes toward risk and nonmonetary aspects of a job, (measured in 1972 by asking about reasons for choosing an occupation much earlier) were related to earnings.

The results are presented in the form of percentage differences from some "standard" group, with *t* tests.

COMMENTS ON THE ANALYSIS OF EARNINGS

I have no objections to ransacking, and do a lot of it myself. I am concerned, however, with the use of a single-stage linear model in this situation. It seems likely, and some theories even call for it, that the factors affecting earnings are not additive. (The dummy variable regressions take care of the nonlinearity of the relationships but not of interaction effects.) Some interaction checks were made, mostly for levels of ability, and by rerunning regressions for some occupation groups.

More important, we do not have here a single-stage causal path, but something calling for a more systematic attention to the possible causal paths.[2] The inclusion of occupation and education and I.Q. in the same regression (which we all tend to do) can be taken as a simple example. If education is an essential prior requirement for some occupations, and there is little later formal education, then our analysis should not assess their influence simultaneously, but attempt to answer one of two questions: Is there anything about occupational choice that explains earnings over and above its role as the channel through which education works? (For this, we need the partial correlation of occupation with earnings.) Is there anything about education that affects earnings over and above what could be explained by occupation? (For this, we need the partial correlation of education with earnings.) And since both have nonlinear effects and/or no neat metric, assessing marginal contributions really requires rerunning whole sets of dummy variable regressions.

The sociologists have recently leapfrogged over most economists in the development of more sophisticated procedures for analyzing data, borrowing from Sewall Wright, a geneticist, and his "path analysis."[3] If we were to analyze the present problem in their terms, we might have a diagram like Figure 1. Not only does such a diagram reveal problems like the dangers of simultaneous use of sequential explanatory forces, but it also alerts us to such other possible difficulties as: (a) the possibility that the attitudes (reasons for occupational selection) reported in 1972 might have been the result of success rather than its

FIGURE 1   Paths of Influence Leading to Earnings

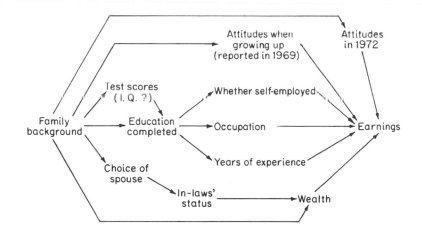

NOTE: Exogenous forces affect each of the variables, and are customarily indicated by arrows coming to them from empty space. I have left them off for simplicity. The system is recursive—no feedback arrows, though some could be justified.

cause or may work *through* other things; (b) the possibility that what appears to be an effect of well-educated in-laws may reflect mate selection and the individual's own background and ambition, rather than nepotism.

Even path analysis makes restrictive assumptions, the most powerful, of course, being that of recursivity—no feedback loops to demand structural equation models. And most path analysis has to assume measurability and linearity, or at least some uniform arbitrary scaling of categorical variables. It is not the statistics but the attention to modeling the world that is important.

The additivity assumption is, however, also a problem. And spelling out the possible effects of combined extremes on whole sets of predictors is probably an exaggeration. Indeed, it is testably so. One should look at the cases which combine such extremes and examine their residuals. I submit that they would prove nonadditivity—by being mostly less extreme than the additive model predicts.

I am particularly concerned with the use and interpretation of 1972 reports on reasons for occupational selection to explain 1955 and 1969 incomes. It is quite possible that attitudes are far more the result of economic experience than a cause of it. We're looking at our own panel data now to check this.

Finally, while there are various caveats about the meaning of both occupation and education, let me reinforce them. What does an occupational title represent? It can represent salary, responsibility, education required, training, supervision of others, whether supervised and by how many levels, skills, clean or dirty work (white collar), size of organization, type of industry (farmer), prestige, whether you serve others personally, whether on annual salary, amount and kind of capital equipment used, entrepreneurial activities, work for a government, and in the words of Eliot Jacques, how often you are evaluated by others.

If it shrewdly incorporates many of these, it should, of course, relate well to earnings. We find it difficult to keep coders from looking at earnings when they categorize occupations! Sociologists' occupation scales are *based on* correlations with earnings and education, so if we use those codes we are likely to reproduce their methods, just as analysis of quarterly time series may rediscover the seasonal adjustment.

And education has problems of spurious correlation with things other than investment in human capital. It can represent self-selection by perseverance, willingness to hew to the line, ambition, or selection by others by obedience, memory, adulation, intelligence, or acquired knowledge, or even acquired skills (physical, cognitive, psychological, or affective). It can represent simple correlation with parental background, inheritance, standards, or actual help, or the friends met in school and later help from them. It can even mean credentials which are substantively meaningless but open a lot of doors. In other words, attributing earnings to education is probably always a somewhat fruitless and dangerous undertaking. We have no adequate natural experiments, only spurious correlations.

Finally, I must urge that we have results presented in forms closer to the original data. Coefficients representing percent difference (logs) from some excluded group are affected by the earnings of that excluded group, as are the t-tests. What we want are departures from *average* and the significance of those. There is no reason why dummy variable regressions cannot be presented in that form. What the reader really needs is the unadjusted subgroup means for each dummy variable subclass, such as religious group, the adjusted coefficients or means, the subgroup frequencies, and some measure of the importance of the whole set of subclasses. For the unadjusted, gross effect, the correlation ratio, beta-squared, is clearly the appropriate measure of importance. We have been using an analogue for the adjusted coefficients, which is also analogous to the partial beta coefficient (the normalized regression coefficient if one thinks of the coefficients as a new scale, scaling a variable called religion). If the adjusted coefficients are in the form of deviations from the grand mean (have a weighted sum of zero instead of having one coefficient constrained to zero) then it is easy to assess their individual significance, since it is largely affected by the number of cases in that subgroup and the overall standard deviation (reduced if the multiple R-squared is large). But t-tests of individual coefficients expressed as deviations from an excluded class are difficult to interpret. It is useful to see both the gross and net effects, to see what the adjustment for intercorrelation by the regression actually does. Sometimes, the effect of a predictor is *greater* after the adjustments, indicating a spurious lack of association in the crude data.[4]

When we compare R-squares from regressions explaining the log of earnings, what are we doing? True, extreme cases may affect things, but models which seem best with logs can differ from those which explain the actual earnings best.

Which brings me, because it is related, to an even more difficult statistical problem, that of weighting. Logs are a kind of weighting, emphasizing the importance of differences at the lower end of the scale. Several times the author argues that weights for differential sampling or response rates are not required because unequal weighting will not affect the unbiasedness of coefficients estimated from the data. This is true *only if the model is correctly specified*, and our models are never correctly specified. We have rather good evidence that failure to use weights makes appreciable differences in coefficient estimates even in generally accepted models.

DISTRIBUTION OF EARNINGS

A second strand of analysis deals with variance, skewness, and kurtosis, finding the distributions not log-normal, but with skewness, and stretched-out-tails (platykurtic). Between 1955 and 1969, variance increased more than the mean; skewness and kurtosis got smaller. If one looks at residuals from various regressions, all three, of course, get a little smaller, but not much. The failure of the regressions to reduce skewness reraises the possibility of nonaddivities. One difficulty in comparing skewness and kurtosis between years, and between original data and residuals, is that most of us have no intuitive sense for the size of sampling errors or third and fourth moments. I have the uneasy feeling that most of the differences are random and do not call for much sophisticated explanation. The apparent finding that what the author calls the "self-employment variables" reduce variance and skewness most when their effect is removed, may well be the removal of the effects of business assets in a few extreme cases, where there is a conceptual problem to boot, that "earnings" are partly a return to capital.

Some of Taubman's speculation about late recognition of talent is potentially testable by seeing whether the relative importance of ability compared with education is greater in 1969 than in 1955. Such a comparison is made difficult by the absence of any way of looking at the importance of sets of dummy variables, as distinct from the range of their coefficients. I recommend to users of such regression the partial beta analogue we use, or else the actual calculation of the partial R-square for each crucial set of predictors, by rerunning the regression without that set and then looking at (R-square full − R-square without)/(1 − R-square without), which estimates the partial R-square.

However, in our experience, the analogue to the partial beta coefficient (normalized regression coefficient) is close enough and can easily be calculated from the dummy variable regression material.

TRENDS IN EARNINGS

The third section deals with trends in earnings for individuals from 1955 to 1969, taking maximal advantage of the panel data. Starting with transition matrices, and with such matrices separately for different levels of education, several regressions are presented where the dependent variable is the percent increase in income ($Y69 - Y55$)/$Y55$. The initial income is used as one of the explanatory variables in some regressions, representing "the effects of all the unmeasured variables." Our interpretation would be different—namely, that we are really looking at regression, in the old-fashioned sense of that term, and of two types: real and statistically spurious, resulting from errors in measurement.

In general, and this has been our experience, too, it proves to be difficult to explain changes in earnings. Change is mildly associated with ability, and with education (at these upper levels of education), and with a number of the same variables that explained level. The R-squares are deceptively large, of course, because of the lagged dependent variable format—$Y - 1$ as a "predictor"; we need a more modest estimate of how much of the *change* we have explained!

The author then goes on to examine whether some of the results can be simplified and interpreted as reflecting a single effect, such as investment in on-the-job training.

Change is found to be related to education, having gone to a private elementary school, minority religion (though there is a disturbing inconsistency in the "Jewish" effect depending on which equation was used), engaging in sports or work as a youth, not doing chores (farm background?), and self-employment.

The data do not seem to be easily interpretable as differences in on-the-job training (Mincer), and the author suggests they may represent choices of careers with more risk and more payoff, and a sorting over time for those who take the risks.[5]

COMMENTS ON CHANGE

Studying change separately from level is always a difficult task. Attempts to assess experimental programs have recently made this even more clear. Change and level are intimately related in fact, and in statistical artifact. Let us take statistical artifact first. The term regression arose because of a discovered tendency for things subject only to random shocks to appear to regress toward the mean. In other words, any individual whose initial measure was unusually high (low) tended to move down (up) subsequently. If the initial departure was a measurement error, then the regression was a spurious result of measurement problems. If the departure was real (the result of some shock), then a real regression phenomenon was occurring, but neither of these reflect long-term real differences in trends. The problem is exacerbated, of course, by taking increases as a percent of the initial year. If two people whose normal income is $10,000 have initial incomes, from random shock or measurement error, of $5,000 and $15,000, respectively, one has a 100 percent increase and the other, a 33 percent decrease. And if on the average there are increases, those with initial low levels will have larger percentage increases.

Using the initial level as one of the predictors is Taubman's solution. It is equivalent to using both the level and the square of the initial level to explain the change, and all other variables shift that *relation* by a fraction of the initial level. In some of our work, we take the change as a percent of the middle years, or as a percent of the average (beginning and end) years. Even better, perhaps, would be to find the relationship of change to average level, and explain the deviations from that, since even our measure tends to have some remaining (usually positive) relation to level.

Take the interpretation of education: People whose education was high relative to their 1955 earnings had a larger increase in earnings. Is this anything more than "regression to the mean" again? And is this why age seems to have an effect?

Finally, why do the results vary so much across the four equations?

TESTING THEORIES OF INCOME DISTRIBUTION

The final section of Taubman's paper asks whether some of the simpler theories of income-distribution dynamics fit the data. It is a valiant attempt, since as the author points out, most theories are not easily refuted, being so general that with some adjustments they can fit almost any set of data—like the "permanent income hypothesis." They are a way of looking at data rather than a testable proposition. But by imposing some additional reasonable assumptions, it can be shown that the data do *not* fit a stochastic theory of independent random changes in earning levels (the R-squared increases from 1955 to 1969, and there *is* a correlation of change with level).

The on-the-job training theory, or a variant which simply talks about willingness to trade a low start for a promise of more rapid increases in earnings later, is examined by assuming that 1955 may represent the "overtaking point," and that

1969 may represent the peak earnings year. In this case the R-square should be largest in 1955, when the "investments in job training" are least distorting. (It is assumed that anyone who earns less than expected is investing the difference in job training, something which surely must take some prize for special interpretation of data.) Since R-square does go up rather than down, the data do not fit this theory better, either. The author concludes that markets may not function that well, even for this special upper-level population.

Finally there are sorting-uncertainty models, even more difficult to test. In general, the author concludes, we may need a collection of theories and explanations to fit the complex world in which we live. I agree.

FOR ALL FOUR PARTS

I have some strong feelings about presentation of data. We need better estimates of the explanatory power not of individual subgroups of explanatory characteristics—such as one occupational class—but of each characteristic as a whole. We want to know how much education matters, for instance.

And we all need to cast a wider net when we search for the reasons why our measured variables make a difference. A significant relationship can have a variety of explanations. Ultimately the proof of any one explanation must consist of discrediting all the alternative explanations of the same relationship. There had not been time today to engage in that exercise extensively, but the kind of data we have here surely invite it.

In summary, I really think that the analysis of earnings levels needs a model that pays more attention to levels of causation, to explanatory variables that can affect other explanatory variables but that cannot be affected by them, in other words, directional relationships. And the analysis of changes in earnings needs to face up, in addition, to the problems of separating level from trend. This is a discouraging road, of course, since we can explain level a lot better than changes. I am not convinced that studies of the higher moments of distributions are useful, except as indicators that our additive models are not working (or that some better transformation of the dependent variable is called for). And finally, we must all come to terms with the strategy of research. Are we actually testing models or engaging in what Ed Leamer calls "Post Data Model Construction"? And if we are doing the latter, with any ingenuity whatever, even the most sophisticated methods of penalizing ourselves for looking at the data are not likely to suffice.

I suggest that we develop some protocols about research reporting which require that the author clearly state whether he is constructing models (has run more than one regression), or is testing some particular model or set of models. If the latter is the case, Taubman's exercise in asking what in the data could possibly refute a particular model is a good example. But it is also revealing, in that most theories and models are not testable without imposing additional assumptions.

Given the rich bodies of microdata becoming available, and the ransacking capacity that some of us have been developing on computers, I predict an explosion of "findings" and a rediscovery of what other social sciences have long since found, that the "aha" factor can lead to many "significant," but contradictory, findings. We can reduce the confusion if we all make clear what we are doing, but we really should ransack only part of the data, and use the other part to fit and test the preferred model that resulted from the searching process.

NOTES

1. That was the base for Thorndike's original study: R. L. Thorndike and F. Hagen, *Ten Thousand Careers* (New York: Wiley, 1959).
2. Z. Griliches and W. Mason have shown that it is possible to assess more complex models in "Education, Income, and Ability," *Journal of Political Economics* 80 (May-June supplement 1972): S74–S103.
   See also Paul Wachtel, "The Effect of School Quality on Achievement, Attainment Levels, and Lifetime Earnings," *Explorations in Economic Research* 2 (Fall 1975), pp. 502–536.
3. Sewall Wright, "The Method of Path Coefficients," *Annals of Mathematical Statistics* 5 (1934): 161–215.
   P. R. Heise, "Problems in Path Analysis and Causal Inference," in E. F. Borgatta, ed., *Sociological Methodology (San Francisco:* Jossey-Bass, 1969); Arthur Goldberger and O. D. Duncan, eds., *Structural Equation Models in the Social Sciences* (New York: Seminar Press, 1973).
4. For documentation of a computer program that does all these things, see Frank Andrews, John Sonquist, James Morgan, and Laura Klem, *Multiple Classification Analysis (Ann Arbor, Mich.:* Institute for Social Research, 1973).
5. See Duncan's paper in this volume.

Jacob Mincer
National Bureau of Economic Research and Columbia University

This is a partial comment on Taubman's paper in response to the section entitled "Investment in On-the-Job Training Models" (in Section VI), which purports to test a job-training theory ascribed to me. I will not elaborate on a number of perhaps unavoidable shortcomings in Taubman's brief summary of this model, as my actual detailed specification and analysis are now available to the reader in the monograph *Schooling, Experience, and Earnings*, published by the NBER in 1974, just after this Conference. It will suffice to stress several points which are relevant to the purported tests:
1. There is no prediction in my analysis to the effect that persons who invest more in their early work experience will later earn more than persons who invest less. This would be true only when the postschool earnings capacity Y_i^* is the same for each individual i. Holding years of schooling

fixed is not sufficient. In my work I found that 40 percent of the variance is due to variation in $Y*$ among men with the same schooling who, moreover, worked the same number of weeks per year.

2. The coefficient ρ in Taubman's expression (4) refers to the correlation between dollar investments and dollar earning capacity $Y*$. This should be positive, and the implications for dollar growth and for growth of dollar variances are consistent with the findings. However, in the analysis of relative (percent) growth of earnings and of variances of logarithms of earnings, ρ is a correlation between time-equivalents of investment with levels of earning capacity (ln $Y*$). The latter ρ can be zero or negative, when the former is positive.

3. The fact that a near-zero value of ρ can give rise to a structure which is *in part* similar to the predictions of stochastic theories does not warrant a rejection of the investment (job-training) theory. Indeed, other parts of the structure are shown to be inconsistent with "random shock" theories in my monograph (Chapter 7), and the stochastic theory rejected in favor of the investment theory which is consistent with the observed structure.

4. Some approximations are better than others, but it is particularly far-fetched in the Thorndike sample to assume that persons in it had the same number of years of work experience in a given calendar year (1955), even if the persons had the same education. In this sample, there is a large variation among individuals in the chronology of their schooling, military service, and job experience. Taubman's tests are of doubtful value in view of this variation.

5. Taubman's brief sketch of human capital analysis suggests a flavor of monomania to it. This is a misunderstanding of the concept of human capital and of the function of parsimonious models. Apart from this objection I do accept the proposition that labor markets function well enough for the purposes of my analysis, as the predicted tendencies in the wage structure do appear in the observations. I am not aware of a better definition of "functioning well."

13

C. RUSSELL HILL
University of South Carolina

and

FRANK P. STAFFORD
University of Michigan

Family Background and Lifetime Earnings

I. INTRODUCTION

Family background, as measured by variables such as education of parents, income of parents, and family size, is generally believed to be an important direct or indirect determinant of lifetime economic capacity and earnings of individuals. In the case where background is a direct determinant of earnings, family variables can be thought of as measures of marketable human capital which exists apart from that represented by education and training on-the-job. This view has relatively weak empirical support to date and the major issues are now: Which parental

NOTE: We should like to thank Harvey Brazer, Lois Hoffman, Jan Kmenta, John Marsh, Myra Strober, Paul Taubman, and Finis Welch for helpful comments. Our analysis of the Panel Study of Income Dynamics was supported by a grant from the Office of Economic Opportunity to the University of Michigan's Survey Research Center.

background variables represent forces that are important in determining a child's ability to develop later economic capacities? Are these variables measures of environmental or genetic factors? How does background influence the paths of lifetime training and earning as well as their levels?

In this paper, we advance the hypothesis that many of these background variables which have been used reflect, to a large extent, environmental forces, and that these environmental forces are in fact quite well measured, as a first approximation, by time inputs to the children particularly prior to grade school and particularly by the mother. We also argue that background factors influence ability to learn economic skills and that a particular pattern of life-cycle earnings is implied. Namely, persons from backgrounds where there is a greater input to child care will have greater attainment of education and training, and hence will have earnings which, over the life cycle, diverge from the earnings of those in whose backgrounds less emphasis has been placed on child care.

Belief in the importance of environmental influences or, more generally, experience, on the development of economic capacities of individuals has a long as well as distinguished history. If we consider capacities which require learning one must include in a history John Locke's well-known *Essay Concerning Human Understanding* (1689). Locke argued, in an unequivocal fashion, for the importance of experience in individual learning.[1] Locke's theme was certainly acceptable to later writers such as David Hume and Adam Smith. It is (or should be) well-known that Smith believed that "the difference ... between a philosopher and a common street porter, for example, seems to arise not so much from nature as from habit, custom, and education."[2] In fact, Smith ascribed such importance to environmental influences that he attributed the great beauty he perceived in London prostitutes to their diet of potatoes![3]

The experience theme emphasized by Smith is still very much a part of thought in research on lifetime earning capacity by economists who utilize the human capital framework. To date the forms of experience which have received most emphasis in the human capital literature are those relating to formal schooling and on-the-job training. More recently, there has been increased research on the influence of parental preschool investments in children on the child's subsequent educational attainment and earnings. While ability to acquire economic skills is often discussed in the human capital literature, until recently very little effort has gone toward distinguishing whether an acquired or inherited ability is being discussed.

A more extensive literature exists in sociology and psychology with respect to the influence of parental characteristics and child-rearing practices on child development. This literature contains a running debate about the relative importance of innate abilities versus acquired abilities and motivation. While a comprehensive review of this literature is not possible within the scope of this paper, we can comment on some of the most well-known work. This will provide some basis for comparison of our approach and findings with those in other disciplines, as well as with those of other economists.

What we plan to do is, first, to review a general framework for interpreting the influence of background on lifetime earnings (Section II). The basic model relies on multiple forms of human capital: inherited ability, early human capital produced by investments of time and money by the parents directed to the child's ability to learn, and later on, marketable human capital which is used by the child from the point in time when he is making his own decisions about training and labor market participation. The reason for introducing several forms of human capital and particularly early human capital rests on the empirical fact noted earlier that the most important parental influences on the adult earnings of their children have been consistently shown to be indirect rather than direct. That is, parental inputs (often measured only by father's education or occupation) appear to be related to such measures of later human capital as educational attainment but are typically found not to have a major direct impact on adult earnings. This evidence is reviewed in Section III. In terms of the psychological literature, the debate on the relative importance of environmentally versus genetically determined abilities cannot be resolved simply by noting that parental variables in some way affect ability to learn, which, in turn, affects adult skills and earning capacity. What is needed is a classification of background influences into those that can be considered genetic and those that can be considered environmental. Further, which early environmental variables are most important in determining ability to learn?

We do not have some ideal data set (such as a large lifetime panel of relevant variables for monozygotic twins raised under widely varying conditions) but plan to demonstrate the potential influence of home inputs of parental time by using data from a recent panel study conducted for the Office of Economic Opportunity (OEO) by the Survey Research Center (SRC) of the University of Michigan (Section IV). This survey provides information on housework time, and through regression analysis, we infer the amounts of husband's and wife's time in child care for preschool children across various socioeconomic groups. We then relate these different levels of child care time to what is known about educational attainment and lifetime earnings of adults with parents in the different socioeconomic groups.

II. A GENERAL APPROACH TO LIFETIME INVESTMENT IN SKILLS

A. A Life-Cycle Model with Home Inputs Exogenous

To begin our discussion, we can specify a model of lifetime skill acquisition beginning with the individual's inherited or genetic endowment and going through two time periods. During the first time period, the individual's parents or other adults invest in his ability to learn. In this stage the individual is not making explicit decisions about his own "career" but, rather, is having these decisions made for him. In our discussion, we will first treat these investments as simply given. This is partly because complete specification of the process would be very difficult even if there were clear evidence on the factors influencing childhood development as it pertains to acquisition of economically productive learning capacities. More importantly, we choose not to address ourselves to the problem here, since a proper specification would also imply specification of a model of inter-generational transfers of money and time. Given the current rather limited knowledge of parental behavior in providing time and money to young children, a large number of fairly general models could be proposed, and hence, it seems prudent to postpone such a project to a later date. As will become apparent, even our less ambitious approach rests on many easily contended elements.[4]

To illustrate our approach we start by defining three types of human capital and four time points which define two time intervals.

K_0 = initial inherited endowment of ability;

K_1 = early human capital from home investments;

K_2 = later or "marketable" human capital;

and

T_0 = initial time period (birth);

T_1 = point in time ending the home investment process (given);

T_2 = point in time beginning the self-investment or training process and market earnings (given) $T_2 \leqq T_1$;

T_3 = end of the training and market earning period.

During the home interval ($T_0 \leqq T < T_1$), a stock of skills relating to the ability to learn (K_1) is built up by parental investments of time (h) and market inputs (M). In a more general specification, time paths of these variables as well as the end of the home interval (T_1) could be made endogenous. We shall discuss some of the economic forces which determine h, M, and T_1 in part B. To simplify the discussion, we shall treat T_1 as given, and, during the home period, the stock of early human capital is accumulated by the following equation of motion:

(A1) $\dot{K}_1 = Q_1 = Q_1(K_0, h_1, h_2, M, K_1; t)$ $T_0 \leq t < T_1$

   $h_1 =$ home time on child by wife;

   $h_2 =$ home time on child by husband; and

   $t =$ a time index to portray age of child or time-dependent developmental process.

The presence of the fixed factor, K_0, generates rising marginal costs of producing increments to early human capital per unit time. Here we ignore possible depreciation. Note also that, in general, positive output should not require a positive level of K_1. At time T_2 and beyond, the individual makes his own decisions about training time, consumption time and (labor) market time. The financial assets available for consumption (and market inputs to investment) can be defined by $R(T_2)$ or in the form of an interest rate. Individuals from high-income backgrounds have more financial assets available for consumption and out-of-pocket costs of training, or they can be viewed as having the opportunity to borrow at a lower interest rate.[5]

During the later period marketable capital is produced with own time (s), market inputs (D) and human capital of all three types.

(A2) $Q_2 = Q_2(K_0, K_1, K_2, s, D; t)$

The equation of motion for capital is:

(A3) $\dot{K}_2 = Q_2 - \delta K_2$

The production function, $Q_2(\cdot)$, has the fixed factors K_0 and K_2 which assures rising marginal costs, and in general, positive output need not require a positive level of K_2. A unit budget of own time is divided between training (s) and labor supply ($l = 1 - s$) in models where the objective function is simply maximum present value of lifetime earnings. In a somewhat more general approach, maximization of a utility function with arguments of leisure time and market expenditures can be developed.[6] Still more ambitiously, one can specify leisure time, market expenditures on own consumption, and child care (produced by time and market expenditures on children) as arguments of the objective function. Specification of this third possibility would provide a partial representation of an inter-generational model; a model which we shall forgo at this point, since we are treating parental decisions in a limited context.

Let us consider the case where the objective function is the integral of utility over the later period. Given levels of R, K_0 and K_1 at T_2 the preference function to be optimized by the individual is[7]

(A4) $\quad J = \int_{T_2}^{T_3} U(c, X)\, dt$

subject to the equations of motion for financial assets and human capital which are

(A5) $\quad \dot{R} = (1 - c - s)\alpha K_2 - pX + rR$

(A6) $\quad \dot{K_2} = Q_2(s, K_2; K_0, K_1, D, t) - \delta K_2$

and the condition that $R \geqq 0$ at $t = T_3$. The definitions of new variables and parameters are:

c = leisure time;

X = market goods (physical quantities);

p = price of market goods;

α = rental value of a unit of K_2; and

r = interest rate.

The Hamiltonian for this control problem is

(A7) $\quad H = U(\cdot) + \lambda_{K_2}[Q_2(\cdot) - \delta K_2] + \lambda_R[(1 - s - c)\alpha K_2 - pX + rR]$

For the individual, an optimal path of the control variables $(\hat{X}, \hat{s}, \hat{c},$ and, by our budget identity, $1 - \hat{s} - \hat{c} = \hat{l})$ should be chosen to maximize the performance index given an inherited ability level, K_0, and home human capital, K_1. If the parents have as an argument in their utility the welfare of their children, then in choosing a level of home training they will "look at" the incremental value of the optimized performance index for each of their N children in determining their decision to increase the amount of home inputs. That is, they consider

(A8) $\quad \Delta J^* = J^*(K_1^2) - J^*(K_1^1)$

where

K_1^1 = some given level of home training;

K_1^2 = some higher level of home training; and

$J^*(\cdot)$ = the value of the performance index as optimized by the offspring for given levels of K_1.

Thus, a person's lifetime welfare is partly produced by his parents through home training, and usual arguments about consumer behavior apply to the actions of the parents. That is, a higher level of "wealth," or what Becker has termed "full income," of the parents will induce them to purchase more offspring welfare (J) via child care, on the assumption that children's lifetime welfare is a normal good. Also, the substitution effect of a higher price of offspring welfare (as embodied in the price of market goods for child care and, more importantly, the price of time of the parents) will induce them to buy less child care. The effects of income and prices on time inputs to children within the context of a static model of time allocation are analyzed further in Section IIB.

Up to this point, the discussion has been very general. To be more explicit is difficult, because we are discussing a complex dynamic process. From previous work in the area, however, we can illustrate some basic points concerning life-cycle earnings patterns and home background. To begin, we ignore market inputs in the production of human capital, restrict the human capital production function (A2) to the simple functional form of Cobb-Douglas [$O_2 = A_1(sK_2)^\beta$], introduce parental inputs and inherited genetic endowment as a neutral technical shift in efficiency in producing human capital, and set $T_1 = T_2$. Further, if we impose a particular simple functional form on the utility function [$U = \ln(A_0 c^{\theta_1} X^{\theta_2})$] then in a recent paper Stafford and Stephan have shown that for interior solutions and for a zero interest rate and no time preference, the equations of motion for human capital and its shadow value are[8]

(A9) $\quad \dot{\lambda}_{K_2} = \lambda_{K_2} \delta - \lambda_K \alpha + \theta_1/K_2$

(A10) $\quad \dot{K}_2 = A_1[\beta\lambda_{K_2}A_1/(\lambda_R\alpha)]^{\beta/(1-\beta)} - \delta K_2$

To determine the qualitative behavior over the interval $T_2 < t \leq T_3$ the loci for $\dot{\lambda}_{K_2} = \dot{K}_2 = 0$ can be plotted in λ_{K_2}, K_2 space. For these loci, it is apparent that if one specifies A_1 as being a measure of ability to learn which is increased by parental inputs during $T_0 < t \leq T_2$ the individual would, for an initial endowment of K_2, choose a more extended training period as part of his optimal strategy in maximizing lifetime consumption.[9] Alternatively, if one were to specify the parental function as teaching the child directly marketable skills (a high level of K_2 at time T_2) but not increasing ability to learn (produce human capital), the children from backgrounds with more parental inputs would then initially train less and rent out a higher proportion of their human capital stock, but later in life have earnings which converged toward those who initially received less home training. This basic result holds as well for models which specify discounted lifetime earnings as the objective function.[10] Thus, existing theoretical work can be interpreted as consistent with the view that parental inputs to early training (and/or genetic ability) which increase ability to augment one's own marketable skills will result in lifetime human capital and net earnings profiles which are more precipitous. That is, age-market capital profiles of those who receive much home inputs will fan out from (or even cross) profiles of those with less home investment.

B. The Allocation of Time and Market Inputs to Children

If parents derive satisfaction from the expected level of child welfare as suggested by (A8), household time allocation models of demographic behavior which are addressed to the question of "child quality" can be used to portray parental investment in children's home or early human capital. In this section of our paper, we shall review a model of consumer choice as applied to intrafamily time allocation. The object here is to determine what, if any, implications such a model has regarding differentials among socioeconomic status groups in the time allocated to the care of children. The basic model discussed here has been developed in detail by Willis and Becker and Lewis.[11] The reader should, therefore, consult these papers for detailed derivations. Basically, the household can be viewed as maximizing a utility function of the following form

(B1) $U = U(N, Q, S)$

where N is the number of children, Q can be interpreted as their quality or early home investment (assumed to be the same for all children), and S is the rate of consumption of all other commodities. While N and Q enter as separate arguments in the parent's utility function via their determination of number of children and their lifetime welfare, it is "child services," $C = NQ$, whose production and consumption we are interested in here. We will assume that both C and S are produced according to the following linearly homogeneous household production functions

(B2) $C = C(h_c, M_c)$

(B3) $S = S(h_s, M_s)$

where h_i and M_i $(i = C, S)$ are, respectively, vectors of time and goods devoted to the production of the two commodities.

We will view the time inputs to household production as being those of the wife and, consequently, view the husband as devoting his entire time budget to labor market activity. While this is a strong restriction on the general model as well as somewhat of a departure from reality, empirical evidence from several time-use surveys suggests that it is not far from the truth. Finally, the family maximizes (B1) subject to the following full income, F, constraint

(B4) $F = \pi_c C + \pi_s S = H + wT$

where the π_i are the full prices of the two commodities, H is the sum of the family's nonlabor wealth and the husband's income from earnings, $T = h_c + h_s + L$ is the total amount of time available to the wife which is divided between household production ($h = h_s + h_c$) and labor market activity, L, and w is the average market wage received by the wife. We will assume here that the wife's price of time is equal to w and this, in turn, is independent of her hours spent at work in the market. For the wife who does not allocate time to L, the price of time is quite likely understated by w. We shall ignore this important point here, for it is not central to our discussion. The reader should, however, consult two recent papers by Reuben Gronau for the implications of this point for a more general model of intrafamily time allocation.[12]

The importance of Becker and Lewis' model is that it makes clear the importance of the interaction between the quantity (N) and quality (Q) of children in understanding both cross-sectional and time-series data on fertility. A central point of their paper concerns the difference between "true" and "observed" income and price elasticities of the demand for N and Q. They demonstrate that observed income elasticities, which are derived by changing F while holding π_c and π_s constant, are on the average, smaller than the true elasticities, which are derived by changing the total expenditure on N, Q, and S, holding constant their respective shadow prices. Further, if it is assumed, as seems plausible, that the true income elasticity with respect to Q is larger than that with respect to N, then the observed Q elasticity will exceed the observed N elasticity. Just the opposite is true for observed compensated (negative) price elasticities, however. Here the observed income-compensated elasticity of N tends to be numerically greater than the corresponding Q elasticity. These relationships provide consistent interpretations of the empirical work of economic demographers and, in particular, fully explain the anomaly of zero or negative income elasticities with respect to the number of children, observed in much of the literature. The implication of these points for our analysis is that socioeconomic status groups which are characterized by relatively high prices of time and full income are likely to produce child services (C) through a process of relatively large resource investments in the quality of existing children, rather than increasing the number of children.

The effects of changing income and prices on the allocation of time to child services (h_c) can be analyzed in a straightforward way, given the model sketched in above. If full income is held constant, the compensated price (wage) elasticity of child-care time can be shown to be the following

(B5) $\qquad \left| \dfrac{\partial h_{hc}}{\partial_w} \cdot \dfrac{w}{h_c} \right|_F \equiv \varepsilon = -(1-\alpha_c)\gamma_c + (1-k)\sigma(\alpha_s - \alpha_c)$

where $\alpha_c = wh_c/\pi_c C$ is the time intensity parameter for the production of $C = NQ$ (α_s is analogously defined for the production of S); γ_c is the elasticity of substitution between h_c and M_c in the production of C, $k = \pi c C/F$ and σ is the elasticity of substitution in consumption between C and S. The first term on the right-hand side of (B5) indicates that a compensated increase in w will lead to a reduction in h_c reflecting the substitution of M_c for h_c in production. The algebraic sign of the second term on the right-hand side of (B5) depends on the difference in time intensity parameters in the production of C and S. We shall argue here (as does Willis) that particularly in the preschool years, $\alpha_s - \alpha_c < 0$. While an increase in w raises the marginal cost of producing both S and C, it raises it relatively more for the commodity which is most time intensive. For $\sigma > 0$ this will lead to a substitution away from C.

An increase in the wife's price of time also increases real full income and, consequently, leads to increases in the demand for all commodities and inputs, assuming the existence of no inferior factors. The sign of the uncompensated price elasticity for C is, therefore, unknown a priori. However, if we find (as we do in Section IV) that high-status mothers allocate a larger amount of time to child care than do low-status mothers, and if socioeconomic status serves as a reasonable index of the wife's price of time, then the consumption of C must be relatively income elastic. Further, as distinct from other household activities, the production of C (at least during the preschool years) probably exhibits a smaller elasticity of substitution (γ_c) between goods and time and accounts for a larger fraction of the family's full income (k). Both of these phenomena will lead to a smaller absolute value of ε for given values of α_c, α_s, and σ, thereby increasing the relative importance of the income effect in assessing the effects of changes in w on h_c.

Families of differing socioeconomic status differ both in terms of full income (F) and in the prices of their members' time. The model outlined above makes it clear that increased full income (through, say, an increase in H) leads to increased consumption of all commodities (assuming no inferiority) and the inputs used to produce them. The effects of changes in w on the allocation of time are more problematic. However, the characteristics of preschool child care give one some reason to expect the income effect to be dominant. Consequently, the model outlined above suggests that differentials in family background which are typically measured by some type of socioeconomic status index should be associated with differentials in the consumption (production) of child care (*C*) and in its time and goods inputs.

To summarize our discussion in Section II of the role of family background on lifetime earning capacity, we can note four basic points.

1. The parents' motivation to care for children (demand high quality) can be developed by treating the child's lifetime welfare as one argument in the parents' own lifetime utility function. Parents' contribution to early human capital provides part of the means by which their offspring can develop adult capacities, including marketable skills. Thus, parental choices regarding this consumer good can be analyzed within a broadened household decision-making model. Recent work along these lines has been the focus in much of the development of an economic theory of demographic behavior, and we have shown a relation between this literature and the issues of investments in early human capital.

2. The influence of parental inputs (of either the inherited type [K_0] or home inputs to early human capital [K_1]) on adult earning capacity is primarily indirect. Parents determine the ability to learn much more than the directly marketable skills of their offspring.

3. Whether the individual's (lifetime) utility function has as its argument simply market earnings net of investment costs, or has leisure and consumption of market goods, the life-cycle human capital accumulation models support, or are at least consistent with, the view that the lifetime earnings of more able persons will diverge from those of less able persons.

4. While 3 holds without explicit regard to the relative importance of genetic factors or home investments in determining ability, there is the issue of which inputs matter. Is ability to learn a genetically fixed capacity at the one extreme or is it something which, as Smith argued, is largely determined by habit and custom? How important is the input of parental time? We now turn to a review of the existing social-science literature as it pertains to these four topics.

III. BACKGROUND VARIABLES AND PERSONAL DEVELOPMENT

A. A Sample of the Sociological and Psychological Literature

The sociological work which appears to have the most direct bearing on the topic of family variables and their influence on adult earnings and economic status is that of O. D. Duncan and his associates. The basic framework used is a recursive model wherein: "father's occupation, the number of siblings, and the early intelligence level of the respondent are taken to be 'predetermined' variables with respect to the later achieved statuses and intelligence as measured at maturity . . . . It would be much more difficult to represent the correlation of early intelligence with parental status as an outcome of a causal process. The solution to this problem would be tantamount to a solution of the 'heredity-environment' problem with respect to measured intelligence."[13] These background variables relate to education, later intelligence, occupation, and earnings as represented by a path diagram, which is given by Duncan and is presented as Figure 1.

FIGURE 1   Path Diagram Representing Dependence of Status Achievement on Family Background and Intelligence (Path Coefficients Estimates for U.S. White Men 25–34 Years Old, 1964)

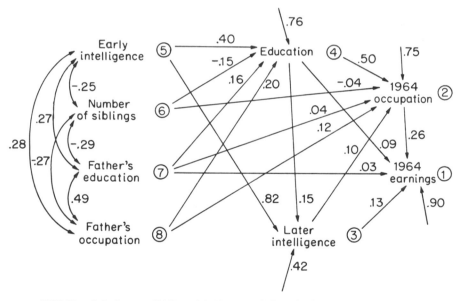

SOURCE: O. D. Duncan, "Ability and Achievement." *Eugenics Quarterly* (Mar. 1968), p. 7.

While there are numerous differences between the approach we have set forth in Section II and that of the Duncan model, the points of comparability are in the emphasis on parental characteristics and number of siblings on educational attainment, and the very minor magnitude assigned to the *direct* influence of background variables on adult economic capacity (occupation and earnings).[14] This basic model has been used in subsequent studies by economists, as will be discussed below, but in most of the research to date the actual predetermined parental variables used have been *father's* education and occupation rather than education and occupation of *both* parents. Another feature of the Duncan specification is that "Figure 1 merely shows [the background] variables 5–8 as intercorrelated among themselves—the correlations are depicted by the curved lines with arrowheads at both ends—and it is not considered as part of the task at hand to explain how these correlations arise."[15] By using recent work on economic demography, we have shown that it is possible to include in a general framework a specification of how parental time and money inputs vary across families and how these, in turn, can influence the stock of early human capital (early intelligence and ability). In our life-cycle model of Section IIA, educational attainment and lifetime training are heavily dependent on these behavioral patterns in the home, and the influence of educational policies is presumably dependent on the "initial conditions" which children bring with them into the school system.[16]

When one turns to the psychological literature for help in specifying the way in which genetic endowments versus family environmental factors influence early development, several features are apparent. First, the literature is enormous. Second, the literature is certainly as controversial as it is large. Third, the literature is of some use to economists. The piece by Arthur Jensen contains all three elements.[17] The paper, while itself lengthy (123 pages), refers the reader to 153 references and argues that no less than 80 percent of the variation in basic intelligence can be explained by genetic factors, leaving environmental influences 20 percent. The minor role of environmental factors as well as Jensen's argument for genetic differences by race are of little comfort for those who believe that Adam Smith was by and large correct.

This psychological research should be of interest to economists, because it does deal with the role of parental and other inputs in the intellectual development of children. The key empirical studies focus on the comparison between monozygotic twins reared apart and reared together. Such data, as one can readily imagine, are rather scarce and hence the studies are subject to the criticism that they are not based on consistently collected sample points. Also a question of great importance is how one measures the variation in environments between those reared together and those reared apart. In the approach which we follow, one of the critical measures is time input by the parents and, particularly, by the mother. If variations in father's education or family income are used (the latter measured by "the material conditions of their homes"),[18] these may serve as only poor measures of variations in home inputs.

Even relying on Jensen's work, we can find some support for the importance of inputs of time into child care. In his discussion of the importance of educational intervention for development of children who are disadvantaged, he notes that "ordinary nursery school attendance, with a rather diffuse enrichment program but with little effort directed at development of specific cognitive skills, generally results in a gain of 5 or 6 I.Q. points in typical disadvantaged preschoolers. If special cognitive training, especially in verbal skills, is added to the program, the average gain is about 10 points. . . . Average gains rarely go beyond this, but when the program is extended beyond the classroom into the child's home, and there is instruction in specific skills under short but highly attention-demanding daily sessions . . . about a third of the children have shown gains of as much as 20 points."[19] The potential importance of early home inputs in influencing I.Q. exists because ". . . I.Q. is not constant, but, like all other developmental characteristics, is quite variable early in life and becomes increasingly stable throughout childhood."[20] Recent work by psychologists which supports the view that development is influenced substantially by parent-infant interaction will be discussed more fully in relation to our own empirical findings in Section IV.

Quite apart from the extent to which I.Q. is subject to change through parental and other inputs, there is the issue of the economic significance of I.Q. Many of the studies which deal with I.Q. or achievement seem to have a ring of "score for score's sake" to them. The issue of whether I.Q., especially adult I.Q., has strong implications for adult economic capacities is never really treated adequately. For example, while Jensen does at some points distinguish between generalized intelligence and marketable skills,[21] he apparently feels it is sufficient to note that average I.Q. scores of high-status, high-paying occupations are also high.[22] This problem of "score for score's sake" characterizes much of the work by sociologists and economists who have concerned themselves with whether different educational programs raise achievement scores (or I.Q.). This is a major failing of the work by Christopher Jencks.[23] Apart from his failure to understand the distinction between goodness of fit and importance, there is the issue of whether achievement scores really measure economic capacities, including the capacities necessary to develop marketable skills.

Within the field of research on I.Q., there is a serious debate as to whether important dimensions to basic mental ability are measured by even the most sophisticated of current I.Q. tests. Work on the physiological level demonstrates that there is important functional specialization of the two hemispheres of the brain with respect to different types of mental tasks; "the hemispheric specializations have been described as 'gestalt-synthetic' for the right hemisphere and 'logical-analytic' for the left. . . . In a culture where most individuals are exposed to intensive education of the left hemisphere potential for reading, writing, grammar, and so on, we could reasonably expect a tendency for the propositional mode to dominate, even when dealing with problems for which it is less appropriate. Conversely, persons raised in a nonliterate culture emphasizing different training, in spatial skill for example, should exhibit a reverse [appositional] tendency."[24]

This research implies that there is more to intelligence or ability to learn than what is measured by conventional tests, but the relative importance of propositional versus appositional skills in developing earning capacities is certainly not clear at this point. However, it is quite clear that environmental or background influences can be viewed as important in developing the different kinds of abilities. Bogen et al. found that when given a Street test, which involves identification of silhouettes that have been partially obliterated so as to make their recognition difficult, and which is interpreted as measuring appositional skills, Hopi Indians and blacks scored higher than middle-class whites. Conversely, middle-class whites performed better on a standard I.Q. test (WAIS similarities, a similarities test), which is believed to serve as a measure of propositional skills. One reason given for observing these differences is that "subdominant groups in a technological society are provided less access to propositionising and consequently must rely more often upon the alternative appositional strategy."[25]

Family background and associated early environment can be important not only for their influence on learning ability, but also as representative of a set of factors which influences motivation. Willingness to learn new skills can obviously be of great importance in human capital formation. Representation of this willingness could be aggregated with ability-to-learn parameters of our general model in Section IIA, but may require particular types of inputs to young children by the parents. Qualitative aspects of parent-child interaction are stressed in the literature on achievement motivation, which concerns itself with how people acquire an interest in improving their capabilities in areas where a standard of performance can be identified.

Heckhausen, in his review of the parental influences in achievement motivation, emphasizes the influence of parental approval, affection, and encouragement of trust as important determinants of motivation.[26] The role of quantity of time by parents in developing achievement motivation is left as a more open question. It seems possible that in addition to qualitative aspects of the parent-child interaction, actual quantity of time per child may be important as well. Thus, our empirical work on quantity of time to children in Section IV may be worth considering for future work on achievement motivation.

To summarize our brief review of the sociological and psychological literature as it relates to the development of economic capacities as influenced by early or background factors, we can note five points:

1. The work by Duncan is consistent with the view that parental inputs have an important but indirect influence on adult earning capacity, but his empirical work does not attempt to identify the separate influences of background, such as time inputs by the mother and father. In Section IV, as a supplement to our own findings, we review the recent evidence of education of mother and father on children's educational attainment.

2. The role of environmental factors or home inputs can be seen in psychological research, even if one relies on the work of those who assign the least importance to home or other environmental influences vis-à-vis genetic endowment of mental abilities. As we shall argue in Section IVC, for low-income families, a larger number of children results in lower input of time per child. Hence, lower I.Q. (which is associated with family size), insofar as I.Q. is important in developing economic capacities, can be viewed as subject to important environmental influences.

3. There is no clear evidence of the extent to which I.Q. measures basic mental skills. Recent research demonstrates that another important skill—the ability to extract an integrated image from a variety of fragmented inputs—appears to be more closely related to the facility of the right hemisphere of the brain, or integrative thinking, whereas standard I.Q. measures relate to facility with left brain, or propositional, thinking.

4. The relation between various mental abilities as measured by achievement test scores and subsequent economic capacities—or, in terms of the model in Section II, the capacity to learn economic capacities—is not obvious.

5. The achievement motivation literature is consistent with our human capital approach but has tended to emphasize qualitative aspects of parent-child interaction. It seems reasonable that some quantity of time is required to develop achievement motivation as well as learning abilities.

B. A Review of the Economic Literature

Many of the empirical studies by economists on the influence of background variables on adult earnings are basically consistent with the work of Duncan in two ways. First, the model used is recursive, and second, the major influence of parental background is indirect, through its influence on acquired marketable human capital, as indexed by years of schooling. The work of Bowles[27] and Griliches and Mason[28] provides examples of what has been done, and here we find that the variables used as background measures include father's occupation and father's schooling. The empirical findings of the Griliches and Mason study are diverse, because they are based on a very complex data set. For our purposes, their central findings include the following: a measure of adult I.Q., the Armed Forces Qualification Test (AFQT), though positively correlated with personal background variables, has a small net contribution to earnings (p. S-88). Second, there were rather large effects of religion, color, and schooling before service on AFQT, and minor effects of parental status variables (p. S-91). The first point provides additional support for the work of Duncan, which emphasizes the indirect role of ability. The second point emphasizes environmental influences on one measure of ability but is inadequate for our purposes, because the status variables may be only poor measures of time inputs by the parents. The model of household production and demand for child quality, as measured by inputs to children, demonstrates the role of family income potential (Section IIB). From the model and previous empirical work, we know that father's status variables should influence time to children via the implied income effects on the wife's time allocation. Thus, it is somewhat surprising that there is such a minor influence of status variables. However, if time inputs are important and the wife is the major provider of these inputs, then sole reliance on measures of father's status will provide only a rough measure of time inputs.

The work of Sam Bowles also uses the recursive framework and provides strong support for the importance of indirect effects of background on adult earning capacity. He argues as well for a strong *direct* influence of background on adult earnings through his attempt to correct, via an errors-in-variables approach, for the response error in reporting background. This finding has been criticized by Gary Becker, who noted that successful persons could have an upward bias in the recall of their parents' status,[29] and, in any event, the finding is dependent on the accuracy of the correction, which Bowles admits is quite imperfect.[30] The major problem of the Bowles study, like that of Griliches and Mason, is that variables for father's status were included but not mother's status.[31]

Another way of providing support for our general specification of background as influencing ability to learn marketable skills is to examine the shape of the capital and earnings paths for individuals. For a given initial level of marketable skills, individuals with greater ability or motivation to learn should have capital and earnings profiles which diverge from those who are less able.

In studies of the general labor force, John Hause has found that persons with higher initial ability to learn (as indexed by tests prior to formal schooling) have earnings profiles which diverge from those of less initial ability.[32] In Hause's studies, the question of whether ability to learn is environmentally determined is answered only weakly, if at all, but the importance of environmental inputs is given some potential support. Within educational attainment categories and accounting for test score, those whose religion was Catholic or Jewish had higher current earnings.[33] The results are not well suited to our purposes, since measured ability and years of schooling attained are in our view influenced by background. Therefore, important indirect effects of parental time inputs through their influence on acquired ability and education cannot be identified. At this stage, the Hause study seems to provide potential evidence for the influence of time allocation. If Catholic and Jewish families allocate more time per child to child care than other families, then we shall have some confidence that our approach is valid.

Using a very specialized panel of children who had an I.Q. of 140 or higher in the early 1920s and who were followed into adult life over a period of almost forty years, Arleen Leibowitz has reported several pertinent results.[34] If only heredity determined the ability of children, then one could expect *either* parent's education (as a proxy for ability) to be equally important in determining ability of the children. From the results of Bogen et al., there is reason to believe that I.Q. is, at best, only a proxy for acquired general ability. Subject to this qualification, it is still significant to note that mother's education has a greater influence on educational attainment of children than does father's education. This is important because prior work by Leibowitz and Hill and Stafford has demonstrated that mothers, and particularly those who are highly educated, change their market and nonmarket time allocation to care for young children, whereas fathers, by and large, do not. Leibowitz also found that parental background variables had a minor *direct* influence on earnings even though they have important indirect effects through increasing ability to learn (as measured by I.Q.) and through their influence on years of schooling attained.

While the study by Leibowitz relies on a very special sample, a recent study by Richard Morgenstern[35] uses data from the 1968 Urban Problems Survey conducted by the Survey Research Center of the University of Michigan. Morgenstern also relies on a recursive model to analyze the data and consequently has a regression of educational attainment on various personal background variables. Mother's education and father's education are both found to be important in determining education attained. This is certainly consistent with the time allocation approach, and for blacks, mother's education was found to be more important than father's education in affecting educational attainment. This is consistent with Leibowitz's finding of greater influence of mother's education and provides some additional support for the importance of environmental inputs and particularly time inputs. However, for whites, Morgenstern did not find a greater influence of mother's education and, in fact, claims that while "mother's education is a better predictor of educational attainment among blacks, . . . father's educational attainment is a better predictor for whites." Two explanatory points seem appropriate. First, as noted earlier in Section II, father's education, via income effects, can have an important influence on mother's time devoted to children. Second, the Urban Problems Survey, being restricted to central cities, is less likely to represent a cross section of whites than of blacks, because successful whites (those with large time inputs from their mothers?) can more easily obtain housing outside the central city.

To summarize our review of the use of background factors in the studies of lifetime earnings by economists, we can note first that the indirect nature of the influence seems to be observed universally and explains the popularity of the recursive model. Second, there does seem to be evidence, particularly from the work of Hause, that the earnings of those with greater ability diverge over time from those with less ability, rather than being higher by a constant proportion throughout the working life.[36] These results we take as support for the ability-to-learn interpretation of background influences (equations [A2] and [A10]). Third, there is scattered evidence that background variables which correlate with likely variables in parental time inputs to children during early years in the home have a bearing on earnings through their influence on ability to develop marketable capacities. What we hope to encourage is work on an explicit link between time inputs, ability to learn, and subsequent lifetime earnings. One issue in this work is the future role of recursive model building.

The recursive model is attractive primarily because of its statistical simplicity, which permits single-equation estimation and provides fairly straightforward interpretation. This simplicity is desirable and probably warranted, given the enormous data problems in studying lifetime earnings. It can be argued that under these circumstances, there is a high marginal payoff to better data as compared with better model specification. Indeed, given the data problems, it seems difficult to have great confidence in checking any structural phenomenon, a fact which is not without strong empirical implications. Nonetheless, the recursive model does have some problems which should be kept in mind.

Use of a recursive system is justified by arguing that there is an unequivocal causal ordering to events: what happens to you as a preschooler is prior to what happens to you while in school, which is prior to what happens to you as an adult. However, it seems reasonable to suppose that parents derive satisfaction from the child's lifetime welfare, and they know that what the child will choose to do as an adult will depend in part on what they do for him while he is still a preschooler. Therefore, while there is a temporal ordering to activities, it is still not correct to look at these activities as if they were independent of one another in their effect on lifetime earning capacity. Consider the analogy of a crop with the three inputs of land, seed and fertilizer, and harvesting effort. Even though there is an obvious temporal sequence of: first the land, then the seed and fertilizer, and then the harvesting effort, the marginal products of each are, in general, interdependent and the relative contribution of each factor cannot be assessed simply by noting a temporal ordering.

IV. TIME INPUTS TO CHILDREN

In an earlier section of this paper, we presented a model of lifetime skill acquisition that is initiated through parental time and goods investments in the children. We have also reviewed empirical evidence from economists and other social scientists regarding the effect of family background on subsequent earnings and occupational achievement. In this section, we shall demonstrate that there is a striking relationship between the family background variables as they are usually measured (education and occupation of parents) and the amount of time allocated to preschool children. Indeed, we shall argue that the environmental forces which the family background variables are measuring in earnings functions are, in fact, largely a reflection of differentials in parental time inputs to children. And while we do not have any direct evidence concerning the effects of the preschool child-care time we measure here on the child's future economic and social status, we do present some provocative, though indirect, evidence from child psychologists and others that this time is important.

The measurement of parental time inputs to children requires a data source with detailed time-use information. Such data sets are, unfortunately, still rather rare. While the Office of Economic Opportunity (OEO) *Panel Study of Income Dynamics* we use here does provide data on the time spent on housework as well as in the labor market, it is not as detailed as we should like. In particular, housework time spent on children is not available directly from the data but must be estimated, and nonhousework time allocated to the children is not available at all. We have discussed our method of estimation in detail elsewhere and so will not review it at length here.[37] Suffice it to say that our basic method is to regress hours of housework on the number of children in different age categories. The estimated coefficients then represent the increment to housework due to the presence of a child of specified age; it is this increment which we interpret as child care time.

Our sample consists of families headed by a male with wife present where both were between the ages of 21 and 45 in 1969. In addition, the head was employed in that year in one of seven occupational groups discussed below. The specification of the regression model is very simple with the only independent variables being the number of children within specified age ranges. Nevertheless, the results are very robust, changing little with the inclusion of additional regressors. In addition, our basic methodology has now been used to estimate preschool time inputs from two quite different data sets and the results have been reassuringly consistent.[38] Regressions were initially estimated for both male family heads and wives within groups defined by the male head's occupation or the educational attainment of the head and wife. As noted in the previous sections of this paper, both occupation and educational attainment are commonly used indicators of family background or socioeconomic status. Consequently, our technique is to estimate time inputs to children within socioeconomic status groups and then make comparisons across groups.

The first result of interest was that fathers allocate little time to preschool children within any of the socioeconomic status groups. Our regressions do not reveal any consistent pattern of change of the head's child-care time as the child grows older and indicate that the head spends only about 10 to 20 percent of the time spent by the mother in child-care time in the preschool years. To the extent, then, that family background variables in earnings functions reflect early environmental influences, they would probably be more accurately measured by variables relating to the mother's, rather than the father's, characteristics.[39]

The regressions were initially estimated using as independent variables the number of children aged 0–2, 3–4, 5–6, and 7–17, and the annual hours of housework and labor market work as dependent variables. These regressions indicated a strong response in terms of time allocation away from market work and toward housework by the wife when preschool children were present. Generally, the increase in housework was greater than the corresponding reduction in market work within each of the socioeconomic status groups. This occurs because child-care time can come not only out of market time but also leisure time. We found that in low-status groups (defined by the head's occupation) there was a sharp fall in housework time for older preschool children (ages 3–4 and 5–6) in comparison with the time allocated to infants. High-status mothers, however, allocated a relatively steady and high level of time throughout the preschool years. The reasons for this differential age-of-child-dependent shape to housework time between social classes are discussed in detail though not conclusively in our earlier work. As our main interest here is with the total time allocated to the preschool child and how it differs across social classes, the regressions we report here use only the number of children 0–6 and 7–17 as independent variables, and only the annual hours of housework time as the dependent variable. While this hides some interesting age-specific detail, it does yield the information we seek. Estimates of time spent in the physical care of children by social class and several related topics are presented below.

A. Allocation of Time to Preschool Children by Head's Occupation and Parent's Education

Our sample consists of 1,261 families with the characteristics discussed above. The male head's occupation in 1969 was used to define three status groups which closely compare to the socioeconomic status groups derived by O. D. Duncan, particularly for the high and low groups. Regression of the wife's annual hours spent on housework on the number of children 0–6 and 7–17 within each of these three groups are presented in Table 1.[40] These regressions exhibit the basic pattern that we have found consistently: striking "social class" or "full income" differentials

TABLE 1 Regressions of Annual Hours of Housework for Married Women, 21–45, by Occupation of Head, 1969

Variable	Professionals, Managers, Self-Employed	Clerical, Craftsmen	Operatives, Laborers
CHILDREN 0–6	445	219	200
	(88)	(72)	(70)
CHILDREN 7–17	108	90	42
	(50)	(46)	(25)
Constant	1,198	1,534	1,517
	(79)	(87)	(88)
Number of observations	403	430	428
S.E.E.	899	995	1,019
R^2	.188	.056	.049

NOTE: The data source for this and all subsequent regressions is the *Panel Study of Income Dynamics* collected by the University of Michigan's Survey Research Center under contract from the Office of Economic Opportunity. In this and all subsequent tables, estimated standard errors are found in parentheses below the estimated coefficient.

in the time allocated to preschool children. The coefficients indicate, for example, that a preschool child in a high-status family has 445 hours of maternal time allocated to him during each of the preschool years. In contrast, the low-status child is the recipient of only 200 hours per preschool year. Again, we would point out that these numbers obscure interesting patterns of time use within the preschool years (ages 0–6), but the basic character of class differentials is unchanged. The ratio of time inputs to preschool children between high- and low-status groups is 2.25 : 1 and this is significantly different from unity.[41]

Much the same pattern exists when we stratify the sample on the basis of the head's and wife's educational attainment. A stratification by educational attainment seems particularly meaningful in the context of a study of the allocation of time. The head's education is a useful proxy for a family's "permanent" income, while the wife's education is a stong predictor of her price of time and potential market wage rate.[42] The total sample size is smaller in Table 2 than in Table 1, for we have deleted families in which the wife's education was a missing variable.

TABLE 2   Regressions of Annual Hours of Housework for Married Women, 21–45, by Education of Head and Wife, 1969

Variable	LOLO	LOHI	HILO	HIHI
CHILDREN 0–6	156	299	343	434
	(33)	(104)	(72)	(74)
CHILDREN 7–17	49	119	45	128
	(20)	(74)	(47)	(50)
Constant	1,566	1,106	1,584	1,078
	(68)	(189)	(130)	(108)
Number of observations	805	65	179	165
S.E.E.	1,020	866	990	842
R^2	.031	.131	.118	.186

NOTE: The educational strata are defined as follows:
LOLO: both head and wife have not attended college;
LOHI: head has not attended college but the wife has;
HILO: head has attended college but the wife has not;
HIHI: both head and wife have attended college.

The income elasticity of preschool child-care time is clearly evident when the educational strata are employed. Comparing groups in which the wife's price of time is held "constant" and family permanent income increases (comparing, e.g., LOLO with HILO and LOHI with HIHI), there is a pronounced increase in the mother's time allocated to preschool children. The income effect resulting from an increase in the wife's price of time, holding constant other family income through the head's education, also appears to dominate the substitution effect when one compares the time allocation between LOLO and LOHI and also between HILO and HIHI.

B. Time Allocation by Sex of Child

A persisting and well-documented earnings differential is that between men and women. Even after standardizing for differences in labor market participation and other factors, women still receive earnings which are about 71 percent of those received by men.[43] There are several reasons that can be, and have been, offered for this phenomenon; we are concerned here with how this differential might relate to environmental forces in the home via sex differentials in the time allocated to preschool children. This was investigated by regressing annual housework hours on the number of sons and the number of daughters 0–6 and 7–17 in each of the four head-wife education groups defined above. The comparison of most interest is between the estimated coefficients of the variables SONS 0–6 and DAUGHTERS 0–6. Systematic differences between these two coefficients by parents' educational attainment may give some insight into one effect of family background on earnings differentials by sex. The regression results are found in Table 3.

TABLE 3 Allocation of Time to Housework for Married Women, 21–45, by Age and Sex of Child, 1969

Variable	LOLO	LOHI	HILO	HIHI
DAUGHTERS 0–6	100	526	278	551
	(48)	(152)	(111)	(106)
DAUGHTERS 7–17	31	−148	8	133
	(32)	(127)	(80)	(87)
SONS 0–6	210	174	410	334
	(46)	(117)	(106)	(99)
SONS 7–17	67	326	87	127
	(32)	(116)	(77)	(85)
Constant	1,568	1,089	1,570	1,070
	(68)	(179)	(131)	(108)
Number of observations	805	65	179	165
S.E.E.	1,019	821	993	841
R^2	.035	.244	123	.198

NOTE: For definition of educational strata see NOTE to Table 2.

There are two interesting implications of these results. First, holding the wife's education constant and moving from low to high levels of the head's education (comparing, e.g., LOLO with HILO and LOHI with HIHI), it is clear that the total time allocated to preschool children increases for both sexes of children. Second, holding father's education constant reveals that wives with at least some college education spend more time with their preschool daughters than with their sons, while the reverse is true for non-college-educated mothers. Further, these differences are, for the most part, statistically significant.[44] Again, as in the results shown in Table 2, the husband's education apparently served primarily as an income proxy leading to increased consumption (production) of the child services commodity and a resultant increase in its time inputs. The mother's education serves to determine the allocation of time by sex within the total determined by the head's "income."

Given the results of Table 3 and the presumption that family background factors operating through parental time inputs to children influence the child's ability to learn, we would now expect that daughters of well-educated mothers would receive substantially more formal schooling than daughters of less-educated women, holding constant the father's income or education. Testing this hypothesis is, in general, difficult, for in most data sources only the male has been interviewed, and he is presumed to be the head of household. As a consequence the surveys obtain detailed information on only his family background and subsequent schooling. Fortunately, however, a recent paper by Greg Duncan, using the panel data that we employ here, was able to investigate in some detail the effects of family background on daughter's educational attainment.[45] Duncan obtained a sample of children between the ages of 18 and 30 who had completed their formal education, and who had lived in one of the panel's interviewed families in 1968 but had become heads or wives in their own households by 1972. Information on the educational attainment of the children was obtained from them directly in 1972, while information on their parents' characteristics were obtained from the parents themselves during the years 1968–72.

Duncan finds that the effects of parental education on the educational attainment of their children differ considerably between males and females. While father's education is predominant in affecting the son's education, this is not the case for daughters. Holding constant family income, family size, and several other factors, the effects of father's education on the educational attainment of daughters is negligible. The net effect of mother's education on the daughter's attainment is strong and significant, however, and shows that having a college-educated mother rather than a grade-school educated mother is associated with slightly more than one extra year of schooling for daughters.

Duncan's results seem to be generally consistent with those of Sewell and Shaw.[46] Using logitudinal data for a sample of Wisconsin high school seniors, they find that the mother's education has a stronger independent effect in influencing her daughter's, rather than her son's, educational plans and attainment. In addition, they find that in discrepant situations where one parent has some college education but the other does not (as in our LOHI and HILO groups), mother's, rather than father's, education seems to exert the greater influence on the educational aspirations and achievements of their childen, and especially their daughter.

We would suggest that our results on parental time allocation by sex of child give additional insights into the effects of family background on educational attainment reported by Duncan and Sewell and Shaw. While the evidence is still, given the lack of the requisite data, somewhat fragmented, there is now considerable circumstantial evidence that the ability to learn and the educational aspirations and achievements of the children are affected by environmental forces within the household. Further, it appears that there are sex differentials in the effects of these forces and they are initially a reflection of differential time investments in the children by the mother.

C. Time Allocation to Preschool Children by Size of Family

The number of a child's siblings has consistently been shown to have an important and adverse effect on the child's educational attainment.[47] The environmental explanation usually offered for this phenomenon is one associated with the financial burden a large number of children imposes on the family and the consequent disability of the family head to finance investments in formal schooling for his children.[48] It now seems reasonable to expect that the allocation of time to a preschool child, as well as market-purchased resources, may be influenced by the number of other children in the family. In this section we shall offer some additional results on this topic, using data from the 1969 wave of the panel, and shall discuss their implications for inequality of educational attainment.

A test for the presence of diminishing marginal time inputs to preschool children is provided by including a quadratic term in CHIL-DREN 0–6 in our regressions. Table 4A illustrates the results of this addition when the data are stratified by the head's occupation. In contrast to the occupational stratification used above, the HIGH SES (Socioeconomic Status) group includes only professionals, managers, and self-employed businessmen. LOW SES includes every other coded occupation. The data are again stratified by head's and wife's educational attainment in Table 4B.

Variable	HIGH SES	LOW SES
CHILDREN 0–6	331	294
	(132)	(83)
CHILDREN 7–17	98	60
	(30)	(19)
(CHILDREN 0–6)^2	41	−46
	(47)	(24)
Constant	1,258	1,498
	(90)	(72)
Number of observations	389	825
S.E.E.	908	1,020
R^2	.179	.037

NOTE.   Occupations included in these SES strata are as follows:
   HIGH SES: Professionals, managers, and self-
               employed businessmen
   LOW SES: Clerical, craftsmen, operatives, and laborers

TABLE 4B: **Tests for Diminishing Marginal Time Inputs to Preschool Children, by Education of Head and Wife, 1969**

Variable	LOLO	LOHI	HILO	HIHI
CHILDREN 0–6	262	919	524	282
	(85)	(314)	(199)	(190)
CHILDREN 7–17	50	111	54	120
	(20)	(73)	(49)	(51)
(CHILDREN 0–6)^2	−33	−233	−62	63
	(24)	(112)	(64)	(73)
Constant	1,526	973	1,514	1,118
	(74)	(194)	(149)	(118)
Number of observations	805	65	179	165
S.E.E.	1,019	843	990	843
R^2	1.033	.189	.122	.189

NOTE: For definition of educational strata, see NOTE to Table 2.

In the strata in which the head is relatively well educated or employed in a high-status job (HIGH SES in Table 4A and HILO, HIHI in Table 4B), there is no evidence of significant diminishing time input to preschool children as their number increases. In contrast, the three strata containing less-educated or low-status heads do indicate a significant decline in the time input per preschool child as the number of these children increases. It would be difficult to argue, we believe, that low-status families are more efficient in the provision of child services and that this is reflected in the existence of "economies of scale." What the results do indicate is that the wives in high-status (as defined by the head's education and/or occupation) families spend essentially a constant amount of time per preschool child regardless of their number, while very young children in low-status households receive a smaller amount of parental time than did their older preschool siblings.[49] To the extent that preschool time inputs do have a positive influence on educational attainment and subsequent earnings, the results of Tables 4A and 4B have important implications for studies of inter-generational income inequality.

In a recent paper, Johnson and Stafford have shown again that the level of educational attainment on the part of individuals is systematically determined by a set of economic and demographic variables pertaining to early childhood development. In particular, for a sample of white males in 1964 taken from the *Productive Americans* data source, they have demonstrated that the number of brothers and sisters (BROSIS) has a negative effect on individuals' educational attainment (ED), other things being equal.[50] Our results imply that if the individual is raised in a family whose head has a high level of education, he will receive a constant and relatively large level of preschool time inputs independent of the number of his siblings. Given this result, the negative effect of BROSIS on ED should be attenuated for these high-status families. To test this, we have estimated a regression explaining ED much like that appearing in Johnson and Stafford, except that we have added a dummy variable HIEDFATHER (=1 if the respondent's father graduated from high school) and an interaction term between this variable and BROSIS. High school rather than college education of the father has been used as the variable "breakpoint" given that high status and/or high educational attainment is more properly reflected by this level of educational attainment in the first half of this century. The results of the regression are as follows[51]

$$
\begin{aligned}
ED = \ &1.03 \ln (EXP) + 1.42 \text{ HIEDFATHER} - 0.046 \text{ AGE} \\
&(0.283) \qquad\quad (0.301) \qquad\qquad\qquad (0.006) \\
&-\ 0.375 \text{ BROSIS} + 1.05 \text{ GRURB} \\
&\ \ (0.043) \qquad\qquad (0.170) \\
&+\ 0.136 \text{ OLDBR} + 0.174 \text{ HIEDFATHER} \times \text{BROSIS} \\
&\ \ (0.047) \qquad\qquad (0.083) \\
&+\ 8.02 \\
&\ \ (1.60)
\end{aligned}
$$

with $R^2 = 0.311$ and S.E.E. $= 2.52$. The positive and significant coefficient of the interaction term indicates that the negative effect of BROSIS on ED is substantially weakened for individuals from high-status families.[52] While we do not have direct evidence that this is due to the constancy of preschool time inputs in these households, this regression result together with Tables 4A and 4B provides circumstantial evidence for this.

D. Religious Preferences

In Section IIIB of this paper we described some recent evidence that Catholics have higher earnings than Protestants for a given level of formal schooling. In the context of our investigation, this fact leads us to test for the presence of differentials in preschool time inputs by parents' religious preference. In the context of our discussion in Section II, religion can serve as an index of parental preferences for child development, and to the extent that we find such differentials, it will provide us with an appealing explanation of the observed subsequent earnings differentials by religious background. Hopefully, this result and the others presented above will lead to an interpretation of the background variables which are usually included in earnings functions in a manner which is consistent with their relationship to preschool investments in human capital.

TABLE 5 Allocation of Time to Market Work and Housework, Married Women 21–45, by Religious Preference, 1969

Variable	Housework	Market Work
CHILDREN 0–6	182	−155
	(32)	(26)
CHILDREN 7–17	66	−13
	(17)	(13)
CATH	87	−0.15
	(99)	(80)
CATH 0–6	111	−76
	(62)	(50)
Constant	1,451	846
	(56)	(46)
Number of observations	1,111	1,111
S.E.E.	976	976
R^2	.075	.058

Using our same basic sample—husband/wife families between the ages of 21 and 45 where the husband was employed in 1969—we have eliminated all families with religious preference other than Protestant and Catholic.[53] Our basic functional form is by now familiar, given the previous discussion; we add here a dummy variable CATH (=1 if the family is Catholic) and the interaction between CATH and CHILDREN 0–6 (CATH 0–6). A positive sign on the estimated coefficient of CATH 0–6 would indicate that, across our sample, Catholic mothers allocate more housework time to preschool children than do Protestants. As is apparent from Table 5, this is precisely what we observe with the null hypothesis that the coefficients of the Catholic dummy and interaction variable are both zero being rejected at the 1 percent level in the housework regression ($F = 6.57$). We cannot reject this hypothesis in the market work regression at the 5 percent level where the calculated $F = 2.35$. In conjunction with the work of Hause,[54] Table 5 again provides some evidence of the relationship between preschool time inputs into children and postschool economic well-being.

E. Educational Expectations

In Section II, we hypothesized that in choosing a level of home training or quality for their children, parents "look at" the incremental effect of their time and goods inputs to the children in the home on the child's lifetime welfare, given the child's initial inherited endowment of ability and family wealth. The model implies, then, that parental home investments in the child's training are influenced by their expectations and aspirations concerning the child's future educational attainment and market earnings. In this section, we provide some empirical evidence of the effect of educational expectations on the mother's time allocated to preschool children.

A variable, COLEXP, was constructed on the basis of the answer to the following question in the 1969 wave of the panel: "About how much education do you think the children will have when they stop going to school?" If the parents answered that some or all of their children will go to college, the variable COLEXP was set equal to one. The relative importance of the mother's characteristics is again shown here through a simple regression of COLEXP on the head's and wife's educational attainment. The wife's education was a much stronger indicator of the parents' educational expectations for their children.[55] The variable, COLEXP, and an interaction term between it and the number of children 0–6 was added to our basic regression model. If parents view time inputs as important in influencing the child's future economic and social well-being, this should be reflected by way of a positive coefficient on the interaction term in the regressions explaining annual hours of housework and a negative coefficient in the market work regressions. The sample was again stratified by head's occupation and grouped into HIGH SES and LOW SES (see Table 4A). The mean value of COLEXP was 0.38 and 0.25 in the two subsamples, respectively. The regression results are found in Table 6.

TABLE 6 Allocation of Time to Housework and Market Work, Married Women, 21–45, by Educational Expectations, 1969

Variable	——HIGH SES——		——LOW SES——	
	Housework	Market Work	Housework	Market Work
CHILDREN 0–6	388	−162	118	−125
	(60)	(48)	(36)	(29)
CHILDREN 7–17	102	−13	33	6
	(40)	(32)	(23)	(18)
COLEXP	−159	354	340	260
	(164)	(133)	(129)	(103)
COLEXP*CHILD 0–6	163	−242	126	−130
	(99)	(180)	(71)	(57)
Constant	1,262	682	1,676	761
	(124)	(100)	(84)	(67)
Number of observations	403	403	858	858
S.E.E.	896	723	1,009	807
R^2	.194	.121	.045	.054

NOTE: For definition of SES strata, see NOTE to Table 4A.

The regression results confirm the hypothesis that we maintained regarding the effect of college expectations held by the parents for their children on the mother's allocation of time to preschoolers. They also, we believe, provide support for the life-cycle model we presented above, in that home investments in children are determined, in part, by a lifetime planning process in which educational expectations play a part. In addition, the work of Harvey Brazer and Martin David[56] has shown that the educational expectations held by parents are an important determinant of the children's subsequent educational attainment, so we again have a link between preschool home investments and investments in formal schooling.[57]

F. Time Inputs and Child Development[58]

In the previous pages, we have presented a considerable amount of evidence on the relationship between family background variables as they are typically measured (e.g., occupation, education, family size, and religion) and preschool time investments in children. We have, in effect, argued that while the usual family background variables do describe the general characteristics of the home environment, they are most importantly an index of preschool home investments made in the children by the parents, and it is this investment which is the important environmental force in influencing the child's subsequent economic and social well-being. In this section, we present some evidence from child psychologists on the effects of parental time on the child's cognitive and affective abilities. Again, we would point out that a lifetime panel of representative individuals is not available to us, so that a direct link between preschool time inputs and subsequent educational attainment and earnings cannot be shown. Nevertheless, we have presented a considerable body of circumstantial evidence of this link and here present a brief review of experimental research on the relationship between parental time and child development.

The traditional view in the child development literature attributed the child's intellectual ability largely to genetic factors. However, recent research has consistently shown the importance of parent-infant interaction as a source of stimulation, emotional satisfaction, and reinforcement for the child.[59] The interaction between parent and child develops within the infant the expectancy that his behavior can affect his environment and this, in turn, motivates the infant to produce and utilize behaviors and skills not reinforced in his past experience.[60] The most dramatic effects resulting from the lack of parental time during the preschool years have been demonstrated among children in grossly deprived circumstances. This research has demonstrated that the infant needs a one-to-one relationship with an adult or he may suffer cognitive and affective loss that may never be recouped.[61] Within the normal range of parent-child interaction, a few studies have shown that the expressive and vocal stimulation and response that the mother gives to the infant affects its development. Of particular interest here is the fact that while attempts to increase cognitive performance through day care programs have not been very successful, increasing the mother-infant interaction in the home does appear to have more enduring positive effects.[62] Arleen Leibowitz, using the longitudinal data on high I.Q. individuals discussed in Section IIIB, has shown that the quantity of time allocated to them as preschool children was a significant determinant of their I.Q. as measured at age eleven. I.Q., in turn, had a significant positive effect on the years of schooling completed, holding constant several other family economic and demographic characteristics. The work of James Guthrie et al.[63] reviews evidence that suggests that the lack of parental time devoted to the physical care of preschoolers is closely associated with both physical and mental deficiencies and a consequent reduction of the child's ability to succeed in school.

There is no evidence that the time devoted to preschool children must be that of the mother, or that this role is better filled by a male or a female. There is some evidence that the child benefits from predictability in handling, but it is not clear whether different handling has any long-lasting effects. Thus, while our data indicate that it is only the mother's housework time which responds to the presence of preschool children, the evidence from the research of child psychologists suggests that if it were supplied, the father's time could be as important as the mother's in affecting the child's future well-being.

The evidence presented above concerning the importance of the parent-child interaction is not, it should be pointed out, conclusive. The problem of not having comparable groups plagues studies of the effects of the intensity of maternal care on the child's cognitive development. In particular, there are no studies available which have permitted intensity of maternal contact to vary while controlling for other factors (such as maternal personality and amount and type of paternal contact) which might affect the results. Nevertheless, the child development literature does provide some useful and important insights into how environmental factors in the home, as measured by maternal time devoted to children, influence the child's ability to learn.

V. CONCLUSION

In this paper, we have tried to set forth a consistent explanation of the role of family background variables in the earnings functions estimated by economists. These variables have generally been entered in a rather ad hoc manner, with little justification for their inclusion. It is clear, however, that influences of family background, particularly as measured by parental time inputs to the care of children, fit well into the theory of investments of human capital (although our preliminary efforts to integrate these and subsequent investments into a lifetime human capital model can certainly be improved upon). In particular, we have shown here that besides the well-known relation between investments in formal schooling and family of origin variables, investments of time in preschool human capital are also related to these variables (e.g., parental education, occupational status, family size, religion).

Preschool investments in time and goods are, according to the work of child psychologists, associated with a child's ability to learn (as partly indexed by I.Q.). In our interpretation, this ability to learn results in a larger sustainable adult human capital stock as well as more extensive investment of time in learning new skills early in life and over a longer period of one's lifetime. Greater ability to learn is reflected in greater educational attainment and lifetime earnings profiles which are more precipitous and fan out with age (and possibly experience) from those with less investments.

The achievement literature of psychologists implies that parental orientation or *qualitative* aspects of the parent-child interaction are important in developing the child's motivation and ability. The research which we have presented, while not inconsistent with this view, suggests that the *quantity* of time is also important in child development. It would seem that future research ought to be directed toward measurement of both quantity and quality of parental time as it influences child development. In addition, the extent to which variations in quantity and quality of parent-child interaction (per child) influence development *within* a given occupational grouping of the parents should be determined.

It is often alleged that parental social status (or occupation) per se determines subsequent adult status of the child. Yet, we have evidence consistent with the view that parental time makes a difference within occupational grouping of the parents. First, within admittedly broad SES groups, those parents who expect their children to attend college put in more time on these children while they are preschoolers. Second, larger families within the lower SES group put in less time per child. This effect of family size results in lower educational attainment of the children. Although this can be partly rationalized by smaller financial resources per child as well as less time per child, these findings are consistent with the view that time is important. Third, cultural differences as indexed by religion are related to differences in time per child. If the findings of Hause on earnings and education differentials by religious preference are substantiated by further research, this will provide additional support for our hypothesis of home time as an important input to children. Fourth, women who are more educated put in more time with their preschool daughters and this appears to influence the daughters' educational attainment. These results obtain for a given status of the father and suggest that highly educated women succeed in teaching their daughters how to learn even in the case where the husband is of moderate to low educational attainment.

Another aspect of the study of parental time to preschoolers is the potential role it has in effecting inter-generational links in education and income. While parental income allows greater money expenditure on children (e.g., greater educational quality), inter-generational influences through quantity and quality of time inputs are likely to be important as well. In this regard our finding on time differentials by sex, if substantiated by additional research, is important. Suppose women who are highly educated grew up in homes where they as preschool daughters were "high quality" children and received sizably larger inputs of time than did sons. Then, the fact that these women put in more time on their own daughters suggests that familial patterns of time input to children can be an important source of inter-generational stability in economic capacities. More generally, if inputs by parents are important in influencing lifetime achievement of their children, it is not surprising that in examining demographic behavior a high quality elasticity with respect to family income is observed. If parents adopt the child-rearing practices they themselves experienced and if quality matters for later development then this provides an apparent explanation for the high elasticity.

Our study also suggests that high parental income, by inducing a greater demand for child quality (inputs of time and money), contributes to inter-generational correlation in economic capacities. Consequently, income effects inducing greater child care may be one of the important benefits of income maintenance programs.

NOTES

1. As one example of his argument he cited the following problem posed and answered by a friend: "Suppose a man born blind, and now adult, and taught by his touch to distinguish between a cube and a sphere [and] . . . suppose then the cube and sphere [to be] placed on the table, and the blind man be made to see: *quaere*, whether *by his sight, before he touched them*, he could now distinguish and tell which is the globe, which the cube? . . . Not. For though he has obtained the experience of how a globe, how a cube affects his touch, yet he has not yet obtained the experience that what affects his touch so or so must affect his sight so or so . . ." (John Locke, *An Essay Concerning Human Understanding* [New York: World Publishing Co., Meridian Books Edition, 1964], pp. 121–122).
2. Adam Smith, *The Wealth of Nations* (New York: Random House, Modern Library Edition, 1937), p. 15.
3. Ibid., p. 161.
4. As Duncan notes: "The presumption is that improvements in knowledge [of the socioeconomic life cycle] will result in modifications and complications of the models" (O. D. Duncan, "Inheritance of Poverty or Inheritance of Race?" in *On Understanding Poverty*, D. P. Moynihan, ed. [New York: Basic Books, 1964]), p. 89.
5. See G. S. Becker, *Human Capital and the Personal Distribution of Income* (Ann Arbor: University of Michigan, 1967).
6. Some work along these lines has been done recently. See Gilbert Ghez and Gary S. Becker, "The Allocation of Time and Goods Over the Life Cycle," processed,

University of Chicago, Apr. 1972; Michael Landsberger and Ury Passy, "Human Capital, Its Shadow Price and Labor Supply," mimeograph series No. 138, Israel Institute of Technology, 1973; Frank Stafford and Paula Stephan, "Labor, Leisure and Training Over the Life Cycle," paper presented at the 1972 Meetings of the Econometric Society (revised November 1973).

7. To introduce time preference or other age-dependent changes in preferences one can specify the general function as $U = U(c, X, t)$.

8. Stafford and Stephan, "Labor, Leisure and Training," p. 12. With a zero interest rate, the shadow value of financial assets, λ_R, is a constant throughout.

9. If parents' home training increases β, this will also motivate an earnings profile which rises dramatically over time.

10. See Paula Stephan, "Life Cycle Training Paths Subsequent to Formal Schooling" (Ph. D. diss., University of Michigan, 1971), pp. 22–24 and 126–127. See also her "Human Capital: A Productive Function with Factor Substitution" (Working Paper No. 7374-17, Department of Economics, Georgia State University, February 1974). Jacob Mincer discusses this issue in *Schooling, Experience, and Earnings* (New York: NBER, 1974), pp. 11–23.

11. Robert J. Willis, "A New Approach to the Economic Theory of Fertility Behavior"; and Gary S. Becker and H. Gregg Lewis, "On the Interaction Between the Quantity and Quality of Children"; both appearing in *Journal of Political Economy* 81 (March/April 1973); Willis, pp. S14–S64; Becker and Lewis, S279–S288.

12. R. Gronau, "The Effect of Children on the Housewife's Value of Time," *Journal of Political Economy* 81 (March/April 1973): S168–S199; and "The Intra-family Allocation of Time: The Value of the Housewife's Time," *American Economic Review* 63 (Sept. 1973): 634–651.

13. Otis Dudley Duncan, "Ability and Achievement," *Eugenics Quarterly* 15 (Mar. 1968), pp. 1–11.

14. Henry Levin has called to our attention one recent sociological study which does report substantial direct influences of parental background (as measured by income) on son's earnings. See William Sewell and Robert Hauser, "Causes and Consequences of Higher Education: Models of the Status Attainment Process," *American Journal of Agricultural Economics* 54 (Dec. 1972): 851–861. They report that son's income ten years subsequent to high school graduation is $93 higher for each $1,000 of parents' income. However, it is well known that richer parents purchase higher quality schooling for their children and we would expect higher earnings for graduates of higher quality school systems (given *years* of schooling).

15. Otis Dudley Duncan, "Ability and Achievement," p. 6.

16. See J. S. Coleman, "Equal Schools or Equal Students," *The Public Interest*, no. 4 (Summer 1966): 70–75.

17. Arthur R. Jensen, "How Much Can We Boost I.Q. and Scholastic Achievement," *Harvard Educational Review* 39 (Winter 1969): 1–123.

18. Jensen, "How Much Can We Boost I.Q.," p. 52.

19. Ibid., p. 97.

20. Ibid., p. 18. This result is consistent with the negative influence of number of siblings on early intelligence reported by Duncan. Also, a recent article by Joe D. Wray ("Population Pressure on Families: Family Size and Child Spacing," in National Academy of Sciences, *Rapid Population Growth* [Baltimore: Johns Hopkins Press, 1971]) demonstrates the influence of family size on children's I.Q.

21. Jensen, "How much Can We Boost I.Q.," pp. 16, 17.

22. Ibid., pp. 13–15.

23. Christopher Jencks et al., *Inequality* (New York: Basic Books, 1972).

24. J. E. Bogen, R. DeZure, W. D. Tenhouten, and J. F. Marsh, "The Other Side of the Brain and the A/P Ratio," *Bulletin of the Los Angeles Neurological Societies* 37 (Apr. 1972): 49–61.

25. Bogen et al., "Other Side of the Brain," p. 50.

26. See Heinz Heckhausen, *The Anatomy of Achievement Motivation* [New York: Academic Press, 1967], pp. 150–162.

27. Samuel Bowles, "Schooling and Inequality from Generation to Generation," *Journal of Political Economy* 80 (May/June 1972): S219–S251. See also his "The 'Inheritance of I.Q.' and the Intergenerational Reproduction of Economic Inequality," *Review of Economics and Statistics* 56 (Feb. 1974): 39–51.

28. Zvi Griliches and William Mason, "Education, Income and Ability," *Journal of Political Economy* 80 (May/June 1972): S74–S103.

29. G. S. Becker, "Comment," *Journal of Political Economy* 80 (May/June 1972): S-253. Also see Sewell and Hauser, "Causes and Consequences," p. 858.

30. E.g., Bowles, "Schooling and Inequality," p. S-235.

31. Father variables but not mother variables are also used in Ritchie H. Reed and Herman P. Miller, "Some Determinants of the Variation in Earnings for College Men," *Journal of Human Resources* 5 (Spring 1970): 177–190.

32. See John C. Hause, "Ability and Schooling as Determinants of Lifetime Earnings or If You're So Smart, Why Aren't You Rich?" *American Economic Review* 61 (May 1971): 289–298. See also John C. Hause, "Earnings Profile: Ability and Schooling," *Journal of Political Economy* 80 (May/June 1972): S108–S136. Taubman and Wales, using some of the same data which Hause used, found that with an alternate measure of ability the interaction between ability and subsequent earnings was weakened considerably. They do comment that "ability initially has little effect on earnings but that over time the effect grows, and perhaps grows more rapidly for those with graduate training and high ability." See Paul Taubman and Terence J. Wales, "Higher Education, Mental Ability and Screening," *Journal of Political Economy* 81 (Jan./Feb. 1973): 28–55.

33. Hause, "Earnings Profile," pp. S134–S137. See also Daniel C. Rogers, "Private Rates to Return to Education: A Case Study," *Yale Economic Essays* 9 (Spring 1969): 89–134.

34. Arleen Leibowitz, "Home Investments in Children," *Journal of Political Economy* 82 (Mar./Apr. 1974): S111–S131.

35. Richard Morgenstern, "Direct and Indirect Effects on Earnings of Socioeconomic Background," *Review of Economics and Statistics* 55 (May 1973): 225–233.

36. See George E. Johnson and Frank P. Stafford, "Lifetime Earnings in a Professional Labor Market: Academic Economists," *Journal of Political Economy* 82 (May/June 1974): 549–569, for the influence of graduate school "quality"/personal "ability" on lifetime earnings.

37. See "Allocation of Time to Preschool Children and Educational Opportunity," *Journal of Human Resources* 9 (Summer 1974): 324–341, and "Time Inputs to Children," in J. N. Morgan, ed., *5000 American Families—Patterns of Economic Progress,* Vol. II (Ann Arbor: Institute of Social Research, 1974).

38. Our initial efforts were with the *Productive Americans* data from 1964 (*Productive Americans,* James N. Morgan et al., Survey Research Center Monograph No. 43 [Ann Arbor: Institute for Social Research, 1966]) and more recently with the OEO panel data from 1969. The results from these two data sets are compared in Hill and Stafford, "Time Inputs to Children."

39. Due to the tendency of people of similar characteristics (education, for example) to marry (G. S. Becker, "A Theory of Marriage: Part I," *Journal of Political Economy* 81

[July/Aug. 1973]: 813–846) the errors involved in using the father's characteristics alone are probably not large. However, it is clear that especially in the case of status discrepancy between the husband and wife (see W. H. Sewell and V. P. Shah, "Parents' Education and Children's Educational Aspirations and Achievement," *American Sociological Review* 33 [Apr. 1968]: 191–209) and in several more general instances discussed below, the characteristics of the mother have an independent effect on the child's educational attainment and earnings.

40. In our regressions we present only one or two independent variables at a time. In principle, we have run one large regression with all independent variables but we chose to look at one or two for the purpose of more simply describing the level of time inputs as a function of the particular independent variables.

41. A Chow test was performed to test for equality of regression slopes between the high- and low-status groups. The null hypothesis of status equality was rejected at the one percent level with an $F = 5.88$.

42. See Gronau, "The Effect of Children," and "The Intra-family Allocation of Time."

43. See, e.g., Ronald Oaxaca, "Sex Discrimination in Wages," in *Discrimination in Labor Markets*, A. Rees and O. Ashenfelter, eds. [Princeton: Princeton University Press, 1973].

44. Using a one-tailed test at the 0.05 level, the estimated difference between the coefficients of DAUGHTERS 0–6 and SONS 0–6 is significantly *greater* than zero for LOHI ($t = 1.98$) and HIHI ($t = 1.53$) and significantly *less* than zero for LOLO ($t = 1.64$). The null hypothesis that the coefficients are equal could not be rejected for HILO ($t = 0.82$). The existence of substantial differences in inputs across children (by sex) is not consistent with the Willis and Becker/Lewis quality models in Section IIB, which assume constant quality for each child. This was pointed out to us by Dennis DeTray.

45. G. Duncan, "Educational Attainment," in *5000 American Families—Patterns of Economic Progress*, J. N. Morgan, ed. [Ann Arbor: Institute of Social Research, 1974]. See p. 321 (Table 7-2) of Volume I.

46. Sewell and Shaw, "Parents' Education."

47. See, e.g., O. D. Duncan, "Inheritance of Poverty" and "Ability and Achievement," and S. Bowles, "Schooling and Inequality."

48. It has been shown that I.Q. is related to birth order, with earlier parities scoring higher on standard I.Q. tests. That this reflects more than the obvious fact that firstborns are also more likely to be in small families can be seen in Lillian Belmont and Francis A. Morolla, "Birth Order, Family Size, and Intelligence," *Science* 182 (Dec. 1973): 1096–1100.

49. The lowered "quality" per child as number of children increases in low-income families is not consistent with the assumed constant quality level across children in the Willis and Becker/Lewis models.

50. Johnson and Stafford, "Social Returns to Quantity and Quality of Schooling," *Journal of Human Resources* 8 (Spring 1973): 139–155.

51. The variables are defined as follows: EXP = per pupil educational expenditure by region of origin, AGE = age of respondent in 1964, GRURB = dummy variable if grew up in an urban area, OLDBR = number of older brothers and sisters. Numbers in parentheses are standard errors. For additional details, see Johnson and Stafford, "Social Returns" (pp. 142–147).

52. Belmont and Marolla in "Birth Order" demonstrate that larger family size results in a lower I.Q. but that this family-size effect is attenuated for nonmanual workers and is greater for manual workers.

53. A separate analysis of Jewish families was undertaken but the sample size was too small (N = 33) to provide meaningful estimates of the parameters.

54. Hause, "Earnings Profile." However, he shows an effect of religion beyond the influence of years of schooling. To be fully consistent with our view, the time input should have an influence on years of schooling attained as well.

55. The estimated regression is as follows

$$COLEXP = -.101 + .024 \ EDW + .009 \ EDH$$
$$(.058) \ (.006) \qquad (.004)$$

with $R^2 = .039$ and S.E.E. $= .443$ and where EDW (EDH) is the educational attainment of the wife (head). The hypothesis that the coefficient of EDW is greater than that of EDH could not be rejected at the 1 percent level ($t = 3.06$).

56. "Social and Economic Determinants of the Demand for Education," in *Economics of Higher Education*, S. Mushkin, ed. [Washington, D.C.: Government Printing Office, 1962].

57. It should be noted that college expectations in the *absence* of preschool children induces a reallocation of time away from housework and into the labor market. This is consistent with research on how families pay for college. See John B. Lansing, Thomas Lorimer and Chikashi Moriguchi, *How People Pay for College* [Ann Arbor: Survey Research Center, 1960].

58. The authors are indebted to Lois W. Hoffman of the University of Michigan's Department of Psychology for her help in guiding us through the child development literature.

59. In some work currently under way at Stanford University, Eleanor Maccoby and Carol Jacklin are attempting to assess the relation between hormonal balance, early physical and emotional interaction, and subsequent development through a panel study of children starting at infancy. There is some evidence that direct physical contact with infants alters the hormonal balance and influences development.

60. M. Lewis and S. Goldberg, "Perceptual-Cognitive Development in Infancy: A Generalized Expectancy Model as a Function of the Mother-Infant Interaction," *Merrill-Palmer Quarterly* 15 (Jan. 1969): 81–100.

61. L. J. Yarrow, "Separation from Parents During Early Childhood," in *Review of Child Development Research*, M. L. Hoffman and L. W. Hoffman, eds. [New York: Russell Sage Foundation, 1964].

62. P. Levenstein, "Cognitive Growth in Preschoolers through Verbal Interaction with Mothers," *American Journal of Orthopsychiatry* 40 (Apr. 1970): 426–432.

63. *Schools and Inequality* [Cambridge: Massachusetts Institute of Technology Press, 1971], pp. 140–144.

13 ‖ COMMENTS

Jacob Mincer
National Bureau of Economic Research and Columbia University

I. INTRODUCTION

Hill and Stafford devote half of their paper to a conceptual mapping of the link from family background to individual lifetime earnings. That this link appears to be long, indirect, and intricate may surprise some who view income as a largely inherited characteristic. This is not to say that genetic and economic inheritance is unimportant, but the view of earnings as a rental on the human capital stock does shift the focus of attention from direct transfers to parental efforts toward accumulation of the human capital stock of their children. This leads to research questions about (1) the nature and scope of parental efforts, (2) the productivity of these efforts in adding to the human capital stock of children, and (3) the relative importance of parental contributions in the ultimate level of the capital stock achieved by the children.

The empirical work reported by Hill and Stafford relates to the first research question, and only to a partial measure of parental efforts, namely the *time* aspect of parental inputs in early child development. On the second question, the effects of these inputs, the authors cite fragmentary evidence related to educational attainment of children. The last step, the ultimate connection with lifetime earnings, is not attempted at all. So, the itinerary charted in the first half of the paper is traversed only a small part of the way, but this is not for lack of imagination or courage. The problem is that available data fade out long before the destination is in sight.

Even if short, I find this excursion into a large and ramified subject very interesting, not only in the negative sense of highlighting the need for kinds of data economists rarely dream about, but also positively in terms of the findings, particularly as they complement the authors' previous findings and those of other explorers who are very much on the same trail.

II. FINDINGS ON PARENTAL TIME INPUTS

Hill and Stafford visualize the early production function of a child's human capital as consisting of three inputs: the genetic endowment of the child, parental contributions of market goods, and parental inputs of their own time. Their research is confined to the estimation of parental time inputs, and of their relation to parental characteristics. No attempt is made to study the other inputs and the relations among them.

It is worth noting, at this point, that interest in the mere quantity of time, which Hill and Stafford focus on, was originally provoked by observations of labor force data. These showed not only that mothers of preschool children withdraw from the labor market, but that the more educated mothers tend to withdraw from market work to a greater extent than less educated mothers, despite their higher market wage rates and, on average, stronger lifetime attachment to the labor force. Here was a tip of an iceberg that appeared to promise a cluster of riches below the surface; such as: insights into fertility behavior, especially its quantity-quality tradeoff or interaction, and human capital transfers within the family, particularly from mothers to children, with implications for the earnings of each.

In her 1972 Columbia doctoral dissertation Arleen Leibowitz has drawn the attention of economists to these facts and promises. The intimation of measurability of opportunity costs of child care and of their relation to parental characteristics opened the door to (a) a better understanding of the role of forgone market experience in the earnings functions of women, and (b) to an enrichment of the human capital earnings function by the inclusion of "home investments," along with schooling and postschool investments, as determinants of earning capacity. However, for such research leads to be taken seriously, it is first necessary to ascertain whether the time patterns suggested by the labor force data do, indeed, reflect child care activities in the household. This is where Hill and Stafford come in.

In the present paper, they report results of an analysis of the Office of Economic Opportunity (OEO) Panel Study of Income Dynamics, which replicates and extends their previous work on the *Productive Americans* data. Both the 1964 (*Productive Americans*) and the 1969 (OEO Panel) surveys provide reports by parents of hours of housework and of market work during the preceding year. Reports from close to a thousand husband-wife families were studied in each survey. In both Hill and Stafford studies, the method of estimating time parents devoted to their children was indirect: a regression of hours of housework on the number of children in particular age intervals yielded coefficients which represent the increment to housework associated with the presence of a child of specified age. This coefficient was interpreted as child care time.

In the 1964, but not the 1969, study the same analysis was performed for market time as well as for housework time. Also father's housework was studied in addition to that of the mother.

In terms of the regression coefficients of housework time, in 1964 fathers apparently contributed very little time to preschool children, so they were evidently not worthy of attention in the 1969 study. Related work (by H. Ofek and J. Smith) showed that fathers' market work actually increases when there are preschool children in the household, as mothers' market earnings diminish or vanish—an example of intrafamily substitution in the household production function.

I shall return to the matter of father's time and market time of mothers after reviewing the findings in the present paper in which the authors report only on housework time of mothers.

Very briefly, the findings—as interpreted from the regression coefficients—are:

1. Maternal child-care time devoted to a preschool child amounts to several hundred hours per year.
2. The amount of time devoted per child by mothers is almost twice as large in families with professional and college educated parents than in other families. Time inputs into *preschool* children are larger by similar amounts when either the father's or the mother's education increases. However, and this is something the authors did not note: for school-age children (age 7–17) time inputs increase with mother's, but not with father's, education (Table 2).
3. The panel feature of the OEO data makes possible an attempt to verify the inferences from cross sections in observing changes over time in the same families. It appears that in families who did not have children (age ≤2) in 1969 but had them in 1971, mothers increased their housework by amounts comparable to those observed in the cross section. Also, the differences by occupational status of fathers are comparable. The new finding here is that presence of older children reduces housework of mothers at the lowest socioeconomic levels, but not elsewhere (Table 2).
4. Child care time declines as the child ages, but significant time inputs continue to be provided to school-age children of more educated parents, particularly of more educated mothers—as noted before (point 2).
5. Child care time is less per child in families with more children—mainly at the lower, not the higher, socioeconomic levels.
6. At given levels of father's education, more educated mothers devote more time to preschool daughters. While for given levels of mother's education, more time is devoted to preschool sons (by mothers always) as father's education rises.

III. DISCUSSION OF RESULTS AND OF SOME COMPARATIVE FINDINGS

Now, how do the estimates of incremental housework time compare with differentials in market work associated with the presence of children? As already noted, in the 1964 study, Hill and Stafford ran regressions of mothers' time in market work in addition to the housework time regressions. It appeared that mothers' market time reductions associated with additional children paralleled the estimates of additional housework time by socioeconomic status of parents and by age of children, but no findings were shown for numbers of siblings or sexes of children. Also, the reduction of market work time was, on average, half the size of the increase in housework, with greater reductions in market work at higher socioeconomic level per unit increase in housework time.

If these findings are reliable, they encourage research based on market work statistics which are much more abundant than time budgets. They suggest, however, that reliance on market work data would lead to an underestimate of time inputs to children. Regrettably, Hill and Stafford do not replicate or do not show the market time regressions in the present paper, particularly with respect to their more provocative findings on effects of sexes and number of children.

There are, of course, problems with the meaning of the indirect measures of child care time, as the authors surely realize but do not spell out in the present paper. To list a few:

1. Any time not reported as housework, but spent with children in joint consumption or leisure activities, is left out. Clearly, both estimates of time inputs and of opportunity costs would change if joint consumption time were included, as it ought to be.

2. Substitution of child care for other categories of housework is likely to impart a downward bias to the regression estimates of time inputs to children. On the other hand, housing space and "household production" surely increase concurrently with the number of children as income grows in the life cycle, particularly in the middle and upper socioeconomic strata families. This imparts an upward bias to the coefficients, and may account for the attenuation of the negative effect of siblings on child care time which Hill and Stafford observe in the more affluent families.

3. The quality of familial interactions obviously cannot be gauged by the quantitative measures alone. If they could, the implication would be that fathers could be replaced by money disbursing agencies. Perhaps this is happening, and the nature or absence of effects is a testable hypothesis. But, even in quantitative terms, part of the problem with the Hill and Stafford data is that they tend to emphasize physical care of children and largely leave out the recreational, social, and educational interactions, in which both parents tend to participate.

Indeed, this distinction is observed by Arleen Leibowitz, who analyzed the details of child care more directly in time budgets collected from over 1,000 Syracuse, New York, families by Kathryn Walker at Cornell. Leibowitz calculated time per day devoted to physical and "other" child care—the latter defined as time spent with parents in social and educational activities. Her estimates translated to an annual basis show roughly similar orders of magnitude as those of Hill and Stafford, but the differences by education of mother seem much smaller. Those differences are more pronounced in "other care" than in physical care. Incidentally, Leibowitz finds that fathers, while contributing little (about 10 percent of total) to physical care, contribute as much as 30 percent of total time to "other" child care. Both high- and low-education groups spend decreasing amounts of time as children age, but the lesser decline in higher education groups found by Hill and Stafford is not clearly confirmed in the Syracuse data. The other findings of Hill and Stafford were not replicated as shown.

IV. INFERENCES AND CONJECTURES

Having learned something about parental time allocation to children, we must still relate these inputs to the output, from which the significance of the inputs presumably derives. Returning to the production function and assuming we can define the output, we must hold the other inputs fixed to observe the effects of parental time in increasing the early human capital of children. If the other factors, genetic endowment, parental money expenditures, and the quality of time inputs are ignored, we must be assuming that the observed time inputs are positively correlated with the others, or dominating their effects, so as to constitute an index of scale of production.

Actually, Hill and Stafford show no direct relation between parental time inputs and measures of child's development or achievement. Some evidence to that effect was shown by Arleen Leibowitz in the very special Terman sample in a simplified recursive scheme. Briefly, she found that (1) parental time inputs as well as education of the mother affected the child's I.Q. measure, (2) once I.Q. and both parental educations are taken into account, the time-input measures have no further effect on educational attainment of the child, and (3) once education and experience of the adult son or daughter are taken into account, none of the parental variables are of much consequence in affecting earnings.

The evidence which Hill and Stafford cite on the relation between family background variables and educational attainment of children is indirect. It utilizes the positive correlation they found between time inputs and education of each of the parents. But since parental education variables represent factors such as income and quality of child care, it is difficult to read their effects as being primarily reflections of time inputs, since these other things are factors of production in their own right.

Nevertheless, Hill and Stafford are right to emphasize that since mothers spend more time in child care than fathers, the traditional focus on father's socioeconomic level in analyses of family background effects on education should be broadened to include the characteristics of the mother. Indeed, effects of mother's education tend to be more pronounced than that of father's in several studies which hold family income constant. On the other hand, the evidence on differences in these effects by sex of children or by number is quite tenuous.

Other studies, and especially a recent one by Rosenzweig based on state urban populations, contradict the notion of a stronger effect of mother's education on the educational attainment of daughters than of sons. And the Population Council survey by Wray on the effects of numbers of siblings on various measures of child quality (such as health and I.Q.) does not exempt the upper socioeconomic levels from the observed negative correlations.

In sum, the findings are, as yet, fragile, and the power of statistical evidence tends to diminish as we try to move along the progression of links between family background and lifetime earnings. All the more should the efforts of Hill, Stafford, and Leibowitz be encouraged, especially by economists. Their work makes a strong case for an economic analysis of the role of family in the formation of economic capacities of children. It also lays the groundwork for an economic analysis of social mobility, an important aspect of income distribution, and a problem on which, thus far, only some light of sociologists and much heat of ideologues has been brought to bear.

REFERENCES

Hill, R., and Stafford, F. "Allocation of Time to Preschool Children and Educational Opportunity." *Journal of Human Resources* 9 (Summer 1974): 323–341.

Leibowitz, Arleen. *Women's Education and Allocation of Time*. Ph.D. dissertation, Columbia University, 1972.

————. "Production in the Household." Meetings of the American Economic Association, Dec. 1973.

————. "Home Investments in Children." *Journal of Political Economy* 82, Part II (May 1974): S111–S131.

Ofek, H. "Labor Supply in the Family Context." Ph.D. dissertation, Columbia University, 1971.

Rosenzweig, M. "Differential Investment in Children." Yale University Growth Center Discussion Paper 193, Nov. 1973.

Smith, J. P. "Family Labor Supply over the Life Cycle." Mimeographed. New York: NBER, 1977.

Wray, J. D. "Population Pressure on Families." *Population Council Report* 9, Aug. 1971.

14

LEE A. LILLARD
National Bureau of
Economic Research

The Distribution of Earnings and Human Wealth in a Life-Cycle Context

INTRODUCTION AND SUMMARY

Economists have long been interested in individual earnings differences and in the dispersion of earnings within populations. Recent development of explicit theoretical and empirical earnings functions from life-cycle human capital investment models increases the potential to explain existing earnings distributions and to predict changes in them. Life-cycle models suggest that current earnings are not a good index of well-being if choices about intertemporal transfers are available. Under certain conditions, the present value of earnings net of investments in human capital, human wealth, is an index of economic well-being. The purpose of this paper is to outline a set of conditions under which human wealth is an index of well-being in a life cycle, prefatory to empirical estimates of earnings and human wealth distributions for the 1960 Census population. Some tentative remarks on the interpretation of economic well-being in a life-cycle context when these conditions are not met are included. The basic conditions which allow human wealth to index well-being include the existence of a loan market for consumption

NOTE: This research was sponsored by National Science Foundation grant GS–31334 and U.S. Department of Labor grant L73-135 to the NBER. I have benefited from the comments of T. D. Wallace and Finis Welch. I wish to thank Christy Wilson for drawing the original figures.

557

expenditures, a fixed leisure-work time pattern, and no consumption of education or investment. If these are relaxed, appropriate adjustments to human wealth must be made.

The basic earnings equation used to predict earnings and human wealth is estimated on the NBER-Thorndike sample described later. Earnings are a function of age, schooling, and ability. This earnings function is used to predict earnings and human wealth distributions for the 1960 Census population, based on the joint distribution of age, schooling, and ability, as seen in age and schooling data from the 1960 Census of Population, and ability data within schooling classes from the NBER-Thorndike sample.

The purpose of this exercise is essentially to point out how earnings functions, which have been studied quite extensively, can be made more useful—that is, by predicting human wealth and by generating earnings distribution. Researchers often state: "If the distribution of such and such an independent variable has been this, then . . . ." These statements can be considered more formally, as I am trying to illustrate here. Even if the Thorndike sample is not like the 1960 Census (differences are noted later), the earnings function estimated from it can reproduce the general characteristics of the 1960 Census observed earnings distribution. In a previous paper, I have presented in more detail the statistical distribution theory necessary to go from the joint density of a population with respect to those characteristics which determine earnings through the estimated earnings function to a predicted earnings distribution. Even without any restrictive assumptions such as log-normality, the predicted distributions are positively skewed and the moments for subpopulations, such as schooling and age groups, behave similarly in actual and predicted distributions. The many caveats are pointed out in the paper.

Predicted earnings distributions are derived for the overall population, for schooling classes, for age groups, and for ability classes. Both the actual distribution and the distribution of earnings corrected for variation not explained by age, schooling, and ability are presented for each, along with selected summary statistics and Lorenz Curves. The predicted distributions reproduce the characteristics of the actual distributions for the 1960 Census population quite well, except for differences which can be explained between the 1960 Census population and the NBER-Thorndike sample.

Recognizing the degree of "fit" between predicted and observed 1960 Census earnings distributions and the reason for it, we then proceed to predict the distributions of mean human wealth, based on the same equations. This section attempts to estimate "What would be the distribution of the expected value of human wealth for employed men in the 1960 Census if they were like the NBER-Thorndike sample?"

Detailed mean human wealth distributions and selected statistics are presented, assuming a retirement age of sixty-six for several rates of discount. The sensitivity of the selected statistics, especially the mean, to discount rate and retirement age assumptions are then considered. Finally, some rough estimates of the variance of human wealth, rather than the variance of the mean, are constructed.

A lower bound on the variance of human wealth is defined as the variance in the present value of predicted earnings plus an error component which is completely transitory and independent from period to period. An upper bound is defined as the variance of the present value of predicted earnings plus a completely persistent error component which is constant over the life cycle but varies randomly over individuals, independently of the level of ability and schooling. Intermediate cases can be considered as combinations of these when the transitory and persistent variations are independent.

We study the effect of schooling level and of ability level on the distributions and on measures of inequality. These estimates are especially sensitive to discount rate assumptions. The effect of increased schooling level, for example, is to increase mean human wealth at discount rates below some level and to decrease mean human wealth at discount rates above that level. If this rate is below what we believe to be an appropriate discount rate—say, the rate appropriate to consumption loans or the real rate of return on physical assets—then the discrepancy could be accounted for by, for example, the consumption value of schooling or education discussed earlier. In this case, then, the human wealth measure is not a good index of economic well-being and the distribution of mean human wealth is not a good measure of the distribution of mean economic well-being. We may gain some insight into the partial effect of other attributes such as ability if they do not affect the consumption value of schooling. Ability increases the mean human wealth almost uniformly. Some inferences are made about the effect of retirement age on mean human wealth, but these results are tenuous, due to the limited upper age range in the sample.

MEASURING ECONOMIC WELL-BEING IN A LIFE-CYCLE CONTEXT

The life-cycle model is developed by assuming an individual maximizes lifetime utility, represented by an intertemporal utility function[1] within his opportunity set. Three components of the opportunity set are distinguished: endowment, market opportunities, and productive opportunities. All of these are relevant to an index of economic well-being.

Human capital investment models[2] assume that the individual has a homogeneous—across individuals and units within an individual—initial endowment of human capital, E_o, which can be rented in the labor market at the constant rate R per unit of time. This stock of human capital is subject to a given constant exogenous rate of deterioration δ, but the opportunity is available to use purchased inputs D, at price, P, and own human capital K to produce new human capital, according to the production function $Q(K, D)$. The net change in the stock of human capital at any point in time or age is then represented by $\dot{E}_a = Q(K_a, D_a) - \delta E_a$. These conditions relate to endowment and productive possibilities. Other endowments might include an initial endowment of nonhuman capital, an exogenous time stream of receipts or debts, and an exogenous time stream of educational inputs.[3]

Utility-maximizing behavior is clearly influenced by the existence or availability of market opportunities for intertemporal transfer of funds. When such funds are available, clearly earnings in a given time period cannot be considered an index of well-being.

There are many possible sets of assumptions. Consider market opportunities as they affect consumption, investment in human capital, and interperiod transfers of nonhuman wealth. The possibility of borrowing and loaning funds, endowed or earned, expands the permissible set of time paths of investment and consumption decisions. For example, there may be no market opportunities for borrowing or lending at all, in which case the individual must finance current investment in human and/or nonhuman capital and consumption out of current market earnings and exogenous receipts.

It is illustrative to introduce the concept of perfectly separable market opportunities—that is, funds borrowed for one purpose, consumption, investment in human capital, or investment in nonhuman capital, cannot be used for any other purpose. This is primarily introduced to capture the notion that investment in human capital accesses a different funds market, because (1) human capital is embodied in the individual, thus not subject to confiscation, which would imply a higher borrowing rate; and (2) there exist government-subsidized loan programs available only for educational investment at a lower rate. The nature of a perfectly separable funds market for financing direct educational expenditures, PD_a, will then affect only productive possibilities. Many additional constraints may also be imposed on the model, such as compulsory school attendance, and various school subsidy formulas.

Define:

$$Y_a^* = R \cdot E_a \qquad \text{Earning capacity at age } a$$

$$Y_a = R(E_a - K_a) \qquad \text{Gross earnings at age } a$$

$NY_a = R(E_a - K_a) - PD_a$ Earnings at age a net of direct educational investment

$I_a = RK_a + PD_a$ Total investment in human capital at age a

$N =$ Age at which working life and life cycle end, exogenous

$HW = \int_{t=0}^{N} e^{-rt} NY_t \, d_t$ Human wealth, present value of net earnings discounted at a rate dependent upon market opportunities

This development of the human capital model has ignored one sense of the time concept and has implicitly assumed that human capital is embodied in the individual, so that time and human capital enter the human capital production function in the same way. That is, $Q(K_a, D_a) = Q(SE_a, D_a)$, where S is the fraction of total time allocated to the production of new human capital. An equivalent model can be developed in terms of the use of time. A fuller discussion of the time interpretation is attempted in Ben-Porath (1967), Ghez (1972), Heckman (1974), and Lillard (1973).

The relevant index of lifetime economic well-being is lifetime utility. Consider a pedagogical construction under which human wealth defined as the present value of earnings net of educational investment is a relevant measure of economic well-being and the effect of failure to satisfy those conditions.

Human Wealth as an Index of Lifetime Well-Being

Human wealth is an index of economic well-being when the individual behaves in such a way as to maximize the present value of net earnings and there are no exogenous endowments of initial wealth or time stream of receipts or debts. The individual then maximizes his lifetime utility by arranging intertemporal consumption in an optimal manner, subject to the wealth constraint represented by human wealth. When exogenous endowments are present but do not affect the criteria of maximizing human wealth, their present value (positive for a time stream of receipts and negative for a time stream of debts) should be added to the wealth constraint and correspondingly to the index of economic well-being.

Under what conditions then will an individual behave in such a way as to maximize human wealth. We have already assumed the individual has perfect knowledge of himself and the world and faces no uncertainties. There is a fixed constant amount of time in each period to be allocated to either the labor market to produce earnings or to human capital production.[4] The utility function of the individual does not include as arguments either the stock of human capital or the use of time allocated to either the labor market or human capital production. This condition excludes the possibility that either investment or work is a more desirable activity, that obtaining education or going to school could be a consumption activity, and that the individual might derive utility directly from being more educated or highly trained. The individual has available a source of unlimited borrowing and lending at a constant rate of interest, r, for the purpose of consumption. This source of funds may or may not be available to finance educational expenditures as long as the loan markets are perfectly separable as defined earlier. If the unlimited funds are available for human capital investment, then the funds markets need not be separable and the model corresponds to the Ben-Porath (1967) specification. However, the loan market for human capital may contain any sort of imperfection as long as it is separable. This loan market may include low interest loans from parents or government agencies, high interest loans due to the embodied nature of human capital, or in the extreme no loan market for human capital investment expenditures at all. Under these conditions, clearly the relevant rate of discount of net earnings is the interest rate, r, on loans for consumption purposes.

The particular life cycle of earnings model specified by these conditions, assuming no loan market for direct educational expenditures and a Cobb-Douglas production function,[5] is capable of being fully solved analytically, which illustrates the simultaneity of schooling and earnings while providing an exact functional form for earnings and human wealth. This solution is exposited fully in Lillard (1973) and only summary results are presented here.

The solution implies that in the early period the individual specializes in the production of new human capital, full-time schooling, using all of his earning capacity for investment.[6] The period of specialization is

$$0 \leqq a \leqq a^*$$

where a^* denotes the age at which the individual stops specializing and begins investing only a fraction of his earning capacity. Specialization ends when earning capacity ceases to be an effective constraint on investment. One implication of assuming no loan market for educational expenditures, and the only qualitative difference from the Ben-Porath perfect loan market case is the prediction of positive labor force participation during the period of specialization. The individual supplies a constant fraction[7] of his human capital to the market to finance expenditures for direct educational expenditures, i.e., $R(E_a - K_a) = PD_a$.

Specialization with no loan market means investing exactly all of earnings capacity in the form of forgone earnings and purchased inputs. Specialization with the same perfect loan market available means using all of human capital in production and borrowing to finance purchased inputs. There are many intermediate assumptions, including availability of special loan markets, scholarships, and so on,[8] which may be available only during the period of specialization or formal full-time schooling. The effect of these conditions is summarized in the stock of human capital, earning capacity, at a^*. This earning capacity at a^* depends upon initial earning capacity, RE_o. It is important to note that the solution for earnings after the period of specialization takes earning capacity at a^* as a datum, both earnings and a^* are endogenous state variables and any exogenous change which affects earnings will also affect the length of time in specialization, and both must be considered jointly.

The length of the period of specialization is endogenous to the model. The optimum age to stop specializing in production and begin positive net earning is that point where the investment paths of the two regions cross. That is, the individual will invest according to the rule K_a and D_a for nonspecialization, except when he is constrained by his earning capacity, during which period he will invest all of his earning capacity. The solution for a^* as a function of the parameters and initial endowment of human capital, but not age, is an implicit simultaneous structural relationship which must be satisfied for each solution. The implicit solution for a^* must be considered simultaneously with earnings function to make any inferences. The expression allows inferences about the direction of effect of each characteristic on the length of the period of specialization.

For the particular solution reported in Lillard (1973), the length of the specialization period varies directly with N, R, and β, and inversely with E_o, P, and r. The effect of all other characteristics is ambiguous.[9]

For the rest of the life cycle, after the period of specialization ends, $a^* \leq a \leq N$, the individual invests some fraction of his earning capacity in producing more human capital. Neither forgone earnings nor direct educational expenditures, and thus investment in human capital, is a function of the initial stock of human capital E_o.[10] Gross investment declines with age after the period of specialization, reaching zero at retirement age N.[11] Earning capacity, observed earnings, and net earnings at any age after a^* depend upon the stock of human capital and the investments at that age. All of these results for the specific solution are presented in greater detail in Lillard (1973).

Given these assumptions so that human wealth is an index of well-being, what then does human wealth depend upon? As we have noted, it depends upon access to borrowing funds to finance human capital investment. Clearly access to such a loan market expands investment possibilities and enhances human wealth. Also, individuals may differ in the efficiency with which human capital is produced, the production parameters β, β_1, and β_2 in the specific model above. More efficiency in producing new human capital clearly increases human wealth. An empirical counterpart to β is introduced later.

An increase in the retirement age N, or a decline in the rate of interest, will clearly increase human wealth. A decline in the rate at which human capital deteriorates, δ, will clearly increase human wealth. Individuals may differ in some or all of these parameters. For empirical purposes, we shall assume that they differ only in ability representing efficiency of production, and schooling representing a^*. The effect of increased schooling on human wealth is less clear, since it represents the effect of all other differences between individuals, and these differences must satisfy the implicit simultaneous schooling relationship.

When Human Capital Is Not an Index of Well-Being

The life-cycle model makes it clear that when individual inter-temporal choice is available, individual period earnings are a myopic measure of well-being. Under certain conditions, when inter-temporal consumption choices are perfectly free, human wealth is a measure of lifetime well-being, and individual-period earnings observations and the age-earnings profile itself merely illustrate the optimal timing of a separable process. When these very stringent conditions are not met, the problem of indexing well-being falls ultimately back to considerations of the inter-temporal utility function. Human wealth and the lifetime pattern of earnings become variables of choice. Constructing an index based on observable values becomes extremely complex. The relevant models of life-cycle behavior have not yet been fully developed or analyzed. The problem is not solved here but relaxation of certain conditions one at a time may lend some additional insight into the problem. Let us begin with relatively simple deviations with the clearest implications.

The first potential problem is that schooling or education or the level of investment in human capital may enter the utility function directly. Alternatively, utility may be a function of the stock of human capital held by the individual—say, as a status measure, or by affecting the efficiency of consumption (see Michael [1972]). In these cases an investment in human capital yields returns not measured in the present value of net earnings. Human wealth will understate return to education. Human wealth may decline with increased schooling, discounted at the consumption borrowing rate, while total inter-temporal utility rises.

Secondly, consider the effect of allowing leisure time, as well as investment and work time, to be a subject for choice. This is the most widely considered generalization and has not yet been satisfactorily treated. Heckman (1973) and Stafford and Stephan (1973) attempt to model this generalized problem. Few specific conclusions have been obtained. Smith (1973) analyzes the problem of labor-leisure choice, assuming wages are exogenous. In the more general model, the individual must make inter-temporal choices about consumption of leisure and goods. The leisure-investment-work choice makes earnings endogenous and the result of previous decisions. We cannot say whether the present value of net earnings overstates or understates economic well-being. This depends on the individual's relative valuation of goods and leisure and their timing over the life cycle. What is needed is a measure of "full wealth." The usual suggestion is to value leisure time at the market wage and consider the net worth of total time. This approach seems to be inappropriate if the wage is endogenous. The individual will "choose" a low investment and wage pattern "because" he values his leisure time more. The full wealth at market-wage correction works in the wrong direction. What is needed in this situation is an index of initial endowments—say, of human capital—and the constraints the individual faces. A larger initial endowment makes an individual unambiguously better off, even if he chooses a lower value of human wealth than an individual beginning with less. This does not get us very far empirically but is meant as food for thought.

Another obvious omitted concept is nonhuman wealth, which must be included in any wealth calculations. The existence of initial nonhuman wealth clearly affects the access of the individual to funds for financing educational investments.

The effect of risk and uncertainty on investment in human capital is considered briefly by Levhari and Weiss (1973) and Razin (1973). Again the problem is exceedingly difficult and clear implications are few.

These tenuous statements are meant only as caveats in the interpretation of the empirical estimates which follow.

1960 CENSUS: PREDICTED EARNINGS DISTRIBUTIONS AND THE DISTRIBUTION OF HUMAN WEALTH

The previous sections considered the appropriateness of certain measures of economic well-being. This section considers the distribution of well-being if it is measured by either earnings or human wealth. Both the overall distributions and distributions within schooling and ability classes and age classes, where appropriate, will be considered. The format is to consider an earnings equation estimated using the NBER-Thorndike sample data, then to predict aggregate earnings distributions for the 1960 Census. The estimated age-earnings equations are a function of schooling and ability levels. This section may be characterized as answering the query, "What would be the distribution of earnings of the men in the NBER-Thorndike sample if they had the distribution of age and schooling present in the 1960 Census?" or "What would be the distribution of earnings of employed men in 1960 if they were like the men in the NBER-Thorndike sample?" As will be pointed out later, several caveats are in order in using one group to predict the other. Predicted and actual 1960 distributions are compared when possible.

Recognizing the degree of "fit" between predicted and observed 1960 Census earnings distributions and the reason for it, we then proceed to predict the distributions of mean human wealth based on the same equations. This section attempts to estimate "what would be the distribution of the expected value of human wealth" either "of the men in the NBER-Thorndike sample if they had the schooling distribution present in the 1960 Census" or "of employed men in the 1960 Census if they were like the NBER-Thorndike sample." Detailed mean human wealth distributions and selected statistics are presented, assuming a retirement age of sixty-six for several rates of discount. The sensitivity of the selected statistics, especially the mean, to discount rate and retirement age assumptions are then considered. Finally, some rough estimates of the variance of human wealth, rather than the variance of the mean, are constructed.

A lower bound on the variance of human wealth is defined as the variance in the present value of predicted earnings plus an error component which is completely transitory and independent from period to period. An upper bound is defined as the variance of the present value of predicted earnings plus a completely persistent error component which is constant over the life cycle but varies randomly over individuals, independently of the level of ability and schooling. Intermediate cases can be considered as combinations of these when the transitory and persistent variations are independent.

The primary conclusions are that aggregate earnings distributions can be reproduced reasonably well even with the crude calculations made here, and that it is possible to generate estimates of human wealth distributions. In doing so, we can study the effect of schooling level and of ability level on the distributions and on measures of inequality. These estimates are especially sensitive to discount rate assumptions. The effect of increased schooling level, for example, is to increase mean human wealth at discount rates below some level and to decrease mean human wealth at discount rates above that level. The cutoff rate is in the neighborhood of 5.5 percent. If 5.5 percent is below what we believe to be the appropriate discount rate—say, the rate appropriate to consumption loans or the real rate of return on physical assets—then the discrepancy could be accounted for by, for example, the consumption value of schooling or education discussed earlier. In this case, then, the human wealth measure is not a good index of economic well-being and the distribution of mean human wealth is not a good measure of the distribution of mean economic well-being. We may gain some insight into the partial effect of other attributes, such as ability, if they do not affect the consumption value of schooling. Ability increases the mean human wealth almost uniformly. Some inferences are made about the effect of retirement age on mean human wealth, but these results are tenuous, due to the limited upper age range in the sample.

A Specific Earnings Function and Estimates

It is well founded theoretically and empirically that earnings depend upon schooling, ability, and age or experience.[12] The earnings function estimated and used here results from a life cycle of earnings model which is discussed elsewhere in detail, along with the empirical estimates.[13] The estimated earnings function is cubic in age, quadratic in schooling, and cubic in ability, including all interactions. This is the "best equation," in the sense that the age, schooling, and ability polynomials were determined by error variance criteria.[14] The estimated earnings function is[15]

$$Y(A, S, B) = 21108.50 - 3921.20A + 877.25S + 148.02SA + 206.09A^2$$
$$- 794.20S^2 + 6.87SA^2 + 116.42S^2A - 7.82S^2A^2 - 45197.00B$$
$$+ 11015.00BA + 4721.40BS - 1820.80BSA - 594.93BA^2$$
$$+ 1065.00BS^2 + 83.51BSA^2 - 122.05BS^2A + 8.56BS^2A^2$$
$$+ 28134.00B - 6738.40B^2A - 5035.20B^2S + 1435.20B^2SA$$
$$+ 371.38B^2A^2 - 240.65B^2S^2 - 72.59B^2SA^2 + 5.86B^2S^2A$$
$$+ 0.99B^2S^2A^2 - 2.99A^3 - 0.31A^3S + 0.15A^3S^2 + 9.09BA^3$$
$$- 1.04BA^3S - 0.17BA^3S^2 - 5.74B^2A^3 + 1.04B^2A^3S$$
$$+ 0.03B^2A^3S^2$$

where A = age, S = years, and B = ability index. The resulting age-earnings profiles are presented in Figures 1A, 1B, and 1C for various ability and schooling levels. Both schooling and ability raise earnings at

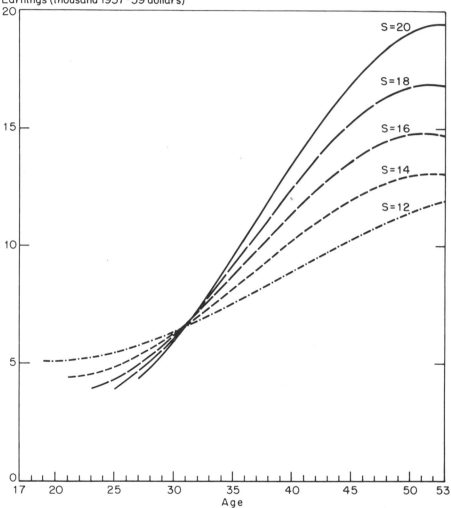

FIGURE 1A Cubic Estimated Age-Earnings Profiles Based on the NBER-Thorndike Sample for Several Schooling Levels at the Average Ability Level

Earnings (thousand 1957–59 dollars)

S=20

S=18

S=16

S=14

S=12

Age

NOTE: All earnings are in 1957–59 dollars.

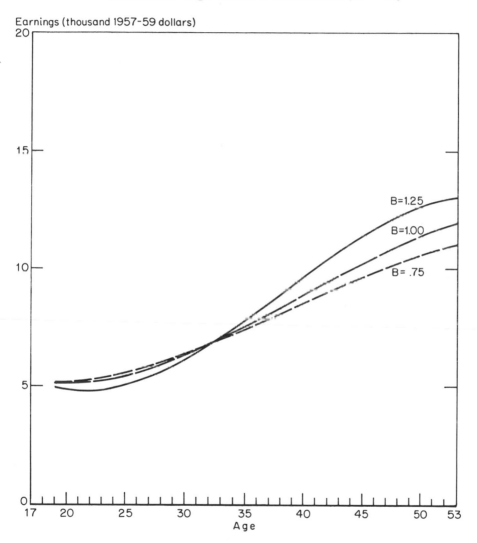

FIGURE 1B Cubic Estimated Age-Earnings Profiles Based on the NBER-Thorndike Sample for Average Ability and One Standard Deviation (.25) Above and Below for High School Graduates (S = 12)

Earnings (thousand 1957-59 dollars)

B=1.25

B=1.00

B= .75

Age

FIGURE 1C Cubic Estimated Age-Earnings Profiles Based on the NBER-Thorndike Sample for Average Ability and One Standard Deviation (.25) Above and Below for College Graduates (S = 16)

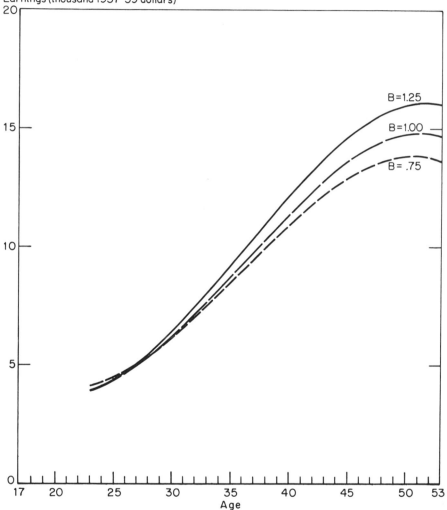

Earnings (thousand 1957-59 dollars)

every age in the life cycle after some initial period.[16] Earnings estimated beyond age fifty-six are a pure prediction, in the sense that there are no individuals in the sample beyond that age. The resulting estimates of human wealth, defined as the present value of predicted earnings, are presented in Figures 2A and 2B for discount rates of 3, 5, and 7 percent.[17]

Consider the characteristics of the NBER-Thorndike sample which may make it different from the general population described in the 1960 Census. The NBER-Thorndike sample is based on a group of males volunteering for Air Force pilot, navigator, and bombardier programs in the last half of 1943. These volunteers were given initial screening tests and a set of seventeen tests to measure various abilities[18] in 1943. Thorndike and Hagen sent a questionnaire to a sample of 17,000 of these men in 1955, which included a question on 1955 earnings. In 1969, the NBER sent to a subset of these men a subsequent questionnaire, which included additional questions on earnings in later years and questions on schooling and initial job earnings.

The data include five separate approximately equally spaced points[19] on the age-income profile as well as the year of initial job, year of last full-time schooling, years of schooling, and seventeen separate measures of ability. The age-income points are approximately initial job, 1955, 1960, 1964, and 1968. The individuals in the Thorndike sample differ from the U.S. male population as a whole in several ways.[20] First, the sample includes a high-ability group. All of the men completed high school or high school equivalency examinations and passed the initial screening for the Air Force flight program. Their general health was better than the general population[21] in 1969. They were more homogeneous in height and weight due to military qualifications. They seem to have a high degree of self-confidence, self-reliance, and risk preference. They tend to be entrepreneurs. An unusual 20 percent work longer hours. Some of these factors may, however, be related to the high ability. The observed age range is nineteen to fifty-seven years but with less than 1 percent outside the range nineteen to fifty-five. The cubic earnings equation is quite a poor prediction above this range, since predicted earnings drop rapidly to large negative values; therefore, earnings are assumed constant at their peak level after the peak occurs.[22]

Earnings Distributions from the Estimated Earnings Function

The distribution of earnings derives from the distribution of the population with respect to age, ability, and schooling. Our predictions use 1960 U.S. Census of Population data on the distribution of the United States

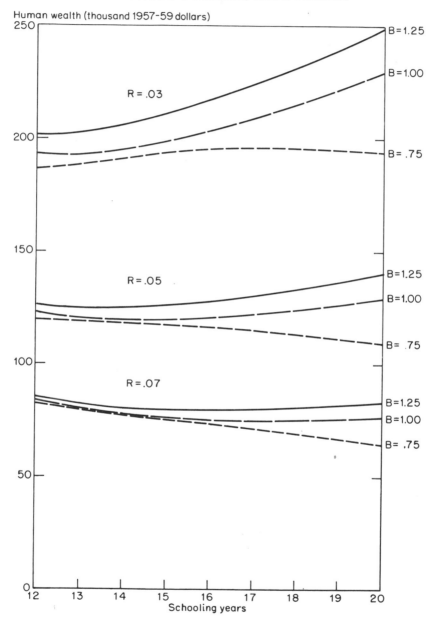

FIGURE 2A   Present Value of Predicted Observed Earnings from the Estimated Age-Earnings Profiles Based on the NBER-Thorndike Sample as a Function of Schooling (N = 66); Discounted at 3 Percent, 5 Percent, and 7 Percent

Human wealth (thousand 1957–59 dollars)

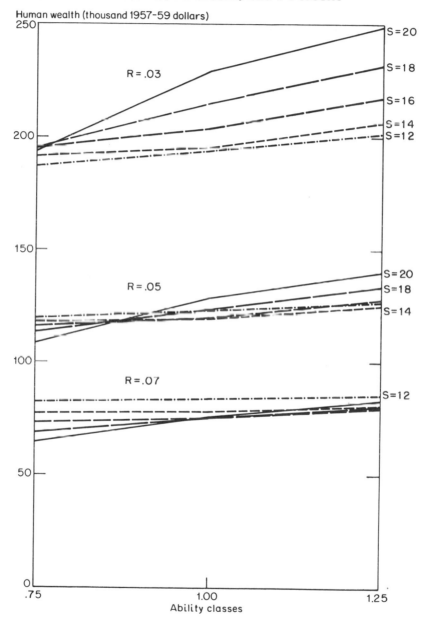

FIGURE 2B Present Value of Predicted Earnings as a Function of Ability from the Estimated Age-Earnings Profiles Based on the NBER-Thorndike Sample (N = 66); Discounted at 3 Percent, 5 Percent, and 7 Percent

Human wealth (thousand 1957-59 dollars)

S=20
S=18
S=16
S=14
S=12

R = .03

S=20
S=18
S=14

R = .05

R = .07

S=12

.75   1.00   1.25

Ability classes

population of males eighteen years old and over by labor force status, years of school completed, and age to predict earnings distributions based on the estimated earnings function.[23] A general framework for translating the joint density of age and characteristics which determine earnings through the earnings function into earnings or human wealth density is presented in Lillard (1973a).

Since the earnings function predicts earnings only after the end of full-time schooling, the distribution of the population by age and schooling is taken only for persons employed and in the civilian labor force. The joint and marginal distributions of age and schooling are presented in Table 1. Since all persons in the NBER-Thorndike sample

TABLE 1 Joint and Marginal Distributions of Age and Schooling for Employed Males Eighteen to Sixty-Four Years of Age with at Least a High School Education, from the 1960 Census of Population

| | Years of Schooling | | | | Age Marginal |
	12	13–15	16	17+	
18–19	.0247	—	—	—	.0247
20–21	.0280	.0146	—	—	.0426
22–24	.0455	.0182	.0080	—	.0716
25–29	.0803	.0313	.0215	.0148	.1480
30–34	.0793	.0306	.0241	.0194	.1534
35–44	.1670	.0560	.0361	.0330	.2920
45–54	.0980	.0405	.0218	.0216	.1819
55–64	.0399	.0227	.0123	.0108	.0858
Schooling marginal	.5628	.2139	.1237	.0996	1.0

have at least a high school education, predictions are restricted to that population. That is, the distribution of yearly earnings is predicted for persons who are between the ages of eighteen and sixty-four, have at least a high school education and are employed.[24] The distribution of the population with respect to ability is assumed to be the same as the NBER-Thorndike sample on which the earning function was estimated, since no ability data are reported in the 1960 Census of Population. Statistics for the distribution of ability by schooling class used is presented in Table 2.[25] For calculation of predicted yearly income, it is assumed that all individuals in an age or schooling class are at the midpoint of that class.[26]

TABLE 2 **Selected Statistics for the Distribution of the Ability Index Overall and by Schooling Level from the NBER-Thorndike Sample for Schooling Interval Midpoints**

	Mean	Standard Deviation
Overall	1.00	.25
By schooling:		
12 years	0.910	.219
14 years	0.971	.229
16 years	1.063	.255
18 years	1.071	.261

Yearly earnings are calculated for each age, schooling, ability combination corresponding to midpoints of class intervals. Each calculated yearly income assumes the relative frequency of the corresponding age, schooling, ability combination. The relative frequency of any (A, B, S) combination is calculated as the joint relative frequency of the age, schooling combination reported by the Census of Population times the relative frequency of the ability level within that schooling class.[27] These relative frequencies are then summed into relative frequencies of yearly earnings for intervals of a thousand dollars.[28]

The resulting predicted overall distribution of earnings and the predicted distribution for various subpopulations effectively represent distributions of mean earnings allowing no variation around the predicted value. However, only about 28 percent of the variation in earnings is explained by variation in age, schooling, and ability.

Consider the problem of correcting the distribution of earnings for variation not accounted for by variation in age, schooling, and ability. The error variance of the estimating equation is $\hat{\sigma}^2 = 36,593,472$ (standard error $= 6,049.25$). It is assumed that the errors are identically and independently[29] distributed, with mean zero and standard deviation 6,049.25. The obvious first-order approximation is simply to correct the standard deviations of the various distributions by using, for example

$$Y = \sqrt{\mathrm{Var}_{A,S,B}[Y(A, S, B)]} = \sqrt{\mathrm{Var}_{A,S,B}[Y(A, S, B)] + \hat{\sigma}^2}$$

This correction is unsatisfactory, however, because of the possibility of assigning a positive frequency to negative earnings, and it is desirable to see the effect on statistics other than the variance. Another simple approximate procedure based on the truncated normal is used to construct the distributions themselves, then selected statistics are calculated from these distributions.[30] This procedure is not entirely satisfactory either, since the truncation increases the mean and decreases the dispersion, but it allows a crude approximation. The probability density for any individual age, schooling, ability combination is calculated as before, but the density is allocated to earnings intervals according to the above-normal distribution centered on the midpoint of the interval in which the predicted value falls. This is an admittedly crude but simple correction. Better corrections can no doubt be obtained through more complex calculations. The interval in which the predicted earnings value falls receives an incremental relative frequency of .0662 times the relative frequency of that age, schooling, ability combination. Intervals adjoining the central interval receive an incremental relative frequency of .0643 times the relative frequency of (A, S, B) each, and so forth, until all relative frequency of the error is exhausted.

Finally, the actual distribution of earnings for employed males sixteen to sixty-four yours old with at least a high school education is calculated from more general distributions reported in the 1960 Census of Population.

All three overall earnings distributions and the corresponding Lorenz curves are presented in Figures 3A and 3B. Selected statistics and relative frequency tables are included in the tables of individual type distribution subsections.

The major caveats may be summarized as follows. The NBER-Thorndike sample and the population of employed males in 1960 differ in several ways, the most important of which is the high level of ability present in the NBER-Thorndike sample. Even though ability distributions by schooling class are used, the distribution of ability especially in lower schooling classes will overstate ability relative to the actual distribution in the 1960 population. The 1960 population is heavily concentrated at lower levels of schooling, especially high school, which is at the lower end of the range of observation for the Thorndike sample and thus subject to less confidence in estimation. Interval midpoints with respect to schooling are used for schooling classes 13–15 (14) and 17+ (18). More precise information about the distribution within these intervals would sharpen the prediction.

Predictions beyond age fifty-six are made assuming earnings constant after peak earnings. This is necessary due to the data limitations in the NBER-Thorndike sample. The age distribution used from the 1960 Census assumes individuals are at the midpoint of age intervals that increase in length from two years at early ages to ten at late ages. Approximately 10 percent of the 1960 population falls in the least reliable age interval, 55–64.

The unequal intervals also cause problems in comparing predicted and actual earnings distributions. Predicted distributions can be made for any interval groups and are made for equal $1,000 intervals here. The Census of Population earnings distributions are unequal beyond $7,000. Statistics are computed using interval midpoints and will vary with

FIGURE 3A   Predicted Mean Earnings, Predicted Corrected Earnings, and Actual Income Distributions for Employed Males between the Ages of 18 and 64 with at Least a High School Education

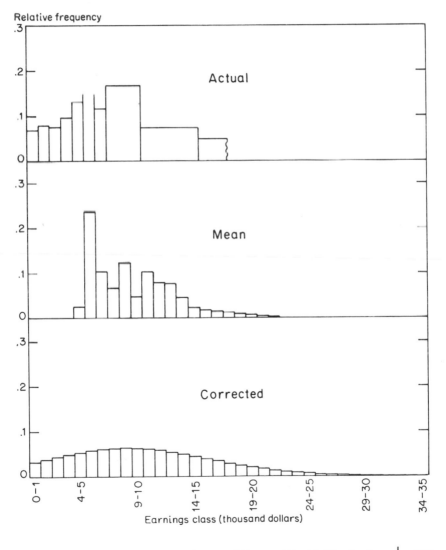

Earnings class (thousand dollars)

Lorenz Curves for Predicted Mean Earnings, Predicted Corrected Earnings, and Actual Income Distributions for Employed Males between the Ages of 18 and 64 with at Least a High School Education

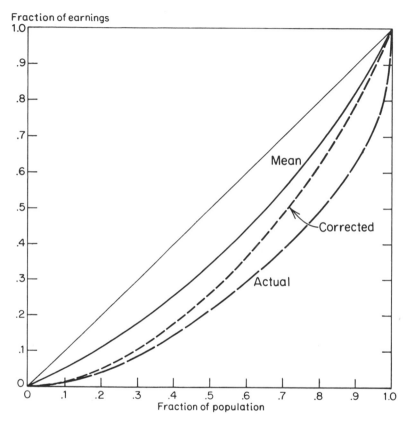

different groupings. Interval midpoints predicted by the Pareto method were used for the interval fifteen thousand dollars and over in the Census of Population, while equal 1,000 intervals up to 90,000 are used for predicted distributions.

Several important differences remain. The 1960 Census figures are for total income, whereas the predicted figures are for earnings in the labor market. There may be important differences in weeks worked during the year, and hours worked during the week, between the sample and the population. There are indications that the men in the NBER-Thorndike sample tend to work longer hours and to spend less time unemployed.

Another very important difference is that the 1960 Census figures include employed students, whereas these persons are excluded in estimating the earnings function. This contributes to the large relative frequency of very low income at early ages in the actual Census distribution. For example, 53 percent of eighteen and nineteen year olds earned less than $1,000. These are likely to be employed students.

Predicted Mean Earnings Distributions

These earnings distributions are derived by transforming probability density from three-dimensional (age, schooling, ability) space through the estimated earnings function into the earnings dimension. Since age, schooling, and ability are not the only characteristics of an individual which determine earnings, these may be termed expected or mean earnings distributions. They are the distribution of the expected value of earnings.

Selected statistics relating to the earnings distributions are presented in Table 3. The relative frequency distributions for selected subgroups are in Figures 4A, 4B, 4C, and 4D.

Predicted Earnings Distributions Corrected for Unexplained Variation

These earnings distributions are mean earnings distributions corrected for variation in earnings not explained by age, schooling, and ability. Instead of transforming density from (age, schooling, ability) space into a single earnings point, it is spread over the positive real line in a manner proportional to the normal probability density, with its center at the predicted mean value and standard deviation equal to the estimated standard error of the regression.

Selected statistics are presented in Table 4. Relative frequency distributions for selected subgroups are presented in Figures 5A, 5B, 5C, and 5D.

Actual Earnings Distributions

These earnings distributions are those actually observed in the 1960 Census. Again they include total income and include employed students. Selected statistics are presented in Table 5. Relative frequencies for selected subgroups are presented in Figures 6A, 6B, and 6C.

TABLE 3 **Selected Statistics for Predicted Mean Earnings Distributions for Employed Males Eighteen to Sixty-Six with at Least a High School Education, Based on an Earnings Function from the NBER-TH Sample**

	Mean ($)	Median ($)	Standard Deviation ($)	Coefficient of Variation	Skewness	Gini Coefficient
Overall	9,182	8,545	3,530	.38	0.86	.21
By schooling:						
12 years	8,188	8,214	2,412	.29	0.50	.16
14 years	9,478	10,246	3,344	.35	0.11	.20
16 years	10,607	11,188	4,281	.40	0.20	.23
18 years	12,391	12,799	5,185	.42	0.03	.24
By age:						
19 years	5,679	5,582	506	.09	3.95	.03
21 years	5,556	5,518	503	.09	2.57	.03
23 years	5,457	5,455	585	.11	1.52	.04
27 years	5,528	5,504	484	.09	2.35	.03
32 years	7,011	6,921	622	.09	1.24	.04
39 years	9,992	9,617	1,632	.16	0.99	.09
49 years	13,283	12,479	2,681	.20	1.08	.11
59 years	13,833	12,917	2,599	.19	1.51	.10
By ability:						
<.75	8,359	8,313	2,537	.30	0.34	.17
.75–1.00	8,732	8,310	3,062	.35	0.65	.19
1.00–1.25	9,474	9,223	3,738	.39	0.62	.22
>1.25	11,241	10,739	4,892	.44	0.51	.25

NOTE: Skewness is measured by the square root of $E(X - \bar{X})^3/S^3$. Coefficient of variation is $S/\bar{X}$. The ability index is distributed with mean 1.0 and standard deviation .25.

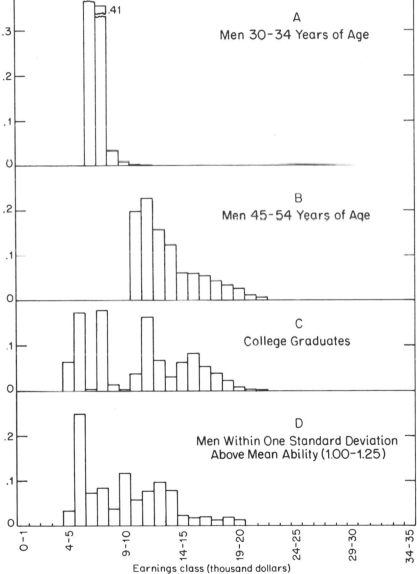

TABLE 4 Selected Statistics for Predicted Mean Earnings Distributions Corrected for Unexplained Variation

	Mean ($)	Median ($)	Standard Deviation ($)	Coefficient of Variation	Skewness	Gini Coefficient
Overall	10,201	9,652	5,971	.59	.53	.33
By schooling:						
12 years	9,343	8,883	5,433	.58	.48	.33
14 years	10,423	9,989	5,902	.57	.42	.32
16 years	11,435	10,959	6,447	.56	.42	.32
18 years	13,041	12,663	7,102	.54	.34	.31
By age:						
19 years	7,535	7,016	4,703	.62	.57	.35
21 years	7,460	6,935	4,678	.63	.58	.35
23 years	7,403	6,871	4,663	.63	.59	.35
27 years	7,442	6,917	4,672	.63	.58	.35
32 years	8,394	7,955	4,959	.59	.49	.33
39 years	10,658	10,373	5,574	.52	.33	.30
49 years	13,538	13,336	6,257	.46	.24	.26
59 years	14,032	13,859	6,283	.45	.24	.25
By ability:						
<.75	9,443	9,125	5,527	.59	.46	.33
.75–1.00	9,813	9,311	5,716	.58	.50	.33
1.00–1.25	10,457	9,912	6,081	.58	.50	.33
>1.25	12,015	11,420	6,864	.57	.48	.33

FIGURE 5A **Predicted Earnings Distribution Corrected for Unexplained Variation for Men 30–34 Years of Age**
FIGURE 5B **Predicted Earnings Distribution Corrected for Unexplained Variation for Men 45–54 Years of Age**
FIGURE 5C **Predicted Earnings Distribution Corrected for Unexplained Variation for College Graduates**
FIGURE 5D **Predicted Earnings Distribution Corrected for Unexplained Variation for Men within One Standard Deviation Above Mean Ability (1.00–1.25)**

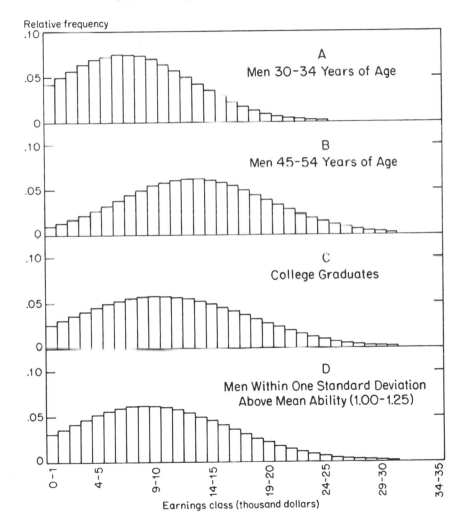

TABLE 5 Selected Statistics for the Actual Distribution of Earnings for Employed Males between the Ages of Eighteen and Sixty-Four with at Least a High School Diploma

	Mean ($)	Median ($)	Standard Deviation ($)	Coefficient of Variation	Skewness	Gini Coefficient
Overall	6,429	5,358	5,356	0.83	2.24	.39
By schooling:						
12 years	5,346	4,933	3,696	0.69	1.42	.34
13–15 years	6,181	5,212	5,464	0.88	1.47	.42
16 years	8,756	6,424	7,650	0.87	1.48	.39
17+ years	12,334	7,258	12,475	1.01	1.26	.47
By age:						
18–19	1,399	993	1,315	0.94	3.36	.43
20–21	2,313	1,889	1,774	0.77	2.16	.39
22–24	4,023	4,109	2,299	0.57	1.03	.31
25–29	5,092	4,884	2,726	0.54	1.62	.27
30–34	6,674	5,940	3,839	0.58	2.01	.28
35–44	7,900	6,471	5,482	0.69	2.09	.33
45–54	9,050	6,529	8,006	0.88	2.01	.40
55–64	9,704	6,164	10,424	1.07	1.99	.48

NOTE: The interval means for the open-ended interval, $15,000 and above, are calculated separately for each class by the Lorenz procedure.

FIGURE 6A **Actual Distribution of Total Income Reported in the 1960 Census of Population for Men 30–34 Years of Age**
FIGURE 6B **Actual Distribution of Total Income Reported in the 1960 Census of Population for Men 45–54 Years of Age**
FIGURE 6C **Actual Distribution of Total Income Reported in the 1960 Census of Population for College Graduates**

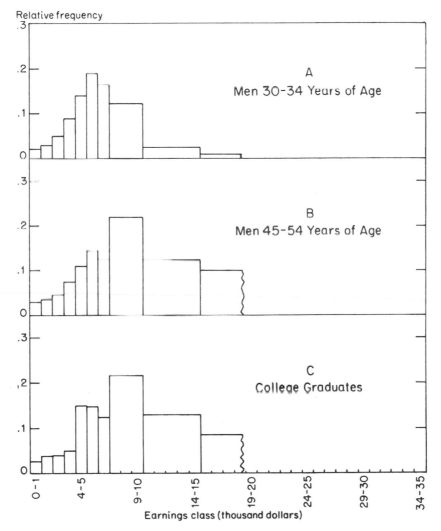

Comparison of Mean Earnings, Corrected Earnings, and Actual Earnings Distributions

It should be remembered that any comparisons between predicted and actual distributions are subject to the qualifications implied by earlier comments. Another important factor in comparing actual and predicted statistics is the unequal 1960 Census income intervals, especially the open-ended interval "greater than $15,000." Better comparisons could be obtained from more detailed intervals, since the selected statistical estimates are quite sensitive to the interval midpoint chosen for the "greater than $15,000" interval.

Both the mean and corrected earnings distributions display the general characteristic of the actual distribution but tend to "overstate" earnings. All of the distributions display positive skewness, and have center and dispersion positively related to age and schooling. The predicted distributions also indicate increased center and dispersion with increased ability. The distributions corrected for unexplained variation tend to "overcorrect" in the sense that the resulting distributions are more smooth than the actual distribution.

The mean earnings distributions obviously have less dispersion than either the corrected or actual distributions, and the corrected distributions tend to overpredict mean earnings relative to the actual distribution, especially at young ages. The procedure used for "correcting" the mean earnings distribution to account for error variation seems to be inadequate. Evidence cited later with respect to human wealth will indicate that the error is not purely transitory, but has a persistent element that is related to age. That is, there are unobserved variables which may be uncorrelated with schooling and ability but which are not uncorrelated with age. An individual's profile may lie wholly above or wholly below the estimated profile and this is not captured in the correction to earnings distribution. Further evidence indicates that the distribution of this persistent component of earnings is itself positively skewed, which would further enhance the positive skewness of earnings as evidenced by the underprediction of positive skewness in the predicted, as opposed to actual, earnings distributions. These problems could be partially alleviated by a more complete accounting of the variation in earnings than is present in this earnings function. It should be remembered, however, that a source of the discrepancy in skewness is the large number of employed students at very low income level. The students' problem also partially explains the overprediction of the mean at young ages. For example, note the $1,000–$2,000 mean income of eighteen through twenty-one year olds. Fully employed males should have mean earnings greater than this even at young ages. The inclusion of these students will also pull down the mean of the overall actual distribution and the mean of the lower schooling groups. It should be noted, also, that the correction procedure by truncating the normal distribution at zero earnings and using conditional densities causes the corrected means to be too large.

Consider the properties of these distributions in more detail. With respect to central tendency, both the mean and median are overstated by the predicted distribution. Even so, the mean and median move in the right direction between age and schooling classes. The mean increases within higher schooling classes for both predicted and actual distributions. Mean and median earnings rise continuously with age in the actual distributions but decline very slightly before rising continuously after age twenty-four in both predicted distributions. The dip in mean earnings is clearly evident in the age-earnings profiles in Figure 1A. In the actual distribution, this property would be hidden by the inclusion of employed young students with very low earnings. Both mean and median earnings are predicted to rise sharply as the ability level of a subgroup rises. Again, the high ability level of the NBER-Thorndike sample itself is a source of the overstatement of earnings. It should be noted that the overall mean of the population is a weighted average[31] of individual subgroup means, whether grouped by age, schooling, or ability.

Dispersion is overstated in the corrected predicted distribution when measured by the standard deviation, but understated when measured by the coefficient of variation. The standard deviation increases continuously with schooling. As age increases, it dips slightly before age twenty-four in the predicted distributions, then rises continuously as it does throughout in the actual distribution. It is interesting to note here that the variance of overall earnings is the sum of the average of the variances of the subgroups and the variance of average earnings of subgroups.[32]

Another characteristic of earnings distributions widely discussed in the literature is concentration represented by the Lorenz curve and its summary statistic, the Gini coefficient.[33] The Gini coefficient is roughly the same between the corrected predicted and actual distributions, except that the predicted distributions always understate inequality at the extremes of age and schooling and overstate it in the middle range. This is partially caused by the large unequal income intervals in the actual distributions. Since the Lorenz curve is approximated by joining chords, the Gini is always understated but the understatement is much larger for the actual distributions.

The predicted distributions tend to indicate less skewness than the actual distribution, but this statistic is very sensitive to the unequal broad earnings classes in the actual distribution, and the results are not directly comparable. This statistic, as mentioned, is especially sensitive to the normality assumption used for the correction.

Predicted Human Wealth Distributions from the Estimated Earnings Function

The purpose of this section is to predict the distribution of human wealth overall, by schooling class, and by ability class for several interest rates and retirement ages. Human wealth is defined here as the present value of earnings, net of educational or human capital investments over the individual's lifetime. The earnings function and corresponding age-earnings profiles estimated from the NBER-Thorndike sample correspond to earnings somewhere between net and gross values, depending upon what fraction of investment is obtained on-the-job. The empirical measure of mean human wealth is then the integral of the discounted estimated earnings function with respect to age from the end of formal schooling to the retirement age.

Since the estimated earnings function corresponds to mean earnings, the estimated human wealth corresponds accordingly to the mean present value of observed earnings. Since the mean error for any age is zero and the estimation error is assumed to be uncorrelated with age, schooling, or ability, the expected discounted sum of errors over the life cycle is also zero. That is

$$PV(S, B) = \hat{P}V(S, B) + \int_{a=S}^{N} e^{-ra} u(a, S, B)\, da$$

where

$$\hat{P}V(S, B) = \int_{a=S}^{N} e^{-ra} \hat{Y}(a, S, B)\, da$$

so that

$$E_u[PV(S, B)] = \hat{P}V(S, B)$$

The predicted distributions presented in this section are the distributions of $\hat{P}V(S, B)$ and thus correspond to mean human wealth distributions. This should be carefully noted in observing the small measures of dispersion and inequality. Corrections for other sources of variation are considered later. The means should be unbiased estimates but the variation should be interpreted as variation in the mean, which obviously has much less dispersion. Thus, overall variation is due to differences in expected human wealth due to schooling and ability. Variation within a subgroup—say, schooling—is due to differences in expected human wealth due to the other factor, ability.

Everyone in the population is assumed to have the same discount rate and the same working life, but individuals differ in schooling and ability. Density is transformed from two-dimensional (schooling, ability)—space into human wealth—space through the integral function. The same schooling and ability distribution and midpoints are used as before.

Detailed selected statistics for mean human wealth are presented in Tables 6 and 7 for the overall population and for schooling and ability subgroups for discount rates three through seven and retirement age sixty-six and a retirement age that is a function of schooling level. The expected retirement ages as a function of schooling level, $N(S)$, are taken from Mincer (1973) and are reproduced in Table 8.

The relative frequency distributions for discount rates 3, 5, and 7 percent and retirement age sixty-six are presented in Figures 7A though 7G.

The most striking result is that there is much less inequality in mean human wealth than in mean earnings. Both the coefficient of variation and the Gini coefficient drop drastically. To the extent that perfect capital markets for consumption are available to everyone, the human wealth variation is a more appropriate index of the variation in expected economic well-being.

The clearest result of a more detailed study of the effect of schooling, ability, retirement age, and the discount rate is that an increased retirement age unambiguously raises mean human wealth, see Figure 8, and an increased discount rate unambiguously lowers it, see Figure 9. It is interesting to note that a 1 percent change in the rate of discount, within the range 3 to 7, has a much larger effect on mean human wealth than an increase of four years in retirement age from sixty-six to seventy. As expected, retirement age has an increasingly smaller effect at higher discount rates but the rate of discount has an increasingly greater effect for later retirement ages.

The effect of the discount rate on variation in human wealth is more ambiguous and is intimately related to the effect of schooling on human wealth. It is important to note that due to the year of forgone earnings and the short initial period of lower earnings associated with more schooling, increased schooling does not unambiguously increase predicted human wealth or mean human wealth averaged over ability levels. Predicted human wealth increases with increased schooling only if the discount rate is below the internal rate of return.[34] Figures 10 and 11 clearly illustrate this result for mean human wealth at various schooling levels. The reversal occurs at approximately 5.75 percent, except that high school graduates pass those with some college at approximately 4.5 percent. The effect of schooling declines as the discount rate increases up to the crossover, then has a negative effect on mean human wealth. Thus, an increased rate of discount decreases variation up to about 6 percent, at which point it causes the variation within ability groups, due to schooling, to increase. That is, at high discount rates, schooling differences cause variation, but because of their increasing negative effect on human wealth.

TABLE 6 Selected Statistics for the Predicted Distribution of Human Wealth for the Overall Population, by Schooling Class, and by Ability Class for Several Rates of Discount, Assuming Retirement Age Sixty-Six

	Discount Rate	Mean (Dollars)	Median (Dollars)	Standard Deviation (Dollars)	Coefficient of Variation	Skewness	Gini Coefficient
Overall	.03	198,240	193,759	15,264	.08	2.08	.04
	.04	154,150	150,940	9,762	.06	2.75	.03
	.05	121,943	120,145	6,236	.05	3.23	.02
	.06	97,965	97,846	4,651	.05	2.66	.02
	.07	79,948	80,847	4,479	.06	1.09	.03
By schooling:							
12 years	.03	190,969	189,523	7,262	.04	3.14	.02
13–15 years		197,873	194,327	8,932	.05	1.89	.02
16 years		211,515	206,880	15,669	.07	1.24	.04
17+ years		223,619	221,086	20,058	.09	0.74	.05
12 years	.04	150,781	149,527	5,501	.04	4.72	.02
13–15 years		153,052	150,484	6,152	.04	2.16	.02
16 years		160,407	156,880	11,277	.07	1.36	.04
17+ years		167,770	165,086	15,646	.09	1.14	.05
12 years	.05	121,389	120,418	3,850	.03	8.25	.01
13–15 years		120,215	118,660	4,525	.04	2.00	.02
16 years		123,504	120,880	8,480	.07	1.22	.04
17+ years		126,852	125,086	11,740	.09	1.07	.05
12 years	.06	99,121	98,727	3,078	.03	11.28	.01
13–15 years		96,294	95,422	2,960	.03	2.28	.01

16 years		96,145	94,457	6,226	.06	1.34	.03
17+ years		97,282	96,454	8,851	.09	0.97	.05
12 years	.07	82,418	82,023	2,562	.03	13.72	.01
13–15 years		77,941	77,352	1,961	.03	2.60	.01
16 years		75,866	74,464	4,662	.06	1.39	.03
17+ years		75,367	74,454	6,651	.09	0.98	.05
By ability:							
<.75	.03	186,977	134,817	7,085	.04	9.13	.01
.75–1.00		191,716	190,109	6,136	.03	1.49	.02
1.00–1.25		202,595	197,755	11,113	.05	1.45	.03
>1.25		227,941	224,668	19,376	.09	0.82	.05
<.75	.04	147,298	146,797	5,565	.04	14.35	.01
.75–1.00		149,638	149,141	2,685	.02	2.00	.01
1.00–1.25		156,840	155,143	6,063	.04	1.58	.02
>1.25		174,308	171,107	13,006	.07	1.70	.04
<.75	.05	118,572	118,841	5,184	.04	11.81	.01
.75–1.00		118,824	118,930	1,729	.01	−.026	.01
1.00–1.25		123,440	123,058	3,269	.03	1.24	.01
>1.25		134,963	132,833	8,120	.06	2.05	.03
>.75	.06	96,133	95,774	5,438	.06	7.26	.02
.75–1.00		96,214	95,943	2,977	.03	−1.00	.02
1.00–1.25		98,501	98,776	2,506	.03	−0.19	.01
>1.25		106,223	105,131	5,135	.05	2.16	.02
<.75	.07	79,640	80,835	5,744	.07	4.00	.03
.75–1.00		78,755	80,461	3,883	.05	−1.13	.03
1.00–1.25		80,159	82,073	3,631	.05	−0.39	.02
>1.25		84,605	84,128	3,922	.05	1.41	.02

TABLE 7 Selected Statistics for the Predicted Distribution of Human Wealth for the Overall Population, by Schooling Class, and by Ability Class for Several Rates of Discount, Assuming Retirement Age $N(S)$

	Discount Rate	Mean (Dollars)	Median (Dollars)	Standard Deviation (Dollars)	Coefficient of Variation	Skewness	Gini Coefficient
Overall	.03	202,736	196,074	18,243	.09	1.95	.04
	.04	156,950	153,159	11,451	.07	2.77	.03
	.05	123,653	121,659	6,925	.06	3.41	.02
	.06	98,887	98,590	4,803	.05	3.16	.02
	.07	80,423	81,106	4,345	.05	1.60	.03
By schooling:							
12 years	.03	193,662	192,990	7,587	.04	2.48	.02
13–15 years		200,873	197,066	9,342	.05	1.83	.02
16 years		218,248	214,880	16,304	.07	1.20	.04
17+ years		238,737	237,086	20,755	.09	0.49	.05
12 years	.04	149,053	147,672	5,757	.04	13.14	.01
13–15 years		152,212	151,192	3,996	.03	2.36	.01
16 years		159,845	156,777	8,313	.05	1.76	.03
17+ years		178,992	174,776	16,261	.09	1.75	.05
12 years	.05	122,403	121,705	4,080	.03	7.25	.01
13–15 years		121,573	119,928	4,223	.03	2.35	.02
16 years		125,920	123,430	8,553	.07	1.36	.04
17+ years		132,369	131,086	12,532	.09	1.26	.05
12 years	.06	99,705	99,202	3,171	.03	10.23	.01
13–15 years		96,699	95,623	2,991	.03	2.23	.01
16 years		97,682	95,605	6,412	.07	1.34	.03
17+ years		100,464	99,086	9,267	.09	1.18	.05
12 years	.07	82,658	82,393	2,626	.03	12.74	.01

13–15 years		78,010	77,386	2,067	.03	2.52	.01
16 years		77,032	75,605	4,695	.06	1.54	.03
17+ years		77,193	76,454	6,969	.09	1.10	.05
By ability:							
<.75	.03	189,966	186,817	8,337	.04	5.62	.02
.75–1.00		195,552	193,638	9,006	.05	2.00	.02
1.00–1.25		207,867	201,755	15,046	.07	1.55	.04
>1.25		234,869	230,440	23,534	.10	0.67	.06
<.75	.04	149,053	147,672	5,757	.04	13.14	.01
.75–1.00		152,212	151,192	3,996	.03	2.36	.01
1.00–1.25		159,845	156,777	8,313	.05	1.76	.03
>1.25		178,992	174,776	16,261	.09	1.75	.05
<.75	.05	119,297	119,037	4,914	.04	14.82	.01
.75–1.00		120,541	120,356	1,797	.01	0.79	.01
1.00–1.25		125,321	124,176	4,106	.03	1.70	.02
>1.25		137,616	134,300	10,018	.07	2.08	.04
<.75	.06	96,849	97,183	5,122	.05	8.75	.02
.75–1.00		96,881	97,913	2,457	.03	-0.76	.01
1.00–1.25		99,608	99,912	2,710	.03	-0.03	.01
>1.25		107,891	105,278	5,939	.06	2.57	.03
<.75	.07	79,873	83,835	5,434	.07	4.94	.03
.75–1.00		79,214	80,615	3,653	.05	-0.84	.02
1.00–1.25		80,553	82,073	3,202	.04	-0.30	.02
>1.25		85,822	85,776	4,273	.05	1.55	.03

TABLE 8 Estimated Average Retirement Age by Years of Schooling, from Mincer (1974)

Years of Schooling	Estimated Average Retirement Age
8 years	65
9–11 years	66
12 years	67
13–15 years	67
16 years	68
17+ years	70

The effect of increased ability is to increase unambiguously mean human wealth as illustrated in Figures 12 and 13. The magnitude of the effect of ability declines at higher discount rates, since the returns to higher ability come late in the life cycle.

The human wealth distributions are corrected for error variation by decomposing the error into purely random or transitory and persistent components. A lower bound on the variance of human wealth is defined as the variance of the present value of predicted earnings plus an error component which is completely transitory and independent from period to period. An upper bound is defined as the variance of the present value of predicted earnings plus a completely persistent error component which is constant over the life cycle but varies randomly over individuals independently of the level of ability and schooling. Intermediate cases can be considered as combinations of these when the transitory and persistent variations are indepedendent. The upper and lower bounds allow no comparisons of inequality in human wealth versus earnings, since the human wealth coefficient of variation lower bound lies below, and the human wealth coefficient of variation upper bound lies above, the earnings coefficient of variation. The answer lies in the "persistence" of the error over an individual's lifetime. The standard deviation of the persistent component is estimated and used to estimate standard deviation and coefficient of variation for human wealth. Corresponding estimates are also made by calculating the actual present value of the residuals for each individual.

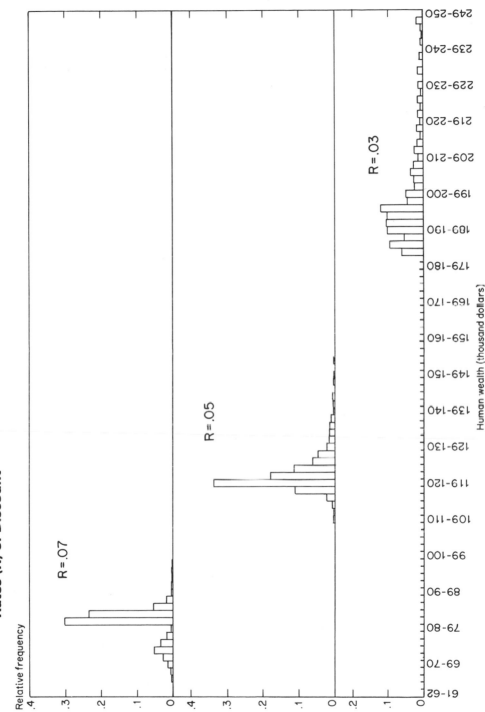

FIGURE 7A Predicted Distribution of Mean Human Wealth for the Overall Population for Several Rates (R) of Discount

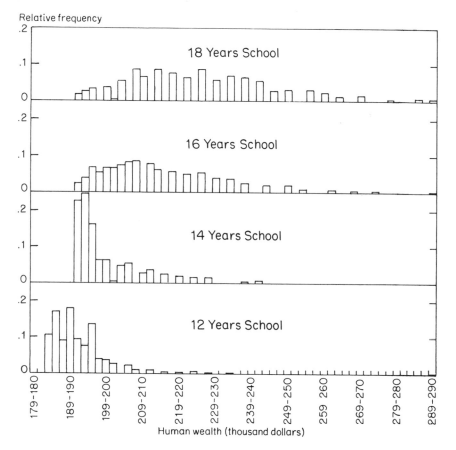

FIGURE 7B   Predicted Distribution of Mean Human Wealth by Schooling Level, Discounted at 3 Percent

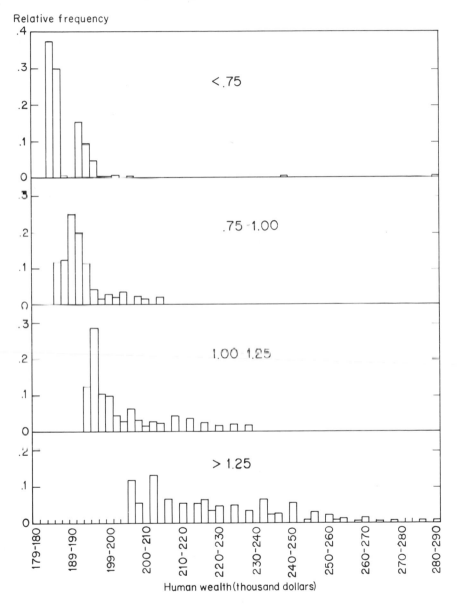

Human wealth (thousand dollars)

FIGURE 7D Predicted Distribution of Mean Human Wealth by Schooling Level, Discounted at 5 Percent

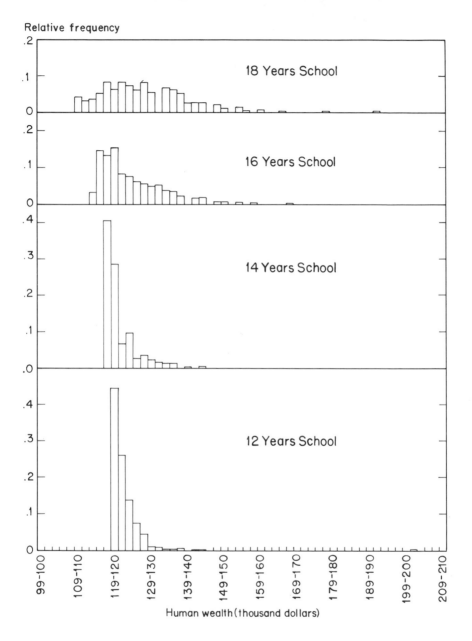

FIGURE 7E   Predicted Distribution of Mean Human Wealth by Ability Group, Discounted at 5 Percent

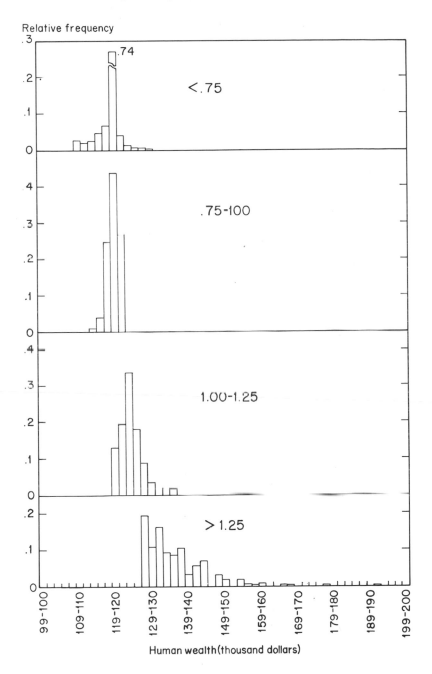

Human wealth(thousand dollars)

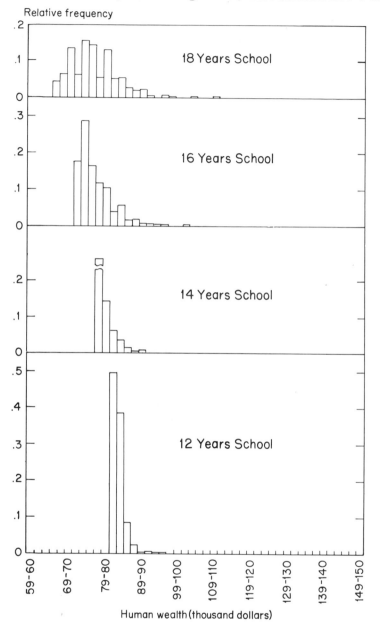

FIGURE 7F **Predicted Distribution of Mean Human Wealth by Schooling Level, Discounted at 7 Percent**

Relative frequency

18 Years School

16 Years School

14 Years School

12 Years School

Human wealth (thousand dollars)

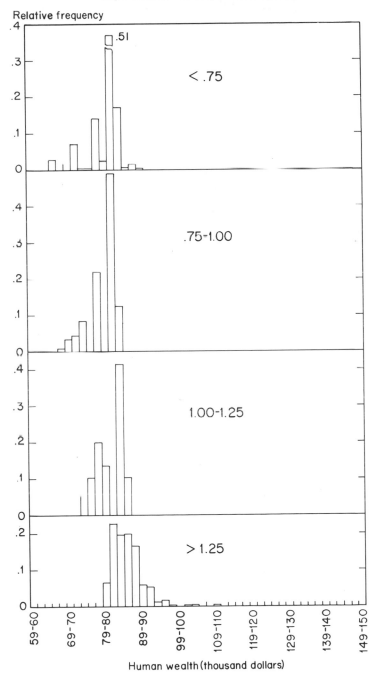

FIGURE 7G Predicted Distribution of Mean Human Wealth by Ability Group, Discounted at 7 Percent

FIGURE 8 Overall Mean Human Wealth as a Function of Retirement Age for Several Rates of Discount

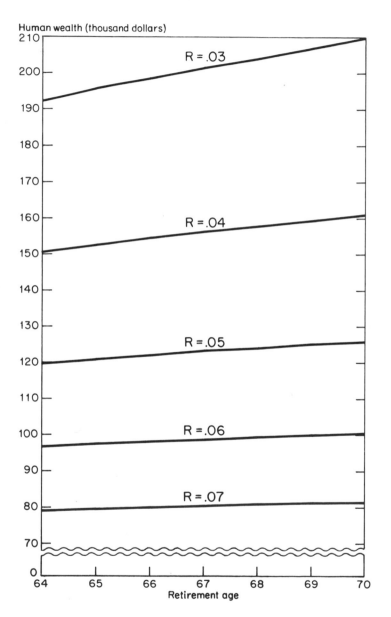

Human wealth (thousand dollars)

R = .03

R = .04

R = .05

R = .06

R = .07

Retirement age

FIGURE 9 **Overall Mean Human Wealth as a Function of the Discount Rate for Retirement Ages 66 and 70 and Retirement Age as a Function of Schooling Level, N(S)**

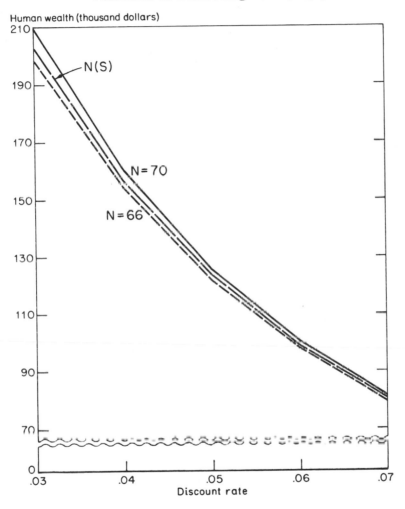

FIGURE 10 Mean Human Wealth by Schooling Level as a Function of the Rate of Discount for Retirement Age 66

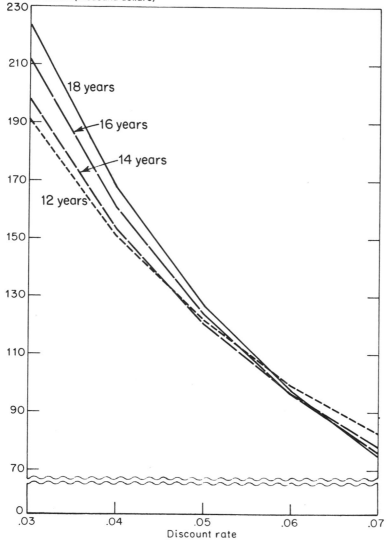

Human wealth (thousand dollars)

FIGURE 11 Mean Human Wealth as a Function of Schooling Level for Several Discount Rate and Retirement Combinations

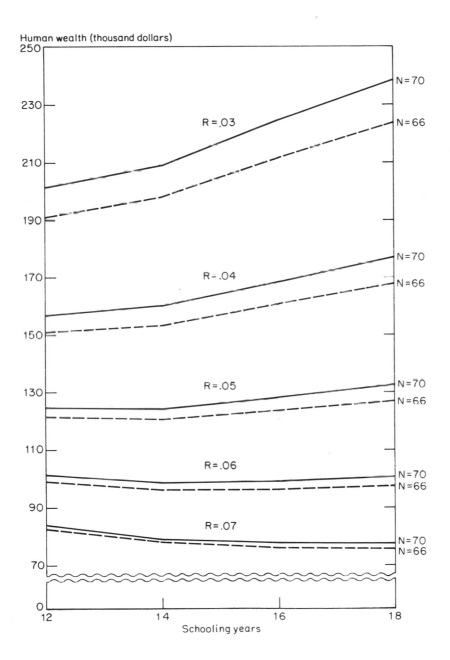

Human wealth (thousand dollars)

FIGURE 12 Mean Human Wealth by Ability Class as a Function of the Rate of Discount for Retirement Age 66

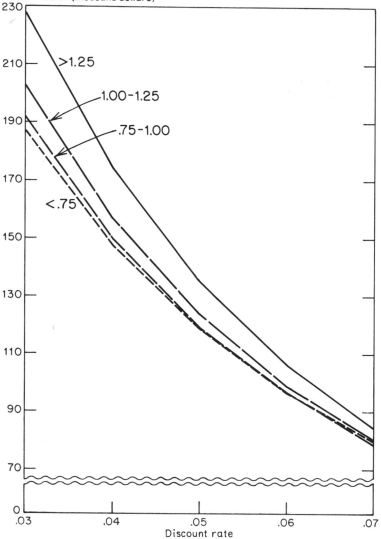

Human wealth (thousand dollars)

>1.25

1.00-1.25

.75-1.00

<.75

Discount rate

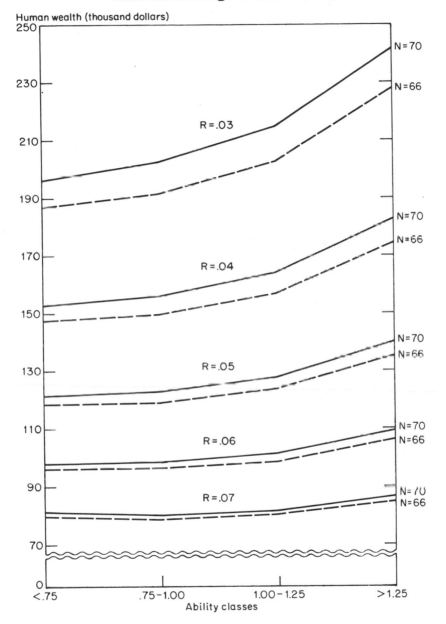

FIGURE 13 Mean Human Wealth as a Function of Ability Class for Several Discount Rate and Retirement Age Combinations

Human wealth (thousand dollars)

R = .03

R = .04

R = .05

R = .06

R = .07

N = 70
N = 66
N = 70
N = 66
N = 70
N = 66
N = 70
N = 66
N = 70
N = 66

250

230

210

190

170

150

130

110

90

70

0

<.75   .75 - 1.00   1.00 - 1.25   >1.25

Ability classes

Consider the more general combination of these two variance components.

$$Y_i(a, S, B) = \hat{Y}(a, S_i, B_i) + \delta_i + \eta_{ia}$$

where i indicates individual.

The error components δ_i and η are assumed independent of each other and over i and are uncorrelated with a, S, and B; therefore $\delta \sim (0, \sigma_\delta^2)$ and $\eta_a \sim (0, \sigma_\eta^2 I)$ where I is of dimension equal to the number of age points specified. We still obtain

$$E_{\delta,\eta}[Y(a, S, B)] = \hat{Y}(a, S, B)$$

and

$$E_{\delta,\eta}[\hat{P}V(S, B)] = \int_{a=S}^{N} e^{-ra}\hat{Y}(a, S, B)\, da$$

Consider the variance for fixed values of schooling; that is, for both ability and schooling fixed or simply within a schooling class.

$$\text{Var}_{\delta\eta}[PV(S, B)] = \text{Var}_{\delta\eta}\left[\int_{a=S}^{N} \delta e^{-ra}\, da + \int_{a=S}^{N} \eta_a e^{-ra}\, da\right]$$

$$= E_{\delta\eta}\left[\int_{a=S}^{N} \delta e^{-ra}\, da + \int_{a=S}^{N} \eta_a e^{-ra}\, da\right]^2$$

$$= E_{\delta\eta}\left[\int_{a=S}^{N} \delta e^{-ra}\, da\right]^2 + E_{\delta\eta}\left[\int_{a=S}^{N} \eta_a e^{-ra}\, da\right]^2$$

$$+ 2E_{\delta\eta}\left[\left(\int_{a=S}^{N} \delta e^{-ra}\, da\right)\left(\int_{a=S}^{N} \eta_a e^{-ra}\, da\right)\right]$$

$$= \sigma_\delta^2(e^{-rS} - e^{-rN})^2/r^2 + E_\eta\left[\int_{a=S}^{N} \eta_a e^{-ra}\, da\right]^2$$

Since δ and η are independent

$$= \sigma_\delta^2(e^{-rS} - e^{-rN})^2/r^2 + \sigma_\eta^2(e^{-2rS} - e^{-2rS})/2r$$

since

$$E_\eta\left[\int_{a=S}^{N} \eta_a e^{-ra}\, da\right]^2 = \sigma_\eta^2 \int_{a=S}^{N} e^{-2ra}\, da$$

Similarly

$$\text{Var}_{B,\delta,\eta}[PV(S)] = \text{Var}_B[\hat{P}V(S, B)] + \sigma_\delta^2(e^{-rS} - e^{-rN})^2/r^2$$
$$+ \sigma_\eta^2[e^{-2rS} - e^{-2rN}]/2r$$

However, when schooling varies as within ability classes, or in the overall distribution, we must take an expected value with respect to the lower limit of the present value integral.

$$\text{Var}_{S,\delta,\eta}[PV(B)] = \text{Var}_S[\hat{P}V(S, B)] + \sigma_\delta^2[E_S(e^{-2rS}) - 2e^{-rN}E(e^{-rS}) + e^{-2rN}]/r^2$$
$$+ \sigma_\eta^2[E(e^{-2rS}) - e^{-2rN}]/2r$$

TABLE 9 Error Variance Lower and Upper Bound Correction Factors for Retirement Age Sixty-Six

	Discount Rate				
	.03	.04	.05	.06	.07

Overall, $[E_S(e^{-2rS}) - e^{-2rN}]/2r$ and $E_S(e^{-rS} - e^{-rN})^2/r^2$

	.03	.04	.05	.06	.07
	12.7594	9.3207	7.1006	5.5911	4.5180
	514.3049	341.5083	234.0726	165.1963	119.7322

By schooling, $(e^{-2rS} - e^{-2rN})/2r$ and $(e^{-rS} - e^{-rN})/r^2$

	.03	.04	.05	.06	.07
12 years	13.9522	10.4229	8.1199	6.5346	5.3919
	573.8171	387.8743	270.7686	194.6646	143.7127
14 years	12.2807	8.8479	6.6358	5.1359	4.0736
	489.5750	321.1340	217.0589	150.8151	107.4442
16 years	10.7982	7.5058	5.4207	4.0356	3.0771
	416.3503	265.1138	173.5719	116.6002	80.1921
18 years	9.4833	6.3622	4.4259	3.1701	2.3241
	352.8105	218.1631	138.4082	89.9325	59.7336

By ability, $[E_{S|B}(e^{-2rS}) - e^{-2rN}]/2r$ and $[E_{S|B}(e^{-2rS}) - 2E_{S|B}(e^{-rS})e^{-rN} + e^{-2rN}]/r^2$

	.03	.04	.05	.06	.07
<.75	13.2224	9.7462	7.4921	5.9515	4.8501
	537.3420	359.3718	248.1428	176.4407	128.8384
.75–1.00	12.9530	9.4981	7.2633	5.7404	4.6552
	523.9226	348.9463	239.9150	169.8519	123.4912
1.00–1.25	12.5895	9.1648	6.9576	5.4597	4.3971
	505.8616	334.9714	228.9324	161.0955	116.4171
>1.25	11.8130	8.4522	6.3029	4.8578	3.8432
	467.2546	305.0703	205.4099	142.3217	101.2336

NOTE: Upper figure lower bound. Lower figure upper bound.

The lower bound obtains when $\sigma_\delta^2 = 0$, and the upper bound obtains when $\sigma_\eta^2 = 0$, for a given total variation $\sigma_\delta^2 + \sigma_\eta^2$ from the estimated earning function. The coefficients of the variance components are presented in Table 9 for discount rates 3 through 7 percent and retirement age sixty-six. The upper and lower bounds on variance of human wealth overall and within subgroups are presented in Table 10. The corresponding coefficients of variation are presented in Table 11.

Both the standard deviation and the coefficient of variation differ widely between the lower and upper bound. The inequality in mean human wealth is much less than either the lower bound or upper bound. This indicates that the error component is very important in determining human wealth inequality and indicates that the persistent component is

TABLE 10   Lower and Upper Bounds on the Standard Deviation of Human Wealth and the Standard Deviation of the Mean

	Discount Rate				
	.03	.04	.05	.06	.07
			Mean		
Overall	$ 15,264	$ 9,762	$ 6,236	$ 4,651	$ 4,479.09
By schooling:					
12 years	7,262	5,501	3,850	3,078	2,562.40
14 years	8,932	6,152	4,525	2,960	1,961.16
16 years	15,669	11,277	8,480	6,226	4,662.79
18 years	20,058	15,646	11,740	8,851	6,651.07
By ability:					
<.75	7,085	5,565	5,184	5,438	5,744.34
.75–1.00	6,136	2,685	1,729	2,977	3,883.49
1.00–1.25	11,113	6,063	3,269	2,506	3,631.12
>1.25	19,376	13,006	8,120	5,135	3,922.32
			Lower Bound		
Overall	26,456	20,890	17,284	15,041	13,616.00
By schooling:					
12 years	23,734	20,290	17,662	15,767	14,279.00
14 years	23,004	19,017	16,227	14,025	12,366.00
16 years	25,311	20,046	16,440	13,655	11,591.00
18 years	27,374	21,855	17,314	13,941	11,370.00
By ability:					
<.75	23,110	19,688	17,351	15,728	14,508.00
.75–1.00	22,620	18,836	16,394	14,796	13,617.00
1.00–1.25	24,170	19,291	16,288	14,355	13,194.00
>1.25	28,421	21,874	17,222	14,288	12,491.00
			Upper Bound		
Overall	138,033	112,215	92,760	77,889	66,344.00
By schooling:					
12 years	145,089	119,264	99,615	84,457	72,564.00
14 years	134,146	108,578	89,238	74,348	62,734.00
16 years	124,424	99,139	80,147	65,617	54,371.00
18 years	115,382	90,709	72,130	58,046	47,224.00
By ability:					
<.75	140,404	114,811	95,432	80,537	68,903.00
.75–1.00	138,599	113,033	93,714	78,894	67,335.00
1.00–1.25	136,509	110,881	91,587	76,820	65,370.00
>1.25	132,189	106,455	87,078	72,349	60,991.00

NOTE: The assumptions underlying these bounds are outlined in the text.

TABLE 11 Coefficient of Variation for Mean, Lower Bound and Upper Bound for Human Wealth Distributions

			Discount Rate		
	.03	.04	.05	.06	.07
			Mean		
Overall	.08	.06	.05	.05	.06
By schooling:					
12 years	.04	.04	.03	.03	.03
14 years	.05	.04	.04	.03	.03
16 years	.07	.07	.07	.06	.06
18 years	.09	.09	.09	.09	.09
By ability:					
<.75	.04	.04	.04	.06	.07
.75–1.00	.03	.02	.01	.03	.05
1.00–1.25	.05	.04	.03	.03	.05
>1.25	.09	.07	.06	.05	.05
			Lower Bound		
Overall	.13	.14	.14	.15	.17
By schooling:					
12 years	.12	.13	.15	.16	.17
14 years	.12	.12	.13	.15	.16
16 years	.12	.12	.13	.14	.15
18 years	.12	.13	.14	.14	.15
By ability:					
<.75	.12	.13	.15	.16	.18
.75–1.00	.12	.13	.14	.15	.17
1.00–1.25	.12	.12	.13	.15	.16
>1.25	.12	.13	.13	.13	.15
			Upper Bound		
Overall	.70	.73	.76	.80	.83
By schooling:					
12 years	.76	.79	.82	.85	.88
14 years	.68	.71	.74	.77	.80
16 years	.59	.62	.65	.68	.72
18 years	.52	.54	.57	.60	.63
By ability:					
<.75	.75	.78	.80	.84	.87
.75–1.00	.72	.76	.79	.82	.85
1.00–1.25	.67	.71	.74	.78	.82
>1.25	.58	.61	.65	.68	.72

very important in determining inequality in human wealth. We can note, however, that inequality in mean values before correcting for error variation is much less for human wealth than for earnings—in the overall values, the difference being 38 percent for earnings as opposed to about 5 or 6 percent for human wealth. When the correction for error variation is made, the lower and upper bound on the coefficient variation for human wealth brackets the coefficient of variation for either the predicted distribution of earnings or the actual coefficient of variation observed for earnings. It is necessary, then, to estimate the variance of the persistent component in revising our estimate of the standard deviation and coefficient of variation of human wealth.

The standard deviation of the persistent component of the error term is estimated in the following way. For each individual of the roughly 5,000 in the sample, the persistent component is measured as that value of a constant error, deviation from the predicted profile, such that the present value of deviations from it, the purely transitory part, is zero, i.e.,

$$\delta = \frac{\sum \mu(a)e^{-ra}}{\sum e^{-ra}}$$

The standard deviation of the error term is \$6,048 and the standard deviation of the persistent component, $\hat{\sigma}_\delta$, is roughly \$4,000, depending on the discount rate. The corresponding estimates of the standard deviation and coefficient of variation of human wealth based upon this estimate of the standard deviation of the persistent component are presented in Table 12 under the heading "Estimated for 1960 Census Groups Using $\hat{\sigma}_\delta$."

Corresponding estimates are made by calculating the actual present value of the residuals in the sample and inflating them to the equivalent of a working life of observations,[35] and taking the standard deviation. These are presented as the "directly estimated" values also shown in Table 12. These estimates correspond quite closely to those of the previous procedure and are larger probably because of the greater schooling present in the Thorndike sample than in the 1960 Census of Population.

The estimated inequality in human wealth is slightly less than the inequality in the predicted earnings distributions corrected for unexplained variations, the coefficient of variation being 60 percent for earnings and 50 percent for human wealth. The actual distribution of earnings is even more unequally distributed, with the coefficient of variation of 83 percent. It should be noted that the coefficient of variation for the actual distribution of earnings is larger than even the upper bound of the coefficient of variation for the human wealth distributions.

These crude estimates seem to indicate that human wealth is more equally distributed over individuals than is earnings, but that the varia-

TABLE 12   Estimated Standard Deviation of Human Wealth and Coefficient of Variation

	.03	.04	.05	.06	.07
			Discount Rate		
Standard Deviation of the Persistent Component					
σ_δ	$ 4,102	$ 3,943	$ 3,799	$ 3,671	$ 3,559
Standard Deviation of Human Wealth					
Directly Estimated from Present Value of Sample Residuals					
Overall	98,760	78,292	62,640	50,612	41,319
Estimated for 1960 Census Groups Using $\hat{\sigma}_\delta$					
Overall	95,617	74,847	59,795	48,764	40,562
By schooling:					
12 years	99,938	79,254	64,061	52,772	44,233
14 years	92,539	72,234	57,455	46,483	38,245
16 years	86,414	66,391	51,941	41,279	33,339
18 years	80,800	61,410	47,266	36,933	29,270
By ability:					
<.75	96,730	76,318	61,443	50,456	42,208
.75–1.00	95,461	75,056	60,220	49,309	41,124
1.00–1.25	94,274	73,747	58,906	48,003	39,918
>1.25	92,056	71,351	56,312	45,358	37,283
Coefficient of Variation					
From Direct Estimate					
Overall	.49	.50	.51	.51	.51
From Estimate Using $\hat{\sigma}_\delta$					
Overall	.47	.48	.48	.49	.50
By schooling:					
12 years	.52	.53	.52	.53	.54
14 years	.46	.47	.47	.48	.49
16 years	.40	.42	.41	.42	.43
18 years	.34	.34	.36	.37	.38
By ability:					
<.75	.51	.51	.52	.52	.53
.75–1.00	.49	.49	.50	.51	.52
1.00–1.25	.45	.46	.47	.48	.50
>1.25	.39	.40	.41	.42	.43

NOTE: $\hat{\sigma}_\mu = \$6,048$

tion in these measures due to factors other than schooling and ability are quite important, and that much further analysis is necessary to really pinpoint sources of human wealth inequality. This analysis is meant to be suggestive of the procedure by which more precise implications can be obtained. This general type of analysis can be carried out using any earnings function describing age-earnings profiles, or alternatively, experience-earnings profiles, as a function of characteristics for which data is available on the joint distribution of those characteristics.

NOTES

1. The individual is also assumed to have perfect knowledge of himself and the world and faces no uncertainties.
2. Many aspects of the following discussion are considered in more detail in the growing literature on this subject, including Rosen (1972), Rosen (1973), Mincer (1974), Stafford and Cohen (1973), Stafford and Stephan (1972), Heckman (1973), Smith (1973), Weiss (1971), Razin (1971). The original works of Becker (1962, 1967) and Ben-Porath (1967) are obviously important.
3. The effect of educational doles on the length of the schooling period are considered by Wallace and Ihnen (1972).
4. Time spent in on-the-job training is considered in human capital production, as is investment time off-the-job, rather than in the labor market. The distinction of where investment occurs, on or off the job, has no implication for total investment, assuming a single production function, but does have empirical implications for the interpretation of earnings per unit time for time intervals within a period. They may represent net or gross earnings or even earning capacity. More detail on this issue is considered in Lillard (1973b).
5. $Q(K_a, D_a) = K_a^{\beta_1} D_a^{\beta_2}$

   such that $(\beta_1 + \beta_2)\epsilon(0, 1)$ and $\beta_1 > 0$. It is also assumed in the equation presented here that $\delta\epsilon(0, 1)$.
6. A general proof that if specialization occurs, it occurs in the initial periods is provided by Ishikawa (1973).
7. The constant fraction result is due to the Cobb-Douglas production function.
8. Becker (1967) provides a discussion of loan markets.
9. For a more detailed discussion of these implicit partials see Wallace and Ihnen (1972).
10. Even though the level of investment is not a function of initial earning capacity, the fraction of earning capacity invested, I_a/RE_a, will be, since earning capacity is.
11. This result obtains from the assumption of no bequest and no restriction on the objective function at N.
12. See for a review, Mincer (1970).
13. Lillard (1973b).
14. Additional polynomial terms were added until they failed to significantly reduce error variance.
15. $R^2 = .2759$. Age and schooling in this equation are years beyond age sixteen. No individual in the sample had less than a high school education. Caution should be taken for predicting below this schooling level, especially late in the life cycle. The

estimates are based on observation of 15,578 age-earnings points from 4,956 individuals. The upper age range of the sample is 54 years and the age-earnings profiles turn down sharply, because there are four men who are three to four years older than the rest of the sample, older when applying in 1943, who have unusually low earnings. All predictions of earnings are restricted as closely as possible to the age range observed.

16. Again, these results are discussed in detail in Lillard (1973b).

17. Due to the data limitations in age mentioned earlier for human wealth predictions, it was assumed that the earnings profiles are flat after the end of the sample range where the profiles peak. I prefer this to either the quadratic or linear profile estimates. For example, in the quadratic estimates, the profiles rise parabolically, since the convexity at early ages dominates the concavity at older ages, which is even more unrealistic.

18. The ability index used in this paper is the first principal component of a subset of the ability test scores corresponding approximately to I.Q.-type attributes. The effect of each individual ability measure and their interactions on earnings and schooling is also discussed in Lillard (1973).

19. Any observation which might cause special problems is omitted. These include those individuals disabled, unemployed, in the military, or who are pilots as their major occupation. Particular year observations for an individual are omitted if, for example, the year of initial job was questionable.

20. Many of these comments originated with F. T. Juster, who directed the data collection for the NBER.

21. The model response was excellent, with 57 percent; 38 percent were good; 3 percent, fair; and less than 1 percent each were poor or nonresponse.

22. When mean earnings predicted distributions are also derived with this assumption.

23. U.S. Census of Population: 1960 (Final Report PC(a)-5A) Subject Reports, School Enrollment: Personal and Family Characteristics of Persons Enrolled in School or College and of Persons Not Enrolled (U.S. Bureau of the Census, 1963, Table 4, page 54).

24. The age is extended to sixty-four because it corresponds to the closest Census of Population age classification, 35–64 years old. The distributions do include persons employed while going to school full time and are correspondingly incorrectly estimated.

25. Forty ability intervals were actually used in calculations.

26. Any assumption about how observations are distributed within reported class intervals is arbitrary. This assumption facilitates calculation of earnings but adds a source of error in the predicted distribution of earnings. The predicted relative frequencies are created in a discrete rather than a continuous manner.

27. Assuming this distribution of ability is a source of error in the predicted distribution to the extent that the distribution of ability of Air Force pilot and navigator school candidates in 1943 is different from the distribution of ability of employed males in 1960.

28. The equal intervals of $1,000 are used to allow the greatest perspective and skewness, since the discrete and widely spaced midpoints of the age and schooling intervals distort the continuity of the predicted distribution. The predicted distributions with unequal interval lengths for higher incomes used in Census of Population tabulations are presented later for comparisons with the actual distributions calculated from Census of Population data.

29. Each individual observations error is distributed independently of age, schooling, ability and the error in any other observation.

30. All interval probabilities are corrected according to the truncated normal, so that only positive earnings are counted and the total relative frequency of all positive earnings is unity.
31. The weights are obviously the relative frequency of the subgroups.
32. Both the average of variances and the variance of averages are calculated weighted by the relative frequency of the subgroups. Formally, $\text{Var}(Y) = E[\text{Var}(Y/\text{subgroup})] + \text{Var}[E(Y/\text{subgroup})]$.
33. The Gini coefficient is the area between the diagonal and the Lorenz curve relative to the area of the triangle, one-half. A larger Gini coefficient implies more inequality. The extremes are zero when every individual gets an equal share of total income and one when one individual holds total income.

    An alternative interpretation of the Gini coefficient is the mean absolute difference between all possible pairs of values relative to their mean, i.e.

    $$\frac{\int_{-\infty}^{+\infty} \int_{-\infty}^{+\infty} |X - Y| f(X) f(Y) \, dX \, dY}{2\bar{X}}$$

    X and Y represent all possible pairs of values, earnings, and the numerator is the coefficient of mean difference. The mean difference due to Gini (1912) is dependent on the dispersion of the values among themselves and not on deviations from the mean as in the case of the standard deviation and thus coefficient variation. The Lorenz curve and Gini coefficient are unambiguous measures of concentration only if the Lorenz curves do not cross. An infinite number of Lorenz curves may have the same Gini concentration coefficient if they cross. If two Lorenz curves cross once, say at the point (.7, .3) and have the same Gini coefficient, the population underlying the Lorenz curve which is beneath in the region bounded by (0, 0), (0, .3), (.7, 0), and (.7, .3) may be said to have income distributed more unequally among low income holders (lower 70 percent) than among high income holders, relative to the other population. This says nothing about location of high and low, only about the concentration of low relative to high income holders. This may be thought of as if populations have the same Gini coefficient, and thus, their Lorenz curves must cross, and the same variance and mean, the population with the largest positive skew having its Lorenz curve above the other in the lower earnings region.
34. More detailed comments on calculations of an internal rate of return for the NBER-Thorndike data based on both log equations and present value equalization are presented in Lillard (1975).
35. A maximum of 5 and an average of 3.2 age-earnings points are observed. These are then inflated by the factor $(N - S)/\text{Number of Points}$. These estimates are slightly different from the others in that the underlying schooling distribution is that of the Thorndike sample rather than the 1960 Census population.

REFERENCES

Becker, G., 1964. *Human Capital*. Columbia University Press, New York.
———. 1967. *Human Capital and the Personal Distribution of Income*. W. S. Woytinsky Lecture No. 1, Department of Economics, Institute of Public Administration, University of Michigan, Ann Arbor.
Becker, G., and Chiswick, B. R., 1966. "Education and the Distribution of Earnings." *American Economic Review* 56 (2): 358–369.
Ben-Porath, Y., 1967. "The Production of Human Capital and the Life Cycle of Earnings." *Journal of Political Economy* 75 (4): 352–365.

Ghez, G., and Becker, G. S., 1976. *The Allocation of Time and Goods Over the Life Cycle.* NBER, New York.

Haley, W. J., 1973. "Human Capital: The Choice Between Investment and Income." *American Economic Review* 63 (5):929–944.

Heckman, J. J., 1974. "Estimates of a Human Capital Production Function Embedded in a Life Cycle Model of Labor Supply." Processed. NBER, New York.

Ishikawa, T., 1973. "A Simple Jevonian Model of Educational Investment Revisited." Harvard Institute of Economic Research, Discussion Paper 289, April.

Johnson, T., 1970. "Returns from Investment in Human Capital." *American Economic Review* 60 (4):546–560.

Levhari, D., and Weiss, Y., 1972. *The Effect of Risk on Investment in Human Capital.* Foerder Institute for Economic Research, Tel Aviv University, October.

Lillard, L. A., 1973b. "An Essay on Human Wealth." NBER Working Paper No. 4.

———. 1973a. "From Age-Earnings Profiles to the Distribution of Earnings and Human Wealth." NBER Working Paper No. 9, September.

———. 1975. "Ex Post Rates of Return to Schooling When There Are Interactions Among Variables in the Earnings Function." Processed, April.

Mincer, J., 1970. "The Distribution of Labor Incomes: A Survey with Special Reference to the Human Capital Approach." *Journal of Economic Literature* 8 (1):1–26.

———. 1974. *Schooling, Experience, and Earnings.* NBER, New York.

Morgan, J., 1962. "The Anatomy of Income Distributions." *Review of Economics and Statistics* 44 (3):270–283.

Razin, A., 1973. "On Investment in Human Capital Under Uncertainty." University of Minnesota, processed, March.

Rosen, S., 1973. "Income Generating Functions and Capital Accumulation." Harvard Institute of Economic Research, Discussion Paper 306, June.

———. 1972. "Measuring the Obsolescence of Knowledge." University of Rochester, Working Paper, June.

Schultz, T. W., 1971. *Investment in Human Capital: The Role of Education and of Research.* Free Press, New York.

Smith, James P., 1973. "Family Labor Supply over the Life Cycle." Processed. NBER, New York.

Stafford, F. P., and Stephan, P. E., 1973. "Labor, Leisure, and Training Over the Life Cycle." Working Paper, Georgia State University, November.

Stafford, F. P., and Cohen, M. S., 1973. "A Life Cycle Model of the Household's Time Allocation." Working Paper, University of Michigan, June.

Taubman, P., and Wales, T., 1972. *Mental Ability and Higher Educational Attainment in the Twentieth Century*, Carnegie Commision Technical Report.

U.S. Bureau of the Census, 1963. *Census of Population: 1960.* Final Report PC(2)-5A. U.S. Government Printing Office, Washington, D.C.

Welch, F., 1970. "The NBER Approach to Human Resource Problems." NBER monograph.

14 | COMMENTS

Zvi Griliches
Harvard University

This is a long and difficult paper, the result of much research, only part of which is described in the paper at hand. I found it hard going and some of my comments may be based on a misunderstanding or misreading of the paper.

The paper does four things: (1) it presents a brief summary of the state of the optimal-investment-in-human-capital theory and outlines a special version of it to be used further on; (2) it reports on the results of estimating an earnings function (as a function of age, schooling, and ability) based on this theory and on the NBER-Thorndike data; (3) it adjusts these estimates to correspond to the 1960 Census data for the population as a whole; and (4) it computes estimates of the distribution of human wealth as a function of different discount rates and discusses the sources of its variance and alternative measures of inequality. Since I have difficulties with all four of the steps, I shall discuss them in turn.

We need a theory to interpret our data and we must make simplifications and "unrealistic" assumptions to be able to comprehend the world. However, assumptions must be chosen so that they do not eliminate the essence of the problem. Lillard assumes a perfect consumption loan market, implying that one can borrow enough to eat no matter how long one is in school or who one is. This essentially removes any short-term investment funds constraint from the model. (It is true that he must finance tuition and other direct costs from current earnings, but the bulk of investment costs are forgone earnings, not direct costs.) In this model, then, maximizing individuals will differ in their schooling attainment only because they differ in the productivity of learning (ability) and for no other reason. Moreover, no allowance is made in this (or other similar models) for the fact that schooling is subsidized, primarily by parents but also by various public bodies, implying a rather different calculus of the optimal amount of investment in human capital than is assumed by the model and by the interpretation of the estimates.

The version of the model actually computed takes formal schooling as predetermined and concentrates on the effects of postschooling on-the-job training on the age-earnings profiles of individuals. In this version, the family background variables do not appear explicitly, since they are assumed to work entirely via the previously achieved formal schooling levels. Also one should note that ability enters only to the extent that it represents individual differences in the productivity of *equal* amounts of time spent on on-the-job training. It does not reflect the total (reduced form) contribution of ability differences to observed differential in earnings, since it does not allow for the effects of ability on achieved schooling levels or on the supply of hours of work.

Another, more specific difficulty of this type of model is the assumption of the same production function of human capital both in school and in on-the-job training. First, the fact that specialization occurs would make one suspect that the technology of human capital accumulation may not be the same in these rather different pursuits. More importantly, since schooling is largely accomplished in the nonprofit public sector, it is not obvious that one can assume that the observations are "on" the production function or that behavior can be described in terms of it. Of course, one might want to interpret this "production function" just as a summary device describing the constraints facing an individual, but there is no market mechanism then which would force the technology of the public sector to be similar to, and as efficient as, that of on-the-job training, which presumably is occurring largely in the private sector of the economy.

When all is said and done, Lillard estimates earnings as a cubic function, with interactions, of age, schooling, and ability. The relationship of that to the particular theory outlined earlier is obscure. There are a number of practical difficulties with these estimates. Imposing a cubic age structure is a mixed blessing, producing rather strange age-earnings profiles. It is quite clear that in the "real" world earnings of highly educated people do not turn down at age 50, Figure 1A notwithstanding. Also, the prediction that at age 27 high school dropouts earn more than high school or college graduates is inconsistent with all other data known to me. Since the original age distribution of this sample is rather narrow, the estimated effect of age is confounded with that of time, a problem that is not really solved by deflating the earnings series by a general price index. Finally, the estimated ability effects, the primary reason for using the NBER-Thorndike data, are surprisingly small. Moreover, they seem to account for little of the observed dispersion in schooling, mean ability differing by little over one-half of a standard deviation between the lowest and highest schooling levels (see Table 2). This leaves most of the schooling dispersion to be thought of as exogenous, a reasonable but unfortunate conclusion in the context of an *investment* theory of human capital.

It is not clear to me, really, what the purpose is of adjusting the estimated distribution to the 1960 Census levels. The discrepancy between it and the NBER-Thorndike sample is so large, that any extrapolation to the whole population appears to be unwarranted. To recapitulate, the NBER-Thorndike sample covers only the union of the upper half of the schooling and the ability distributions. Extrapolating it to the other quadrants on the assumption that the equations are the same there seems rather farfetched. Moreover, both the schooling of this population and the correlation of ability with schooling are based on economic and institutional conditions as they were in the 1930s and early forties. Much of the 1960 population was educated and selected (by others and itself) in the late 1940s and the 1950s, a much different time period, with different conditions of access to schooling opportunities and economic resources (such as the G.I. bill). There are many peculiarities in the actual tables which may be due to the extrapolation procedure. For example, in Table 3, the mean of predicted earnings is below the median in the highest schooling class, a not very likely occurence. The situation improves in Table 4, when the residuals are put back into the tables, but the estimates still remain rather unrealistic. Comparing the overall predicted results in Table 4 to the actual figures in Table 5, one finds that Lillard's extrapolation procedure significantly underestimates the dispersion and skewness of the actual earnings distribution. If I understand Figures 5A through 5D, they tell us that because the original earnings function accounts for very little of the observed variation in earnings, adjusting the observed distributions for differences in the arguments of this function does not change our view of the inequality of earnings by much (which is a point already made by Jencks, among others).

This problem, the interpretation of the residual variance, also affects the major product of this paper—the estimated dispersion of human wealth. The reasons why wealth distributions would be less unequal than earnings distribution are: (1) the averaging out of the life-cycle inequality of income over time; and (2) the averaging out of the transitory components of earnings over time. Since in Lillard's model, the effects of schooling and ability persist over time, the dispersion due to these sources should not cancel out. The role of unexplained sources of variation is illustrated in my Table 1, culled from Lillard's paper.

TABLE 1   Overall Coefficients of Variation

| | Earnings | ———— Human Wealth ———— | |
		At .03 Discount Rate	At .07 Discount Rate
Predicted	.38	.09	.05
Adjusted for unexplained variation	.59		
Lower bound		.13	.17
Upper bound		.70	.83

Whether human wealth is really more equally distributed than earnings depends on our assumption about the persistence of the random unexplained components. If "luck" or unobserved characteristics persist, then it is not true that wealth dispersion is much smaller than earnings dispersion. This is clearly an important area for further research. Even within Lillard's own data, it would have been possible to estimate the fraction of the random variance that persists and get a narrower bound.

Finally, I am not sure that the computed wealth distributions have much operational content, since the human capital market is far from perfect and the average twenty-six year old cannot really borrow $70,000 plus solely on the basis of his human capital.

15

JAMES D. SMITH
Pennsylvania State University

STEPHEN D. FRANKLIN
Pennsylvania State University

GUY H. ORCUTT
Yale University

The Inter-generational Transmission of Wealth: A Simulation Experiment

I. INTRODUCTION

Better government data and greater access to them have spurred a renewed interest in the analysis of income and wealth distributions. For the most part, this interest picked up where the work of the late thirties and early forties left off—with cross-sectional distributions. Of growing interest, however, has been the inter-generational transmission of wealth. Questions of how much of the observable cross-sectional distribution can be accounted for by inheritance and how much by saving out of earnings have been matters of speculation and some empirical work by Soltow,[1] Morgan,[2] and Projector.[3] However, as Brittain points out, research has not been well structured to capture the importance of inheritance.[4] The issue of inheritance has been, for the most part, a peripheral one in studies concerned with other economic behavior.

In the work reported here, extant data from several sources were used to simulate the transmission of wealth at death. To measure the influence of death taxes and inheritances on inter-generational wealth distributions, simulation experiments were conducted with four death-tax systems. Two tax systems use estate wealth as a base and two use inheritances as a base. An experiment without taxes was also run.

In brief, the procedure followed was to: (a) modify the 1962 Survey of Financial Characteristics of Consumers (SFCC) file from a family file to a file of persons identified as members of specific family units; (b) stochastically attribute to families members living away from home; (c) allocate to individuals all wealth not specifically identified with individual family members in the original file; (d) pass the file and subject each individual to a Monte Carlo death process based upon age-sex-race-marital status-specific mortality rates for 1962; (e) distribute estates of decedents stochastically in accordance with estimated probability patterns of bequests and other transfers to family members at home and away from home, and to nonfamily members and to charity; (f) tax estates or inheritances in accordance with four tax "statutes"; and (g) calculate the before and after characteristics of the distribution of wealth and the yield to the Treasury.

II. RESULTS OF SIMULATION EXPERIMENTS

Simulation 1. Current Estate Tax

The first simulation experiment employs a tax statute which approximates the current federal estate tax law. The tax statute captures the essential features of the present federal estate tax. It provides for a personal exemption of $60,000 for each decedent's estate and a marital deduction of the actual amount bequeathed a spouse or one-half the estate (whichever is less). Charitable bequests, costs of last illness, legal fees, and administrator's commissions are deductible in arriving at taxable estate. After exemptions and deductions are subtracted from the net worth of estates, the remainder is taxed in accordance with current federal estate tax rates (see Table 1).

Features of the federal estate tax which were not captured are the credits for state and foreign death taxes and the reduction in rates applicable to assets which have been taxed in another estate within 10 years. Also missed are assets given away in contemplation of death and certain other lifetime transfers which are constructively part of the estate for federal estate tax purposes.

TABLE 1   Federal Estate Tax Schedule

Taxable Estate Equal to or More than— (1)	Taxable Estate Less than— (2)	Tax on Amount in Column (1) (3)	Rate of Tax on Excess over Amount in Column (1) (Percent) (4)
$ 0	$ 5,000	$ 0	3
5,000	10,000	150	7
10,000	20,000	500	11
20,000	30,000	1,600	14
30,000	40,000	3,000	18
40,000	50,000	4,800	22
50,000	60,000	7,000	25
60,000	100,000	9,500	28
100,000	250,000	20,700	30
250,000	500,000	65,700	32
500,000	750,000	145,700	35
750,000	1,000,000	233,200	37
1,000,000	1,250,000	325,700	39
1,250,000	1,500,000	423,200	42
1,500,000	2,000,000	528,200	45
2,000,000	2,500,000	753,200	49
2,500,000	3,000,000	998,200	53
3,000,000	3,500,000	1,263,200	56
3,500,000	4,000,000	1,543,200	59
4,000,000	5,000,000	1,838,200	63
5,000,000	6,000,000	2,468,200	67
6,000,000	7,000,000	3,138,200	70
7,000,000	8,000,000	3,838,200	73
8,000,000	10,000,000	4,568,200	76
10,000,000	—	6,088,200	77

SOURCE: Federal Estate Tax Return, Form 706 (Re. Sept. 1963).

Using the weighted SFCC sample, slightly modified to represent better the upper tail of the wealth distribution (see Section III), a test of the simulation model was made using the federal estate tax statute. If the simulation model captures behavior in the real world, simulated taxes for decedents with gross assets of $60,000 or more should approach those reported for 1963 by the Internal Revenue Service (IRS). Simulated taxes and those reported by the IRS are compared in Table 2. The comparison shows similar numbers of returns filed for estates with gross

TABLE 2   Comparison of Simulated Results with Internal Revenue Service Data for Returns Filed in 1962

Size of Gross Estate	Simulation	IRS
	Number of Returns	
≥ $2,000,000	803	618
$1,000,000 < 2,000,000	858	1,151
500,000 < 1,000,000	3,493	3,232
100,000 < 500,000	52,701	42,989
60,000 < 100,000	64,133	30,999
Total returns	121,988	78,989
	Taxes	
Tax collected	$2.1 billion	$2.1 billion[a]

[a]Before tax credits. The actual IRS tax collected on 1963 returns amounted to $1.8 billion. See *Statistics of Income: Fiduciary Gift and Estate Tax Returns, 1962*, p. 51

assets above $100,000, but the model generates 64,133 estate tax returns in the range between $60,000 and $100,000 gross assets, compared to only 30,999 returns reported by the IRS. We believe two factors account for the difference. First, there is a lag in filing, and returns filed with the IRS in 1963 are largely for persons who died before 1963, whereas the returns "filed" in the simulation model are only for persons who "died" in 1963.[5] The population and its mean wealth have increased steadily; consequently, IRS filings in a given year understate the number of returns which will ultimately be filed for decedents who die in that year. Secondly, there is strong evidence of noncompliance with the filing provision of the law near the filing threshold.[6] Our purpose at this point is not to test for compliance with the law (a potential use of the model), but to establish the credibility of the model for assessing the impact of alternative tax systems on the distribution of wealth. It does appear, however, that the simulated number of tax returns may be closer to the number of estates with gross assets between $60,000 and $100,000 than that reported by the IRS (see note 6).

In the simulation, 1.75 million persons died.[7] This compares very favorably with the official reported number of 1.76 million deaths in 1962 or the 1.81 million deaths in 1963.[8]

The assets of the simulated decedents totaled $40.4 billion. Estate taxes collected came to $2.1 billion. After allowance for decedents' debts, attorneys' fees, administration costs, last medical costs, funeral expenses, and estate taxes, $32.4 billion of their assets devolved to their heirs and beneficiaries. The simulation logic of inheritance is described in detail in the methodology section, but basically wealth is transmitted along familial lines revealed in the SFCC data.

The question we would answer is: Does this process of death transfers and death taxes alter the distribution of wealth?

It appears (Table 3) that the present estate tax contributes very little to reducing the concentration of wealth. A slight reduction of the number of families at the very bottom of the distribution occurs (see "all units" column in Table 3), but above a net worth of $2,000 no changes are revealed. The changes at the bottom of the distribution are attributable to the deaths of poor older families and the inheritance of wealth by "poor" families from those with substantial wealth.

Distributions by age of head, Table 3, reveal that although the shape of overall distribution is stable, families are moving around within the distribution. For instance, families with a head 65 or older decline in numbers all along the distribution. On the other hand, the numbers of families headed by a person age 30 to 65 and with a net worth of over $15,000 increases. There are also increases in the number of families near the top of the distribution with heads under 30. In the simulation there is no saving function, so all the changes are the result of wealth transfers. It appears, then, that wealth is transmitted from older to younger families who have at least a minimal net worth (more than $1,000) before inheriting. Families also lose wealth because family members die and their wealth is depleted by the cost of dying and taxation before it is inherited by survivors. Just as there is no saving in the model to move families up the wealth distribution, there is no consumption to move them down. So, again, it is the pure effect of death transfers which is observed.

It can be argued that family net worth understates the immediate wealth effect of death on a family. The death of a family member may concentrate wealth in the hands of a smaller number of persons, so average net worth of family members would then increase. The increase in average member wealth could be quite significant if the life of the decedent was well covered with life insurance. The value of human capital is not part of the wealth concept used here. Were human capital to be included, a different view of the wealth effect of death would be in order. To examine the interaction of changing family size and wealth transfers, the before and after tax distributions were tabulated on a per capita family basis, e.g., family net worth divided by family size. The results are shown in Table 4.

Whatever dramatic changes may occur to the average wealth of family members because of changes in family size and inheritances, they do not reveal themselves in the per capita family wealth tabulations of Table 4. If anything, the table suggests more stability on a per capita basis than on an aggregate family basis.

TABLE 3 Distribution of Families by Net Worth and Age of Head Before and After Current Estate Tax, 1962 (Numbers in thousands)

Net Worth		All Units	Head's Age		
			<30	30<65	≧65
Before Taxes					
	< $ 1,000	8,712.7	2,217.3	5,314.1	1,181.3
$ 1,000 <	2,000	5,704.6	1,859.9	3,047.6	797.2
2,000 <	3,000	2,697.0	727.0	1,808.7	161.3
3,000 <	4,000	2,339.6	405.4	1,492.8	441.4
4,000 <	5,000	2,161.1	266.5	1,432.7	461.9
5,000 <	6,000	1,688.7	179.0	1,222.5	287.2
6,000 <	7,000	1,216.6	139.6	907.8	169.2
7,000 <	8,000	1,781.5	183.2	1,245.8	352.5
8,000 <	9,000	1,350.4	23.9	1,047.0	279.6
9,000 <	10,000	1,742.3	288.8	972.1	481.4
10,000 <	15,000	6,381.4	417.6	4,549.0	1,414.8
15,000 <	20,000	4,717.8	197.3	3,715.2	805.3
20,000 <	25,000	3,507.6	79.9	2,911.0	516.6
25,000 <	50,000	7,838.8	269.0	5,678.2	1.891.6
50,000 <	100,000	3,970.8	6.7	2,953.3	1,010.8
100,000 <	200,000	1,226.7	46.1	877.1	303.5
≧	200,000	889.4	2.6	556.9	329.8
After Taxes					
	< $ 1,000	8,464.2	2,156.6	5,218.0	1,091.3
$ 1,000 <	2,000	5,429.4	1,799.8	2,898.0	732.2
2,000 <	3,000	2,646.9	769.6	1,718.2	159.2
3,000 <	4,000	2,261.8	421.1	1,436.1	404.6
4,000 <	5,000	2,198.6	325.7	1,449.8	423.1
5,000 <	6,000	1,727.4	212.5	1,246.6	268.3
6,000 <	7,000	1,238.4	153.8	923.5	161.2
7,000 <	8,000	1,782.4	195.1	1,262.8	324.5
8,000 <	9,000	1,374.1	48.6	1,036.6	288.8
9,000 <	10,000	1,637.5	266.8	927.3	443.4
10,000 <	15,000	6,398.4	467.0	4,577.9	1,354.6
15,000 <	20,000	4,801.9	221.7	3,787.5	793.2
20,000 <	25,000	3,575.6	105.4	2,939.4	530.8
25,000 <	50,000	7,877.9	287.2	5,772.8	1,819.3
50,000 <	100,000	3,964.2	12.8	3,016.2	935.3
100,000 <	200,000	1,230.5	46.2	887.3	297.1
≧	200,000	884.3	2.9	561.1	320.4

TABLE 4 **Distribution of Families by Per Capita Net Worth and Age of Head Before and After Current Estate Tax, 1962**
(Numbers in thousands)

Net Worth		All Units	<30	Head's Age 30<65	≥65
		Before Taxes			
<$	1,000	19,551.1	4,907.5	12,667.8	1,975.8
$ 1,000<	2,000	7,450.7	1,398.4	5,098.7	953.5
2,000<	3,000	5,371.0	537.2	4,317.5	616.2
3,000<	4,000	3,622.1	76.6	2,791.7	753.8
4,000<	5,000	2,514.6	62.4	2,068.2	383.9
5,000<	6,000	2,084.4	57.0	1,284.5	743.0
6,000<	7,000	2,011.5	15.5	1,592.7	403.3
7,000<	8,000	1,613.2	88.3	1,008.7	516.2
8,000<	9,000	1,395.3	65.5	932.0	397.8
9,000<	10,000	761.5	46.7	446.4	268.4
10,000<	15,000	4,005.5	55.7	2,715.0	1,234.8
15,000<	20,000	2,322.6	91.3	1,548.3	682.9
20,000<	25,000	1,345.8	0.0	855.1	490.7
25,000<	50,000	2,446.2	0.0	1,628.7	817.5
50,000<	100,000	748.1	6.8	389.5	351.8
100,000<	200,000	460.2	0.5	286.8	172.9
≥	200,000	223.3	0.4	99.8	123.0
		After Taxes			
<$	1,000	16,096.3	4,258.3	10,342.5	1,498.2
$ 1,000<	2,000	6,685.3	1,321.8	4,590.8	774.0
2,000<	3,000	4,876.3	706.1	3,611.6	559.0
3,000<	4,000	3,802.2	413.3	2,986.6	402.3
4,000<	5,000	3,244.7	167.3	2,347.3	730.1
5,000<	6,000	2,273.8	99.9	1,873.4	300.6
6,000<	7,000	1,555.5	46.8	1,162.8	345.9
7,000<	8,000	1,793.6	43.7	1,210.8	539.2
8,000<	9,000	1,359.8	9.6	1,101.1	249.2
9,000<	10,000	1,429.9	77.4	921.1	431.5
10,000<	15,000	4,352.1	197.4	2,957.2	1,197.6
15,000<	20,000	2,497.1	33.2	1,683.4	780.5
20,000<	25,000	2,032.5	94.2	1,332.0	606.3
25,000<	50,000	3,446.0	15.7	2,320.9	1,109.5
50,000<	100,000	1,119.4	6.8	654.0	458.6
100,000<	200,000	620.2	0.6	391.9	227.7
≥	200,000	308.0	0.7	170.3	137.0

To examine better the dynamics within the distributions suggested by Tables 3 and 4, a decile matrix of before and after tax rank was constructed (Tables 5 and 6). Families are found to experience considerable decile movement even though the aggregate distribution is stable.

So far, we have demonstrated that our simulation model (a) stochastically generates deaths which are almost identical in number to those reported in the official vital statistics for the U.S.; (b) generates tax collections by the Treasury (with a tax algorithm which replicates the present federal estate tax rules) which are quite comparable to those reported in the official Treasury statistics; and (c) generates estate sizes which are in essential agreement with the size distribution of estates reported by the IRS in the range above $100,000 gross assets. (Below $100,000, we find many more estates than the IRS reports, and there is strong reason to believe the IRS is wrong and the model's results are very close to correct; see note 6). On the basis of the above results we are prepared to use the model to form judgments about the process of inter-generational wealth transfers and death taxes.

By measuring events which occur in the simulation population, it is possible to gain insights into the inter-generational distribution of wealth which are not available from natural data. In Tables 3 and 4, it is shown that when saving and consumption are held constant (set to zero), the distribution of wealth after one year's deaths and associated taxes is little different from that before the events occurred. However, there is a widely held belief that the transmission of wealth at death results in increasing its concentration and that the federal estate tax lessens the concentration by whittling down large estates before they devolve to already rich persons. Both beliefs are intuitive, since there is no empirical data to support either of them. To measure the independent effects of death transfers and estate taxes on the distribution of wealth, the simulation was rerun setting the tax rate to zero for all estates. After the simulation, family distributions of net worth were produced and are shown in Table 7, along with the net worth distributions for families before simulation and after the simulation, using the federal estate tax. The results are rather startling. Taken alone, the transfer of wealth at death does not tend to increase the concentration of wealth but to decrease it slightly. In the first three columns of Table 7, the before-simulation distribution of net worth on December 31, 1962, the percentage change in the intervals of the distribution due to death transfers in the absence of a death tax, and the resultant distribution on December 31, 1963 are shown. There is a pronounced net movement of families out of the four lowest net worth classes and a slight decrease, or no net change, in the numbers of families at the top of the size distribution. The overall effect, then, of death transfers in the absence of a death tax is to

TABLE 5 Before and After Death Tax Family Net Worth Position, Current Federal Estate Tax, 1962
(Figures represent numbers of families in thousands)

Before Tax Family Net Worth Position in Thousands of Dollars (by deciles)	After Tax Family Net Worth Position in Thousands of Dollars (by deciles)									
	1	2	3	4	5	6	7	8	9	10
1	5,630.5	92.3	0.5	0.0	9.5	11.3	0.0	4.8	0.0	0.2
2	129.0	5,381.4	210.3	10.4	0.0	10.9	16.7	0.0	0.0	0.0
3	0.0	261.6	5,043.9	432.8	0.0	6.4	7.2	0.0	0.0	0.0
4	0.0	26.2	431.3	4,637.1	627.0	3.9	0.0	8.9	0.0	1.7
5	0.0	4.5	47.4	565.6	4,338.9	792.3	0.0	0.0	2.3	0.0
6	0.0	0.0	18.5	81.7	688.8	4,263.5	678.6	12.2	0.0	0.0
7	0.0	0.0	11.5	20.2	64.5	575.1	4,418.6	654.2	4.7	3.5
8	0.0	0.0	0.2	17.1	19.6	65.0	474.4	4,389.0	795.1	4.4
9	0.0	0.0	0.0	0.0	12.1	30.6	85.0	313.7	4,563.1	675.6
10	0.0	0.0	0.0	0.4	6.5	4.4	85.2	381.5	401.5	4,929.3
Total	5,759.5	5,766.0	5,763.6	5,765.3	5,766.9	5,763.4	5,765.7	5,764.3	5,766.7	5,614.7

NOTE: Dollar figures in thousands for deciles are as follows:

Decile 1 = 52.3   Decile 6 = 6.1
Decile 2 = 29.3   Decile 7 = 3.3
Decile 3 = 20.2   Decile 8 = 1.4
Decile 4 = 14.2   Decile 9 = 1.0
Decile 5 = 9.9   Decile 10 = Less than 1.0

TABLE 6 Before and After Death Tax Family Per Capita Net Worth Position, Current Federal Estate Tax, 1962

(Figures represent numbers of families in thousands)

Before Tax Family Per Capita Net Worth Position in Thousands of Dollars (by deciles)	After Tax Family Per Capita Net Worth Position in Thousands of Dollars (by deciles)									
	1	2	3	4	5	6	7	8	9	10
1	5,570.4	109.7	14.6	6.1	0.0	4.8	0.0	0.0	0.0	0.2
2	171.2	5,328.3	168.6	18.0	9.6	0.0	0.0	0.0	0.0	0.0
3	13.7	227.0	5,172.6	334.0	4.9	0.0	0.0	0.0	0.0	0.0
4	6.8	64.2	331.6	4,922.9	414.9	4.9	5.6	2.3	1.7	0.0
5	0.0	18.7	39.6	360.2	4,685.8	657.0	5.6	0.0	0.0	0.0
6	0.0	11.9	21.9	49.8	550.6	4,571.1	566.6	6.6	0.0	0.0
7	0.0	5.4	3.5	46.6	75.0	429.2	4,582.3	570.9	0.0	0.0
8	0.0	0.0	7.2	25.8	7.8	57.6	514.1	4,537.1	550.1	0.0
9	0.0	0.0	0.0	0.0	8.3	30.4	65.9	534.1	4,519.8	655.9
10	0.0	0.0	5.0	0.4	8.8	10.9	25.0	112.5	690.7	4,953.1
Total	5,762.1	5,765.2	5,764.6	5,763.8	5,765.7	5,765.9	5,765.1	5,763.5	5,762.3	5,618.6

NOTE: Dollar figures in thousands for deciles are as follows:

Decile 1 = 24.4   Decile 6 = 2.0
Decile 2 = 13.1   Decile 7 = 1.1
Decile 3 = 7.9   Decile 8 = 0.6
Decile 4 = 4.9   Decile 9 = 0.6
Decile 5 = 3.2   Decile 10 = Less than 0.3

TABLE 7 Simulation of Independent Effects of Bequests and Current Estate Tax on the Size Distribution of Family Wealth, 1962

Family Net Worth	Distribution of Families before Simulation (Thousands)	Change due to Bequests (Percentage change)	Distribution of Families after Deaths with Zero Tax (Thousands)	Change due to Current Estate Tax (Percentage change)	Distribution of Families after Current Estate Tax (Thousands)	Change due to Bequests and Estate Tax (Percentage change)
< $ 1,000	8,712.7	−2.9	8,461.9	0.0	8,464.2	−2.9
$ 1,000 < 2,000	5,704.6	−5.0	5,419.0	0.2	5,429.4	−4.8
2,000 < 3,000	2,697.0	−2.5	2,630.1	0.6	2,646.9	−1.9
3,000 < 4,000	2,339.6	−3.2	2,265.7	−0.2	2,261.8	−3.3
4,000 < 5,000	2,161.1	2.1	2,206.9	−0.4	2,198.6	1.7
5,000 < 6,000	1,688.7	1.2	1,708.6	1.1	1,727.4	2.3
6,000 < 7,000	1,216.6	2.5	1,246.5	−0.6	1,238.4	1.8
7,000 < 8,000	1,781.5	0.1	1,783.9	−0.1	1,782.4	0.1
8,000 < 9,000	1,350.4	1.9	1,375.8	0.1	1,374.1	1.8
9,000 < 10,000	1,742.3	−4.8	1,658.2	−1.2	1,637.5	−6.0
10,000 < 15,000	6,381.4	0.0	6,333.2	0.2	6,398.4	0.3
15,000 < 20,000	4,717.8	1.8	4,804.4	−0.1	4,801.9	1.8
20,000 < 25,000	3,507.6	1.8	3,570.7	0.1	3,575.6	1.9
25,000 < 50,000	7,838.8	0.8	7,899.2	−0.3	7,877.9	0.5
50,000 < 100,000	3,970.8	−0.2	3,964.2	0.0	3,964.2	−0.2
100,000 < 200,000	1,226.7	0.3	1,230.5	0.0	1,230.5	0.3
≧ 200,000	889.4	−0.5	884.3	0.0	884.3	−0.5
Total	57,927.0		57,493.0		57,493.0	

lessen concentration. This apparently comes about for several reasons. First, some one-person families, which have a higher probability of being at the bottom of the distribution than do larger families, die off. Secondly, most decedents (over 95 percent in 1962) have estates of less than $60,000 net worth. When these estates are distributed to surviving children and to other families' members, they are parceled into rather small bequests, so that most inheritors are not moved a long way up the wealth distribution. Thirdly, inheritors, contrary to popular opinion, are often at the lower end of the wealth distribution. This is particularly relevant for the findings in the case of children of wealthy parents. The children of the rich are likely to have above-average levels of human capital, because they have longer than average periods of schooling, but that very fact increases the probability that they will inherit wealth before they have accumulated significantly out of their own earnings. In the methodology section, it will be found that one's own wealth is a poor predictor of inheriting; educational level was found to be a much better one.

In column 5 of Table 7, the distribution of families by size of net worth after simulation, with the current estate tax rates in effect, is shown. The difference between the distribution shown in column 3 (zero tax rates) and column 5 is the pure distributional impact of the current estate tax, i.e., independent of the pretax devolution pattern. The tax can, of course, do nothing to move families out of the lower reaches of the distribution, so one would not expect to find negative changes (column 4), but there appears to be a slight increase in the numbers of families at the lower end. This suggests that some of the smaller parcels of wealth intended for families in the range above the lowest three net worth intervals were diminished when the tax was applied. These families who would have ended in richer classes with a zero death tax find themselves at the bottom with the current tax. Such families must have come from some other part of the distributions, and they presumably came from the middle range where the net impact of the tax is to reduce the number of families. Oddly enough, the tax has no measurable impact at the top of the distribution. Whatever gross outflows of families occurred from the intervals above a net worth of $50,000 were offset by movement into the classes by inheritors who were nearer the middle of the distribution. There are a number of reasons for this unexpected result. First, bequests are more often made to persons of less wealth than the decedent than the converse. Secondly, the tax on intrafamily wealth transfers is less than the rates alone would suggest. (When the decedent is married, up to 50 percent of his estate is exempt. The first $60,000 of net worth of all estates is also exempt.) Thirdly, estate planning removes from the purview of the tax law certain assets and distributes them constructively or, in fact, prior to death. Fourthly, the base of the current federal death tax is the net worth after deductions and exemptions of the estate, not the wealth of the inheritor. Thus, the share of the pretax estate inherited by an indigent heir is diminished by the same percentage as that share inherited by an affluent heir.

We are left then with the paradox that a tax whose philosophical foundation is to mitigate a natural process toward inequality is apparently obstructing a natural process toward greater equality.

At this point, we turn to the simulation of three alternative tax structures which differ from the current tax by varying degree.

Simulation 2. Reform Estate Tax

It was noted that the current estate tax had little effect on the distribution of wealth at the top of the distribution, because the generous marital and personal exemptions permit the transfer of substantial amounts of untaxed wealth. Also, the marital exemption discriminates among heirs. We have structured a tax which eliminates discriminatory features, increases the personal exemption of all estates to $100,000, and provides for higher rates on estates over $100,000. The rates are 50 percent on the first $400,000 of taxable estate and 100 percent on amounts in excess of $400,000. It is assumed, of course, that appropriate measures to insure against tax avoidance, such as placing appropriate taxes on inter-vivos gifts, would be implemented.

This simulation was run in exactly the same manner as the first experiment. The same persons selected to die by the Monte Carlo draws in the first experiment were selected again, so, although the selection of deaths is stochastic, the same stochastic selection was used for all experiments to avoid inter-experiment Monte Carlo variation.

This tax reduces inequality on both a straight family basis and on a per capita family basis (see Tables 8 and 9). Although the one-year reduction in equality is very slight, it would, over a number of years, compress the distribution of wealth.

In Table 10 the pure tax effect on the distribution of family wealth is shown. The tax results in a diminution of persons at the top of the distribution, but also increases the number at the bottom. In addition, it results in an increase in the number of families in the middle range. Although there is only a slight difference in the distribution of wealth resulting from this tax, the yield to the Treasury is much greater, $7.2 billion compared to $2.1 billion, under the current federal tax system.

TABLE 8 Distribution of Families by Net Worth and Age of Head Before and After Reform Estate Tax, 1962 (Numbers in thousands)

Net Worth		All Units	<30	30 < 65	≧65
				Head's Age	
Before Taxes					
< $	1,000	8,712.7	2,217.3	5,314.1	1,181.3
$ 1,000 <	2,000	5,704.6	1,859.9	3,047.6	797.2
2,000 <	3,000	2,697.0	727.0	1,808.7	161.3
3,000 <	4,000	2,339.6	405.4	1,492.8	441.4
4,000 <	5,000	2,161.1	266.5	1,432.7	461.9
5,000 <	6,000	1,688.7	179.0	1,222.5	287.2
6,000 <	7,000	1,216.6	139.6	907.8	169.2
7,000 <	8,000	1,781.5	183.2	1,245.8	352.5
8,000 <	9,000	1,350.4	23.9	1,047.0	279.6
9,000 <	10,000	1,742.3	288.8	972.1	481.4
10,000 <	15,000	6,381.4	417.6	4,549.0	1,414.8
15,000 <	20,000	4,717.8	197.3	3,715.2	805.3
20,000 <	25,000	3,507.6	79.9	2,911.0	516.6
25,000 <	50,000	7,838.8	269.0	5,678.2	1,891.6
50,000 <	100,000	3,970.8	6.7	2,953.3	1,010.8
100,000 <	200,000	1,226.7	46.1	877.1	303.5
≧	200,000	889.4	2.6	556.9	329.8
After Taxes					
< $	1,000	8,464.2	2,156.6	5,218.0	1,091.3
$ 1,000 <	2,000	5,436.0	1,799.8	2,904.6	732.2
2,000 <	3,000	2,644.6	769.6	1,715.9	159.2
3,000 <	4,000	2,310.3	446.2	1,454.7	409.4
4,000 <	5,000	2,192.5	313.6	1,460.6	418.3
5,000 <	6,000	1,720.3	203.1	1,244.0	273.3
6,000 <	7,000	1,253.5	150.2	941.2	162.2
7,000 <	8,000	1,755.0	195.1	1,236.5	323.3
8,000 <	9,000	1,374.6	61.9	1,017.4	295.4
9,000 <	10,000	1,657.6	253.9	964.8	438.9
10,000 <	15,000	6,384.9	476.8	4,561.1	1,348.0
15,000 <	20,000	4,824.1	220.6	3,794.7	809.2
20,000 <	25,000	3,529.7	96.3	2,918.9	514.4
25,000 <	50,000	7,872.5	287.2	5,767.5	1,819.3
50,000 <	100,000	3,959.5	12.8	3,011.5	935.3
100,000 <	200,000	1,233.0	46.3	889.2	297.6
≧	200,000	881.0	2.7	558.6	319.9

TABLE 9 Distribution of Families by Per Capita Net Worth and Age of Head Before and After Reform Estate Tax, 1962
(Numbers in thousands)

Net Worth		All Units	<30	Head's Age 30 < 65	≧ 65
		Before Taxes			
< $	1,000	19,551.1	4,907.5	12,667.8	1,975.8
$ 1,000 <	2,000	7,450.7	1,398.4	5,098.7	953.5
2,000 <	3,000	5,371.0	537.2	4,317.5	616.2
3,000 <	4,000	3,622.1	76.6	2,791.7	753.8
4,000 <	5,000	2,514.6	62.4	2,068.2	383.9
5,000 <	6,000	2,084.4	57.0	1,284.5	743.0
6,000 <	7,000	2,011.5	15.5	1,592.7	403.3
7,000 <	8,000	1,613.2	88.3	1,008.7	516.2
8,000 <	9,000	1,395.3	65.5	932.0	397.8
9,000 <	10,000	761.5	46.7	446.4	268.4
10,000 <	15,000	4,005.5	55.7	2,715.0	1,234.8
15,000 <	20,000	2,322.6	91.3	1,548.3	682.9
20,000 <	25,000	1,345.8	0.0	855.1	490.7
25,000 <	50,000	2,446.2	0.0	1,628.7	817.5
50,000 <	100,000	748.1	6.8	389.5	351.8
100,000 <	200,000	460.2	0.5	286.8	172.9
≧	200,000	223.3	0.4	99.8	123.0
		After Taxes			
< $	1,000	16,118.6	4,265.8	10,357.3	1,498.2
$ 1,000 <	2,000	6,687.6	1,324.6	4,590.2	774.0
2,000 <	3,000	4,880.8	707.0	3,606.9	567.3
3,000 <	4,000	3,815.3	420.4	3,001.0	394.0
4,000 <	5,000	3,218.0	148.9	2,339.0	730.1
5,000 <	6,000	2,273.0	102.1	1,865.5	305.3
6,000 <	7,000	1,581.9	44.6	1,189.8	347.5
7,000 <	8,000	1,787.5	43.7	1,200.6	543.1
8,000 <	9,000	1,345.7	12.9	1,094.0	238.8
9,000 <	10,000	1,436.0	74.4	916.6	445.0
10,000 <	15,000	4,340.8	197.0	2,959.8	1,184.0
15,000 <	20,000	2,499.4	33.2	1,675.9	790.3
20,000 <	25,000	2,015.1	94.2	1,324.3	596.6
25,000 <	50,000	3,450.7	15.7	2,325.6	1,109.5
50,000 <	100,000	1,114.9	6.9	649.0	459.1
100,000 <	200,000	623.3	0.7	395.4	227.2
≧	200,000	304.4	0.5	166.9	137.0

TABLE 10 **Percentage Change in Family Wealth Size Distribution Due to Pure Tax Effect of Reform Estate Tax, 1962**

Net Worth	Percentage Change Due to Tax
< $ 1,000	0.0
$ 1,000 < 2,000	0.3
2,000 < 3,000	0.6
3,000 < 4,000	2.0
4,000 < 5,000	−0.7
5,000 < 6,000	0.7
6,000 < 7,000	0.6
7,000 < 8,000	−1.2
8,000 < 9,000	−0.1
9,000 < 10,000	0.0
10,000 < 15,000	0.0
15,000 < 20,000	0.4
20,000 < 25,000	−1.1
25,000 < 50,000	−0.3
50,000 < 100,000	−0.1
100,000 < 200,000	0.2
≥ 200,000	−0.4

Simulation 3. Inheritance Tax, Modest Reform

The historical justifications of U.S. death taxes have been wealth redistribution and an impediment to plutocracy. In recent years, however, the annual Treasury yield from the tax has approached $2 billion. Whether redistributive or revenue raising, the burden of the tax would best be distributed on the ability to pay of natural persons with a beneficial interest in the estate. Clearly, there is no beneficial interest of a decedent in his estate. The only persons having beneficial interests are the potential heirs. Two simulation experiments taxing heirs were run.

The first experiment taxes *heirs*, using the current estate tax schedule (Table 1), but the base of the tax is the sum of one's inheritance plus his own net worth. An inheritor is not taxed on any part of his own wealth but the tax rates applicable to his inheritance begin with the marginal rate applicable to the first dollar of inherited wealth in excess of his own net worth. For instance, if the inheritor had a net worth of $60,000, the first $5,000 of his inheritance would be taxed at a 3 percent rate, the next

$5,000 at a 7 percent rate, and so on (see Table 1, page 623). If the total inheritance of this heir were to amount to $20,000, his total tax bill would amount to $1,600 on the $20,000 inheritance. A richer individual receiving the same $20,000 would be taxed at higher rates. For instance, should the inheritor have a net worth of $500,000, entry into the tax table would be at the 35 percent rate. Since the tax rate for amounts between $500,000 and $750,000 is 35 percent, the entire $20,000 would be subject to a 35 percent rate, or a total of $6,000. An heir whose net worth was $12,000 would pay no tax on his $20,000 inheritance. Tables 11 and 12 show the before and after distributions of the tax.

The pure tax effect of this inheritance tax results in greater reductions at the top and smaller increases at the bottom of the wealth distribution than do the present or reform estate tax. Apparently, the high marginal rates on wealthy heirs have a significant impact on affluent heirs within the same family as the decedent, while the exemption for heirs results in a smaller bite being taken from relatively less affluent inheritors (see Table 13).

Simulation 4. Severe Inheritance Tax Reform

To test the effect of a severe inheritance tax, a $50,000 limit was placed on the amount one could inherit from one estate. The tax has almost no direct effect on the distribution of wealth except at the very highest wealth levels (see Table 14). The top two wealth classes are slightly diminished and the third from the top class picks up the few families which are bumped down. The reasons for the small direct redistributive effect of such a severe tax are that (a) very few people inherit amounts in excess of $50,000, and (b) there is no provision in the model for a behavioral change in the bequeathing practices of individuals.

If wealth holders were confronted with either of the inheritance taxes we have simulated, they would presumably change their wills to minimize tax erosion of their estates. If they carried this behavior to its limit, they would avoid all inheritance taxes by bequeathing amounts no greater than $60,000 and $50,000 to individual heirs respectively in the third and fourth simulation experiments. If they were to do so, it would achieve substantial redistribution.

In the modest reform inheritance tax, inheritors are subject to progressive tax rates when the sum of the heirs' prior wealth and inheritance exceed $60,000. The rate will never, however, exceed 77 percent. Under such a tax, testators would evaluate how much they were willing to have their total distribution diminished by inheritance taxes in order to benefit specific heirs. If testators' aversion to having their bequests

TABLE 11 Distribution of Families by Net Worth and Age of Head before and after Modest Reform Inheritance Tax, 1962
(Numbers in thousands)

Net Worth	All Units	Head's Age <30	Head's Age 30<65	Head's Age ≧65
		Before Taxes		
< $ 1,000	8,712.7	2,217.3	5,314.1	1,181.3
$ 1,000 < 2,000	5,704.6	1,859.9	3,047.6	797.2
2,000 < 3,000	2,697.0	727.0	1,808.7	161.3
3,000 < 4,000	2,339.6	405.4	1,492.8	441.4
4,000 < 5,000	2,161.1	266.5	1,432.7	461.9
5,000 < 6,000	1,688.7	179.0	1,222.5	287.2
6,000 < 7,000	1,216.6	139.6	907.8	169.2
7,000 < 8,000	1,781.5	183.2	1,245.8	352.5
8,000 < 9,000	1,350.4	23.9	1,047.0	279.6
9,000 < 10,000	1,742.3	288.8	972.1	481.4
10,000 < 15,000	6,381.4	417.6	4,549.0	1,414.8
15,000 < 20,000	4,717.8	197.3	3,715.2	805.3
20,000 < 25,000	3,507.6	79.9	2,911.0	516.6
25,000 < 50,000	7,838.8	269.0	5,678.2	1,891.6
50,000 < 100,000	3,970.8	6.7	2,953.3	1,010.8
100,000 < 200,000	1,226.7	46.1	877.1	303.5
≧ 200,000	889.4	2.6	556.9	329.8
		After Taxes		
< $ 1,000	8,461.9	2,154.3	5,218.0	1,091.3
$ 1,000 < 2,000	5,422.4	1,802.1	2,888.8	732.2
2,000 < 3,000	2,639.7	753.2	1,724.0	162.5
3,000 < 4,000	2,258.7	425.5	1,431.9	401.3
4,000 < 5,000	2,207.1	330.2	1,453.8	423.1
5,000 < 6,000	1,725.7	220.0	1,237.5	268.3
6,000 < 7,000	1,244.6	150.0	933.4	161.2
7,000 < 8,000	1,791.4	198.9	1,267.9	324.5
8,000 < 9,000	1,369.6	48.6	1,025.5	295.4
9,000 < 10,000	1,645.4	266.8	941.9	436.8
10,000 < 15,000	6,407.3	467.0	4,586.8	1,354.6
15,000 < 20,000	4,818.1	226.6	3,789.9	802.1
20,000 < 25,000	3,560.2	102.3	2,931.6	526.3
25,000 < 50,000	7,900.1	285.4	5,801.3	1,814.9
50,000 < 100,000	3,936.2	12.8	2,985.3	938.2
100,000 < 200,000	1,224.3	46.4	883.3	294.6
≧ 200,000	880.7	2.7	558.2	319.9

TABLE 12 Distribution of Families by Per Capita Net Worth
and Age of Head before and after Modest Reform
Inheritance Tax, 1962
(Numbers in thousands)

Net Worth	All Units	Head's Age		
		<30	30<65	≧65
Before Taxes				
< $ 1,000	19,551.1	4,907.5	12,667.8	1,975.8
$ 1,000 < 2,000	7,450.7	1,398.4	5,098.7	953.5
2,000 < 3,000	5,371.0	537.2	4,317.5	616.2
3,000 < 4,000	3,622.1	76.6	2,791.7	753.8
4,000 < 5,000	2,514.6	62.4	2,068.2	383.9
5,000 < 6,000	2,084.4	57.0	1,284.5	743.0
6,000 < 7,000	2,011.5	15.5	1,592.7	403.3
7,000 < 8,000	1,613.2	88.3	1,008.7	516.2
8,000 < 9,000	1,395.3	65.5	932.0	397.8
9,000 < 10,000	761.5	46.7	446.4	268.4
10,000 < 15,000	4,005.5	55.7	2,715.0	1,234.8
15,000 < 20,000	2,322.6	91.3	1,548.3	682.9
20,000 < 25,000	1,345.8	0.0	855.1	490.7
25,000 < 50,000	2,446.2	0.0	1,628.7	817.5
50,000 < 100,000	748.1	6.8	389.5	351.8
100,000 < 200,000	460.2	0.5	286.8	172.9
≧ 200,000	223.3	0.4	99.8	123.0
After Taxes				
< $ 1,000	16,096.3	4,258.3	10,342.5	1,498.2
$ 1,000 < 2,000	6,690.1	1,321.8	4,590.7	778.8
2,000 < 3,000	4,868.9	706.1	3,599.1	564.2
3,000 < 4,000	3,799.1	401.4	3,005.4	392.3
4,000 < 5,000	3,245.9	171.8	2,344.0	730.1
5,000 < 6,000	2,282.0	109.1	1,872.3	300.6
6,000 < 7,000	1,566.9	41.2	1,179.8	345.9
7,000 < 8,000	1,785.8	47.5	1,199.2	539.2
8,000 < 9,000	1,374.1	11.3	1,113.7	249.2
9,000 < 10,000	1,431.0	78.2	912.4	440.4
10,000 < 15,000	4,346.6	194.9	2,958.5	1,193.3
15,000 < 20,000	2,501.0	35.6	1,689.4	776.1
20,000 < 25,000	2,029.7	91.8	1,326.8	611.1
25,000 < 50,000	3,451.0	15.7	2,330.8	1,104.5
50,000 < 100,000	1,105.2	6.8	636.9	461.5
100,000 < 200,000	614.9	0.7	389.3	224.9
≧ 200,000	304.5	0.5	167.1	136.9

TABLE 13 Percentage Change in Family Wealth Size Distribution Due to Pure Tax Effect of Modest Reform Inheritance Tax, 1962

Net Worth	Percentage Change Due to Tax
< $ 1,000	0.0
$ 1,000 < 2,000	0.1
2,000 < 3,000	0.4
3,000 < 4,000	−0.3
4,000 < 5,000	0.0
5,000 < 6,000	1.0
6,000 < 7,000	−0.2
7,000 < 8,000	0.5
8,000 < 9,000	−0.5
9,000 < 10,000	−0.8
10,000 < 15,000	0.4
15,000 < 20,000	0.3
20,000 < 25,000	−0.3
25,000 < 50,000	0.0
50,000 < 100,000	−0.7
100,000 < 200,000	−0.5
≧ 200,000	−0.4

taxed were stronger than their preference to benefit specific heirs, they would distribute their estate so that no inheritor ended up with more than $60,000 when his prior wealth and inheritance were summed. It is unlikely that all testators have such strong aversions, and many would accept some diminution of their distributed estates in order to benefit preferred heirs at lower marginal tax rates. At higher marginal rates, which come about with increasing size of bequests and increasing prior wealth of heirs, it is suspected that testators' aversion to taxes would overtake their preference for benefiting specific heirs, and they would parcel out some of their bequests in smaller amounts and to less affluent heirs.

The manner in which the modest reform inheritance tax simulation (experiment 3 above) was run has decedent's estates distributed according to patterns observed under the present federal estate tax, that is, without penalty for giving bequests in excess of $60,000 or benefiting heirs whose prior net worth equalled or exceeded $60,000. Consequently, we can think of the experiment as reflecting a limit at which

TABLE 14 **Percentage Change in Family Wealth Size Distribution Due to Pure Tax Effect of Severe Inheritance Tax, 1962**

Net Worth	Percentage Change Due to Tax
< $ 1,000	0.0
$ 1,000 < 2,000	0.0
2,000 < 3,000	0.0
3,000 < 4,000	0.0
4,000 < 5,000	0.0
5,000 < 6,000	0.0
6,000 < 7,000	0.0
7,000 < 8,000	0.0
8,000 < 9,000	0.0
9,000 < 10,000	0.0
10,000 < 15,000	0.0
15,000 < 20,000	0.0
20,000 < 25,000	0.0
25,000 < 50,000	0.0
50,000 < 100,000	0.4
100,000 < 200,000	−0.7
≥ 200,000	−0.6

testators were insensitive to a tax penalty for contributing to the concentration of wealth.

At the other limit, testators would not make bequests which resulted in an heir's after-inheritance wealth exceeding $60,000. We can approximate the results of such behavior by redistributing the taxes collected by the Treasury in experiment 3. We have no empirical basis for estimating how testators would parcel out their assets, but will arbitrarily assume that testators are indifferent to the wealth of heirs so long as the total inheritance tax remains zero for heirs other than those they would favor under an estate tax. It is also assumed that all taxes are redistributed on a per capita basis. These assumptions make it easy to compare the results of all four tax systems. The effect of the taxes under these assumptions can be measured by redistributing on a per capita basis taxes collected in each of the experiments.

A tax which redistributes net worth toward greater equality will reduce the numbers of family units in the intervals at the tails of the distribution and increase them near the mean of the distribution. In Table

TABLE 15 Percentage Change in Number of Families in Intervals of the Distribution of Net Worth due to the Taxation of Death Transfers and the Redistribution of Treasury Yield

Net Worth	Before Simulation Distribution (Thousands)	No Tax	Current Estate Tax	Reform Estate Tax	Modest Inheritance Tax	Severe Inheritance Tax
< $ 1,000	8,712.7	-2.9	-43.6	-52.1	-52.0	-52.0
$ 1,000 < 2,000	5,704.6	-5.0	55.6	61.2	61.7	61.7
2,000 < 3,000	2,697.0	-2.5	-1.4	10.6	9.5	9.2
3,000 < 4,000	2,339.6	-3.2	-3.7	-6.5	-7.3	-7.3
4,000 < 5,000	2,161.1	2.1	4.1	0.8	1.1	-0.5
5,000 < 6,000	1,688.7	1.2	-6.7	1.7	-2.3	-0.8
6,000 < 7,000	1,216.6	2.5	18.2	23.5	27.7	28.4
7,000 < 8,000	1,781.5	0.1	0.5	-3.7	-3.4	-5.1
8,000 < 9,000	1,350.4	1.9	-0.7	6.7	6.2	6.9
9,000 < 10,000	1,742.3	-4.8	-7.0	-22.0	-20.5	-19.8
10,000 < 15,000	6,381.4	0.0	0.0	4.0	3.7	3.4
15,000 < 20,000	4,717.8	1.8	1.1	2.2	2.3	1.9
20,000 < 25,000	3,507.6	1.8	2.1	-0.2	0.6	1.1
25,000 < 50,000	7,838.8	0.8	1.4	1.9	2.1	2.2
50,000 < 100,000	3,970.8	-0.2	0.5	0.4	-0.1	0.9
100,000 < 200,000	1,226.7	0.3	0.3	0.5	-0.2	-0.4
≥ 200,000	889.4	-0.5	-0.5	-0.9	-0.9	-1.2
Mean net worth	$29,714	$29,930	$29,930	$29,932	$29,934	$29,923
Standard deviation	$446,823	$446,060	$445,615	$445,879	$445,566	$446,544
Relative standard deviation	15.04%	14.90%	14.89%	14.90%	14.88%	14.92%

15, the percentage change in the number of families within intervals due to the joint effect of taxation and redistribution of Treasury collections is shown. The "no tax" column shows the changes due solely to the devolution choices made by testators, and the law, for intestate decedents.

The three hypothetical tax systems which we structured result in greater equality than the current estate tax. It will be recalled that the pure tax effect of the current estate tax is toward inequality, so what is observed in column 3 is mostly the redistribution of Treasury yield (about $2 billion). We have assumed that all citizens benefit equally from Treasury expenditures, so families benefit in proportion to their size. In the case of the modest inheritance tax or the severe inheritance tax, the redistribution of Treasury tax collections is equivalent to a behavioral change on the part of testators to bequest to heirs so as to avoid death taxes. Since the tax yield of the modest inheritance tax, the reform estate tax, and the severe estate tax are all about three and one-half times larger than the current estate tax yield (see Table 16), they all produce greater

TABLE 16   Treasury Yield under Four Simulated Death Tax Systems, 1962 (Millions of dollars)

Current estate tax	2,127
Reformed estate tax	7,214
Modest reform inheritance tax	6,572
Severe reform inheritance tax	6,672

redistributive effects than does the current estate tax. Both of the inheritance taxes result in greater redistribution than does the current reform estate tax. This is apparent from the percentage changes in the number of families within net worth intervals at the tails of the distribution.

When the redistributive effect of government expenditures is taken into account, it becomes apparent that reforms in death taxes can perceptibly change the distribution of wealth even in the short run. Longer-run simulations using the more flexible Orcutt model at the Urban Institute will permit tests of the longer-run consequences of these prototype death tax reforms.

As noted in the beginning of this section, the model takes account of the costs of dying—medical expenses, lawyer's fees, executor's commissions, and funeral expenses. Because these expenses are greater than the total taxes collected under the present estate tax system, some importance attaches to them in considering the impact of death on the distribution of wealth. Many low-wealth families may be driven into debt to bury a family member and settle his estate. In Table 17 we show the simulated costs of dying and related information.

TABLE 17 Characteristics of Decedents and Simulated Costs of Dying, Charitable Bequests and Assets Available for Distribution

Number of decedents	
Gross estate < $60,000	1,625,245
Gross estate ≥ $60,000	121,988
All decedents	1,747,333
Gross assets of decedents	$40,394,000,000
Net assets of decedents	$38,524,000,000
Costs of dying	
Last illness medical expenses	$529,000,000
Attorney's fees	$1,009,000,000
Executor's commisions	$544,000,000
Funeral expenses	$1,944,000,000
Total	$4,026,000,000
Charitable contributions	$1,706,000,000
Net assets available for distribution and taxes	$32,792,000,000

The cost of last illness is estimated at $529 million or about $301 per decedent. Attorney's fees amounted to $1 billion or over 3 percent of the wealth passing from decedent to beneficiary at death. Funeral expenses constituted an even greater share of the total wealth transmitted at death, $1.9 billion out of $38.5 billion, or almost 5 percent. Taking the total estimated cost of dying, $4.0 billion, we find that it amounts to about 10 percent of the total assets left for distribution.

III. METHODOLOGY

To operate the simulation model, a suitably organized sample representation of the U.S. population and a set of behavioral relations characterizing the devolution of wealth at death, by bequest or otherwise, were required. The Survey of Financial Characteristics of Consumers (SFCC) file was modified to that end. Patterns of wealth devolution were estimated using federal estate tax files and files of Washington, D.C., estate tax returns. We turn first to the modification of the SFCC file and then to a discussion of the simulation logic, bringing in the behavioral estimates in approximately the order in which they are used in the simulation.

Modifying the SFCC File

The SFCC file contains observations on 2,557 sample families representing 57.9 million family units in the population on December 31, 1962. The survey in which the information was gathered is the most detailed survey inquiry into family financial data available. Nevertheless, it contains a number of deficiencies which had to be remedied for the purpose to which we put it.

1. Family Composition The SFCC file contains limited information on family members living at home, but none for children who have left home. Since the main inter-generational flow of wealth is from parent to child, it is important to have a basis of simulating the flow of wealth to children who have left home.

Information in the SFCC file combined with information available about the number of children ever born to married women permitted a rough assignment of the number of children living away from home.

The SFCC file contained the following relevant information.
1. Marital status of head
2. Age of head
3. Age of spouse
4. Age of youngest child at home
5. Age of oldest child at home
6. Number of years since marriage

From the 1960 Census of Population, the number of children ever born by age of married women was obtained:

Age of Woman	Number of Children Ever Born
15–19	1.3
20–24	1.8
25–29	2.5
30–34	2.8
35–39	2.9
40–44	2.9
45–49	2.9
50+	3.4

SOURCE: Irene B. Taeuber and Conrad Taeuber, *People of the United States in the 20th Century*, Census Monograph Series, p. 429.

Above age thirty-five the average number of children born appears to be very close to 3.

The following rules were used to expand the family composition information on the SFCC record:

   i.   It was assumed the first child was never born before mother's age 17.
   ii.   Mothers under 35 were assumed to have all children living at home. Those 35 and over were eligible to have children living away from home.
   iii. All mothers 35 and older were assumed to have no away from home children older than the number of years since their marriage.
   iv.   The number of children over 18 living away from home were assumed to be equal to the number of years since last marriage minus 18, but women were assumed *never more than 3 living children including those at home.*
   v.   The number of children living at home was set equal to the number of persons in the family minus 2 for "married couples" and minus 1 in families in which the head was widowed, divorced or separated.
   vi.   For all families headed by a divorced, widowed, or separated head, the number of children away and at home was calculated as though there were a wife present of the same age as the head. Further it was assumed that the marriage took place at the "wife's" age 20.
   vii. When a family was assigned children living away from home, a shadow record for each such child was created in the file.

2. Treatment of Asset Composition   The SFCC file provides far more detail of the composition of family wealth than is needed in the model. Consequently, assets were compressed into two categories: (1) life insurance face value minus policy loans; and (2) all other assets. All debts except life insurance policy loans (which were netted out of gross assets) were lumped together. The only reason for identifying life insurance as a separate category is the particular role that it plays in inter-generational transfers. Only the cash surrender value of the policy is appropriately considered a part of the assets of the living, but the event of death creates an asset equal to the face value less policy loans. (In reality, the owner of a life insurance policy and the insured need not be the same person, but we have not tried to deal with this distinction in the model.)

The SFCC file identifies three classes of persons: (1) family head (always male in a family including a husband and wife), (2) wife of head,

(3) other family members. The file identifies separately the values of the following assets and debts belonging to heads or wives:

1. Checking account balances
2. U.S. savings bonds (face value)
3. Mortgage assets
4. Nonmortgage loans to individuals
5. Life insurance (face value)
6. Savings account balances (includes amounts in savings and loan associations, credit unions, commercial banks, mutual savings banks and other savings institutions not specifically identified)

Each of the above assets held by other family members as a group was also identified. Other family members included both children and other persons living with the family. For our purposes, we assumed that all other family members were children of the head and wife and that they shared equally in the ownership of all assets and debts designated as belonging to other family members.

The following assets were not reported in the file as belonging to a class of persons, but simply as family assets.

1. Treasury bills (par value)
2. Treasury notes (par value)
3. Treasury certificates (par value)
4. Treasury bonds (par value)
5. State and local bonds (par value)
6. Foreign government and corporation bonds (par value)
7. Domestic corporation bonds (par value)
8. Loans to businesses
9. Corporate stock (market value)
10. Value of business assets (book)
11. Loans to business not elsewhere classified
12. Withdrawable amounts in profit-sharing plans
13. Value of family's residences
14. Value of investment real estate
15. Net value of brokerage accounts
16. Automobile value (market)
17. Oil royalties, patents, and commodity contracts

Lacking any data with which reliable estimates of the relative shares of total family assets held by husbands and wives could be made, we summed the values of the above seventeen categories and arbitrarily assigned 65 percent of the sum to the head and 35 percent to the wife, if present, or allocated it entirely to the family head when no wife was present. This procedure reduces some of the variation in relative shares of total family wealth held among husbands and wives and increases each of their shares relative to that of other family members. Since the value of assets held by other family members is relatively very small when compared to that held by the head and wife, the latter adjustment appears to be of little consequence.

Loans against life insurance policies were identified in the original file as obligations of the head, wife, or other family members as a group. The same treatment was applied to these debts in our model as was given assets similarly identified.

The following were designated family debts in the original file:
1. Loans secured by stock (other than margin accounts)
2. Loans secured by bonds
3. Installment debt
4. Noninstallment debt not elsewhere classified

The same treatment was accorded these debt items as was accorded family assets.

3. Pareto Adjustment of Upper Tail of SFCC Wealth Distribution
The Survey of Financial Characteristics file is a stratified sample of U.S. noninstitutional population on December 31, 1962. High-income families were relatively overselected in the sample design, a feature particularly appropriate to our use of the file. Nevertheless, it is extremely difficult for a sample survey to capture the elongated upper tail of the wealth distribution. In practice what happens is that one ends up with a sample of a truncated tail. Because the tail of the distribution is of critical importance in a model of death transfers, we fitted a Pareto function to the weighted observations of families with net worth over $25,000 and spread the 57 (unweighted) richest families out across the function, retaining their original weights so that they continued to represent the same proportion of the total number of U.S. families as in the original file, but they were assigned the midpoint of the net worth interval in which they fell on the net worth argument of the function.

The Pareto function, $P_{nw} = b(NW)^{-\alpha}$ was estimated to have the following parameter values: $b = 213.8$ and $\alpha = 0.74$, where P_{nw} is the percent of the population with net worth (measured in thousands) in excess of NW. Once the parameters of the function were estimated, it was possible to derive the value of NW which is exceeded by any proportion of the population.

$$NW = \sqrt[-\alpha]{\frac{P_{nw}}{b}}$$

The sum of the weights in the file are equal to the 1963 population of families. If the distribution of wealth were Paretian and the sample were adequate, we would expect the observations on net worth to follow the estimated values of the function. The richest 57 cases in the file had a combined weight of 23,501. This represented 0.0406 percent of the total sum of weights, and hence the lower end of the interval in which the entire 57 cases fell was estimated as $2.24 million. Taking each of the cases and sequentially cumulating their weights, the lower limit of the interval on the Pareto function was calculated.

$$NW_i = \sqrt[-\alpha]{1 - Z_n - \frac{\sum\limits_{i=n+1}^{m} \gamma_m / \sum \gamma}{b}}$$

where Z_n is the ratio of the sum of the weights of the first 2,500 cases to the total sum of weights $\Sigma\gamma$. i runs from 2,501 to 2,557 (the 57 richest cases). The midpoint of the interval within which each case fell was substituted for the reported net worth of the case, and all the asset values of the cases were adjusted in accordance with the ratio of the assigned/original net worth values. Figure 1 and Table 18 show the details of this adjustment.

4. Adjustment of SFCC Wealth to National Balance Sheet Totals It is characteristic of field surveys that they underestimate the value of assets held in the society. In the case of the SFCC file, consumer durables were not measured and had to be assigned, using 1962 balance sheet figures. The value of consumer durables in 1962 was $150.3 billion. This value was distributed among families as follows: one-half of the $150.3 billion was distributed in proportion to all other assets. The other half was distributed in equal shares to each family.

The value of assets other than consumer durables reported in the SFCC file was $1.41 trillion, while that reported in national balance sheets was $1.92 trillion. The Pareto function adjustment, described above, brought the SFCC total to $1.45 trillion. The difference, $510 billion, was assigned to families (heads and wives) in the same proportion as reported assets were held.

Simulation Procedures

Figure 2 is a schematic of the overall simulation model. The following procedures were carried out in the simulation process.

1. Replication of File The SFCC is a small sample, 2,557 cases. To overcome such Monte Carlo variability, all cases in the file with net worth under $2,000,000 were replicated 10 times and all cases with a net worth of $2,000,000 or more were replicated 100 times and the weights were adjusted accordingly.

FIGURE 1   Log of Percentage of Population Having Greater Than Specified Net Worth Versus Log of Net Worth

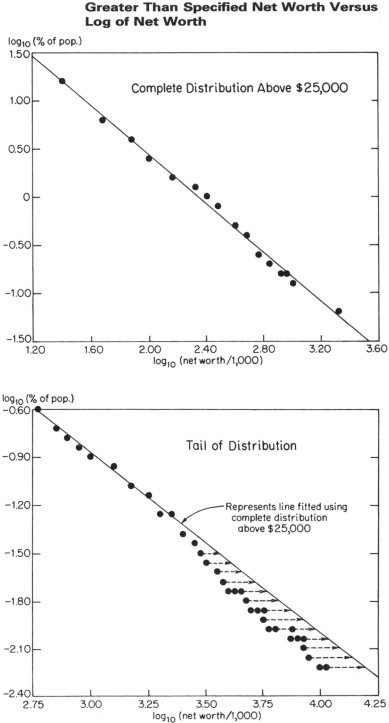

TABLE 18 Adjustment of Upper Tail to Conform to Pareto Function, 1962 SFCC File (Thousands of dollars)

	Original Value	Predicted Value		Original Value	Predicted Value
1.	23,438	180,504	40.	3,005	3,190
2.	14,862	77,327	41.	2,870	3,163
3.	14,491	53,647	42.	2,851	3,139
4.	10,084	11,729	43.	2,738	3,068
5.	9,846	11,115	44.	2,718	3,046
6.	7,943	10,625	45.	2,695	2,993
7.	7,690	10,285	46.	2,598	2,740
8.	7,378	9,318	47.	2,591	2,699
9.	7,098	8,797	48.	2,533	2,649
10.	6,951	8,236	49.	2,486	2,626
11.	6,923	7,722	50.	2,454	2,611
12.	6,714	7,563	51.	2,433	2,569
13.	6,610	7,418	52.	2,381	2,406
14.	6,380	7,262	53.	2,293	2,392
15.	6,013	6,976	54.	2,254	2,361
16.	5,503	6,807	55.	2,249	2,352
17.	5,010	6,694	56.	2,225	2,319
18.	4,886	6,330	57.	2,221	2,308
19.	4,673	6,099	58.	2,198	2,165
20.	4,667	6,016	59.	2,183	2,156
21.	4,389	5,184	60.	2,178	2,143
22.	4,362	5,051	61.	2,158	2,133
23.	4,266	4,981	62.	2,120	2,112
24.	4,228	4,914	63.	2,120	2,102
25.	4,163	4,819	64.	2,101	2,086
26.	4,139	4,723	65.	2,060	2,075
27.	3,903	4,672	66.	2,060	1,980
28.	3,574	4,608	67.	2,057	1,975
29.	3,571	4,552	68.	2,024	1,964
30.	3,450	4,492	69.	1,986	1,954
31.	3,401	4,433	70.	1,967	1,947
32.	3,351	4,390	71.	1,934	1,928
33.	3,341	3,963	72.	1,892	1,921
34.	3,228	3,851	73.	1,871	1,912
35.	3,143	3,818	74.	1,866	1,904
36.	3,112	3,787	75.	1,854	1,898
37.	3,073	3,688	76.	1,842	1,888
38.	3,054	3,657	77.	1,825	1,881
39.	3,010	3,560	78.	1,811	1,875

TABLE 18 (concluded)

	Original Value	Predicted Value		Original Value	Predicted Value
79.	1,788	1,789	90.	1,611	1,688
80.	1,788	1,783	91.	1,597	1,682
81.	1,783	1,776	92.	1,585	1,611
82.	1,762	1,770	93.	1,573	1,605
83.	1,755	1,756	94.	1,572	1,591
84.	1,729	1,744	95.	1,567	1,580
85.	1,729	1,737	96.	1,556	1,574
86.	1,726	1,731	97.	1,556	1,561
87.	1,663	1,726	98.	1,548	1,547
88.	1,658	1,710	99.	1,546	1,534
89.	1,629	1,705	100.	1,483	1,529

2. Mortality Probabilities and Death The modified SFCC file was passed and each person's record was interrogated by the Stochastic Death Generator to determine the age, sex, race, and marital status of the person. From a set of 1962 age-sex-race-marital status-specific mortality rates, the probability of death was determined. A Monte Carlo draw and the ascertained probability determined if the person died or lived. If the person was to live, the next person's record in the family was interrogated. If it was determined a person was to die, death was effected immediately and his family's record was reconstructed to reflect only the surviving members. If more than one death took place in a family, the family record was reconstructed after the last death. Following the death of a family member as much of the economic process of dying and transfering wealth was captured as data permitted.

3. Cost of Last Illness Nearly all deaths impose medical costs on the estates of the decedents. In cases where there is a terminal illness of prolonged length, the medical costs may be substantial. The deductibility of these costs for purposes of calculating taxable estate on the federal estate tax return provided a data base to estimate the relation of the cost of last illness to other characteristics of decedents. The cost of last illness was analyzed using AID-III.[9]

In Figure 3 the result of the AID analysis is shown. The five final groups explain 5.4 percent of the variance in the cost of terminal illnesses as reported on federal estate tax returns. One would not expect to explain a great deal of the variance with the variables available to us, but there is a systematic, positive relationship between net worth and cost of last

FIGURE 2 Generalized Schematic of Simulation Model

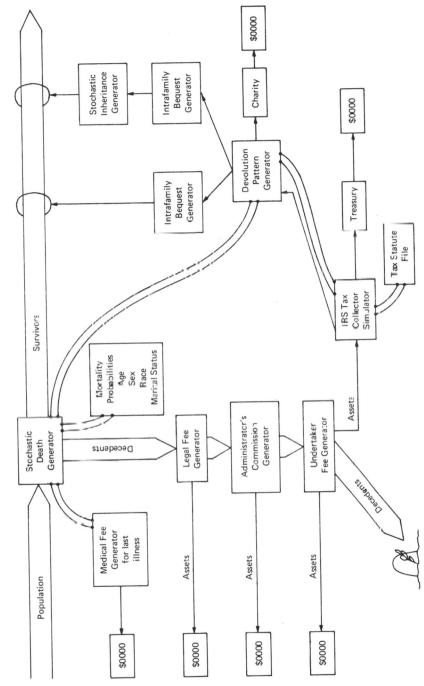

FIGURE 3 Medical Expenses of Last Illness ($\bar{m}$ = Mean Cost in Dollars)

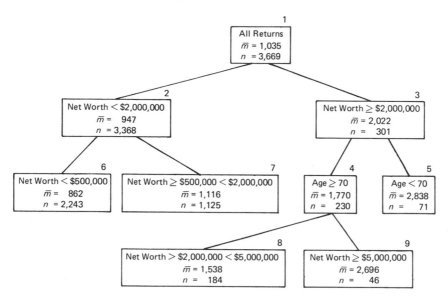

NOTE: Variation explained = 5.4%. Sex was an eligible variable but did not contribute to a significant reduction in variance. n = number of observations in group.

illness. The only other variable which contributed significantly to reducing the original variance was age of decedent. Thus, only these two characteristics of decedents were used in the attribution of last-illness costs. The actual attribution of the cost was unsophisticated, the expected value was assigned within each characteristic class.

4. Attorney's Fees Attorney's fees are a deductible item in the federal estate tax. Consequently, they are available from the estate tax return. Using AID to split the population into groups such that a regression of attorney's fees on gross estate within groups would produce the greatest reduction of variance relative to a regression on the total set of observations, 51.1 percent of the variance was explained. Age and marital status of decedent were the only other variables which were able to provide a basis for splitting the population with a significant reduction in variance. In Figure 4 it can be seen that a simple regression of attorneys' fees on gross assets (measured in thousands of dollars) would produce coefficients of $a = \$549, b = 15.66$. The predicted value $\$3,645$ is the expected attorney's fee when the mean value of the group's gross assets ($\$198,000$) is plugged into the equation.

FIGURE 4 Attorney's Fees AID with Regression on Gross Estate (Dollars)

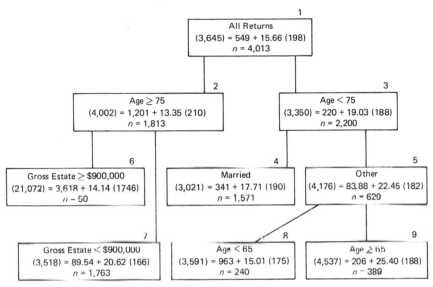

NOTE: For the overall regression, $R^2 = 46.8\%$. Marginal variance explained by subgroup regression = 4.3%. Total $R^2 = 51.1\%$. Sex was also an eligible variable but could not produce a significant reduction in variance. The predicted value of the equation in each group is the value of attorney's fees estimated when gross estate measured in thousands of dollars was at its mean for the group. n = number of observations in group.

5. Executor's Fees The cost of executor's fees was estimated using two regression equations and data from the 1962 federal estate tax file.

$$EXCOM + = a + b_1(NET\ WORTH) + b_2(MS1) + b_3(MS2) + b_4(MS3)$$

where net worth is measured in thousands of dollars, $MS1$ is a dummy for married decedents, $MS2$ is a dummy for never married decedents, and $MS3$ is a dummy for all other marital statuses. The equation was fitted separately for decedents with net worth under $200,000 and those with net worth of $200,000 or more. The estimated coefficients for the two equations are:

	Net Worth < $200,000	Net Worth ≧ $200,000
a	$172.50	$2,517.80
b_1	14.8	17.3
b_2	−843.5	−3,575.0
b_3	575.5	4,223.4
b_4	268.0	−648.1
	$R^2 = 17.9$	$R^2 = 32.2$

6. *Funeral Expenses* In the simulation, they are attributed to decedent's estates on the basis of 8 regression equations fitted in the process of an AID run on the 1962 estate tax file. The combined splitting of the population into eight final groups, and the simple regression of funeral expenses on net worth within each final group, explained 19.2 percent of the variance of funeral expenses. In Figure 5 we show the results of the AID run with group regressions.

In some cases, the total costs of dying exceed the assets of the decedent. This is frequently the case with children. Although they will not generally incur legal or administration fees of any significance, the cost of last illness and funeral will diminish estates of children as well as those of adults. Whether a child or an adult, the cost of last illness, administration fees, lawyer's fees, and funeral expenses are all deducted from their estates in accordance with the AID analyses above. When these costs result in a negative estate, it is transferred to the decedent's heirs in the same manner as a positive valued estate. This conceptualization is consistent with the actual process of cost bearing for decedents.

7. *Bequest Patterns* Little information is available about the pattern of transfers set in motion by death. Data available from the IRS identify amounts going to charity and in some years to spouse, but no information about the division of bequests between members of the decedent's family living at home or, for that matter, the total amount remaining in the decedent's family versus that going to noncharitable legatees outside the immediate family. In order to estimate the pattern of estate distribution, a file constructed by Smith from estate tax returns filed in the District of Columbia in 1967 was used.[10] The statutes of the District of Columbia require an estate tax return to be filed for the estates of all decedents with gross assets of $1,000 or more. Thus, the file provided nearly the complete range of estate sizes. Further, the file was constructed to provide information about the distribution of assets among spouse, children, other relatives, nonrelatives and charities (including gifts to governments). The processes of estimating the pattern of estate distribution in a form suitable for Monte Carlo applications is depicted in Figure 6.

The first step was to use AID to estimate the probability that a bequest was made outside the family. A family is defined for this purpose as a head, wife, and children, wherever they live. All never married persons were excluded from the estimation on the grounds that we would follow the arbitrary rule that never married persons had neither spouse nor children and that all their wealth would flow outside the family as defined. The results of the AID analysis are shown in Figure 7. The combination of being married and having a net worth of under $100,000 resulted in a

FIGURE 5 Funeral Expenses AID with Regression on Net Worth

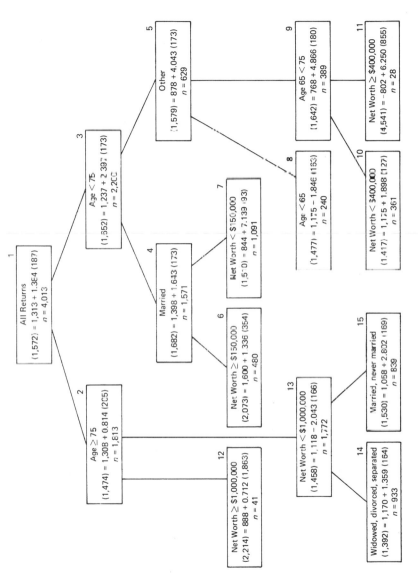

NOTE: The overall regression R^2 = 9.3%. Marginal explained by subgroup regression = 9.9%. Total R^2 = 19.2%. Dependent variable in parentheses is the estimated value of funeral expenses when the independent variable is net worth, measured in thousands of dollars is at the mean for the group.

FIGURE 6 Estimation Sequence for Identifying Patterns of Wealth Flows at Death

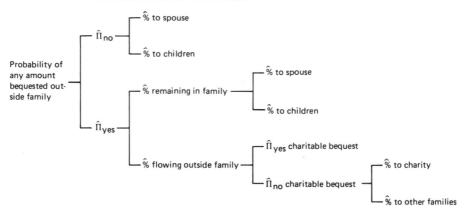

FIGURE 7 Probability of Making a Bequest Outside Family

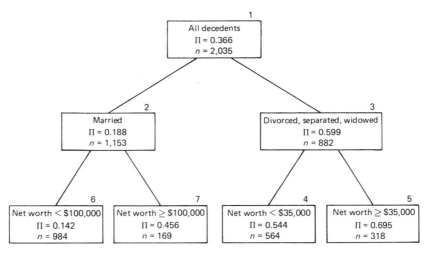

NOTE: Variance explained = 22.4%. Age and sex were also eligible variables but did not contribute to a significant reduction in variance.

probability of .142 of making a bequest outside the family. If a decedent were not married and had $35,000 or more, on the other hand, the probability of making an outside bequest was .695. The four end groups shown in Figure 7 accounted for 22.4 percent of the variance around the mean probability of outside bequests for all decedents.

In order to estimate the mean share of assets going to a spouse, a sample of 1,090 decedents who were residents of the District of Columbia and married at the time of their death in 1967, was used to calculate the proportion that the value of assets passing to spouse was of the total value of assets passing to children plus spouse, by sex and value of estate. The mean of the ratio was also calculated:

$$\sum_{i=1}^{n} \frac{\dfrac{\text{spouse}_i}{\text{spouse}_i + \text{children}_i}}{n}$$

These values are shown in Table 19.

TABLE 19 Wealth Bequeathed to Spouse as a Percent of Total Wealth Bequeathed to Spouse and Children by Sex and Value of Total Net Estate of Decedents, Washington, D.C., 1967

Value of Net Estate (Thousands of dollars)	Mean of Ratio: Spouse / (Spouse + Children)		Ratio of Aggregates of Wealth: Σ Spouse / (Σ Spouse + Children)	
	Males	Females	Males	Females
< 5	86.7	79.0	85.7	82.7
5 < 10	90.4	87.3	90.9	86.1
10 < 15	91.7	82.3	92.1	82.9
15 < 20	90.6	86.3	90.9	86.9
20 < 25	95.5	79.9	95.1	80.5
25 < 30	90.7	90.9	91.0	89.7
30 < 35	97.7	83.4	97.7	82.9
35 < 50	96.0	81.3	96.3	81.6
50 < 75	82.9	75.2	82.3	75.6
75 < 100	91.0	66.6	90.9	63.0
100 < 250	79.4	59.0	79.8	55.8
≥ 250	72.1	52.7	75.3	41.8

Females consistently transfer less to their surviving spouse, as a proportion of total transfers to spouse and children, than do males, and the distribution of estates between wives and children shifts in favor of children as the total value of estates increases. The observed patterns with respect to value of estate are consistent with estate planning strategies to minimize repeated taxation of the same bundle of wealth.

Given that we had a basis for predicting the probability that a bequest would be made outside the family, it was necessary to estimate the share of one's estate which would flow outside (or, conversely, remain inside) the family. AID was used again, this time to estimate the proportion of a decedent's assets which were bequested outside the family if any outside bequests were made (see Figure 8).

FIGURE 8 Percent of Decedent's Assets Bequeathed Outside Family for All Decedents Making Outside Bequests

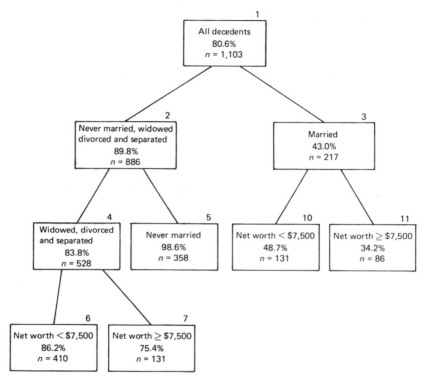

NOTE: Variance explained = 38.4%. Age and sex were eligible variables but did not contribute significantly to the reduction of variance.

As might be expected, married decedents give a smaller share outside their family than do decedents who are other than married. The proportion of one's assets given beyond the bounds of the family decreases with increased wealth, but the absolute amount most likely increases, given the relative small change in the percentage increase associated with increased wealth.

We next estimated the probability that those decedents transferring wealth outside their family made a bequest to charities or governments. The AID tree shown in Figure 9 explained 11.3 percent of the variance in the probability that a charitable transfer took place. The second step in the estimation of charitable bequests was to estimate the share of assets

FIGURE 9 **Probability That Bequest is Made to Charity or Government, Given That Some Wealth Was Bequeathed Outside Family**

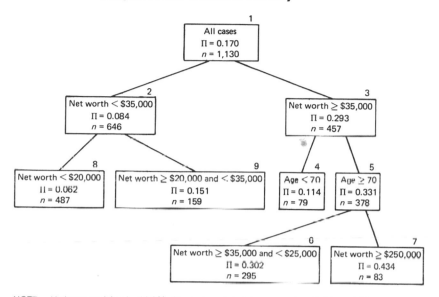

NOTE: Variance explained = 11.3%. Sex and marital status were also eligible variables, but could not contribute to a significant reduction in variance.

leaving the family which went to charities (including gifts to government) for all decedents making charitable bequests. We were able to explain 13.6 percent in the variance in the share of wealth flowing away from decedents which went to charities. The AID tree of Figure 10 shows the result of the AID analysis.

Estimation of Inheritances from Outside Family Unit

The sum of inheritances and gifts received by 113 families are contained in the SFCC file. The ratio of inheritances generated by estates over $60,000 to the value of gifts greater than $3,000 reported in *Statistics of Income, 1962*, is about seven to one. On this basis, the value of gifts and inheritances in the SFCC file was treated as inheritances only. Estimation of an inheritance pattern was done in two stages. First, the probability that a family will receive an inheritance during the simulated year was estimated using AID. The results of the AID analysis shown in Figure 11 indicate that inheritance from outside the family unit cannot be predicted very well ($R^2 = 2.3\%$) with the information that was available. For the

FIGURE 10 Percent of Estate Leaving Family That is Bequeathed to Charity for Decedents Making Bequests to Charity

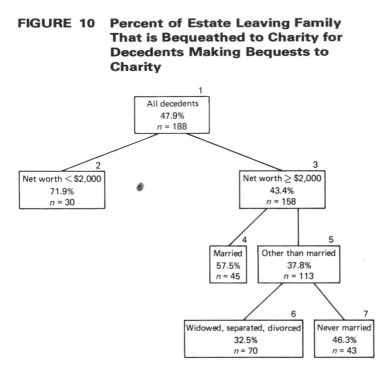

NOTE: Variance explained = 13.6%. Age and sex were eligible variables, but could not significantly reduce the unexplained variance. The category of charity includes donations to government.

FIGURE 11 Probability of Receiving an Inheritance

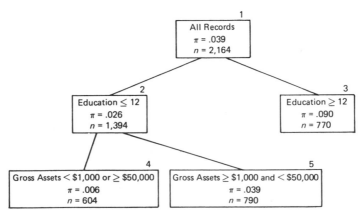

NOTE: Variance explained = 2.3%. Income, age, marital status, sex and race were also eligible variables but did not contribute to a significant reduction in variance.

simulation, each family was assigned an inheritance probability π equal to one of four values in the final AID groups. The second stage was to estimate an equation to predict the size of inheritance using the 113 SFCC families which received an inheritance. The resulting equation has the form:

$$\log_e (INHERITANCE) = a + b_1 (GROSS\ ESTATE) + b_2 (AGE) + b_3 (ED)$$

where *GROSS ESTATE* is measured in thousands of dollars, *AGE* and *ED* are the age and number of years of education of the head, respectively. The estimated coefficients are

$a = 3.58$

$b_1 = 0.0007 \qquad R^2 = 21.9\%$

$b_2 = 0.027$

$b_3 = 0.17$

NOTES

1. Lee Soltow, *Toward Income Equality in Norway* (Madison, Wis.: University of Wisconsin Press, 1965).
2. Robin Barlow, Harvey E. Brazer, and James N. Morgan, *Economic Behavior of the Affluent* (Washington, D.C.: Brookings Institution, 1966).
3. Dorothy Projector and Gertrude S. Weiss, *Survey of Financial Characteristics of Consumers*, Federal Reserve Technical Papers, Aug. 1966.
4. John A. Brittain, "The Intergenerational Transmission of Wealth: Prospects for a Research Program," Dec. 1971, processed.
5. Conceptually, the model can most accurately be said to reflect death between July 1, 1962 and June 30, 1963. This comes about because the SFCC sample represents the U.S. population on December 31, 1962. Official mortality rates are available using a July 1, 1962 or July 1, 1963 base. We arbitrarily chose the 1962 base.
6. The number of estates filing tax returns in 1963 are graphed by size of gross assets in the chart below. In contrast to all other evidence about the size distribution of assets, the frequency of estates below about $70,000 declines rapidly. The failure of estates to file is believed to result from the fact that most such estates have a zero tax liability. Discussions with employees of the Internal Revenue Service indicate that they believe substantial nonfiling occurs for estates with "gross" assets of less than $70,000. See figure on next page.
7. No attempt was made to capture the incidence of fetal deaths or deaths of infants at birth, since the SFCC file would not readily provide a basis for such events.
8. U.S. Department of Health, Education, and Welfare, *Vital Statistics of the United States*, Mortality, Part A, 1963.
9. AID-III is a data-searching algorithm which sequentially splits a population into pairs such that the sum of the variance around the mean of the pair or the expected value of a regression is the smallest possible proportion of the variance around the expected values of the group from which the pair was derived. The technique has the advantage

over regression in not requiring an additive set of independent variables. It also imposes no linearity restrictions on relations between variables. For a detailed discussion on AID-III, see John A. Sonquist, Elizabeth L. Baker, and James N. Morgan, *Searching for Structure* (Ann Arbor, Mich.: Institute for Social Research, 1971).

10. James D. Smith, "White Wealth and Black People: The Distribution of Wealth in Washington, D.C., 1967," in James D. Smith, ed., *Personal Distribution of Income and Wealth* (New York: NBER, 1975).

Figure for Footnote 6

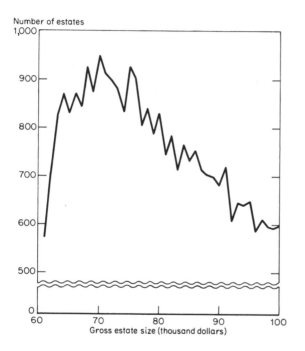

15 | COMMENTS

John A. Brittain
The Brookings Institution

The role of the inheritance of personal wealth in the perpetuation of economic inequality is an intriguing and important question. A related puzzle is the apparent failure of nominally high death-tax rates to curb inheritance or alleviate inequality to any significant degree. This paper by Smith, Franklin, and Orcutt initiates an interesting and stimulating microsimulation approach to these issues. Their objective is to portray the net direct effect on the wealth distribution of a four-step sequence: deaths, associated costs, the intervention of taxation, and distributions to heirs. While the authors may have raised more questions than they have answered, particularly with respect to the reliability of the output of these simulations, this is a useful pioneering effort.

(It should be noted here that my comments originally presented at the conference have been substantially rewritten because the authors have since revised practically their entire empirical presentation. The main changes here are in Section 2, from which tabulations of my own derivative computations have been dropped; some tentative generalizations from those estimates have been retained, however, in the belief that they are still valid.)

Smith et al. speak modestly of a simulation "experiment," but they also cautiously suggest that its results point to weak tax and inheritance effects, at least in the short run. They also find considerable short-run mobility within the wealth distribution. I shall try to give the gist of their model and findings, along with some running comments on both. A few general observations are reserved for Section 3.

I. THE SIMULATION SCHEME

It may be useful to turn at once to the second half of this paper for details on the underlying simulation model. There is time, however, to convey only its general flavor.

Mortality in the Initial Population

Like the Watergate literature, simulation seems to have an eerie language of its own. There is the usual initial population that is manipulated by operating

---

NOTE: The views expressed are those of the author and should not be attributed to the trustees, officers, or other staff members of the Brookings Institution.

characteristics. In the present paper, there is reference to a complex algorithm which drives the system, but, for brevity, the readers must settle for a flow chart. Even so, the initial population, scenario, and time frame are clear enough. It is New Year's Eve, 1962. The curtain rises to reveal 59 million consumer units, their wealth and other aspects of their private lives. Actually our view of this huge initial cast of characters is provided by a projection of a broad sample known as the "modified SFCC file," and described in detail in the paper. Enter the Stochastic Death Generator, who is nothing more than an objectively selective executioner. He is offered his choice from the modified file of consumer units. Guided by the Census probability of death during 1963 for a person of given age, sex, race, and marital status, the Stochastic Death Generator invokes a Monte Carlo draw to do away with about 400,000 consumer units and 1.7 million individuals. The Generator's victims are not replaced, nor is any adjustment made for growth or inflation in 1963.

Adjustments and Deductions from Gross Estates

The received 1962 Projector-Weiss sample of 2,557 families (SFCC) is adjusted by adding flows to children who have left home and compressing asset categories. The face value of life insurance is removed from the SFCC wealth variants for the living, which clearly understates their wealth by ignoring current cash values. An attempt is made to enrich the information on top wealth holders by extrapolation of a Pareto fit to data on families with net worth under $25,000; the 57 richest families were spread out to conform with this Pareto distribution, but with their relative weight unchanged. This reliance on the Pareto line greatly increases estimated wealth at the top, and a rationale for the procedure seems essential. In any case, to stabilize the Monte Carlo estimates, the modified sample is then replicated tenfold below $2,000,000 and one-hundred-fold above, with weights being adjusted accordingly.

After the rubbing out of each individual, his family record is reconstructed to include only surviving members, and revised to reflect expenses, taxes, and inheritances. This requires an elaborate system of behavioral relationships to portray the main costs of dying (including federal estate taxes), and the effect of wealth transfers at death. For example, medical costs of the last illness deducted on federal estate tax returns are related to net worth and age; attorney's fees are regressed on gross assets within various age groups. Executor's fees are regressed on net worth and marital status dummies within estate size classes; funeral expenses were estimated similarly. The four behavior models were only modestly successful, with the variance explained ranging from 5 percent for medical expenses to 51 percent for attorney's fees. Whether good fits or bad, they were used to estimate the net estates left by 1.7 million individuals tapped by the electronic Grim Reaper. Further deductions, based on various estate tax structures, are presumed to yield the amount available for distribution.

In their lengthy methodological section, the authors do not discuss the role of taxes explicitly. Presumably each federal estate tax structure discussed early in the paper is built into the model to form the link between taxable estate and the amount available for distribution. However, there apparently was no way of allowing for the effect of state death taxes on federal tax liabilities and on the net amount available for distribution. Nor could any account be taken of gift taxes that may have been paid essentially in lieu of estate taxes.[1]

The Pattern of Bequests

Given the estimated amount available for distribution from the 1.7 million estates, the next step was to develop a model to estimate individual bequests. This is a complex problem, involving leakages from the family unit as well as inheritances from without; it also requires a model of the distribution among spouse and children. The last fifth of the paper discusses the estimation procedure, utilizing District of Columbia data on 1957 estates as low as $1,000. It is extremely difficult to appraise the reliability of these inheritance equations and probability distributions, but in general their explanatory power does not seem very great. It would be useful to compare the results to those from simple hypothetical assumptions such as: everything to spouse, if any; otherwise, equal division among children, if any; otherwise, everything to charity. This might indicate how much these manipulations are accomplishing.

An appraisal of the reliability of this microsimulation model is extremely difficult for me (and, no doubt, for the authors themselves). The extermination of 1.7 million consumer units according to a four-way demographic classification is a fairly persuasive beginning. However, the explanatory models of deductions and inheritances seem rather rough, since they do, on the average, no more than about 20 percent of the job. One is, at least, left to wonder how the results from this experiment would compare to the results if more reliable operating characteristics were available.

II. THE FINDINGS: TAX EFFECTS AND REFORMS

The effects of the current and three other tax structures were studied via four simulations. That is, the basic simulation model with a given set of operating characteristics was run repeatedly, with only the tax structures being changed. While useful, it should be noted that this approach stresses the comparative effects of different tax structures, as distinct from an explicit analysis of the effect of inheritance (as modified by these tax structures).

Current Estate Tax

The authors check the size distribution of gross estates generated by their model against returns reported to the Internal Revenue Service in 1963. In this range of estates (over $60,000) the agreement on frequencies seems satisfactory, even though in the range below $100,000 the IRS falls far short; this is presumably due to nonfiling on behalf of nontaxable estates. Thus, the more realistic and larger number of units in the simulation should not seriously undermine its tax estimates, since most of the marginal wealth units would show zero estimated tax liability.

In their Table 3, the authors next compare wealth distributions before and after simulation.[2] A reduction in numbers in the bottom class suggests a slight reduction of overall wealth concentration for which the estate tax can claim little credit; it was probably largely due to the disappearance of elderly poor from the distribution. It is clear that this in itself represents no fundamental change. What one would like to know is the shape of the distribution after the decedents have been replaced by increases in other demographic categories, and after allowance for growth and inflation.[3] In any case, the authors appear to have overlooked an offsetting peculiarity in the table. The postdeath simulation yields higher numbers in four of the six size classes over $15,000—about 1 percent more altogether; this works against any decline in concentration suggested by the reduced number of the poor.

A breakdown of the distribution by age shows, not surprisingly, a general decline in frequencies all along the wealth distribution for those over 65. More significantly, the number of relatively well-off persons under 30 also appears to have increased slightly; 47 percent are above $2,000 after simulation, compared to 44 percent before, and the number in every class above $2,000 increased, with one exception. This seems to indicate inheritance by already relatively well-off young families; this conclusion must be qualified here and in later discussions, however, by the perplexing fact that the number of consumer units in this age group rose from 7.31 to 7.49 million, despite a plausible overall decline of .40 million among all age groups.

It would be interesting to learn how the conflicting tendencies in Table 3 add up in terms of standard measures of inequality. I have made rough estimates of the standard deviation of the logarithmic of wealth based on these distributions. If valid, these confirm some of the authors' points, raise some new questions, and clarify the effects of tax reforms discussed later.[4] My highly tentative figures support the authors' impression of a slight decline in overall concentration under the simulation; it appears that the increased numbers in the top classes did not completely offset the effect of a reduction in numbers at the bottom. Although young people who were already relatively well-off appear to have fared well, the reduction in the numbers at the bottom also suggests some of them may have been moved well up the scale; their gains at the bottom may have outweighed gains at the top. In any case, these developments among young families probably account for most of the overall increase in numbers at the top.

The figures also indicate a plausible 6 percent decline in the numbers of families headed by the aged, and my rough estimate suggests an overall decline in wealth concentration in that group. This decline in concentration among the elderly appears due to a concentration of deaths at the top and bottom, for which I have no ready explanation. My computations also point to one interesting statistical artifact. Despite taxes, expenses, charitable contributions, and other leakages, and with no income growth or inflation in the model, the simulation of deaths yields estimated increases in the overall mean net worth and the mean for each age category. If this is correct, the decline in the number of family units and the increased value of life insurance after death apparently offset the effect of death taxes and other leakages. However, it would be prudent to check the individual results for an explanation.

Smith et al. also present their estimates on a per capita basis to offset the effect of decreased family size. However, the figures reported in Table 4 are quite implausible; for example, after simulation, more than 25 percent of families with heads under 30 had a per capita net worth of $2,000 and above compared to only 15 percent before; about one out of every eight families with net worth under $2,000 was moved up from that class, and the relative frequency in the $3,000–$4,000 class increased from 1 percent to nearly 6 percent. The questionable nature of the figures in Table 4 is perhaps even better illustrated by the data on *all* families with per capita net worth under $1,000. The simulation reduced the number of families in this wealth class by 3.5 million, or 18 percent. Deaths reduced the total number of families by 0.4 million, but it is unlikely that more than 0.2 million of these were among the one-third of families with per capita wealth below $1,000. The authors report that about 1 percent of the population died that year. It is difficult to conceive that they concentrated sufficient bequests among the poorest third of the wealth distribution to raise the per capita wealth of nearly 18 percent of these families above $1,000. If they really did so, the inheritance process would have to be counted as a most remarkable antipoverty institution!

Obviously the data underlying Table 4 should be reinvestigated, but it is possible that the results in the upper ranges are valid. Of course, any substantial overall gain by the better-off young would be an important finding, but it would also be difficult to attribute it all to inheritance; only about 1 percent of the population of *individuals* died and nearly half of them presumably left most of their estate to an elderly spouse. Clearly, the indicated relative gains by well-off young families are rather implausible and deserve further analysis.

A useful attempt is made with 10 × 10 transition matrixes to display the movement among wealth classes. The lack of smoothness in the results is bound to raise some doubts. For example, in Table 5 only 500 families starting in the top tenth fell into the third and fourth "deciles," but 20,800 fell all the way to the fifth or sixth. The matrixes would also be more interesting if an age breakdown were provided as before. The sums of rows and columns are also rather far from checking out. Nevertheless, some aspects of these rank switches are interesting. For example, the table suggests a much greater tendency to rise from the bottom tenth as a result of the death simulation than to fall from the top. About 880,000 families (18 percent) rose at least one notch from the bottom tenth compared to 119,000 (2 percent) who fell from the top. This finding and virtually the same result in Table 6 may, however, be related to the implausible gains by poor families already discussed in connection with Tables 3 and 4.

To sum up, the indicated overall effect of simulated taxes and inheritance is minuscule, but plausible, except for the gains in the lower ranges of Table 4. The key, but unexplained, finding is a relative gain by the wealthier young families, but the *amounts* of wealth involved are small, and the tabulations seem questionable on some counts.

Alternative Tax Structures

Three reforms are studied:
   a. Estate Tax Reform: $100,000 exclusion, 50 percent marginal rate on the first $400,000 taxable, 100 percent marginal rate above that.
   b. Inheritance Tax, Modest Reform: heirs taxed by estate tax rates, but base equals inheritance plus prior net worth.
   c. Inheritance Tax, Severe Reform: first $50,000 of inheritance is exempt, remainder is taxed at a 100 percent rate.

No philosophical cases are presented for these reforms, although some interesting probable consequences are discussed in the authors' concluding observations. In any case, the menu is broad enough to make an empirical study of their effects interesting. From the simulations emerge the most important conclusion of this study. That is the virtually total impotence of even substantially more progressive death taxation as regards moving the wealth distribution toward equality, at least in one year. Despite the importance of this finding, very little time need be spent on it here; the computations based on the simulations of tax reforms (Tables 8–12) yield results only slightly different from those under the current tax. When Smith et al. allocate tax proceeds equally per capita (Table 15) the taxes are found to have a greater effect, especially on the lower wealth classes. However, the differences in effect *among* the alternative taxes remain small. Thus the reforms have no significant effect on the wealth distribution in one year.

The short-run redistributional impotence of death-tax reform also has an important corollary. If so radical a departure from the estate tax as the "severe" inheritance model produces about the same overall results as the estate tax itself, it can be inferred that the latter has little short-run impact on the overall wealth distribution. In fact, none of these tax structures has much effect, even at the top. As a further inference, it is apparent that even the modest changes between "before" and "after" revealed in the many tables of this paper can be attributed more to the decedents' dropping out of the distribution, to inheritance, and to factors other than taxation.

It seems safe to attribute the indicated impotence of estate taxation to two major factors. First, not many individuals die in a given year. Second, of these decedents, only a small fraction have any substantial amounts of material wealth to leave behind.

III. CONCLUDING REMARKS

One experiment always leads to others, so I hope I will not appear insatiable if I mention some thoughts for the future.

Tests of Simulation Model

The minimal redistributive effects observed are important, so further checks of the reliability of the model are in order. There could be more checking of changes in aggregates, such as overall wealth, against components of the change, like taxes, expenses, and charitable contributions; such estimates could be checked against other sources. In the case of the operating characteristics, tests of some alternative or extreme assumptions might be tried, such as primogeniture against equal division.

Broadening the Scope

Integrating this model with a broader one embodying savings, consumption, and growth, as well as feedback effects, will inspire more confidence. This would also allow for new entries into the population replacing the decedents, without which the meaning of the experiment is rather clouded. Behavioral effects of the tax, such as the use of avoidance techniques, need further consideration, especially gifts, insurance, and trust devices and estate-planning strategies in general.

It is vital for any inheritance model to consider also marital selection patterns. Obviously men do not marry women of equal wealth, but neither is the pairing random. It would be useful to estimate the correlation and analyze its effect on the wealth distribution.

Extension of the Model over Time

The above suggestions may be overambitious. Less grandiose and, I should think, readily implemented, would be repeated annual simulations carrying the initial population many years ahead. Perhaps there is suspicion that the operating characteristics will drift, but I am surprised that it has not been tried here. Is the computer already groggy? Is the Stochastic Generator exhausted or finding his work distasteful? I should think the long-run effect of death taxes and inheritance taxes may be fairly substantial despite short-run stability. One might expect inheritance to help perpetuate inequality, whereas the estate tax works to alleviate it. A projection of the model might show which force is stronger. When all is said and done, however, I suspect that the inheritance of *human* wealth will be found to be the major force maintaining the overall inequality of economic status. On the other hand, material wealth undoubtedly does have a powerful influence at the top of the distribution.

NOTES

1. The marital and charitable deductions for estate tax purposes, unlike the previously mentioned expenses, were not treated as expenses out of gross estate. They were allowed for in estimating the tax, however, and their effects on inheritance were also taken into account.

2. The table refers to "Before Taxes" and "After Taxes," but the meaning is actually "Before Deaths" and "After Deaths," with the full effects of costs and inheritances being measured, not tax effects alone. In later tabulations, the authors attempt to separate the two effects.
3. The more elaborate simulation model at the Urban Institute may ultimately offer some insight on this.
4. The logarithmic transformation was used to achieve symmetry, and, consequently, more accurate approximations to the mean and standard deviation. The transformation also yielded approximate normality and a direct comparability of the concentration measures for different age groups, despite their difference in means. The results of my extremely rough approximations are summarized here for what they are worth. The authors, of course, need not depend on frequency distributions and could obtain exact results from the individual observations.

Index

446, 458, 468, 469, 471-76, 478, 483,
493n, 494n, 498n
Morgan, James N., 191, 621
Morgenstern, Richard, 425, 528-29
Moriguchi, Chikashi, 549n
Morolla, Francis A., 548n
Mortensen, D., 385
Mueller, D.C., 13
Murray, Michael P., 42n, 64n
Musgrave, Richard, 47
Muth, Richard F., 58, 63n, 69

Nagda, M.L., 205-06, 231
National Association of Social Workers, 49
National Bureau of Economic Research, 6,
204-05, 492n
National Emissions Data System, 226
National Income Accounts, 1, 9, 45. *See also*
Government Receipts and Expenditure
Account; Income and Product Account;
Personal Income and Outlay Account
National Institute for Occupational Safety
and Health, 357
National Opinion Research Center, 416
National Science Foundation, 427, 492n
NBER-Thorndike sample, 381, 416, 426-28,
474, 494n, 501, 510, 558, 566, 571, 574,
576, 578, 587, 588, 612, 616n, 618, 619
Neighborhood Characteristics 15 percent
sample, 313, 330
New York *Times*, 164, 185
1970 California polls, 86-97, 103n, 104n,
109-10
Niskanen, William, 104-05n
Nixon, Richard, 105n
Nonpecuniary work rewards, 355-76, 413-14;
control over overtime, 369-71; and earnings
distribution, 425-26, 442-44, 480; and education, 356-57, 363-76; employment
stability, 371-72; fringe benefits, 365-67;
healthy and safe working conditions,
367-68; job autonomy, 372-75; methodology, 359-62; model of, 357-59; and
occupation, 360-75, 376; and race, 358-59,
363-76, 377-78n; and sex, 361-76, 377-78n;
and work experience, 356-57, 363-76
Nordhaus, William D., 10, 214

Oaxaca, Ronald L., 305, 356
Occam's razor, 49
Occupation: and black/white male earnings,
276-78, 300-01; and earnings distribution,

384-85, 389-90, 392-94, 430-31, 481; and
male/female earnings, 311-12, 324-29,
345; and nonpecuniary work rewards,
360-75, 376; and uncertainty, 384-85,
389-90, 392-94
Occupational dissimilarity index, 312, 326
Ofek, H., 551
Office of Business Economics, 203
Office of Economic Opportunity, 513, 530,
551
Oi, Walter, 249
Olsen, Edgar O., 58
On-the-job training, 471-76, 483, 507-08,
509-10
Orcutt, Guy H., 643
Overtime hours, control over, 369-71

Panel Study of Income Dynamics, 415, 530,
547n, 551, 552
Parnes, H., 415, 428
Pauly, M.V., 102n
Personal income, 10-11
Personal Income and Outlay Account, 9-50;
and cash transfers, 13-15, 45-46; and food
stamps, 16; and government capital con
sumption, 11, 16, 18, 20; and government
capital formation, 11; and in kind transfers,
15-20, 46; and medical care, 15-16; modifi-
cation of, 11-12, 13-20, 45-46, 48
Phillips curve, 324
Population Council survey, 554
Post, A. Alan, 172
Productive Americans data source, 538,
547n, 551
Projector, Dorothy S., 410n, 416, 621, 666
Project Talent sample, 491n
Public housing, 16-20, 33, 51-69; effect of,
on consumption patterns, 55, 58-60; indifference curves, 52-57; market rent of, 57;
value of, to occupants, 54-55, 58-63, 67.
See also In-kind transfers
Public Housing Authorities, 42n

Quality of Employment Survey, 357, 365,
377n

Race: and air pollution damage, 213, 229;
and earnings, 120-21, 129-34, 135-45,
150-53, 155-56, 159-60, 363-64; and male/
female earnings, 318, 319-28, 344-45, 347,
350, 353; and nonpecuniary work rewards,
358-59, 363-76, 377-78n. *See also* Black/

Uncertainty: and ability, 392-94; causes of, 382-83, and demographic groups, 386-89; and earnings distributions, 379-95, 414-16; and immobility, 389-92; methodology, 385-86; and occupation, 384-85, 389-90, 392-94; types of, 381-82
University of Michigan Survey Research Center, 357, 413, 513, 528
Urban Institute, 643, 672n
Urban Problems Survey, 528, 529

Von Furstenberg, G.M., 13
von Neumann, John, 425
Vroman, Wayne, 299

Wachtel, P., 424
Waddell, Thomas E., 226n, 230
Wales, T., 381, 382, 422, 426-27, 429-30, 432, 433, 435, 442, 493n, 494n, 547n
Walker, Kathryn, 553
Wedgewood, Josiah, 412n
Weisbrod, Burton A., 173, 195
Weiss, Gertrude S., 410, 666

Weiss, Y., 385, 565
Welch, Finis R., 242, 243-244, 261
Welfare programs, 95-98
West, P., 494n
Willis, Robert J., 518, 548n
Wilson, J.Q., 86, 103n
Wise, D., 422, 497n
Wolfe, B., 428, 443
Work experience: and lifetime distribution of earnings, 440-42, 480-81; and nonpecuniary work rewards, 356-57, 363-76
Work history: and change in total earnings, 145-47; changes in, 142-45; and earnings, 121-22, 134-47; and percentage employed, 135-42, 156-57
Working conditions, 367-68
Wray, J.D., 554
Wright, Sewall, 503
Wykoff, Frank C., 178, 179-80, 183, 192n, 196

Zupan, Jeffrey M., 165, 212-13, 227n, 230

About the Editor

F. Thomas Juster is Director of the Institute for Social Research and Professor of Economics at The University of Michigan. His research interests include economic and social accounting systems, the measurement of economic welfare and the distribution of welfare, the role of expectational measures in analysis of the spending and saving behavior of consumers, and the analysis of non-market time and time allocation generally among households.

He has published extensively in all of these areas, including "A Framework for the Measurement of Economic and Social Performance," (in *The Measurement of Economic and Social Performance*) Milton Moss, ed., Columbia, 1974; *Education, Income and Human Behavior*, McGraw-Hill, 1975; *Anticipations and Purchases*, Princeton University Press for NBER, 1964; and *Household Capital Formation and Financing*, Columbia University Press for NBER, 1966.

Juster is a member of the American Statistical Association Advisory Committee to the U.S. Census Bureau, a Senior Advisor to the Brookings Panel on Economic Activity, a member of the Advisory Committee to the Congressional Budget Office, and Chairman of a recent National Academy of Sciences Committee on the measurement of energy consumption.